New Urban Spaces

ALSO BY NEIL BRENNER

Critique of Urbanization: Selected Essays

Implosions/Explosions: Towards a Study of Planetary Urbanization (editor)

Cities for People, Not for Profit: Critical Urban Theory and the Right to the City (coeditor, with Peter Marcuse and Margit Mayer)

New State Spaces: Urban Governance and the Rescaling of Statehood

Spaces of Neoliberalism: Urban Restructuring in North America and Western Europe (coeditor, with Nik Theodore)

NEIL BRENNER is Professor of Urban Theory, Graduate School of Design, Harvard University.

For Ignacia,
Ivan, and Izar

TABLE OF CONTENTS

LIST OF FIGURES

LIST OF ABBREVIATIONS

APS	Advanced producer services
BRI	Belt and Road Initiative
BRICS	Brazil, Russia, India, China, South Africa
COSIPLAN	South American Council of Infrastructure and Planning (*Consejo Suramericano de Infrastructura y Planeamiento*)
DMIC	Delhi-Mumbai Industrial Corridor
EU	European Union
GIS	Geographic information systems
GLC	Greater London Council
ICTs	Information and communications technologies
IFCs	International financial centers
IIRSA	Initiative for the Integration of Regional Infrastructure in South America (*Iniciativa para la Integración de la Infraestructura Regional Suramericana*)
IMF	International Monetary Fund
ISI	Import-substitution industrialization
OECD	Organisation for Economic Co-operation and Development
NAFTA	North American Free Trade Agreement
NGOs	Nongovernmental organizations
NIDL	New international division of labor
nNIDL	*New* new international divisions of labor
NUA	New urban agenda
RCSRs	Rescaled Competition State Regimes
SDGs	Sustainable Development Goals
SEM	Single European Market
SEZ	Special economic zone
SMEs	Small and medium-sized enterprises
STS	Science and technology studies
TNCs	Transnational corporations
TPSN	Territory place scale network

UN	United Nations
UNESCO	United Nations Educational, Scientific, and Cultural Organization
UPDs	Urban development projects
USD	Uneven spatial development
WCA	World city archipelago

New Urban Spaces

1
Openings: The Urban Question as a Scale Question?

FOR MUCH OF THE TWENTIETH CENTURY, the field of urban studies defined its research object through a series of explicit or implied geographical contrasts. Even as debates raged regarding how best to define the specificity of urban life, this realm was almost universally demarcated in opposition to two purportedly nonurban zones—the suburban and the rural. Labels have changed for each term of this opposition, as have researchers' understandings of how best to conceptualize its basic elements and the nature of their articulation. Yet, across otherwise divergent epistemological, methodological, and political traditions, most of twentieth-century urban studies rested upon the underlying assumption that cities represent a particular type of territory that could be defined in opposition to other, differently configured territories that lay beyond or outside its boundaries.

This vision of the urban was famously and precisely crystallized in Ernest Burgess's classic concentric rings diagram from 1921, in which "the" city (actually a cipher for early twentieth-century Chicago) was defined as a series of neatly delineated territorial zones stretching outward from a geometrically positioned center into suburbia and, ultimately, toward an empty horizon of the countryside.[1] Beginning almost immediately after its publication,

---

[1] Robert Park and Ernest Burgess, eds., *The City* (Chicago: University of Chicago Press, 1967 [1925]).

Burgess's model was criticized and reformulated. Some scholars redrew the contours of the diagram to capture more accurately the internal spatial patterning of city life; others questioned the theory of human ecology on which it was grounded. Nonetheless, even amid these variegated research initiatives, Burgess's vision of urban space epitomized the metageographical unconscious—a hidden yet nearly all-pervasive framework of assumptions regarding spatial organization—that underpinned much of twentieth-century urban studies. Across otherwise divergent politico-intellectual traditions, the city was conceived, at core, as a bounded territorial area whose specificity could be most effectively grasped by contrasting it to other areas from which it was presumed to be distinct. Until relatively recently, this underlying assumption served as an epistemological bedrock for the entire field of urban studies, not only within the venerable Chicago school tradition that Burgess helped to establish, but even within more radical or critical scholarly traditions, including Marxism, that sought explicitly to transcend this tradition.[2]

In effect, this amounted to a *horizontal* cartography of the urban question. Modern capitalism was envisioned as an extended territorial landscape on which different types of settlement space (urban, suburban, rural) were juxtaposed, with greater or lesser degrees of coherence, discretenesss, and boundedness, to create a patchwork quilt of areal differentiation. This mapping can be understood as territorial in the specific sense that, like the political jurisdictions of the modern Westphalian interstate system, its components were assumed to be bounded, contiguous, nonoverlapping, and encompassing.[3] The demarcations separating urban, suburban, and rural spaces were understood to shift historically, but the spaces themselves

---

[2] Neil Brenner and Christian Schmid, "Towards a New Epistemology of the Urban?," *CITY* 19, no. 2–3 (2015): 151–82; Neil Brenner and Christian Schmid, "The 'Urban Age' in Question," *International Journal of Urban and Regional Research* 38, no. 3 (2013): 731–55; Neil Brenner, "Urban Revolution?," in *Critique of Urbanization: Selected Essays* (Basel: Bauwelt Fundamente/Birkhäuser Verlag, 2016), 192–211; and Neil Brenner, ed., *Implosions/Explosions: Towards a Study of Planetary Urbanization* (Berlin: Jovis, 2014).

[3] The classical theorization of this Westphalian conception of territory is John Gerard Ruggie, "Territoriality and Beyond: Problematizing Modernity in International Relations," *International Organization* 47, no. 1 (1993): 139–74. See also, foundationally, John Agnew and Stuart Corbridge, *Mastering Space: Hegemony, Territory, and International Political Economy* (New York: Routledge, 1995). For further elaborations on the rich, polyvalent, and contested concept of territory in modern social, political, and spatial theory, see Stuart Elden, "Land, Terrain, Territory," *Progress in Human Geography* 34, no. 6 (2010): 799–817; Stuart Elden, "Missing the Point: Globalisation, Deterritorialisation and the Space of the World," *Transactions of the Institute of British Geographers* 30 (2005): 8–19; Neil Brenner and Stuart Elden, "Henri Lefebvre on State, Space, Territory," *International Political Sociology* 3, no. 4 (2009): 353–77; and Christian Schmid, "The

were assumed to remain discreet (defined with reference to their internally specific features), distinct (geographically separated from one another), exclusive (encompassing the entirety of a zone), and universal (abiding, transcontextual features of human settlement).

During the mid- to late twentieth century, as the field of urban studies matured and evolved, several subterranean theoretical explorations began to unsettle the prevalent metageographical unconscious of urban studies, and thus to suggest the possibility of alternative conceptualizations of the field, its research focus, and its methods. One of the most important strategies to this end, which had been pioneered as early as the 1930s but which was not broadly consolidated until the early 1990s, entailed demarcating the urban not as a territory, but as a *scale*. In this alternative approach, urban space was delineated not through a horizontal contrast of cities to other (suburban or rural) settlement zones, but instead through a *vertical* positioning of urban scales within dynamically evolving, multitiered organizational-geographical configurations. In addition to the urban scale, such configurations were generally assumed to include at least three other key scales—the regional, the national, and the worldwide or global. Sometimes other scales were also considered—for instance, the body, the neighborhood, the local, the metropolitan, the supranational, and the continental.

In each case, the urban was conceptualized less as a bounded areal unit—the container of the city—than as a sociospatial *relation* embedded within a broader, dynamically evolving whole. It was constituted not through the demarcation of a territorial area, but through the crystallization of a sociospatial *positionality* within a broader, multiscalar framework of relationships. As such, the urban was understood to entail determinate sociospatial operations, practices, contours, and parameters, but these were thought to evolve fluidly, sometimes dramatically, within the larger framework of interscalar relationships in which they were enmeshed. The relationships in question—economic, institutional, political, cultural, ecological—encompassed many scales while also provisionally weaving them together to forge historically specific, temporarily stabilized interscalar configurations. To be sure, these emergent scalar explorations diverged, sometimes drastically, in their specific definitional framings of the urban phenomenon. Despite this, they shared a basic concern to conceptualize the urban not as a unit or type of settlement space, but as a vibrant force field of sociospatial practices defined through its relational embeddedness and shifting positionality within

Urbanization of the Territory: On the Research Approach of ETH Studio Basel," in *Territory: On the Development of Landscape and City*, ed. ETH Studio Basel (Zurich: Park Books, 2016), 22–48.

a broader, interscalar framework of patterned, regularized sociospatial interdependencies.

Early experiments with a scalar approach to urban questions, articulated from diverse politico-epistemological standpoints, were implicit within several heterodox traditions of midcentury and postwar urban geography, planning, and regional science, from Walter Christaller's central place theory, Robert Dickinson's studies of urban settlement systems, and Jean Gottmann's approach to megalopolis formation to the wide-ranging studies of urban boundaries, systems, and hierarchies produced by scholars such as Brian Berry, John Friedmann, and Allan Pred.[4] Whatever their differences of conceptual grammar, methodology, and research focus, such approaches shared a concern to transcend narrowly territorialist, areal, or localist understandings of the urban, and thus to explore the broader sociospatial configurations produced through the dynamics of urbanization. However, even as they tentatively began to explore the implications of a scalar *problematique*, the spatial imaginaries of these broadly heterodox postwar explorations were mainly focused on other dimensions of urbanization processes—nodality and agglomeration, for instance, or connectivity and networking, or the functional differentiation of territories. It was only in the 1980s, with the development of a new "lexicon of geographical scale" (Neil Smith) in the field of historical-materialist geopolitical economy, that scholars began directly, systematically, and reflexively to elaborate the elements of a "scalar turn" for urban theory.[5]

---

[4] See, for example, Walter Christaller, *Central Places in Southern Germany*, trans. Carlisle W. Baskin (Englewood Cliffs, NJ: Prentice Hall, 1966 [1933]); Robert E. Dickinson, *City and Region: A Geographical Interpretation* (London: Routledge and Kegan Paul, 1964); Jean Gottmann, *Megalopolis: The Urbanized Northeastern Seaboard of the United States* (Cambridge, MA: MIT Press, 1961); Brian Berry and Frank E. Horton, eds., *Geographic Perspectives on Urban Systems* (Englewood Cliffs, NJ: Prentice Hall, 1970); John Friedmann and Clyde Weaver, *Territory and Function: The Evolution of Regional Planning* (Berkeley: University of California Press, 1979); and Allan Pred, *City-Systems in Advanced Economies* (London: Hutchinson, 1977).

[5] Neil Smith had begun to elaborate the elements of this scalar turn in his classic volume, *Uneven Development Nature, Capital and the Production of Space* (New York: Blackwell, 1984). He subsequently elaborated some of its key elements in a series of essays and articles, including Neil Smith, "Homeless/Global: Scaling Places," in *Mapping the Futures*, ed. Jon Bird, Barry Curtis, Tim Putnam, and Lisa Tickner (New York: Routledge, 1993), 87–119; Neil Smith, "Geography, Difference and the Politics of Scale," in *Postmodernism and the Social Sciences*, ed. Joe Doherty, Elspeth Graham, and Mo Malek (New York: St. Martin's Press, 1992), 57–79; Neil Smith, "Remaking Scale: Competition and Cooperation in Prenational and Postnational Europe," in *Competitive European Peripheries*, ed. Heikki Eskelinen and Folke Snickars (Berlin: Springer Verlag, 1995), 59–74; and Neil Smith and Dennis Ward, "The Restructuring of Geographical Scale: Coalescence and Fragmentation of the Northern Core Region," *Economic Geography* 63, no. 2 (1987): 160–82. Another early engagement with scale questions in historical-geographical materialist social theory was by Peter J. Taylor, especially in his book, *Political*

Scale had, of course, long been a key concept in human geography, but its intellectual foundations were reinvented as of the 1980s in conjunction with emergent concerns with worldwide capitalist restructuring and associated debates on "globalization."[6] Within this emergent literature on the "new political economy of scale," all scales, whether urban or supraurban, were understood to be socially produced, politically contested, and thus historically malleable.[7] Moreover, such scaling and rescaling processes were now shown to be closely intertwined with broader processes of political-economic restructuring, including geoeconomic integration, the remaking of statehood, and the production of new patterns of urban and regional development. This meant that any scalar hierarchy—and, indeed, any putatively fixed unit, level, stratum, or tier within it—had a rich historical geography that was (1) mediated through power relations, state regulatory strategies, and sociopolitical struggles and (2) potentially mutable through sociopolitical contestation. Deciphering such volatile scalar geographies of power and struggle was thus an essential task for critical research, not least within the field of critical urban studies. Subsequently, alongside recently reinvigorated notions of place, territory, and space, the new lexicon of geographical scale came to offer urbanists a powerful new conceptual tool through which to investigate, in rigorously relational terms, the changing geographies of urbanization, both historically and under contemporary conditions.

The explosion of interest in the new political economy of scale dovetailed with the development of what is today known as global city theory and, more generally, with the elaboration of critical approaches to globalized

---

Geography: World-Economy, Nation-State and Locality (New York: Longman, 1985). See also Peter J. Taylor, "A Materialist Framework for Political Geography," *Transactions of the Institute of British Geographers* 7 (1982): 15–34; and Peter J. Taylor, "Geographical Scales within the World-Economy Approach," *Review* 5, no. 1 (1981): 3–11.

[6] See, for example, Erik Swyngedouw, "The Mammon Quest: 'Glocalisation,' Interspatial Competition, and the Monetary Order: The Construction of New Scales," in *Cities and Regions in the New Europe*, ed. Mick Dunford and Grigoris Kafkalas (London: Belhaven Press, 1992), 39–68; Erik Swyngedouw, "The Heart of the Place: The Resurrection of Locality in an Age of Hyperspace," *Geografiska Annaler B* 71 (1989): 31–42; Erik Swyngedouw, "Neither Global nor Local: 'Glocalization' and the Politics of Scale," in *Spaces of Globalization*, ed. Kevin Cox (New York: Guilford Press, 1997), 137–66; Alain Lipietz, "The Local and the Global: Regional Individuality or Interregionalism?," *Transactions of the Institute of British Geographers* 18, no. 1 (1993): 8–18; and Jamie Peck and Adam Tickell, "Searching for a New Institutional Fix: The After-Fordist Crisis and the Global-Local Disorder," in *Post-Fordism: A Reader*, ed. Ash Amin (Cambridge, MA: Blackwell, 1994), 280–315.

[7] For a useful overview of this literature and associated debates, see Roger Keil and Rianne Mahon, eds., *Leviathan Undone? The New Political Economy of Scale* (Vancouver: University of British Columbia Press, 2010).

urbanization.[8] Insofar as the connections between geoeconomic restructuring and the remaking of urban space have figured crucially in studies of globalizing cities, questions of scale have been central to key aspects of theory, methodology, and concrete research in this field of inquiry. Initially, this took the form of investigations of the so-called global/local nexus, in which scholars debated how best to conceptualize and investigate the changing modes of insertion of urban spaces into global circuits of capital, commodities, and labor. Subsequently, more differentiated approaches to scalar questions, rescaling processes, and the politics of scale were developed. In contrast to then-prevalent discourses predicting the end of geography and the construction of a borderless world, the process of "globalization" was now recast as an uneven, contested, and ongoing rearticulation of interscalar relations in conjunction with the destabilization of historically entrenched, nationally organized formations of capitalism and their associated regulatory institutions. This conceptual reorientation enabled scholars to investigate how cities and urban systems were being (re)inserted into worldwide divisions of labor and their changing positionalities in relation to a broad range of political-economic rescaling processes, including the restructuring of national states and national economies. Questions of territorial regulation—a key terrain and medium of rescaling—were thus now also systematically integrated into debates on emergent scalar geographies of urban life. Against this background, scholars of contentious politics also began to explore the implications of ongoing rescaling processes for patterns of sociopolitical mobilization and, more specifically, for the dynamics of urban social movements.

With the further refinement of scalar concepts during the 1990s, major subfields of urban research—including studies of urban hierarchy, urban form, urban politics, urban governance, urban economic restructuring, gentrification, sociospatial polarization, urban social movements, and urban political ecology—were being recast in reflexively scalar terms. Scale was now recognized as a key dimension of urbanization, and meanwhile there was an impressive outpouring of research on cities as arenas and targets for diverse forms of rescaling. The classic concern with urban place-making and urban territorial organization remained robust, of course, and an emergent research agenda on worldwide interurban connectivity likewise began to generate considerable interest, perhaps most famously due to Manuel Castells's

---

[8] For a general overview of this literature, see Neil Brenner and Roger Keil, eds., *The Global Cities Reader* (New York: Routledge, 2006). Key contributions to this literature are discussed at length in Chapter 4.

influential theories of the network society.[9] Nonetheless, by the early 2000s, the question of scale had become a pervasive conceptual and methodological reference point in major strands of urban theory and research, across otherwise quite diverse fields of investigation. Was the urban question being transformed into a scale question?

Threads of a Problematique

This book is devoted to a systematic exploration of the broad *problematique* associated with the reflexive mobilization of scalar narratives, scalar categories, and scale-attuned methods in the field of critical urban studies since the early 1990s. Its guiding questions are the following: In what sense can the urban question be reframed as a scale question? What conceptualizations of scale—and of the urban scale in particular—are most appropriate for such an exploration? What are the theoretical, methodological, and empirical consequences of such a scalar reframing? How does a scalar analytics transform our understanding of the unit, site, and object of urban research? To what degree, and in what ways, can and should "the city" remain a central analytical construct and empirical focal point in a scale-attuned approach to the urban question? What are the implications of scale-attuned approaches to urban theory and research for interpretations of contemporary patterns of urban restructuring? What are the implications of such approaches for the investigation of restructuring processes within specific places, regions, and territories? Finally, what are the appropriate conceptual parameters for scalar approaches to urban questions? In other words, are there limits to scale as an explanatory, interpretive, and descriptive category?

Aside from this opening chapter, earlier versions of the writings included in this book have been published previously, mostly in journals of urban studies, geography, sociospatial theory, and geopolitical economy, as well as in edited volumes devoted to those research fields. Chapters 2, 9, and 10 have been completely rewritten and significantly expanded. All other chapters have also been revised substantially to enhance analytical precision, to improve stylistic clarity, and to weave together more tightly the common threads of argumentation, conceptualization, and inquiry that connect them. New bibliographic references have also been selectively added to reflect more recent research and lines of scholarly debate. However, I have resisted the temptation to modify the main substantive arguments of the texts included

---

[9] Manuel Castells, *The Rise of the Network Society* (Cambridge, MA: Blackwell, 1996).

here, to update the empirical investigations upon which they build, or to present them in the form of an encompassing theoretical synthesis. In thus proceeding, I have sought to preserve the analytical integrity and contextual specificity of each text while also highlighting the fluid, exploratory nature of my own, still-ongoing efforts to develop appropriate conceptual tools, scalar and otherwise, for deciphering emergent urban transformations and, more generally, for demarcating the relentlessly mutating terrain of the urban question.

This procedure reflects two intentions. First, this book brings together an otherwise widely dispersed series of writings that have explored a shared theoretical *problematique* on scale questions in contemporary urban theory while also seeking to reconceptualize the spatial parameters of urban re-search in ways that help illuminate the rapidly mutating landscapes of ur-banization that have been crystallizing in recent decades. In so doing, my goal is to put into clear relief the main intellectual concerns, conceptual orientations, methodological commitments, and research agendas that have animated my explorations of this *problematique*, and that continue to guide my work. Accordingly, I have selected texts that most clearly articulate the key elements of my evolving approach to such issues in relation to specific terrains of investigation and arenas of conceptual experimentation. Many of these studies have involved more concrete modes of investigation, especially in relation to the remaking of urban, regional, and territorial governance in the North Atlantic zone. Others have involved engagements with parallel theoretical or methodological debates in urban studies on, among other topics, post-Fordism, territorial regulation, global cities, neoliberalization, comparative methods, the politics of space, the right to the city, and, most recently, planetary urbanization. All have entailed a systematic elaboration of scalar epistemologies, concepts, methods, and cartographies to decipher key aspects of emergent urbanization processes.

Second, the organizational architecture of this volume reflects my un-derstanding, and my practice, of urban *theorizing*.[10] Consistent with the di-alectical traditions of social theory in which I situate my work, I have never intended my contributions to debates on the urban question to "lock in" a fixed, complete, or comprehensive interpretive framework.[11] Indeed, because

---

[10] On the practice, process, and stakes of theorizing in urban studies, see Jennifer Robinson, "New Geographies of Theorizing the Urban: Putting Comparison to Work for Global Urban Studies," in *The Routledge Handbook on Cities of the Global South*, ed. Susan Parnell and Sophie Oldfield (London: Routledge, 2014), 57–70.

[11] Neil Brenner, *Critique of Urbanization: Selected Essays* (Basel: Bauwelt Fundamente/Birkhäuser Verlag, 2016).

they are thoroughly enmeshed within the contradictory, restlessly mutating sociospatial relations they aspire to illuminate, dialectical conceptualizations of urban questions are not, and cannot ever be, a definitive "capture" of an ontologically fixed condition. Rather, they represent dynamically evolving, partial, and incomplete efforts to decipher the endlessly churning maelstrom of capitalist urbanization in which theorists, like all social researchers, are ineluctably situated. Consequently, as Jennifer Robinson explains, urban theory "should be practiced and conceptualized as radically revisable," not least because its site and focal point, the urban, is "a political and practical achievement . . . made through political contestation."[12] In precisely this sense, my writings on scale and the urban question are intended as part of what Robinson has appropriately characterized as a collective endeavor to "destabilize the terms of the urban and set in motion conversations towards its on-going reinvention."[13] They offer no more than an exploratory theoretical *orientation*—a basis for posing and investigating a range of questions related to conceptualizations of the urban, and for tracking their variegated methodological, interpretive, and political implications across sites, contexts, and territories. For this reason, it seems most consonant with my own particular way of "doing theory" to present some of its main results to date in the relatively fluid, open-ended format of this book.

Several chapters intersect in their articulation of certain core theoretical arguments—for instance, regarding the specificity of scale (or, more precisely, scaling/rescaling processes) as one among several key dimensions of sociospatial relations under capitalism; on the intensification of rescaling processes since the geoeconomic crises of the 1970s; on the limits and blind spots of methodologically localist or city-centric approaches to urban research; on the consequences of reflexively multiscalar epistemologies, concepts, and methods for the demarcation of urban studies as a research field; on the key role of state spatial strategies in mediating and animating the production of new urban spaces; on the dialectical interplay between post-1970s patterns of urban restructuring and the production of post-Keynesian state spaces; on the continued forward motion and ongoing, crisis-induced reconstitution of political strategies to rescale urban space; and on the methodological dangers of overextending scalar concepts beyond their proper domain of application. Rather than being merely repeated, however, these and other key strands of argumentation are interwoven across the

---

[12] Robinson, "New Geographies of Theorizing the Urban," 67.

[13] Ibid.

book's chapters, in relation to a range of scholarly literatures and research foci, in order to build—and to *apply*—a scale-attuned approach to contemporary urban questions. In this way, the book's main arguments emerge less through a linear unfolding than through the layering together of distinct yet interconnected critical investigations of a core *problematique*.

State Rescaling and the Urban Question

In exploring the centrality of scale questions in urban theory, this book devotes considerable attention to the role of state spatial strategies (and their changing scalar articulations) in mediating, managing, animating, and canalizing the remaking of urban space during successive cycles of capital accumulation and crisis formation. This analysis stands in stark contrast to influential strands of contemporary urban studies that bracket or background the state's pervasive, multiscalar role in shaping and reshaping the urban process under capitalism—whether due to a one-sided methodological localism (often connected to an empirical focus on municipal governance arrangements), an embrace of problematic "state decline" arguments (often derived from uncritical discourses on "globalization"), or an equally questionable belief in the neoliberal ideology of self-regulating markets (which still pervades much of mainstream global urban discourse). Against such "state denialist" approaches, the conceptual framework developed in this book treats urban space and state space as intricately entangled, mutually co-constituting and conflictually coevolving formations of scale-differentiated sociospatial relations under modern capitalism.[14] Building especially on the work of radical sociospatial theorists David Harvey and Henri Lefebvre, Chapter 2 develops this argument in abstract, theoretical terms while also broadly contextualizing it in relation to the historical geographies of capitalist development during the last 150 years, in which the institutional, infrastructural, and interscalar mesh connecting urban space and state space has been thickened considerably. Subsequent chapters explore the various ways in which state spatial strategies have shaped the production and transformation of urban space during the last four decades, in conjunction with multiscalar processes of neoliberal regulatory creative destruction.[15]

---

[14] The concept of "state denial" is derived from Linda Weiss, *The Myth of the Powerless State* (London: Policy, 1998).

[15] David Harvey, "Neoliberalism as Creative Destruction," *Annals of the American Academy of Political and Social Science* 610 (2007): 22–44; Neil Brenner and Nik Theodore, "Cities and the

This is a theme I have explored extensively in earlier work, particularly in a previous book, *New State Spaces*.[16] In that context, I was likewise concerned with the interplay between urban restructuring and state restructuring, but the main *explanandum* of my investigation was the rescaling of state space. Accordingly, urban governance was treated as an analytical window through which to decipher the changing spatial and scalar selectivities of modern state power during the Fordist-Keynesian period and, subsequently, with the development of what I termed Rescaled Competition State Regimes (RCSRs). Several texts included in the present volume (especially Chapters 4, 5, and 6) are closely connected to that line of investigation, but their analytical focus here is precisely inverted. As its title indicates, the central concern of this book is the production of new *urban* spaces. Accordingly, processes of state rescaling (the "new state spaces" of my previous work) are considered mainly with reference to their variegated impacts on the capitalist urban fabric. As several chapters of this book argue, these impacts have been profound. New urban spaces have been actively forged through the aggressive, and often socially and politically regressive, rescaling of state space during the last four decades. More specifically, the production of neoliberalized regimes of urbanization has occurred in large measure through spatial and scalar transformations of statecraft that have extended, institutionalized, and normalized market discipline across the urban fabric while also targeting certain strategic sites within each territory for intensified transnational investment, advanced infrastructure development, and enhanced global connectivity. This has permitted certain metropolitan "islands," as well as selected inter-metropolitan logistics corridors and enclaves of emergent hinterland industrialization, to be much more tightly interlinked across planetary space. However, it has also entailed an increasing splintering of the capitalist urban fabric as a whole, generally in ways that have eroded the isomorphic articulation of national territories and national urban systems that had been pursued within earlier regimes of spatial Keynesianism, national developmentalism, and urban managerialism.[17]

Geographies of 'Actually Existing Neoliberalism,'" in *Spaces of Neoliberalism*, ed. Neil Brenner and Nik Theodore (Oxford: Blackwell, 2002).

[16] Neil Brenner, *New State Spaces: Urban Governance and the Rescaling of Statehood* (New York: Oxford University Press, 2004).

[17] The paradigmatic account of this "splintering" of the planetary urban fabric is Stephen Graham and Simon Marvin, *Splintering Urbanism: Networked Infrastructures, Technological Mobilities and the Urban Condition* (New York: Routledge, 2001).

One major consequence of this tendential scalar disarticulation of state space and the capitalist urban fabric has been to destabilize the entrenched centrality of the national scale as the encompassing "power container" of modern political-economic life, leading to a situation Chris Collinge has aptly described as a "relativization of scales."[18] Under conditions of scale relativization, as Bob Jessop has explained, the taken-for-grantedness of national space is undermined as the relations between global, supranational, national, and subnational scales of political-economic activity are systematically reshuffled; there is no hegemonic or dominant scale of sociospatial relations.[19] Instead, the scalar configuration of key political-economic processes—including capital accumulation, territorial regulation, social reproduction, and political mobilization—becomes more fluid, more immediately subject to intense contestation, and thus more susceptible to the prospect of being reorganized, whether in incremental or in radical ways. This, in turn, undermines any isomorphism or convergence that may have, at least in tendential form, previously characterized the scalar geographies of such processes and associated patterns of uneven development, especially during the North Atlantic Fordist, national-developmentalist period in the second half of the twentieth century. Consequently, particularly since the 1980s, the vision of hierarchically structured, precision-nested scalar arrangements serving as a shared sociospatial meta-architecture for major political-economic processes has become increasingly obsolete. Instead, we have been experiencing a proliferation of more tangled, haphazardly intercalated, and unevenly patterned scalar arrangements across the planetary sociospatial landscape, each connected to specific political-economic operations, strategies, and struggles. Under these conditions, the capitalist urban fabric is no longer organized as an encompassing, worldwide grid of national city-systems, neatly subdivided into internal central place hierarchies, but is instead unevenly differentiated among variegated places, regions, territories, and landscapes whose mottled connective tissue more closely resembles that of an intricately stitched latticework than a simple pyramid, hierarchy, or grid.

---

[18] See Chris Collinge, "Spatial Articulation of the State: Reworking Social Relations and Social Regulation Theory" (unpublished manuscript, Centre for Urban and Regional Studies, Birmingham, 1996). On the notion of the national state (and thus the national scale) as a power container, see Anthony Giddens, *A Contemporary Critique of Historical Materialism* (Berkeley: University of California Press, 1985).

[19] Bob Jessop, "The Crisis of the National Spatio-Temporal Fix and the Ecological Dominance of Globalizing Capitalism," *International Journal of Urban and Regional Research* 24, no. 2 (2000): 323–60.

Despite their apparently unstructured complexity, their intense institutional differentiation, their spatially fragmenting impacts, and their aggressively polarizing, market-disciplinary logics, these processes of scale relativization have not been associated with a diminished role for state institutions in the shaping and reshaping of the capitalist urban fabric. The scalar geographies of state power have shifted in epochally significant ways, but state spatial strategies continue to mediate, animate, and canalize urbanization, and its associated crisis tendencies, in pervasively powerful ways, across contexts and territories, worldwide. A key challenge for urban theorists, therefore, is to develop new conceptual frameworks through which to decipher the state's intensive, if perpetually evolving, roles in the structuration of urbanization processes under the scale-relativized worldwide conditions of the post-1980s period. This requires not only a spatialized, scale-attuned reconceptualization of statehood—a task to which I devoted much of *New State Spaces*—but also, as I contend in what follows, a rather fundamental retheorization of urbanization itself.

The Fabric of Urbanization

One of the most essential, if also controversial, epistemological implications of the combined scale-theoretical and state-theoretical approach developed here is further to decenter what geographer Terry McGee concisely described nearly a half century ago as "city dominant" approaches to the modern urban condition.[20] In more recent years, such approaches have been aptly characterized under the rubric of "methodological cityism": their hallmark is (1) to presuppose unreflexively the "city"—generally understood as a territorially bounded, sociologically distinctive spatial cluster—as a pregiven, self-evident, or universal unit of analysis and, concomitantly, (2) to conceive the entirety of non-*city* space, by definition, as a non-*urban* or "rural" zone.[21]

---

[20] Terry McGee, "The Urbanization Process: Western Theory and Third World Reality," in *The Urbanization Process in the Third World* (London: Bell and Sons, 1971), 12–34.

[21] The concept of methodological cityism was developed by Hillary Angelo and David Wachsmuth in their critical reformulation of recent work in urban political ecology. See their foundational article, "Urbanizing Urban Political Ecology: A Critique of Methodological Cityism," *International Journal of Urban and Regional Research* 39, no. 1 (2015): 16–27. As conceived here, this methodological tendency entails not only a naturalization of the "city" as a unit of analysis but the unreflexive separation of that unit, both in analytical and in geographical terms, from a putatively exterior, "non-city" domain. For additional reflections on the ideological dimensions of the city concept, see Hillary Angelo, "From the City Lens toward Urbanisation as a Way of Seeing: Country/City Binaries on an Urbanising Planet," *Urban Studies* 54, no. 1 (2016): 158–78; David Wachsmuth, "City as Ideology: Reconciling the Explosion of the City

One of the more unorthodox, if not downright heretical, arguments of this book, which builds strongly upon a thesis proposed by Henri Lefebvre in the 1970s, is that the urban condition—and, more generally, the process of urbanization under modern capitalism—cannot be reduced to the sociospatial entities that are conventionally labeled as "cities."[22]

The city, I argue, is only one element within, and expression of, the multiscalar, polymorphic, and restlessly mutating geographies of capitalist urbanization. These are constituted through the relentless *implosion* of sociospatial processes into dense centers of population, infrastructure, and economic activity and through the equally dynamic *explosion* of sociospatial relations across vast territories, landscapes, and ecologies that are likewise being perpetually enclosed, operationalized, industrialized, and creatively destroyed in support of capital's voracious, profit-driven metabolism, whether for purposes of industrialized agriculture, extraction, energy generation, logistics, waste processing, environmental management, or otherwise.[23] Consequently, especially with the intensifying, accelerating, and increasingly worldwide industrialization of capital during the course of the twentieth century, the city and the urban—two of the foundational keywords of urban studies—must be analytically distinguished. Doing so, I submit, permits a more theoretically precise, historically and contextually nuanced understanding of both terms of this relationship and its ongoing historical evolution under modern capitalism.

While several chapters of this book devote extensive attention to the globally networked metropolitan islands of the "world city archipelago," the scalar analytics thereby developed also subvert the conventional definitional equation of urbanization with the growth of cities as specific, distinct, bounded, and localized spatial units, as well as the ontology of "naïve objectivism" that

---

Form with the Tenacity of the City Concept," *Environment and Planning D: Society and Space* 32, no. 1 (2014): 75–90; David Cunningham, "The Concept of Metropolis: Philosophy and Urban Form," *Radical Philosophy* 133 (September/October 2005): 13–25; and Kanishka Goonewardena, "The Urban Sensorium: Space, Ideology and the Aestheticization of Politics," *Antipode* 37, no. 1 (2005): 46–71. More generally, on the production of spatial ideologies, see Henri Lefebvre, "Reflections on the Politics of Space," in *State, Space, World*, ed. Neil Brenner and Stuart Elden (Minneapolis: University of Minnesota Press, 2009 [1970]), 167–84.

[22] Henri Lefebvre, *The Urban Revolution*, trans. Robert Bononno (Minneapolis: University of Minnesota Press, 2003 [1970]).

[23] See Brenner and Schmid, "Towards a New Epistemology"; Brenner, "Urban Revolution?"; Brenner, *Implosions/Explosions*; Martín Arboleda, "In the Nature of the Non-City: Expanded Infrastructural Networks and the Political Ecology of Planetary Urbanisation," *Antipode* 48, no. 2 (2016): 233–51; and Martín Arboleda, "Spaces of Extraction, Metropolitan Explosions: Planetary Urbanization and the Commodity Boom in Latin America," *International Journal of Urban and Regional Research* 40, no. 1 (2016): 96–112.

is generally presupposed within such definitions.[24] To the degree that studies of urban questions focus primarily or exclusively on these metropolitan islands and their translocal connections, they tend to bracket the broader, politically mediated transformations of interscalar relations from which such apparently localized spaces have been wrought, and which they have, in turn, actively accelerated and intensified. Crucially, however, the point of this critique of methodological cityism is not to deny the importance of agglomeration economies, nodal connectivity, spatial density, or local politics to the dynamics of urbanization, or to suggest that large, dense metropolitan areas do not exist or do not matter for political-economic processes under capitalism. The claim, rather, is that such conditions, processes, and terrains of struggle can only be understood adequately within a broader, multiscalar field of sociospatial relations that constitutes and continually reweaves the capitalist urban fabric as a whole. We need, in other words, a multiscalar yet territorially differentiated conceptualization of urban space itself, and of the geographies of urbanization, to decipher (1) the variegated patterns and scales in which the sociospatial relations of agglomeration are produced, contested, and reworked and (2) the evolving supralocal crystallizations, parameters, and consequences of urbanization processes under capitalism.

The Lefebvrian notion of the capitalist urban fabric (*le tissu urbain*), which is elaborated at length in Chapter 2, offers a solid foundation for such a multiscalar reconceptualization, one that includes agglomeration processes (the moment of *implosion*) as well as the construction and continual reorganization of operational landscapes that support and, quite literally, metabolize such processes (the moment of *explosion*). Subsequent chapters investigate the fluidly mutating, constitutively uneven geographies of the capitalist urban fabric in the North Atlantic zone and beyond since the 1970s and the role of state spatial strategies in mediating and animating those mutations. In thus proceeding, I also critically engage some of the major strands of methodological cityism that have infused prominent approaches to contemporary urban studies, especially within the scholarly literatures on global cities, urban entrepreneurialism, informational cities, the new regionalism,

---

[24] On the world city "archipelago," see Peter J. Taylor, *World-City Network: A Global Urban Analysis* (London: Routledge, 2004); and, more recently, David Bassens and Michiel van Meeteren, "World Cities and the Uneven Geographies of Financialization: Unveiling Stratification and Hierarchy in the World City Archipelago," *International Journal of Urban and Regional Research* 40, no. 1 (2016): 62–81. On the problem of naïve objectivism in social science, see Andrew Sayer, *Method in Social Science*, 2nd ed. (London: Routledge, 1992). As Sayer explains, such approaches ignore the conceptual mediation of social life and presuppose the capacity of social researchers to capture the "facts" through pure induction.

urban regimes, and urban growth machines. Those explorations reveal that each of these terrains of research and debate contains contradictory methodological tendencies, some of which reinforce the localist, territorialist, and naïve-objectivist precepts of methodological cityism, while others open up alternative, potentially productive methodological horizons for broader, relationally multiscalar imaginaries of urbanization processes, their variegated geographical crystallizations, and their fluid, contradictory metabolism. Through a series of critical readings of these approaches, I develop a more reflexively scale-attuned, state-theoretical approach to the capitalist urban fabric, with particular reference to the tumultuous, if constitutively uneven, sociospatial transformations of the last four decades. This approach is intended to help illuminate emergent patterns and pathways of urban restructuring, both within and beyond the sites of agglomeration (and associated settlement "units"), that have long monopolized the attention and imagination of urban researchers.

Contours of an Exploration

In sum, then, this book charts the contours of a multifaceted, open-ended, and still-ongoing exploration. Its chapters follow a pathway of focused questioning, defined by the scalar *problematique* outlined previously, and by the concerted search for conceptual tools and methodological strategies adequate to deciphering emergent rescalings of the worldwide urban fabric under late twentieth- and early twenty-first-century capitalism. They offer a variety of concepts, methods, and analytical openings in relation to specific sites, patterns, and trajectories of urban transformation, and they propose some interpretive inroads through which to decipher the latter, particularly in the North Atlantic context but also, potentially, in other global regions. They also present an alternative vision of urban studies that destabilizes the naturalized emphasis on the "city" as the field's exclusive, self-evidently necessary geographical focal point, offering instead a reconceptualization of capitalist urbanization as a process that includes the moments of city building and city *un*building, as well as the production and ongoing transformation of a multiscalar, territorially variegated urban fabric: an unevenly extended matrix of sociospatial relations, territorial configurations, infrastructural relays, and metabolic circuits that support or result from capitalist industrialization.[25] In thus proceeding, these writings also trace the process of theorizing

---

[25] The concept of unbuilding (*Abbau*) is derived from Lewis Mumford's classic analysis of the "paleotechnic" city in *The City in History* (New York: Harcourt, 1961), 446–81. This key concept

that grounds and animates my work—its abiding commitments, but also its continuous adaptation, mutation, and reconstitution in relation to ongoing urban transformations and shifting terrains of scholarly debate regarding the latter.

When I first began exploring the rescaling of the capitalist urban fabric in the mid- to late 1990s, debates on "globalization"—a "geographical euphemism" par excellence, as Neil Smith then observed—were in full bloom across the social sciences.[26] In that context, nascent conceptualizations of rescaling and reterritorialization, along with the more general notion of capitalist uneven spatial development inherited from previous decades of historical-geographical materialist theorizing, offered powerful methodological antidotes to then-popular visions of an increasingly borderless world economy, dominated by deterritorialized, putatively hypermobile capital whizzing across the "hyperspace" of postmodern capitalism. The elegantly simple yet far-reaching insight, initially developed by Neil Smith and Erik Swyngedouw, was that emergent forms of geoeconomic integration actually entailed new scalar crystallizations of capitalist territorial organization, and a new pattern of worldwide uneven spatial development, rather than the death of distance, the end of geography, the consolidation of a borderless world, and the smoothing out of entrenched sociospatial inequalities, as many academics, journalists, and policymakers were then proposing. My own subsequent theorizing about the shifting scalar dimensions of urbanization under capitalism built upon those intellectual foundations, and has been strongly energized by a concern to deconstruct some of the closely related spatial ideologies that have proliferated across the field of urban studies, planning, and policy in the wake of the globalization debates. These include a variety of ideas, assumptions, and narratives about global cities, urban regeneration, place marketing, the new localism, the new economy, interurban competition, the new regionalism, and the urban age.[27] As with any critique

---

underscores a far-reaching insight that also lies at the heart of David Harvey's approach to capitalist urbanization (discussed at length in Chapter 2): the same forces that construct large-scale urban sociospatial configurations may also deconstruct and destroy them, thus laying the groundwork for subsequent rounds of urban development. As I argue in subsequent chapters, this observation is also highly salient for exploring the scalar construction and deconstruction of the capitalist urban fabric.

[26] Neil Smith, "The Satanic Geographies of Globalization: Uneven Development in the 1990s," *Public Culture* 10, no. 1 (1997): 174. For a useful synthesis of critical approaches to the *problematique* of globalization, see Richard Appelbaum and William L. Robinson, eds., *Critical Globalization Studies* (New York: Routledge, 2005).

[27] Other currently popular urban spatial ideologies include contemporary discourses on smart cities, creative cities, eco-cities, urban sustainability, and urban resilience. While not explored

of urban ideology, the key task of such explorations is to deconstruct the claims to economic, cultural, and spatial hegemony that define, naturalize, and reproduce a particular urban condition or project and, in so doing, to demarcate the possibility for alternative forms of urbanization that inhere within, but are suppressed by, existing sociospatial arrangements, practices, and modes of understanding.[28]

Just as importantly, my pathway of theorizing has also been forged through a range of critical engagements with some of the diverse scholarly approaches to the urban question that have crystallized in recent decades, including those produced by other critically oriented urbanists. Whatever differences of epistemology, conceptual apparatus, methodological orientation, and analytical program have underpinned such exchanges, they have generally been animated by a shared concern to confront the wide-ranging challenges associated with deciphering emergent patterns and pathways of urban restructuring.[29] In my own work, this historically embedded, sociopolitically positioned understanding of critical urban theory is grounded upon a specific understanding of the relationship between (urban) theory and (urban) historical change.[30] Critical urban theory, I have long argued, develops in significant measure through the continual reinvention of its own concepts, methods, and concerns, in direct relation to the restlessly mutating spaces of urbanization in which it is embedded. Crucially, however, the radical revisability of critical urban theory stems not from some fixed ontological property of urban space—for instance,

---

in this book, these discourses likewise require careful critical deconstruction—see, for instance, Adam Greenfield, *Against the Smart City* (New York: Do projects, 2013); Jamie Peck, "Struggling with the Creative Class," *International Journal of Urban and Regional Research* 29, no. 4 (2005): 740–70; Timothy Luke, "Neither Sustainable nor Development: Reconsidering Sustainability in Development," *Sustainable Development* 13 (2005): 228–38; Lawrence J. Vale, "The Politics of Resilient Cities: Whose Resilience and Whose City?," *Building Research & Information* 42, no. 2 (2014): 191–201; and Susan Fainstein, "Resilience and Justice," *International Journal of Urban and Regional Research* 39, no. 1 (2015): 157–67. For further elaborations on the critique of spatial ideology as a key element within the project of critical urban theory, see Brenner, *Critique of Urbanization*, and the works cited in note 21.

[28] See Neil Brenner, "The *Problematique* of Critique" and "Critical Urban Theory, Reloaded? Dialogue with Martín Arboleda," in *Critique of Urbanization*, 16–24, 268–89.

[29] In this sense, my approach resonates with Ananya Roy's recent engagement with Edward Said's concept of "traveling theory" to situate the heterodox, heterogeneous projects of critical urban studies: they emerge and evolve as embedded yet oppositional responses to historically specific sociopolitical formations of urbanization. See Ananya Roy, "Worlding the South: Toward a Post-Colonial Urban Theory," in Parnell and Oldfield, *The Routledge Handbook on Cities of the Global South*, 16; and Edward Said, "Traveling Theory," in *The World, the Text and the Critic* (Cambridge, MA: Harvard University Press, 1983).

[30] See Neil Brenner, "What Is Critical Urban Theory?," in *Critique of Urbanization*, 25–41.

as being too complex or indeterminate to grasp in conceptual terms—but from the relentless sociohistorical *dynamism* of the "urban phenomenon" itself.[31] In other words, urban theory must be constantly reinvented because the geographies it seeks to illuminate, and in which it is itself situated, are continually being transformed. Hegel's famous early nineteenth-century invocation of the "owl of Minerva" in the preface to his *Philosophy of Right* (1820) presumably refers to this same dilemma: abstract concepts are always already outdated, because the dynamism of modern life continually transforms their conditions of possibility and fields of application by reworking the social worlds from which they emerge, and which they aspire to grasp.[32] In characterizing our urbanizing planet as a "virtual object," Henri Lefebvre evidently had something similar in mind: the field of urban theory is derived from historical geographies which it must constantly transcend in order to grasp emergent sociospatial transformations that continually appear on the horizon of practice, representation, thought, and imagination.[33]

One of the abiding challenges of critical urban theory is to chart an intellectual course that productively combines these distinct yet interwoven epistemological imperatives: (1) to maintain maximal reflexivity regarding the sociohistorical situatedness of all urban concepts, narratives, and representations; (2) to deconstruct dominant ideologies of urbanism that naturalize hegemonic sociospatial arrangements and the forms of domination, exclusion, marginalization, and social suffering they support; and (3) to anticipate emergent urban conditions, practices, and transformations and their wide-ranging implications for knowledge formations, everyday life, and the politics of space. This anticipatory epistemological orientation represents a notable, if generally overlooked, point of intellectual convergence between the Lefebvrian vision of the urban as a virtual object and contemporary postcolonial critiques of hegemonic urban knowledge formations.[34] Both

---

[31] The phrase is from Lefebvre, *Urban Revolution*, 45–76.

[32] On this reading of Hegel, see Fredric Jameson, *The Hegel Variations: On the Phenomenology of Spirit* (New York: Verso, 2014). The Minerva reference is from G. W. F. Hegel, "Preface," in *The Philosophy of Right*, trans. Alan White (Indianapolis: Focus-Hackett, 2002 [1820]), 10: "As the thought of the world, [philosophy] always appears only in the time after actuality has completed its process of cultivation, after it has finished. . . . When philosophy paints its grey in grey, then has a shape of life grown old . . . it cannot be rejuvenated, it can only be known; the owl of Minerva begins its flight only with the falling of dusk."

[33] Lefebvre, *Urban Revolution*, 16–17.

[34] On the latter, see Jennifer Robinson, "Comparative Urbanism: New Geographies and Cultures of Theorizing the Urban," *International Journal of Urban and Regional Research* 40, no. 1 (2016): 187–99; Ananya Roy, "Who's Afraid of Postcolonial Theory?," *International Journal*

positions require precisely an openness to—and, indeed, a reflexive anticipation of—the obsolescence and thus transcendence of the very conceptual frameworks upon which emergent urban processes, formations, and contestations are understood.

The studies presented in this book illustrate one analytical pathway through which such an epistemological orientation may be mobilized to track the vicissitudes of the urban question during a period of particularly tumultuous planetary transformation. Indeed, the following chapters endeavor not only to assemble the elements of a scalar approach to critical urban theory, but to critically assess the limits of such an approach. On this basis, especially in the book's final chapters, I also explore the possibility of further reinventing, and even superseding, the scalar concepts and methods initially proposed. The guiding question that animates these explorations— *Is the urban question a scale question?*—thus leads not only to a critique of city-centric approaches to the urban, to a series of closely associated conceptual recalibrations and methodological realignments, and to an alternative, constitutively multiscalar conceptualization of urban space, but eventually, to a fundamental reformulation of that initial framing of the urban question itself. Specifically, my explorations of the *problematique* of scale in urban theory generate a series of autocritical reflections that bring into focus some of the limitations of scalar—or, more precisely, scale-*centric*—interpretations of the urban question. This leads, on the one hand, to a respecification of the proper conceptual parameters for scale-attuned modes of interpretation in the face of the rich variegation, unevenness, and polymorphism of contemporary sociospatial transformations, including those associated with place-making, reterritorialization, and networking. More radically still, these autocritical reflections open up a new horizon of epistemological exploration that is embodied in a dramatically rescaled formulation of the urban question itself: *Is the urban question a scale question?* thus mutates into *Has urbanization become planetary?*

The reframing of the urban question outlined in the book's final two chapters is closely connected to a collaborative investigation of planetary urbanization with Christian Schmid.[35] This approach systematically builds upon, and yet in some ways also supersedes, the scalar framing that underpins the foregoing analyses. However, my supersession of scale in

---

of Urban and Regional Research 40, no. 1 (2016): 200–209; and Ananya Roy, "The 21st Century Metropolis: New Geographies of Theory," *Regional Studies* 43, no. 6 (2009): 819–30.

[35] See, especially, Brenner and Schmid, "Towards a New Epistemology"; Brenner and Schmid, "The 'Urban Age' in Question"; as well as the contributions to Brenner, *Implosions/Explosions*.

the book's final chapters must be understood not as a simple negation, but in the Hegelian-Marxian sense of an *Aufhebung* that at once preserves *and* transcends the framework from which it was formed. The book's main line of argumentation is thus configured as a spiral movement across levels of abstraction and several interconnected terrains of inquiry. It flows from a relatively abstract, reflexively scalar formulation of the urban question under modern capitalism (Chapters 2 and 3) toward a series of critical engagements with several major approaches to contemporary urban studies in conjunction with more concrete-complex pathways of investigation of post-1980s urban transformations in various zones of Euro-America (Chapters 4 to 7). This leads to a series of autocritical maneuvers that produce a relativization and *Aufhebung* of my initial scalar formulation of the urban question (Chapter 8) and that, finally, facilitate a reformulation of that question around the *problematique* of planetary urbanization, which simultaneously builds upon and transfigures the scalar analytics that were forged and deployed in earlier chapters (Chapters 9 and 10). The main elements of this spiral movement are summarized in Figure 1.1.

Outline of the Argument

Following this introductory overview, the subsequent two chapters assemble the theoretical foundations for an exploration of the urban question as a scale question. Chapter 2 excavates the distinctive scalar analytics that are embedded within several key ideas of David Harvey and Henri Lefebvre, with particular reference to the fixity/motion contradiction under capitalism, the concept of the urban fabric, the scalar intermeshing of urban space and state space, and the process of rescaling. This analysis generates a scale-attuned theorization of the capitalist urban fabric, as well as a state-theoretical under-standing of the process Lefebvre famously described as the "planetarization of the urban." Chapter 3 considers the ways in which, especially since the 1990s, the scalar dimensions of global urban restructuring have been re-flexively explored within several major streams of critical urban studies. Against the background of earlier rounds of debate on the spatiality of the urban question, I take stock of this apparent scalar turn in urban studies. What, I ask, is the theoretical specificity of a scalar approach to the produc-tion of new urban spaces? What are potential contributions and hazards of such an approach? A relatively narrow, but analytically precise, definitional proposal is offered, which destabilizes methodologically localist, city-centric understandings of the urban while also distinguishing processes of scalar structuration from other key dimensions of sociospatial relations related to

	THEORETICAL FOUNDATIONS	CRITICAL ELABORATIONS AND APPLICATIONS	AUTOCRITIQUE AND THEORETICAL RENOVATION
1	The urban question as a scale question: debates on scale and the urban question; foundations for a scale-attuned, state-theoretical approach to the capitalist urban fabric		
2			
3			
4		Political and economic geographies of rescaling: studies of the interplay between state rescaling and the rescaling of the capitalist urban fabric; critical engagement with the scalar imaginaries of major approaches to contemporary urban restructuring; critique of methodological cityism via the development of a relationally multiscalar, state-theoretical approach to capitalist urbanization	
5			
6			
7			
8			Toward a polymorphic theorization of urbanization and uneven spatial development; contemporary mutations of the urban question; debates on the variegated and uneven geographies of urbanization; critique of scale-centrism and city-centrism via an emergent theorization of extended/planetary urbanization; new rounds of rescaling related to "mega-urbanization" strategies
9			
10			

FIGURE 1.1 Organizational structure and logic of the book.

place-making, territorialization, and networking. This relatively abstract definitional foray is the first of several efforts in this book to demarcate and investigate the proper conceptual parameters of scale in relation to specific terrains of urban studies.

The core scalar explorations of this book are elaborated over the next four chapters, which seek to illuminate the interplay between urban restructuring and rescaling processes, particularly the rescaling of state space, during the post-1980s period (Chapters 4 to 7). These studies build upon the conceptual foundations developed in the opening chapters in order (1) to critically interrogate and, in some cases, to respecify and rework the scalar assumptions articulated within several major fields of contemporary urban theory and research; (2) to develop scale-attuned, state-theoretical analyses of post-1980s patterns and pathways of urban restructuring in the North Atlantic context; and (3) to demarcate some of the specific interpretive consequences that flow from approaches to the urban question that transcend inherited city-centric framings.

Chapter 4 interprets debates on global city formation through a reflexively scalar, state-theoretical lens. As a critical counterpoint to canonical metanarratives of global city formation, which have generally been grounded upon the proposition that state power is eroding under global capitalism, I argue that (rescaled) state institutions have figured centrally as animators and mediators of post-1970s urban sociospatial restructuring, including within putatively "global" or "globalizing" cities. The so-called new localism is, therefore, not the outgrowth of endogenous, bottom-up economic development but, in an important respect, the political expression of multiscalar state spatial strategies that seek to (re)position metropolitan regions in relation to emergent transnational spaces of accumulation. On this basis, I explore various ways in which the proliferation of multiscalar state strategies to reorganize the capitalist urban fabric has, in turn, engendered significant post-Keynesian, neoliberalizing transformations of state spatial and scalar organization. In this way, I present one of the key theses of this book: new urban spaces are produced through the rescaling of state space, and vice versa. This chapter also destabilizes the deeply entrenched assumption that cities represent the necessary, proper, or default unit of analysis for approaches to the urban question. The scalar units of urbanization processes are themselves produced and continually rewoven through the creatively destructive forward motion of capital and the intricate mediations of the latter through state spatial strategies and sociopolitical mobilization.

Chapters 5, 6, and 7 continue this line of argumentation with reference to several key terrains of debate on contemporary urban governance restructuring. Chapter 5 develops a scalar reinterpretation of contemporary political strategies to promote urban regeneration through the clustering of so-called new economy industries specialized in the production and deployment of advanced informational and communications technologies. In contrast to much of the hype and hyperbole that has surrounded the new economy concept, this analysis of European trends suggests that urban growth strategies oriented toward such firms and sectors have generally involved rescaled, broadly neoliberalized approaches to the regulation of uneven spatial development that seriously exacerbate, rather than resolve, the crisis tendencies of contemporary capitalism. However, despite their destabilizing macroeconomic consequences, and the often vague, ideologically slippery spatial visions attached to projects to promote a new economy, such neoliberalizing regulatory rescalings continue to play a key role in the production of new urban spaces and new forms of urbanization.

Chapter 6 presents a critical perspective on the "new regionalism" debate that has swept through important streams of urban and regional studies and economic geography since the 1980s. As in Chapter 5, I here mobilize a scalar analytics to question mainstream political metanarratives regarding the prospects for putatively endogenous, bottom-up political strategies to stimulate urban industrial regeneration. My analysis suggests that, at core, new regionalist programs have entailed a scalar recalibration of local financial, institutional, and regulatory failures, but without significantly impacting their underlying macrospatial causes, within or beyond major cities. Consequently, rather than counteracting the crisis tendencies and contradictions of post-Keynesian, neoliberalizing capitalism, the competition-oriented, market-disciplinary spatial politics of the new regionalism have perpetuated or exacerbated the latter. Its enduring consequences, to date, have been deepening economic crises, a further splintering of urban governance arrangements, intensifying territorial polarization, and pervasive regulatory disorder, rather than stable capitalist industrial growth or coherent territorial development.

Chapter 7 builds upon the scalar analytics developed in earlier chapters to decipher contemporary debates on urban growth machines and the post-1980s "entrepreneurial" remaking of local economic governance. In what sense, I ask, are urban growth machines, in fact, *urban*? Is it really "the city," as most of the scholarly literature suggests, that serves as the optimal or natural spatial locus for urban regime formation and growth machine strategies? To address such questions, I excavate several key arguments from John Logan and Harvey Molotch's seminal work on this topic. This analysis raises some doubts regarding an influential contemporary critique of Logan and Molotch's work for its putative methodological localism, suggesting instead that their framework is, in fact, explicitly attuned to the role of interscalar politico-institutional relays in the construction and transformation of local (or urban) governance systems. This leads to a dynamically multiscalar reading of the national institutional frameworks that have facilitated the formation of growth machines at the urban scale during the course of US territorial development, including during the post-1980s period. While this chapter focuses on the US case, its argument has broader methodological implications for the comparative-historical investigation of urbanization, territorial alliance formation, and urban governance in other contexts as well.

Chapter 8 presents a series of metatheoretical reflections on the scalar framework of analysis developed in the preceding chapters while also outlining several major challenges for subsequent rounds of research on the spatialities of urbanization. Here I return to the definitionally narrow conceptualization of scale proposed in Chapter 3 and further elaborate some of its implications for investigations of uneven spatial development, a *problematique* that has long been a key focal point for urban researchers. Drawing on Henri Lefebvre's striking metaphor of social space as a *mille feuille*, a flaky dessert pastry composed of "a thousand layers," this chapter argues that the geographies of uneven development and, by implication, those of the capitalist urban fabric are best conceived as a multifaceted superimposition and interpenetration of sociospatial relations. In contrast to scale-centric or methodologically territorialist approaches, I thus propose that the morphologies of sociospatial relations under capitalism are too densely and intricately interwoven to be represented through a single geometrical image or spatial metaphor, whether scalar, territorial, or otherwise. From this point of view, scalar approaches to urban theory will be most productive when their conceptual and explanatory parameters are precisely circumscribed in the context of a multidimensional, polymorphic approach to critical geopolitical economy that also systematically explores processes of place-making, territorialization, and networking.

These metatheoretical reflections on uneven spatial development and urbanization preserve the core elements of a scalar approach to the urban question, but they also present some strong methodological cautions regarding the hazards of overextending or underspecifying scalar concepts. To be sure, especially in the context of contemporary patterns of worldwide sociospatial restructuring, which are profoundly transforming inherited interscalar configurations, it has proven hugely productive to frame emergent urban questions through a reflexively scalar theoretical lens. Nonetheless, it is essential to avoid applying that lens beyond its proper domain of application, either (1) by treating scale as a generic conceptual metaphor for sociospatiality as such or (2) by conflating scale with other dimensions of sociospatial relations, such as place, territory, or networks. Proceeding otherwise risks embracing a problematic scale-centrism in which all aspects of sociospatial relations are subsumed under, or interpreted through, an undifferentiated, overgeneralized scalar analytic. Certainly, in the relational, processual sense elaborated in this book, the urban *is* a scale, and this aspect of urban space is indeed today being fundamentally reconfigured. Nonetheless, scalar categories require very precise specification in order to remain coherent analytical tools of theorization, investigation, interpretation, and critique.

In a final argumentative maneuver, Chapters 9 and 10 connect these metatheoretical reflections to a new round of theorizing on the urban question that, much like previous cycles of debate on such issues, has been provoked by the challenge of deciphering emergent patterns and pathways of urban restructuring. It is here that my guiding question regarding the possibility of a scalar reframing of the urban question is transformed into a more explicit, systematic concern with the *problematique* of planetary urbanization. These chapters propose such a reframing through a critical assessment of contemporary "urban age" discourses, which are viewed as narrowly city-centric simplifications of a constitutively uneven, territorially differentiated, and spatially extended landscape of planetary urbanization. Through a series of critical reflections, epistemological reorientations, conceptual proposals, and conjunctural arguments, an alternative vision of urban theory is presented that transcends such universalizing, homogenizing spatial ideologies while directing attention to the intensely variegated new geographies of urban-industrial, infrastructural, and ecological transformation that are emerging beyond major population centers, in close conjunction with new spatial strategies of large-scale industrial resource extraction, agroindustrial land-use intensification, logistical acceleration, marketized techno-environmental management, and territorial enclosure. The consolidation of such mega-urbanization strategies has been manifested in a bewildering array of colossal spatial configurations designed to support the metabolism of the global metropolitan network, as well as the planetary supply chains and industrializing hinterlands upon which the latter depend. In this way, the dialectical interplay between concentrated and extended urbanization—agglomeration processes and the construction/transformation of industrialized operational landscapes in support of the latter—comes to occupy center stage in a reformulated framing of the contemporary urban question.[36] The concept of the capitalist urban fabric—elaborated in previous chapters with reference to the scale question, scale relativization processes,

---

[36] The distinction between concentrated and extended urbanization is developed at greater length in Brenner and Schmid, "Towards a New Epistemology"; and in the contributions to Brenner, *Implosions/Explosions*.

and the evolution of state spatial strategies—now acquires new layers of meaning, and additional sociospatial dimensions, in relation to emergent investigations of the operational landscapes of extended urbanization.

This theoretical reframing of the urban question directly builds upon, yet in some respects also transcends, the scalar analytics developed in earlier chapters. On the one hand, my approach to the study of planetary urbanization is firmly grounded upon many of the same conceptual foundations and methodological orientations that have long underpinned my studies of the rescaling of urban space:

- It involves the rejection of localist, city-centric approaches to the urban, emphasizing instead the relationally multiscalar, variegated, and uneven geographies of the capitalist urban fabric.
- It emphasizes the key role of state spatial strategies in constituting, stratifying, and reorganizing the capitalist urban fabric across places, territories, and scales.
- It is concerned with the contradictory dynamics of sociospatial creative destruction—the production and deconstruction of territorial organization—that animate and mediate the capitalist form of urbanization.
- It further elaborates upon the planetarization of the urban, a process that is initially explored in Chapter 2 with reference to the state-theoretical and interscalar dimensions of Henri Lefebvre's influential hypothesis regarding the contemporary urban revolution.
- It theorizes emergent forms of urban restructuring as a medium and expression of political strategies to construct new, rescaled urban spaces in a geoeconomic context of deepening, if intensely variegated, processes of scale relativization and neoliberalization.
- It emphasizes the polymorphic character of urban geographies under capitalism—their differentiation and stratification by scale, but also through processes of place-making, territorialization, and networking.

My endeavor to develop and deploy a scalar approach to urban theory has thus flowed directly into my more recent explorations of planetary urbanization, at once as a new way of theorizing the capitalist form of urbanization and as an emergent historical-geographical configuration of the capitalist urban fabric that requires further investigation.[37] Indeed, in an important sense,

---

[37] There are, of course, many other routes into such explorations. For Christian Schmid's account of his own intellectual itinerary in relation to the latter, see his "Journeys through Planetary Urbanization: Decentering Perspectives on the Urban," *Environment and Planning*

planetary urbanization represents the latest in a series of market-disciplinary rescaling projects that have been reshaping the capitalist urban fabric since the global economic crises of the 1970s. As such, it encompasses not only the globalizing cities, metropolitan regions, and regional growth alliances that were analyzed in previous chapters as force fields and outcomes of rescaling processes but also a variety of emergent mega-territorial formations of infrastructure investment, land-use intensification, and metabolic transformation that crisscross erstwhile hinterlands, rural zones, and even wilderness areas, and which now appear to have become strategic new spatial frontiers for combined urban transformation, regulatory reorganization, and rescaling. In short, as I argue in the final two chapters, the construction of these significantly upscaled zones of extended urbanization, which now encompass entire continents, as well as diverse intercontinental, interoceanic, and even planet-spanning infrastructural configurations, has become a major (geo)political strategy of capitalist expansion and state developmentalism under contemporary conditions. A scalar analytics thus remains an essential methodological tool for any effort to decipher such spaces, their politico-institutional mediations, their crisis tendencies, and their consequences, across the variegated landscapes of both concentrated and extended urbanization.

In other ways, however, the reflections on planetary urbanization presented in the book's final chapters also entail a significant autocritique, relativization, and indeed a kind of *Aufhebung* of the specific scalar analytics mobilized in this book and elsewhere to frame the urban question. The key issue here involves the meaning(s) attached to the concept of the "urban" itself, whether as an adjectival label qualifying other terms (urban space, urban restructuring, urban development, urban governance, and so forth) or as the differentiating lexical element in the superordinate concept of urbanization. In my scalar explorations of the urban question, the main critique of city-centric, localist approaches involves the elaboration of a conceptual framework that embeds cities, and agglomeration processes more generally, within broader, multiscalar configurations of sociospatial relations, institutional organization, and territorial regulation. However, despite my explicit concern to supersede city-centric approaches to urban studies,

D: *Society and Space* 36, no. 3 (2018): 591–610; as well as "The Urbanization of the Territory." Other possible intellectual pathways into such an investigation are presented in Brenner, *Implosions/Explosions*, as well as in Michelle Buckley and Kendra Strauss, "With, against, and beyond Lefebvre: Planetary Urbanization and Epistemic Plurality," *Environment and Planning D: Society and Space* 34, no. 4 (2016): 617–36; and Stefan Kipfer, "Pushing the Limitations of Urban Research: Urbanization, Pipelines and Counter-Colonial Politics," *Environment and Planning D: Society and Space* 36, no. 3 (2018): 474–93.

and my persistent insistence on the Lefebvrian distinction between the city and the urban, much of that work remains, in concrete-historical and empirical terms, focused on relatively familiar, methodologically conventional research sites: large population centers, densely settled built environments, and metropolitan systems of infrastructure development, capital investment, and governance. To be sure, throughout my investigations, these terrains of urban life are reframed in consistently relational, multiscalar terms, as arenas and outcomes of urbanization processes, rather than being circumscribed within discrete, bounded settlement units. Nonetheless, it may be argued that, insofar as they are still largely focused upon the dynamics of (what I would now term) concentrated urbanization, such scalar explorations entail no more than a partial transcendence of entrenched urban epistemologies: they involve an expansively multiscalar framing of city-building and agglomeration processes, but they tend to avoid excavating what is arguably a more foundational layer of the urban question—namely, the first-order, ontological problem of demarcating exactly what kind of process or phenomenon the urban actually *is*. This fundamental question can be helpfully illuminated through scalar explorations, but the latter might also have the unintended consequence of masking it, insofar as they risk reducing the urban to a theoretically self-evident entity, whose "complexity" consists chiefly in its shifting, variegated sociospatial patterns and scalar articulations.[38]

During my early studies in urban theory, it was my interest in scale questions that drew my attention to Lefebvre's theorization of the urban fabric, which I appropriated as a basis for developing a relationally multiscalar, state-theoretical approach to urban restructuring under conditions of deepening scale relativization. Today, however, I would not reduce the concept of the urban fabric to its function in reframing the urban question as a scale question, even though it has proven quite salient for that purpose. Perhaps more important, the concept of the urban fabric points toward what is arguably a more radical conceptual reorientation in urban theory, one that entails a

---

[38] As Ross Exo Adams has brilliantly argued in a series of provocative writings, this problem is pervasive within both historical and contemporary urban discourse, from the social sciences to planning, urban design, and architecture: "Indeed, as it happens in many discourses . . . wherever the urban is raised as the site of inquiry, the problem always tends to be something else that it contains. Assumed to be a transhistorical background of human life, the urban appears never to constitute a problem in and of itself." See Ross Exo Adams, "The Burden of the Present: On the Concept of Urbanisation," *Society and Space*, February 11, 2014, http://societyandspace.org/2014/02/11/the-burden-of-the-present-on-the-concept-of-urbanisation-ross-exo-adams. See also Ross Exo Adams, "Natural Urbans, Natural Urbanata: Ecological Urbanism, Circulation and the Immunization of Nature," *Environment and Planning D: Society and Space* 32, no. 1 (2014): 12–29.

foundational rethinking of the historically specific content of the "urban" itself under modern capitalism.[39] It is precisely such issues that recent reframings of the urban question around the *problematique* of planetary urbanization productively open up for further theoretical debate and concrete exploration. This requires us to revisit, on a rather foundational level, the nature of urbanization itself as a specific kind of spatiotemporal, metabolic, and political process under capitalism. Indeed, as Christian Schmid and I have argued elsewhere, such considerations generate the need for a "new epistemology of the urban," a framework of analysis that can more directly confront the urban question as such, without reducing it to the permutations of urban spatial form, morphology, or typology while also providing a conceptual basis on which to decipher emergent, early twenty-first-century patterns and pathways of urban restructuring.[40]

The book's concluding chapters suggest, then, that a purely scalar reframing of the urban question can only partially address that challenge. The major theoretical imperative that flows from such autocritical arguments is to reconceptualize the capitalist urban fabric not simply as a territorially differentiated, multiscalar geography of urban centers and agglomeration processes embedded within broader, dynamically evolving interscalar configurations, but as the medium and outcome of the relentless processes of implosion/explosion that, as I would now argue, represent the spatiotemporal core of the capitalist form of urbanization. It should be emphasized, however, that the scalar analytics developed herein may also be readily integrated into studies of planetary urbanization. Much like the geographies of concentrated urbanization on which I focus much of my attention in this book, the terrain of extended urbanization can be productively investigated through a relationally scale-attuned, state-theoretical mode of analysis— albeit one that must also be equally concerned with the role of place-making,

---

[39] This is an argument that Stefan Kipfer, among others, has been making for a long time, and which has been strongly reinforced in recent "third wave" readings of Lefebvre's urban theory, for instance, by Kanishka Goonewardena and Christian Schmid, among others. See, in particular, Stefan Kipfer, "Why the Urban Question Still Matters: Reflections on Rescaling and the Promise of the Urban," in Keil and Mahon, *Leviathan Undone?*, 67–86; and Christian Schmid, "Henri Lefebvre, the Right to the City and the New Metropolitan Mainstream," in *Cities for People, Not for Profit: Critical Urban Theory and the Right to the City*, ed. Neil Brenner, Margit Mayer, and Peter Marcuse (New York: Routledge, 2012), 42–62. See also, more generally, Kanishka Goonewardena, Stefan Kipfer, Richard Milgrom, and Christian Schmid, eds., *Space, Difference and Everyday Life: Reading Henri Lefebvre* (New York: Routledge, 2008). These highly suggestive interpretations and appropriations of Lefebvre's approach to the urban question assume renewed significance, I believe, in the context of contemporary debates on planetary urbanization.

[40] Brenner and Schmid, "Towards a New Epistemology."

territorialization, and networking processes in its construction and ongoing transformation. In this sense, the scalar explorations elaborated in the main body of this book are intended to help form the methodological and conceptual groundwork for the research agenda on planetary urbanization that is outlined in the concluding chapters.

The Location of Theory

The pathway of theorizing forged in this book offers only one set of strategies through which to confront the challenges of deciphering the production of new urban spaces under early twenty-first-century capitalism. My intention in these studies is hardly to resolve such challenges; I certainly do not believe that any single theory, framework, or methodology could do so. My more modest goal here is to put forward some potentially useful epistemological perspectives, conceptual proposals, and methodological strategies, the results of my own explorations in a series of interlinked research endeavors, through which at least some dimensions of emergent geographies of urbanization might be illuminated.

Looking back on my intellectual pathway since the late 1990s, I can immediately recognize a number of significant limitations, missing links, and blind spots connected to the theoretical framework I have been elaborating. For instance, my approach to urban questions—whether as scale questions or, more recently, in relation to the emergent *problematique* of planetary urbanization—is very much focused on the dynamics, contradictions, and crisis tendencies of capitalism, primarily through the analytical lens of spatialized political economy and state theory. There is no doubt that such methodological orientations may be productively connected to a range of closely interrelated *problematiques* within the broad fields of radical geography, critical urban studies, and spatial humanities that are not effectively explored here—for instance, the structuration of urban scalar configurations through diverse sociospatial positionalities (especially of race, gender, ethnicity, sexuality, and citizenship); the role of colonialism, war, geopolitics, and empire in the production and deconstruction of scalar fixes; the scalar logics and illogics of social reproduction, financialization, accumulation by dispossession, territorial enclosure, depeasantization, transnational migration, and informalization; and the politics of scale associated with patterns of social mobilization, political insurgency, and struggles to (re)appropriate the city (and the urban) as a commons. Would engagement with such essential issues require a comprehensive deconstruction or even abandonment of the theoretical approach elaborated in my writings? Could at least some of the latter agendas be further explored in productive directions in relation to the scalar analytics and lines of interpretation I have proposed? To what degree, and in what ways, would other analytical, empirical, locational, or political entry points into the urban question and/or into the scale question transform the specific conceptual, methodological, and interpretive commitments elaborated here? These are questions on which, for the moment, I can only speculate; they are certainly legitimate ones to pose of any approach to critical social theory, urban or otherwise. My hope is that at least some of the heterodox theoretical offerings assembled here might prove fruitful in terrains of conceptualization and investigation beyond those on which I have focused my efforts.

Another urgently important but underexplored *problematique* in this book concerns the interplay between the rescaling of the capitalist urban fabric and the evolving scalar geographies of the "web of life"—the nonhuman life forms and material geographies of the so-called earth system upon which capitalism depends, and which capital has relentlessly transformed throughout its *longue durée* world-historical ecology.[41] To some degree, this set of issues is brought into more reflexive focus in the book's final chapters, in conjunction with my incipient reflections on planetary urbanization as an uneven and combined process of rescaling and politico-territorial, infrastructural, and ecological creative destruction. For the most part, however, the analytic lens developed here is so concertedly focused on the challenges of superseding unreflexively localist, city-centric approaches to the urban question that it neglects to engage the parallel, and indeed tightly interconnected, methodological hazards associated with inherited conceptions of the city (and of the urban) as being ontologically separate from a putatively external realm of nonhuman "nature."

Of course, there is now an entire field of critical urban studies, urban political ecology (UPE), that has been systematically exploding such Cartesian dualisms since the early 2000s.[42] Much recent work in UPE has been explicitly concerned with questions of scale and rescaling processes, and there have certainly been ample opportunities for conceptual cross-fertilization regarding scale questions across various terrains of urban and ecological

---

[41] On which, see Jason W. Moore, *Capitalism in the Web of Life: Ecology and the Accumulation of Capital* (New York: Verso, 2016); Noel Castree, "The Anthropocene and the Environmental Humanities: Extending the Conversation," *Environmental Humanities* 5 (2014): 233–60; and Nik Heynen, Maria Kaika, and Erik Swyngedouw, eds., *In the Nature of Cities: Urban Political Ecology and the Politics of Urban Metabolism* (New York: Routledge, 2006).

[42] See, above all, Heynen et al., *In the Nature of Cities*.

research.[43] However, despite its broadly effective transcendence of the city/ nature divide and its consistent embrace of a relational conception of scale, key streams of UPE research have been framed in ways that privilege cities as sites of analysis and equate the urban with processes of sociospatial concentration.[44] Consequently, the broader implications of a UPE approach for rethinking the variegated, uneven geographies of planetary urbanization, and of the "capitalocene" more generally, have only just begun to be systematically explored.[45] Clearly, the relation between the capitalist urban fabric and the web of life under the capitalocene requires further exploration, at once as a problem of social ontology, as a question of conceptualization, as a focal point for historical and contemporary investigation, and as a terrain for future politico-institutional experimentation. Perhaps, in facing such wide-ranging challenges, some of the scalar analytics developed here may also help facilitate a more systematic transcendence of inherited and still deeply entrenched Cartesian dualisms—including urban/rural, society/nature, city/ nature, interior/exterior, and human/nonhuman—that continue to obscure our understanding of, and our ability to shape, the wide-ranging, planet-transforming sociometabolic transformations that have been unleashed under the capitalist form of urbanization.[46]

To what degree, finally, is the approach to urban theory presented in this book limited in its sphere of application to the regionally specific (North Atlantic) research context in which many of its major elements were elaborated? Can there be—indeed, *should* there be—a more general theorization of the urban question, whether as a scale question or otherwise, under modern capitalism? Or, does the endeavor to develop such an approach

---

[43] See, paradigmatically, Erik Swyngedouw and Nik Heynen, "Urban Political Ecology, Justice and the Politics of Scale," *Antipode* 35, no. 5 (2003): 898–918; and Nathan Sayre, "Ecological and Geographical Scale: Parallels and Potential for Integration," *Progress in Human Geography* 29, no. 3 (2005): 276–90.

[44] Angelo and Wachsmuth, "Urbanizing Urban Political Ecology." See also Martín Arboleda, "In the Nature of the Non-City: Expanded Infrastructural Networks and the Political Ecology of Planetary Urbanization," *Antipode* 48, no. 2 (2016): 233–51.

[45] See, for example, Erik Swyngedouw, *Liquid Power: Contested Hydro-Modernities in Twentieth Century Spain* (Cambridge, MA: MIT Press, 2015); Matthew Gandy, *The Fabric of Space: Water, Modernity and the Urban Imagination* (Cambridge, MA: MIT Press, 2016). On the capitalocene, see Moore, *Capitalism in the Web of Life*; Jason W. Moore, ed., *Anthropocene or Capitalocene? Nature, History and the Crisis of Capitalism* (Oakland, CA: PM Press/Kairos, 2016); and Jason W. Moore, "The Capitalocene, Part I: On the Nature and Origins of our Ecological Crisis," *Journal of Peasant Studies* 4, no. 3 (2017): 594–630.

[46] For further reflections on such issues, see Martín Arboleda, "Revitalizing Science and Technology Studies: A Marxian Critique of More-Than-Human Geographies," *Environment and Planning D: Society and Space* 35, no. 2 (2017): 360–78 as well as Brenner, "Critical Urban Theory, Reloaded?"

always require "provincialization"—that is, contextual embedding and locational particularization?[47]

At first glance, this book's commitment to developing a theorization of *the* urban question—a formulation that is, of course, derived from the work of Marxian authors such as Manuel Castells, Henri Lefebvre, and David Harvey—may appear to stand in flagrant contradiction to the project of developing locationally inscribed, contextually embedded, epistemologically situated approaches to urban theory and research. Surely, one might object, the insistence on theorizing "the" urban question, apparently as a singular *problematique*, exemplifies the very form of universalizing, totalizing, and "metrocentric" thought (whether of a Eurocentric, neocolonial, masculinist, or heteronormative variety) that has been critically deconstructed by urban theorists working in postcolonial, feminist, and queer-theoretical traditions.[48] How could any conceptualization of "the" urban illuminate the extraordinary multiplicity of sociospatial conditions, processes, life worlds, and struggles that underpin contemporary urbanization processes?

Such questions are fundamental; they have important epistemological and political stakes. The emphasis on situated knowledge—the sociohistorical embeddedness of ways of knowing, including those used in all forms of theory and research—offers an appropriately strong counterpoint to hegemonic knowledge formations, urban and otherwise, that assert, and often attempt to impose, universalizing, normalizing truth claims. The latter are problematic not only because they homogenize the complexities of social life based upon generic "legibility projects" but because the simplifications they promulgate are operationalized in spatial practice to consolidate, reproduce, and naturalize forms of domination, oppression, exclusion, and social suffering: neoliberalism, colonialism, white supremacy, patriarchy, heteronormativity, authoritarianism, xenophobia, and various combinations thereof.[49]

---

[47] Debates on such questions have been intensifying in recent years, in significant measure due to the productive politico-epistemological questions posed by postcolonial urban scholars regarding the limits of inherited Western, Euro-American, or North Atlantic approaches to urban theory. For key contributions and overviews, see Susan Parnell and Sophie Oldfield, eds., *The Routledge Handbook on Cities of the Global South* (London: Routledge, 2014), as well as the works cited in note 34. Another useful recent reflection on such issues is Helga Leitner and Eric Sheppard, "Provincializing Critical Urban Theory: Extending the Ecosystem of Possibilities," *International Journal of Urban and Regional Research* 40, no. 1 (2016): 228–35.

[48] The concept of metrocentrism is productively developed in Tim Bunnell and Anant Maringanti, "Practicing Urban Research beyond Metrocentricity," *International Journal of Urban and Regional Research* 34, no. 2 (2011): 415–20.

[49] On legibility projects, see James C. Scott, "State Simplifications: Nature, Space and People," *Journal of Political Philosophy* 3, no. 3 (1995): 191–233.

In this context, the invocation of contextual specificity may have a powerful rhetorical, political, and substantive function: it signals a critically oriented researcher's concern to produce locationally inscribed ways of knowing that are more attuned to the underlying complexities of the social fabric, and which can thus serve a counterhegemonic purpose in academic research and public discourse alike. It is for this reason that debates on the status of what is often described as "general theory" in urban studies are often quite heated. Their stakes are at once scholarly and normative; they connect directly to the questions about positionality, knowledge, power, and possible urban worlds that animate so much of the most creative, politically relevant work being produced in this vibrant research field today.

My own commitments in such debates resonate strongly with such concerns, since they likewise emphasize the socially embedded, politically mediated character of all forms of urban theory and research, including those that are under critical examination or constructive development in this book. While my own theorization of epistemic positionality is more strongly rooted in heterodox Marxian frameworks (especially in the work of Frankfurt school philosophers and Lefebvre) than in poststructuralist or postcolonial traditions, there is arguably much intellectual common ground among them. Indeed, despite the proliferation of sometimes divisive debates that antagonistically counterpose Marxian-inspired geopolitical economists against poststructuralists (including feminists, neo-Foucauldians, neo-Deleuzians, postcolonial scholars, and queer theorists), I believe that their epistemological and political common ground springs into clear focus when their core concern with linking the critique of knowledge to the critique of power is contrasted to the instrumentalist, accommodationist, and triumphalist agendas of hegemonic forms of "authoritative" social knowledge, such as social science positivism, neoclassical economics, conventional approaches to geographic information systems (GIS), technocratic modes of policy science, or mainstream global urban policy discourse. This observation is not intended to deny, ignore, or dismiss the divergent understandings of positionality, knowledge/power, and critique, and the wide-ranging politico-normative concerns, that animate the field of critical urban studies today. The point is simply to suggest that internal divisions among critically oriented theorists, whether of an epistemological or political nature, are considerably less profound or consequential than those that distinguish them from mainstream, hegemonic approaches to social knowledge.[50]

---

[50] This is a broad generalization, but I believe it is a defensible one, both intellectually and politically. Clearly, the classical distinction between "traditional" and "critical" theory introduced by

At the same time, however, I reject the simplistic opposition between situated knowledges and so-called "general theory" that is still widely invoked or presupposed by many poststructuralist scholars who are concerned to deconstruct modes of interpretation that aspire, in some way, to transcend the immediate locational contexts in which they emerge. Some version of this binarism (along with several parallel dualisms: local/global, particular/universal, heterogeneity/homogeneity, fragment/whole, inside/outside, exception/norm) has framed or underpinned a variety of key debates in the field of critical urban studies over the decades, on topics such as post-Fordism, postmodernism, localities, gentrification, globalization, and neoliberalization, among others, and it continues to serve as an important reference point in many contemporary academic skirmishes around assemblage urbanism, feminist urban theory, postcolonial urbanism, planetary urbanization, and other emergent theoretical explorations. Four broad observations may serve to clarify further the specific epistemic position that grounds my investigations, arguments, proposals, and speculations in this book.

First, local and contextual conditions are not pregiven or self-evident, but are mediated through supralocal, intercontextual processes, interconnections, and interdependencies, which likewise require interpretation, conceptualization, and investigation. For this reason, the invocation of "specificity," whether with reference to locality, place, region, or context, requires systematic engagement not only with the particularities of a site but with its relational connections, articulations, and mediations, across various spatial scales. To proceed otherwise is to risk embracing an ontology of particularism in which experiential, localized, contextual, or socially embedded forms of evidence are taken for granted; viewed as privileged, uncontestable, and transparent windows into the real; or conceived as untheorizable singularities. As feminist social historian Joan Scott paradigmatically argued in the early 1990s, such neopositivistic methodologies actually weaken the project of developing histories (and, we might add, geographies) of difference, because

Frankfurt school cofounder Max Horkheimer in the 1930s requires further elaboration in relation to contemporary constellations of social knowledge, but I believe it still offers an essential intellectual reference point on which basis to differentiate critically oriented approaches to urban knowledge from mainstream, technocratic, and market-triumphalist knowledge formations. See Max Horkheimer, "Traditional and Critical Theory," in Critical Theory: Selected Essays, trans. Matthew O'Connell (New York: Continuum, 1982 [1937]), 188–243. For a powerful contemporary reflection on such issues that also productively complicates Horkheimer's midcentury view of positivism, see Elvin Wyly, "Positively Radical," International Journal of Urban and Regional Research 35, no. 5 (2011): 889–912. For a strong indictment of contemporary formations of urban "science" and a concomitantly energetic call for a renewal of critical approaches, see Brendan Gleeson, "What Role for Social Science in the 'Urban Age'?," International Journal of Urban and Regional Research 37, no. 5 (2013): 1839–51.

they relegate the experiential, the contextual, and the local to a realm of putative facticity that is claimed to be insulated from the very processes of social (and spatial) construction and interpretive mediation that are under investigation.[51] Reflecting on the limits of purely immanentist, methodologically localist approaches to the urban question, Jamie Peck reaches a closely parallel conclusion, suggesting that they often rest upon highly problematic, naïve empiricist epistemic foundations that occlude a researcher's capacity to decipher the manifold ways in which apparently "local" and "proximate" conditions are in fact mediated through supralocal formations of power, strategy, and struggle:

> The primacy of the empirically observable and the locally proximate, at the expense of longer-distance, structural relations, can invite confusion or conflation with that class of endogenizing, internalist and victim-blaming accounts, say, of the local political "causes" of urban fiscal crises that inappropriately responsibilize or even pathologize those actors visibly on the scene. This means that recurrent urban processes—the kind that are realized, in a mediated and contingent fashion, in site after site—are unlikely to be understood or even recognized as such. Instead, the reluctance to trace common processes across multiple sites, or to acknowledge structural patterns (even in a non-structuralist way), is reflected in a tendency for such recurrent phenomena either to be (re)described, *de novo*, to be mistaken for endogeneously produced or *sui generis* formations, or to be characterized as deviations from a better-known norm. Rich description of individual city-sites substitutes for the tracing of urbanization processes across cases and places—a form of methodological isolation which can be likened to an attempt to understand fluvial dynamics by first removing a bucket of water from the stream.[52]

This is hardly to dismiss the local as an essential site and category of analysis; on the contrary, it remains, in principle, as fundamental as any other site or scale of inquiry into the capitalist urban fabric. The task, rather, is to decipher how experience, locality, and context are actively produced and understood as such, including through relationally multiscalar, intercontextual sociospatial processes that transcend the site under investigation, and that may also be generating parallel transformations, modes of differentiation,

---

[51] Joan Scott, "The Evidence of Experience," *Critical Inquiry* 17, no. 4 (1991): 773–97.

[52] Jamie Peck, "Cities beyond Compare?," *Regional Studies* 49, no. 1 (2015): 177. For a closely parallel critique of localist epistemologies in science studies and social history, see Peter Galison's brilliant meditation, "The Limits of Localism: The Scale of Sight," in *What Reason Promises: Essays on Reason, Nature and History*, ed. Wendy Doniger, Peter Galison, and Susan Neiman (Berlin: De Gruyter, 2016), 155–70.

and contestations elsewhere. In this way, scholars can more effectively avoid the methodological blind spots associated with what Saskia Sassen has aptly described as the "endogeneity trap," in which local (or regional, national, or global) outcomes are explained exclusively with reference to phenomena or processes considered to be internal to, or spatially coextensive with, that scale of analysis.[53]

Second, the notion of "general theory," especially when counterposed to an unreflexivelyaffirmativenotionoflocaldifferenceorcontextualexceptionalism, is an unhelpful simplification of the differentiated, dynamically evolving palette of epistemological strategies that have been mobilized by critical urban theorists to investigate the intercontextual geographies of urbanization, as well as their constitutively uneven, variegated, and restlessly mutating crystallizations across places, territories, and scales. To be sure, researchers as diverse as Geoffrey West, Edward Glaeser, and, most recently, Allen J. Scott and Michael Storper have prominently embraced orthodox, monist visions of urban theory as offering, or aspiring to offer, universally valid propositions regarding the intrinsic nature of urban processes and outcomes.[54] However, this rigidly nomothetic, monist conception of theory as a disembodied mode of scientific inquiry and as a means to produce universally valid covering laws hardly exhausts the quite varied terrain of epistemological positions through which intercontextual approaches to urban theory may be envisioned. On the contrary, across the Marxism/poststructuralism divide, there are rich seams of heterodox, nominalist, immanentist, and critical realist urban theorizing that, whatever their differences, (1) insist on the socially embedded, historically situated, and politically mediated nature of urban knowledge while also (2) aspiring to produce generalizable knowledge regarding historically constituted, constitutively uneven patterns and pathways of urbanization.[55] Historical sociologist Fouad Makki's dialectical reconceptualization of

---

[53] Saskia Sassen, *Territory, Authority, Rights: From Medieval to Global Assemblages* (Princeton, NJ: Princeton University Press, 2006).

[54] See, for example, Luis Bettencourt, José Lobo, Dirk Helbing, Christian Kühnert, and Geoffrey West, "Growth, Innovation, Scaling and the Pace of Life in Cities," *Proceedings of the National Academy of Sciences* 104, no. 17 (2007): 7301–6; Edward Glaeser, *Cities, Agglomeration and Spatial Equilibrium* (New York: Oxford University Press, 2008); and Allen J. Scott and Michael Storper, "The Nature of Cities: The Scope and Limits of Urban Theory," *International Journal of Urban and Regional Research* 39, no. 1 (2015): 1–15.

[55] For useful overviews of diverse approaches to "theory" in contemporary critical urban studies, see Robert Beauregard, "What Theorists Do," *Urban Geography* 33, no. 4 (2012): 477–87; Ozan Karaman, "An Immanentist Approach to the Urban," *Antipode* 44, no. 4 (2011): 1287–306; Roy, "21st Century Metropolis"; Robinson, "New Geographies of Theorizing the Urban"; Gleeson, "What Role for Social Science"; and Peck, "Cities beyond Compare?"

combined and uneven development offers a concise summary of such a methodological orientation, which has extremely robust applications in the field of critical urban studies:

> As an explanatory procedure, this requires a back and forth movement from epochal analysis towards greater historicity and the grounding of variant patterns of social change in the inter-societal constellation of power relations. This is an approach that is inimical to schematic formulas that can be mechanistically applied everywhere against recalcitrant historical realities, or turned into fetishized abstractions that substitute the simplicity of an idea for the complexity of the world.[56]

There is, in other words, a fundamental difference between a universalizing theory and a generalizing one: the former denies its own sociohistorical positionality and claims to advance infallible, encompassing, transcendent truths; the latter, by contrast, may be grounded upon a perspectival realism that self-reflexively emphasizes its own embeddedness in sociospatial relations while simultaneously seeking to illuminate the emergent (that is, historically formed and always evolving) properties, regularities, and interconnections that structure sociospatial relations within *and* across contexts, territories, ecologies, and scales.[57] It is this latter, perspectival realist epistemology that underpins my explorations here: it insists upon the situatedness, immanence, incompleteness, and revisability of all knowledge claims while simultaneously seeking to develop historically specific concepts, methods, and modes of explanation that can illuminate the constitutively relational, structurally patterned dynamics, transformations, contradictions, and contestations associated with urbanization processes.[58]

Third, the approach to urban theorizing developed in this book is fundamentally committed to the need for abstraction—that is, to the elaboration,

---

[56] Fouad Makki, "Reframing Development Theory: The Significance of the Idea of Combined and Uneven Development," *Theory and Society* 44 (2015): 491. For further reflections, see also Jamie Peck, "Macroeconomic Geographies," *Area Development and Policy* 1, no. 3 (2016): 305–22.

[57] For a productive explication of this key distinction in the context of a rigorously sociological approach to postcolonial theory, see Julian Go, *Postcolonial Thought and Social Theory* (New York: Oxford University Press, 2016). The distinction between universalization and generalization is also productively developed in Roy, "Who's Afraid of Postcolonial Theory?"

[58] The concept of perspectival realism is productively developed in Go, *Postcolonial Thought.* See also Gillian Hart, "Denaturalizing Dispossession: Critical Ethnography in the Age of Resurgent Imperialism," *Antipode* 38, no. 5 (2006): 977–1004; and Gillian Hart, "Relational Comparison Revisited: Marxist Postcolonial Geographies in Practice," *Progress in Human Geography* 42, no. 3 (2018): 371–94.

deployment, and continual reinvention of concepts that permit us to distinguish surface appearances (the empirically given; the world as it is immediately perceived) from the underlying mechanisms, relations, processes, and strategies that produce the latter. As Andrew Sayer explains, abstract concepts are an essential basis on which to "grasp the differentiations of the world . . . of individuating objects, and of characterizing their attributes and relationships. . . . Even where we are interested in wholes we must select and abstract their constituents."[59] In this sense, the process of abstraction is essential to any mode of conceptualization, since it is on this basis alone that the essential or defining elements of the entity, relation, process, or transformation under analysis can be specified as such. Crucially, as Sayer's formulation underscores, abstract concepts are not meant to provide a comprehensive description or complete "capture" of every concrete aspect of the social world that exists or that may be of analytic, political, or normative interest. Instead, such concepts offer a means of delineating the essential, constituent properties of the specific types of phenomena or sites that are being investigated.

This is one important sense in which debates on "the" urban question are recurrently taken up. Rather than arbitrarily subsuming the manifold determinations, mediations, and manifestations of urban life under a universal definition, the preposition "the" in references to "the urban question" refers to the process of theoretical abstraction upon which such debates necessarily hinge. Across diverse politico-intellectual and locational terrains, explorations of this *problematique* involve precisely the attempt to delineate the concept of the urban on a level of abstraction that helps illuminate key dimensions of emergent sociospatial relations, patterns, configurations, and struggles, across contexts, territories, ecologies, and scales. The major stake, then, in divergent theoretical approaches to the urban question is not whether they grasp the full complexity of urban life or whether, due to their abstract generality, they neglect certain issues, elements, or dynamics that may be of intellectual, political, or normative significance. Insofar as the function of abstraction is precisely to differentiate the essential, primary, or necessary properties of a particular phenomenon from its superficial, secondary, or contingent elements, such a reproach is logically indefensible. Abstraction is, by definition, a partial, one-sided depiction of a constitutively multifaceted, overdetermined social world. The salient question, rather, is whether the specific kinds of conceptual abstractions proposed by urban

---

[59] Sayer, *Method in Social Science*, 86. See also, foundationally, Andrew Sayer, "Abstraction: A Realist Interpretation," *Radical Philosophy* 28 (Summer 1981): 6–15.

theorists offer a "practically adequate" basis on which to demarcate, in analytically precise yet situated, historically determinate, politically informative terms, the constituent properties of the urban question as it is expressed, contested, and transformed in and through sociospatial relations.[60]

This brings us, finally, to a fourth core element of the approach to the urban question elaborated in these pages. The abstractions proposed here to theorize the capitalist form of urbanization are understood not simply as ideal-typical proposals for more precisely delineating the constituent features of urban spaces, processes, transformations, and struggles; they also represent historically specific expressions of the abstract spatial practices that underpin, animate, and result from the capitalist form of urbanization itself. In this sense, the abstractions mobilized here to theorize the urban question as a scale question and the *problematique* of planetary urbanization are understood as "real abstractions": their emergence and intelligibility as modes of thought are directly connected to the de facto modes of sociospatial abstraction that are unleashed, generalized, and entrenched through the urbanization process under capitalism.[61] As Marx foundationally argued in the *Grundrisse*, a specific mode of abstraction associated with the commodity form is produced and naturalized through the value relations of capitalism; its hallmark is to impose a logic of calculation, quantification, interchangeability, and profit maximization upon diverse regimes of concrete social practice, whether in the sphere of production, reproduction, politics, science, or everyday life.[62] As Łukasz Stanek has expertly demonstrated, a parallel line of argumentation underpins Henri Lefebvre's theorization of the urban as a specific modality of *spatial* abstraction that is likewise consolidated and generalized under capitalism, especially in the wake of twentieth-century processes of global industrialization.[63] This entails not only the construction

---

[60] The concept of practical adequacy is from Sayer, *Method in Social Science*, 86.

[61] On the concept of "real" or "concrete" abstractions, see Stuart Hall, "Marx's Notes on Method: A 'Reading' of the '1857 Introduction,'" *Cultural Studies* 17, no. 2 (2003): 113–49; and Alberto Toscano, "The Open Secret of Real Abstraction," *Rethinking Marxism* 20, no. 2 (2008): 273–87.

[62] See, classically, Karl Marx, "Introduction," in *Grundrisse: Foundations of the Critique of Political Economy*, trans. Martin Nicolaus (New York: Penguin Books, 1973 [1857]). For extensive discussion of this text and its possible uses for critical social theory, see Hall, "Marx's Notes on Method."

[63] See Łukasz Stanek, *Henri Lefebvre on Space: Architecture, Urban Research and the Production of Theory* (Minneapolis: University of Minnesota Press, 2011). See also Chris Butler, "Abstraction beyond a 'Law of Thought': On Space, Appropriation and Concrete Abstraction," *Law Critique* 27, no. 3 (2016): 247–68; and Alex Loftus, "Violent Geographical Abstractions," *Environment and Planning D: Society and Space* 33 (2015): 366–81.

of specifically capitalist forms of territorial organization to facilitate, accelerate, and expand the accumulation process, but the continual creative destruction of such territorial configurations as they are rendered obsolete through capital's own relentless pursuit of new horizons of profitability (see Chapter 2). In precisely this sense, as Lefebvre emphasizes, the spatial abstractions produced through the capitalist form of urbanization are not simply oriented toward homogenization, the obliteration of concrete differences; they also continually push toward the hierarchization, fragmentation, and (re)differentiation of the very sociospatial configurations that, at least under certain spatiotemporal conditions, permit expanded capital accumulation to occur. Indeed, the spatial abstractions that permeate the capitalist urban fabric actively feed upon and intensify sociospatial differentiation while dramatically, often violently, transforming the broader territorial frameworks in and through which local "specificity" and "differences" are articulated.[64]

Thus understood, the need for abstract (and, by implication, intercontextual) modes of conceptualization in the field of urban theory is not simply a methodological orientation or a generic ontological commitment; it flows directly from the monstrously complex challenges of deciphering the contradictory dynamics of urbanization under capitalism, which entail the production of a world-encompassing spatiotemporal grid for the production and circulation of capital while also accentuating the strategic importance of distinctive, place-based conditions and ongoing processes of territorial and scalar differentiation within the maelstrom of capitalist expansion. How to understand a regime of sociospatial practices that is, simultaneously, generalizing and particularizing, equalizing and differentiating, valorizing and devalorizing, explosive and implosive, connecting and fragmenting, assembling and yet pulverizing? How to decipher a mode of global territorial development that requires, simultaneously, the systematic consolidation of colossal, increasingly planet-spanning investments in relatively fixed, immobile infrastructures for the metabolism of capital *and* their recurrent dismantling and reconstruction in pursuit of the grim imperative of endless, profit-driven growth?

Abstractions are not the only methodological tool through which to analyze such tendencies and countertendencies, but they arguably represent an indispensable—necessary but not sufficient—basis on which to decipher

---

[64] See Christian Schmid, "Specificity and Urbanization: A Theoretical Outlook," in *The Inevitable Specificity of Cities*, ed. ETH Studio Basel (Zurich: Lars Müller Publishers, 2014), 282–97. A version of this argument also underpins Neil Smith's classic analysis of capital's dialectic of equalization and differentiation in *Uneven Development*.

key dimensions of the capitalist form of urbanization and its kaleidoscopic, often catastrophic, sociospatial and ecological consequences. Clearly, abstract theoretical maneuvers must always be complemented through concrete-complex analytical strategies, including those that are attuned to place-based conditions, and that thereby illuminate the specificity and even contingency of emergent histories, strategies, and struggles. I would insist, however, that "real" or "concrete" abstractions, including those proposed in these pages, represent an essential, if constitutively incomplete, element within any critical approach to the capitalist urban fabric, its developmental tendencies and countertendencies, its explosive contradictions, and its variegated consequences. Without them, we risk losing sight of the broader "context of context," or *metacontext*, in which urban life emerges and evolves, and which co-constitutes its very conditions of possibility in the modern world through, as Jamie Peck notes, "substantive connections, recurrent processes and relational [modes of] power."[65]

Just as importantly, the real abstractions mobilized in these investigations are intended to underscore the historically specific, growth- and profit-oriented mode of industrial development that so powerfully animates and mediates the urban process under capitalism. As such, they are also meant to facilitate another important task of critical urban theory, that of demarcating the possibilities—extant, latent, anticipated, imagined—for what I have elsewhere termed "*alter*-urbanizations": alternative pathways for the production and collective appropriation of the urban worlds upon which planetary life now depends.[66] In this sense, perhaps paradoxically, my commitment to abstract modes of urban theorizing is intrinsically connected to a radical political project, that of envisioning the prospects for postcapitalist urban futures, even amid the continued consolidation of speculative, hyperfinancialized, aggressively profit-based and militarized patterns and pathways of urban restructuring across the planet as a whole.[67]

---

[65] Peck, "Cities beyond Compare," 162. On the notion of a "context of context" and the systemic production of institutional and spatial variegation, see Neil Brenner, Jamie Peck, and Nik Theodore, "Variegated Neoliberalization: Geographies, Modalities, Pathways," *Global Networks* 10, no. 2 (2010): 182–222.

[66] See Brenner, *Critique of Urbanization*. Several powerful inroads into such a project are elaborated in David Harvey, *Rebel Cities: From the Right to the City to the Urban Revolution* (London: Verso, 2012); Stavros Stavrides, *Common Space: The City as Commons* (London: Zed, 2016); and Massimo De Angelis, *Omnia Sunt Communia: On the Commons and the Transformation to Postcapitalism* (London: Zed, 2017).

[67] For a powerful meditation on the connection between abstract theorizing and the politics of emancipation, see Theodor Adorno, "Resignation," in *Critical Models: Interventions and Catchwords*, trans. Henry W. Pickford (New York: Columbia University Press, 2005), 289–93.

What, then, is the location of theory? How can the vibrantly heterodox politico-intellectual currents that together constitute the field of critical urban theory illuminate the interplay between abstraction and specificity, patterned structuration and immanent emergence, path dependence and path shaping, across the capitalist urban fabric? From my perspective, the most generative contemporary approaches to critical urban theorizing occupy a space of contradiction: they strive to grasp, in immanent, historically specific ways, the generalizing, patterned dynamics of capitalist urbanization, across places, territories, ecologies, and scales, while also attempting to illuminate the intensely variegated, contextually embedded, and dynamically emergent sociospatial relations in which urban worlds are lived, imagined, contested, appropriated, and transformed. And, through the mobilization of diverse epistemological strategies, they seek to confront this task while also reflexively locating themselves—their core categories of analysis, methods, research questions, and politico-normative orientations—within the very fabric of urban history, struggle, and mutation they aspire to illuminate.

Certainly, as postcolonial urban theorists have effectively argued, the project of "locating" theory requires a relentless critical reflexivity regarding the ways in which even the most abstract categories of urban analysis are mediated through contextually embedded, place-specific experiences of urbanization.[68] It is for this reason that any reflexively located approach to critical urban theory must remain ever open to the prospect of conceptual destabilization and reinvention through the exploration of diverse urban "elsewheres," not as incommensurable particularities that somehow lie beyond the scope of theoretical analysis, but precisely as an impetus toward new modes of conceptual generalization and new spatial vectors of urban comparativism.[69] At the same time, however, the studies assembled in this book suggest that the challenge of locating urban theory is not exhausted by that endeavor, but requires parallel strategies of conceptual reinvention that critically interrogate the underlying metageographical assumptions that necessarily underpin all forms of urban research, no matter where they are situated in concrete locational terms.

Here, reflexivity entails locating a theoretical framework not only in relation to the specific contexts of its emergence but with reference to the abstract

---

[68] For a parallel exploration of hidden, place-based influences on putatively "general" theory, see Thomas Gieryn's study of the Chicago school of urban sociology: "City as Truth-Spot: Laboratories and Field-Sites in Urban Studies," *Social Studies of Science* 36, no. 1 (2006): 5–38.

[69] This argument is forcefully articulated in Robinson, "New Geographies of Theorizing the Urban"; and Roy, "Who's Afraid of Postcolonial Theory?"

conceptual demarcations regarding the spatial site, imprint, and impact of urbanization that frame the very project of urban studies, whether in the social and ecological sciences, the spatial humanities, or the planning, policy, and design disciplines. In this sense, reflexive engagement with questions of location in urban theory is never simply a matter of revealing the contextual influences on processes of concept formation; it always also entails the ongoing critical interrogation of the modes of conceptual abstraction through which the urban is delineated, defined, visualized, mapped, and analyzed as a distinctive kind of space that requires sustained investigation.

From this perspective, then, a reflexively situated urban theory requires attention not only to an immense variety of locations around the world as potentially generative sources of theoretical innovation and comparative insight, but equally, a continued critical interrogation of the relentlessly churning, multiscalar geographies—economic, political, cultural, ecological—that underpin, animate, and result from the planetary metabolism(s) of capitalist urbanization. These dimensions of reflexivity in critical urban theory are not only compatible, but can mutually reinforce and animate one another in productive ways. As the location of urban theory continues to mutate in relation to the restlessly transformative, contradictory, and intensely contested dynamics of urbanization it seeks to decipher, we do indeed need to construct new geographies of urban theorizing. That project will clearly require the systematic exploration of diverse "elsewheres" that have previously been peripheralized, black-boxed, or ignored in debates on the historical and emergent geographies of our rapidly urbanizing planet, whether in the global South, the postsocialist world, or the planetary hinterlands to which I direct attention in this book's final chapters. Just as importantly, the project of critical urban studies will also require continued engagement with the urban question itself—whether as a scale question; a question of place-making, territorialization, or network formation; a *problematique* of implosion/explosion; or otherwise. The collective work of critical urban theory thus continues to hinge, in essential yet constitutively incomplete ways, on the development, deployment, refinement, and continual reinvention of abstract concepts—of the urban, of urbanization, of the urban fabric, and, ultimately, of *alter*-urbanizations.

2
Between Fixity and Motion: Scaling the Urban Fabric

DURING THE EARLY 1970S, the "urban question" (*la question urbaine*) formulated in Manuel Castells's classic book became a lightning rod for critical analyses of the production of space under capitalism.[1] Shortly thereafter, in his neglected work *De l'État*, Henri Lefebvre proposed to embed the urban question—to which he had himself already devoted several books—within the still-broader question of geographical scale, its social production, and its sociopolitical contestation. As Lefebvre declared, "Today the question of scale (*la question d'échelle*) inserts itself at the outset—at the foundation, as it were—of the analysis of texts and the interpretation of events."[2]

More than a decade later, however, when the theme of the production of space had stimulated a considerable body of innovative research, Edward Soja noted that geographical scale remained an "understudied" subject, despite the "initial probes" of several critical geographers.[3] Indeed, with a few notable exceptions—including Lefebvre's own studies of state space

---

[1] Manuel Castells, *The Urban Question: A Marxist Approach*, trans. Alan Sheridan (Cambridge, MA: MIT Press, 1977 [1972]).

[2] Henri Lefebvre, *De l'État: De Hegel à Marx par Staline*, vol. 2 (Paris: Union Generale d'Editions, 1976), 67.

[3] Edward W. Soja, *Postmodern Geographies* (New York: Verso, 1989), 149.

in the four volumes of *De l'État*; David Harvey's analysis of "hierarchical arrangements" in the concluding chapter of *Limits to Capital*; Neil Smith's "see-saw" theory of uneven geographical development; and Peter J. Taylor's respatialization of world-system analysis—the *problematique* of spatial scale and its social production was still generally neglected.[4] In most approaches to sociospatial theory, scales were viewed as discrete, nested, stable units within which the production of space occurred, rather than as mutually constitutive, intermeshed, and mutable elements of this process.

Today, the "scale question" posed by Lefebvre over four decades ago is still acknowledged more frequently in the mainstream social sciences through implicit, uninterrogated assumptions than through explicit theorization or reflexive analysis. Nevertheless, especially since the 1990s, there has been a remarkable explosion of research on the "difference that scale makes" among critical sociospatial theorists working within and beyond the disciplinary parameters of geography.[5] As the territorial foundations of the Fordist-Keynesian, national-developmentalist configuration of capitalism have been deconstructed and reworked, spatial scales are no longer conceived as fixed, pregiven arenas of social life. Instead, the full spectrum of spatial scales, from the body, the neighborhood, the local, and the regional to the national, the continental, and the global, are now being recognized as historical products, at once socially constructed, institutionally mediated, politically contested, and therefore malleable.[6] Under these circumstances, the scale question has acquired an unprecedented methodological salience, if not urgency, in diverse fields of social-theoretical debate and in a vast range of sociospatial investigations.

---

[4] See David Harvey, *The Limits to Capital* (Chicago: University of Chicago Press, 1982); Neil Smith, *Uneven Development* (New York: Blackwell, 1984); Peter J. Taylor, *Political Geography: World-Economy, Nation-State and Locality* (New York: Longman, 1985); Peter J. Taylor, "A Materialist Framework for Political Geography," *Transactions of the Institute of British Geographers* 7 (1982): 15–34; and Peter J. Taylor, "Geographical Scales within the World-Economy Approach," *Review* 5, no. 1 (1981): 3–11.

[5] Kevin Cox, "The Difference That Scale Makes," *Political Geography* 15 (1996): 667–70.

[6] See, foundationally, Neil Smith, "Homeless/Global: Scaling Places," in *Mapping the Futures*, ed. Jon Bird, Barry Curtis, Tim Putnam, and Lisa Tickner (New York: Routledge, 1993), 87–119; Neil Smith, "Geography, Difference and the Politics of Scale," in *Postmodernism and the Social Sciences*, ed. Joe Doherty, Elspeth Graham, and Mo Malek (New York: St. Martin's Press, 1992), 57–79; Neil Smith, "Remaking Scale: Competition and Cooperation in Prenational and Postnational Europe," in *Competitive European Peripheries*, ed. Heikki Eskelinen and Folke Snickars (Berlin: Springer Verlag, 1995), 59–74; Erik Swyngedouw, "Neither Global nor Local: 'Glocalization' and the Politics of Scale," in *Spaces of Globalization*, ed. Kevin Cox (New York: Guilford Press, 1997), 137–66; and Peter J. Taylor, "Embedded Statism and the Social Sciences: Opening Up to New Spaces," *Environment and Planning A* 28 (1996): 1917–28.

In methodological and substantive terms, these discussions have been extraordinarily multifaceted, and they continue to evolve rapidly across the interstitial terrain of critical sociospatial analysis, as well as within environmental studies, the spatial humanities, and the design disciplines.[7] As these explorations have gained momentum, several major lines of research on the production and politics of scale have crystallized. On an epistemological level, scholars have critically interrogated geographical scale in the context of debates on the appropriate spatiotemporal unit of analysis and level of abstraction for historical, sociological, cultural, and environmental research.[8] In the field of critical geopolitical economy, strategies to reconfigure scalar organization have been analyzed as essential dimensions of the post-1970s wave of worldwide capitalist restructuring, whether with reference to the rescaling of capital accumulation, financial circuits, state power, governance networks, urbanization, social reproduction, or sociometabolic flows.[9] The politics of scale have also been explored in relation to the

---

[7] For helpful overviews, see Roger Keil and Rianne Mahon, eds., *Leviathan Undone? The New Political Economy of Scale* (Vancouver: University of British Columbia Press, 2010); Andrew Herod, *Scale* (New York: Routledge, 2011); Sallie Marston, "The Social Construction of Scale," *Progress in Human Geography* 24, no. 2 (2000): 219–42; and Nathan Sayre, "Ecological and Geographic Scale: Parallels and Potential for Integration," *Progress in Human Geography* 29, no. 3 (2005): 276–90.

[8] See, for instance, Sayre, "Ecological and Geographic Scale"; John Agnew, "The Territorial Trap: The Geographical Assumptions of International Relations Theory," *Review of International Political Economy* 1, no. 1 (1994): 53–80; John Agnew, "Representing Space: Space, Scale and Culture in Social Science," in *Place/Culture/ Representation*, ed. James Duncan and David Ley (London: Routledge, 1993), 251–71; Kevin Cox and Andrew Mair, "Levels of Abstraction in Locality Studies," *Antipode* 21 (1989): 121–32; Andrew Sayer, "Behind the Locality Debate: Deconstructing Geography's Dualisms," *Environment and Planning A* 23, no. 3 (1991): 283–308; Neil Smith, "Dangers of the Empirical Turn," *Antipode* 19 (1987): 59–68; Immanuel Wallerstein, *Unthinking Social Science: The Limits of 19th Century Paradigms* (Cambridge: Polity, 1991); and David Palumbo-Liu, Nirvana Tanoukhi, and Bruce Robbins, eds., *Immanuel Wallerstein and the Problem of the World: System, Scale, Culture* (Durham, NC: Duke University Press, 2011). More recent debates on climate change, the "Anthropocene," and the historical social sciences have generated a new wave of such debates. See, in particular, Dipesh Chakrabarty, "The Climate of History: Four Theses," *Critical Inquiry* 35, no. 2 (2009): 197–222.

[9] See, for instance, Philip Cerny, "Globalization and the Changing Logic of Collective Action," *International Organization* 49, no. 4 (1995): 595–625; Erik Swyngedouw, "The Mammon Quest: 'Glocalisation,' Interspatial Competition, and the Monetary Order: The Construction of New Scales," in *Cities and Regions in the New Europe*, ed. Mick Dunford and Grigoris Kafkalas (London: Belhaven Press, 1992), 39–68; Erik Swyngedouw, "The Heart of the Place: The Resurrection of Locality in an Age of Hyperspace," *Geografiska Annaler B* 71 (1989): 31–42; Erik Swyngedouw, "Reconstructing Citizenship, the Re-Scaling of the State and the New Authoritarianism: Closing the Belgian Mines," *Urban Studies* 33 (1996): 1499–521; Bob Jessop, "Post-Fordism and the State," in *Post-Fordism: A Reader*, ed. Ash Amin (Cambridge, MA: Blackwell, 1994), 251–79; Alain Lipietz, "The National and the Regional: Their Autonomy Vis-à-Vis the Capitalist World Crisis," in *Transcending the State-Global Divide*, ed. Ronen P. Palan and Barry K. Gills (Boulder, CO: Lynne Rienner Publishers, 1994), 23–44; Alain Lipietz, "The

ongoing remaking of democracy, the territory/sovereignty nexus, hegemony, geopolitics, and regulatory space under globalizing, neoliberalizing, post-Westphalian capitalism.[10] And finally, among scholars of social movements and cultural politics, scale has been productively explored as a medium and stake of sociopolitical contestation. Across diverse sites and contexts, these research endeavors demonstrated that scalar configurations serve not only as structural dimensions of domination, but may also become key strategic parameters in struggles for empowerment and, consequently, may be subjected to radical reorganization.[11]

As David Delaney and Helga Leitner have suggested, a broadly shared methodological agenda underpins these otherwise heterogeneous theoretical explorations and topical investigations: "Geographic scale is conceptualized as being socially constructed rather than ontologically pre-given. . . . [T]he geographic scales constructed are themselves implicated in the constitution

Local and the Global: Regional Individuality or Interregionalism?," *Transactions of the Institute of British Geographers* 18, no. 1 (1993): 8–18; Jamie Peck and Adam Tickell, "The Social Regulation of Uneven Development: 'Regulatory Deficit,' England's South East, and the Collapse of Thatcherism," *Environment and Planning A* 27 (1995): 15–40; Jamie Peck and Adam Tickell, "Searching for a New Institutional Fix: The After-Fordist Crisis and the Global-Local Disorder," in Amin, *Post-Fordism: A Reader*, 280–315; and Neil Smith and Dennis Ward, "The Restructuring of Geographical Scale: Coalescence and Fragmentation of the Northern Core Region," *Economic Geography* 63, no. 2 (1987): 160–82.

[10] See, for instance, William E. Connolly, "Democracy and Territoriality," *Millennium* 20, no. 3 (1991): 463–84; David Held, *Democracy and the Global Order: From the Modern State to Cosmopolitan Governance* (Cambridge: Polity, 1995); Bob Jessop, *The Future of the Capitalist State* (London: Polity, 2002); Neil Brenner, *New State Spaces: Urban Governance and the Rescaling of Statehood* (New York: Oxford University Press, 2004); Leo Panitch, "Globalization and the State," in *Socialist Register 1994*, ed. Ralph Miliband and Leo Panitch (London: Merlin Press, 1994), 60–93; Peter Marden, "Geographies of Dissent: Globalization, Identity and the Nation," *Political Geography* 16 (1997): 37–64; and Helga Leitner, "The Politics of Scale and Networks of Spatial Connectivity," in *Scale and Geographic Inquiry*, ed. Eric Sheppard and Robert McMaster (Malden, MA: Blackwell, 2004), 236–55.

[11] See, for instance, Peter J. Taylor, "The Paradox of Geographical Scale in Marx's Politics," *Antipode* 19 (1994): 387–91; Andrew Herod, "Labor's Spatial Praxis and the Geography of Contract Bargaining in the US East Coast Longshore Industry, 1953–1989," *Political Geography* 16, no. 2 (1997): 145–69; Andrew Herod, "The Production of Scale in United States Labour Relations," *Area* 23 (1991): 82–88; Andrew E. G. Jonas, "The Scale Politics of Spatiality," *Environment and Planning D: Society and Space* 12 (1994): 257–64; Philip F. Kelly, "Globalization, Power and the Politics of Scale in the Philippines," *Geoforum* 28 (1997): 151–71; Lynn Staeheli, "Empowering Political Struggle: Spaces and Scales of Resistance," *Political Geography* 13 (1994): 387–91; Neil Smith and Cindi Katz, "Grounding Metaphor: Towards a Spatialized Politics," in *Place and the Politics of Identity*, ed. Michael Keith and Steve Pile (London: Routledge, 1993), 67–83; Byron Miller, "Political Action and the Geography of Defense Investment," *Political Geography* 16 (1997): 171–85; Helga Leitner, "Reconfiguring the Spatiality of Power," *Political Geography* 16 (1997): 123–43; and Helga Leitner, Eric Sheppard, and Kristin Sziarto, "The Spatialities of Contentious Politics," *Transactions of the Institute of British Geographers* 33, no. 2 (2008): 157–72.

of social, economic and political processes."[12] From this perspective, spatial scale is not to be construed as a timeless, asocial container of sociospatial relations, but—much like "structures" in sociological theories of practice—as their historical presupposition, medium, and outcome.[13] As Neil Smith classically argued in the early 1990s, scales must be viewed at once as the "materialization of contested social forces" and as their active "progenitors"; they are continually produced, contested, reconfigured, and transformed as the "geographical organizer and expression of collective social action."[14] "Scale," Smith proposed, "demarcates the sites of social contest, the object as well as the [spatial] resolution of the contest."[15] In Erik Swyngedouw's similarly foundational formulation, "Geographical scales are both the realm and the outcome of the struggle for control over social space."[16] In closely parallel terms, cultural anthropologist Anna Tsing has more recently argued that "scale is not just a neutral frame for viewing the world; scale must be brought into being. . . . Scales are claimed and contested in cultural and political projects."[17]

These social- and political-constructionist methodological injunctions provide an essential foundation for any critical approach to the scale question under historical and contemporary capitalism. Building upon these approaches, this chapter develops a more specific, historical-geographical materialist analytical lens through which to explore the vicissitudes of the scale question under capitalism. Clearly, geographical scales and interscalar configurations are produced through an immense range of sociopolitical, institutional, cultural, ecological, and discursive-representational processes that cannot be derived from any single, encompassing dynamic or causal mechanism. Nevertheless, this chapter sets out to decipher the pervasive

[12] David Delaney and Helga Leitner, "The Political Construction of Scale," *Political Geography* 16 (1997): 93.

[13] On structurationist theories, see Pierre Bourdieu, *Outline of a Theory of Practice* (Cambridge: Cambridge University Press, 1977); Anthony Giddens, *The Constitution of Society: Outline of the Theory of Structuration* (Cambridge: Polity, 1984); and William Sewell, "A Theory of Structure: Duality, Agency and Transformation," *American Journal of Sociology* 98, no. 1 (1992): 1–29.

[14] Smith, "Remaking Scale," 61; Smith, "Homeless/Global," 101.

[15] Smith, "Homeless/Global," 101.

[16] Swyngedouw, "Mammon Quest," 60.

[17] Anna Lowenhaupt Tsing, *Friction: An Ethnography of Global Connection* (Princeton, NJ: Princeton University Press, 2005), 58. See also Anna Lowenhaupt Tsing, "On Nonscalability: The Living World Is Not Amenable to Precision-Nested Scales," *Common Knowledge* 18, no. 3 (2012): 505–24.

implications of one of capitalism's core geographical contradictions—that between fixity and motion in the circulation of capital—for the production and transformation of scalar arrangements.

It was David Harvey who, during over four decades of theorizing on capitalist urbanization, uneven spatial development, and crisis formation, proposed what is arguably still the foundational account of the fixity/motion contradiction.[18] In Harvey's theorization, the process of capital accumulation is necessarily dependent upon territorial organization (fixity); yet capital's relentless pursuit of surplus value perpetually destabilizes and supersedes its own territorial preconditions (motion). The fixity/motion contradiction is thus articulated, as Harvey explains, "between the rising power to overcome space and the immobile spatial structures required for such a purpose" during the course of capitalist development.[19]

This chapter treats the fixity/motion contradiction as a key analytical reference point for theorizing the production of scale and interscalar configurations under capitalism. The core argument is that the fixity/motion contradiction and the unstable territorial landscapes whose production it mediates are articulated in determinate scalar patterns: they are *scaled* in historically specific ways, and they are periodically *rescaled* during periods of crisis-induced sociospatial restructuring. The claim here is not that formations of scalar organization could somehow be functionally derived from circuits of capital, or that overaccumulation crises mandate a specific pattern of scalar deconstruction or interscalar reconstitution. As emphasized earlier with reference to recent theoretical contributions, the production of scale is always institutionally mediated and shaped through intense, contextually specific sociopolitical struggles, some of which may be destructive, disruptive, or only incoherently articulated to processes of capital accumulation. Nonetheless, such mediations and contestations can be productively deciphered by being analytically situated in relation to the broader structural (il)logics associated with capitalism as a contradictory, dynamic, endemically crisis-prone, and unevenly developed historical-geographical system. In other words, the scalar selectivities of crisis formation and strategies of crisis resolution are structurally embedded, but they are not structurally

---

[18] See Harvey, *Limits to Capital*; David Harvey, "The Geopolitics of Capitalism," in *Social Relations and Spatial Structures*, ed. Derek Gregory and John Urry (London: Macmillan, 1985), 128–63; David Harvey, *The Urban Experience* (Baltimore: Johns Hopkins University Press, 1989); David Harvey, *Spaces of Capital: Towards a Critical Geography* (New York: Routledge, 2001); David Harvey, *Spaces of Global Capitalism* (London: Verso, 2006); and David Harvey, *The Seventeen Contradictions of Capitalism* (New York: Oxford University Press, 2014).

[19] Harvey, "Geopolitics of Capitalism," 150.

preordained. This interscalar "context of context" provides an essential, if incomplete, interpretive reference point for more concrete-complex, strategically oriented modes of investigation into scale-making strategies and the politics of scale under capitalism.[20]

To develop this line of argumentation, I first scrutinize the largely implicit scalar dimensions of Harvey's account of the fixity/motion contradiction, which offers several essential, if somewhat undertheorized, insights. I then turn to some of the key scalar analytics that are embedded within Henri Lefebvre's approach to sociospatial theory, urbanization, the capitalist urban fabric, and state space. As with Harvey's theorization, a powerful scalar imagination pervades Lefebvre's approach, but it likewise mainly crystallizes as a background framing for other conceptual maneuvers. A scale-attuned reading of several of Lefebvre's key ideas yields a number of fruitful interpretive proposals regarding the intrinsically relational character of scale; the shifting scalar geographies of urbanization; the strategic role of state institutions in mediating the fixity/motion contradiction and its sociospatial expressions in the capitalist urban fabric; and the progressively more intricate intermeshing among the scales of urbanization and those of state space during the course of twentieth-century capitalist development.

These considerations generate some solid methodological foundations for confronting the scale question under capitalism, and for connecting it to the (re)conceptualization and investigation of capitalist urbanization. In particular, a scale-attuned reading of Harvey and Lefebvre generates an analytical perspective from which to investigate the interplay between successive rounds of state spatial intervention and the shifting scalar geographies of the capitalist urban fabric during the last four decades. More generally, these conceptual maneuvers provide analytic mediations between the strategic, agency-centric arguments emphasized in the contemporary literature on the politics of scale and the more structural modes of analysis that are arguably required to grasp the scalar crystallizations of the fixity/motion contradiction. This chapter thus situates contemporary rescaling processes in a broader geohistorical context while also assembling the conceptual grounding for the scale-attuned approach to the capitalist urban fabric that is developed in this book.

---

[20] On the "context of context," see Neil Brenner, Jamie Peck, and Nik Theodore, "Variegated Neoliberalization: Geographies, Modalities, Pathways," *Global Networks* 10, no. 2 (2010): 182–222; Neil Brenner, Jamie Peck, and Nik Theodore, "After Neoliberalization?," *Globalizations* 7, no. 3 (2010): 313–30.

The Fixity/Motion Contradiction and the Scale Question

The problem of territorial organization under capitalism, as theorized by David Harvey, grounds my approach to the production of scale and interscalar configurations.[21] According to Harvey, the contradictory interplay between fixity (the need for territorial organization) and motion (the equally foundational drive toward sociospatial restructuring) has underpinned the continuous reshaping of territorial landscapes throughout capitalism's long-term global history. Exploration of this contradiction thus provides considerable analytical leverage, he argues, in relation to diverse aspects of sociospatial relations under capitalism.

On the one hand, building on Karl Marx's classic analysis in the *Grundrisse*, as well as on Rosa Luxemburg's closely related theory of imperialism, Harvey argues that capital is inherently globalizing, oriented toward the continual acceleration of turnover times and the overcoming of all geographical barriers to accumulation. In Marx's well-known formulation, "the tendency to create the world market is inherent to the concept of capital itself. Every limit appears as a barrier to be overcome."[22] In Marx's view, this "annihilation of space by time" must thus be viewed as one of the core spatiotemporal expressions and projects of capital:

> While capital must on the one side strive to tear down every spatial barrier to intercourse, i.e. to exchange, and conquer the whole earth for its market, it strives on the other to annihilate this space with time, i.e. to reduce to a minimum the time spent in motion from one place to another. The more developed the capital, therefore, the more extensive the market over which it circulates, which forms the spatial orbit of its circulation, the more does it strive simultaneously for an even greater extension of the market and for greater annihilation of space by time.[23]

Harvey has occasionally described this spatiotemporal tendency within the capital relation through the concept of "space-time compression," which usefully underscores the mutually recursive relations between capital's drive to expand its spatial field of operations and its concomitant acceleration

---

[21] See note 18.

[22] Karl Marx, *Grundrisse: Foundations of the Critique of Political Economy*, trans. Martin Nicolaus (New York: Penguin Books, 1973 [1857]), 408.

[23] Ibid.

of turnover times in pursuit of maximal surplus value extraction.[24] In addition to these tendencies, however, the concept of "motion" in Harvey's theorization also refers to the spatial deconstruction of any sociotechnical, locational, institutional, political, or ecological barriers to the accumulation process. Accordingly, for my purposes here, the more general concept of *deterritorialization* will be used to reference capital's triple-pronged drive toward spatial expansion, temporal acceleration, and relentless spatiotemporal restructuring.[25]

On the other hand, Harvey argues that capital's moment of deterritorialization is contingent upon a wide range of relatively fixed and immobile spatial infrastructures. These include, among other elements, customized equipment for production, circulation, and social reproduction; urban-regional agglomerations; state regulatory configurations; large-scale sociotechnical networks; infrastructuralized landscapes for metabolizing materials, food, water, energy, and waste; logistical grids; and so forth. This, then, is the dialectical "other" of deterritorialization: capital's equally endemic moment of *territorialization*, which is embodied in historically specific frameworks of *territorial organization*.

According to Harvey, as the process of global capitalist industrialization has been accelerated and expanded, the spatial infrastructures associated with capital's moment of territorialization have been more comprehensively designed, choreographed, and coordinated, especially through the instruments of large-scale state spatial planning. Nonetheless, these variegated landscapes of territorialization have remained chronically volatile due to capital's endemic crisis tendencies. Faced with persistently disruptive overaccumulation crises, inherited formations of territorial organization may be subjected to dramatic waves of "creative destruction," the spatial analogs to those explosive bursts of technological innovation to which Austrian economist Joseph Schumpeter famously applied this suggestive Nietzschean term in the early 1940s.[26] Under such conditions, as capital strives to extricate

---

[24] See, for example, David Harvey, *The Condition of Postmodernity* (Cambridge, MA: Blackwell, 1989).

[25] On the scalar politics of deterritorialization, see Neil Brenner, "Beyond State-Centrism: Space, Territoriality and Geographical Scale in Globalization Studies," *Theory & Society* 28 (1999): 39–78.

[26] For discussion of Schumpeter's position, as well as several closely related formulations in Marx's writings, see David Harvey, *The Enigma of Capital: And the Crises of Capitalism* (New York: Oxford University Press, 2010), 45–47. On the Nietzschean roots of the application of "creative destruction" to economics by Schumpeter, as well as by Werner Sombart, see Hugo Reinert and Erik Reinert, "Creative Destruction in Economics: Nietzsche, Sombart, Schumpeter," in *Friedrich Nietzsche 1844–2000: Economy and Society*, ed. Jürgen Georg Backhaus and Wolfgang Drechsler (Boston: Kluwer, 2006), 55–85.

itself from the spatial prison of investments previously sunk into the built environment and large-scale infrastructural configurations, far-reaching devalorization processes are unleashed. Inherited forms of territorial organization, including their technoscientific foundations, infrastructural supports, institutional-regulatory scaffolds, and sociopolitical bases, are radically reorganized as dominant factions of capital and place-based political alliances seek out new spatial horizons for pursuing a fresh round of capital accumulation. In the wake of intense sociopolitical conflicts, this generally leads to the construction of new spatial divisions of labor and to a significant reconstitution of territorial organization itself.

For Harvey, therefore, the fixity/motion contradiction lies at the heart of each successive configuration of capitalist development: its geographies at once internalize (temporarily contain) and express (explosively articulate) that contradiction, generating discontinuous rhythms of expanded accumulation, followed by sustained periods of stagnation, instability, crisis, devalorization, and accelerated sociospatial restructuring. Configurations of territorial organization are continually produced as the geographical preconditions for capital's expansionary dynamism, only to be creatively destroyed during recurrent rounds of systemic crisis. In short, in Harvey's laconic but precise formulation, "spatial organization is necessary to overcome space."[27] The contradictory interplay between fixity and motion—between the need for territorial organization (territorialization) and the equally foundational drive toward sociospatial creative destruction (deterritorialization)—thus offers a powerful analytical basis for deciphering the production and perpetual reorganization of sociospatial configurations under capitalism.

In a much-debated conceptual maneuver, Harvey refers to the provisionally stabilized configurations of territorial organization that support capital's globalizing, accelerationist dynamic as a "spatial fix"—understood as a "tendency towards . . . a structured coherence to production and consumption within a given space."[28] A spatial fix is secured, Harvey argues, through "the conversion of temporal into spatial restraints to accumulation."[29] On a definitional level, the notion of a "fix" in Harvey's work connotes several intertwined meanings: (1) the relatively stabilized, long-term nature of

---

[27] Harvey, "Geopolitics of Capitalism," 146.

[28] Ibid., 141, 145, 146. Among the many texts in Harvey's vast corpus that develop this concept, the most essential are *The Limits to Capital, The Urban Experience,* and *Spaces of Capital* (see notes 4 and 18). For several useful critical evaluations, see Noel Castree and Derek Gregory, eds., *David Harvey: A Critical Reader* (Malden, MA: Blackwell, 2006).

[29] Harvey, *Limits to Capital,* 416.

investments that are sunk into the built environment and associated infra-structural configurations; (2) the spatially immobilized character of those investments; and (3) their role as a potential resolution for capital's crisis tendencies, albeit one that is tightly circumscribed in both temporal and spatial terms.

This latter aspect of the spatial "fix" deserves special emphasis, since it illuminates the contradictory spatial (il)logic that inheres at the heart of the capital relation. Much like the ephemeral feelings of satisfaction or "fix" ex-perienced by the drug addict or alcoholic as he or she attempts, in vain, to satiate a self-destructive "habit," capital's fixation on space—its voracious need for territorial organization—can meet with no more than fleeting grati-fication within the endless cycle of accumulation. Indeed, since no spatial fix could resolve the endemic problem of overaccumulation under capitalism, each configuration of territorial organization is only provisionally stabilized; its eventual devalorization is unavoidable. In this sense, in Harvey's analysis, each spatial fix for capital amounts to no more than a chronically unstable "dynamic equilibrium" within a chaotic see-saw of perpetual sociospatial cre-ative destruction.[30]

Capital, then, is addicted to territorial organization; yet no formation of territorial organization could permanently satisfy its ravenous appetite for accumulating surplus value or, for that matter, effectively insulate itself from the persistent threat of devalorization. This generates the famous "knife edge" structural dilemma "between preserving the values of past commitments made at a particular place and time, or devaluing them to open up fresh room for accumulation."[31] This dilemma, Harvey has shown, is expressed precisely through "the restless formation and re-formation of geographical landscapes," the historically specific configurations of territorial organiza-tion in which the fixity/motion contradiction is fought out.[32]

Harvey focuses his analysis on the general conditions under which rel-atively stabilized forms of territorial organization may crystallize within the capitalist maelstrom. As he develops the elements of his theoretical ap-proach, the central agenda is to demonstrate, on a relatively abstract-logical level, how and why spatial fixes may be structurally ossified relative to cycles of accelerated capital devalorization and crisis-induced sociospatial restruc-turing. Harvey is, correspondingly, only secondarily concerned with the

---

[30] Harvey, "Geopolitics of Capitalism," 136.

[31] Ibid., 150.

[32] Ibid.

specific patterns of territorial organization that are thereby formed. For this reason, his analyses are ambiguous regarding the question that most centrally concerns us here—the scalar composition of each historical spatial fix and its associated architecture of territorial organization. Several competing accounts appear to coexist somewhat uneasily in his classic writings from the 1980s on the fixity/motion dialectic.

First, in his major writings on cities, Harvey implies that the *urban* scale has been the fundamental geographical foundation for every historical spatial fix. From this point of view, spatial fixes are rooted in long-term investments in the built environments of cities; agglomeration is viewed as the locational anchor for capitalist industrial growth. In this vein, Harvey pinpoints four distinct forms of urban built environment that have, he suggests, offered spatial fixes for capital during successive waves of industrialization—mercantile cities, industrial cities, Fordist-Keynesian cities, and post-Keynesian cities.[33] In the wake of each cycle of crisis-induced restructuring, Harvey argues, urban built environments have been devalorized and reorganized to acquire new roles within a reconstituted spatial division of labor, and thus to reinvigorate the accumulation process.

Second, in various writings on uneven development and crisis theory, Harvey elaborates various discussions of the spatial fix that transcend this rather physicalist, agglomeration-centric conception of geographical fixity, highlighting instead its socio-organizational aspects, above all with reference to the *regional* scale. To this end, building on the work of French industrial geographer Philippe Aydalot, Harvey introduces a more formal, capital-theoretical definition of structured coherence as "that space within which capital can circulate without the limits of profit within socially-necessary turnover time being exceeded by the cost and time of movement."[34] In several closely related analyses, Harvey emphasizes the importance of interfirm relations, local labor markets, class struggle, territorial alliances, state regulatory institutions, and technological capacities in defining the precise scalar parameters and institutional architecture of each regionalized spatial fix.[35] In such discussions, Harvey implies that spatial fixes are established above all through the *"regional spaces* within which production and consumption, supply and demand (for commodities and labor power), production and

---

[33] Harvey, *Urban Experience.* See also, more recently, David Harvey, *Rebel Cities: From the Right to the City to the Urban Revolution* (London: Verso, 2012).

[34] Harvey, "Geopolitics of Capitalism," 146. See also Philippe Aydalot, *Dynamique spatiale et développement inégal* (Paris: Economica, 1976).

[35] See, for instance, Harvey, *Urban Experience,* 125–64, especially 139–44.

realisation, class struggle and accumulation, culture and life style, hang to-gether . . . within a totality of productive forces and social relations."[36] Here, then, the key issue is not spatial agglomeration as such, but the "hanging to-gether" of diverse socio-organizational elements—industries, technologies, institutions, regulations, and class relations—in a manner that coherently, cumulatively, and durably supports capital accumulation. Harvey thereby implies that the regional scale—rather than the urban, the national, or otherwise—is the privileged spatial locus in and through which such a structured coherence for the accumulation process may be constructed and tendentially reproduced.

Third, Harvey also deploys the notion of the spatial fix to describe the role of interscalar configurations in animating, supporting, and regulating the sociospatial relations of capital. This conceptualization underpins several of Harvey's major writings on urbanization, urban restructuring, and uneven spatial development from this period, but it is elaborated most explicitly in the "third cut" approach to crisis theory he developed at the end of *Limits to Capital*.[37] Here, rather inconspicuously woven into his discussion of "hier-archical arrangements," Harvey connects a distinctive theorization of scale questions—or, more precisely, of *inter*scalar configurations—to his concep-tualization of the fixity/motion contradiction.

Harvey accomplishes this, in a first step, by exploring the implications of the fixity/motion contradiction and several closely associated spatial tensions (concentration/dispersal, globalization/fragmentation, standardization/customization) for the scalar organization of several major sociospatial processes—including production, exchange, circulation, state regula-tion, urbanization, and sociopolitical struggle. On this basis, Harvey also suggests that key actors and organizations within the capitalist geopolitical economy—transnational corporations, states, territorial alliances, and social movements—may attempt to reorganize their scales of operation to manage, displace, or instrumentalize the threat or reality of devaluation. In this way, Harvey articulates a dynamically relational, multiscalar conceptualization of the spatial fix. In a two-pronged conceptual maneuver, he further suggests (1) that each spatial fix crystallizes through the regularized intermeshing of sociospatial processes across multiple, relationally interconnected spatial scales and (2) that this interscalar "meshing" of sociospatial processes creates

---

[36] Harvey, "Geopolitics of Capitalism," 146 (italics in original). For a closely related conceptu-alization, see Erik Swyngedouw, "Territorial Organization and the Space/Technology Nexus," *Transactions of the Institute of British Geographers* 17 (1992): 417–33.

[37] Harvey, *Limits to Capital*, 413–45, especially 422–24, 429–31.

a distinctively scalar layering of territorial organization.[38] The resultant scalar architecture, Harvey argues, is composed of relatively durable, "nested hierarchical structures of organization" that mediate, and are in turn shaped by, the fixity/motion contradiction:

> The tensions between fixity and motion in the circulation of capital, between concentration and dispersal, between local commitment and global concerns, put immense strains upon the organizational capacities of capitalism. The history of capitalism has, as a consequence, been marked by continuous exploration and modification of organizational arrangements that can assuage and contain such tensions. The result has been the creation of nested hierarchical structures of organization which can link the local and particular with the achievement of abstract labor on the world stage.[39]

Thus, in marked contrast to his suggestion elsewhere that spatial fixes are anchored within a single or primary scale, this aspect of Harvey's theory indicates that the construction of each spatial fix at urban or regional scales is itself a multiscalar process in which—to repeat his key formulation—"various hierarchically organized structures . . . mesh awkwardly with each other to define a variety of scales—local, regional, national and international."[40] Geographical scales are viewed here as relationally intertwined organizational-territorial matrices acting as "transmission devices" between locally and regionally embedded sociospatial relations, national political-institutional configurations, and the global space of abstract labor and the world market: they mediate the core operations of capital circulation, its endemic crisis tendencies, and the sociopolitical conflicts they provoke.[41] In effect, these arguments entail an explicit recognition that spatial fixes are also—in the terminology later introduced by Neil Smith—*scalar fixes*: they hinge not only upon scale-specific forms of territorial organization, but upon the relatively durable territorial organization of *interscalar* configurations.[42]

This theorization of the spatial fix as an interscalar architecture is actually implicit in Harvey's periodization of capitalist urbanization, albeit largely as a backdrop to his discussion of changing forms of urban built environment

---

[38] Ibid., 422–23.

[39] Ibid., 422.

[40] Ibid., 423.

[41] Ibid., 424.

[42] Smith, "Remaking Scale."

and regional spatial configuration.[43] If the mercantile form of urbanization was premised upon a key role for city-states as basic territorial units of economic life, the industrial and Fordist-Keynesian forms of urbanization entailed an increasingly centralized role for national states in organizing capital accumulation, territorial regulation, and class relations across spatial scales. Harvey also suggests that the post-1970s round of urban restructuring has dissolved the nationally scaled spatial isomorphism between capital accumulation, economic regulation, and social reproduction that had been pursued under the postwar, national-developmentalist growth regime, causing urban regions around the world to be exposed more directly to the volatility associated with global capital flows, unfettered financial speculation, and aggressive interspatial competition. Likewise, Harvey's classic analysis of the entrepreneurial city, developed in the late 1980s, emphasizes the role of rescaled, post-Keynesian forms of national state power in animating the proliferation of local and regional economic initiatives and the consequent neoliberalization of urban governance across the North Atlantic zone.[44] Thus, although it remains largely implicit within his major theoretical manifestos of the 1980s, important strands of Harvey's work during this period offer the lineaments of a scale-attuned approach to the fixity/motion contradiction and a dynamically multiscalar conceptualization of the spatial fix.

Building upon Harvey's theorization, we thus arrive at several generative methodological propositions for exploring the vicissitudes of the scale question:

- Territorial organization under capitalism is scaled within historically specific interscalar configurations, "hierarchical structures of organization" that offer provisional stability within the maelstrom of sociospatial creative destruction.[45]
- The resultant scale configurations, or scalar fixes, are essential organizational and operational elements within each spatial fix. Spatial fixes are not merely enclosed within pregiven spatial scales or positioned upon a fixed scalar ladder, but entail the construction of specific interscalar hierarchies, divisions of labor, patterns of stratification, relays, circuits, and operations in support of capital accumulation.

[43] Harvey, *Urban Experience*, 17–58.

[44] David Harvey, "From Managerialism to Entrepreneurialism: The Transformation in Urban Governance in Late Capitalism," *Geografiska Annaler: Series B Human Geography* 71, no. 1 (1989): 3–17.

[45] Harvey, *Limits to Capital*, 422.

- Cycles of devalorization and accelerated sociospatial restructuring are frequently associated with rescaling processes, which destabilize and rework inherited scalar fixes and the configurations of territorial organization with which they are intermeshed.

Harvey's approach to the fixity/motion contradiction offers a productive methodological starting point for investigating the rescaling of territorial organization, and thus of the urbanization process, under capitalism. However, because it is largely focused on the abstract tendencies and countertendencies associated with capital circulation, Harvey's theorization veers dangerously close to an ex post facto functionalism in which pathways of institutional restructuring are interpreted solely or primarily with reference to their role in securing the sociospatial conditions for capital accumulation. For example, Harvey posits that, during periods of crisis, the tension between fixity and motion "is bound to snap," and thus that "the nested hierarchical structures [of scalar organization] have to be reorganized, rationalized and reformed." In this way, he suggests, "institutional arrangements grown profligate and fat" can be "brought into tighter relation to the underlying requirements of accumulation," and thus serve to absorb overaccumulation and stave off the threat of devalorization.[46]

While plausible enough as abstract generalizations regarding the *longue durée* cycles of sociospatial creative destruction and rescaling that animate the landscape of capitalism, such formulations could easily be misunderstood as functionalist simplifications implying that scalar arrangements will be recalibrated, quasi-automatically, to meet the "underlying requirements" of capital accumulation. Aside from these methodological hazards, Harvey's conceptually elegant but relatively abstract engagement with the scale question in *Limits* tends to bracket the politico-institutional mediations, strategic expressions, and variegated sociospatial consequences of the fixity/motion contradiction, and thus of rescaling processes. Despite their essential role as modes of crisis displacement and crisis resolution, rescaling processes cannot be reduced to a single, coordinated scale-making project, capitalist or otherwise, and their impacts cannot be derived directly from the "underlying requirements" of the accumulation process. Rather, scalar fixes are produced through the politically negotiated, often haphazard coalescence, or "meshing," of multiple sociospatial relations, projects, and struggles. They articulate, mediate, and rework the sociospatial dynamics of the fixity/

---

[46] Ibid., 431.

motion contradiction, sometimes in incoherent, disruptive, dysfunctional, destructive, or even disastrous ways. In this sense, the scalar configuration of territorial organization is not only ensnared within the fixity/motion contradiction, but is simultaneously an arena, stake and product of sociopolitical conflict. Rescaling is, in this sense, a *political strategy*.

To confront such issues, and to elaborate the conceptualization of scalar fixes, rescaling processes and the politics of scale used in this book, I turn now to another foundational approach to radical sociospatial theory that is permeated with suggestive, if mainly implicit, scalar insights—that developed by Henri Lefebvre in his major sociospatial writings from the late 1960s through the late 1970s.

Henri Lefebvre and the Scale Question

Henri Lefebvre is among the most influential contemporary sociospatial theorists, and his writings from the 1970s, in particular, have powerfully shaped several subsequent generations of scholarship in radical geography, geopolitical economy, and critical urban studies on a diverse range of epistemological, methodological, thematic, and political issues.[47] For present purposes, I consider his approach to the "scale question" which, as noted at the outset of this chapter, he had posed and begun to explore in his spatial investigations of this period.[48]

---

[47] For general overviews and critical interpretations of Lefebvre's sociospatial theory, the most essential studies are Stuart Elden, *Understanding Henri Lefebvre: Theory and the Possible* (New York: Continuum, 2004); Łukasz Stanek, *Henri Lefebvre on Space: Architecture, Urban Research and the Production of Theory* (Minneapolis: University of Minnesota Press, 2011); Christian Schmid, *Stadt, Raum und Gesellschaft: Henri Lefebvre und die Theorie der Produktion des Raumes* (Stuttgart: Franz Steiner Verlag, 2005); and Kanishka Goonewardena, Stefan Kipfer, Richard Milgrom, and Christian Schmid, eds., *Space, Difference, Everyday Life: Reading Henri Lefebvre* (New York: Routledge, 2008). On Lefebvre's approach to state theory, see Neil Brenner and Stuart Elden, "Introduction: State, Space, World. Lefebvre and the Survival of Capitalism," in Henri Lefebvre, *State, Space, World: Selected Essays*, ed. Neil Brenner and Stuart Elden (Minneapolis: University of Minnesota Press, 2009), 1–50.

[48] Lefebvre, *De l'État*, 2:67. Before proceeding further, one point of clarification is needed regarding Lefebvre's terminology. Lefebvre discusses the scale question on the basis of two key terms—*niveau* (level) and *échelle* (scale). Whereas the former term refers to different levels or dimensions of social reality, the latter term captures the notion of scale in its spatial meaning, as a stratum of sociospatial organization. On the one hand, Lefebvre refers to three key "levels" or *niveaux* of social reality: the global (*global*) level, the "mixed" or the urban level, and the "private" or everyday level. On the other hand, Lefebvre refers as well to multiple "scales" or *échelles*: the body, the local, the urban, the regional, the national, the supranational, the worldwide (*mondial*), and the planetary. Given the specific conceptions of scale and rescaling under development in this book, this discussion focuses primarily on Lefebvre's account of scale as *échelle*. Clearly, a more systematic consideration of the intricacies of Lefebvre's theory would require a careful

Throughout two of his major books of the 1970s, *The Production of Space* and *De l'État*, Lefebvre argues that geographical scales operate at once as boundaries and as hierarchies of sociospatial relations (in his terms, "spatial practices").[49] On the one hand, Lefebvre suggests that scales circumscribe sociospatial relations within determinate organizational-territorial parameters, or "space envelopes."[50] In an extended methodological discussion of scale in volume 2 of *De l'État*, Lefebvre elaborates this point, suggesting that each geographical scale must be conceptualized in terms of three intertwined conditions—those of its historical formation, those of its provisional stabilization, and those of its possible rupture or transformation.[51] In this sense, Lefebvre suggests, geographical scales under capitalism canalize sociospatial relations into determinate but potentially malleable frameworks of patterned interdependence. In so doing, Lefebvre insists, scales are directly implicated in those relations, contributing to the vicissitudes of their historical reproduction, reconfiguration, and potential transformation.

On the other hand, Lefebvre is equally insistent that geographical scales can never be understood in isolation; they are constitutively relational patternings of sociospatial relations that are at once embedded within and shaped through broader interscalar architectures. It is, in other words, through interscalar relations that distinctive, durable, and operationally significant scalings of sociospatial practice are forged. As Lefebvre argues in a classic formulation, "*Social spaces interpenetrate one another and/or superimpose themselves upon one another. They are not things, which have mutually limiting boundaries and which collide because of their contours or as*

---

analysis of his conception of scale as level. For an insightful exploration of these issues, with particular reference to the urban question, see Stefan Kipfer, "Why the Urban Question Still Matters: Reflections on Rescaling and the Promise of the Urban," in Keil and Mahon, *Leviathan Undone?*, 67–86. For one of my own early attempts to excavate the scalar analytics of Lefebvre's writings on globalization, albeit mainly from a geopolitical economy perspective, see Neil Brenner, "Global, Fragmented, Hierarchical: Henri Lefebvre's Geographies of Globalization," *Public Culture* 10, no. 1 (1997): 135–67.

[49] See Lefebvre, *De l'État*, vol. 2; as well as Henri Lefebvre, *The Production of Space*, trans. Donald Nicholson-Smith (Cambridge: Blackwell, 1991 [1974]); Henri Lefebvre, *De l'État: l'État dans le monde moderne*, vol. 1 (Paris: Union Générale d'Éditions, 1976); Henri Lefebvre, *De l'État: Le Mode de Production Étatique*, vol. 3 (Paris: Union Générale d'Éditions, 1978); Henri Lefebvre, *De l'État: Les Contradictions de l'État Moderne*, vol. 4 (Paris: Union Générale d'Éditions, 1978). While Lefebvre's key writings on state theory have not been comprehensively translated, a selection is available in Henri Lefebvre, *State, Space, World: Selected Essays*, ed. Neil Brenner and Stuart Elden (Minneapolis: University of Minnesota Press, 2009).

[50] Lefebvre, *Production of Space*, 329, 351.

[51] *De l'État*, 2:69.

a result of inertia."[52] This "principle of superimposition and interpenetration of social spaces," which Lefebvre develops at length in *The Production of Space*, is closely related to the conception of a "hierarchical stratified morphology" (*une morphologie hiérarchique stratifiée*), which he subsequently elaborates in *De l'État*. Through the latter concept, Lefebvre aims to deconstruct the everyday understanding of scales as precision-nested "blocks" of space defined in terms of absolute territorial size. In contrast to such ideological projections, the notion of a hierarchical stratified morphology advances a conception of scales as relationally intertwined levels within a dynamically evolving, unevenly developed, polarized, world-encompassing, and endemically crisis-riven sociospatial totality.[53] For Lefebvre, then, it is through an analysis of these two closely intertwined aspects of geographical scale—its role as a relatively circumscribed "space envelope" and its relational embeddedness within a "hierarchical stratified morphology"—that differential scalar configurations and associated rescaling processes under capitalism may be distinguished.

In some contexts, Lefebvre appears to present this conception of scale in primarily methodological terms, as an epistemological realignment devised to advance his proposed approach to the production of space. However, as Lefebvre unfurls his wide-ranging analyses in *The Production of Space* and *De l'État*, many concepts that are initially framed as methodological interventions are soon revealed as "concrete abstractions": their emergence is not a reflection of some underlying ontological essence that has now been discovered or revealed, but is conditioned directly by concrete sociospatial transformations that have rendered them essential as interpretive tools. As Łukasz Stanek has brilliantly demonstrated, this proposition applies to the very concept of "space" (*l'espace*) as used by Lefebvre during this period.[54] It also clearly applies to the major ancillary concepts through which Lefebvre approaches the scale question. In this sense, neither the principle of superimposition and interpenetration of social spaces nor the notion of

---

[52] Lefebvre, *Production of Space*, 86 (italics in original).

[53] Lefebvre, *De l'État*, 2:67–69; *De l'État*, 4:293–97; Henri Lefebvre, "Space and the State," in *State, Space, World: Selected Essays*, ed. Neil Brenner and Stuart Elden (Minneapolis, University of Minnesota Press, 2009 [1978]), 235–36. Lefebvre borrows this concept from French mathematician René Thom, his colleague at the University of Strasbourg in the early 1960s, from whose writings on chaos theory and catastrophe he took considerable inspiration. See René Thom, *Modèles Mathématiques de la Morphogénèse: Recueil de Textes sur la Theorie des Catastrophes et ses Applications* (Paris: Union Générale d'Editions, 1974), translated by W. M. Brookes and D. Rand as *Mathematical Models of Morphogenesis* (New York: Halsted Press, 1983).

[54] Stanek, *Henri Lefebvre on Space*.

a hierarchical stratified morphology is merely a methodological proposal. Both have become urgent in epistemological terms, Lefebvre suggests, due to the construction of historically specific formations, layerings and circuits of interscalar organization which they help to illuminate. Lefebvre's conceptualization of the scale question, therefore, is inextricably intertwined with an analysis of the production and periodic reshuffling of interscalar configurations under modern capitalism.

In several key passages of *The Production of Space*, Lefebvre theorizes the historical geographies of capitalism with reference to an epochal transformation from the production of individual commodities *in* space ("competitive capitalism") to the production *of* space itself, a "second nature" of abstract sociospatial infrastructures, landscapes, networks, and ecologies ("neocapitalism").[55] Among the diverse elements of these industrially produced geographies of neocapitalism, Lefebvre draws particular attention, in several vivid formulations, to their unevenly overlapping, conflictually interwoven, and dynamically coevolving scalar morphologies:

> We are confronted not by one social space but by many—indeed, by an unlimited multiplicity or uncountable set of social spaces. . . . No space disappears in the course of growth and development: *the worldwide does not abolish the local.*[56] The *places* of social space are very different from those of natural space in that they are not simply juxtaposed: they may be intercalated, combined, superimposed—they may even sometimes collide. Consequently the local . . . does not disappear, for it is never absorbed by the regional, national or even worldwide level. The national and regional levels take in innumerable "places"; national space embraces the regions; and world space does not merely subsume national spaces, but even (for the time being at least) precipitates the formation of new national spaces through a remarkable process of fission. All these spaces, meanwhile, are traversed by myriad currents. The hypercomplexity of social space should now be apparent, embracing as it does individual entities and peculiarities, relatively fixed points, movements, and flows and waves—some interpenetrating, others in conflict, and so on.[57]

> It is impossible, in fact, to avoid the conclusion that space is assuming an increasingly important role in supposedly "modern" societies. . . . Space's hegemony does not operate solely on the "micro" scale (*á l'échelle "micro"*), effecting the arrangement of surfaces in a supermarket, for instance, or in

---

[55] Lefebvre, *Production of Space*, 37. On the notion of "second nature," see ibid., 109–10, 345, 348, 376, 409.

[56] Ibid., 86 (italics in original).

[57] Ibid., 88 (italics in original).

a "neighborhood" of housing-units (*une unité de voisinage*); nor does it apply only on the "macro" scale (*á l'échelle "macro"*), as though it were responsible for the ordering of "flows" within nations or continents. On the contrary, its effects may be observed on all levels (*niveaux*) and in all the scales of their interconnections (*á tous les échelons et dans leurs connexions*). . . . Today our concern must be with space on a worldwide scale (and indeed—beyond the surface of the earth—on the scale of interplanetary space), as well as with all the spaces subsidiary to it, at every possible scale (*á tous les échelons*). No single space has disappeared completely; and all spaces without exception have undergone metamorphoses.[58]

In these passages and elsewhere, Lefebvre emphasizes the apparently volatile, fractured, disorderly, and even chaotic character of the interscalar configurations upon which neocapitalism's survival hinges. He suggests, for instance, that such scalar geographies evoke the "instant infinity" depicted in Mondrian's paintings; he considers, but then quickly discards, analogies derived from astronomy, mathematics, quantum physics, and fluid dynamics to depict their internal patternings and evolutionary pathways; and he playfully suggests that they most directly resemble the convoluted, flaky texture of a popular French dessert pastry, the *mille-feuille*.[59] Clearly, Lefebvre intends such experiments with spatial metaphor to advance his assertive critique of totalizing, colonizing, technoscientific, and phallocentric approaches that subsume social space under a singular cartographic lens, semiotic framework, or codification system.

Crucially, however, Lefebvre is equally insistent that the intricately layered scalings of social space described in the previously quoted passages cannot be envisioned as a kaleidoscope of random, haphazardly intersecting processes that defy theoretical analysis or rational comprehension. For Lefebvre, the hypercomplex, interlayered qualities of space and scale are not transparently given aspects of social life; but nor are they too opaque, obscure, or mysterious to be decoded through critical investigation. Such misrecognitions are, he argues, the surface expressions, or forms of appearance, of the "fetishized abstract space" of modern capitalism, the defining characteristic of which is precisely to occlude the variegated spatial practices, power relations, struggles,

---

[58] Ibid., 412, translation modified. Nicholson-Smith uses the term "scale" for *l'échelle, les échelons* and *niveaux*; I have rendered the latter term "levels" since this is likewise a specific technical-philosophical term in Lefebvre's work (see note 48). See Henri Lefebvre, *La production de l'espace*, 4th ed. (Paris: Anthropos, 2000 [1974]), 473–74.

[59] Lefebvre, *Production of Space*, 85–87. The *mille-feuille* analogy is revisited at length in Chapter 8.

and ideologies involved in its own production.[60] Consequently, one of the key tasks of the "critique of space" advocated by Lefebvre is to illuminate the historically specific operations of several key sociospatial processes—capitalist industrialization, urbanization, state regulation, techno-environmental management, and sociopolitical contestation—in producing the abstract but fractured geographies of modern capitalism, including those associated with the hierarchical stratified morphologies outlined previously.[61]

In developing his approach to the scale question, Lefebvre confronts this broader challenge by advancing an elegantly simple theoretical-historical proposition. Across various texts and investigations, he interprets the relational properties of scale (as a category of analysis) not as an ontological truism, but as the expression of a historically specific tendency: the progressive, if constitutively uneven, thickening and intermeshing of interscalar relations (in the sphere of spatial practice) during the course of worldwide capitalist development. In the transition from the production of commodities in space to the production of space itself, Lefebvre argues, interscalar linkages have been dramatically intensified, not only in operational terms, but through their material interweaving across the fabric of social space as a whole. Consequently, as Lefebvre emphasizes, "the space engendered [under neocapitalism] is 'social' in the sense that it is not one thing among other things, but an ensemble of links, connections, communications, networks and circuits."[62] Within this vortex of unevenly thickening yet ultimately world-encompassing sociospatial relationality, the various scales of spatial practice are ever more tightly intermeshed; they are mutually embedded within one another and, increasingly, they coevolve and cotransform. Lefebvre develops this proposition with reference to diverse terrains of spatial practice under capitalism, but he devotes particularly comprehensive attention to the increasingly intricate intermeshing among the scalar geographies of urbanization and state space during the course of twentieth-century capitalist development. As I discuss later, in Lefebvre's account, this process culminates with the formation of the comprehensively urbanized, state-managed, hierarchically administered, territorially parcelized, and tendentially nationalized interscalar formation to which he somewhat ponderously refers to as the "state mode of production" (*le mode de production étatique*).

---

[60] Ibid., 93, 306–8. For further elaborations of this key point, see Stanek, *Henri Lefebvre on Space*.

[61] Lefebvre, *Production of Space*, 92.

[62] Lefebvre, "Space and the State," 241.

In a suggestive parallel to Harvey's account of the "meshing" together of hierarchical arrangements, Lefebvre likewise argues that scalar configurations result from the path-dependent accretion of superimposed layerings and relayerings of spatial practice. As the core spatial practices of capitalism are increasingly interwoven, he argues, the distinctive, durable scalar architectures of the hierarchical stratified morphology are crystallized and consolidated; the latter provide a relatively fixed interscalar architecture— a "spatial support"—for the restless flow of sociospatial relations.[63] These interscalar configurations frame, mediate, and animate the further scalar differentiation and (co)evolution of sociospatial relations, and they are in turn periodically creatively destroyed through the contradictory, conflictual spatial practices thereby produced.

Indeed, much like Harvey in his account of the fixity/motion contradiction, Lefebvre repeatedly underscores the extremely delicate, always precarious balance between stabilization and destabilization tendencies within the interscalar geographies of capitalism. Whereas Harvey views devaluation as a perpetual threat to established scalings of territorial organization, Lefebvre views the possibility of systemic rupture—in his terminology, the "space of catastrophe"—as omnipresent within the hierarchical stratified morphology that undergirds capitalism's "second nature" of industrially constructed, institutionally programmed, and territorially managed spaces. Lefebvre is coldly, almost grimly, precise on this point: he defines the "space of catastrophe" as the "corollary" of the hierarchical stratified morphology; it refers to "the conditions under which the space [of capital] might explode."[64] Elsewhere, in an ominous formulation, Lefebvre argues that the capitalist space of catastrophe may inflict considerable violence upon inherited interscalar formations and the sociospatial relations they enframe: "it unsettles, atomizes, and pulverizes preexisting space, tearing it into pieces."[65]

This, then, is the hypercomplex, hierarchized, stratified, meshlike, and volatile scalar architecture of capitalism that Lefebvre is concerned to decipher as he develops his distinctive theoretical approach to the scale question. Investigating such variegated, tangled, and only apparently opaque scalar

---

[63] Ibid., 225.

[64] Ibid., 235–36. As with the notion of hierarchical stratified morphology, Lefebvre's concept of the "space of catastrophe" is derived from the work of mathematician and chaos theorist René Thom. See note 53.

[65] Ibid., 249.

geographies requires systematic, reflexive recognition of several key insights that flow from Lefebvre's scalar analytics:

- Because scales are produced through the tendential intensification, thickening, and intermeshing of interscalar linkages (among actors, institutions, infrastructures, and ecologies), scale can only be understood in relational terms.
- Interscalar relations evolve historically under capitalism, often in discontinuous, contested, and unforeseen ways, through diverse spatial practices, conflicts, and struggles.
- As the fabric of interscalar relations is more thickly, densely, and comprehensively interwoven, scalar configurations have become strategically essential as supports, arenas, outcomes, and stakes of capitalism's core spatial practices.
- As such, inherited scalar arrangements may also be more directly ensnared within, and transformed through, capital's endemic crisis tendencies: they may be destabilized, ruptured, or creatively destroyed in conjunction with successive waves of crisis-induced sociospatial restructuring.

These propositions usefully complement the scalar analytics embedded within Harvey's approach to the fixity/motion contradiction: they illuminate the shifting scalar geographies of capitalism not only as an expression of capital's internal sociospatial contradictions, but as a variegated material, political-institutional, and ecological fabric that supports, mediates, and indeed embodies the urbanization process itself. These considerations point, in turn, toward a subtle but even more analytically essential dimension of Lefebvre's conceptualization—namely, his elaboration of a reflexively state-theoretical approach to the urban question as a scale question, and his corresponding account of the mutually constitutive yet conflictually interwoven scalar geographies of state space and urbanization that crystallized under twentieth-century capitalism.

An Interscalar Mesh: Urbanization, State Space, and Spatial Logistics

On various occasions, Lefebvre describes capitalist urbanization as a process of "implosion-explosion" that unfolds unevenly across places, territories, and scales while also extending across the variegated zones of terrestrial, subterranean, fluvial, oceanic, and aerial space to encompass the entire planet.[66] In contrast to conventional, city-centric approaches, Lefebvre conceives urbanization as a multifaceted transformation of sociospatial relations to support the industrial accumulation of capital on a planetary scale. As such, it dismantles and reconstitutes historically inherited urban centers and political ecologies to create new, specifically capitalist forms of urban territorial organization and sociometabolic transformation. These include metropolitan concentrations, industrial corridors, extractive landscapes, logistical grids, and systems of techno-environmental management, as well as infrastructures of agro-industrial production, energy generation, and waste processing. The resultant "urban fabric" (*le tissu urbain*) is a "net of uneven mesh" in and through which the spatial practices, territorial infrastructures, and technoscientific operations of capitalist industrialization are stretched unevenly among local, metropolitan, and regional centers, across national, transnational, and intercontinental hinterlands to the worldwide scale of the international division of labor and the planet as a whole.[67] It is this encompassing but fractured process of "massive industrialization on a world scale . . . with its consequence of an equally massive urbanization" that underpins Lefebvre's much-debated notions of the "generalization of urban society," "complete urbanization," and "the planetarization of the urban" (*la planétarisation de l'urbain*).[68]

Whereas Harvey offers a precisely sequenced periodization of city development that mirrors broader regimes of accumulation (mercantile, industrial, Fordist-Keynesian, post-Keynesian), Lefebvre's wide-ranging analyses emphasize, on a more general level, the scalar mutations, territorial interventions, colossal infrastructural projects, ecological transformations,

---

[66] See, above all, Henri Lefebvre, *The Urban Revolution*, trans. Robert Bononno (Minneapolis: University of Minnesota Press, 2003 [1970]); and Henri Lefebvre, "The Right to the City," in *Writings on Cities*, ed. and trans. Eleonore Kofman and Elizabeth Lebas (Cambridge: Blackwell, 1996 [1968]). For critical discussion and appropriation of Lefebvre's urban theory, see Łukasz Stanek, Christian Schmid, and Ákos Moravánszky, eds., *Urban Revolution Now: Henri Lefebvre in Social Research and Architecture* (London: Routledge, 2014); and Neil Brenner, ed., *Implosions/Explosions: Towards a Study of Planetary Urbanization* (Berlin: Jovis, 2014).

[67] Lefebvre, "Right to the City," 71. See also, more generally, *The Urban Revolution*, where Lefebvre elaborates his concept of the urban fabric in detail.

[68] These phrases are drawn, variously, from Lefebvre, *De l'État*, 4:265; Lefebvre, "Right to the City," 71; Lefebvre, *Urban Revolution*, 1, 4; and Henri Lefebvre, "Dissolving City, Planetary Metamorphosis," in *Implosions/Explosions*, ed. Neil Brenner (Berlin: Jovis, 2014), 569, originally published as "Quand la ville se perd dans une métamorphose planétaire," *Le monde diplomatique*, May 1989. The contemporary *problématique* of planetary urbanization is explored at length in Chapters 9 and 10.

and technoscientific visions that have undergirded the generalization of capitalist urbanization, especially following the intensification of industrialization processes in the late nineteenth century. In this sense, for Lefebvre, the urban question under capitalism has always been, simultaneously, a scale question: the "planetarization" of capitalist urbanization necessarily entails historically specific scalings of the implosion-explosion process and its unevenly woven fabrics of urban centrality, industrial organization, infrastructural extension, logistical circuitry, socioecological metabolism, and sociospatial polarization. Scalar configurations, in Lefebvre's analysis, serve at once as inherited socioterritorial, institutional, infrastructural, and metabolic frameworks within which capitalist urbanization unfolds and as the contested arenas and results of ongoing strategies to shape, regulate, appropriate, and transform the urbanized sociospatial relations it has produced.

Of particular importance for my analysis is Lefebvre's account of how urbanization processes under capitalism are actively shaped through, and increasingly intermeshed with, the variegated geographies of state space. According to Lefebvre, state space (*l'espace étatique*) under capitalism is not a static territorial container, nor is it an aspatial institutional apparatus that may be instrumentally harnessed to manipulate the capitalist urban fabric from some neutral, external, or dimensionless position. Rather, much like the restlessly mutating geographies of urbanization it aspires to manage, the state is itself an unevenly developed, spatially polymorphic, and dynamically evolving institutional-territorial configuration, a "spatial framework" (*cadre spatial*) that serves at once as a site, medium, and stake of ongoing political strategies and struggles.[69] As Lefebvre explains:

> Each new form of state, each new form of political power, introduces its own particular way of partitioning space, its own particular administrative classification of discourses about space and about things and people in space. Each such form commands space, as it were, to serve its purposes.[70]

Lefebvre conceptualizes the state's sociospatial architecture, or *cadre*, with reference to three fundamental elements—the national territory, an internally differentiated sociospatial scaffolding, and the space of political ideology.[71] First, in a broad parallel to the Weberian tradition of political sociology,

---

[69] Lefebvre, *Production of Space*, 281, translation slightly modified from *La production de l'espace*, 324.

[70] Ibid.

[71] Lefebvre, "Space and the State," 224–25.

Lefebvre analyzes the national state as territorial matrix characterized by the domination of a centralized administrative apparatus over a relatively bounded, internally interconnected zone in which commodity production, circulation, and economic "growth" take place.[72] The territorial form associated with modern statehood is, he argues, linked inherently to violence: through its monopolization of the means of violence, the state seeks to impose a "political principle of *unification*" upon sociospatial relations, including those associated with the implosions and explosions of capitalist urbanization.[73] For Lefebvre, however, the state's territory is analytically distinct from a second dimension of state space, which comprises its own internally differentiated institutional apparatuses; the geographies, infrastructures, and built environments of political regulation, law, public administration, surveillance, and repression; and the symbolic power embodied in monuments, governmental buildings, public spaces, and other architectural or infrastructural displays of state authority.[74] Third, Lefebvre suggests that state space occupies, colonizes, and transforms everyday consciousness to generate a "mental space" through which social consensus is promoted and more or less cohesive political subjectivities are established.[75]

It is against the background of this general conceptualization of state space that Lefebvre explores the "spatial logistics" (*logistique spatiale*) of state power—that is, the proliferation of state techniques for shaping the dynamically evolving, multiscalar urban fabric of capitalism.[76] In a key passage of

---

[72] Ibid., 224.

[73] Lefebvre, *Production of Space*, 281 (italics in original). See also Neil Brenner and Stuart Elden, "Henri Lefebvre on State, Space, Territory," *International Political Sociology* 3, no. 4 (2009): 353–77.

[74] Lefebvre, "Space and the State," 224–25.

[75] Ibid., 225.

[76] The phrase "spatial logistics" is from "Space and the State," 224; the text in question is a partial translation of a key chapter in *De l'État*, vol. 4. The state's role in spatial regulation, management, planning, and logistics is a hugely complex, sometimes obscure, element of Lefebvre's writings of the 1970s: it is one of the major themes explored in the sprawling argument of *De l'État*, especially volumes 3 and 4; it is an omnipresent concern in each of Lefebvre's major urban works, as well as in several striking passages of *Production of Space*; and it is woven across the wide-ranging discussions of space and politics assembled for translation in *State, Space, World*. Yet, in part due to the heterogeneity of his theoretical framework, which draws upon diverse philosophical, political-theoretical, social-scientific, historical, literary, strategic-conjunctural, and journalistic influences, generalizing about Lefebvre's spatialized approach to state theory is a treacherous endeavor. For an overview of some of the key issues and arguments in Lefebvre's body of work on the state, see Brenner and Elden, "Introduction: State, Space, World"; as well as Brenner and Elden, "Henri Lefebvre on State, Space, Territory"; and Alberto Toscano, "Lineaments of the Logistical State," *Viewpoint Magazine*, September 27, 2014, https://viewpointmag.com/2014/09/28/lineaments-of-the-logistical-state/. For one of my own earliest

De l'État, volume 4, Lefebvre poses a powerfully suggestive rhetorical question about such techniques: "Is not the secret of the State, hidden because it is so obvious, to be found in space?"[77] Lefebvre attempts to illuminate this "secret" through an analysis of the state's spatial-logistical operations. His claim, simply put, is that state space provides an institutional-territorial basis for the mobilization of diverse state spatial strategies—including anticipatory planning (*planification*) and forecasting, spatiotemporal programming, territorial management (*aménagement*), and urban planning (*urbanisme*)—that continually produce, manage, regulate, monitor, and reorganize the variegated fabric of capitalist urbanization.[78] Herein, Lefebvre suggests, lies the state's "secret": its comprehensive spatial logistics generate a powerful ideological projection—that the state is administering a pregiven "natural space" or a purely formal territorial geometry, devoid of political significance, rather than a terrain of violence, enclosure, dispossession, exploitation, and struggle that has been forged through earlier rounds of spatial-logistical intervention.[79] Consequently, as Lefebvre explains:

> If space has an air of neutrality and indifference with regard to its contents and thus seems to be purely "formal," the essence of rational abstraction, it is precisely because this space has already been occupied and planned, already the focus of past strategies, of which we can always find traces. Space has been fashioned and molded from historical and natural elements, but in a political way. Space is political and ideological.[80]

It is, Lefebvre maintains, through this blend of logistical, classificatory, and ideological strategies that the state attempts to "command space . . . to serve its purposes" and thus to manage the "contradictions of space."[81] The politics of space result from the mobilization of such state spatial-logistical strategies

---

attempts to decipher Lefebvre's approach to state space, see Neil Brenner, "State Territorial Restructuring and the Production of Spatial Scale: Urban and Regional Planning in the Federal Republic of Germany, 1960–1990," *Political Geography* 16, no. 4 (1997): 273–306. For a more systematic theoretical appropriation, see Brenner, *New State Spaces*, chap. 3.

[77] Lefebvre, "Space and the State," 228.

[78] Among Lefebvre's most trenchant statements on this issue is his essay "Reflections on the Politics of Space," included in Lefebvre, *State, Space, World*, 167–84.

[79] Lefebvre, "Space and the State," 228. Stuart Elden and I have described this ideological projection as the "territory effect." See Brenner and Elden, "Henri Lefebvre on State, Space, Territory."

[80] Lefebvre, "Reflections," 170–71.

[81] Lefebvre, *Production of Space*, 281; Lefebvre, "Space and the State," 238.

not only to manipulate and reweave the urban fabric, but to mask their own pervasive impacts upon it.[82]

Lefebvre's account of state spatial logistics is not simply an abstract catalog of state functions, but is based upon a nuanced historical analysis of how state institutions have mobilized the techniques of spatial logistics to shape, regulate, and rework the recurrent implosions-explosions of urbanization, especially during the course of twentieth-century capitalist development. His investigations of state spatial logistics range widely across historical moments, institutional contexts, political struggles, and concrete examples, often through idiosyncratic or polemical engagements with debates on Western Marxism, Euro-communism, Maoism, and various strands of post-1968 New Left political philosophy in France and beyond. In so doing, Lefebvre also advances his theorization of the so-called state mode of production (SMP), a world-encompassing but territorially parcelized colossus of state power that, he argues, was consolidated during the second half of the twentieth century to support the planetary intensification and extension of capitalist industrialization.

For present purposes, the evolution of Lefebvre's Cold War philosophical and political-ideological position and the intricacies of his theorization of the SMP are less immediately significant than several core analytical observations regarding the relationship between urbanization and state space that can be extracted from his writings of this period. Four such observations are particularly salient here:

1. *Through its spatial logistics, the state coproduces, manages, and reorganizes the multiscalar fabric of urbanization.* Lefebvre emphasizes the state's role in producing the large-scale forms of territorial organization that undergird the urban fabric of capitalism. "Only the State," he argues, "is capable of taking charge of the management of space 'on a grand scale'—highways, air traffic routes—because only the State has at its disposal the appropriate resources, techniques and 'conceptual' capacity."[83] Lefebvre's writings reference diverse examples of such large-scale state interventions in the infrastructures and "technostructures" of production, reproduction, and circulation—including highways, canals, ports, tunnels, bridges, railroads, airports, and public transport systems; zones of resource extraction, energy generation (coal mines, electric grids, nuclear power stations, dams), and waste disposal; postal, telephone, and telecommunications networks; and growth poles,

---

[82] Lefebvre, "Reflections," 174. In Lefebvre's classic formulation from this text: "There is a politics of space because space is political (*il y a politique de l'espace, parce que l'espace est politique*)."

[83] Lefebvre, "Space and the State," 238.

regional industrial complexes, public housing estates (*Grands ensembles*), and new towns. In short, the variegated, stratified urban fabric of capitalism as a whole is shaped through large-scale state infrastructural investments and colossal landscape interventions, which are in turn products of spatiotemporal forecasting, territorial management, and urban planning strategies.[84]

2. *The logistical infrastructures of state space provide a fixed support for capital circulation.* Lefebvre conceptualizes state space as a relatively fixed institutional-territorial infrastructure that undergirds, supports, and stabilizes the relentlessly pulsating implosions and explosions of capitalist urbanization. Through its "permanent establishments" and "permanent centres of decision and action," states attempt actively to control both "flows and stocks, assuring their coordination"; this applies equally to flows of energy, raw materials, labor power, consumer goods, commerce, and so forth.[85] It is "only the state," Lefebvre writes, that "can control the flows [of the modern economy] and harmonize them with the fixed elements of the economy (stocks) because the State integrates them into the dominant space it produces."[86] In this sense, Lefebvre conceptualizes state space as a key lattice within the variegated architectures of capitalist territorial organization. In significant measure due to their relatively fixed, immobilized, and stabilized character, state spatial configurations provide a more or less coherent institutional, infrastructural, and regulatory matrix for the sociomaterial flows that animate capital's circulation process.[87]

3. *State space and the urban fabric are increasingly intermeshed at all spatial scales.* Lefebvre's argument, however, is not simply that the provisionally stabilized properties of state space offer an infrastructural basis for the circulation of capital. His far more consequential claim is that the architectures of state space and the fabric of urbanization are increasingly woven together and intermeshed, at once in material, infrastructural, institutional, and operational terms, through the forward motion of capitalist

---

[84] Ibid., 238–39 passim.

[85] Lefebvre, *Production of Space*, 388; Lefebvre, "Space and the State," 226.

[86] Lefebvre, "Space and the State," 239–40, 243.

[87] Harvey likewise recognizes this point in his discussion of the "territoriality of social infrastructures" in *Limits to Capital*. Here, he emphasizes that the state's territorial organization is essential to its capacity to channel infrastructural investment among various places and scales: "The state provides the single most important channel for flows of value into social infrastructures. . . . [T]he territorial organization of the state . . . becomes the geographical configuration within which the dynamics of the [infrastructure] investment is worked out." Harvey, *Limits to Capital*, 404. For further elaboration of this line of argumentation, see Kevin Cox, "Territorial Structures of the State: Some Conceptual Issues," *Tijdschrift voor Economische en Sociale Geografie* 81 (1990): 251–66.

industrial development. This means not only that the morphological configuration of the urban fabric is molded according to state spatial agendas and technoscientific visions (for instance, of centralization or decentralization, regional redistribution, national resource management, mass consumption, nuclear energy development, or cybernetic monitoring), but that the state's own sociospatial hierarchies, matrices, and operations are ever more intricately intercalated with the meshwork of urbanization, which is itself constantly thickening and expanding at all spatial scales, from the local to the planetary. Thus, in one programmatic formulation, Lefebvre invokes the large-scale logistical infrastructures that were produced during successive cycles of capitalist urbanization—"roads, canals, commercial and financial circuits, motorways and air routes"—as the defining contours of the modern state's own territorial configuration. Elsewhere, Lefebvre insists that the state has not only "presided over" the progressive integration of apparently "once unoccupied" spaces—peripheries, the underground, the skies, mountains, oceans—into the capitalist urban fabric but also that it has provided a "calibrated spatial support" for that constitutively uneven, volatile process of worldwide territorial enclosure.[88] In instrumentalizing and operationalizing such terrains of putative "first nature" within capitalist relations of production, and thereby producing "a kind of unification of world space," the "planetary state system" becomes an essential politico-infrastructural circuitry for the "planetarization of the urban."[89] The capitalist urban fabric, in other words, is not simply a product of state spatial strategies, but serves as an important infrastructural scaffolding, medium, and expression of state power—and, indeed, of state space itself—as it is unevenly extended across the entire planet.

4. *Through its spatial strategies, the state becomes more directly engaged in managing the contradictions, dislocations, and crisis tendencies that pervade the capitalist urban fabric.* Throughout his spatial writings, Lefebvre emphasizes that the geographies of capitalist urbanization are permeated by contradictions—including exchange value/use value, work/leisure, liberation/repression, need/desire, production/consumption, territorialization/deterritorialization, center/periphery, and homogenization/fragmentation—whose disruptive sociospatial consequences the state is tasked with alleviating, or at least

---

[88] Lefebvre, "Space and the State," 225.

[89] Henri Lefebvre, "Space and Mode of Production," in *State, Space, World: Selected Essays*, ed. Neil Brenner and Stuart Elden (Minneapolis: University of Minnesota Press, 2009 [1980]), 212–14; Lefebvre, "Dissolving City, Planetary Metamorphosis."

managing.[90] "In the chaos of relations among individuals, class factions and classes," he explains, "the State tends to impose a rationality, its own, that has space as its privileged instrument."[91] According to Lefebvre, then, the spatial logistics of state power involve not only the production of a more or less coherently coordinated, well-functioning urban fabric to support the metabolism of capital, but diverse forms of territorial, ecological, and interscalar management that are intended to repair the enclosure, fragmentation, degradation, and destruction of everyday social space induced through the (il) logics of capital accumulation. As Lefebvre notes, "The state intervenes in multiple, increasingly specific ways. . . . It seeks . . . to regularize the relations that result from the unequal character of growth. . . . It transforms virtually destructive conflicts into catalysts of growth. . . . It preserves the conditions of a precarious equilibrium."[92] In this way, state spatial strategies mediate the simultaneously homogenizing/pulverizing, fragmenting/fracturing, and hierarchizing/polarizing tendencies within the capitalist urban fabric.[93] In so doing, they also impose "a certain cohesiveness if not a logical coherence" upon the chaotic flow and uneven development of sociospatial relations, and thus contribute directly to the construction of spatial and scalar fixes for the accumulation process.[94]

It is clear, then, that Lefebvre's approach to the intermeshing of state space and the capitalist urban fabric builds directly upon the relational scalar analytic outlined in the previous section. It is precisely through this resolutely dialectical approach to sociospatial theory that Lefebvre is able to theorize the state space/urbanization relationship not simply as a functional articulation among pregiven units or contingently interacting entities, but as a dynamic interweaving and thickening superimposition among mutually interdependent, conflictually coevolving sociospatial processes. On the most general level, therefore, Lefebvre's analysis adds an essential state-theoretical dimension to the scale-attuned theorization of territorial organization developed in the preceding discussion. Lefebvre's account of state spatial logistics puts into relief an argument mentioned but not systematically elaborated in Harvey's work—namely, that state spatial configurations and strategies of infrastructural, logistical, and environmental management mediate the

---

[90] Lefebvre, *Production of Space*, 47, 292–356, 363–65; Lefebvre, "Space and the State."

[91] Lefebvre, "Space and the State," 226.

[92] *De l'État*, 1:56.

[93] Lefebvre, "Space and Mode of Production," 212–16.

[94] Lefebvre, *Production of Space*, 378.

production of territorial organization, and thus of urbanization processes, under capitalism. The fixity/motion contradiction, in short, crystallizes within landscapes of urbanization that are comprehensively shaped and reshaped through state spatial strategies, which in turn directly impact its contextually specific expressions, vicissitudes, and consequences.

State Space, Scalar Fixes, and the Fabric of Urbanization

Lefebvre's analysis of state space and the implosions-explosions of the capitalist urban fabric has far-reaching implications for conceptualizations of the scale question. In particular, Lefebvre's analytical framework illuminates the central role of state spatial strategies in constructing, managing, and reshaping the stratified scalar scaffolding around which the fabric of capitalist urbanization is woven. From this point of view, the architecture of scalar configurations cannot be derived directly from the operational imperatives of capital or from the scalar strategies of any other single actor, institution, or process; it is, at core, a *political mediation*.[95] In Lefebvre's analysis, it is the state, through its pursuit of the territorial "principle of unification," that strives to impose a certain "rationality"—a "precarious equilibrium"—upon the explosive volatility of interscalar relations, and thereby to lock in a provisional "cohesiveness if not coherence" within the pulsating, restlessly mutating urban fabric of capitalism.[96] It is precisely in this context, Lefebvre argues, that scale becomes politically strategic for state operations. By constructing scalar fixes—in Lefebvre's precise formulation, "a hierarchical ensemble (*un ensemble hiérarchisé*) of places, functions and institutions"—the state attempts at once to support and to regulate the constitutively uneven, variegated, dynamic, and crisis-prone sociospatial metabolism of capitalist urbanization.[97]

Lefebvre's work thus draws attention to the key role of state institutions and spatial strategies (which are themselves scale differentiated) in the

---

[95] This argument contrasts sharply to that advanced in some of the founding texts on the production of scale from the 1980s by Peter J. Taylor and Neil Smith, which interpreted scalar organization as a direct functional expression of capitalist economic or ideological imperatives. See, for instance, Taylor, "Geographical Scales"; and Smith, *Uneven Development*. For a sophisticated regulationist meditation on this constellation of issues see Chris Collinge, "Self-Organization of Society by Scale: A Spatial Reworking of Regulation Theory," *Environment and Planning D: Society and Space* 17 (1999): 557–74.

[96] Lefebvre, *Production of Space*, 281, 378; Lefebvre, "Space and Mode of Production," 212; Lefebvre, "Space and the State," 226; Lefebvre, *De l'État*, 1:56.

[97] Lefebvre, "Space and the State," 242; original text from *De l'État*, 4:306, translation slightly modified.

establishment, reproduction, and reworking of scalar fixes, which in turn assume progressively more intricate patterns as the urban fabric is extended across the planetary landscape. The scalar implosions and explosions of capitalist urbanization are mediated through state spatial strategies that seek to enframe, enclose, canalize, and manage them within relatively coherent, territorially cohesive, or even provisionally "unified" scalar configurations—a "hierarchical ensemble" of sociospatial infrastructures, institutions, and relations. In subsequent chapters, I build extensively upon this conceptualization of states as orchestrators, mediators, and regulators of interscalar relations and, by consequence, of the scalar configuration of urbanization. Accordingly, the *problematique* of state spatial strategies, and their shifting scalar articulations, is central to our exploration of the rescaled geographies of urbanization that have crystallized in the post-Keynesian era of neoliberalization and planetary sociospatial restructuring.[98]

But these considerations open up a further constellation of questions regarding the durable impacts of state spatial strategies upon the imploding-exploding scalar landscapes of capitalist urbanization. If, as Lefebvre's work suggests, the capitalist urban fabric and the geographies of state space have been more tightly intermeshed during the last century, then we might plausibly expect their scalar architectures likewise to become mutually entangled, and thus to coevolve. And if, moreover, state spatial strategies figure crucially in the management and tendential stabilization of interscalar relations, then we might also expect the geographies of urbanization to be not only intercalated with those of state space but directly *imprinted* by the state's distinctive spatial configurations—for instance, by its territorially centralized form, its hierarchically structured frameworks of intergovernmental organization, its scale-differentiated institutional apparatuses, its developmentalist modes of spatial intervention, and its specific strategies of logistical-infrastructural management and environmental engineering. To what degree, then, is the morphology of the capitalist urban fabric tendentially shaped into sociospatial patterns that are broadly isomorphic with those of state space?

Lefebvre's concept of the SMP can be interpreted as an argument precisely to this effect. Lefebvre develops the concept in *De l'État* in pursuit of

---

[98] In Chris Collinge's terms, state spatial strategies are oriented simultaneously toward *regulation* (the coordination of sociospatial relations), *super-regulation* (the coordination among diverse strategies of spatial regulation), and *metaregulation* (the reorganization of regulatory and super-regulatory arrangements). See Collinge, "Self-Organization of Society by Scale," 559. Thus understood, state strategies to create scalar fixes primarily involve super-regulation, whereas strategies to reorganize scalar fixes (rescaling strategies) involve metaregulation.

several distinct politico-analytical agendas, but he recurrently suggests that one of the SMP's core regulatory aspirations is, indeed, to establish a spatial isomorphism between state space and the urban fabric. For instance, Lefebvre argues that the rationalizing logistical strategies of developmental industrial states "collide" with inherited, preindustrial, or protoindustrial geographies of extraction, farming, commerce, and craft labor. In his view, this collision results not only in a "rational and scientific space produced and administered by the state" but in the crystallization of a "new space" of urbanization that is at once homogeneous (based upon parcelized, commodified, interchangeable units), fractured (oriented toward tightly circumscribed functions within the ensemble of spatial practices), and hierarchized (based upon the systemic production of sociospatial inequality and exclusion).[99] A parallel line of argumentation underpins Lefebvre's discussion of post–World War II regional industrial policies and technocratic urbanism, which he interprets as a constellation of state strategies to subordinate sociospatial relations to the imperatives of capital accumulation, and thus as the embodiment of a new formation of urbanization oriented toward "the indefinite expansion of the centres, nuclei and growth poles" to cover "space as a whole."[100] By "regulating flows, coordinating the blind forces of growth, and by imposing its law onto the chaos of 'private' and 'local' interests," Lefebvre argues, the SMP seeks to impose "chains of equivalence" onto the atomized, fragmented, and pulverized urban fabric.[101] Especially during the second half of the twentieth century, the SMP has aimed to harness the "instrument of logistical space" to sculpt the unruly urban fabric into a "homogeneous, logistical, optico-geometrical, quantitative space" while also suppressing, neutralizing, or at least managing the "differential" impulses of transgression that are immanent within it.[102]

It is, then, through the worldwide consolidation of the SMP, with its aggressively growth-oriented, developmentalist approach to planetary infrastructural expansion (the *planétarisation* of the urban), national territorial management (*aménagement*), and urban planning (*urbanisme*), that the geographies of urbanization have been pervasively sculpted into a "hierarchical stratified morphology"—a term that is now revealed to have more than merely methodological content. In fact, for Lefebvre, the hierarchically

---

[99] Lefebvre, "Space and the State," 239. See also Lefebvre, "Space and Mode of Production."

[100] Henri Lefebvre, *The Survival of Capitalism*, trans. Frank Bryant (New York: St. Martin's Press, 1976 [1973]), 111–12.

[101] Lefebvre, "Space and the State," 240.

[102] Ibid., 238.

configured properties of interscalar relations are not the expression of a fixed, ontological essence but have crystallized through the cumulative impacts of post–World War II political strategies of (national) centralization, administrative rationalization, logistical coordination, and infrastructural standardization. It is the latter, he argues, that have progressively woven a distinctively "statist" morphological pattern—the aforementioned "hierarchical ensemble of places, institutions and functions"—into the intricately layered, twisted, and tangled *mille feuille* of the capitalist urban fabric. On this basis, Lefebvre postulates, "the state defines itself as the most general form—the *form of forms*—of society. It encompasses and develops all other forms. . . . In this manner the state becomes coextensive with society."[103]

Lefebvre's argument here is not, however, that the capitalist urban fabric is in fact effectively controlled by or subordinated to state projects of territorial and interscalar management; it remains volatile, precarious, uneven, and prone to rupture—always vulnerable to the "space of catastrophe" and to the insurgent rhythms of differential space, which produce "effects that tend to dissolve the extant space and thus to constitute a new space defined in a different way."[104] His claim, rather, is that the morphological architecture of urbanization is increasingly imprinted by the hierarchical, territorially centralizing and standardizing projects of state spatial regulation that were pursued by the national developmentalist states of the postwar epoch. These projects shape and reshape the urban fabric, but they also generate disruptions, conflicts, and dislocations that further destabilize the urbanization process. In this sense, Lefebvre suggests, the state's spatial imprinting of the capitalist urban fabric occurs as much through its grandiose visions of territorial management as through the recurrent regulatory failures, contradictions, and unintended sociospatial consequences thereby engendered. The space of catastrophe, in other words, is as politically mediated as the capitalist urban fabric through which it is woven.

We thus arrive at a seemingly paradoxical but far-reaching conclusion: the production of state space (*l'espace étatique*) represents a strategic moment in the planetarization of the urban. For Lefebvre, the notion of state space is not simply an analytical tool for decoding the spatial dimensions of modern statehood; it is a historically specific concept on which basis he aims to decipher the concerted politico-spatial strategies—in his terms, the "politics

---

[103] Lefebvre, *De l'État*, 3:179 (italics added).

[104] Ibid., 240.

of space"—through which a planetary formation of the capitalist urban fabric has been envisioned, promoted, consolidated, and generalized.[105] The tendential hierarchization and stratification of interscalar relations through state spatial logistics is thus now revealed as an essential element—at once a temporal rhythm and a spatial layer—within the planetarization of the urban fabric.

Lefebvre's spatial isomorphism hypothesis—embodied in his concept of the state as the spatial "form of forms"—provides a helpful interpretive reference point for analyzing the interplay between state space and the urban fabric under postwar, Fordist-Keynesian, national developmentalist capitalism. In several chapters that follow, I build upon Lefebvre's conceptualization to characterize the tendentially nationalized, internally hierarchized, and territorially centralized formation of state spatial regulation and urban development that was consolidated in the North Atlantic zone during this period, and which was embodied in various politico-institutional arrangements (for instance, the redistributive intergovernmental and policy relays of spatial Keynesianism) and urbanization patterns (for instance, nationalized urban hierarchies, standardized national logistics infrastructures, and national strategies of industrial development and regional policy). But to what extent can Lefebvre's spatial isomorphism hypothesis illuminate the production of new urban spaces in the post-1980s period, whether in Euro-America or elsewhere? Are the scalar strata of the capitalist urban fabric still being patterned to resemble the "homogenous, logistical, optico-geometrical, quantitative space" of the SMP, with its "hierarchical ensemble" of interscalar circuitry and its tendentially centralized, territorially unifying regulatory project? Can (national) states still be viewed as an encompassing spatial unity, the "form of forms," a meta-architecture of institutions, infrastructures, and ideologies enframing the patterns and pathways of capitalist urbanization?

The studies assembled in this book suggest that Lefebvre's spatial isomorphism hypothesis cannot, in fact, be sustained with reference to the post-1980s wave of neoliberalizing regulatory reform, territorially splintered infrastructure investment, rescaled state strategies, accelerated sociospatial enclosure, and planetary urban restructuring. On the one hand, even in the radically transformed geographies of post-Keynesian, neoliberalizing, and planetary capitalism whose contours he could only begin to envision in his final writings, Lefebvre's emphasis on the pervasive role of state spatial strategies in shaping the patterns and pathways of urbanization remains

---

[105] Lefebvre, "Reflections on the Politics of Space."

as salient as ever.[106] State spatial-logistical strategies continue to impact the scalar configuration of the capitalist urban fabric in comprehensive, durable ways; they also continue to figure crucially in the management of interscalar relations, in the pursuit of scalar fixes for urbanization, and in the regulation of insurgent political mobilizations. On the other hand, however, the centralized, nationally territorialized, and precision-nested scalar hierarchies of postwar state space have been significantly reterritorialized and rescaled during the last four decades, producing increasingly splintered, scale-relativized political geographies that no longer privilege a primary regulatory level or neatly converge around a single, encompassing territorial center, national or otherwise.[107] This still-ongoing creative destruction of state space has occurred in close conjunction with, and has directly animated, the construction of newly rescaled geographies of urbanization. A major concern of this book is to decipher the emergent geographies of these rescaled urban spaces, even as their tendentially isomorphic articulation to (national) state space has been destabilized and rewoven.

Despite Lefebvre's assumption that the pursuit of such a spatial isomorphism was structurally inscribed within the SMP, and thus that the capitalist urban fabric would be progressively "statified" (at once hierarchized and territorialized) on a planetary scale, his theoretical approach productively illuminates the dialectical coevolution of state spatial-logistical operations and the unevenly extended, intricately tangled meshwork of the capitalist urban fabric. As such, it provides an essential methodological anchor for investigating the production of new urban spaces since the 1980s. The post-1980s rescaling of urbanization has been powerfully mediated through strategies of state spatial regulation that seek to reshape, activate, and regulate the urban fabric under post-Keynesian conditions. Just as crucially, Lefebvre's approach underscores the central role of state rescaling as a political strategy for reweaving and reactivating the fabric of urbanization itself.

Rescaling the Urban Fabric: Toward an Investigation

We thus return to the problem of geographical scale, its social production, its historical reconfiguration, and its sociopolitical contestation—in short, to Lefebvre's "scale question" as it has crystallized in the opening decades of

---

[106] See Lefebvre, "Dissolving City, Planetary Metamorphosis," written in 1989, in which Lefebvre briefly but rather pessimistically reflects on the dynamics of planetary urbanization nearly two decades after his initial hypothesis of this process in his urban writings of the late 1960s.

[107] Brenner, *New State Spaces*; Jessop, *Future of the Capitalist State*.

the twenty-first century. Even more dramatically than from Lefebvre's vantage point in the 1970s, the spatial scales of capital accumulation, territorial regulation, urbanization, and sociopolitical struggle are today shifting under our very feet. It is this recognition that scales have become sites of accelerated reshuffling, institutional volatility, and intense sociopolitical contestation that underpinned Erik Swyngedouw's eloquent plea in the late 1990s for a new discourse of scale attuned above all to its fluidity and mutability as the "product of processes of sociospatial change."[108]

In stark contrast to the methodologically nationalist, regionalist, or localist tendencies that have long prevailed in the social and historical sciences, this radically constructionist approach to the politics of scale has proven hugely generative across an interdisciplinary terrain of critical sociospatial analysis, from state theory and geopolitical economy to urban studies, social movement research, and cultural geography. Rather than relegating scalar organization to a static background parameter or reducing it to a fixed platform for sociospatial relations, such approaches have productively illuminated the variegated processes through which scalar configurations have been produced, contested, and transformed across spatiotemporal contexts. In thus proceeding, studies of the politics of scale have also directed attention to the diverse scale-making projects that have animated contemporary rescaling processes and their implications for key dimensions of political-economic life.

This chapter has likewise emphasized the socially produced, politically contested, and historically mutable character of geographical scales, scalar configurations, and interscalar relations. Yet, by connecting the scale question to the vicissitudes of the fixity/motion contradiction under capitalism, I have elaborated a somewhat different methodological orientation than that which underpins much of the scholarly literature on the politics of scale. By excavating the scalar analytics that are embedded within the writings of Harvey and Lefebvre, I have argued that the politics of scale cannot be analytically reduced to the strategic orientations, evolutionary pathways, and impacts of scale-making projects themselves. Instead, this analysis has suggested that the dynamics of rescaling must be embedded within broader historical geographies that are profoundly shaped by the spatiotemporal (il) logics of capital's fixity/motion contradiction—its fundamental reliance upon relatively fixed, provisionally stabilized frameworks of territorial organization and its equally powerful impulsion to promote sociospatial creative

---

[108] Swyngedouw, "Neither Global nor Local," 140.

destruction. Insofar as both moments of the fixity/motion contradiction are scale differentiated, the politics of scale are directly ensnared within the (il)logics of capital's problematic relation to territorial organization. To be sure, contextually specific scale-making projects and rescaling strategies cannot be functionally derived from the fixity/motion contradiction or from any other abstract operations of capital. However, in broad geohistorical perspective, the establishment and dismantling of scalar fixes appear to have unfolded in close conjunction with successive accumulation regimes, modes of territorial regulation, and cycles of crisis-induced restructuring.[109] This suggests that contextually embedded forms of the politics of scale are themselves embedded within, and profoundly shaped by, a broader "context of context." This *metacontext* is a densely layered fabric of capitalist territorial organization that has been forged through the geohistorical interplay between provisionally stabilized scalar fixes and successive waves of crisis-induced rescaling.

To develop this analytical orientation, this chapter has elaborated a conceptual grammar through which to investigate the continual scale differentiation and rescaling of territorial organization under capitalism, with specific reference to (1) the thickening interconnections among scales and the relational intermeshing among scalar configurations; (2) the scalar extension, territorial consolidation, and internal stratification of the capitalist urban fabric; (3) the scalar differentiation of state space and territorial regulation; (4) the mobilization of state spatial strategies (state spatial logistics) designed to consolidate or rework the scalar configuration and layout of territorial organization; and (5) the progressively more densified interweaving of the capitalist urban fabric and state space during the course of capitalist development. While Lefebvre's approach to the state mode of production postulates an intensifying statification, nationalization, and territorialization of the urban fabric under modern capitalism, this analysis has reinterpreted his concept in more historically specific terms, as an account of the tendentially isomorphic crystallization of urban space and state space that was unevenly consolidated in the North Atlantic zone during the postwar period up through the 1970s. My critical appropriation of key categories and methods from Harvey and Lefebvre thus also provides a basis on which to investigate the variegated processes and political strategies through which, since that time, the nationalized meshwork of urban space and state space that was

---

[109] Edward W. Soja, "Regions in Context: Spatiality, Periodicity and the Historical Geography of the Regional Question," *Environment and Planning D: Society and Space* 3 (1985): 175–90; Collinge, "Self-Organization of Society by Scale."

inherited from the Fordist-Keynesian, national-developmentalist formation of capitalism has been ruptured, restructured, and rewoven. Such an approach can productively guide our exploration of the contradictory, uneven, and volatile interplay between post-Keynesian projects of state rescaling and the planetary remaking of the capitalist urban fabric during the post-1980s period.

From this perspective, then, the explosive politics of scale that has proliferated under contemporary capitalism must be viewed not only as an attempt to dismantle the tendentially nationalized scalar configurations that prevailed during the postwar accumulation regime and to resolve its cascading crisis tendencies, but as a series of relatively uncoordinated yet concerted politico-spatial strategies to establish stabilized, rescaled formations of the capitalist urban fabric that might support a new wave of expanded capital accumulation. As Neil Smith productively emphasized in one of his pioneering texts on scale, it is precisely through the role of scalar fixes in provisionally *freezing* social, economic, and political interaction within relatively stabilized, coherent frameworks of territorial organization that "highly contentious and contested social relationships become anchored if not quite in stone at least in landscapes that are, in the short run, fixed."[110] The contemporary rescaling of the capitalist urban fabric is occurring, in large measure, through a proliferation of political strategies to impose new forms of territorial fixity upon an intensely polarized, endemically crisis-riven, and relentlessly mutating planetary landscape, in significant part through the reorganization of state space and state scalar organization. The connection between strategies of state rescaling and the spatial politics of fixing capital is, accordingly, a central focus in the chapters that follow.

---

[110] Smith, "Remaking Scale," 62.

3
Restructuring, Rescaling, and the Urban Question

WRITING IN THE LATE 1970s, Henri Lefebvre declared that a "generalized explosion of spaces" was occurring in which inherited geographies of capitalism and state power were being dramatically rewoven.[1] The phrase "explosion" (*l'éclatement*) appears frequently in Lefebvre's writings of this period and connotes a radical unsettling not only of established practices, institutions, and ideologies, but of the spaces in and through which the latter are constituted. Thus, alongside the generalized societal eruption (*l'irruption*) associated with the May 1968 movements in Paris, Lefebvre speaks of any number of explosions that were, he argued, ricocheting across world capitalism during this period—for instance, of the historic city, the town, big cities, metropolitan spaces, the regions, core-periphery relations, inherited spaces, borders, and frontiers; of reason, the family, the nation, the economy, and history; and of Stalinism and Marxism.[2] Elsewhere, Lefebvre proposed that a dynamic of simultaneous "implosion-explosion" (*l'implosion-explosion*) was transforming inherited urban geographies in conjunction with the

---

[1] Henri Lefebvre, *State, Space, World: Selected Essays*, ed. Neil Brenner and Stuart Elden (Minneapolis: University of Minnesota Press, 2009 [1979]), 190.

[2] Ibid., 90, 104, 109, 118, 186, 214, 236, and 264. See also Henri Lefebvre, "The Right to the City," in *Writings on Cities*, ed. and trans. Eleonore Kofman and Elizabeth Lebas (Cambridge: Blackwell, 1996 [1968]).

increasing generalization of urbanization processes across spatial scales, from the body, the city, and the territory to the worldwide and the planetary.[3]

In the early twenty-first century, following several decades in which critical urbanists and geographers have worked energetically to refine and reinvent the lexicon of sociospatial theory, Lefebvre's use of terms such as *l'irruption*, *l'éclatement*, and *l'implosion-explosion* may seem somewhat chaotic, imprecise, and perhaps overly apocalyptic. And yet, even as the discourse of sociospatial theory has become more conceptually differentiated, Lefebvre's insight still rings true to the creatively destructive, endemically crisis-prone dynamics of late modern capitalism. The fabric of urbanization continues to be rewoven through diverse processes of crisis-induced restructuring at all spatial scales. As Lefebvre recognized during the crises of the Fordist-Keynesian geopolitical order in the early 1970s, social space is always being produced and transformed under capitalism; it is never fixed, static, or pregiven. In this sense, Lefebvre's notion of an "explosion of spaces" and more recent writings on urban-regional restructuring are oriented toward the same intellectual and political *problematique*. Several decades ago, radical geographer Edward Soja summarized this constellation of issues in the following paradigmatic terms:

> Restructuring is meant to convey a break in secular trends and a shift towards a significantly different order and configuration of social, economic and political life. It thus evokes a sequence of breaking down and building up again, deconstruction and attempted reconstitution, arising from certain incapacities or weaknesses in the established order which preclude conventional adaptations and demand significant structural change instead. . . . [R]estructuring is rooted in crisis and a competitive conflict between the old and the new, between an "inherited" and a "projected" order. It is not a mechanical or automatic process, nor are its results predetermined. . . . Restructuring implies flux and transition, offensive and defensive postures, a complex mix of continuity and change.[4]

Since the early 1980s, much of the most insightful work in the broad, heterogeneous field of critical urban studies has attempted to decipher the "complex mix of continuity and change" associated with such restructuring processes in the tumultuous aftermath of North Atlantic Fordism, national developmentalism, and (as of the 1990s) state socialism, along with their

---

[3] Lefebvre, *State, Space, World*, 123.

[4] Edward W. Soja, "Economic Restructuring and the Internationalization of Los Angeles," in *The Capitalist City*, ed. Michael Peter Smith and Joe Feagin (Cambridge: Blackwell, 1987), 178.

causes, expressions, and implications. As this body of research indicates, the problematic of restructuring intersects with a range of fundamental theoretical, empirical, and political questions in urban and regional studies, as well as in critical planning practice. For instance: Do contemporary restructuring processes herald a new configuration of global capitalist development or a continued politics of crisis management, regulatory experimentation, and muddling-through? Do such restructuring processes assume territory-, place-, and scale-specific forms, and if so, what are their causes, contours, and ramifications? How are such processes, in their spatially selective, unevenly developed and variegated forms, shaped by institutional configurations, political strategies, and social forces? Can restructuring processes be harnessed by progressive institutions, coalitions, and social movements to promote more radically democratic, socially just, territorially coherent, and environmentally sane forms of urbanization?

Given the importance of spatial considerations to each of these questions, their persistent intellectual and political urgency helps explain much of the "reassertion of space in critical social theory" that was famously declared in the mid-1980s by Soja.[5] To be sure, debates on the conceptualization of social space since that time have been influenced by diverse philosophical and social-theoretical currents, including Hegelian dialectics, Marxism, critical realism, phenomenology, hermeneutics, structuralism, feminism, psychoanalysis, poststructuralism, actor network theory, queer theory, posthumanism, and postcolonialism. But the appropriation of such legacies has been powerfully mediated through the innumerable challenges of deciphering the explosive processes of sociospatial restructuring and urban transformation that have been ricocheting across the world economy since the breakdown of the North Atlantic Fordist, national-developmentalist georegulatory configuration. In the wake of more recent, equally explosive crisis tendencies in the early twenty-first century, which have further redifferentiated the already deeply unstable, polarized, and variegated geographies produced through earlier rounds of restructuring, the task of deciphering the restlessly changing landscapes of capitalist urbanization remains as urgent as ever.

But how, precisely, are these constantly, unevenly churning spaces of restructuring to be conceptualized? This issue is as contested today as it was in the 1980s, when debates on the *problematique* of restructuring gathered momentum among urbanists and other critical geographers. On the one hand, there now exist several weighty shelfloads of books and edited collections

---

[5] Edward W. Soja, *Postmodern Geographies* (New York: Verso, 1989).

that grapple productively with the question of theorizing social space, its production, and its transformation under modern capitalism.[6] On the other hand, much of the most theoretically reflexive research in critical urban studies during the post-1980s period has been focused less on the problematic of social space as such than on several, more specific dimensions and dynamics of contemporary sociospatial restructuring. These include, for instance, processes of place-making, agglomeration, localization, decentralization, and the reworking of spatial divisions of labor; the tension between geographical fixity and mobility, and the concomitant construction and dismantling of spatial fixes; processes of territorialization, deterritorialization, and reterritorialization; the extension and thickening of interspatial networks; regionalization tendencies and the uneven spatial development of political-economic relations; and, most centrally here, the production of geographical scale and the associated process of *rescaling*.

Questions of scale gained increasing prominence in diverse fields of critical geopolitical economy and critical urban studies as of the 1990s, not only through emergent studies of rescaling processes by global city theorists and regulationist urban researchers, but through the reflexively scalar conceptual frameworks put forward by radical geographers such as Neil Smith and Erik Swyngedouw.[7] These interventions, and a subsequent outpouring of theoretical and empirical contributions within critical geopolitical economy,

---

[6] For an overview, see Edward W. Soja, *Postmetropolis* (Cambridge: Blackwell, 2000), as well as, classically, Derek Gregory and John Urry, eds., *Social Relations and Spatial Structures* (New York: Palgrave, 1985) and Jennifer Wolch and Michael Dear eds., *The Power of Geography: How Territory Shapes Social Life* (London: Unwin Hyman, 1989).

[7] On global city theory, see John Friedmann and Goetz Wolff, "World City Formation: An Agenda for Research and Action," *International Journal of Urban and Regional Research* 6 (1982): 309–44; and Peter J. Taylor, "World Cities and Territorial States: The Rise and Fall of Their Mutuality," in *World Cities in a World-System*, ed. Paul L. Knox and Peter J. Taylor (New York: Cambridge University Press, 1995), 48–62. On regulationist approaches to spatial restructuring and rescaling, see Alain Lipietz, "The National and the Regional: Their Autonomy Vis-à-Vis the Capitalist World Crisis," in *Transcending the State-Global Divide*, ed. Ronen P. Palan and Barry K. Gills (Boulder, CO: Lynne Rienner Publishers, 1994), 23–44; Jamie Peck and Adam Tickell, "Searching for a New Institutional Fix: The *After*-Fordist Crisis and the Global-Local Disorder," in *Post-Fordism: A Reader*, ed. Ash Amin (Cambridge, MA: Blackwell, 1994), 280–315; and Bob Jessop, "The Crisis of the National Spatio-Temporal Fix and the Ecological Dominance of Globalizing Capitalism," *International Journal of Urban and Regional Research* 24, no. 2 (2000): 323–60. For early contributions to a historical-geographical materialist theory of scale production, see Neil Smith, "Geography, Difference and the Politics of Space," in *Postmodernism in the Social Sciences*, ed. Joe Doherty, Elspeth Graham, and Mo Malek (New York: St. Martin's Press, 1992), 57–79; and Erik Swyngedouw, "The Mammon Quest: 'Glocalization,' Interspatial Competition and the Monetary Order: The Construction of New Scales," in *Cities and Regions in the New Europe: The Global-Local Interplay and Spatial Development Strategies*, ed. Mick Dunford and Grigoris Kafkalas (London: Belhaven Press, 1992), 39–68.

have significantly enhanced our capacity to decipher the scalar dimensions of restructuring, and of urbanization processes more generally, under both historical and contemporary capitalism. Rather than conceiving the scalar constitution of modern capitalism—its differentiation and stratification among local, regional, national, supranational, and global geographical units—as a pregiven feature of social life, such scalar configurations were now understood as produced, contested, and therefore malleable arenas and products of political-economic relations. Accordingly, key contributions to geopolitical economy, state theory, urban studies, social movement studies, political ecology, and environmental geography have scrutinized diverse forms of contemporary scalar transformation, or rescaling, in which inherited scalar arrangements are being progressively challenged, destabilized, and reworked.[8] Of course, the social and ecological sciences have long contained implicit assumptions regarding the scalar constitution of political-economic and environmental processes, from capital accumulation and state regulation to urbanization, sociopolitical mobilization, and land-use change. However, these more recent interdisciplinary developments indicate that the scale question is now being confronted with unprecedented methodological reflexivity across important streams of critical sociospatial analysis. Consequently, scalar considerations now figure explicitly within most spatially attuned accounts of contemporary capitalist restructuring.

Against the background of such investigations, this chapter examines some of the core contributions and potential limits of scale-attuned interpretations of post-1970s patterns of urban restructuring. Whereas the preceding chapter considered the conceptualization of scale production and rescaling processes under capitalism from a broad geohistorical perspective, my concern here is to explore the appropriate parameters for scale-theoretical conceptualizations of *urban* conditions, processes, and transformations, especially in the contemporary formation of post-Keynesian, neoliberalizing capitalism. Accordingly, I begin by excavating the scalar presuppositions that underpinned debates on what Manuel Castells famously termed "the urban question" during the course of the 1970s and 1980s.[9] This discussion suggests that, especially as of the 1990s, the urban question was productively reconceptualized in reflexively scalar terms in the context of

---

[8] For a foundational overview and critical interrogation of this literature, see Roger Keil and Rianne Mahon, eds., *Leviathan Undone? Towards a Political Economy of Scale* (Vancouver: University of British Columbia Press, 2009); and Eric Sheppard and Robert McMaster, eds., *Scale and Geographic Inquiry* (Malden, MA: Blackwell, 2004).

[9] Manuel Castells, *The Urban Question: A Marxist Approach* (Cambridge, MA: MIT Press, 1977 [1972]).

debates on worldwide urban restructuring, uneven spatial development, and geoeconomic integration. Subsequent sections affirm the usefulness of a scalar perspective on contemporary urban transformations but under-score the persistent difficulty of defining its distinctive analytical content. This problem is then confronted directly through the elaboration of nine general propositions that specify the determinate conceptual parameters of scale questions and, by implication, of rescaling processes, as analyzed here.

The proposed theorization entails two far-reaching analytical consequences—first, a destabilization of the long entrenched assumption that "cities" are the most appropriate or default unit of analysis and scalar reference point for urban studies; and second, an explicit conceptual narrowing of scale questions, such that they are not conflated with questions related to other dimensions of sociospatial relations under capitalism, such as place-making, territorialization or networking. Each of these propositions and their wide-ranging methodological implications is further elaborated in sub-sequent chapters, across several terrains of theoretical debate and concrete research in the field of critical urban studies.

Space, Scale, and the Urban Question

Since the early 1970s, debates on the urban question have centered closely around the conceptualization of space in research on cities.[10] However, in their efforts to conceptualize urban spatiality, urban theorists have neces-sarily introduced diverse assumptions concerning the distinctiveness of the urban scale of sociospatial organization (as opposed to, for instance, the re-gional, the national, or the global scales). To unpack this assertion and its implications for contemporary urban theory, let us reconstruct briefly some of the scalar assumptions upon which previous rounds of debate on the urban question have been grounded.

In his classic 1972 work, *The Urban Question*, Marxist sociologist Manuel Castells attacked the Chicago school of urban sociology for its failure to grasp the historical specificity of the urban form under capitalism.[11] Against this uni-versalistic "urban ideology," Castells set out to delimit the role of the "urban system" as a determinate structure within the capitalist mode of production. In so doing, Castells implicitly distinguished two basic dimensions of the

---

[10] Mark Gottdiener, *The Social Production of Urban Space*, 2nd ed. (Austin: University of Texas Press, 1985).

[11] Castells, *Urban Question*.

urban, which for present purposes can be termed its scalar and its functional aspects. The scalar aspect of the urban concerned the materiality of social processes organized on the urban scale as opposed to supraurban scales. In Castells's terminology, scales are understood as the differentiated "spatial units" of which the capitalist system is composed.[12] The functional aspect of the urban, Castells's most explicit focus in *The Urban Question*, concerned not merely the geographical setting or territorial scope of social processes, but their functional role or "social content."[13] According to Castells's famous argument, the specificity of the urban "spatial unit" could be delimited theoretically neither with reference to its ideological, its political-juridical, or its production functions, but only in terms of its role as a site for the reproduction of labor-power.[14] The essence of Castells's position, then, was the attempt to define geographical scale in terms of its social function. Castells repeatedly acknowledged the existence of multiple social processes within capitalist cities but argued that only collective consumption was functionally specific to the urban scale. Castells's attempt to spatialize Althusserian structuralism was thus premised upon an understanding of geographical scales as spatial expressions of social functions.

Castells began to modify this position almost immediately after the publication of *The Urban Question*, but throughout the 1980s, the latter work continued to exercise a massive influence upon conceptualizations of geographical scale within urban studies. Peter Saunders's widely discussed critique of Castells's early work usefully illustrates the extent of this influence.[15] The core of Saunders's critique was a rejection of the notion that any of the social processes located within cities are, in a necessary sense, functionally specific to that geographical scale. This observation led Saunders to view urban spatial organization as a merely contingent effect, and thus as a flawed conceptual basis for confronting the urban question. However, in reaching this conclusion, Saunders implicitly embraced Castells's own criterion of functional specificity as the theoretical linchpin of the urban question. It was this underlying assumption that enabled Saunders to invoke the supraurban character of the social processes located within cities as grounds for dismissing the possibility of a coherent spatial definition of the urban. Saunders's alternative proposal to define urban sociology

---

[12] Ibid., 445–50.

[13] Ibid., 89, 235.

[14] Ibid., 235–37, 445.

[15] Peter Saunders, *Social Theory and the Urban Question*, 2nd ed. (London: Routledge, 1986 [1981]).

as the study of consumption processes preserved the label "urban" only as a "matter of convention."[16] Saunders thereby rendered the urban dimension of urban sociology entirely accidental, a random choice of geographical scale.

Despite their diametrically opposed conclusions, both positions in the Castells/Saunders debate were premised upon two shared assumptions regarding the role of geographical scale in the urban question. First, both authors viewed the urban scale as the self-evident empirical centerpiece of the urban question. Because of their overarching concern with the functional content of the urban, Castells and Saunders reduced its scalar aspect, the existence of distinctively urbanized "spatial units" within an unevenly developed global capitalist system, to a pregiven empirical fact rather than conceptualizing it as a theoretical problem in its own right. Consequently, neither author could explicitly analyze the ways in which the urban scale is itself socially produced or, most crucially from the vantage point of the post-1980s period, the possibility of its rupture or transformation. Second, the arguments of both Castells and Saunders were grounded on what might be termed a "zero sum" conception of geographical scale—the notion that scales operate as mutually exclusive rather than as relationally intermeshed, coevolving frameworks for sociospatial relations. On this basis, both Castells and Saunders implied that supraurban geographical scales were merely external parameters for the urban question. By contrast, as I will discuss below, a subsequent round of theoretical experimentation in global urban studies interpreted the fluidly evolving interlinkages between urban and supraurban scales as intrinsic to the very content of the urban question.

Various alternatives to Castells's early work were elaborated during the late 1970s and early 1980s, as many urban scholars attempted to redefine the specificity of the urban. The key task from this perspective was to delineate social processes that were tied intrinsically, but not exclusively, to the urban scale. Thus, cities were now analyzed as multidimensional geographical sites in which, for instance, industrial production, local labor markets, infrastructural configurations, interfirm relations, urban land-use matrices, and household-level consumption processes were clustered together. From David Harvey's capital-theoretic account of urban built environments and Allen J. Scott's neo-Ricardian theorization of the urban land nexus to Michael Storper and Richard Walker's post-Weberian analysis of industrial agglomeration and territorial development, these approaches replaced Castells's

---

[16] Ibid., 289.

criterion of functional specificity with that of scale specificity.[17] The analytical core of the urban question was no longer the presumed functional unity of the urban process, but the evolving role of the urban scale as a multifaceted materialization of capitalist sociospatial relations. In effect, Castells's early position was inverted. Against his conception of scales as the spatial expressions of social functions, the sociospatial relations of capitalism were now analyzed in terms of their distinctive materializations at the urban scale.

These multifaceted analyses of urban sociospatiality soon flowed into broader explorations of the production of space and spatial configuration under capitalism. David Harvey's historical-geographical materialist conceptualization of the spatial fix exemplified this tendency.[18] In his writings of the 1980s, Harvey continued to view the urban scale as a key geographical foundation for the accumulation process, and he elaborated an influential periodization of capitalist development focused on successive historical waves of urbanization. At the same time, as discussed in the previous chapter, Harvey now began more explicitly to conceptualize the role of supraurban spaces and processes—for instance, regional divisions of labor, national institutional constellations, supranational regimes of accumulation, and world market conditions—as central geographical preconditions for each historical spatial fix under capitalism. Closely analogous methodological strategies were elaborated by other radical geographers such as Doreen Massey, Neil Smith, and Edward Soja, who embedded their respective engagements with the urban question into broader theoretical accounts of capitalist sociospatiality on supraurban scales, whether with reference to changing spatial divisions of labor, patterns of uneven spatial development, or forms of crisis-induced restructuring.

Three aspects of these debates deserve emphasis here. First, insofar as these analyses of urban space flowed directly into a range of supraurban questions—the regional question, the problematic of uneven development, the core-periphery debate, and so forth—the coherence of the urban question was severely unsettled.[19] Whereas explorations of the urban question had contributed crucially to this broader spatialization of Marxian geopolitical

---

[17] See, for example, David Harvey, *The Urban Experience* (Baltimore: Johns Hopkins Press, 1989); Allen J. Scott, *The Urban Land Nexus and the State* (London: Pion, 1980); Michael Storper and Richard Walker, *The Capitalist Imperative: Territory, Technology and Industrial Growth* (New York: Basil Blackwell, 1989). For a general overview of these discussions, see Soja, *Postmetropolis*.

[18] Harvey, *Urban Experience*; and David Harvey, *The Limits to Capital* (Chicago: University of Chicago Press, 1982).

[19] Soja, *Postmodern Geographies*, 94–117.

economy, the latter trend now appeared to be supplanting the urban question itself, relegating urban space to a mere subtopic within the more general issue of capitalism's uneven historical geographies. Second, these analyses introduced more multidimensional conceptions of geographical scale than had previously been deployed. Scales were no longer equated with unitary social functions but were viewed increasingly as crystallizations of diverse, overlapping political-economic processes. Third, despite this methodological advance, the historicity of geographical scales was recognized only in a relatively limited sense. Capital was said to jump continually between the urban, regional, national, and global scales in pursuit of new sources of surplus value, but the possibility that entrenched scalar hierarchies and interscalar relations might themselves undergo restructuring and be creatively destroyed was not systematically explored. It was not until the early 1990s, with the proliferation of research on the urban dimensions of geoeconomic restructuring, that more historically dynamic conceptualizations of geographical scale and interscalar configurations were elaborated within critical urban studies.

(Re)scaling the Urban Question?

Since the 1990s, the urban question has continued to provoke intense debate and disagreement, but its parameters have been significantly redefined in conjunction with a new wave of research on worldwide processes of urban and regional restructuring. In contrast to previous conceptions of the urban as a relatively self-evident scalar entity, urban researchers have been confronted with major transformations in the social, institutional, infrastructural, and geographical organization not only of the urban scale, but of the worldwide scalar hierarchies and interscalar networks in which cities are embedded. Under these circumstances, researchers have reconceptualized the urban question with direct reference to a range of supraurban rescaling processes.

This methodological reorientation can be illustrated with reference to several important streams of post-1990s urban and regional research. First, global city theorists and industrial geographers explored the enhanced strategic importance of place-specific social relations, localization processes, and territorial concentration as basic preconditions for global economic interdependencies.[20] From this perspective, the urban scale operates as a localized node within globally organized circuits of capital accumulation,

---

[20] Paul L. Knox and Peter J. Taylor, eds., *World Cities in a World-System* (New York: Cambridge University Press, 1995).

whereas the global scale is in turn constituted through networks of interlinked cities and metropolitan regions. Second, many urban scholars analyzed dramatic shifts in both the vertical and horizontal relations among cities, as manifested, for instance, in the consolidation of new global urban hierarchies; in accelerated informational, financial, and migratory flows among cities; in the construction of new planetary interurban telecommunications infrastructures; in intensified interurban competition; and in countervailing forms of interurban cooperation and coordination.[21] From this perspective, the urban is not only a nested stratum within supraurban political-economic hierarchies but also a medium and product of dense interscalar networks linking dispersed locations across the world economy. Third, regulationist-inspired analyses linked processes of urban restructuring to ongoing transformations of state spatial organization that were recalibrating the forms and functions of national regulatory institutions and giving new importance to both supranational and subnational forms of governance.[22] From this perspective, the urban scale is not only a localized arena for global capital accumulation, but a strategic regulatory coordinate in which a multiscalar restructuring of state spatiality has been unfolding.

Of course, the appropriate interpretation of urban transformations during this period was, and remains, a matter of considerable debate. Nonetheless, three core propositions emerged through this wave of theorizing regarding the "transformed form" of the urban question under the new geopolitical and geoeconomic conditions:

1. *The destabilization of nationalized scalar fixes.* The nationalized formation of capital accumulation, state regulation, urbanization, and sociopolitical struggle that prevailed during the Fordist-Keynesian, national-developmentalist period was being destabilized. Under the volatile conditions of the post-1980s period, therefore, the "institutional arrangements that at one time were congruent at the national level are now more dispersed at multiple spatial levels"; meanwhile, a "multifaceted causality runs in virtually all directions among the various levels of society: nations, sectors, free trade zones, international

---

[21] Stephen Graham, "Cities in the Real-Time Age: The Paradigm Challenge of Telecommunications to the Conception and Planning of Urban Space," *Environment and Planning A* 29 (1997): 105–27; and Peter J. Taylor, *World-City Network* (London: Routledge, 2004).

[22] Neil Brenner, *New State Spaces: Urban Governance and the Rescaling of Statehood* (New York: Oxford University Press, 2004); Bob Jessop, *The Future of the Capitalist State* (London: Polity, 2002).

regimes, supranational regions, large cities and even small but well-specialized localities."[23]

2. *The proliferation of rescaling strategies.* Following the crisis of North Atlantic Fordism in the 1970s, diverse sociopolitical strategies were mobilized to reorganize inherited interscalar configurations in key realms of political-economic organization and everyday life, including urbanization.[24] Within and beyond major metropolitan regions, these rescaling strategies were widely viewed as a means to resolve crisis tendencies, to manage regulatory problems, to recalibrate power relations, and to establish a new geographical basis for economic growth, territorial governance, and political identities. Consequently, in this context, cities and metropolitan regions were becoming increasingly strategic sites of regulatory experimentation, institutional innovation, and sociopolitical contestation.[25]

3. *The relativization of scales.* The forms, functions, institutional configuration, and spatial organization of the national scale were being significantly recalibrated, generally with major consequences for patterns and pathways of urban development. This situation was aptly described by Chris Collinge, and later by Bob Jessop, as a "relativization of scales."[26] From this point of view, the sociospatial transformations of the post-1980s period were not unleashing a unidirectional process of globalization, triadization, Europeanization, decentralization, regionalization, or localization, in which a single scale (be it global, triadic, European, regional, or local) would replace the national as the primary level of political-economic coordination. Instead, inherited scalar hierarchies and interscalar relations were being rearticulated across the world economy as a whole, but without producing a new privileged, dominant, or hegemonic scale of political-economic organization. The nationalized scalar fixes of earlier decades

---

[23] Robert Boyer and J. Rogers Hollingsworth, "From National Embeddedness to Spatial and Institutional Nestedness," in *Contemporary Capitalism: The Embeddedness of Institutions*, ed. J. Rogers Hollingsworth and Robert Boyer (New York: Cambridge University Press, 1997), 472, 470.

[24] Erik Swyngedouw, "Neither Global nor Local: 'Glocalization' and the Politics of Scale," in *Spaces of Globalization*, ed. Kevin R. Cox (New York: Guilford Press, 1997), 137–66.

[25] Allen J. Scott, *Regions and the World Economy* (London: Oxford University Press, 1998).

[26] Chris Collinge, "Spatial Articulation of the State: Reworking Social Relations and Social Regulation Theory" (unpublished manuscript, Centre for Urban and Regional Studies, Birmingham, 1996); Jessop, "Crisis of the National Spatio-Temporal Fix."

of capitalist development were thus now superseded by a situation of pervasive interscalar flux and scale relativization.

In sum, then, as indicated by the proliferation of terms and phrases such as the "local-global interplay," the "local-global nexus," and "glocalization," many urban researchers during the 1990s and subsequently were conceptualizing emergent processes of geoeconomic restructuring as a contested rearticulation of scalar organization. In this way, the *problematique* of geographical scale—its spatial organization, social production, political contestation, and historical reconfiguration—was now reflexively positioned at the very heart of the urban question. Whereas the urban question had previously crystallized in the form of debates on the functional specificity or scale specificity of the urban within relatively stable interscalar hierarchies, it was now being rearticulated, across major currents of critical urban studies, in the form of *a scale question.*

Challenges and Pitfalls of Scalar Analysis

Even as urbanists have come to mobilize scalar concepts with increasing reflexivity, significant methodological challenges have been associated with the tasks of (1) deciphering the tangled scalar hierarchies, mosaics, and networks of urban life that have been emerging in the wake of post-1980s geoeconomic and geopolitical transformations; (2) specifying the role of cities, metropolitan regions, and intercity networks within emergent political-economic geographies; (3) understanding the implications of scale relativization for patterns and pathways of urban development; and (4) theorizing the variegated patterns and pathways of rescaling that are currently reshaping the capitalist urban fabric itself. Central to confronting each of these challenges is the need to construct an appropriate conceptual grammar for representing the dynamic, politically contested character of geographical scales and interscalar relations under conditions of deepening scale relativization.

However, despite the energetic explorations of radical sociospatial theorists in recent decades, a rigorously processual scalar lexicon remains elusive. A reification of scale appears to be built into everyday scalar terms (such as local, regional, national, and global) insofar as they represent dynamic processes of sociospatial and institutional creative destruction (localization, regionalization, nationalization, and globalization) as if they were neatly enclosed within fixed, bounded territorial containers. Relatedly, existing scalar vocabularies are poorly equipped to grasp the tangled, perpetually mutating historical interconnections and interdependencies among geographical scales. Insofar as terms such as "local," "urban," "regional," and so forth are used to demarcate purportedly separate territorial "islands" of sociospatial relations, they obfuscate the profound mutual imbrication of all scales and the densely interwoven, overlapping interscalar networks through which the latter are constituted. It is the failure to excavate such interscalar entanglements that leads to the pervasive "endogeneity trap" diagnosed by Saskia Sassen, in which scales of analysis and explanation are assumed to converge.[27] These difficulties are exacerbated still further by the circumstance that much of the mainstream social scientific division of labor is still organized according to distinctive scalar foci—for instance, urban studies, regional studies, comparative politics, area studies, international relations, and so forth—that tend to reify historically specific forms of territorial and scalar organization, and thus to obstruct efforts to explore the dynamics of interscalar relations and rescaling processes.

Even among those who are concerned to develop a reflexively scale-attuned approach to the production of space, the conceptualization of scale itself has become increasingly contentious. Theorists differ, for instance, on how best to delineate the essential properties of scale, on the analytical and empirical scope of the concept, on its relation to other key sociospatial concepts, and on its appropriate application to the study of concrete sociospatial relations, processes, and transformations. While some theorists have tended to extend the concept of scale so broadly that it becomes synonymous with sociospatiality as such, others have argued for its complete eradication in favor of a "flat ontology" that avoids any analytical engagement with the vertically stratified dimensions of territorial organization. Consequently, amid the many scholarly exchanges, debates, and polemics regarding such issues that have transpired since the 1990s, theorists have struggled to find ways of coherently distinguishing the ontological, epistemological, cartographic, political, and experiential dimensions of scale, such that processes of scaling and rescaling might be analyzed through a broadly shared sociospatial lexicon.[28]

---

[27] Saskia Sassen, *Territory, Authority, Rights: From Medieval to Global Assemblages* (Princeton, NJ: Princeton University Press, 2006).

[28] For useful overviews of such debates, see Andrew Herod, *Scale* (New York: Routledge, 2011), as well as the contributions to Keil and Mahon, *Leviathan Undone?*; and Sheppard and McMaster, *Scale and Geographic Inquiry*. For a sampling of various additional important positions in the debate, see, for instance, Harriet Bulkeley, "Reconfiguring Environmental Governance: Towards a Politics of Scales and Networks," *Political Geography* 8 (2005): 875–902; Chris Collinge, "Flat Ontology and the Deconstruction of Scale," *Transactions of the Institute of British Geographers* 31 (2006): 244–51; Arturo Escobar, "The 'Ontological Turn' in Social Theory," *Transactions of the Institute of British Geographers* 32 (2007): 106–11; Andrew E. G. Jonas, "Pro

Given this, it would seem appropriate to ask, with Bryon Miller, whether scale is in danger of becoming a "chaotic concept" that lumps together "a diverse range of objects and processes, many of them unrelated."[29] As productive as the contemporary "scalar turn" has been in illuminating important dimensions of post-1970s capitalist restructuring, its contributions will be significantly blunted in the absence of analytical precision regarding the concept of scale and other, equally essential keywords of sociospatial theory, such as place, territory, and networks.

For present purposes, I will not attempt to review the somewhat convoluted vicissitudes of recent theoretical debates on the scale question, which have advanced diverse politico-epistemological agendas and have been oriented toward a range of concrete inquiries across diverse fields of social science, humanities, and design research. Instead, in order to provide an analytical orientation for the studies presented in subsequent chapters of this book, the task here is to present a concise statement of the key elements in the conceptualization that guides this analysis. As will immediately become evident, the position developed here diverges sharply from several prominent methodological tendencies that have crystallized in recent debates on the scale question among critical sociospatial theorists, including (1) the treatment of scale as a general metaphor for sociospatiality as such,[30] (2) the equation of scale with territorialist understandings of space,[31] (3) calls to abandon scalar concepts in favor of topological modes of analysis and "flat ontologies,"[32] and (4) the construction of sociospatial theory on the basis of transhistorical or ontological claims regarding the nature of social life as

Scale: Further Reflections on the 'Scale Debate' within Human Geography," *Transactions of the Institute of British Geographers* 31 (2006): 399–406; Richard Howitt, "Scale as Relation: Musical Metaphors of Geographical Scale," *Area* 30, no. 1 (1998): 49–58; and Nathan Sayre, "Ecological and Geographic Scale: Parallels and Potential for Integration," *Progress in Human Geography* 29, no. 3 (2005): 276–90.

[29] Bryon Miller, "Is Scale a Chaotic Concept? Notes on Processes of Scale Production," in Keil and Mahon, *Leviathan Undone*, 52.

[30] Sallie Marston, "The Social Construction of Scale," *Progress in Human Geography* 24, no. 2 (2000): 219–42.

[31] Ash Amin, "Regions Unbound: Towards a New Politics of Place," *Geografiska Annaler* 86 (2003): 33–44; Ash Amin, "Spatialities of Globalization," *Environment and Planning A* 34 (2002): 385–99.

[32] Sallie Marston, John Paul Jones, and Keith Woodward, "Human Geography without Scale," *Transactions of the Institute of British Geographers* 30 (2005): 416–32; Amin, "Spatialities of Globalization."

such.[33] In thus proceeding, however, my goal is not to expound upon the philosophical limitations of such positions, but to offer a concise overview of the conceptualization of scale that underpins my own explorations of rescaling processes. From this point of view, the essential issue is not the absolute ontological "truth" of a particular conceptualization, but its relative usefulness to the specific analytical, interpretive, and/or political task at hand—for my purposes here, that of deciphering post-1970s patterns and pathways of urbanization. This pragmatic criterion of concept validity is, I believe, a more productive basis for scholarly investigation, exchange, and debate than the a priori, quasi-metaphysical constructions that continue to inform many important strands of contemporary sociospatial theory.

While the following propositions initially deploy the term "scale," they quickly transcend this relatively static, generic terminology and elaborate a reformulated conceptual grammar based on processual, contextually embedded notions of scaling and rescaling. Scales, in this framework, are no more than the temporarily stabilized crystallizations of historically specific sociospatial processes, which must be theorized and investigated on their own terms. It is, in short, geohistorical processes of scaling and rescaling, rather than scales themselves, that must be the main analytical focus for approaches to the scale question.[34] This conceptualization, which is strongly influenced by Erik Swyngedouw's powerful formulations on the topic, is intended to provide a basis for further inquiry into the rescalings—whether of urbanization, capital accumulation, state regulation, socioecological metabolism, or sociopolitical contestation—that have been of particularly central concern to contemporary urban researchers. I begin with epistemological foundations before turning to second- and third-order problems of conceptualization and analysis.

Nine Propositions on Rescaling

1. *A critical realist epistemology of scale.* What are the conditions of possibility for describing the social world in scalar terms? I rely here upon a critical realist epistemology in which the intelligibility of a scalar lens into social life is understood to be derived from a prior state of affairs—namely,

---

[33] Escobar, "'Ontological Turn'"; Chris Collinge, "The *Différance* between Society and Space: Nested Scales and the Returns of Spatial Fetishism," *Environment and Planning D: Society and Space* 23 (2005): 189–206.

[34] Swyngedouw, "Neither Global nor Local."

the differentiation of sociospatial relations among distinct yet interconnected scalar strata, which in turn structure perception, experience, understanding, representation, and practice.[35] Whatever they might signify—and,
as indicated, this is a matter of considerable disagreement—scalar concepts
are not simply categories of analysis imposed by the researcher on the unstructured complexity of life (ideal types or conceptual abstractions, in Max
Weber's sense). Rather, as understood here, the lexicon of geographical scale
emerges as a "real abstraction" of historically specific patterns, regularities,
interdependencies, and systems of relations that crystallize through, and
impact, sociospatial relations.[36] Under contemporary capitalism, therefore,
the persistent assertions of the scale question have been linked intrinsically to the changing organizational and spatial configuration of this historically specific social formation and its associated crisis tendencies. While
versions of a scale question assumed determinate forms within earlier historical configurations of capitalist territorial development, their conditions
of possibility—and therefore, their intellectual foundations, conceptual
orientations, and concrete reference points—differed qualitatively from those
that have crystallized during the post-1980s conjuncture of restructuring.[37]

2. *Scales result from the vertical ordering of social relations.* But what is
the specificity of scalar categories, and to what do they properly refer? As
conceived here, building upon a precise formulation by Chris Collinge, scale
results from the "vertical ordering" of social formations.[38] In addition to the

---

[35] Andrew Sayer, *Method in Social Science*, 2nd ed. (London: Routledge, 1992).

[36] On the latter term, see Sayer, *Method in Social Science*. The notion of geographical scale as
a conceptual "lexicon" is from Neil Smith, "Remaking Scale: Competition and Cooperation in
Prenational and Postnational Europe," in *Competitive European Peripheries*, ed. Heikki Eskelinen
and Folke Snickars (Berlin: Springer Verlag, 1995), 59–74.

[37] On earlier versions of the scale question under capitalism, see Neil Smith, *Uneven
Development: Nature, Capital and the Production of Space* (New York: Blackwell, 1984); and Neil
Smith, "Scale Bending and the Fate of the National," in Sheppard and McMaster, *Scale and
Geographic Inquiry*, 192–211. For a radically opposed, ontological starting point, see Marston,
Jones, and Woodward, "Human Geography without Scale," and Amin, "Spatialities of
Globalization."

[38] Chris Collinge, "Self-Organization of Society by Scale: A Spatial Reworking of Regulation
Theory," *Environment and Planning D: Society and Space* 17 (1999): 557–74. In Collinge's key
formulation (557):

A comprehensive approach to spatial organization will address the axes of place and scale
in a unified manner. It will acknowledge that the global social formation has a "horizontal" structure in which the same activities are organised at similar scales in different
places. But it will also acknowledge that this formation has a "vertical" structure too, in
which different activities are organised at different scales and in which those at certain
scales tend to dominate the rest. An appreciation of both axes of social organisation is especially important in understanding the formation of societies.

"horizontal" (areal, topological, or networked) differentiation of sociospatial relations across places, regions, and territories, there is also a process of "vertical" ordering in which sociospatial relations are differentiated and stratified among global, supranational, national, regional, metropolitan, local, household, and/or bodily levels (among others). It is this vertical structuration of sociospatial relations that makes scalar concepts intelligible in everyday life, and essential as tools of sociohistorical inquiry. Only in the absence of such a vertical differentiation of sociospatial relations could the ascalar vision of a "flat ontology" postulated by actor-network theorists and other contemporary theorists of topological spatiality become plausible. Crucially, however, as I argue below and in subsequent chapters, the spatialities of scale cannot be reduced to this vertical dimension. Depending on the specific sociospatial process that is under investigation, several equally foundational dimensions of sociospatial relations may also be of considerable significance and will require parallel theorization and analysis. Scale is defined by vertical differentiation, but its variegated spatialities exceed this dimension.[39]

3. *Scales exist because social processes are scaled.* Geographical scales—the discrete tiers, strata, or levels within vertically ordered sociospatial configurations—are not static, fixed, or permanent properties of political-economic life. They are best understood, rather, as socially produced, and therefore malleable, dimensions of specific sociospatial processes—such as capitalist production, social reproduction, state regulation, urbanization, socioenvironmental metabolism, sociopolitical struggle, and so forth. Insofar as any social, political, economic, or environmental process or institutional configuration is vertically differentiated among relatively individuated spatial tiers, the problem of its scalar organization (and, by implication, that of its potential reorganization, or rescaling) arises. It is more precise, therefore, to speak of the scaling (scale differentiation) and rescaling (scale reordering) of specific sociospatial processes and institutional forms rather than of scales

---

[39] In emphasizing the verticality of scalar relations, the approach proposed here does not deny the importance of horizontal forms of interscalar interaction and interdependence—for instance, networks of relations between actors, coalitions of actors, or organizations located within geographically dispersed metropolitan regions, territories, and so forth. I argue, however, that interscalar configurations and networks of spatial connectivity are mutually constitutive rather than mutually exclusive dimensions of sociospatial relations. Indeed, networks of spatial connectivity are arguably directly structured by scaling and rescaling processes insofar as the latter are likely to play a key role in demarcating (1) the specific spatial units between which the networks in question are interconnected and (2) the spatial orbits of the networks in question. However, while scaling processes may mediate such relations of horizontal connectivity, scalar categories cannot, in themselves, offer a full description of the multidimensional spatialities associated with networks and several other key dimensions of sociospatial relations. This issue is further explored in subsequent chapters.

per se. Scales are but the provisionally stabilized outcomes of scaling and rescaling processes; the former can be grasped only through an analysis of the latter.

4. *Scales can only be grasped relationally.* Scales cannot be construed adequately as fixed units within a system of nested territorial containers defined by absolute geographic size (a "Russian dolls" model of scale). The institutional configuration, functions, histories, and evolutionary dynamics of any one geographical scale can only be grasped relationally, in terms of its changing links to other geographical scales situated within broader interscalar configurations.[40] Consequently, the meanings of scalar terms such as "global," "national," "regional," "urban," and "local" are likely to differ qualitatively depending on the specific sociospatial processes being described, which are likely to produce distinctive scalar morphologies, interscalar articulations, and choreographies of scalar evolution. Thus, despite the substantialist spatial lens that is imposed by grammatical convention, it is actually quite misleading to characterize scale in singular terms—as, for instance, in discourses about "the" local, "the" regional, "the" national, "the" global, and so forth. Such formulations imply that individual scales contain a pregiven coherence, and thus deflect attention away from the ineluctably relational co-constitution of scalar levels through the flow of sociospatial processes within and among interscalar configurations.

5. *Forms of interscalar organization represent mosaics, not pyramids.* The institutional landscape of capitalism is not characterized by a single, encompassing scalar pyramid into which all sociospatial relations and institutional configurations are neatly enfolded. Rather, each major sociospatial process under modern capitalism is likely to be associated with a distinctive pattern of scalar ordering, generally manifested in a variegated crystallization of institutional arrangements, material infrastructures, regulatory configurations, patterns of sociospatial interdependence, sociometabolic flows, and so forth. The pattern of scalar differentiation associated with national states, for instance, may only partially correspond to that of

---

[40] An important corollary to this argument—productively emphasized by Helga Leitner and Byron Miller—is the recognition that the vertical orderings of sociospatial relations associated with scaling processes may or may not assume a hierarchical, top-down form. As Leitner and Miller argue, hierarchy is only one among many possible forms of verticality; various modalities of stratification are possible within any given interscalar configuration. Consequently, emphasizing the verticality of scaling processes does not entail the belief that "the global sets the rules and the local accommodates. . . . Power asymmetries between different scales are always contested and subject to struggle." See Helga Leitner and Byron Miller, "Scale and the Limitations of Ontological Debate: A Commentary on Marston, Jones and Woodward," *Transactions of the Institute of British Geographers* 32 (2007): 117.

national urban hierarchies, which may in turn only tendentially correspond to that of nationalized patterns of energy generation, financial circulation, commodity exchange, or political subjectivity. Consequently, the scalar architectures of capitalism as a whole are composed of mosaic-like, geohistorical accretions of tangled, crosscutting, asymmetrically stratified, and only partially overlapping interscalar configurations. The latter are likely to evolve along spatially uneven, temporally discontinuous, and nonisomorphic pathways.

6. *Interscalar configurations are embedded within polymorphic geographies.* Processes of scaling and rescaling occur in close conjunction with other geohistorical forms of sociospatial patterning, such as territorialization (enclosure, bounding), place-making (agglomeration, clustering), and network formation (interspatial linkage). The scalar differentiation of any given sociospatial process is thus only one among many potentially significant dimensions of its geographical configuration. While sociospatial relations are often scaled, their geographies are generally differentiated along several other important axes that cannot be completely subsumed under an encompassing scalar umbrella. For this reason, as I argue throughout this book, studies of scaling and rescaling must avoid the hazard of "scale-centrism" in which the scalar attributes of social, political-economic, or metabolic processes are privileged to the neglect of other dimensions of sociospatial relations that may be equally or even more significant in relation to specific research questions.[41]

7. *Interscalar rule regimes may crystallize.* Even as successive geohistorical waves of scaling and rescaling unfold, the scalar architectures of capitalism cannot be conceived simply as a haphazard bricolage of superimposed layerings of interscalar organization. Indeed, despite the relationality, unevenness, polymorphism, mutability, and evolutionary dynamism emphasized previously, macrospatial rule regimes are frequently consolidated under capitalism in which a (relatively) coherent interscalar architecture is (provisionally) stabilized that may entail the crystallization of (1) a dominant scale of political-economic power; (2) specific modalities, relays, and circuits of interscalar stratification; and/or (3) distinctive patterns and pathways of interscalar metagovernance, conflict, and evolution. These are precisely the scalar fixes discussed in the preceding chapter with reference to the work of David Harvey and Henri Lefebvre. By constructing a determinate

---

[41] Bob Jessop, Neil Brenner, and Martin Jones, "Theorizing Socio-Spatial Relations," *Environment and Planning D: Society and Space* 26 (2008): 389–401. The implications of this argument are revisited at length in Chapter 8.

configuration of interscalar organization and regularizing sociospatial relations among its major tiers, such rule regimes impose operational parameters around important dimensions of political-economic life, including capital accumulation, political regulation, socioenvironmental metabolism, and sociopolitical contestation.[42] Under these circumstances, in Roger Keil and Rianne Mahon's precise formulation, "while there may be a plurality of hierarchies, pluralism does not prevail."[43] A key challenge for studies of scaling and rescaling processes under capitalism, therefore, is to explore the establishment, consolidation, destabilization, or dismantling of such interscalar rule regimes. More generally, it is essential to investigate the variegated sociospatial processes through which the meta-architecture of such rule regimes evolves in relation to systemic cycles of capital accumulation, geohistorical waves of institutional-regulatory restructuring, patterns of political contestation, and pathways of crisis formation.

8. *Rescaling processes are frequently path dependent.* The bulk of the literature on scale production and rescaling, with its empirical focus on the tumultuous post-1970s period, has emphasized the cataclysmic forms of scalar transformation that have ensued during and following waves of systemic crisis. Under these conditions, extant scalar configurations are dismantled and rejigged; and amid intense sociopolitical struggles and organizational experiments, new orderings of interscalar relations are established. However, even during phases of intensified restructuring, scalar configurations are not infinitely malleable. Processes of crisis-generated rescaling do not entail the complete replacement of one interscalar configuration by another, fully formed scalar order or the total disappearance of some scales as others supersede them. Rather, rescaling processes generally occur through the path-dependent, mutually transformative interaction of inherited interscalar arrangements with emergent strategies to reimagine and recalibrate the latter. This means that, even in the midst of intense pressures to restructure a given interscalar order, entrenched scalar configurations may close off certain pathways of rescaling by circumscribing the production of new scales within determinate institutional, political-economic, and geographical

---

[42] On the theorization of rule regimes and their implications, see Brenner, *New State Spaces*; Jamie Peck, "Political Economies of Scale: Fast Policy, Interscalar Relations and Neoliberal Workfare," *Economic Geography* 78, no. 3 (2002): 332–60; Neil Brenner, Jamie Peck, and Nik Theodore, "Variegated Neoliberalization: Geographies, Modalities, Pathways," *Global Networks* 10, no. 2 (2010): 182–222; Neil Brenner, Jamie Peck, and Nik Theodore, "After Neoliberalization?," *Globalizations* 7, no. 3 (2010): 313–30; as well as Swyngedouw, "Neither Global nor Local"; and Jessop, "Crisis of the National Spatio-Temporal Fix."

[43] See Roger Keil and Rianne Mahon, "Introduction," in Keil and Mahon, *Leviathan Undone?*, 18.

parameters. The differential modalities of scalar restructuring—incremental, conjunctural, tendential, systemic, cataclysmic, and so forth—therefore deserve careful investigation.[44]

9. *Rescaling processes recalibrate the geographies and choreographies of power relations.* The scaling and rescaling of sociospatial processes mediates, and is in turn shaped by, asymmetrical and conflict-laden social power relations.[45] On the one hand, the establishment of relatively stable scalar configurations may serve to entrench geographies and choreographies of domination/subordination, inclusion/exclusion, and normalization/othering that empower some social actors, identities, coalitions, forces, and organizations at the expense of others, generally on the basis of structurally inscribed positionalities such as class, gender, sexuality, race, ethnicity, and citizenship. In this sense, scaling processes are likely to figure strategically within what Doreen Massey has famously termed the "power-geometries" of social life—that is, the contested materialization of unequal relations of class, gender, sexuality, ethnicity, race, empire, and citizenship within historically specific sociospatial arrangements.[46] On the other hand, however, scalar configurations may operate not merely as materializations and arenas of social power struggles, but as their very objects and stakes: their reorganization can also profoundly reshape power geometries themselves, across sites, places, and territories.

---

[44] Chris Collinge (in "Self-Organization of Society by Scale") implies that the selection of a dominant scale and, more generally, the evolution of scalar hierarchies are calibrated to be optimal for purposes of accumulation. However, while Collinge's analysis provides a useful structuralist critique of certain voluntarist tendencies within regulation theory, the assumption that scalar evolution will reflect the changing historical requirements of capital accumulation is problematic. As the literature on path dependency suggests, suboptimal institutional configurations are frequently locked in due to their progressively higher payoffs ("increasing returns") as they become more prevalent. See W. Brian Arthur, *Increasing Returns and Path Dependence in the Economy* (Ann Arbor: University of Michigan Press, 1994). Additionally, it is crucial to explore the ways in which rescaling processes are also conditioned by (1) the (relative) sclerosis or (apparent) inertia of extant scalar configurations and (2) the evolution of political strategies and sociopolitical contestation.

[45] This claim is one of the core insights developed by Neil Smith and Erik Swyngedouw in their foundational writings on the production of scale. See also, among other contributions, Christian Berndt, "The Rescaling of Labour Regulation in Germany: From National and Regional Corporatism to Intrafirm Welfare," *Environment and Planning A* 32, no. 9 (2000): 1569–92; Noel Castree, "Geographic Scale and Grass-Roots Internationalism: The Liverpool Dock Dispute, 1995–1998," *Economic Geography* 76, no. 3 (2000): 272–92; Andrew Herod, "Labor's Spatial Praxis and the Geography of Contract Bargaining in the US East Coast Longshore Industry, 1953–1989," *Political Geography* 2 (1997): 145–69; and Neil Smith, "Homeless/Global: Scaling Places," in *Mapping the Futures*, ed. Jon Bird, Barry Curtis, Tim Putnam, and Lisa Tickner (New York: Routledge, 1993), 87–119.

[46] See Doreen Massey, *Space, Place and Gender* (Minneapolis: University of Minnesota Press, 1996); as well as, more generally, Eric Sheppard, "The Spaces and Times of Globalization: Place, Scale, Networks and Positionality," *Economic Geography* 3 (2002): 307–30.

As Swyngedouw explains, "the continuous reshuffling and reorganization of spatial scales is an integral part of social strategies and struggles for control and empowerment."[47] Concomitantly, in Smith's classic formulation: "The scale of struggle and the struggle over scale are two sides of the same coin."[48] The specification of the particular geohistorical, institutional, and political conditions under which inherited interscalar orders may become stakes rather than mere settings of social struggles over the configuration of power-geometries is clearly among the central tasks for any critical theory of scaling processes.

Given my emphasis, in the preceding propositions, on (1) the pluralized, polymorphic character of sociospatial relations; (2) the inherent relationality of each tier or stratum within interscalar configurations; and (3) the profoundly dynamic, processual character of scaling and rescaling processes, the conventional discourse of scale appears strikingly inadequate to the analytical tasks at hand. We are confronted not with a simple hierarchy of fixed, stable, discrete, singular, and nested scales, but with a multiplication of politically mediated, socially contested, unevenly tangled, nonisomorphic, and dynamically evolving patterns of scale differentiation and scale redifferentiation, all of which are in turn thoroughly intermeshed with other key dimensions of sociospatial relations.

In their important synthesis of recent debates on scale, Keil and Mahon have proposed the notion of a "political economy of scale" as a shorthand reference to recent scholarly efforts to decipher the relentless scaling and rescaling of political-economic life under modern capitalism.[49] However, the concept of a *scaled political economy* more precisely describes the specific theoretical approach proposed here. This terminology explicitly underscores that the focal points for scalar inquiry are not scales "in themselves," but the geohistorically variegated processes of scaling and rescaling that underpin, mediate, and result from the restless, conflictual flux of sociospatial relations. The methodological challenge, therefore, is not merely to recognize the scale-differentiated and scale-stratified character of sociospatial relations under capitalism, but, more generally, (1) to explore the diverse geohistorical processes through which scaled political-economic configurations (including interscalar rule regimes) are actively produced, contested, destabilized, and transformed and (2) to trace the ways in which such vertically ordered

---

[47] Swyngedouw, "Neither Global nor Local," 141.

[48] Smith, "Homeless/Global: Scaling Places," 101.

[49] See Keil and Mahon, *Leviathan Undone?*

sociospatial configurations shape, and are in turn shaped by, the evolving geographies of power, domination, exploitation, normalization, contestation, and insurgency.

Toward a Scale-Attuned Approach to Urban Theory

The propositions presented previously are intended to offer conceptual and methodological orientation for concrete research forays on the scalar dimensions of urban restructuring, as well as, more generally, for studies of other terrains of sociospatial restructuring in which scaling and rescaling processes may be significant. In particular, the conceptualization proposed here is meant to offer an analytically precise, robust alternative to recent writings that blunt or overextend scalar concepts and an equally strong counterpoint to deconstructive proposals to abolish scalar concepts entirely in favor of a "flat ontology" of networks.

Perhaps most fundamentally for this book's main line of argumentation, the conceptualization of scaling as a vertical ordering of sociospatial relations has the rather far-reaching methodological consequence of exploding any approach to the urban question that conceives its object as a self-enclosed local, metropolitan, or regional "unit" within which restructuring processes occur. In contrast to such entrenched conceptual assumptions and naturalized habits of mind, my analysis here suggests that the urban cannot be conceived effectively as a fixed arena or generic site "in" which restructuring unfolds; it is, rather, itself continuously produced and reconstituted through such processes. To speak of urban restructuring, therefore, is not to reference a process of transformation that is occurring within familiar, stable, ahistorical, or transhistorical units of analysis—cities, city regions, metropolitan regions, or otherwise. Rather, within the framework proposed here, *it is the urban itself* that is being reconstituted in and through the spatiotemporal dynamics of urban restructuring. It is, in other words, the very nature of urban spaces—their very coherence, operationality, and intelligibility as such, and their corresponding relationships to other, equally dynamic scales of political-economic activity—that is transformed through restructuring processes. In this sense, the constitutive properties, elements, and parameters of urban spaces are never pregiven but are continually made and remade through the broader, multiscalar sociospatial transformations that animate and continually disrupt the dynamics of capitalist industrial development.

Clearly, further theoretical explorations and concrete investigations are required in order to grapple with any number of key analytical tasks that flow from this approach. Most urgent among these are (1) theorizing the mechanisms through which urbanization processes under capitalism are scale differentiated and scale stratified; (2) exploring the geohistorical conditions under which apparently stabilized interscalar configurations of the capitalist urban fabric have been shaken up, rejigged, and transformed; (3) analyzing the patterns and pathways through which, across various contexts, inherited configurations of urban life have been rescaled; (4) deciphering the diverse political strategies, social forces, and territorial alliances that mobilize around, or against, strategies to rescale urbanization processes and their politico-regulatory geographies; and (5) examining the interplay between processes of scaling/rescaling and other dimensions of sociospatial relations—including place-making, territorialization, and networking—during the geohistories of capitalist urbanization, and especially in the current conjuncture of intensified interscalar volatility, scale relativization, and scalar experimentation. These are among my core concerns in the chapters that follow.

The explosion of reflexive debates on geographical scale and rescaling since the 1990s has entailed an important extension and fine-tuning of the spatialized approaches to urban and regional political economy that had been consolidated during the preceding decade, and which had been provoked in no small measure by the post-1970s shaking up of the interscalar configurations associated with Fordist-Keynesian, national-developmentalist capitalism and Cold War, postcolonial geopolitics. Subsequently, and not only within urban studies, discussions of the scale question generated a more precise conceptual lexicon for investigating the ongoing vertical redifferentiation of sociospatial relations during a particularly volatile period of crisis-induced capitalist restructuring. Whereas a sophisticated spatial vocabulary had already been developed in the 1980s for grasping key horizontal dimensions of capitalist historical geographies (including place, region, and territory), the subsequent elaboration of reflexively scale-attuned sociospatial theories, concepts, and methods has enabled urban researchers more effectively to denaturalize, historicize, and critically interrogate the scaling and rescaling processes that have figured centrally in the spatiotemporal dynamics of capitalist urbanization. Consequently, debates on the scale question have inspired many urbanists, as well as other critical geopolitical economists, to explore the intense contestations of interscalar relations that animate the contemporary remaking of the capitalist urban fabric.

As I argue in subsequent chapters, recent contributions to the analysis of scale production and scale transformation have particularly massive implications for the field of urban studies, whose site, object, and unit of analysis remain deeply ambiguous even after nearly a century of sustained, often contentious debate. In particular, as the preceding discussion underscores, scalar approaches to the urban question seriously problematize the naturalized assumption that "cities"—however those sociospatial entities might be defined—are the most appropriate units of analysis and scalar focal points for urban research. The argument suggested here, and which I elaborate in detail later, is *not* that processes of sociospatial agglomeration do not exist or that such processes do not engender distinctive, highly consequential zones of concentration and intensification, whether of population, economic activity, social interaction, infrastructure, institutional organization, connectivity, or otherwise. The claim, rather, is that such clustering processes and their variegated consequences cannot be deciphered coherently though an exclusive analytical focus on cities as self-propelled, self-enclosed, territorially bounded, and putatively distinctive units of settlement space. Instead, a reflexively scalar approach to the urban question requires us to conceive city building, and the dynamics of sociospatial agglomeration more generally, in relationally multiscalar terms, and on this basis, to embed them analytically within interscalar configurations that involve vast regional, national, supranational, and ultimately planetary geographies of urban transformation. In this way, cities and metropolitan regions, as well as still-larger zones of agglomeration, can be reconceptualized as recurrent yet highly variegated sociospatial patterns that have been woven and rewoven into the capitalist urban fabric during its geohistorical evolution. Such an approach explodes the long taken-for-granted definitional equation of the city and the urban while also opening up new analytical horizons for a rigorously relational, multiscalar theorization and analysis of capitalist urbanization, both historically and in the current period of accelerated planetary urban restructuring.[50] Such horizons of reconceptualization involve, among other tasks, (1) exploring the interplay between the (multiscalar) dynamics of agglomeration and broader, but similarly multiscalar, geographies of territorial and ecological transformation that support and result from the latter and (2) deciphering the role of state spatial strategies and spatial politics, across places, territories, and scales, in producing, shaping, and reshaping the capitalist urban fabric as a whole.

---

[50] It was, of course, Henri Lefebvre who offered the classic critique of the entrenched equation of the city and the urban—and, more generally, of the conceptualization of urbanization as city growth. See, above, all, *The Urban Revolution*, trans. Robert Bononno (Minneapolis: University of Minnesota Press, 2003 [1970]). Lefebvre's position and its contemporary analytical implications are revisited in more detail in Chapters 9 and 10.

As generative as a scalar perspective may be for urban theory and re-search, the propositions elaborated previously also entail a strongly cautionary warning against the prevalent tendency to overextend scalar concepts, whether in urban studies or any other branch of sociospatial theory. This is because scalar structurations of social space, with their modalities of vertical ordering and redifferentiation, are analytically distinct from other dimensions of sociospatial relations, such as place-making, localization, territorialization, and networking; each of latter also figures centrally in processes of urbanization, whose geographies are at once uneven, variegated, and polymorphic. The lexicon of geographical scale is most powerful, therefore, when its analytical limits are explicitly recognized in the course of sociospatial analysis.[51] Paradoxically, then, a narrower conceptualization of scale facilitates a broader but more precise application of this concept to the challenges of investigating emergent patterns and pathways of sociospatial restructuring, including those associated with emergent forms of urbanization. In other words, while a rigorously multiscalar approach to urban studies can indeed open up new analytical horizons for the investigation of urbanization processes, such an approach will be most productive when scalar epistemologies are reflexively intertwined with sociospatial concepts that illuminate other key dimensions of urban life, transformation, and struggle.

Capitalism has, of course, long been scale differentiated, but the post-1970s period of crisis-induced global restructuring has been marked by particularly far-reaching and tumultuous interscalar transformations. In particular, the geoeconomic project of neoliberalization, with its relentless promotion of capital mobility, unfettered market relations, and intensified commodification, has entailed a major redefinition of established scales of sociopolitical regulation and an aggressive attempt to forge new interscalar hierarchies in which the (il)logics of beggar-thy-neighbor interspatial competition, deregulation, privatization, enclosure, financialization, and fiscal austerity have been comprehensively institutionalized. These trends have assumed variegated forms across contexts and territories, but they have entailed particularly profound ramifications for urban regions and their associated governance frameworks, which have become key arenas and targets for a wide range of neoliberalization strategies.[52]

---

[51] Neil Brenner, "The Limits to Scale? Methodological Reflections on Scalar Structuration," *Progress in Human Geography* 15, no. 4 (2001): 525–48.

[52] See Neil Brenner and Nik Theodore, eds., *Spaces of Neoliberalism: Urban Restructuring in North America and Western Europe* (Oxford: Blackwell, 2002); as well as Brenner, Peck, and Theodore, "Variegated Neoliberalization."

At the same time, both within and beyond metropolitan regions, and across diverse inter-metropolitan networks, oppositional movements that strive to block or to roll back the onslaught of neoliberalization have likewise been mobilizing geographical scale in strategic, remarkably creative ways—whether by jumping scales to circumvent the hegemony of dominant institutional practices, by mobilizing support for reregulatory projects that aim to (re)socialize capital at particular scales, or by envisioning alternative interscalar rule regimes based upon principles of radical democracy, protection of the commons, or sociospatial justice.[53] It is precisely in this sense that the increasing prominence of scalar concepts in contemporary urban studies represents a "real abstraction" of an intensifying, proliferating politics of scale. As the configuration of interscalar relations has become such an important stake of contemporary sociopolitical strategy and contestation, urbanists and other spatially reflexive scholars have likewise come to view the scale question as an essential dimension of sociospatial relations.

[53] Margit Mayer, "Contesting the Neoliberalization of Urban Governance," in *Contesting Neoliberalism: Urban Frontiers*, ed. Helga Leitner, Jamie Peck, and Eric Sheppard (New York: Guilford, 2007), 90–115; Edward W. Soja, *Seeking Spatial Justice* (Minneapolis: University of Minnesota Press, 2010).

4

Global City Formation and
the Rescaling of Urbanization

SINCE THE 1980s, urban researchers have identified various "global cities" as key spatial nodes of the world economy, the localized basing points for capital accumulation in an age of intensified geoeconomic integration. Since the initial formulation of the "world city hypothesis" by John Friedmann in the early 1980s, global city theory has been consolidated as a major framework for critical research on contemporary urbanization and, more generally, on the changing spatial organization of capitalism.[1] By linking urban

---

[1] John Friedmann and Goetz Wolff, "World City Formation: An Agenda for Research and Action," *International Journal of Urban and Regional Research* 6 (1982): 310–11; John Friedmann, "The World City Hypothesis," *Development and Change* 17 (1986): 69–83; and John Friedmann, "Where We Stand: A Decade of World City Research," in *World Cities in a World-System*, ed. Paul L. Knox and Peter J. Taylor (New York: Cambridge University Press, 1995), 21–26. For overviews of this literature, see Neil Brenner and Roger Keil, eds., *The Global Cities Reader* (New York: Routledge, 2006); and Paul Knox and Peter Taylor, eds., *World Cities in a World-System* (New York: Cambridge University Press, 1995). Throughout this chapter, the terms "global city" and "globalizing city" are used interchangeably. The latter term is arguably more precise insofar as it underscores that the cities in question are not a static "type" but are undergoing specific processes of transformation that require further specification with reference to the dynamics of "globalization." However, insofar as the term "global city" (as well as that of the "world city") is widely used in the literature under discussion here, it is often necessary to rely on this terminology. For further discussion, see Peter Marcuse and Ronald van Kempen, eds., *Globalizing Cities: A New Spatial Order* (Cambridge, MA: Blackwell, 2000); and Neil Brenner and Roger Keil, "From Global Cities to Globalized Urbanization," in Neil Brenner, *Critique of Urbanization* (Basel: Bauwelt Fundamente/Birkhäuser Verlag, 2016), 69–84.

studies directly to international political economy and world system analysis, global city theory has also challenged international political economists to explore the variegated subnational geographies of capitalism that are produced through urbanization processes. More generally, by integrating the divergent scalar foci of these research fields within a reflexively spatialized, dynamically multiscalar analytical framework, global city theory has also contributed to the project of transcending inherited state-centric, methodologically nationalist epistemologies that has been gaining momentum in recent years across the social sciences.[2]

The sustained attention among global cities researchers to what Alain Lipietz has aptly termed the "impassable dialectic of local and global" has generated an extraordinary outpouring of urban research.[3] In analytical terms, one of the major contributions of global cities research has been to relate the dominant socioeconomic trends within major urban regions—for instance, the expansion and spatial concentration of advanced producer services firms, cycles of deindustrialization and reindustrialization, speculative patterns of real estate investment, increasing labor market segmentation, accelerated local and metropolitan governance reform, intensifying sociospatial polarization, and new patterns of class and ethnic conflict—to a new scalar formation of the world urban hierarchy, and to the post-Fordist accumulation strategies that have underpinned its consolidation.[4]

Yet this analytical privileging of the global/local dualism in global cities research has also entailed several major theoretical blind spots—in particular, the tendency to bracket the continued significance of nationally scaled, if dynamically mutating, geographies of accumulation, regulation, and contestation in mediating both global urbanization patterns and local pathways

---

[2] John Agnew, "The Territorial Trap: The Geographical Assumptions of International Relations Theory," *Review of International Political Economy* 1, no. 1 (1994): 53–80; Peter J. Taylor, "Embedded Statism and the Social Sciences: Opening Up to New Spaces," *Environment and Planning A* 28 (1996): 1917–28; Immanuel Wallerstein, ed., *Open the Social Sciences: Report of the Gulbenkian Commission on the Restructuring of the Social Sciences* (Stanford, CA: Stanford University Press, 1996).

[3] Alain Lipietz, "The Local and the Global: Regional Individuality or Interregionalism?," *Transactions of the Institute of British Geographers* 18, no. 1 (1993): 16. On the global/local dialectic in contemporary processes of sociospatial restructuring see also Mick Dunford and Grigoris Kafkalas, "The Global–Local Interplay, Corporate Geographies and Spatial Development Strategies in Europe," in *Cities and Regions in the New Europe*, ed. Mick Dunford and Grigoris Kafkalas (London: Belhaven Press, 1992), 3–38.

[4] For an overview of these connections, see Joe Feagin and Michael Peter Smith, "Cities and the New International Division of Labor: An Overview," in *The Capitalist City*, ed. Michael Peter Smith and Joe Feagin (Cambridge, MA: Blackwell, 1989), 3–34.

of urban development. Indeed, despite their concern to bring into focus the broader scalar geographies that shape the production of urban space, the bulk of global cities research has embraced what might be termed a "zero sum" conceptualization of geographical scale: the growing significance of one geographical scale is said to entail, by definition, the marginalization, fragmentation, or erosion of others. Among its problematic implications, this zero-sum understanding of scale has bolstered a pervasive embrace of "state decline" arguments—the dubious assumption that national state power is eroding under conditions of accelerated "globalization." The national scale is thus said to contract as the global scale putatively expands in operational significance. Consequently, despite its otherwise essential insights into the new scalar geographies of urbanization that have been produced during the post-1970s wave of geoeconomic restructuring, global cities research has generated a truncated analysis of rescaling processes. It brackets the national institutional mediations that co-constitute the contemporary global-local interplay, as well as the essential role of state spatial strategies, at all scales, in animating, managing, and canalizing emergent forms of globalized urbanization. Such approaches have also generally failed to consider the ongoing spatial and scalar reconstitution of national state power that has mediated and, in many cases, directly activated contemporary patterns of urban restructuring. The process of global city formation, then, has not only been shaped by state institutions, at multiple spatial scales, but has also given further impetus—at once in institutional, regulatory, and political terms—to the ongoing remaking of urban, regional, and territorial governance under the broadly post-Keynesian conditions of late twentieth- and early twenty-first-century capitalism.

This chapter seeks to transcend these deficiencies within global cities research by examining the changing historical relationship between urbanization patterns and state spatial strategies, with particular reference to the dynamics of rescaling in the European Union in the 1990s and early 2000s. My methodological starting point is the conceptualization of interscalar relations, scalar fixes, state spatial strategies, and the capitalist urban fabric developed in the preceding chapters. From this point of view, the process of global city formation has not only entailed a rescaling of the capitalist urban fabric but has also been intimately intertwined with a significant spatial and scalar reconfiguration of inherited formations of national state power and territorial regulation. The rescaling of the urban fabric and the rescaling of state space are thus analyzed here as mutually intertwined processes of sociospatial restructuring; neither can be understood adequately except in relation to the other. This mode of analysis also leads to a reconceptualization of the scalar geographies of global city formation itself, not simply as a transformation that specific types of cities (whether "post-Fordist," "post-Keynesian," "global," or otherwise) might undergo, but as a broader, if constitutively uneven, scalar reorganization of the capitalist urban fabric as a whole. This rearticulation of the urban fabric may be understood at once as a medium, expression, and outcome of a new politics of scale in which the scalar organization of sociospatial relations is being actively destabilized, contested, rewoven, and transformed. This chapter thus further elaborates one of my core arguments in this book: the scalar configuration of urban life has today become a highly consequential terrain and stake of sociopolitical struggle.

Debates on global city formation are one among several major streams of contemporary urban research whose critical evaluation, via the approach to scale presented in this book's opening chapters, may help (1) problematize unreflexively city-centric understandings of newly emergent urban spaces and (2) illuminate the interplay between state rescaling and the rescaling of urbanization while also (3) offering an interpretive basis on which to decipher emergent formations of scalar politics, their contradictions, and their mutations. Accordingly, several closely related debates among urban researchers will be explored with similar analytical intentions in subsequent chapters—on cities and the new economy (Chapter 5), on the new regionalism (Chapter 6), and on urban growth machines (Chapter 7).

New Scalings of the Urban: Global City Theory and the World City Archipelago

Global city theory has been deployed extensively in studies of the role of major cities such as New York, London, and Tokyo as international financial centers and headquarters locations for transnational corporations (TNCs).[5] While the theory has proven hugely influential in place-based investigations in these and many other North American, western European, and East Asian cities, its central agenda is best conceived more broadly, as an attempt to analyze the rescaled geographies of capitalist urbanization that have crystallized

---

[5] See, for instance, Saskia Sassen, *The Global City: New York, London, Tokyo* (Princeton, NJ: Princeton University Press, 1991); John Mollenkopf and Manuel Castells, eds., *Dual City: Restructuring New York* (New York: Russell Sage Foundation, 1991); Anthony D. King, *Global Cities: Post-Imperialism and the Internationalization of London* (New York: Routledge, 1990); Takashi Machimura, "The Urban Restructuring Process in Tokyo in the 1980s: Transforming Tokyo into a World City," *International Journal of Urban and Regional Research* 16, no. 1 (1992): 114–28.

following the geoeconomic crises of the 1970s. From this point of view, the core intellectual project of global cities research is not merely to classify cities within world-scale central place hierarchies or to explore the formative dynamics of a particular cohort of global financial centers. Rather, as John Friedmann programmatically proposed in the mid-1980s, global city theory aspires to decipher the changing "spatial organization of the new international division of labor."[6] According to global cities researchers, the key feature of this emergent configuration of world capitalism is that cities—or, more precisely, metropolitan regions—rather than the territorial economies of national states have become its most elementary geographical units and propulsive engines. These urban regions are said to be arranged hierarchically on a global scale according to their differential modes of integration into the capitalist world economy.[7]

In his classic historical study of civilization and capitalism, *The Perspective of the World*, French *Annales* school historian Fernand Braudel famously suggested that the "world-economy always has an urban center of gravity, a city, as the logistic heart of its activity."[8] Accordingly, Braudel's *longue durée* investigation of capitalist development in early modern Europe tracked the epochal shift from the "city-centered economies" of Genoa, Venice, Antwerp, and Amsterdam to the English "territorial economy," based upon an integrated national market clustered around London, from the fifteenth to the eighteenth centuries.[9] During the subsequent two centuries of capitalist development, cities were integrated more tightly into national economic territories and were more comprehensively subordinated to the political power of national states.[10] Although cities continued to operate as central nodes of world trade and imperialist expansion throughout the nineteenth and twentieth centuries, the network geography of interurban flows was increasingly

---

[6] Friedmann, "World City Hypothesis," 69.

[7] See Friedmann and Wolff, "World City Formation"; Feagin and Smith, "Cities and the New International Division."

[8] Fernand Braudel, *The Perspective of the World*, trans. Siân Reynolds (Berkeley: University of California Press, 1984), 27.

[9] Braudel (*Perspective of the World*, 294) attributes this seminal distinction between city-centered economies (*Stadtwirtschaft*) and "territorial economies" (*Territorialwirtschaft*) to Karl Bücher's 1911 work, *Die Entstehung der Volkswirtschaft*. By coupling these terms to his own notion of the world economy (also derived from another German term, *Weltwirtschaft*), Braudel attempted to map the *longue durée* historical geography of capitalism in terms of various forms of interpenetration among cities, state territories, and worldwide divisions of labor.

[10] Charles Tilly, *Coercion, Capital and European States, AD 990–1990* (Oxford: Blackwell, 1990).

subsumed within the territorial geography of states.[11] Early uses of the term "world city" by urban planners such as Patrick Geddes (in 1915) and Peter Hall (in 1966) precisely reflected this tendential territorialization of the urbanization process on a national scale.[12] In their canonical texts, each of these authors interpreted the cosmopolitan character of major metropolitan regions as an expression of their host states' geocultural or geopolitical power.

By contrast, the central hypothesis of contemporary global cities research is that, since the geoeconomic crises of the 1970s, another epochal transformation in the spatial organization of capitalism has been unfolding that has enabled cities to reassert their strategic centrality in the world system. In John Friedmann's crisp formulation from the mid-1990s, global cities are the "organizing nodes" of world capitalism; "articulations" of regional, national, and global commodity flows; and "basing points" in the "space of global capital accumulation."[13] Therefore, Friedmann maintains, the consolidation of a worldwide urban hierarchy since the early 1970s must be understood as a fundamental scalar realignment in the geography of global capitalism, "an historically unprecedented phenomenon" in which cities and interurban networks are increasingly superseding national territorial economies as the geographical bedrock of capitalist development.[14]

In this framework of analysis, then, major cities and metropolitan regions are no longer conceived as the subnational building blocks of relatively self-enclosed, autocentric national space economies. Rather, they are understood as "neo-Marshallian nodes within global networks," as "regional motors of the global economy," and as flexibly specialized locational clusters within a "global mosaic of regions."[15] In effect, alongside its many other influential and controversial lines of argumentation, global city theory posits a major rescaling of contemporary urbanization: it asserts that historically

---

[11] Peter J. Taylor, "World Cities and Territorial States: The Rise and Fall of Their Mutuality," in Knox and Taylor, *World Cities in a World-System*, 48–62; Anthony D. King, *Urbanism, Colonialism and the World Economy* (New York: Routledge, 1991).

[12] Patrick Geddes, "A World League of Cities," *Sociological Review* 26 (1924): 166–67; Peter Hall, *The World Cities* (New York: McGraw-Hill, 1966).

[13] Friedmann, "Where We Stand," 21–26.

[14] Ibid., 26.

[15] See, for example, Ash Amin and Nigel Thrift, "Neo-Marshallian Nodes in Global Networks," *International Journal of Urban and Regional Research* 16, no. 4 (1992): 571–87; Allen J. Scott, "Regional Motors of the World Economy," *Futures* 28, no. 5 (1996): 391–411; and Allen J. Scott, *Regions and the World Economy* (New York: Oxford University Press, 1998). See, more generally, Edward W. Soja, "The Postfordist Industrial Metropolis," in *Postmetropolis: Critical Studies of Cities and Regions* (Oxford: Blackwell, 2000), 156–87.

inherited national urban hierarchies, national urban systems, and national models of territorial development are today being superseded by a dramatically rescaled formation of globalized urbanization in which, it is claimed, variegated local-global linkages bypass or crosscut, and thus progressively decompose, national economic territories. Consequently, in Peter J. Taylor's memorable phrasing, the capitalist world economy is now undergirded by a "world city archipelago," a globe-spanning network of interconnected urban nodal points that provides essential service inputs and customized, high-technology infrastructural capacities in support of transnational corporate accumulation strategies.[16]

Global city theorists have analyzed the consolidation of this world city archipelago (WCA)—and more generally, the rescaling of inherited territories of urbanization—with reference to two intertwined geoeconomic transformations of the post-1970s period: (1) the emergence of a new international division of labor dominated by transnational corporations and (2) the crisis of the postwar North Atlantic Fordist regime of accumulation.

First, global city theorists have interpreted the consolidation of a world city archipelago as a key urban consequence of the new international division of labor (NIDL), a formation of the world economy that had crystallized as of the late 1960s, in conjunction with a massive expansion and geographical reorganization in the operations of TNCs.[17] Whereas the "old" international division of labor was based upon agriculture and raw materials extraction in the colonial periphery and industrial manufacturing in the imperial core, the NIDL entailed the relocation of significant manufacturing industries to semi-peripheral and peripheral states in search of cheaper, less militant sources of labor-power, along with a significant intensification of import substitution industrialization (ISI) strategies in major Third World/postcolonial states.

---

[16] Peter J. Taylor, *World City Network: A Global Urban Analysis* (New York: Routledge, 2004). My concern with the WCA, and not only global cities themselves, as an intellectual construct and *problematique* of global cities research is strongly influenced by the recent work of David Bassens and Michiel van Meeteren. See their fundamental articles, "World Cities under Conditions of Financialized Globalization: Towards an Augmented World City Hypothesis," *Progress in Human Geography* 39, no. 6 (2015): 752–75; and "World Cities and the Uneven Geographies of Financialization: Unveiling Stratification and Hierarchy in the World City Archipelago," *International Journal of Urban and Regional Research* 40, no. 1 (2016): 62–81.

[17] The key text on the NIDL is Folker Fröbel, Jürgen Heinrichs, and Otto Kreye, *The New International Division of Labor: Structural Unemployment in Industrialized Countries and Industrialization in Developing Countries*, trans. Pete Burgess (New York: Cambridge University Press, 1980). For a more recent critical evaluation and reinvention of this concept with reference to early twenty-first century capitalism, see Greig Charnock and Guido Starosta, eds., *The New International Division of Labor: Global Transformation and Uneven Development* (New York: Palgrave Macmillan, 2016).

One of the key insights of first-generation global city theorists was to recognize some of the specifically urban consequences of the NIDL's worldwide consolidation. In addition to the deindustrialization of many First World industrial regions and the concomitant proliferation of new industrial spaces across the Third World, they argued, the NIDL was also associated with a significant spatial concentration of headquarters locations, advanced producer service (APS) firms, and other administrative-coordination functions within a world-encompassing network of major metropolitan regions: the world city archipelago. For global city theorists, the urban nodes of the WCA served as command centers for decision making, financial planning, logistical coordination, and infrastructural control within the globally dispersed commodity chains overseen by TNCs.[18] In subsequent generations of global cities research, especially in the wake of Saskia Sassen's foundational contributions, scholarly attention shifted from TNC headquarters locations themselves to the role of APS firms (in banking, law, consulting, insurance, accounting, advertising, design, and so forth) in producing a "global control capacity" within the WCA's major urban nodes.[19] Just as important to this line of research was the investigation of new information and communications technologies, whose place-specific modes of deployment and highly customized spatial configurations within global cities were viewed as essential preconditions for producing the global control capacity upon which the entire NIDL was grounded.[20]

Second, global city theorists have also connected the formation of a WCA to the obsolescence of the postwar Atlantic Fordist regime of accumulation, which had been grounded upon mass production systems led by vertically integrated firms, state-subsidized formations of mass consumption, nationally configured Keynesian demand management arrangements, nationalized

---

[18] Although economist Stephen Hymer had already recognized this connection in his pioneering studies of TNCs during the 1960s, R. B. Cohen appears to have been the first urbanist to explore it systematically. See Cohen's classic chapter, "The New International Division of Labor, Multinational Corporations, and Urban Hierarchy," in *Urbanization and Urban Planning in Capitalist Society*, ed. Michael Dear and Allen J. Scott (London: Methuen, 1981), 287–315. See also Feagin and Smith, "Cities and the New International Division of Labor."

[19] Sassen, *Global City*.

[20] See, most famously, Manuel Castells, *The Informational City* (Cambridge, MA: Blackwell, 1989); and Stephen Graham and Simon Marvin, *Splintering Urbanism* (New York: Routledge, 2001). For critical reflections on the nature of "command and control" within the WCA, see John Allen, "Powerful City Networks: More Than Connections, Less Than Domination and Control," *Urban Studies* 47 (2010): 2895–911; as well as Bassens and van Meeteren, "World Cities." Chapter 5 considers more systematically the role of new information and communications technologies in contemporary rescaling processes.

frameworks of collective bargaining, and nationally redistributive social welfare, regional, and infrastructural policies.[21] The post-1970s crisis of the Fordist accumulation regime across Euro-America was paralleled by what Michael Storper has termed a "resurgence of regional economies" in zones that were generally located outside the manufacturing heartlands of the previous cycle of industrial development, and where decentralized, vertically disintegrated, and putatively "flexible" forms of industrial organization and interfirm coordination could, it was argued, more readily flourish.[22] These new industrial spaces were said to include, paradigmatically, "sunrise" growth regions such as Silicon Valley, Los Angeles-Orange County, Baden-Württemberg, and the Third Italy, but also the newly consolidated industrial districts associated with the major urban nodes of the WCA. Scholars of post-Fordist industrial geography interpreted these newly ascendant or resurgent global cities not simply as strategic command and control centers for TNCs, but as important sites of industrial dynamism, technological innovation, and new forms of interfirm cooperation, induced in significant measure through the propulsive effects of urban agglomeration. In the influential narrative of Allen J. Scott and Michael Storper from the late 1980s, the major sectors associated with such putatively ascendant flexible production systems (and associated agglomeration economies) were specialized in revitalized craft production, high-technology industries, and advanced producer and financial services.[23] It was, of course, the latter—the APS complex explored at length by Sassen and other scholars of international financial centers—that was thought to underpin the crystallization of the WCA and the core economic operations of its constituent urban nodes. Consequently, as David Bassens and Michiel van Meeteren have more recently observed:

[21] On the concept of Fordism and its breakdown in the 1970s, see Michel Aglietta, *A Theory of Capitalist Regulation* (New York: Verso, 1979); Alain Lipietz, *Mirages and Miracles* (London: Verso, 1987); Elmar Altvater, "Fordist and Post-Fordist International Division of Labor and Monetary Regimes," in *Pathways to Industrialization and Regional Development*, ed. Michael Storper and Allen J. Scott (New York: Routledge, 1992), 21–45; Bob Jessop, "Fordism and Post-Fordism: A Critical Reformulation," in Storper and Scott, *Pathways to Industrialization and Regional Development*, 46–69; and Erik Swyngedouw, "Neither Global nor Local: 'Glocalization' and the Politics of Scale," in *Spaces of Globalization*, ed. Kevin Cox (New York: Guilford Press, 1997), 137–66.

[22] See Michael Storper, "The Resurgence of Regional Economies, Ten Years Later: The Region as a Nexus of Untraded Interdependencies," *European Urban and Regional Studies* 2, no. 3 (1995): 191–221; and Michael Storper, *The Regional World: Territorial Development in a Global Economy* (New York: Guilford, 1997).

[23] Michael Storper and Allen Scott, "The Geographical Foundations and Social Regulation of Flexible Production Complexes," in *The Power of Geography*, ed. Jennifer Wolch and Michael Dear (Boston: Unwin Hyman, 1989), 24–27.

World cities seemed to fit into the new post-Fordist growth theory . . . as sites hosting command and control functions that served as alleviators of transaction costs barring the realization of comparative advantages in the new regional world. Services were interpreted to lubricate the process of flexible specialization in a globalizing economy. . . . APS could be regarded as just another regional specialization as control functions were gradually being externalized to independent APS TNCs that themselves were subject to agglomeration economies in world cities.[24]

In reaction to such rather sweeping generalizations, which were widely embraced in the 1980s and 1990s among many scholars of post-Fordism, subsequent analyses advised a more cautious analytical perspective that acknowledged the dynamism of flexible production systems, within the WCA, new industrial districts, and elsewhere, while situating them within a worldwide context characterized by continued geoeconomic and geopolitical volatility, pervasive and intensifying uneven geographical development, a continued expansion of transnational production networks, and concomitant pursuit of scale economies by large corporate conglomerates, accelerated financialization and associated crisis tendencies, neoliberal ideological hegemony, and, in many major global regions, the persistence of broadly neo-Fordist modes of industrial organization.[25] Nonetheless, the regulationalist conceptualization of flexible production systems developed by Storper, Scott, and other proponents of the new industrial geography resonated closely with, and directly influenced, the scalar analytic that was then being elaborated within global city theory. Beyond the contentious debate on the specific nature of "flexibility" as a feature of "after-Fordist" industrial organization, the core insight that emerged from such studies was that TNC strategies to enhance command and control on a world scale hinge upon the construction

---

[24] Bassens and van Meeteren, "World Cities," 757.

[25] See, for instance, Andrew Sayer, "Postfordism in Question," *International Journal of Urban and Regional Research* 13, no. 3 (1989): 666–95; Amin and Thrift, "Neo-Marshallian Nodes"; Flavia Martinelli and Erica Schoenberger, "Oligopoly Is Alive and Well: Notes for a Broader Discussion of Flexible Accumulation," in *Industrial Change and Regional Development*, ed. Georges Benko and Mick Dunford (New York: Belhaven Press, 1991), 117–33; Jamie Peck and Adam Tickell, "Searching for a New Institutional Fix: The *After*-Fordist Crisis and the Global–Local Disorder," in *Post-Fordism: A Reader*, ed. Ash Amin (Cambridge, MA: Blackwell, 1994), 280–315; Jamie Peck and Adam Tickell, "The Social Regulation of Uneven Development: 'Regulatory Deficit,' England's South East, and the Collapse of Thatcherism," *Environment and Planning A* 27 (1995): 15–40. For an insightful retrospective assessment of this phase of global cities research, framed against the background of subsequent political-economic transformations associated with the financialization of the world economy, see Bassens and van Meeteren, "World Cities."

of place- and region-specific sociospatial arrangements, not least within globalizing city-regions. As Storper programmatically explained:

> There is a dialectical dynamic of globalization and territorialization at work in the construction of city economies today, with many apparently paradoxical dimensions. The organization of reflexivity by local, regional, national and global firms pushes all of them towards cities. Globalization is both the top-down force of organizing markets and production systems according to supranational competitive criteria and resource flows, and the bottom-up pull of territorialization of both market penetration (a process requiring global firms to insert themselves in conventional-relational contexts of their markets, not a simple technocratic operation) and the effort to tap into geographically differentiated producer's capacities. . . . City economies are pulled simultaneously in both these directions by these forces and it is the interrelationship between the two that has to be appreciated in the study of a particular city's economy.[26]

This is, in effect, an elaboration of Harvey's understanding of the problem of territorial organization under capitalism, as explored in detail in Chapter 2. Space-time compression and deterritorialization tendencies under post-Fordist capitalism hinge upon the construction of new forms of territorial organization—including production complexes, technological-institutional systems, infrastructural configurations, and other place-based externalities—especially at the urban scale. Storper's narrative, much like that of Sassen in her major writings of the same period, interprets global cities and other new industrial districts as distinctively post-Fordist forms of urban territorial organization that support—whether through "untraded interdependencies" (Storper), the production of global control "capacity" (Sassen), or otherwise—the more aggressively globalizing accumulation strategies that were being pursued by TNCs following the collapse of the Atlantic Fordist growth regime.

Most crucially for the present discussion, this mode of analysis articulates an explicit conception of rescaling. The post-1980s global upscaling of capitalist control capacities and commodity chains (the rise of the NIDL and, more generally, of global capitalism) is said to be inextricably intertwined with an equally robust downscaling or localization of socioeconomic assets and strategic infrastructural arrangements (the WCA, the formation

---

[26] Storper, *Regional World*, 248–49.

of global cities, and the proliferation of new industrial districts).[27] Insofar as the strategic command and control operations of global cities hinge not only upon the spatial clustering of TNC headquarters functions, but upon decentralized, intensively localized APS complexes, the studies of agglomeration economies developed in post-Fordist growth theory powerfully reinforced and extended the account of rescaling processes that was then being elaborated among global city theorists.

For purposes of this investigation, then, one of the key contributions of global cities research in the 1980s and 1990s was to illuminate the new global-local scalings of urbanization processes that were emerging following the geoeconomic crises of the 1970s, and which were embodied, specifically, in the WCA and its constituent urban nodes. Indeed, as analyzed by global cities researchers in this period, the WCA was said to embody, simultaneously, the globally oriented accumulation strategies of TNCs within the NIDL and the indelible requirement for locally or regionally scaled forms of territorial organization within strategic urban locations to support capital's new strategies of accumulation.

Of course, as first-generation global cities researchers regularly emphasized, this rescaling of the capitalist urban fabric was being articulated in diverse institutional-political crystallizations in each zone of the world economy; its uneven, variegated forms of expression could not be captured adequately through the generic image of the WCA, by singular models of "the" global city, or by universalizing models of global urbanization.[28] Additionally, as Friedmann in particular has repeatedly insisted, the WCA is but one layer within capitalism's intensely differentiated, rapidly mutating, and always contested geographical configuration, which has equally been associated with new geographies of uneven development across places, territories, scales, and ecologies, stretching from the economic "deadlands" of the older industrial core states into a mosaic of differentially peripheralized cities, regions, and hinterland zones stretching across the world economy as a whole.[29] In its most theoretically precise and methodologically reflexive forms, therefore, global city theory aspires to grasp only

---

[27] For a general overview of the scalar metanarratives embedded within the contributions of the new industrial geography in the 1980s, see Erik Swyngedouw, "The Heart of the Place: The Resurrection of Locality in an Age of Hyperspace," *Geografiska Annaler B* 71, no. 1 (1989): 31–42.

[28] On the genealogies, dangers, and limits of such overgeneralizations, see Jennifer Robinson, *Ordinary Cities* (London: Routledge, 2006).

[29] See, for example, Friedmann, "Where We Stand," 41–43. See also Neil Smith, "The Satanic Geographies of Globalization: Uneven Development in the 1990s," *Public Culture* 10, no. 1 (1997): 169–92.

one vector of emergent rescaling processes, albeit a strategically consequential one, within a deeply uneven, variegated, polarized, hierarchized, and volatile global landscape of urban transformation.

Global Cities and National Space: Critique and Reformulation

How are the global-local dynamics explored by global cities researchers articulated to inherited national economic spaces? Even if inherited national space economies are being destabilized and reshaped, the economic geography of post-Fordist capitalism cannot be reduced to the WCA, its urban nodes, interurban networks, and an undifferentiated "outside" of peripheralized zones that putatively lack the strategic centrality and networked connectivity of global cities. Clearly, state territories do not simply disintegrate in the face of accelerated geoeconomic integration; thus, their specific relation to the process of global city formation should be an essential analytical concern for any approach to the changing spatial organization of capitalism as a whole. Indeed, insofar as global city theory is, in Friedmann's programmatic formulation, directly concerned with the "contradictory relations between production in an era of global management and the political determination of territorial interests," an investigation of changing city/state relations—including their shifting scales of organization and their evolving, often contested interscalar articulations—is arguably among its most central tasks.[30]

In practice, however, the challenges of such an investigation have been bypassed or short-circuited rather than being systematically confronted, either in empirical or theoretical terms. Despite the robust conception of rescaling that underpins its theoretical architecture, most concrete research on global cities has been composed largely of monoscalar investigations, generally focusing either on local or on global scales of analysis. Whereas place-based, case-study-oriented studies have privileged the local scale of specific cities (albeit positioned within a broader geoeconomic context), most global-cities-inspired research on urban hierarchies and interurban networks has been framed around the global scale (albeit generally with reference to local implications and outcomes). The evolving role of national political-economic space—whether as a force field of capital accumulation, as an institutional-regulatory arena, or as a site of sociopolitical contestation—has been

---

[30] Friedmann, "World City Hypothesis," 69.

neglected almost entirely among global cities researchers. To the extent that state power and its variegated geographies have been explored in global cities research, these issues have usually been understood with reference to local or municipal institutions, or as sclerotic but increasingly obsolete territorial background structures derived from earlier phases of capitalist development. Consequently, much like the other major academic approaches to "globalization" that gained popularity during the "Clinton boom" of the 1990s, the bulk of global cities research produced during that period exemplified the widely pervasive intellectual-cultural trend of "state denial": the assumption that accelerated geoeconomic integration would logically entail an erosion of national state power.[31] Writing at the end of that decade, Linda Weiss summarized that trend as follows:

> There are many forms of state denial currently in evidence. Most converge on the same set of claims and presuppositions: viz. the loss of national autonomy, the powerlessness of governments in the face of transnational capital, the obsolescence of the nation-state as an organizing principle. Underlying all these "endist" and convergence arguments is the conception of a globalizing economy integrated only by transnational capital and the market. As the twentieth century draws to a close, the notion of a "global" economy, dominated by stateless corporations and borderless finance, has captured the imagination of countless commentators. . . . [T]he regnant view projects an era of global convergence, where transnational corporations stride across the world at random, and where national governments—from Tokyo to Timbuktu—are increasingly irrelevant and powerless to influence the economic welfare of their citizens.[32]

Despite its otherwise nuanced account of localization processes within strategic, globally networked urban spaces, this is the generic spatial imaginary of "globalization"—as placeless, borderless, deterritorialized, unregulated, and ultimately beyond political-territorial control—that has underpinned the major approaches to global city formation. And it is this spatial imaginary that has enabled global cities researchers to focus their studies almost exclusively on local-global dynamics while systematically

---

[31] Influential contributions to the globalization debate of the 1990s that advanced such arguments include, among others, Arjun Appadurai, *Modernity at Large: Cultural Dimensions of Globalization* (Minneapolis: University of Minnesota Press, 1996); Manuel Castells, *The Rise of the Network Society* (Cambridge, MA: Blackwell, 1996); Castells, *The Informational City*; Susan Strange, "The Defective State," *Daedalus, Journal of the American Academy of Arts and Sciences* 124, no. 2 (1995): 55–74; and Scott, *Regions and the World Economy*.

[32] Linda Weiss, *The Myth of the Powerless State* (London: Policy, 1998), 2.

neglecting the national mediations of those processes, especially those associated with (reconstituted) national state spatial strategies. This privileging of the global/local dualism among global cities researchers has also been premised upon a "zero sum" conception of spatial scales: the global and the national scales are viewed as being mutually exclusive—what one gains, the other loses—rather than as being intrinsically related, coevolving layers of territorial organization, derived from mutually entangled, co-constitutive processes (for instance, of urbanization, capital accumulation, state regulation, and sociopolitical contestation).

In contrast to the state-denialist spatial imaginary of global capitalism and the closely associated zero-sum understanding of interscalar relations, this chapter develops an alternative analytics of scale through which to decipher the multifaceted, evolving interplay between global city formation and the remaking of state space. Building upon the theoretical framework introduced in the preceding chapters, the capitalist urban fabric—including the major "islands" forming the WCA—is analyzed here as a site, medium, and outcome of scale-articulated state spatial strategies. This conceptualization immediately brings into view the constitutive role of state institutions, at all spatial scales, in producing, shaping, regulating, and recalibrating the local-global rescaling processes on which global city theorists have focused their attention. On the one hand, despite a range of emergent fissures, fractures, and ruptures in inherited state spatial formations, every global city has remained tightly embedded within its host state's (national) territory in ways that require careful decoding, analysis, and theorization. On the other hand, the process of global city formation has been directly facilitated through the production of new spaces and scales of state power, not least through the operations of (reconstituted) national state institutions in managing multiscalar patterns of urbanization, infrastructural investment, and territorial development. State rescaling thus serves as an important politico-institutional strategy through which new urban spaces and new scales of urbanization are being produced. Because the thesis of state decline and a concomitant zero-sum conception of spatial scale have been embraced so pervasively within the global cities literature, the significance of this interscalar interplay between geoeconomic transformation, national state spatial reorganization, and urban restructuring has not been sufficiently explored, whether on a structural-institutional, politico-strategic, or ideological level. Before we explore the challenges associated with that task, the basic rationale underlying this line of argumentation can be further explicated through a critical examination of the two paradigmatic accounts of global city/national state relations that were developed by first-generation global cities researchers—the work of John Friedmann and Goetz Wolff in the 1980s and that of Saskia Sassen in the early 1990s and subsequently.[33]

Written during a period of accelerating economic globalization and heightening Cold War geopolitical tension in the early 1980s, Friedmann and Wolff's classic, agenda-setting article contained a politically impassioned, insightful discussion of emergent lines of sociopolitical conflict, division, and struggle in global cities.[34] In this context, Friedmann and Wolff embraced a relatively strong version of a state decline argument: in their analysis, global city/territorial state relations are expressed as a geoeconomic battle between globally mobile TNCs and static, immobile state territories. Global cities and territorial states are thus described as diametrically opposed political-economic entities: to the extent that the territorial state operates as a structural impediment to the dominance of global capital, it is said to be debilitated, above all on its local levels. According to Friedmann and Wolff, there is an "inherent contradiction between the interests of transnational capital and those of particular nation states that have their own historical trajectory."[35] This situation, they argue, produces new constellations of sociopolitical struggle within and beyond global cities—for instance, between city inhabitants and TNCs; between city inhabitants and national policymakers; between national and global fractions of the bourgeoisie; and, most fundamentally, between capital and labor. These conflicts are severely exacerbated, in their view, by the fragmented administrative organization of global cities, which generally lack any overarching metropolitan authority.

On this basis, Friedmann and Wolff advance their key thesis on urban governance: global city formation, they suggest, engenders a progressively deepening fiscal crisis of the local state.[36] Whereas global capital requires the construction and maintenance of advanced, customized infrastructural facilities such as roads, ports, airports, and canals, as well as the policing and surveillance of the subaltern classes, the influx of new sources of labor-power into the city, particularly of poor migrant workers, generates "massive needs for social reproduction," including housing, health care, education, transportation, and various social welfare services.[37] This, they argue, triggers an increasingly dire situation in which the social and ecological costs of global city

---

[33] Friedmann and Wolff, "World City Formation"; Sassen, *Global City*.

[34] Friedmann and Wolff, "World City Formation."

[35] Ibid., 312.

[36] Ibid., 326–27.

[37] Friedmann, "The World City Hypothesis," 77.

formation far exceed the revenue streams and regulatory capacities of the local state, which subsequently becomes the "major loser" in a maelstrom of globally induced constraints.[38] Drawing upon Manuel Castells's influential notion of the "space of flows," Friedmann later summarized this state of affairs as follows:

> The more the economy becomes interdependent on the global scale, the less can regional and local governments, as they exist today, act upon the basic mechanisms that condition the daily life of their citizens. The traditional structures of social and political control over development, work and distribution have been subverted by the placeless logic of an internationalized economy enacted by means of information flows among powerful actors beyond the sphere of state regulations.[39]

As prescient and powerful as Friedmann and Wolff's classic article was in the context of urban restructuring processes in the 1980s, its account of the interplay between global city formation and state restructuring was seriously truncated, above all due to its embrace of a rather orthodox state-denialist spatial imaginary, which relegated both national and local state power to a domain of regulatory helplessness, indifference, or ineptitude. While it is evident that the geoeconomic crises of the post-1970s period undermined certain traditional policy instruments through which states have attempted to stimulate, manage, and steer the accumulation process, the narrative of capitalist deterritorialization/state decline conflates the ongoing reconfiguration of the national scale of state regulation with a withering away of state power as such.[40] The post–Bretton Woods georegulatory transformations of the 1970s and 1980s did indeed herald the partial erosion of central state regulatory control over certain types of cross-border capital and monetary flows. Despite this, however, national states have remained key institutional matrices of politico-regulatory power, significant agents of economic governance, and an essential infrastructural scaffolding for the ongoing production, management, and reorganization of the capitalist urban fabric. By conceptualizing state restructuring as a unilinear process of national state demise and cascading local state failure, Friedmann and Wolff's analysis effectively bracketed the ways in which, even as of the early 1980s, state spaces

---

[38] Friedmann and Wolff, "World City Formation," 327.

[39] Friedmann, "Where We Stand," 25.

[40] Leo Panitch, "Globalization and the State," in *Socialist Register 1994*, ed. Ralph Miliband and Leo Panitch (London: Merlin Press, 1994), 60–93.

were being qualitatively transformed at all spatial scales in relation to emergent patterns of globalized urbanization under the NIDL. Thus, as James Anderson notes:

> The presentation of a simplistic "choice" [in debates on the future of the state] between just two alternatives—life or death—obscures the possibility that something else is happening: a qualitative reshaping of states and nations, territoriality and sovereignty, which is not captured by notions of death or decline.[41]

For purposes of this discussion, the key issue is not only the wide-ranging interpretive implications of an analytical distinction between state erosion and state restructuring, but the degree to which many of the very urban transformations that Friedmann and Wolff associated with global city formation were directly mediated through newly emergent, post-Keynesian state institutions and spatial strategies. For instance, the new patterns of international capital mobility associated with the NIDL were being actively facilitated through state policies to liberalize capital controls and to lift various legal and fiscal constraints on foreign direct investment (FDI). Meanwhile, both within and beyond global cities, sociospatial divisions were being seriously exacerbated through the politics of welfare state retrenchment—a trend that intensified in subsequent decades. And most crucially for this analysis, the logistical, informational, technological, and institutional infrastructures required to support global city operations were being directly promoted through "competition state" political strategies and/or actively subsidized through national and subnational public investments—albeit often in the form of "public-private partnerships," which tended to mask state involvement and the corporate appropriation of taxpayer funds behind the ideological veneer of "market led" growth. Moreover, insofar as neoliberalizing state institutions throughout the 1980s were aggressively restructuring themselves, at both national and subnational scales, to *promote* renewed capital accumulation within their most strategically positioned urban spaces, Friedmann and Wolff's hypothesis of an "inherent contradiction" between TNCs and state power cannot be empirically sustained. Since that decade, this still-ongoing neoliberalization of statehood has been intensely variegated, at once in political, institutional, and spatial terms, but it has evidently not entailed a unilinear weakening of state capacities or a simple

---

[41] James Anderson, "The Shifting Stage of Politics: New Medieval and Post-Modern Territorialities?," *Environment and Planning D: Society and Space* 14 (1996): 135.

decomposition of the national scale. What has been crystallizing, rather, are qualitatively reshaped formations of state space and state spatial strategy that have been designed to enhance place-specific socioeconomic assets and competitive advantages, and thereby to fix TNC investment within strategic economic zones in each national territory.[42] In this sense, as I argue below, the new urban spaces that have been produced through global city formation are also, in a fundamental sense, new state spaces as well.

Whereas Friedmann and Wolff's account of global city formation is premised upon the notion of state demise, Sassen's analysis of economic globalization in New York, London, and Tokyo in her widely acclaimed book, *The Global City*, is surprisingly state-centric. Sassen likewise identifies changing city/state relations as one of her central concerns: "What happens to the relationship between state and city," she asks, "under conditions of strong articulation between a city and the world economy?"[43] For Sassen, contemporary global city-territorial state relations are captured through the notion of "systemic discontinuity":

> I posit the possibility of a *systemic discontinuity* between what used to be thought of as national growth and the forms of growth evident in global cities in the 1980s. These cities constitute a system rather than merely competing with one another. What contributes to growth in the network of global cities may well not contribute to growth in nations.[44]

Sassen focuses primarily upon two types of interurban linkages—those among global cities themselves and those between global cities and other cities located within their host states' territories. On this basis, Sassen argues that global city formation in New York, London, and Tokyo has been connected to processes of industrial decline elsewhere within the US, British, and Japanese urban systems:

> Prior to the current phase, there was high correspondence between major growth sectors [in global cities] and overall national growth. Today we see an increased asymmetry: The conditions promoting growth in global cities contain as significant components the decline of other areas of the United States,

---

[42] Neil Brenner, *New State Spaces: Urban Governance and the Rescaling of Statehood* (New York: Oxford University Press, 2004); Bob Jessop, *The Future of the Capitalist State* (Oxford: Wiley, 2002); Aihwa Ong, *Flexible Citizenship: The Cultural Logics of Transnationality* (Durham, NC: Duke University Press, 1999).

[43] Sassen, *The Global City*, 14.

[44] Ibid., 8–9.

the United Kingdom, and Japan and the accumulation of government debt and corporate debt.[45]

Sassen elaborates her "systemic discontinuity" thesis through a systematic, statistically grounded analysis of the changing role of each global city within its *national* urban system.[46] Specifically, Sassen presents data to show that global cities now contain overwhelming locational concentrations of producer and financial service industries relative to the national average in their respective host countries, and she traces various locational and employment shifts within the US, British, and Japanese urban hierarchies that have ensued in conjunction with economic restructuring in New York, London, and Tokyo.[47]

However, it is not readily obvious why nationally organized city systems are the most appropriate empirical reference point for such an investigation, especially since, by Sassen's own account, the consolidation of the NIDL has entailed the formation of transnational urban hierarchies. Indeed, as Peter J. Taylor has argued, each of Sassen's global cities can be viewed not only as the apex of a destabilized, if still nationally scaled, urban hierarchy, but as the major urban articulation point and financial control center for one among the three superregional blocs of the contemporary world economy— North America, the European Union, and East Asia.[48] Whether the urban hierarchy of contemporary capitalism is subdivided into these or other scalar configurations is a question that could be effectively pursued only through a rejection of the notion, which served as an article of faith within twentieth-century urban social science, that national states are the fundamental territorial unit and spatial scale on which city systems are organized.[49]

Sassen's notion of "systemic discontinuity" presupposes two processes whose articulation has become asymmetrical during the course of historical time. In her analysis, however, only one of these processes, the formation of global cities, is understood historically; the other, the national state, is treated as a relatively static, unchanging background structure, the container of a national city system whose territorial coherence is not thought to have been fundamentally altered through ongoing processes of global

---

[45] Ibid., 13.

[46] Ibid., 129–67.

[47] Ibid., 129–39, 139–63.

[48] Peter J. Taylor, "Understanding the 1980s, Part 1a," *Review of International Political Economy* 1, no. 2 (1994): 365–73.

[49] For critical reflections on this entrenched assumption, see Taylor, *World City Network*.

sociospatial restructuring. Oddly enough, then, Sassen's empirical analysis of global city formation replicates the entrenched methodological nationalism inherited from her mid-twentieth-century predecessors in the study of urban hierarchies and systems. In effect, Sassen presupposes that the spatial referent with which global city formation is "discontinuous" remains the national economy, understood as a relatively bounded, territorially self-enclosed, and internally differentiated system of cities.[50] In this sense, despite her emphasis on the various global/national fissures, disjunctures, and dislocations that have been induced through global city formation, Sassen's analytical framework replicates a conventionally territorialist model of global capitalism as an aggregation of national space economies. In this state-centered, territorially bounded universe, global cities can be understood only as zones of exception that are, in georegulatory terms, situated "outside" the world interstate system despite their physical location within national political jurisdictions.[51]

Many of Sassen's subsequent writings in the late 1990s and early 2000s replicate the analytical blind spots associated with her scalar imaginary in *The Global City*, albeit in the context of investigations that are much more explicitly attuned to the politics of territory and place. For example, in one of her key texts of the late 1990s, a slim book of essays that connected her earlier urban research to questions of political sovereignty, Sassen interprets global cities as new sites of "extraterritoriality" that are paradoxically situated "beyond" the state's jurisdictional reach while nevertheless being enclosed within its borders.[52] Despite this deepening engagement with the changing politics of city/state relations, however, Sassen's analysis actually reinforces rather than supersedes the relatively conventional conception of the national territory and, by implication, of the national scale, that underpinned *The Global City*. The metaphor of extraterritoriality is derived from medieval European debates on the right of embassy, and as with Sassen's previous line of argumentation, it presupposes a conception of states as relatively static

---

[50] Sassen's own conclusion regarding the evolving functional and spatial links between manufacturing and service industries indicates the limitations of such a focus: "Yes, manufacturing matters, but from the perspective of finance and producer services, it does not have to be national." Sassen, *Global City*, 328. On the historical construction and deconstruction of the "national" economy as an object of knowledge and practice, see Hugo Radice, "The National Economy: A Keynesian Myth?," *Capital and Class* 22 (1984): 111–40.

[51] See also Saskia Sassen, *Cities in the World Economy* (London: Sage, 1993), xiii–xiv.

[52] Saskia Sassen, *Losing Control? Sovereignty in an Age of Globalization* (New York: Columbia University Press, 1996), 4, 13. See also Saskia Sassen, "Territory and Territoriality in the Global Economy," *International Sociology* 15, no. 2 (2000): 372–93.

territorial background structures that are being selectively perforated, but not otherwise qualitatively transformed, through processes of geoeconomic restructuring. Just as foreign embassies are understood as protected, self-enclosed sites in which the host state's exclusive sovereignty is locally punctured, Sassen here implies that global cities' economic operations circumvent state territorial boundaries in certain tightly circumscribed, legally "exceptionalized" locations while leaving those boundaries otherwise essentially intact and operational. Clearly, this was a more politically inflected version of Sassen's earlier "systemic discontinuity" thesis, but it preserved her underlying conception of global cities as sites of exception to an otherwise universally hegemonic framework of national territorial organization that was said to be left basically unchanged amid processes of geoeconomic restructuring.

It is only in her subsequent book, *Territory, Authority, Rights,* that Sassen makes a more decisive break with such methodologically limiting assumptions.[53] Here, however, her analytical focus shifts away from the *problematique* of global city formation and the concomitant rearticulation of city/state relations toward explorations of various questions related to the historical geographies of territory and sovereignty during the course of modern state formation up through the contemporary moment of accelerated economic globalization. Nonetheless, in the course of her investigations of such issues, Sassen's work generates a number of methodological insights that are of considerable relevance to my efforts here to decipher contemporary rescalings of urbanization.

First, Sassen emphatically underscores the active role of national states in promoting, managing, and regulating geoeconomic integration, as well as the wide-ranging structural transformations of state power that have been associated with that role. Sassen's main concern, in developing this line of argumentation, is to demonstrate that the scalar terrain of the "global" is not positioned outside or beyond the state's purview but is actively constituted through a multiscalar geography of state activities, legal authority, and regulatory intervention. In this way, Sassen's writings on the territory/sovereignty nexus open up the possibility of exploring the ways in which processes of global city formation have likewise been mediated, promoted, and managed through state spatial strategies, and through a multiscalar remaking of the institutional-regulatory spaces in and through which such strategies are deployed.

---

[53] See, above all, Saskia Sassen, *Territory, Authority, Rights: From Medieval to Global Assemblages* (Princeton, NJ: Princeton University Press, 2006).

Second, Sassen's analysis elaborates a methodologically elegant critique of the zero-sum conceptualization of spatial scale—to which she here refers as an "endogeneity trap"—that underpins mainstream, state-denialist approaches to globalization. Specifically, she argues not only that contemporary forms of geoeconomic integration are facilitated by national state institutions, but that such processes are embedded within, and in turn qualitatively transform, inherited nationalized "assemblages" of spatial, territorial, and scalar organization. Although Sassen does not herself directly engage with Lefebvre's sociospatial theory in search of tools for superseding this endogeneity trap, her analysis of institutional assemblages presupposes a fluidly relational conceptualization of scale that is broadly analogous to the Lefebvrian "principle of superimposition and interpenetration of social spaces" that grounds my own approach to the capitalist urban fabric. In such a framework, as Sassen points out, it is possible to explore the interplay between centripetal and centrifugal scaling processes, which may consolidate or deconstruct historically and geographically specific scalar assemblages of institutional organization, whether nationalized or otherwise. Additionally, this approach to scalar assemblages and vectors of institutional rescaling productively supersedes the widely prevalent tendency to treat nationalizing and globalizing processes as mutually exclusive, directing attention instead to the ways in which they are relationally interconnected and even co-constitutive within dynamically evolving configurations of interscalar relations.[54]

Such "analytic pathways," as Sassen terms them, offer a useful methodological basis for overcoming both state-demise arguments and zero-sum conceptions of geographical scale in research on global cities and, more generally, for introducing a more nuanced theorization of the rescaling processes that have underpinned contemporary patterns and pathways of urban restructuring.[55] From this point of view, global cities are not to be conceived as uniquely globalized, transnationally networked urban nodes that are

---

[54] In a very general sense, Sassen's notion of institutional assemblages resonates with the conceptualization of the scalar fix presented in Chapter 2. Despite their divergent theoretical lineages, both concepts refer to the historically variable, politically contested ways in which interscalar orders are consolidated, while also underscoring the politically contentious, and thus malleable, dimensions of scalar configurations. However, in contemporary urban theory, the assemblage concept is laden with a range of philosophical assumptions that strongly diverge from the framework developed in this book. For further elaboration, see Neil Brenner, David J. Madden, and David Wachsmuth, "Assemblage Urbanism and the Challenges of Critical Urban Theory," *CITY* 15, no. 2 (2011): 225–40; and David Wachsmuth, David J. Madden, and Neil Brenner, "Between Abstraction and Complexity: Meta-Theoretical Observations on the Assemblage Debate," *CITY* 15, no. 6 (2011): 740–50.

[55] Sassen, *Territory, Authority, Rights*, 5 passim.

perforating otherwise relatively unchanged national systems of cities and state power; nor do they herald the unilinear erosion or dissolution of such inherited politico-institutional frameworks. Instead, along with the broader infrastructural architectures of the WCA as a whole, global cities may be productively reconceptualized as sites of both institutional and sociospatial restructuring in and through which a broader, multiscalar transformation of the capitalist urban fabric is unfolding.

Post-Keynesian Geographies of Rescaling

Cities are at once basing points for capital accumulation (*nodes* in global flows) and organizational-administrative levels of statehood (*coordinates* of state territorial power). As nodes in global flows, cities operate as loci of industrial production, as centers of command and control over dispersed circuits of capital, and as sites of exchange within local, regional, national, and global markets. This is the dimension of cities that has been analyzed extensively in the vast literature on the political economy and historical geography of capitalist urbanization. Second, as coordinates of state territorial power, cities are regulatory-institutional levels within each state's organizational hierarchy. The term "coordinate" is intended to connote not only the embeddedness of major urban centers within the state's territorial matrix but also their changing structural positions within the multiple, overlapping regulatory networks through which state power is constituted, deployed, and transformed across spatial scales. These coordinates may be interlinked through various means, from legal-constitutional regulations, financial interdependencies, administrative divisions of labor, and hierarchies of bureaucratic command to informal regulatory and coordination arrangements, interurban policy networks, and ad hoc, issue-specific modes of cooperation. This dimension of cities has been analyzed most prominently in studies of the local state, urban regimes, and municipal governance.

This basic distinction has far-reaching interpretive consequences for the analysis of global city formation in relation to rescaling processes. During the Fordist-Keynesian period (circa 1950 to 1970), these two dimensions of city building were spatially coextensive within the boundaries of the national territorial state. As nodes of accumulation, cities were enframed within the same large-scale territorial infrastructures of capitalist production, circulation, and reproduction that underpinned and constituted the national economy. The cities of the older industrialized world, in particular, served as the engines of Fordist mass production and as the core metropolitan expressions of a global economic system that was compartmentalized into nationalized territorial matrices. Though transnational interurban linkages remained crucial to the Atlantic Fordist space economy, especially across the circuits of Cold War geopolitics and emergent pathways of postcolonial development, cities and regions were generally seen to operate above all as the foundations for national economic growth, essentially as the most dynamic territorial subunits within a spatially integrated national economic space. Consequently, across each of the three "worlds" of Cold War national developmentalism, it was widely assumed that the industrialization of major metropolitan areas would generate a propulsive dynamic of employment, investment, and growth that would, in turn, lead to the industrialization of each state's internal peripheries, and thereby counteract the problem of territorial inequality.

Likewise, as coordinates of state territorial power, Fordist-Keynesian regional and local regulatory institutions functioned primarily as transmission belts for central state socioeconomic policies. Their major strategic goal was to stimulate industrial growth and to redistribute its effects as evenly as possible across the national territory. To this end, redistributive, compensatory regional policies were widely introduced to promote industrial development, employment growth, and infrastructure investment within each state's internal peripheries. It was this constellation of regulatory priorities and spatial imaginaries that led postwar regional development theorists such as Gunnar Myrdal and Albert Hirschman to view the national territory as the basic container of spatial polarization between urban cores and internal peripheries; that led urban geographers such as Brian Berry and Allan Pred, among many others, to view national city systems as the primary spatial scale on which rank-size urban hierarchies were organized; and that led state theorists such as Claus Offe to describe municipal politics as a mere "buffer zone" constructed by the central state to insulate itself from proliferating social conflicts and legitimation crises.[56]

Since the 1970s, however, these tendentially nationalized, state-centric geographies of urbanization and territorial regulation have been profoundly

---

[56] For these authors' classic statements on such issues, see Gunnar Myrdal, *Economic Theory and Under-Developed Regions* (London: Gerald Duckworth, 1957); Albert Hirschman, *The Strategy of Economic Development* (New Haven, CT: Yale University Press, 1958); Brian J. Berry, "City Size Distributions and Economic Development," *Economic Development and Cultural Change* 9 (1961): 573–87; Allan Pred, *City-Systems in Advanced Economies* (London: Hutchinson, 1977); Claus Offe, "Zur Frage der "Identität der kommunalen Ebene," in *Lokale Politikforschung*, ed. Rolf-Richard Grauhan (New York: Campus, 1975), 2:303–9. On this period of state regulation and urban governance more generally, see Brenner, *New State Spaces*, chap. 4.

reconfigured as a direct outgrowth of the global crisis of the Fordist-Keynesian developmental model.[57] The crisis of global Fordism was expressed in a specifically geographical form, above all through the contradiction between the national scale of state regulation, with its inherited domestic policy relays, industrialization strategies, and governance mechanisms, and the relentlessly globalizing thrust of postwar capital accumulation, driven by increasingly multilocational, expansionary TNCs seeking to increase their global market share in strategic industrial sectors. In particular, the interscalar configurations that underpinned the Fordist-Keynesian political-economic order, which had been based upon national regulation of the wage relation and international regulation of currency and trade, underwent substantial realignments since the initial geoeconomic shocks and proliferating crisis tendencies of the 1970s. The deregulation of financial markets and the global credit system since the collapse of the Bretton Woods system in 1973 undermined the viability of nationally organized demand management, industrial, and monetary policies. Meanwhile, the accelerated globalization of production, competition, trade, and financial flows in subsequent years compromised the ability of national states to insulate themselves from the world economy as quasi-autarchic economic zones. Thus, as Erik Swyngedouw paradigmatically explained with reference to the scalar realignments of the 1980s:

> Over the last decade or so the relative dominance of the nation state at a scale level has changed to give way to new configurations in which both the local/regional and the transnational/global have risen to prominence. Global corporations, global financial movements and global politics play deciding roles in the structuring of daily life, while simultaneously more attention is paid to local and regional responses and restructuring processes. There is, in other words, a double movement of globalisation on the one hand and devolution, decentralisation or localisation on the other. . . . [T]he local/global interplay of contemporary restructuring processes should be thought of as a single, combined process with two inherently related, albeit contradictory movements and as a process which involves a *de facto* recomposition of the articulation of the geographical scales of economic and of social life.[58]

---

[57] Erik Swyngedouw, "Neither Global nor Local," 137–66; John Agnew and Stuart Corbridge, *Mastering Space: Hegemony, Territory, and International Political Economy* (New York: Routledge, 1995); and Peck and Tickell, "Searching for a New Institutional Fix."

[58] Erik Swyngedouw, "The Mammon Quest: 'Glocalization,' Interspatial Competition and the Monetary Order: The Construction of New Scales," in Dunford and Kafkalas, *Cities and Regions in the New Europe*, 40.

The central geographical consequence of these intertwined political-economic shifts has been a deconstruction of the most elemental territorial building block of the postwar geoeconomic and geopolitical order: the autocentric national economy. This development is at once an expression and an animator of the broader processes of scale relativization that were summarized in the preceding chapter. As Swyngedouw notes:

> What is generally referred to as "post-Fordism" . . . is a series of highly contested, deeply contradictory and variegated processes and power struggles that often revolve around scale, control over particular scales, the content of existing scales, the construction of new scales, and the articulation between scales.[59]

Clearly, then, the tendential spatial isomorphism between the capitalist urban fabric and the nationalized "weave" of state space, which was previously discussed in Chapter 2 with reference to Henri Lefebvre's late Fordist speculations on generalized urbanization, has been underdoing a significant disarticulation, especially since the 1980s. The capitalist urban fabric and state space have remained tightly intermeshed at all spatial scales, but their territorial organization, scalar articulations, and evolutionary pathways no longer coherently coalesce around a single predominant scale, national or otherwise. The central task in the present context is to examine more closely the dynamically mutating geographical-institutional interface between the rescaling of urbanization and the remaking of state spatiality since the collapse of the North Atlantic Fordist growth regime.

First, as global cities researchers have explored at length, the contemporary rescaling of urbanization must be viewed as a multidimensional reorganization of entrenched national urban systems in conjunction with the consolidation of new, worldwide urban hierarchies. To illustrate this ongoing rescaling of the urbanization process, Figure 4.1 schematically depicts the rescaling of the European urban hierarchy since the crisis of the Fordist-Keynesian regime in the early 1970s.

Building upon Stefan Krätke's research, this schematic representation of the contemporary European city system focuses upon the first dimension of urbanization, the role of cities as nodes of capital accumulation.[60] Krätke's model describes contemporary transformations of the European urban

---

[59] Swyngedouw, "Neither Global nor Local," 156.

[60] Stefan Krätke, "Stadtsystem im internationalen Kontext und Vergleich," in *Kommunalpolitik*, ed. Roland Roth and Hellmut Wollmann (Opladen: Leske Verlag, 1993), 176–93.

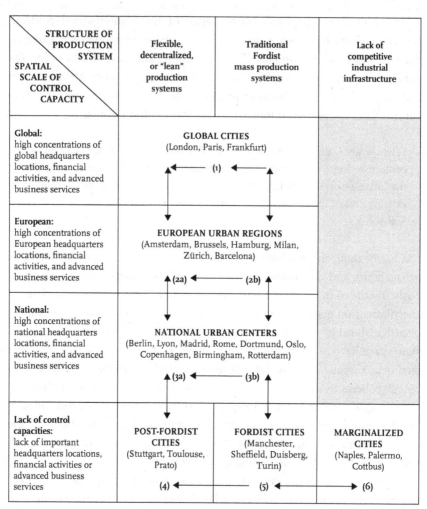

STRUCTURE OF PRODUCTION SYSTEM / SPATIAL SCALE OF CONTROL CAPACITY	Flexible, decentralized, or "lean" production systems	Traditional Fordist mass production systems	Lack of competitive industrial infrastructure
Global: high concentrations of global headquarters locations, financial activities, and advanced business services	**GLOBAL CITIES** (London, Paris, Frankfurt) ◄──── (1) ◄────		
European: high concentrations of European headquarters locations, financial activities, and advanced business services	**EUROPEAN URBAN REGIONS** (Amsterdam, Brussels, Hamburg, Milan, Zürich, Barcelona) ▲(2a) ◄──── (2b) ▲		
National: high concentrations of national headquarters locations, financial activities, and advanced business services	**NATIONAL URBAN CENTERS** (Berlin, Lyon, Madrid, Rome, Dortmund, Oslo, Copenhagen, Birmingham, Rotterdam) ▲(3a) ◄──── (3b) ▲		
Lack of control capacities: lack of important headquarters locations, financial activities or advanced business services	**POST-FORDIST CITIES** (Stuttgart, Toulouse, Prato) (4) ◄────	**FORDIST CITIES** (Manchester, Sheffield, Duisberg, Turin) (5) ◄────	**MARGINALIZED CITIES** (Naples, Palermo, Cottbus) ──► (6)

FIGURE 4.1 Rescaling the European urban hierarchy. (Source: Derived from Stefan Krätke, *Stadt, Raum, Ökonomie* [Basel: Birkhäuser Verlag, 1995], 141.)

hierarchy with reference to two structural criteria—the industrial structure of the city's productive base (Fordist vs. post-Fordist) and the spatial scale of its command and control functions (global, European, national, regional, negligible). The arrows in the figure indicate various possible changes in position among cities within the European urban hierarchy, and various cities have been listed to exemplify each of these levels. As the figure indicates, global city formation has entailed the emergence of a new configuration of the global urban hierarchy, defined through the increasing scale of urban command and control functions, of interurban exchange relations, and of interurban competition. As nodes of accumulation, therefore, cities are no longer enclosed within relatively autocentric national economies, but have been embedded more directly within transnational urban hierarchies, interurban networks, and circuits of capital. Although the cities positioned at the apex of the global, European, North American, and East Asian urban hierarchies present the most dramatic evidence of this transformation, their newly ascendant positions within the global urban system are indicative of a more general scalar rearticulation of urban spaces across the world economy.[61]

Second, the post-1970s wave of global restructuring has also had important implications for the role of cities as coordinates of state territorial power. Despite its tendency to neglect nationally scaled political-economic dynamics, the methodology of global cities research provides a useful starting point for investigating such issues. Much like the place-based sociotechnical infrastructures of global cities, the emergent state spaces of the postwelfare, post-Keynesian era can be productively interpreted as strategically essential layers of the capitalist urban fabric, and as such, as key territorial foundations for emergent, post-Fordist forms of capital accumulation. In this sense, as argued in Chapter 2, state space represents a key infrastructure of capitalist territorial organization that is as tightly enmeshed with the fixity/motion contradiction as are the cities, regions, and sociotechnical networks on which capital most immediately depends for its relentless metabolism of profit-based growth. Edward Soja's influential concept of the "exopolis," originally developed to decipher the tumultuous reconstitution of urban form under post-Fordist capitalism, offers a suggestive spatial metaphor through which to explore this aspect of state spatial restructuring.[62] Like the exopolis, a post-Fordist matrix of industrial agglomeration in which inherited spaces of urbanism are simultaneously turned "inside out" and "outside in," the geographies of post-Keynesian urban governance are likewise being comprehensively rewoven: they are turned *inside out* insofar as state institutions, at various spatial scales, attempt more directly to enhance the global structural competitiveness of strategic subnational spaces, such as cities and regions; and they are simultaneously turned *outside in* insofar as supranational governance agencies, multinational regulatory alliances, and

---

[61] As Peter J. Taylor and his collaborators in the GaWC (Globalization and World Cities) group have comprehensively demonstrated, these rescalings have been tightly intertwined with new geographies of intercity networking, at various spatial scales, throughout the world economy. For an overview and theoretical exploration, see Taylor, *World City Network*.

[62] Edward W. Soja, "Inside Exopolis: Scenes from Orange County," in *Variations on a Theme Park: The New American City and the End of Public Space*, ed. Michael Sorkin (New York: Noonday Press, 1994), 94–122.

transnational corporate and financial organizations now come to play more active, multifaceted roles in the reorganization of each state's national territorial economy, often with profound ramifications for the fortunes of cities and regions.

Under these conditions, urban governance is no longer neatly enframed within nationally centralized hierarchies of state power or oriented primarily toward the balanced distribution of industrial infrastructure and the equipment of collective consumption across the national territory. Instead, the process of urban development is increasingly mediated through a multiscalar architecture of state and nonstate institutions whose overarching goal is, as Alain Lipietz argues, to promote strategic local spaces as "breeding grounds for new productive forces."[63] Rather than focusing primarily on problems of policy coordination and bureaucratic steering within a national administrative framework, this rescaled formation of urban governance is more directly oriented toward establishing supranational and transversal linkages that would help propel metropolitan regions upward within the urban hierarchy depicted in Figure 4.1. This regulatory architecture has also transferred significant decision-making capacities regarding urban planning, infrastructure investment, and land use to certain privileged corporate actors, including transnational firms, banks, and real estate developers. Consequently, as David Harvey presciently recognized during the incipient phase of these wide-ranging politico-institutional realignments, the consolidation of entrepreneurial forms of urban governance has been inextricably intertwined with a fundamental reconstitution of state territorial regulation at all spatial scales.[64]

These post-Keynesian rescalings of urban governance have not only entailed a reconstitution of inherited political geographies of statehood; they have also been associated with a profound transformation of the relationship between states and the urban-territorial infrastructures upon which capital's metabolism depends. As discussed in Chapter 2, territorial organization has long operated as a force of production under capitalism through its infrastructural organization (of productive capacities, land use systems, labor-power, sociotechnical networks, and socioenvironmental relations), its regulatory-institutional constitution, and its assembly of other

---

[63] Alain Lipietz, "The National and the Regional: Their Autonomy Vis-à-Vis the Capitalist World Crisis," in *Transcending the State-Global Divide*, ed. Ronen P. Palan and Barry K. Gills (Boulder, CO: Lynne Rienner Publishers, 1994), 37.

[64] David Harvey, "From Managerialism to Entrepreneurialism: The Transformation in Urban Governance in Late Capitalism," *Geografiska Annaler Series B Human Geography* 71, no. 1 (1989): 3–17.

place-specific externalities.[65] As I argued in that chapter through a reading of Henri Lefebvre's writings, state institutions have figured centrally in the production, regulation, reproduction, and reconstitution of such territorial configurations in relation to historically specific crystallizations of the capitalist urban fabric. During the Fordist-Keynesian period, most older industrial states deployed indirect forms of state spatial intervention oriented toward the reproduction of labor-power (e.g., redistributive social welfare policies), industrial relocation (e.g., subsidies and tax concessions to firms), and other elements of collective consumption (e.g., large-scale investments in the spatial equipment for housing, education, transportation, and urban development). Although the obsolescence of the Fordist-Keynesian regulatory regime has undermined the aspirational unity of national states as territorially self-enclosed containers of socioeconomic activity, this development appears to have intensified rather than diminished the importance of territorial organization as a basis for accumulation strategies and, by implication, as a scale-circumscribing medium of economic governance. As French geographer Pierre Veltz explains:

> Whereas in Taylorist-Fordist mass production, territory mainly appeared as a stock of generic resources (raw materials, labor), nowadays it increasingly underpins a process of *the creation of specialized resources*. Competitiveness among nations, regions and cities proceeds less from static endowments as in classical comparative-advantage theories, than from their ability *to produce new resources*, not necessarily material ones, and *to set up efficient configurations* in terms of costs, quality of goods or services, velocity and innovation.[66]

My hypothesis here is that the rescaled state spaces of the postwelfare, post-Keynesian era have come to play strategically essential roles in the production, coordination, and maintenance of the very "specialized resources" and "efficient configurations" for urban development upon which, according to Veltz's analysis, the post-Fordist process of capital accumulation increasingly depends. Especially as of the 1980s and 1990s, global cities emerged as regulatory leading edges for a range of state spatial strategies that have sought

---

[65] See also Erik Swyngedouw, "Territorial Organization and the Space/Technology Nexus," *Transactions of the Institute of British Geographers* 17 (1992): 417–33; and Mark Gottdiener, "Space as a Force of Production," *International Journal of Urban and Regional Research* 11 (1987): 405–16.

[66] Pierre Veltz, "The Dynamics of Production Systems, Territories and Cities," in *Cities, Enterprises and Society on the Eve of the 21st Century*, ed. Frank Moulaert and Allen J. Scott (London: Pinter, 1997), 79, italics added.

to construct, manage, and sustain such post-Fordist forms of capitalist territorial organization. In contrast to the various incentive-based, indirect, and spatially redistributive policies of the Fordist-Keynesian era, post-Keynesian modes of state intervention have entailed a more direct involvement of state institutions in the promotion of the "productive force of territorial organization."[67] Through a range of spatially selective policies, interventions, and politico-organizational transformations, post-Keynesian states have been attempting to enhance the territorially specific productive capacities of strategically delineated economic spaces and, consequently, to facilitate the production of new urban spaces. When confronted with the apparently increased mobility of capital, money, and commodities across national borders during the post-1970s period, a significant stream of post-Keynesian state spatial strategy has been oriented toward producing and managing the key *immobile* factors of production associated with capital's moment of territorialized fixity, not least within global cities and other delineated territorial zones that are deemed strategic for transnational investment, technological innovation, industrial dynamism, and growth promotion.[68] The overarching goal of such territorializing state spatial strategies, which I have elsewhere characterized as "urban locational policies," has been to establish "territorially rooted immobile assets" and "untraded interdependencies" within strategic local and regional growth zones.[69]

---

[67] Swyngedouw, "Territorial Organization."

[68] For a parallel analysis of the proliferation of such "zoning technologies" in the contemporary East Asian context, see Aihwa Ong, "Graduated Sovereignty in South-East Asia," *Theory, Culture & Society* 17, no. 4 (2000): 55–75; and Aihwa Ong, "The Chinese Axis: Zoning Technologies and Variegated Sovereignty," *Journal of East Asian Studies* 4 (2004): 69–96.

[69] On urban locational policies, see Brenner, *New State Spaces*, chap. 5. On territorially embedded socioeconomic assets and untraded interdependencies, see Ash Amin and Nigel Thrift, "Territoriality in the Global Political Economy," *Nordisk Samheallgeografsk Tidskrift* 20 (1995): 10; and Storper, *Regional World*. With a few exceptions, the literature on the industrial geography of new industrial districts in the 1980s and 1990s focused on the role of associationalist, high-trust practices and cooperative networks in producing these untraded interdependencies. However, such investigations tended to neglect the aggressive ways in which neoliberal, deregulatory policies were also being mobilized during this period in many major urban regions as a means to promote place-specific competitive advantages. Such a reading brackets the ways in which even associationalist regional economies may themselves be periodically subjected to the cost-cutting, competitive pressures promoted through neoliberal policy regimes; and it ignores the possibility that associationalist and neoliberal projects of regulatory transformation mutually condition one another within broader scalar divisions of labor. Such an argument is elaborated at length by Jamie Gough and Aram Eisenschitz, who productively interpret associationalist reregulation and neoliberal deregulation as opposing yet dialectically intertwined strategies to manage capital's crisis tendencies, in part through the rescaling of regulatory space. See, in particular, Aram Eisenschitz and Jamie Gough, "The Contradictions

Even when such territorially embedded assets are not directly produced by the state, a range of governmental and quasi-governmental agencies have become more actively engaged in financing, monitoring, coordinating, and maintaining them. More generally, by adopting growth-oriented, market-disciplinary strategies of urban development, postwelfare state institutions have also come to play more central roles in promoting strategic zones within their territories—financial centers, industrial districts, technopoles, enterprise zones, science and technology parks, innovation hubs, free trade zones, and so forth—as putatively distinctive, innovative, and competitive locational products on the world market. In this way, as Phillip Cerny notes, "the state itself becomes an agent for the commodification of the collective, situated in a wider, market-dominated playing field."[70] The state's role in economic governance is thus no longer merely to reproduce localized production complexes, but continually to protect and enhance their capacities as territorially specific productive forces.[71]

It is in this context that the substantially enhanced operational role of subnational institutional forms in post-Keynesian economic governance is to be understood. Throughout the European Union, local and regional governments have been engaged in a concerted attempt at once to revalorize degraded industrial sites, to promote industrial growth in globally competitive sectors, and to acquire new command and control functions in the world economy by providing various territorial preconditions for transnational capital, including customized transportation and communications links, premium office space, access to appropriate labor markets, digital

---

of Neo-Keynesian Local Economic Strategy," *Review of International Political Economy* 3, no. 3 (1996): 434–58; Jamie Gough and Aram Eisenschitz, "The Construction of Mainstream Local Economic Initiatives: Mobility, Socialization and Class Relations," *Economic Geography* 72, no. 2 (1996): 178–95; and Jamie Gough, "Changing Scale as Changing Class Relations: Variety and Contradiction in the Politics of Scale," *Political Geography* 23, no. 2 (2004): 185–211.

[70] Philip Cerny "Globalization and the Changing Logic of Collective Action," *International Organization* 49, no. 4 (1995): 620.

[71] One major consequence of this rescaled approach to territorial regulation has been an intensification of state-induced uneven spatial development, as relatively brief temporal "bursts" of growth are promoted within carefully delineated territorial zones of major metropolitan regions. This represents a stark contrast to the spatial-Keynesian project of promoting "balanced" patterns of large-scale, long-term territorial development across the national economy as a whole. This tendency of state rescaling and its profound implications for patterns of uneven spatial development were presciently anticipated in the late 1970s by Nicos Poulantzas: "The State's role in favour of foreign or transnational capital heightens the uneven development of capitalism within each country in which foreign capital is reproduced. It does this most notably by designating particular regions as 'development areas' to the detriment of others—a process which . . . produces fissures in the national unity underpinning the bourgeois State." See Nicos Poulantzas, *State, Power, Socialism*, trans. Patrick Camiller (London: New Left Books, 1978), 213.

infrastructure, and other place-specific externalities. It is, then, above all through their intensified mobilization to promote, secure, and sustain a range of putatively place- and region-specific conditions for capital investment that local and regional states, in particular, have gained an enhanced structural significance within the regulatory (and deregulatory) operations of emergent postwelfare competition states.[72]

In the early 1970s, Henri Lefebvre had begun to outline some of the broad contours of an emergent, hyperproductivist state form that would strive to accelerate and intensify capital accumulation through the mobilization of spatially oriented regulatory strategies—a new "politics of space."[73] As Lefebvre noted in the final chapter of *The Production of Space*:

> That relationship [between the state and space] . . . is becoming tighter: the spatial role of the state . . . is more patent. Administrative and political state apparatuses are no longer content (if they ever were) merely to intervene in an abstract manner in the investment of capital. . . . Today the state and its bureaucratic and political apparatuses intervene continually in space, and make use of space in its instrumental aspect in order to intervene at all levels and through every agency of the economic realm.[74]

Reflecting on such trends some two decades later, in the early 1990s, Erik Swyngedouw arrived at the identical conclusion that "the role of the state is actually becoming more, rather than less, important in developing the productive powers of territory and in producing new spatial configurations."[75] This tendency toward an even more direct intermeshing of state institutions

---

[72] On the notion of the competition state, see Jessop, *Future of the Capitalist State*; and Cerny, "Globalization." On the proliferation of local and regional economic initiatives, see, for instance, Margit Mayer, "The Shifting Local Political System in European Cities," in Dunford and Kafkalas, *Cities and Regions in the New Europe*, 255–76; Alan Harding, "Urban Regimes in a Europe of the Cities?," *European Urban and Regional Studies* 4, no. 4 (1997): 291–314; Paul Cheshire and Ian Gordon, "Territorial Competition and the Predictability of Collective (In)action," *International Journal of Urban and Regional Research* 20, no. 3 (1996): 383–99; Tim Hall and Phil Hubbard, "The Entrepreneurial City: New Politics, New Urban Geographies," *Progress in Human Geography* 20, no. 2 (1996): 153–74; and Swyngedouw, "Heart of the Place." On the interplay between reregulation and deregulation in post-Keynesian approaches to local economic governance, see Peck and Tickell, "Searching for a New Institutional Fix"; Gough and Eisenschitz, "Construction of Mainstream Local Economic Initiatives"; and Brenner, *New State Spaces*.

[73] Henri Lefebvre, "Reflections on the Politics of Space," in *State, Space, World: Selected Essays*, ed. Neil Brenner and Stuart Elden (Minneapolis: University of Minnesota Press, 2009 [1970]), 167–84.

[74] Lefebvre, *Production of Space*, 378.

[75] Swyngedouw, "Territorial Organization," 431.

into the spaces of capital has been actively enabled through strategies of state rescaling, which have permitted the core institutions and regulatory instruments of emergent post-Keynesian competition state regimes even more actively to shape and reshape the uneven landscapes of urbanization, generally in customized place-, region-, and scale-specific ways.

In sum, there appears to be a direct connection between post-Keynesian processes of state rescaling and the production of new urban spaces. On the one hand, the accelerated round of urban restructuring induced by the global economic crises of the early 1970s provided much of the impetus for post-Keynesian strategies of state rescaling. The latter first crystallized as a reactive form of crisis management and "endogenous development" in many declining, crisis-stricken Fordist manufacturing regions, before being more comprehensively rolled out as proactive mechanisms of urban locational policy in globalizing city-regions and other emergent industrial spaces of the post-Fordist economy.[76] On the other hand, the rescaled state institutions of the post-Keynesian period have mobilized new forms of urban governance through which to attract and embed transnational capital within their territories. To this end, post-Keynesian states are not only introducing new, territorially differentiated and locationally customized modes of spatial intervention, economic development, and infrastructural planning, but are also reorganizing their own internal scalar architectures in order to facilitate the flow of capital investment toward strategic urban growth zones within their territories. It is for this reason that the link between state rescaling and urban restructuring has been especially consequential within the rapidly globalizing urban spaces—the strategic nodes of the WCA—that have captured the attention of so many critical urban researchers.

Figure 4.2 summarizes these connections in schematic terms, highlighting at once the globalization of the world economy, the post-Keynesian rescaling of state space, and the ramifications of these shifts for the dual rescaling of cities at once as nodes of accumulation and as coordinates of state territorial power.

Globalizing Cities and the New Politics of Scale in Post-Keynesian Europe

We are now in a position to concretize the preceding analysis with reference to the fluidly mutating scalar geographies of global city formation, state

---

[76] Brenner, *New State Spaces*, chap. 5.

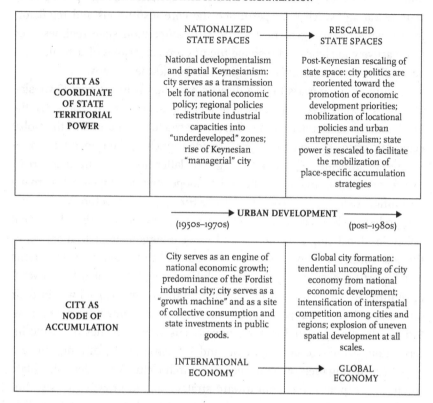

	NATIONALIZED STATE SPACES ⟶	RESCALED STATE SPACES
CITY AS COORDINATE OF STATE TERRITORIAL POWER	National developmentalism and spatial Keynesianism: city serves as a transmission belt for national economic policy; regional policies redistribute industrial capacities into "underdeveloped" zones; rise of Keynesian "managerial" city	Post-Keynesian rescaling of state space: city politics are reoriented toward the promotion of economic development priorities; mobilization of locational policies and urban entrepreneurialism; state power is rescaled to facilitate the mobilization of place-specific accumulation strategies

⟶ **URBAN DEVELOPMENT** ⟶

(1950s–1970s)   (post–1980s)

	City serves as an engine of national economic growth; predominance of the Fordist industrial city; city serves as a "growth machine" and as a site of collective consumption and state investments in public goods.	Global city formation: tendential uncoupling of city economy from national economic development; intensification of interspatial competition among cities and regions; explosion of uneven spatial development at all scales.
CITY AS NODE OF ACCUMULATION	INTERNATIONAL ECONOMY ⟶	GLOBAL ECONOMY

SPATIAL ORGANIZATION OF THE WORLD ECONOMY

FIGURE 4.2 Urban development, state space, and the world economy, 1950–2000.

space, and urban governance in the post-1970s European context. As David Bassens and Michiel van Meeteren have argued, during the 1980s and 1990s, deepening processes of corporate-industrial restructuring, the continued offshoring of labor-intensive manufacturing, accelerated financial deregulation, and the consolidation of a new international financial regime enhanced the importance of global city-regions, a worldwide "network of localization economies" whose specific concentrations of APS firms helped transnational capital reduce transaction costs, optimize investment of surpluses, accelerate technological innovation, adjust to market uncertainties, and manage crises of overaccumulation.[77] Consequently, Bassens and van Meeteren suggest, it was during this period that the key urban nodes of the WCA—including major European financial centers such as London, Paris,

---

[77] Bassens and van Meeteren, "World Cities," 758 passim.

Frankfurt, Amsterdam, and Milan—became "obligatory passage points" in the realization of global circuits of value under post-Fordist capitalism.[78]

The following analysis focuses, in particular, on the new politics of scale that emerged in and around Europe's major globalizing city-regions during the 1980s and 1990s, in close conjunction with the acceleration of European monetary and financial integration. In contrast to mainstream approaches to urban governance, which tend to enclose their investigations within relatively fixed, local or regional scalar frames, this discussion directs attention to (1) the dynamic rescaling of urban governance since the crisis of the European formation of Fordist-Keynesian capitalism and (2) the political strategies through which state institutions and other politico-territorial forces maneuvered to shape these ongoing rescaling processes, within and beyond major metropolitan regions. I focus here upon some of Europe's major globalizing cities, as defined in the literatures discussed previously—the "new industrial districts of transnational management and control" that were consolidated during the last several decades of the twentieth century.[79] However, this analysis embeds such transnationally networked urban nodes within the variegated, increasingly volatile interscalar geographies of the WCA, (European) state space and the capitalist urban fabric.

---

[78] Ibid. According to Bassens and van Meeteren, the subsequent generalization of financialization processes and the concomitant explosion of crisis tendencies in the early twenty-first century at once enhanced and transformed the "class monopoly rent" generated by APS firms within the WCA. These developments have, they argue, broadened the role of the APS complex far beyond the set of global cities that dominated those sectors in the final decades of the twentieth century, while also generating new regulatory challenges and contradictions at every scale of governance (see Bassens and van Meeteren, "World Cities," 756–58 passim). On global city formation in Europe during the late twentieth-century wave of accelerated European integration and global industrial restructuring, see Krätke, "Stadtsystem im internationalen Kontext und Vergleich"; Peter J. Taylor and Michael Hoyler, "The Spatial Order of European Cities under Conditions of Contemporary Globalization," *Tijdschrift voor Economische en Sociale Geografie* 91, no. 2 (2000): 176–89; and Peter J. Taylor and Ben Derudder, "Porous Europe: European Cities in Global Urban Arenas," *Tijdschrift voor Economische en Sociale Geografie* 95, no. 2 (2004): 527–38.

[79] The quoted phrase is from Jennifer Robinson's classic critique of first-wave global cities research, "Global and World Cities: A View from off the Map," *International Journal of Urban and Regional Research* 26, no. 3 (2002): 536. Robinson questions the tendency of global city researchers and global city boosterists alike to fetishize international financial centers as a uniquely powerful class of cities and to ignore the variegated dynamics of global restructuring that are impacting a wide range of cities around the world, including in the global South. In this context, Robinson's use of the phrase "new industrial districts of transnational management and control" rather than the generic shorthand notion of "global cities" is a salient warning against the pervasive tendency of analysts (1) to exaggerate the impacts of global city economic functions on the broader fabric of urban life and (2) to neglect the diverse kinds of transnational relations that have long mediated processes of urban development in cities that do not serve as significant command and control centers for capital.

Globalizing Cities and the Geopolitics of European Integration

The locations of globalizing cities played a major role during the 1990s in the competition among European states to acquire EU government offices within their territories. This form of interspatial competition was mediated directly through global cities' host states as they negotiated the terms and pace of European integration. Such locational decisions resulted in part from strategic compromises among Europe's core powers, as illustrated in the choice of Brussels as the European Union's administrative headquarters. However, the 1998 decision to locate the European Central Bank in Frankfurt was a major turning point in the geopolitical and geoeconomic struggle between the United Kingdom and the Federal Republic of Germany (FRG) to pull Europe's locational center of gravity toward their respective territories; London received only a meager consolation prize, the European Patent Office. The accelerated process of European monetary integration in the 1990s also had major implications for the hierarchy of financial centers within the European Union. Throughout this period, London remained the most important center of financial services within the European Union. However, the introduction of the euro in 1999 provided new opportunities for Frankfurt and Paris, which rolled out new regulatory and technological infrastructures to support global financial markets, and whose surrounding territorial economies were then already participating in the single European currency.[80] For this reason, the supranational geographies of state rescaling that were crystallizing in the European Union during this period appeared to favor the eventual formation of an integrated Frankfurt-Paris-London axis articulating the EU zone to the world economy.[81] Clearly, then, the post-Keynesian rescalings of state space that were pursued across the European Union in the closing decades of the twentieth century had a range of direct ramifications for the scalar geographies of European urban development.

Globalizing Cities and Intergovernmental Relations

Since the early 1980s, central-local relations were significantly transformed throughout western European state territories in the context of pressures associated with accelerating European integration, as well as nationally specific struggles over the appropriate framework for territorial regulation,

---

[80] "Financial Centres Survey," *The Economist*, May 1998, 17.

[81] Peter J. Taylor, "Is the UK Big Enough for Both London and England?," *Environment and Planning A* 29, no. 5 (1997): 766–70.

infrastructure investment, and economic development. Insofar as central or national governments generally treat their territorial subunits as functionally equivalent administrative tiers rather than as geographically distinctive zones of socioeconomic life, processes of global city formation and urban restructuring are rarely discussed in national policy debates on intergovernmental relations. Nevertheless, reconfigurations of intergovernmental relations may have far-reaching, long-term ramifications for the governance of urban regions insofar as they rearrange the local state's administrative, organizational, and financial relays to the central or national government, and thereby affect its regulatory capacities and strategic orientations.[82]

During the course of the 1980s and into the 1990s, several pathways of intergovernmental transformation were forged across the EU's member states that had immediate ramifications for urban development in several of Europe's major financial centers and globalizing city-regions.[83] At one extreme, in the United Kingdom, the Thatcherite wave of central-local restructuring entailed the abolition of the Greater London Council (GLC) and the consolidation of a neo-authoritarian form of centrally imposed local governance in the London region.[84] One of its main goals was to propel London and the South East of England to global city status while suppressing local and regional territorial opposition, including that within London itself. The resultant, centrally imposed forms of urban governance entailed "the removal of subnational state functions to non-electoral local states, while electoral local governments are left formally in position but with much reduced powers."[85]

By contrast, in the German context, processes of state restructuring during the same period entailed an increasingly decentralized role for both the *Länder* and the municipalities in formulating and implementing a range of policies relevant to industrial development, infrastructure planning, and urban growth. These new regulatory geographies enabled the municipal government of Frankfurt am Main, Germany's most important financial center, to roll out a new program of aggressive local boosterism, place marketing,

[82] On this constellation of issues, see Kevin Cox, "Territorial Structures of the State: Some Conceptual Issues," *Tijdschrift voor Economische en Sociale Geografe* 81 (1990): 251–66; Stefan Krätke and Fritz Schmoll, "Der lokale Staat – 'Ausführungsorgan' oder 'Gegenmacht'?," *Prokla* 68 (1987): 30–72; and Simon Duncan and Mark Goodwin, *The Local State and Uneven Development* (London: Polity Press, 1988).

[83] Mayer, "Shifting Local Political System," 255–76.

[84] Duncan and Goodwin, *Local State.*

[85] Ibid., 249.

and economic development policy that profoundly reshaped the city's built environment, development pathway, and socioeconomic landscape.[86] More generally, these decentralizing tendencies in the German federal system helped establish a transformed regulatory environment in which "all *Land* governments . . . behave like the management of a business, attempting to direct their entire policy at the needs and requirements of the *Land* as an industrial location in postfordist world capitalism."[87]

Between these poles was the case of the Netherlands, whose pathway of intergovernmental recalibration combined elements of intensified national state territorial management with localizing and regionalizing reforms. Especially since the mid-1980s, debates on central-local restructuring proliferated on all levels of the Dutch state, leading the national government, the provinces, and the municipalities to promote global city formation in the western Randstad megalopolis (composed of Amsterdam, Rotterdam, Utrecht, and the Hague) as a shared priority for national socioeconomic policy, territorial planning, and infrastructure investment.[88] Under these conditions, the four Randstad provinces (North Holland, South Holland, Utrecht, and Flevoland) acquired major new roles in the coordination of regional and local economic development. The Dutch national government meanwhile rolled out a new repertoire of policy and planning instruments designed to channel investment into the four Randstad cities and more effectively to canalize urban territorial expansion across this polycentric metropolitan region. In effect, a rescaled framework of national, provincial, and local state regulation was viewed as an essential regulatory precondition for protecting and enhancing the Randstad's strategic position as a major metropolitan hub and logistics platform in both the EU and global economies.

Of course, each of the pathways of state rescaling sketched previously was strongly conditioned by inherited institutional, administrative, and legal arrangements, and was also powerfully mediated through contextually

---

[86] See, for example, Roger Keil and Peter Lieser, "Frankfurt: Global City—Local Politics," in *After Modernism: Global Restructuring and the Changing Boundaries of City Life*, ed. Michael Peter Smith (New Brunswick, NJ: Transaction Publishers, 1992), 39–69; and Klaus Ronneberger and Roger Keil, "Ausser Atem—Frankfurt nach der Postmoderne," in *Capitales Fatales: Urbanisierung und Politik in den Finanzmetropolen*, ed. Hansruedi Hitz (Zürich: Rotpunktverlag, 1995), 208–84.

[87] Josef Esser and Joachim Hirsch, "The Crisis of Fordism and the Dimensions of a 'Postfordist' Regional and Urban Structure," *International Journal of Urban and Regional Research* 13, no. 3 (1989): 430.

[88] See, for example, Frans Dieleman and Sako Musterd, eds., *The Randstad: A Research and Policy Laboratory* (Dordrecht: Kluwer, 1992); and Gertjan Dijkink, "Metropolitan Government as Political Pet? Realism and Tradition in Administrative Reform in the Netherlands," *Political Geography* 14, no. 4 (1995): 329–41.

specific territorial alliances and political strategies at all spatial scales of state power. However, as this brief overview indicates, the forms, functions, and strategic orientations of urban governance were being qualitatively remade during the course of the 1980s and 1990s, in direct conjunction with nationally specific pathways of intergovernmental reorganization. While these institutional rescaling processes engendered wide-ranging, if uneven, consequences across the landscape of regulation, they appear to have provided new strategic capacities to a range of governmental agencies, political forces, and territorial alliances, across various scales of state power, through which to promote economic development within the European Union's most globally networked metropolitan regions. It is in this sense that strategies of intergovernmental reorganization decisively conditioned processes of global city formation.

Globalizing Cities and Territorial Politics

As John Friedmann and Goetz Wolff presciently observed in the early 1980s, "Being essential to both transnational capital and national political interests, global cities may become bargaining counters in the ensuing struggles."[89] A decade later, Peter J. Taylor likewise asked: "What would a strong protectionist policy resulting from a popular revolt by industrial America do for New York's role as a world city? Would capital move to a still 'free' Tokyo market?"[90] Taylor's question from the mid-1990s can be quite readily reframed with reference to the June 2016 Brexit vote in the United Kingdom: will Britain's exit from the European Union signal the end of London's long-standing role as Europe's dominant global financial center? How will London-based banks and associated APS firms fare in a post-Brexit world?[91] The crucial issue, then, is how the economic disjuncture between globalizing cities and the territorial economies of their host states is managed politically across contexts and scales.

During the closing decades of the twentieth century, the United Kingdom was the most dramatic European instance of such a disjuncture and an associated polarization of territorial politics. Since the mid-1970s, the dynamism of England's South East as a global city-region was predominantly based

---

[89] Friedmann and Wolff, "World City Formation," 312.

[90] Taylor, "World Cities and Territorial States," 59.

[91] Emma Dunkley, "Six Cities in Search of London's Business after Brexit," *Financial Times*, June 8, 2017; Howard Davies, "Will London Survive as a Financial Centre After Brexit?," *The Guardian*, April 26, 2017; Sarah Lyall, "Will London Fall?," *New York Times*, April 11, 2017.

upon an offshore economy, derived from the city's role as a global financial center, delinked almost entirely from industrial development elsewhere in the United Kingdom. Particularly following the abolition of exchange controls in 1979 and the deregulatory Big Bang of October 1986, the city's role as a global banking and financial center was further consolidated. The "two nations" accumulation strategy of the Thatcher era exacerbated historically entrenched forms of spatial polarization between the Greater London metropolitan area and the rest of the national territory, signaling the alignment of a neoliberal central state with global finance capital and London-based APS firms against the declining manufacturing cities and regions of the North and Scotland. Indeed, the rise of Thatcherism in the 1980s has been interpreted as a "declaration of independence by the south of England, the community dependent on London as a world city."[92] Throughout the 1990s, global city formation in the national capital remained one of the primary priorities of the Major government and, after 1997, of New Labour. Yet, because the United Kingdom remains a national state, and not a city-state clustered around the South East, the tension between global city formation in London and the intensified uneven development of the United Kingdom's territorial economy has remained a recurrent source of intense political conflict in British national politics. Such territorial tensions have only been further exacerbated in the wake of subsequent rounds of financial crisis, austerity policy, and, most explosively, the 2016 Brexit vote.[93]

This situation of an intense polarization of national politics through the process of global city formation has not obtained in Germany due to its decentralized federal system, its polycentric urban structure, and its multiple, internationally networked urban regions. Within this institutional and geographical constellation, it is not politically viable for the federal government to align its socioeconomic, industrial, or spatial policy priorities one-sidedly with any single metropolitan region. Frankfurt represents a partial exception to this situation due to its role as the site of the Bundesbank and the European Central Bank, but even there, urban development has been managed by an ensemble of local authorities and regional institutions that compete with one another, and with other *Länder*, for federal resources. Moreover, in contrast to the city of London, whose financial operations are largely decoupled

---

92 Taylor, "World Cities and Territorial States," 59.

93 Taylor, "Is the UK Big Enough"; Danny Dorling, "Brexit: The Decision of a Divided Country," *British Medical Journal*, July 6, 2016. See also, more generally, Glenn Morgan, "Supporting the City: Economic Patriotism in Financial Markets," *Journal of European Public Policy* 19, no. 3 (2012): 373–87.

from industrial development elsewhere in the United Kingdom, Germany's most globally networked metropolitan regions operate as major articulation points for nationally and regionally embedded industries, and thus remain interwoven in the industrial fabric of a broader territorial economy. As a result, during the course of the 1990s, territorial politics in Frankfurt were articulated predominantly at an *intra*regional scale. Global city formation in Frankfurt's city core generated a spiral of conflicts over administrative organization, financial burdens, living conditions, transportation, ecology, and growth patterns with the cities and towns of the surrounding Rhine-Main region, leading to intense debates on territorial governance reform within the *Land* of Hesse, especially in its most densely urbanized southern zone.[94] Here, then, the territorial politics of global city formation were considerably more regionally circumscribed than in the London/UK context.

A specific form of territorial politics also crystallized around global city formation in the Dutch Randstad region during the course of the 1990s. Although territory-wide forms of core-periphery polarization, interspatial competition, and central-local conflict persisted throughout this period, global city formation in the Randstad became a nearly unchallenged goal for Dutch national planning. The subsequent mobilization of national and local policies around the overarching priority of global city formation entailed the construction of a "national urban growth coalition" that aspired to transform Dutch central cities from providers of public services into the new "spearheads" of economic growth, especially in the Randstad.[95] As in Frankfurt, the politics of global city development in the Randstad generated intense regional conflicts between a range of administrative units, between city cores and suburban fringes, and between diverse sociopolitical factions and territorial alliances that were pursuing divergent regulatory agendas. In other respects, however, the Dutch configuration of territorial politics more closely paralleled the British pattern, insofar as urban governance in the Randstad was coordinated, negotiated, and implemented above all by the *national* government. Amid the many scales on which the Randstad's pathway of urbanization was being forged during this period, it was a national political alliance that proved most decisive for the policy regimes and development strategies that were consolidated.

---

[94] Lorenz Rautenstrauch, "Frankfurt und sein Umland: Planung, Politik, Perspektiven im Bereich des Umlandverbandes Frankfurt," in *Verdichtungsregionen im Umbruch*, ed. Manfred Streit and Hans-Arthur Haasis (Baden-Baden: Nomos, 1990), 233–98; Ronneberger and Keil, "Ausser Atem," 208–84.

[95] Pieter Terhorst and Jacques van de Ven, "The National Urban Growth Coalition in the Netherlands," *Political Geography* 14, no. 4 (1995): 343–61.

Even among global cities situated at the apex of the European urban hierarchy, then, political responses to the post-1980s round of geoeconomic restructuring varied considerably; they hinged substantially upon nationally and regionally specific institutional frameworks, regulatory experiments, lines of territorial contestation, and political strategies. Nonetheless, throughout the 1990s, the process of global city formation across the European Union generated new configurations of political-territorial struggle that at once *pushed* cities toward the adoption of globally oriented accumulation strategies while simultaneously *pulling* them back into the entrenched, multiscalar vortex of national state power. As Taylor explains, "For all their technical prowess in out-flanking the states, global cities remain places within states and this has crucial implications in terms of the politics of representation."[96]

The Rescaling of Spatial Planning

As discussed earlier, since the 1980s, new approaches to economic governance were consolidated across the European Union that promoted cities and regions as the primary "engines" of national territorial development. In most EU states, spatial planning was among the major institutional arenas in which this rescaling of national economic development policy was pursued, in significant measure as a means to facilitate the transformation of national metropolitan centers into globally networked urban regions. This is because, as Colin Crouch and Patrick Le Galès explain, "Advancing favoured places within their national territories has become one of the few forms of substantive economic policy left to national governments within European and global competition regimes."[97]

A particularly noteworthy example of this trend is postunification Germany, where the Spatial Planning Law (*Raumordnungsgesetz*) of 1965 was radically redefined in the early 1990s. The postwar project of "equalizing life conditions" on a national scale was superseded by a new priority: promoting Germany's major metropolitan regions as the most strategically essential levels of spatial intervention.[98] Analogously, in the Netherlands, the postwar project of deconcentration, which had attempted to spread urban

[96] Taylor, "Is the UK Big Enough," 70.

[97] Colin Crouch and Patrick Le Galès, "Cities as National Champions?," *Journal of European Public Policy* 19, no. 3 (2012): 417.

[98] Neil Brenner, "Building Euro-Regions: Locational Politics and the Political Geography of Neoliberalism in Post-Unification Germany," *European Urban and Regional Studies* 7, no. 4 (2000): 319–45.

development more evenly beyond the Randstad core zones, was effectively reversed as of the late 1980s under a new "compact cities" policy. A rescaled framework of Dutch national spatial planning was subsequently rolled out that sought to centralize advanced logistics infrastructure and associated forms of high-technology investment and APS activities within the Randstad region.[99] Analogous rescalings of inherited national spatial planning systems were implemented during the same period in most other EU member states, from Finland and Sweden to France and Italy. Increasingly, metropolitan regions and inter-metropolitan networks replaced the national economy as the key geographical reference points for long-term visions of territorial development.[100] Rather than being embedded within nationally configured spatial divisions of labor and nationalized formations of territorial regulation, these "national champion cities," and the transnational infrastructural configurations that connected them, were now given preferential status in various kinds of spatial policies oriented toward improving their structural positions in European and global circuits of capital.[101]

In parallel, on the EU level, the classical goal of mediating territorial polarization through redistributive regional structural policies was likewise abandoned in favor of a range of decidedly post-Keynesian, tendentially metropolitanized spatial policy frameworks. These involved, among other priorities, promoting local and regional economic competitiveness; incentivizing local and regional governments to lure inward capital investment toward major metropolitan areas, especially from TNCs; and enhancing transnational inter-metropolitan logistics and telecommunications systems.[102] These spatial policy reforms gained momentum during the 2000s, as the European structural funds program was redefined in conjunction with a new round of EU enlargement. This entailed a significant expansion of intra-EU regional revenue transfers, especially to the new member states of Eastern Europe, coupled with an even more extensive consolidation of competitive, growth-first regional policy agendas across the European Union as a whole.

---

[99] Ingeborg Tömmel, "Decentralization of Regional Development Policies in the Netherlands—A New Type of State Intervention?," *West European Politics* 15, no. 2 (1992): 107–25; Andreas Faludi and Arnold Van der Valk, *Rule and Order: Dutch Planning Doctrine in the Twentieth Century* (Dordrecht: Kluwer Academic Publishers, 1994).

[100] Louis Albrechts, ed., *Regional Policy at the Crossroads: European Perspectives* (London: Jessica Kingsley, 1989).

[101] Crouch and Le Galès, "Cities as National Champions?"

[102] Ingeborg Tömmel, "Internationale Regulation und lokale Modernisierung," *Zeitschrift für Wirtschaftsgeographie* 40, no. 1–2 (1996): 44–58.

As of the 1990s, then, the core goal of spatial planning in the European Union and most of its member states was no longer to support "balanced" national development through interregional redistribution, but to position "favored" cities and regions strategically in transnational spatial divisions of labor and infrastructural circuits. In this way, spatial planning was transformed from a broadly Keynesian instrument of redistributive territorial management into a tool of local and regional economic development strategy that actively promoted sociospatial polarization at both European and national scales.[103]

The Scale Politics of Metropolitan Governance Reform

Despite several earlier historical rounds of attempted metropolitan institutional reform, the inherited political geographies of European urban regions have long been fragmented among multiple agencies, departments, and governmental bodies with relatively narrow jurisdictional boundaries. As of the 1990s, however, as the economic "performance" of European city-regions became a major focal point for national debates on macroeconomic growth and industrial restructuring, the governance of metropolitan territorial development acquired an unprecedented (geo)political urgency.[104] Under these circumstances, especially in Europe's most globally networked metropolitan regions, the regional upscaling of urban governance was frequently justified as a means to coordinate economic development agendas, innovation programs, place-marketing strategies, land-use planning, and large-scale infrastructural investment, and on this basis, to bolster territorially embedded competitive advantages. Consequently, entirely new or significantly strengthened metropolitan institutions were widely justified as essential prerequisites for maintaining the competitive advantages of global city-regions in the face of intensifying geoeconomic restructuring and accelerating European integration.

This entrepreneurial, growth-oriented approach to city-regionalism was widely embraced by boosterist national and local politicians, and especially by those factions of capital that had sunk relatively large-scale,

---

[103] Brenner, "Building Euro-Regions"; Brenner, *New State Spaces*, chap. 5.

[104] See Christian Lefèvre, "Metropolitan Government and Governance in Western Countries: A Critical Overview," *International Journal of Urban and Regional Research* 22, no. 1 (1988): 9–25; Willem Salet, Andy Thornley, and Anton Kreukels, eds., *Metropolitan Governance and Spatial Planning* (London: Spon Press, 2003); and Susanne Heeg, Britte Klagge, and Jürgen Ossenbrügge, "Metropolitan Cooperation in Europe: Theoretical Issues and Perspectives for Urban Networking," *European Planning Studies* 11, no. 2 (2003): 139–53; as well as Chapter 6.

fixed investments into metropolitan economies. As Klaus Ronneberger has argued, in the European context, these newly emergent forms of city-regional cooperation were grounded upon a distinctively post-Fordist variant of "spatial solidarity" that privileged an economic logic of maximizing the competitiveness of territorially delimited, metropolitan "battle units," instead of a social logic of redistributing the surplus throughout territorially integrated, national "societies."[105] Crucially, however, these emergent projects of competitive global city-regionalism were often vehemently opposed by politico-territorial alliances seeking to defend extant regulatory geographies. In some European global cities, metropolitan governance reform was aggressively resisted by antigrowth coalitions that sought to protect local investments, to preserve residential amenities, to maintain control over local tax revenues, to bolster property values, and/or to deflect the negative ecological impacts of urban growth toward other locations. Elsewhere, metropolitan reform proposals became lightning rods for struggles regarding the appropriate institutional framework for urban democracy.[106] Thus, in the well-known example of the Labour-dominated GLC prior to its 1986 abolition under Thatcher, metropolitan institutions were viewed as a bulwark of localized control against externally induced bureaucratic, fiscal, and economic constraints. More frequently, the consolidation of new approaches to metropolitan governance was viewed as a technocratic or neoliberal "Trojan horse" that would erode the vitality of local democracy. This perspective was exemplified in the Dutch debate on city-provinces during the 1990s, in which the national government's competitiveness-oriented proposal for a comprehensive reform of metropolitan governance in the Randstad was overwhelmingly rejected in local referenda by the populations of Amsterdam and Rotterdam. Here, expanding the scale of urban governance was widely thought to entail a significant weakening of democratic political accountability and a frontal attack on municipal autonomy.

As these opposed perspectives on metropolitan institutional reform clashed within Europe's globalizing city-regions, struggles for regulatory control over the urbanization process were articulated in the form of intense sociopolitical contestation over the scale(s) of territorial regulation. Clearly, the metropolitan rescaling projects that proliferated during this period

---

[105] Klaus Ronneberger, "Kontrollierte Autonomie und rigide Norm: zur neoliberalen Restrukturierung des Sozialen," *Widersprüche* 69 (1998): 129–50.

[106] Klaus Ronneberger and Christian Schmid, "Globalisierung und Metropolenpolitik: Überlegungen zum Urbanisierungsprozess der neunziger Jahre," in *Capitales Fatales: Urbanisierung und Politik in den Finanzmetropolen Frankfurt und Zürich*, ed. Hansruedi Hitz et al. (Zurich: Rotpunktverlag, 1995), 354–78.

engendered both threats and opportunities for the inhabitants of global cities and surrounding zones; the question was how to develop coherent political strategies and territorial alliances through which to shape their variegated consequences for urban life. In post-Keynesian Europe, then, metropolitan strategies of state rescaling were clearly articulating, and often intensifying, many of the social, political, and ecological contradictions of global city formation, and of post-Fordist urban restructuring more generally. In so doing, they triggered an intricate series of struggles over the scalar organization of state space and the urban fabric that have continued to proliferate well into the 2000s.

The Territorial Organization of Globalizing Cities

It is ultimately on the local scale, however, that the productive force of territorial organization is most directly mobilized, and thus it is here that many of the most consequential sites of combined state rescaling and urban restructuring have been forged during the post-Keynesian era. As of the 1990s, with the consolidation of entrepreneurial approaches to urban governance across the European Union, municipal governments in many of Europe's globalizing city-regions helped to plan, finance, and implement a variety of "flagship" megaprojects that entailed a significant reorganization of the capitalist urban fabric, as well as the construction of new sites, scales, and modes of urban governance.[107] Such strategic urban megaprojects have included, among other iconic sites of neoliberal urbanism, corporate office towers, high-technology innovation districts, advanced logistics terminals (including airports, train stations, and seaports), and various types of retail, entertainment, and cultural facilities (urban shopping malls, museums, stadiums, exhibition centers, concert venues). In many cases, such flagship megaprojects have also been connected to state-supported investments in luxury housing enclaves and hotels, and have been cultivated through spectacular architectural and landscape designs intended to further capitalize upon the potential ground rent of strategic locations within the city. The Docklands redevelopment in London was among the earliest, and most dramatic, European examples of this broadly neoliberalized approach to urban governance, but it quickly became emblematic of a more general

---

[107] Erik Swyngedouw, Frank Moulaert, and Arantxa Rodriguez, "Neoliberal Urbanization in Europe: Large-Scale Urban Development Projects and the New Urban Policy," in *Spaces of Neoliberalism*, ed. Neil Brenner and Nik Theodore (Cambridge, MA: Blackwell, 2002), 195–229; Gilles Pinson, *Gouverner la ville par project: urbanisme et gouvernance de villes européenes* (Paris: Presses de Sciences Po, 2009).

trend in globalizing cities across the European Union and, indeed, much of the world economy. During the course of the 1990s, megaprojects became a seemingly ubiquitous instrument of urban redevelopment and place promotion in the European Union's most globally networked urban regions, as well as in many other major European urban centers that were likewise seeking to enhance their structural positions in transnational circuits of capital.

As David Harvey famously argued, the state-financed megaprojects of the late twentieth century were designed primarily to enhance the global value-generating capacity and speculative potential of relatively circumscribed local sites, rather than directly to improve social conditions for urban populations.[108] Consequently, in stark contrast to the socially and territorially integrationist project of postwar Fordist-Keynesian formations of urban governance, the strategic urban megaprojects of the post-1980s period created "a mosaic of newly constructed built environments with their associated increased rents" and "a patchwork of discrete spaces with increasingly sharp boundaries."[109] Tightly delimited, privately administered enclaves were equipped with highly customized built environments, advanced infrastructures, and patterns of architectural ornamentation that were intended to support specific economic, commercial, cultural, or residential functions while also being increasingly delinked, both operationally and aesthetically, from the broader sociospatial fabric of the city. In this way, the spectacular urban megaprojects of the late twentieth century contributed substantially to the broader splintering, privatization, and polarization of urban space that became increasingly pervasive during this period.[110]

The urban megaprojects of the post-Keynesian era have been premised upon a substantially rescaled approach to urban governance that suspended standard planning procedures and established a host of "exceptionality measures" to permit their relatively unimpeded approval, construction, and subsequent operation. Such quasi-authoritarian regulatory exceptions have included, most notably, "the freezing of conventional planning tools, bypassing statutory regulations and institutional bodies, the creation of project agencies with special or exceptional powers of intervention and

---

[108] Harvey, "From Managerialism to Entrepreneurialism."

[109] Swyngedouw, Moulaert, and Rodriguez, "Neoliberal Urbanization in Europe," 224.

[110] See, for example, Graham and Marvin, *Splintering Urbanism*; Soja, *Postmetropolis*; as well as Martin J. Murray, *The Urbanism of Exception: The Dynamics of Global City Building in the Twenty-First Century* (New York: Cambridge University Press, 2016).

decision-making, and/or a change in national or regional regulations."[111] A major effect of this newly consolidated "urbanism of exception" has been to encourage "a constant proliferation of discretionary, site-specific exceptions and rules that apply only to micro-spaces," a "withering array of special allowances" that "conceal deliberate strategies that serve narrow interests outside the glare of public scrutiny."[112] Indeed, one of the most regressive political consequences of the regulatory rescalings associated with strategic urban megaprojects has been to empower private actors, corporate organizations, rentier elites, a broad array of quasi-governmental/semipublic agencies (such as public/private "partnerships" and urban development corporations), and other immediate "stakeholders" to make strategic land-use and planning decisions while strictly limiting public knowledge, democratic participation, and popular influence over the pathways of urban development that are thereby envisioned, established, and consolidated.[113]

In globalizing city-regions across Europe, then, the proliferation of urban megaprojects has been facilitated by, and in turn further extended, the rescaling of state space. The splintering of the capitalist urban fabric, the proliferation of highly localized regulatory enclaves, the multiplication of site-specific public-private partnerships, the neo-authoritarian fragmentation of urban governance, and the systemic disenfranchisement of local populations have powerfully reinforced one another, not least in the strategically rescaled zones of capital investment and regulatory reorganization in which urban megaprojects were constructed.

* * *

This analysis has offered no more than a general glimpse into the intricacies of late twentieth-century rescaling processes in the European Union, with specific reference to the remaking of urban governance and the closely associated politics of scale that has crystallized in and around Europe's globalizing cities. Amid the confusing, volatile, and contradictory geographies of contemporary geoeconomic restructuring, globalizing cities present a particularly intricate superimposition of social spaces in which inherited configurations of the capitalist urban fabric have been contested, destabilized, and reforged. The rescaling of urbanization has

---

[111] Swyngedouw, Moulaert, and Rodriguez, "Neoliberal Urbanization in Europe," 195, 196 passim.

[112] Murray, *Urbanism of Exception*, 65.

[113] This argument is productively and exhaustively developed in Murray, *Urbanism of Exception*.

been intimately intertwined with a concomitant rescaling of state space through which, simultaneously, (1) cities and metropolitan regions have been mobilized as territorially embedded productive forces in global circuits of capital and (2) distinctively post-Keynesian frameworks of urban governance have been experimentally rolled out and eventually consolidated across the European Union. These rescaled configurations of state space and urban governance have been constructed in close conjunction with the proliferation of political strategies designed to manage emergent urban crisis tendencies, to promote place-specific pathways of urban growth, and, in many cases, to insulate key dimensions of urban development from popular democratic influence. As such, they have also profoundly reshaped the sociospatial relations, strategies, and struggles that at once constitute, animate, and transform the capitalist urban fabric, within and beyond the worldwide archipelago of globalizing city-regions. Whether these disjointed strategies and pathways of interscalar transformation in and around Europe's major metropolitan regions might eventually establish new scalar fixes for some future crystallization of capitalist urbanization is a matter that can only be resolved through the politics of scale itself—that is, through ongoing struggles to reconstruct the scalar configurations in which urban life unfolds.

From the Urban Question to the Scale Question

This chapter has argued for a more sustained exploration of processes of state spatial restructuring in the study of global city formation. Global city formation cannot be adequately understood, I have argued, without an examination of the changing matrices of state spatial organization within which the entire archipelago of globalizing metropolitan regions (the WCA) is embedded. Whereas cities today operate increasingly as localized nodes of economic activity within a global urban hierarchy, post-Keynesian national states are meanwhile restructuring themselves to establish localized, territorially customized institutional capacities for enhancing the global structural competitiveness of major metropolitan regions. In this context, the local, metropolitan, and regional coordinates of state power have acquired a significantly enhanced operational and geopolitical significance through their strategies to enhance place-specific, territorially embedded productive forces. As of the closing decades of the twentieth century, then, the scalar configuration of state power had become a key stake of urban governance restructuring and, by implication, of ongoing struggles to reshape the capitalist urban fabric.

The interscalar transformations examined in this chapter have contributed to an extremely intricate intermeshing of state space and the capitalist urban fabric. However, rather than further consolidating the broadly nationalized, spatially isomorphic patterns of political-economic organization that Henri Lefebvre had associated, in the mid-1970s, with an ascendant "state mode of production," this progressively tighter interweaving of state space and urban space has been advanced precisely through the wide-ranging rescaling processes explored in this chapter. One of the most far-reaching spatial consequences of the latter has been precisely to disassemble the tendential "structured coherence" among national regulatory systems, national economies, and national urban hierarchies that had been at once imagined, naturalized, and actively promoted under the Fordist-Keynesian, national-developmentalist formation of capitalism. Consequently, as Swyngedouw notes:

> The geographical scale of the codification and implementation of institutional-regulatory systems . . . simultaneously defines and circumscribes the power of capital to command space. . . . A reduction in the scale of regulatory-institutional organisation increases the power of capital over space and constrains the command of territorially-organised interests to control territorial organisation. Scale reduction, therefore, reconfigures the boundaries of territorial organisation and intensifies inter-territorial struggle. The struggle over scale and its substantive definition works itself out as a struggle over the command over space and territory.[114]

The rescaling of state power and modes of territorial regulation is but one among many powerful expressions of the explosive politics of scale that has erupted during the last four decades of accelerated, crisis-induced geoeconomic restructuring. Insofar as today neither capital accumulation, state regulation, urbanization, nor economic governance privileges any single, territorially circumscribed spatial scale, the configuration of interscalar relations has become a major stake of sociopolitical contestation. In effect, scale relativization and the new politics of scale have been mutually animating one another, contributing to the further scalar mutation of the capitalist urban fabric, and to a dramatic recalibration of the interscalar configurations and politico-regulatory arrangements through which the latter is woven together. As densely organized sociospatial force fields in which transnational capital, national states, and diverse, territorially

---

[114] Swyngedouw, "Territorial Organization," 61.

embedded sociopolitical forces intersect and often directly clash, globalizing cities are thus strategic sites in which the stakes of this politics of scale are being fought out.

In considering the vast, wide-ranging research *problematique* that is opened up through this approach to contemporary rescaling processes, it is salient to recall Fernand Braudel's vivid description of the early modern world economy as a "jigsaw puzzle" composed of diverse, multiscalar forms of superimposed territorial organization, including cities, territorial states, quasi-states, empires, quasi-empires, zones of market exchange, economic cores, margins, frontiers, and peripheries.[115] In Braudel's historical investigations, the metaphor of the jigsaw puzzle provides a fruitful basis on which to investigate the broadly city-centered economies of early modern Europe in relation to the extended infrastructural configurations and politico-territorial systems in which they were embedded. In his studies, the variegated political-economic geographies of the early modern epoch are understood to have been organized not only on the basis of urban commercial centers and trading networks, but through diverse modes of territorialization (economic, infrastructural, and military) associated with states and empires.

Can Braudel's jigsaw-puzzle metaphor be productively reappropriated to characterize some of the emergent geographies of urbanization, state space, and scale relativization that have been explored in this chapter? As John Ruggie has classically argued, the Westphalian-modernist vision of global political-economic order presupposed tightly bounded, mutually exclusive, formally identical territories and symmetrically patterned, precision-nested scalar hierarchies.[116] To a significant degree, that vision of geopolitical space culminated during the Fordist-Keynesian, national-developmentalist period of world capitalist development, and it has clearly been destabilized and superseded during the post-1980s period. As those familiar, modernist, and nationally territorialized geographies are increasingly superseded and rewoven, might the Braudelian image of a jigsaw puzzle, with its haphazardly shaped pieces, its uneven contours, and its jagged interfaces, offer an alternative metaphorical reference point through which to envision emergent sociospatial transformations? In his foundational analysis of the contemporary "archipelago economy," Pierre Veltz proposes precisely such

[115] Braudel, *Perspective of the World*, 39.

[116] John Gerard Ruggie, "Territoriality and Beyond: Problematizing Modernity in International Relations," *International Organization* 47, no. 1 (1993): 139–74.

a neo-Braudelian methodological perspective on our present moment of restructuring:

> The time is over when it was possible to show, as Braudel did, an economic world organized into clear-cut layers, where big urban centres linked, by themselves, adjacent "slow" economies with the much more rapid rhythm of large-scale trade and finance. Today, everything occurs as if these superimposed layers were mixed and interpenetrated in (almost) all places. Short- and long-range interdependencies can no longer be separated from one another.[117]

Crucially, Veltz's argument is not only that inherited forms of urbanism, territorial bounding, and scale-making are being rearticulated, but that the networked relationships that have long woven together the most elementary units of territorial organization are likewise being reconstituted in profoundly unsettling ways. In this specific sense, Veltz proposes, the contemporary round of accelerated sociospatial restructuring has been manifested not just in a generalized intensification of geoeconomic interdependencies. Perhaps more consequentially, it has also entailed an epochal creative destruction of the very territorial frameworks, interscalar configurations, and socioecological circuits that support capital's everyday metabolism. Consequently, Veltz suggests, classically modernist conceptions of place-making, city/hinterland relations, interurban networks, economic territories, and nested scalar hierarchies are rendered increasingly inadequate and require creative reconceptualization.

For my purposes in this book, such bold declarations are invoked not to dramatize the putative "complexity" of emergent post-Fordist, post-Keynesian, post-welfare, postcolonial, or postmodern geographies; to imply that all inherited sociospatial categories should somehow be abandoned; or to fetishize the contextual specificity or putative exceptionalism of emergent local developmental pathways. The point, rather, is simply to underscore the immense epistemological and conceptual challenges associated with any attempt to decipher contemporary geographies of capitalist urbanization and urban governance restructuring. In a world whose most elementary units of sociospatial organization are being fundamentally reworked, the task of developing an appropriate conceptual lexicon and critical cartography for undertaking urban research is more urgently consequential than ever. In many cases, as with my own continued use of canonical, often taken-for-granted concepts such as city, place, region, territory, and scale—and,

---

[117] Veltz, "Dynamics of Production Systems," 84.

indeed, that of the urban itself—it is necessary to work within inherited analytical vocabularies that are saturated with increasingly problematic sociospatial assumptions, even as we strive to transcend and reinvent them. For this reason, considerable conceptual reflexivity is required in any investigation of contemporary sociospatial restructuring, whether in the field of urban studies or otherwise. In confronting that challenge, the task is not only to construct new sociospatial concepts, but to reappropriate inherited categories, cartographies, and methods of urban research in ways that might more effectively illuminate the volatile, relentlessly mutating worlds of urbanization in which we are situated.

In the early 1970s, Henri Lefebvre, Manuel Castells, and David Harvey radicalized the field of urban theory by presenting the "urban question" as a key analytical window for the critical investigation of capitalism's spatiotemporal dynamics, contradictions, and crisis tendencies. During the course of that decade, Lefebvre's subsequent engagements with what he termed "the scale question" entailed an important extension and state-theoretical elaboration of his earlier, reflexively multiscalar investigations of the capitalist urban fabric.[118] This chapter has connected several insights that are broadly derived from Lefebvre's state-theoretical, scale-attuned theorization of the urban question to more recent scholarly debates on global city formation, especially in the European context. Clearly, research on globalizing cities provides ample evidence that the urban question continues to offer an essential window into the variegated, uneven, and restlessly mutating political-economic geographies of capitalism. However, this analysis indicates various ways in which the urban question, in its contemporary form, is also being articulated in the form of a scale question.

From this point of view, the urban is a medium, mediation, and expression of diverse scaling and rescaling processes through which capitalist formations of territorial organization are produced and creatively destroyed. In post-Keynesian Europe, such rescaling processes have been animated through a range of experimental yet increasingly pervasive state spatial strategies designed to reshape the fabric of urbanization and, in so doing, to rejuvenate the accumulation of capital. In this sense, the urban is not a fixed container or bounded unit in which political-economic restructuring unfolds but is itself actively constituted and continually transformed through the constitutively multiscalar processes, crisis tendencies, strategies, struggles, and conflicts associated with the problem of territorial organization under

---

[118] See Chapter 2; as well as Henri Lefebvre, *De l'État: De Hegel à Marx par Staline*, vol. 2 (Paris: Union Generale d'Editions, 1976), 67.

capitalism. For this reason, contemporary sociospatial transformations present a major methodological challenge to the field of critical urban studies: to integrate analyses of contemporary urban restructuring with an account of the relentlessly mutating scalar configuration of the sociospatial relations. As capital's endemic fixity/motion contradiction is increasingly being articulated in the form of a politics of scale, any confrontation with the urban question leads directly into this broader critical interrogation of what Lefebvre aptly labeled "the scale question."

5
Cities and the Political Geographies of the "New" Economy

THE CONCEPT OF THE "new economy" has been deployed widely since the mid-1990s to refer to a variety of putative transformations in contemporary capitalism.[1] The notion is a slippery one, however, because it has been used in quite divergent ways in journalistic, corporate, political, and academic discourse. Nonetheless, even following the so-called dot-com bubble of 2000–2001 and the far more disruptive global financial crisis of 2007–2009, references to the new economy are still frequently mobilized to denote one or more among five key developments:

1. *Technological transformations.* In some uses, the notion of the new economy refers to the rise and increasing structural importance of various new information and communication technologies (ICTs). These knowledge-driven technologies are said to provide the foundations for a so-called third industrial revolution.

2. *A new growth model.* The notion of a new economy is frequently used to describe an emergent macroeconomic growth model, based upon low inflation and low unemployment, that would supposedly resolve

---

[1] For an excellent critical overview, see Ron Martin, "Making Sense of the 'New Economy': Realities, Myths and Geographies," in *Geographies of the New Economy: Critical Reflections*, ed. Peter Daniels, Andrew Leyshon, Michael Bradshaw, and Jonathan Beaverstock (London: Routledge, 2009), 15–31. The following discussion builds upon Martin's critical geographical analysis of "new economy" discourse and practice.

the economic bottlenecks and crisis tendencies of the 1980s. This new growth regime is usually said to have underpinned the "long Clinton boom" of the 1990s in the United States and to be readily transferable to other national and regional economies.

3. *The death of distance.* In many popular discussions, the notion of the new economy serves as a shorthand reference to the purported organizational flexibility and hypermobility of capitalist firms that rely extensively upon ICTs. In this view, because of their enhanced, space-annihilating technological capacities, new economy industries are no longer subject to traditional geographical constraints such as the need for physical proximity or dependence upon agglomeration economies.

4. *A new phase of capitalism.* Some authors have characterized the new economy in still more encompassing terms, as the manifestation of a new stage of capitalism based upon globalized, flexible production systems; knowledge-driven sectors; the extensive use of ICTs; increasingly flexible forms of labor; a restructured macroeconomic regime; and transformed modes of political-economic regulation.

5. *The transformation of governance.* Finally, many discussions of the new economy have postulated the decline of inherited, hierarchical-bureaucratic forms of national state regulation and the consequent consolidation of more flexible modes of economic governance based upon networked, informal interconnections among entrepreneurial public agencies and diverse private or semiprivate actors. In this view, the rise of the new economy signals the growing obsolescence not only of "old economy" manufacturing industries but also of inherited forms of national state power and hierarchical-bureaucratic organization.

This chapter rejects each of these prevalent assumptions regarding the putative "new economy" in the context of post-1980s patterns and pathways of sociospatial restructuring, state rescaling, and uneven spatial development. In contrast to mainstream assumptions, I argue that the discourse of the new economy generates an oversimplified characterization of contemporary technological, institutional, and sociospatial transformations, one that harmonizes the political-economic contradictions and sociospatial conflicts generated by the latter while deflecting attention away from their territorially uneven, polarizing, and destabilizing effects.[2] In particular, the notion

---

[2] See Martin, "Making Sense of the 'New Economy'"; and the other contributions to Peter Daniels, Andrew Leyshon, Michael Bradshaw, and Jonathan Beaverstock, eds., *Geographies of the New Economy: Critical Reflections* (London: Routledge, 2009).

of the new economy (1) exaggerates the obsolescence of "old economy" manufacturing industries; (2) overestimates the stability, coherence, and interterritorial generalizability of the 1990s "Clinton boom"; (3) brackets the continued embeddedness of ICTs within contextually specific conditions of production, institutional organization, and governance; (4) underestimates the continued structuring role of (rescaled forms of) national state power in urban governance; and (5) masks the role of ICT development in intensifying, not alleviating, sociospatial inequalities within and among urban regions.

Despite these problematic aspects of new economy discourse, the widespread use of this catchphrase to characterize important political-economic trends is indicative of deeper structural changes in the scalar configuration of capitalism since the 1980s. As such, the notion of the new economy should not be dismissed as a purely ideological fantasy. Indeed, much like the notion of neoliberalism, that of the new economy represents what Pierre Bourdieu has termed a "strong discourse" insofar as it "has behind it the powers of a world of power relations which it helps to make as it is, in particular by orienting the economic choices of those who dominate economic relations and so adding its own . . . force to those power relations."[3] From this perspective, a key task for critical studies of the new economy is to decipher the determinate "political operations" through which its core ideological, institutional, and spatial elements are being promulgated in relation to a persistently volatile, unevenly developed, and dynamically evolving landscape of capitalist urbanization.[4]

Accordingly, in contrast to mainstream discourses that connect the new economy to visions of declining state power and decentralized forms of network governance, I argue here that rescaled state institutions and policies have played an important role in promoting ICT development at strategic sites within the capitalist urban fabric. Accordingly, the notion of the new economy is used in this chapter not to describe a self-evident empirical reality or objective trend, but to characterize a variety of political *projects* of technological, regulatory, institutional, and geographical transformation that have been pursued within and among major urban regions since the crisis of North Atlantic Fordism and the subsequent relativization of scales in the 1970s. Specifically, the variegated transformations that are frequently classified under the rubric of the new economy are interpreted here as expressions of historically specific accumulation strategies through which rescaled state

---

[3] Pierre Bourdieu, *Acts of Resistance: Against the Tyranny of the Market* (New York: New Press, 1998), 95.

[4] Ibid.

institutions have been actively promoting and canalizing ICT-led indus-trial growth and, in so doing, have animated and mediated the production of new forms of urbanization.[5] From this point of view, the proliferation of new economy strategies has not entailed the death of distance, the end of geography, the homogenization of industrial landscapes, or the erosion of territorial regulation. Rather, along with regulatory projects oriented toward geoeconomic integration, Europeanization, neoliberalization, and austerity politics, new economy accumulation strategies must be viewed as impor-tant politico-institutional catalysts in generating the rescaled mosaics of un-even spatial development that have been crystallizing during the last four decades.[6]

The proliferation of strategies to promote the urban clustering of ICT-based, post-Fordist sectors has also been linked to a major transformation in the character of territorial regulation itself. In close conjunction with new economy accumulation strategies, the socially and spatially redistrib-utive Keynesian welfare national states of the Fordist-Keynesian, national-developmentalist era have been superseded since the 1980s by rescaled, post-Keynesian state formations that have promoted the geographical con-centration of productive capacities and socioeconomic assets within stra-tegic, putatively self-reliant metropolitan regions. This realignment of territorial regulation away from the traditional Keynesian focus on full em-ployment, demand management, state-subsidized collective consumption, and sociospatial equalization has also been intimately intertwined with un-even yet concerted processes of neoliberalization—manifested, for instance, in successive waves of deregulation, privatization, intergovernmental de-centralization, fiscal retrenchment, entrepreneurial policy experimentation, and place promotion—that have significantly impacted emergent patterns and pathways of urban development.[7] Such post-Keynesian, tendentially

---

[5] Bob Jessop defines an accumulation strategy as "a specific economic 'growth model' complete with its various extra-economic preconditions and . . . a general strategy appropriate to its realiza-tion." See Bob Jessop, *State Theory: Putting the Capitalist State in Its Place* (London: Polity, 1990), 198. To the degree that every accumulation strategy is spatially selective—that is, privileges spe-cific sites and scales of investment, production, employment, exchange, consumption, and so-cial reproduction and at once hinges upon and helps construct distinctive spatial divisions of labor—it generally involves an *urbanization strategy* as well.

[6] For general overviews of such trends, see Philip McMichael, *Development and Social Change* (London: Sage, 1996); Jamie Peck and Adam Tickell, "Neoliberalizing Space," in *Spaces of Neoliberalism*, ed. Neil Brenner and Nik Theodore (Oxford: Blackwell, 2002), 33–57; Ray Hudson, *Producing Places* (New York: Guilford, 2001); and Ray Hudson, *Production, Places and Environment* (London: Routledge, 2014).

[7] Neil Brenner and Nik Theodore, eds., *Spaces of Neoliberalism: Urban Restructuring in North America and Western Europe* (Oxford: Blackwell, 2002). On the variegation of

neoliberalizing rescalings of state spatial regulation are, I contend, a major political medium through which new urban spaces have been produced.[8] While this chapter focuses on the major territorial economies of Western Europe within an unevenly integrating European Union, broadly parallel pathways of state rescaling and urban-regional transformation have been crystallizing in several other major global economic regions, albeit necessarily in place- and territory-specific forms.[9]

To develop this line of argument, the next section discusses the endemic problem of uneven spatial development under capitalism and the changing role of national states in confronting it. On this basis, I consider the dominant spatial strategies through which Western European national states attempted to regulate uneven development at a national scale during the putative "golden age" of Fordist-Keynesian, national-developmentalist capitalism through the late 1970s. Subsequent sections outline the unraveling of such territorially redistributive regulatory strategies through various modalities of rescaling—in particular, through the curtailment of compensatory regional policies and the subsequent proliferation of projects to promote ICT-based sectors and other new industrial specializations within major cities and metropolitan regions. In this context, my analysis emphasizes the rescaling of the institutional arenas, operational strategies, and geographical targets of territorial regulation, and the general consequences of such rescalings for patterns of urban development. A concluding section summarizes the implications of this analysis for scholarly debates on the new economy and on the rescaling of the urban question.

---

neoliberalization processes, see Neil Brenner, Jamie Peck, and Nik Theodore, "Variegated Neoliberalization: Geographies, Modalities, Pathways," *Global Networks* 10, no. 2 (2010): 182–222; and Neil Brenner, Jamie Peck, and Nik Theodore, "After Neoliberalization?," *Globalizations* 7, no. 3 (2010): 313–30.

[8] Neil Brenner, *New State Spaces: Urban Governance and the Rescaling of Statehood* (New York: Oxford University Press, 2004); Erik Swyngedouw, "Neither Global nor Local: 'Glocalization' and the Politics of Scale," in *Spaces of Globalization*, ed. Kevin Cox (New York: Guilford Press, 1997), 137–66.

[9] See, for example, Bae-Gyoon Park, Richard Child Hill, and Asato Saito, eds., *Locating Neoliberalism in East Asia: Neoliberalizing Spaces in Developmental States* (Oxford: Blackwell, 2011); Linda Lobao and Lazarus Adua, "State Rescaling and Local Governments' Austerity Policies across the USA, 2001–2008," *Cambridge Journal of Regions, Economy and Society* 4, no. 3 (2011): 419–35; Kevin Cox, "'Rescaling the State' in Question," *Cambridge Journal of Regions, Economy and Society* 2, no. 1 (2009): 107–21; Julie-Anne Boudreau, Pierre Hamel, Bernard Jouve, and Roger Keil, "New State Spaces in Canada: Metropolitanization in Montreal and Toronto Compared," *Urban Geography* 28, no. 1 (2007): 30–53; and Robert Johnson and Rianne Mahon, "NAFTA, the Redesign, and Rescaling of Canada's Welfare State," *Studies in Political Economy* 76 (Autumn 2005): 7–30.

Urbanization, Territorial Organization, and the Regulation of Uneven Development

The geography of capitalism is polymorphic, multifaceted, and multiscalar, but the process of urbanization is one of its key expressions and products. Since the large-scale industrialization of capital in the nineteenth century, capitalist growth has been directly premised upon the production and continual restructuring of urban spaces.[10]

Across the world economy, the process of capitalist urbanization has been profoundly uneven: it has not entailed a linear expansion or simple diffusion of urban centers, but has produced a "highly disequilibrated form of growth" characterized by continual flux in the fortunes of places, regions, and territories as industries emerge, expand, mature, and decline.[11] While the major propulsive industries of each accumulation regime have generally clustered together within specialized local and regional economies, the maturation of such regimes unleashes significant tendencies toward geographical reorganization and dispersal among firms, workers, and industrial-logistical infrastructures. Indeed, many significant new industries have been initially consolidated in locations that lie outside established agglomeration economies, often in previously marginalized zones that offer emergent sectors important locational advantages and opportunities for innovative activity.[12] In urban and regional economies around the world, therefore, processes of industrial restructuring and technological change have reverberated in powerfully generative but also massively destructive ways. As industries are restructured, so too are cities, regions, and the broader spatial divisions of labor in which they are embedded. In this sense, the evolution of capitalism through successive regimes of accumulation involves not only changing industrial specializations, but recurrent waves of sociospatial restructuring in which (1) the propulsive centers of industrial dynamism are periodically shifted across regions, territories, and scales and (2) urban social, institutional, and infrastructural geographies are creatively destroyed in relation to the evolution of broader spatial divisions of labor and capital's crisis tendencies.[13] The urbanization process thus lies at the heart

---

[10] Henri Lefebvre, *The Urban Revolution*, trans. Robert Bononno (Minneapolis: University of Minnesota Press, 2003 [1970]).

[11] Michael Storper and Richard Walker, *The Capitalist Imperative* (New York: Basil Blackwell, 1989), 8.

[12] Ibid., 70–99.

[13] Ibid.

of the "continuous reshaping of geographical landscapes" that is endemic to capitalism as a uniquely dynamic yet constitutively crisis-prone historical system.[14]

It is apparent, then, that the process of industrial urbanization figures crucially in the production of uneven spatial development under capitalism. In general terms, uneven development refers to the circumstance that social, political, and economic processes under capitalism are not distributed uniformly across the earth's surface or among geographical scales, but are always differentiated among sociospatial configurations characterized by divergent socioeconomic conditions, infrastructural equipment, institutional arrangements, and developmental trajectories. Thus, within a capitalist geopolitical economy, inequalities are not only expressed socially, in the form of class and income polarization, but also spatially, through the polarization of development among different types of places, regions, territories, scales, and landscapes. While these socially produced patterns of core-periphery polarization are always articulated in historically and geographically specific forms, they necessarily entail the systematic concentration of socioeconomic assets, infrastructural investments, and developmental capacities within certain core zones and the chronic exclusion, marginalization, or peripheralization of other places, regions, and territories.[15]

The investigation of uneven spatial development has long been one of the foundational concerns of critical geographical political economy. As Neil Smith has argued in his seminal work on the topic, patterns of uneven geographical development under capitalism are not merely the contingent byproducts of precapitalist geographical differences or of individual, household, or firm-level locational decisions.[16] Rather, they represent systemic expressions of the endemic tension under capitalism between the drive to equalize capital investment across space and the pressure to differentiate such investment in order to exploit place-, region-, territory-, and scale-specific conditions for accumulation. On the one hand, the coercive forces of intercapitalist competition pressure individual firms to replicate one another's profit-making strategies in dispersed geographical locations, and thus to promote a spatial equalization of the conditions for accumulation. On the other hand, the forces of intercapitalist competition engender an equally powerful process of geographical differentiation in which individual firms continually seek out place-specific locational assets that may enable them to protect, maintain, or

---

[14] David Harvey, *The Urban Experience* (Baltimore: Johns Hopkins University Press, 1989), 192.

[15] Storper and Walker, *Capitalist Imperative*.

[16] Neil Smith, *Uneven Development* (New York: Blackwell, 1984).

enhance their competitive advantages. Consequently, each regime of capitalist growth is grounded upon historically specific patterns of uneven geographical development in which the contradictory interplay of equalization and differentiation is materialized. The resultant patterns of sociospatial polarization crystallize not only horizontally, among different types of places, regions, and territories, but also vertically, among various geographical scales stretching from the local, the regional, and the national to the continental and the global. The contours of this uneven geography are thus never inscribed permanently onto the variegated landscapes of capitalism, but are reworked continually through capital's restless, endemically crisis-prone developmental dynamic and through a range of political strategies intended to subject the latter to some measure of regulatory control.

Uneven development is not merely an aggregate geographical effect of differential patterns of capital investment, but engenders a variety of recurrent regulatory problems, both within and beyond the circuit of capital, that may severely destabilize the accumulation process. Indeed, any given historical pattern of uneven geographical development may serve not only as a *basis* for the accumulation process but may also become a serious *barrier* to the latter.[17] For instance, the polarization of territorial development between dynamic urban cores and peripheralized regions may enable certain individual capitals to reap the benefits of scale economies and other externalities, but it may also generate disruptive political-economic effects that threaten to destabilize the space economy as a whole. An erosion of national industrial capacities may ensue as peripheralized regional economies are constrained to adopt cost-based, defensive strategies of adjustment, leading to a premature downgrading of local infrastructures and to worsening life conditions for many local inhabitants.[18] Even within the most economically dynamic urban agglomerations, the problem of uneven development may also "come home to roost" as social polarization, overaccumulation, the perennial threat of capital flight, and various negative externalities (such as infrastructural stress, housing shortages, traffic congestion, and environmental destruction) unsettle established patterns of industrial development.[19] If levels of sociospatial inequality are not maintained within politically acceptable

---

[17] Jamie Peck and Adam Tickell, "The Social Regulation of Uneven Development: 'Regulatory Deficit', England's South East, and the Collapse of Thatcherism," *Environment and Planning A* 27 (1995): 15–40.

[18] Danièle Leborgne and Alain Lipietz, "Two Social Strategies in the Production of New Industrial Spaces," in *Industrial Change and Regional Development*, ed. Georges Benko and Michael Dunford (London: Belhaven, 1992), 27–49.

[19] Harvey, *Urban Experience*, 144.

limits, disruptive sociopolitical conflicts—between classes, class fractions, growth coalitions, social movements, and other place-based alliances—may subsequently arise, often resulting in legitimation crises for ruling political alliances. Uneven geographical development may thus engender not only new profit-making opportunities for capital, but potentially destabilizing, disruptive social and political consequences that, in the absence of effective regulatory management, can seriously erode the institutional preconditions needed for sustained capital accumulation.

While most studies of uneven geographical development have focused on the interplay between capital investment patterns and the evolution of territorial inequalities, the preceding considerations direct attention to the role of state institutions, at various spatial scales, in mediating, shaping, and reacting to these processes. Such an inquiry is of considerable importance because, particularly since the consolidation of organized capitalism during the early twentieth century, national states have mobilized a variety of spatial policies designed precisely to influence the geographies of capital investment and, thereby, to manage the volatile patterns of uneven development that have crystallized within their territorial boundaries. For example, strategies of territorial redistribution and other compensatory regional policies were deployed after World War II to promote the equalization of industry across the national territory, and thus to alleviate the more pernicious, polarizing effects of intranational uneven development. In most Western European countries, some version of this managerial, redistributive, and cohesion-oriented regulatory strategy was mobilized intensively by national states as of the 1930s, and reached its historical highpoint during the mid-1970s, as the Fordist regime of accumulation was being dismantled throughout the North Atlantic zone. Subsequently, however, rescaled strategies of territorial development, regionalization, and place promotion have been rolled out to channel socioeconomic capacities and large-scale infrastructural investments into the most globally competitive locations within each national territory. Since the early 1980s, this entrepreneurial, competitiveness-driven, growth-oriented, and broadly neoliberalizing approach to spatial regulation has largely superseded inherited formations of spatial Keynesianism. One of its major consequences has been to intensify intranational spatial differentiation and territorial inequality across the European Union, and thereby to produce a more splintered pattern of urbanization.[20]

[20] David Harvey, "From Managerialism to Entrepreneurialism: The Transformation in Urban Governance in Late Capitalism," *Geografiska Annaler: Series B Human Geography* 71, no. 1 (1989): 3–17; Stephen Graham and Simon Marvin, *Splintering Urbanism* (New York: Routledge,

It is against this background that we can begin to analyze the interplay between the new economy accumulation strategies of the post-1980s period and the evolution of territorial regulation. In what follows, I trace the changing political strategies through which, since the late 1950s, Western European national states have attempted to manage the problem of uneven development within their territories. Since the era of high Fordism, four successive approaches to the regulation of uneven spatial development have crystallized, each of which has been premised upon historically specific forms of urban and regional governance. The tumultuous, wide-ranging, and still-ongoing rescalings of national state power of the post-1980s period have been intertwined not only with the mobilization of new accumulation strategies intended to promote ICT-led, post-Fordist forms of industrial growth in major metropolitan regions but also, more generally, with the rolling out of new, rescaled approaches to the regulation of uneven spatial development within an increasingly scale-relativized geoeconomic configuration. The new urban spaces of the post-Keynesian epoch have been profoundly shaped through these rescaled state spatial strategies.

Geographies of Territorial Regulation at the Highpoint of Spatial Keynesianism

The economic geography of postwar Fordism in Western Europe was composed of a dispersed yet hierarchical topology in which a functional division of space was imposed at various geographical scales.[21] Spatial divisions of labor emerged within each national territory in the form of hierarchical relationships between large-scale metropolitan regions, in which the lead firms within the major, propulsive Fordist industries were clustered, and smaller cities, towns, and peripheral zones, in which branch plants, input and service providers, and other subordinate economic functions were located. In the Western European context, the geographical heartlands of the Fordist accumulation regime stretched from the Industrial Triangle of northern Italy through the German Ruhr district to northern France and the

---

2001); Michael Dunford and Diane Perrons, "Regional Inequality, Regimes of Accumulation and Economic Development in Contemporary Europe," *Transactions of the Institute of British Geographers* 19 (1994): 163–82; Peter Marcuse and Ronald van Kempen, eds., *Globalizing Cities: A New Spatial Order?* (Cambridge, MA: Blackwell, 2001).

[21] Alain Lipietz, "The National and the Regional: Their Autonomy Vis-à-Vis the Capitalist World Crisis," in *Transcending the State-Global Divide*, ed. Ronen P. Palan and Barry K. Gills (Boulder, CO: Lynne Rienner Publishers, 1994), 23–44.

English Midlands; but each of these regional production complexes was in turn embedded within a nationally specific system of production. Throughout the postwar period, these and many other major European urban regions and their surrounding industrial satellites were characterized by consistent demographic growth and industrial expansion. As the Fordist accumulation regime reached maturity, a major decentralization of capital investment unfolded as large firms began more extensively to relocate branch plants from core regions into peripheral spaces.[22] Under these conditions, urban and regional governance was increasingly nationalized, as Western European states attempted to construct centralized bureaucratic hierarchies, to establish nationally standardized frameworks for capitalist production and collective consumption, to underwrite urban and regional industrial growth, and to alleviate uneven spatial development throughout their national territories.

To standardize the provision of welfare services and to coordinate national economic policies, national states centralized the instruments for regulating urban development, thereby transforming local states into transmission belts for centrally determined policy regimes.[23] Within this managerial framework of urban governance, the state's overarching function at the urban scale was the reproduction of the labor force through public investments in housing, transportation, social services, and other public goods, all of which were intended to replicate certain basic standards of social welfare and infrastructure provision across the national territory.[24] In this manner, local states were instrumentalized "to carry out a national strategy based on a commitment to regional balance and even growth."[25] Insofar as the national economy was viewed as the primary terrain for state action, local and regional economies were treated as mere subunits of relatively autocentric national economic spaces dominated by large-scale corporations. These centrally financed local welfare policies also provided important elements of the social wage, and thus contributed significantly to the generalization of the mass consumption practices upon which the Fordist mode of growth was contingent.[26] As

---

[22] Andrés Rodriguez-Pose, *The Dynamics of Regional Growth in Europe* (Oxford: Clarendon Press, 1998).

[23] Margit Mayer, "The Shifting Local Political System in European Cities," in *Cities and Regions in the New Europe*, ed. Mick Dunford and Grigoris Kafkalas (London: Belhaven Press, 1992), 255–76.

[24] Manuel Castells, *The Urban Question* (Cambridge, MA: MIT Press, 1977 [1972]).

[25] Mark Goodwin and Joe Painter, "Local Governance, the Crises of Fordism and the Changing Geographies of Regulation," *Transactions of the Institute of British Geographers* 21 (1996): 646.

[26] Ibid., 641.

theorists of the dual state subsequently recognized, this pervasive localization of the state's collective consumption functions during the postwar period was a key institutional feature within a broader scalar division of regulation in which production-oriented state policies were generally organized at a national scale.[27] Accordingly, throughout this period, state strategies to manage urban economic development were mobilized primarily at a national scale rather than through independent regional or local initiatives. In this context, a range of national social and economic policy initiatives—including demand management policies, nationalized ownership of key industries (coal, shipbuilding, power, aerospace), the expansion of public sector employment, military spending, and major expenditures on housing, transportation, and public utilities—served to underwrite the growth of major urban and regional economies.[28]

Even though major cities and metropolitan regions received the bulk of large-scale public infrastructure investments and welfare services during the Fordist-Keynesian epoch, such city-centric policy initiatives were counterbalanced through a variety of state expenditures, loan programs, and compensatory regional aid policies designed to spread growth into underdeveloped regions and rural peripheries across the national territory. From the Italian Mezzogiorno and Spanish Andalusia to western and southern France, the agricultural peripheries and border zones of West Germany, the Limburg coal-mining district of northern Belgium, the Dutch northeastern peripheries, the northwestern regions and islands of Denmark, the Scandinavian North, western Ireland, and the declining industrial zones of the English North, South Wales, parts of Scotland, and much of Northern Ireland, each European country had its so-called problem areas or lagging regions, generally composed of economic zones that had been marginalized during previous rounds of industrial development or that were locked into increasingly obsolete technological-industrial infrastructures.[29] Consequently, throughout the postwar period until the late 1970s, a range of regional policies were introduced that explicitly targeted such peripheralized spaces. Generally justified in the name of "balanced national development" and "spatial equalization," these redistributive spatial programs provided various forms of financial aid, locational incentives, and transfer payments

[27] Peter Saunders, *Urban Politics: A Sociological Interpretation* (London: Heinemann, 1979).

[28] Ron Martin and Peter Sunley, "The Post-Keynesian State and the Space Economy," in *Geographies of Economies*, ed. Roger Lee and Jane Wills (London: Arnold, 1997), 280.

[29] Hugh Clout, ed., *Regional Development in Western Europe*, 2nd ed. (New York: John Wiley & Sons, 1981).

to promote industrial growth and economic regeneration outside the dominant city cores, and they often channeled major public infrastructural investments into such locations. Such resource transfers appear to have significantly impacted the intranational geographies of uneven development during the postwar period, contributing to an unprecedented convergence of per capita disposable income within most Western European states.[30] This nationally oriented project of industrial decentralization, urban deconcentration, and spatial equalization was arguably the political lynchpin of spatial Keynesianism, the system of state territorial regulation that prevailed throughout the Fordist-Keynesian period of capitalist development across Western Europe.[31]

Within this nationalized system of urban governance, metropolitan political institutions acquired an important role in mediating between managerial local states and centrally organized, redistributive forms of spatial planning. Particularly between the mid-1960s and the early 1970s, consolidated metropolitan institutions were established in many major Western European city-regions.[32] These region-wide administrative bodies were widely viewed as mechanisms for rationalizing welfare service provision and for reducing administrative inefficiencies within rapidly expanding metropolitan agglomerations. Metropolitan institutions thus served as a key, coordinating administrative tier within the centralized hierarchies of intergovernmental relations that prevailed within the Keynesian welfare state apparatus. As suburbanization and industrial decentralization proceeded apace, metropolitan political institutions were increasingly justified as a means to establish a closer spatial correspondence between governmental jurisdictions and functional territories.[33] By the early 1970s, metropolitan authorities had acquired important roles in guiding industrial expansion, infrastructural investment, and population settlement beyond traditional city cores into suburban fringes, primarily through the deployment of comprehensive land-use plans and other mechanisms intended to influence intrametropolitan locational patterns. In this sense, metropolitan institutions appear to have significantly influenced the geographies of urbanization during the era of high Fordism.

---

[30] Dunford and Perrons, "Regional Inequality."

[31] Martin and Sunley, "Post-Keynesian State"; see also Brenner, *New State Spaces*, chap. 4.

[32] Michael Keating, "The Invention of Regions: Political Restructuring and Territorial Government in Western Europe," *Environment and Planning C: Government and Policy* 15 (1997): 383–98.

[33] Christian Lefèvre, "Metropolitan Government and Governance in Western Countries: A Critical Overview," *International Journal of Urban and Regional Research* 22, no. 1 (1998): 9–25.

In sum, spatial Keynesianism is best understood as a broad constellation of national state strategies designed to promote capitalist industrial growth by alleviating uneven geographical development within each national territory. Spatial Keynesianism intensified the nationalization of state *and* urban space in two senses: first, it entailed the establishment of a well-coordinated system of subnational institutions for the territorial regulation of urban development; second, it entailed the embedding of major local and regional economies within a hierarchically configured, nationally focused political-economic geography. Accordingly, throughout the postwar period, local governments were subsumed within nationally organized institutional matrices defined by relatively centralized control over local socioeconomic policies, technocratic frameworks of metropolitan governance, extensive interregional resource transfers, and redistributive forms of national spatial planning. Taken together, this multiscalar constellation of state institutions and regulatory operations promoted a structured coherence for capitalist industrial growth (1) by transforming urban spaces into the localized building blocks for national economic development and (2) by spreading urbanization as evenly as possible across the national territory (Figure 5.1).

By the early 1970s, however, the aspiration of transcending uneven spatial development within a relatively closed national territory appeared as short-lived as the Fordist accumulation regime itself.

Crisis Management and the New Politics of Endogenous Growth

New approaches to the political regulation of uneven spatial development began gradually to crystallize as of the early 1970s, as the Fordist developmental regime was eroded.[34] A number of major geoeconomic shifts occurred during this era that decentered the predominant role of the national scale as a locus of political-economic coordination and led to the transfer of new regulatory responsibilities upward to supranational institutional tiers such as the European Union and downward to regional and local levels of state organization.

These rescalings of state space were mediated through a range of relatively ad hoc, trial-and-error regulatory responses, crisis management strategies, and political experiments. At a national scale, diverse political alliances mobilized strategies of crisis management to defend the institutional infrastructures of the Fordist-Keynesian order. From the first oil shock

[34] Lipietz, "National and the Regional."

Geoeconomic and geopolitical context
• 1950s–mid-1970s: high Fordism, Cold War, global decolonization • Differentiation of global economic activity among distinct national economic systems under embedded liberalism

Privileged spatial target(s)
• National economy

Major goals
• Deconcentration of population, industry and infrastructure investment from major urban centers into rural peripheries and "underdeveloped," "lagging" or "backward" zones • Replication of standardized economic assets, investments and public goods across the entire surface of the national territory • Establishment of a nationally standardized system of infrastructural facilities throughout the national economy • Alleviation of uneven development within national economies: uneven spatial development is seen as a limit or barrier to stabilized industrial growth

Dominant policy mechanisms
• Locational subsidies to large firms • Local social welfare policies and collective consumption investments • Redistributive regional policies • National spatial planning systems and public infrastructural investments

Spatiotemporality of economic development
• National developmentalism: management of the entire national economy as a relatively integrated, self-enclosed territorial unit moving along a linear developmental trajectory

FIGURE 5.1 Spatial Keynesianism and the political regulation of uneven development.

of 1973 until around 1979, traditional recipes of national demand management prevailed throughout the Organisation of Economic Co-operation and Development (OECD) zone as central governments tried desperately to recreate the conditions for a Fordist virtuous circle of growth. However, as Bob Jessop remarks of the British case, such countercyclical tactics ultimately amounted to no more than an "eleventh hour, state-sponsored Fordist modernisation," for they were incapable of solving, simultaneously, the dual problems of escalating inflation and mass unemployment.[35] Meanwhile, as

---

[35] Bob Jessop, "Conservative Regimes and the Transition to Post-Fordism: The Cases of Great Britain and West Germany," in *Capitalist Development and Crisis Theory*, ed. Mark Gottdiener and Nicos Komninos (New York: St. Martin's Press, 1989), 269.

the boom regions of Fordism experienced sustained economic crises, the policy framework of spatial Keynesianism was further differentiated to include deindustrializing, distressed cities and manufacturing centers as explicit geographical targets for various forms of state assistance and financial aid. In contrast to traditional Keynesian forms of spatial policy, which had focused almost exclusively upon underdeveloped regions and peripheral zones, explicitly urban policies were now introduced in several Western European states to address the specific socioeconomic problems of large cities, such as mass unemployment, deskilling, capital flight, and infrastructural decay. In this manner, many of the redistributive policy relays associated with spatial Keynesianism were significantly expanded. Crucially, however, even though the spatial targets of regional policies were now differentiated to include urban areas as key recipients of state support, the national state's underlying commitment to the project of spatial equalization at a national scale was reinforced throughout the 1970s.

Even as these new forms of state support for urban development were extended, a range of nationally imposed policy initiatives and intergovernmental realignments began to unsettle the entrenched, managerial-welfarist framework that had prevailed throughout the postwar period. Thus, especially as of the late 1970s, the national scale likewise became an important institutional locus for political projects that aimed to dismantle many of the major redistributive policy relays associated with the Keynesian welfare national state. During the post-1970s recession, as national governments were pressured to rationalize government expenditures, central grants to subnational administrative levels, including regions and localities, were diminished. Across Western Europe, these new forms of fiscal austerity caused local governments to become more dependent upon locally collected taxes and nontax revenues such as charges and user fees.[36] In the immediate aftermath of these shifts, many local governments attempted to adjust to the new fiscal conditions by delaying capital expenditures, drawing upon liquid assets, and engaging in deficit spending, but these proved to be no more than short-term stopgap measures. Subsequently, additional local revenues were sought in, among other sources, economic development projects.[37] Whereas the new national urban policies introduced during this period enabled some older industrial cities to capture supplementary public resources, most local governments were nonetheless confronted with major

---

[36] Poul E. Mouritzen, *Managing Cities in Austerity* (London: Sage, 1992).

[37] Joanne Fox-Przeworski, "Changing Intergovernmental Relations and Urban Economic Development," *Environment and Planning C: Government and Policy* 4, no. 4 (1986): 423–39.

new budgetary constraints due to the dual impact of national fiscal retrenchment and intensifying local socioeconomic problems. One of the most significant institutional outcomes of the national fiscal squeeze of the 1970s,
therefore, was to pressure municipalities to seek new sources of revenue
through a proactive mobilization of economic development projects and inward investment schemes.[38]

Under these conditions, a variety of "bootstraps" strategies intended to
promote economic growth "from below," without extensive reliance upon
national subsidies, proliferated in major cities and regions.[39] In contrast to
their earlier focus on welfarist redistribution, local governments now began
to introduce a range of strategies intended to rejuvenate local economies, beginning with land-assembly programs and land-use planning schemes and
subsequently expanding to diverse firm-based, area-based, sectoral, and job
creation measures.[40] Although this new politics of urban economic development would subsequently be diffused in diverse political forms throughout
the Western European city-system, during the 1970s it remained most
prevalent within manufacturing-based cities and regions of the so-called
old economy in which industrial restructuring had generated particularly
serious socioeconomic problems and infrastructural crises.[41] Thus, even
as national governments continued to promote economic integration and
territorial equalization at a national scale, neocorporatist alliances between
state institutions, trade unions, and other community-based organizations
within rustbelt cities and regions from the German Ruhr district to the
English Midlands elaborated regionally specific sectoral, technology, and employment policies to promote what was then popularly labeled "endogenous
growth."[42] The goal of these leftist, neocorporatist, and social democratic
alliances was to establish negotiated strategies of industrial restructuring in
which economic regeneration would be linked directly to social priorities

---

[38] Margit Mayer, "Post-Fordist City Politics," in *Post-Fordism: A Reader*, ed. Ash Amin
(Cambridge, MA: Blackwell, 1994), 316–37.

[39] Udo Bullmann, *Kommunale Strategien gegen Massenarbeitslosigkeit: Ein Einstieg in die
sozialökologische Erneuerung* (Opladen: Leske and Budrich, 1991).

[40] Aram Eisenschitz and Jamie Gough, *The Politics of Local Economic Development*
(New York: Macmillan, 1993); Tim Hall and Phil Hubbard, eds., *The Entrepreneurial
City: Geographies of Politics, Regime and Representation* (London: Wiley, 1998).

[41] Michael Parkinson, "The Rise of the Entrepreneurial European City: Strategic Responses to
Economic Changes in the 1980s," *Ekistics* 350 (1991): 299–307.

[42] Ulf Hahne, *Regionalentwicklung durch Aktivierung intraregionaler Potentiale*, Schriften des
Instituts für Regionalforschung der Universität Kiel, Band 8 (Munich: Florenz, 1985); Walter
Stöhr and David R. Taylor, *Development from Above or Below? The Dialectics of Regional Planning
in Developing Countries* (New York: Wiley, 1981).

such as intraregional redistribution, job creation, vocational retraining initiatives, and class compromise. The basic Fordist-Keynesian priorities of social redistribution, territorial equalization, and class compromise were thus maintained, albeit within the more geographically bounded parameters of regional and/or local economies rather than as a project that would be generalized throughout the national territory.

The 1970s are thus best viewed as a transitional period characterized by intense interscalar struggles among political alliances concerned to preserve the nationalized institutional infrastructures of spatial Keynesianism and other, newly formed political coalitions striving to introduce more decentralized approaches to promoting economic regeneration "from below." Although the new regulatory frameworks sought by such modernizing coalitions remained relatively inchoate, at this time, they shared an explicit rejection of nationally encompassing models of territorial development and a broad commitment to the goal of promoting place-specific trajectories of socioeconomic development. In this sense, the proliferation of local and regional economic initiatives during this period destabilized the nationalizing approach to the regulation of uneven spatial development that had prevailed during the postwar "golden age." While central governments generally continued, throughout the 1970s, to promote such nationalizing, spatially redistributive agendas, the diffusion of this new bootstraps strategy during the same decade appears, retrospectively, to have entailed a major de facto modification of the inherited institutional architecture of spatial Keynesianism. It also opened up a politico-institutional space in which (national, regional, and local) state institutions could, in subsequent decades, mobilize new accumulation strategies oriented toward cultivating and territorializing ICT-based, post-Fordist industrial growth within strategically positioned cities and metropolitan regions.

The Rescaling of State Space and the Quest for a "New" Urban Economy

The crisis of the Fordist developmental model intensified during the 1980s, leading to a new round of state spatial restructuring and urban-industrial transformation under conditions of accelerating scale relativization. The strategies of crisis management introduced during the 1970s had neither restored the conditions for a new accumulation regime nor successfully resolved the deepening problems of economic stagnation, rising unemployment, and industrial decline. Consequently, during the course of the 1980s, most European national governments abandoned traditional Keynesian macroeconomic policies in favor of monetarism; a competitive balance of payments replaced full employment as the overarching goal of monetary and fiscal policy.[43] By the late 1980s, neoliberal political agendas such as welfare state retrenchment, trade liberalization, privatization, and deregulation had been adopted not only in the United Kingdom under Thatcher and in West Germany under Kohl but also in more socially moderate, hybrid forms in many traditionally social democratic or Christian/social democratic countries such as the Netherlands, Belgium, France, Spain, Denmark, and Sweden.[44]

This geopolitical sea change entailed the imposition of additional fiscal constraints upon most municipal and metropolitan governments, whose revenues had already been significantly retrenched during the preceding decade. Political support for large-scale strategic planning projects waned and welfare state bureaucracies were increasingly dismantled, downsized, or restructured, including at metropolitan and municipal levels. Indeed, during the mid-1980s, major metropolitan institutions such as the Greater London Council and the Rijnmond in Rotterdam were summarily abolished. Elsewhere, metropolitan institutions were formally preserved but significantly weakened in practice due to centrally imposed budgetary pressures and enhanced competition between city cores and suburban peripheries for capital investment and public subsidies.[45] The fiscal squeeze upon public expenditure in municipalities and the dramatic weakening of metropolitan governance institutions were thus among the important localized expressions of the processes of post-Keynesian state retrenchment that were gaining momentum in Western Europe during the 1980s. As of this decade, the national preconditions for municipal Keynesianism were systematically eroded. Local and metropolitan governments were now increasingly forced to "fend for themselves" in securing a fiscal basis for their regulatory activities and public investments.[46]

During the same period, a new mosaic of urban and regional development began to crystallize within a tendentially scale-relativized geoeconomic and European constellation. Across the Western European urban system, the crisis of North Atlantic Fordism was triggering the tumultuous decline

---

[43] Fritz W. Scharpf, *Crisis and Choice in European Social Democracy* (Ithaca, NY: Cornell University Press, 1991).

[44] Martin Rhodes, "'Subversive Liberalism': Market Integration, Globalization and the European Welfare State," *Journal of European Public Policy* 2, no. 3 (1995): 384–406.

[45] Max Barlow, *Metropolitan Government* (New York: Routledge, 1991).

[46] Mayer, "Post-Fordist City Politics."

of many large-scale manufacturing regions whose economies had previously been grounded primarily upon Fordist mass production industries. Meanwhile, a number of formerly lagging regions were being transformed into dynamic locations for ICT investment and flexible production systems.[47] Amid this see-saw movement of uneven spatial development, established metropolitan cores such as London, Amsterdam, Paris, Frankfurt, Milan, and Zurich were undergoing significant socioeconomic, infrastructural, and institutional realignments as they acquired a renewed significance as strategic nodal points within global and European financial networks. In this way, as Pierre Veltz explains, the post-1970s period witnessed the consolidation of a European "archipelago economy" in which corporate headquarters, major decision-making centers, and many high-value-added economic activities were concentrated within strategically positioned metropolitan regions.[48] For Veltz, this tendency toward "metropolitanization" embodied a dramatic intensification of territorial divisions across Europe—including an intra-European divide between "winning" and "losing" regions; various intranational divides between booming urban cores and declining manufacturing zones or depressed rural peripheries; intraregional divides between central city cores and their surrounding hinterlands; and intrametropolitan divides between wealthy or gentrified areas and disadvantaged, excluded neighborhoods or peri-urban settlements.[49] Following the consolidation of the Single European Market, the launch of the euro, and various subsequent waves of eastward enlargement, these polarizing tendencies have been further entrenched at European and national scales.[50]

In an influential report prepared for the national French spatial planning agency DATAR in the late 1980s, Roger Brunet famously described the central corridor of European urban development as a "blue banana" whose strategic importance would be further enhanced as global and European economic

---

[47] Allen J. Scott and Michael Storper, "Industrialization and Regional Development," in *Pathways to Industrialization and Regional Development*, ed. Michael Storper and Allen J. Scott (New York: Routledge, 1992).

[48] Pierre Veltz, *Mondialisation, villes et territoires: L'économie d'archipel* (Paris: Presses Universitaires de France, 1993).

[49] Pierre Veltz, "European Cities in the World Economy," in *Cities in Contemporary Europe*, ed. Arnaldo Bagnasco and Patrick Le Galés (New York: Cambridge University Press, 2000), 33–34; see also Stefan Krätke, *Stadt, Raum, Ökonomie* (Basel: Birkhäuser Verlag, 1995); and Stefan Krätke, "Stadtsystem im internationalen Kontext und Vergleich," in *Kommunalpolitik*, ed. Roland Roth and Hellmut Wollmann (Opladen: Leske Verlag, 1993), 176–93.

[50] Peter J. Taylor and Michael Hoyler, "The Spatial Order of European Cities under Conditions of Contemporary Globalization," *Tijdschrift voor Economische en Sociale Geografie* 91, no. 2 (2000): 176–89; Dunford and Perrons, "Regional Inequality."

integration proceeded.[51] Economic activities, technological capacities, and advanced infrastructural investments would, Brunet predicted, be increasingly concentrated within a "vital axis" stretching from the South East of England, Brussels, Paris, and the Dutch Randstad through the German Rhineland southward to Zurich and the northern Italian Industrial Triangle surrounding Milan. Notably, Brunet's famous representation of Western Europe's urbanized boom zone represented a nearly exact inversion of the political geography of development zones that had been supported through compensatory regional policy interventions during the era of spatial Keynesianism. In stark contrast to the notions of cumulative causation upon which earlier regional policies had been based, in which the spatial diffusion of growth potentials was seen to benefit both cores and peripheries, Brunet's model of the blue banana implied that the most globally networked metropolitan regions would be intermeshed into a powerful, relatively autonomous urban network dominated by advanced infrastructural facilities, high-value-added activities, and new economy industries. The consolidation of this core European megalopolis would, Brunet also predicted, leave other European cities, regions, and hinterlands essentially to fend for themselves or risk being further marginalized in the new geoeconomic context.

As Brunet's model dramatically illustrated, the tumultuous political-economic transformations of the 1980s were causing the geographies of postwar spatial Keynesianism to be, in effect, turned inside out. As of this decade, industrial growth was no longer being spread outward from developed, densified urban cores into the marginalized peripheries of each national economy, but was instead being systematically canalized into the most strategically positioned metropolitan regions within European and global spatial divisions of labor. Notably, Brunet depicted these urban cores as the territorially integrated heartlands of new economy industries based upon ICTs, advanced producer and financial services, and other high-technology sectors. In his model, the core European megalopolis was surrounded by, but now increasingly delinked from, a variegated macroterritorial landscape of declining manufacturing regions, marginalized hinterlands, and outlying peripheries that were locked into "old economy" technologies, industries, land-use systems, and institutional forms.

Despite its serious limitations as a social scientific depiction of European political-economic space in the late twentieth century, the wide influence of Brunet's blue banana model was emblematic of a major rescaling of territorial regulation that was gaining momentum throughout Western Europe

---

[51] Roger Brunet, *Les villes 'europeennes'* (Paris: DATAR, 1989).

as of the 1980s.[52] As urban economic restructuring intensified in conjunction with global and European integration, Western European national governments began more explicitly to target major cities and metropolitan regions as the locational keys to national economic competitiveness.[53] In the "Europe of regions"—a catchphrase that became increasingly important in EU-level, national, and subnational policy discussions during this period—cities were no longer seen merely as containers of declining industries and socioeconomic problems, but were now increasingly viewed as dynamic growth engines through which ICT-based, post-Fordist sectors could be fostered and territorially embedded. This view of cities as incubators for the new economy, and thus, as essential national economic assets, became increasingly hegemonic in mainstream policy circles by the late 1980s, as national and local governments prepared for the introduction of the Single European Market.

As Western European states attempted to transform their most economically powerful cities and metropolitan regions into growth engines for ICT-based, post-Fordist industrial growth, they also developed new, rescaled approaches to the regulation of uneven spatial development. Initially, with the ascendancy of neoliberal reform initiatives and the imposition of new forms of fiscal austerity, inherited programs of territorial redistribution were scaled back, thereby exposing local and regional economies more directly to the pressures of Europe-wide and global economic competition.[54] Such policy initiatives were aimed primarily at reducing public expenditures and at undermining traditional forms of *dirigiste*, centralized economic management.[55] As we saw previously, the local economic initiatives of the 1970s emerged in a politico-institutional context in which central governments remained broadly committed to the neo-Keynesian project of promoting national territorial equalization. In stark contrast, the local economic initiatives of the 1980s were articulated under geopolitical, European, and national conditions in which neoliberal policy orthodoxies were acquiring an unprecedented influence, leading to a systematic marginalization or abandonment of inherited compensatory regional policy agendas. In this transformed

---

[52] For an illuminating critique of Brunet's model, see Stefan Krätke, Susanne Heeg, and Rolf Stein, *Regionen im Umbruch* (Frankfurt: Campus, 1997).

[53] Helga Leitner and Eric Sheppard, "Economic Uncertainty, Inter-Urban Competition and the Efficacy of Entrepreneurialism," in Hall and Hubbard, *The Entrepreneurial City*, 285–308.

[54] Martin and Sunley, "Post-Keynesian State."

[55] Chris Ansell, "The Networked Polity: Regional Development in Western Europe," *Governance* 13, no. 3 (2000) 303–33.

geopolitical context, the goal of equalizing economic development capacities across the national territory was increasingly seen to be incompatible with the new priority of promoting place-specific locational assets and endogenous ICT development within major metropolitan regions. Accordingly, in addition to their efforts to undercut inherited redistributive regional policy relays, national governments now also pursued a series of institutional reforms intended to establish appropriate regulatory infrastructures for stimulating post-Fordist forms of industrial growth within their territories.

- As national fiscal transfers to subnational levels were diminished, local governments were granted new revenue-raising powers and an increased level of authority in determining local tax rates and user fees.[56] Such fiscally retrenched, institutionally streamlined local state apparatuses were widely viewed as a key element of the regulatory environment in which new economy industries would flourish.
- New responsibilities for planning, economic development, social services, and spatial planning were devolved downward to subnational (regional and local) governments.[57] This new framework of decentralized, regionalized, or localized policy capacities was frequently justified as an essential means to foster the place-specific conditions of production and regulation required by ICT-based sectors and other new economy industries.
- National spatial planning systems were redefined. Economic priorities such as promoting structural competitiveness, particularly in ICT-based, post-Fordist sectors, superseded welfarist, redistributive priorities such as spatial equalization. In many European countries, the most globally networked metropolitan regions superseded the national economy as the privileged target for major spatial planning initiatives, infrastructural investments, and economic development projects. Although many peripheralized cities, regions, and hinterlands likewise attempted to expand global linkages and to attract high-technology investment, most national policymakers believed that clusters of new economy industries should be promoted especially in those metropolitan regions that were already well endowed with advanced infrastructural facilities, logistics equipment, dynamic labor markets, and a significant legacy of investment by high-technology firms.

---

[56] Fox-Przeworski, "Changing Intergovernmental Relations"; Mayer, "Post-Fordist City Politics."

[57] Alan Harding, "Urban Regimes and Growth Machines: Towards a Cross-National Research Agenda," *Urban Affairs Quarterly* 29, no. 3 (1994): 356–82.

- National, regional, and local governments introduced a range of territory- and place-specific institutions and policies—from enterprise zones, urban development corporations, and airport development agencies to training and enterprise councils, inward investment agencies, and development planning boards—designed to enhance socioeconomic assets and advanced infrastructural investments within strategic urban spaces and to position them competitively in transnational circuits of capital.[58] Such measures were viewed as an important means through which to stimulate and canalize the development of new economy clusters, and to lure ICT investment away from other potential locations within and beyond Western Europe.
- The forms and functions of local states were redefined. Whereas postwar Western European local governments had been devoted primarily to various forms of welfare service delivery and state-financed collective consumption, these institutions now began to prioritize the goals of promoting local economic development and maintaining a "good business environment" within their jurisdictions.[59] Such local economic initiatives, often accompanied by significant tax concessions and other financial incentives to transnational capital, were widely justified as essential regulatory prerequisites for attracting high-technology investment.

In the face of these uneven and combined institutional realignments, inherited frameworks for the political regulation of uneven development were also profoundly rescaled. The nationalizing approach to the regulation of territorial inequalities that had underpinned the Fordist-Keynesian configuration was now superseded by what might be termed a post-Keynesian rescaling strategy, the central goal of which has been to position urban spaces optimally within continent-wide or global circuits of capital.[60] In contrast to postwar strategies of spatial Keynesianism, which had contributed to a tendential alleviation of intranational uneven development, these post-Keynesian rescaling strategies have actively intensified the latter (1) by promoting the concentration of high-technology industrial specializations within each national territory's most globally networked urban spaces;

---

[58] Alan Harding, "Urban Regimes in a Europe of the Cities?," *European Urban and Regional Studies* 4, no. 4 (1997): 291–314.

[59] Mayer, "Shifting Local Political System in European Cities"; Harvey, "From Managerialism to Entrepreneurialism."

[60] Brenner, *New State Spaces*, Chap. 5.

Geoeconomic and geopolitical context
• Late 1970s–present: ongoing processes of regulatory experimentation in the wake of the crisis of North Atlantic Fordism and subsequent cycles of restructuring-induced crisis
• New global-local tensions: global economic integration proceeds in tandem with an increasing dependence of large corporations on agglomeration economies
• The search for a new institutional fix proceeds at all spatial scales in a geoeconomic context defined by variegated, uneven neoliberalization tendencies

Privileged spatial target(s)
• Major urban and regional economies situated within global or supranational circuits of capital

Major goals
• Reconcentration of population, industry and infrastructure investment into strategic urban and regional economies
• Differentiation of national economic space among specialized urban and regional spaces
• Promotion of customized, place-specific forms of infrastructural investment oriented toward global and European economic flows
• Intensification of interspatial competition at all scales: uneven development is now seen as a basis for economic growth rather than as a limit or barrier to it

Dominant policy mechanisms
• Deregulation and welfare state retrenchment
• Decentralization or devolution of intergovernmental arrangements, socioeconomic policies and fiscal responsibilities
• Spatially selective investments in advanced infrastructures, generally within strategic urban spaces
• Place-specific regional and local policies
• Local economic initiatives; proliferation of place-marketing strategies

Spatiotemporality of economic development
• Rescaled approaches to developmentalism: fragmentation of national space into distinct urban-regional economies with their own place-specific locational features and globally oriented developmental trajectories

FIGURE 5.2 Post-Keynesian rescaling strategies and the new politics of uneven development.

(2) by encouraging increasingly divergent, place-specific forms of economic governance, welfare provision, and territorial administration; and (3) by institutionalizing competitive relations, whether for public subsidies or for private investments, among major subnational administrative units. The declared goal of national and local spatial policies is thus no longer to alleviate uneven geographical development, but actively to intensify it through policies designed to strengthen the putatively unique, place-specific socioeconomic assets and infrastructural equipment of transnationally networked

urban regions.[61] The key elements of these post-Keynesian rescaling strategies are summarized in Figure 5.2.

Taken together, then, these wide-ranging rescalings of the Fordist-Keynesian regulatory architecture were seen as a means to establish a new "lean and mean" framework of state regulation that would stimulate growth within specific, high-technology industrial and financial sectors while privileging the strategic urban spaces in which the latter would cluster. In stark contrast to the standardized geographies of state space that prevailed under Fordism, in which national states attempted to maintain minimum levels of service provision throughout the national territory, the establishment of an entrepreneurial, competitiveness-oriented institutional infrastructure for political-economic governance during the 1980s entailed an increasing interscalar differentiation, fragmentation, and polarization of state regulatory activities and a more fine-grained demarcation of their core spatial targets. On the one hand, the consolidation of entrepreneurial forms of urban governance was premised upon the establishment of new subnational layers of state and para-state institutions through which strategic urban spaces could be marketed as customized, competitive locations for key economic functions within global and European spatial divisions of labor.[62] On the other hand, the devolutionary initiatives mentioned earlier reconfigured entrenched intergovernmental hierarchies and scalar divisions of regulation, imposing powerful new pressures upon all subnational politico-administrative units to "fend for themselves" in an increasingly volatile, competitive geoeconomic environment.[63] In this manner, through

---

[61] For a parallel argument, see Jamie Peck, "Political Economies of Scale: Fast Policy, Interscalar Relations and Neoliberal Workfare," *Economic Geography* 78, no. 3 (July 2002): 356. Peck's characterization of the uneven geographies of neoliberal workfarism can be productively applied to newly emergent patterns of spatial, regional, and urban policy in Western Europe:

> Uneven geographic development is being established as an intentional, rather than merely incidental, feature of the delivery of workfare programs, while local experimentation and emulation are becoming seemingly permanent features of the policymaking process. . . . In stark contrast to the aspirations to fair and equal treatment under welfare regimes, when spatial unevenness, local discretion, and instances of atypical . . . treatment were often constituted as policy problems in their own right, or at least anomalies, workfare makes a virtue of geographical differentiation, subnational competition, and . . . circumstance-specific interventions. . . . Although disorder and flux continue to reign, it is becoming increasingly clear that these changes—and the distinctive scalar dynamics that underpin them—are more than simply transitory, but are concerned with a far-reaching, if not systemic, reorganization of the regulatory regime.

[62] Harvey, "From Managerialism to Entrepreneurialism."

[63] Gordon MacLeod, "The Learning Region in an Age of Austerity: Capitalizing on Knowledge, Entrepreneurialism and Reflexive Capitalism," *Geoforum* 31 (2000): 219–36.

successive layerings of post-Keynesian state rescaling and entrepreneurial urban policy reform, a "parallel mosaic of differentiated spaces of regulation" was established within the already increasingly polarized, scale-relativized economic geographies of archipelago Europe.[64]

Of course, the crystallization of these post-Keynesian rescaling strategies has resulted from a variety of economic, political, and geographical dynamics, realignments, and struggles during the last four decades. Even in a broadly post-Keynesian geopolitical context, strategies of state rescaling have been intensely variegated among neoliberal, social democratic, Christian/social democratic, and hybrid forms.[65] However, across territorial contexts and spatial scales, such strategies have served as an important politico-institutional medium through which urban spaces have been qualitatively reshaped, and through which ongoing processes of scale relativization have been at once intensified, deepened, and accelerated. Through their mobilization of post-Keynesian rescaling strategies, national, regional, and local state institutions have attempted to stimulate and canalize the growth of new economy industries within their territories, thereby powerfully contributing to the production of new urban spaces, new patterns of urbanization, and new formations of uneven spatial development.

The Ambiguous Resurgence of Metropolitan Regionalism in the 1990s

A number of critical analysts have emphasized the chronically unstable character of ICT-based approaches to urban redevelopment.[66] First, to the degree that such approaches focus one-sidedly upon ICT-based industries and other new economy sectors, they may neglect to cultivate or rejuvenate extant socioeconomic capacities within particular territories. Second, while ICT-based forms of urban development may successfully unleash short- and medium-term bursts of economic growth within a small group of privileged, "first mover" local and regional economies, the conditions underlying these putative "paradigms" are extremely difficult, if not impossible, to replicate or generalize elsewhere, in geographical contexts characterized by divergent industrial histories, infrastructural configurations, labor markets, and

---

[64] Goodwin and Painter, "Local Governance," 646.

[65] Eisenschitz and Gough, Politics of Local Economic Development; Brenner and Theodore, Spaces of Neoliberalism.

[66] Martin, "Making Sense of the 'New Economy.'" For a critical case study of such issues, see Stefan Krätke and Renate Borst, Berlin: Metropole im Wandel (Berlin: Leske + Budrich, 1999).

regulatory arrangements. Third, due to their relatively circumscribed sectoral, labor market, and spatial impacts, urban development policies oriented toward new economy industries tend to intensify uneven development, sociospatial exclusion, and territorial disparities across spatial scales. In so doing, they are likely to generate significant negative externalities and social costs, and thus to compromise the socioterritorial conditions upon which sustained industrial growth generally depends.

Additional vulnerabilities and crisis tendencies flow from the splintered architecture of post-Keynesian territorial governance itself. As indicated, one of the major effects of post-Keynesian forms of state rescaling has been to enhance competitive pressures upon subnational administrative units and thus to intensify uneven geographical development. While these institutional realignments may temporarily benefit a select number of powerful, globally networked urban regions, where ICT-based industries are disproportionately clustered, they generally inflict a logic of regulatory undercutting upon the broader system of territorial development in which all local and regional economies are embedded. This trend may, in aggregate, seriously erode the territorial coherence of the space economy as a whole and undermine macroeconomic stability. Furthermore, the increasing geographical differentiation of state regulatory activities induced through such post-Keynesian rescaling strategies generates recurrent dilemmas of interscalar coordination within the state apparatus itself, and in relation to the variegated array of private and semiprivate organizations that are involved in economic governance. Indeed, rather than stimulating a more efficient distribution of public resources and investments across places, as predicted by many of their proponents, such rescalings have, in practice, been "as much a hindrance as a help to regulation."[67] Consequently, in the absence of institutional mechanisms of metagovernance capable of coordinating subnational regulatory initiatives and economic development strategies, the state's own organizational coherence and functional unity are likely to be eroded, leading to significant governance failures, political conflicts, and legitimation deficits.[68]

The disruptive, contradictory tendencies unleashed during the post-1980s wave of combined urban-industrial restructuring, urban policy reform, and state rescaling have thus had some important ramifications for the subsequent evolution of post-Keynesian approaches to territorial regulation. Especially as of the 1990s, faced with the pervasive regulatory

---

[67] Painter and Goodwin, "Local Governance," 646.

[68] Bob Jessop, "The Narrative of Enterprise and the Enterprise of Narrative: Place-Marketing and the Entrepreneurial City," in Hall and Hubbard, *The Entrepreneurial City*, 77–102.

deficits of their own predominant strategies of political-economic governance, many Western European states began to pursue further rounds of
rescaling, institutional reorganization, and policy experimentation in an attempt to manage the disruptive socioeconomic consequences of previous
urban regeneration initiatives. Whereas the rescaling of political-economic
governance in the 1970s and 1980s had consisted primarily in strategies
to manage the immediate crisis of Fordism, to rejuvenate urban-industrial
growth, and to promote and canalize ICT-led forms of urban redevelopment,
the rescaling projects of the post-1990s period have also been powerfully
animated by the problem of managing the pervasive governance failures
engendered through these earlier rounds of regulatory restructuring. As of
this period, the politics of rescaling began increasingly to encompass not
only new approaches to stimulating and territorializing urban economic development, but a variety of political-institutional responses to what Claus
Offe famously termed "the crisis of crisis management."[69] The goal of such
rescaling initiatives has been to establish new local and supralocal "flanking
mechanisms and supporting measures" that would more effectively manage
the wide-ranging tensions, conflicts, and contradictions generated across
the urban landscape during earlier rounds of sociospatial and institutional
restructuring.[70]

It is in this context that the widespread proliferation of regionally focused regulatory projects since the 1990s must be understood. As indicated,
the first wave of post-Keynesian rescaling strategies focused predominantly
upon the downscaling of formerly nationalized administrative capacities
and regulatory arrangements toward local tiers of state power. It was under
these conditions that many of the metropolitan institutional forms inherited
from the Fordist-Keynesian period were abolished or downgraded. Since
the 1990s, however, the metropolitan and regional scales have become
strategically important sites for a new round of institutional realignments.
From experiments in metropolitan institutional reform and decentralized
regional industrial policy in Germany, Italy, France, and the Netherlands
to the Blairite project of establishing a patchwork of regional development
agencies (RDAs) in the United Kingdom, these developments led many
commentators to predict that a "new regionalism" was superseding the
rapidly eroding geographies of spatial Keynesianism *and* the more recently

---

[69] Claus Offe, "'Crisis of Crisis Management': Elements of a Political Crisis Theory," in
Contradictions of the Welfare State, ed. John B. Keane (Cambridge, MA: MIT Press,1984), 35–64.

[70] Jessop, "Narrative of Enterprise," 97–98.

consolidated approaches to local economic development that had been pursued during the 1970s and 1980s.[71]

Against such arguments, however, this analysis points toward a crisis-theoretical interpretation of the so-called new regionalism as an important evolutionary modification of earlier rescaling strategies in response to governance failures, dislocations, and crisis tendencies that were largely of their own making. Although the politico-institutional content of contemporary metropolitanization and regionalization strategies continues to mutate, not least through ongoing politico-ideological contestation, such strategies have generally combined two intertwined regulatory projects:

- *Metropolitan entrepreneurialism.* This entails transposing ICT-based strategies of local economic development upward onto a metropolitan or regional scale, leading to a further intensification of uneven spatial development throughout each national territory. The contradictions of ICT-led growth are thus to be resolved through an upscaling of local economies into larger, regionally configured territorial units, which are in turn to be promoted as integrated, competitive locations for globally competitive ICT investment. The scalar configuration of territorial regulation is modified to emphasize regions rather than localities, yet the basic politics of ICT promotion, spatial reconcentration, interspatial competition, and intensified uneven development is maintained.
- *Metropolitan equalization.* This entails countervailing the destructive effects of unfettered interlocality competition by promoting selected forms of social redistribution, territorial cohesion, and spatial equalization *within* delineated metropolitan or regional spaces. Although such initiatives generally do not significantly undermine uneven spatial development between regions, they have attempted to modify some of the most disruptive intraregional impacts of earlier, ICT-based rescaling strategies, with particular reference to intensifying city-suburban conflicts, zero-sum interspatial competition for capital investment, and regulatory fragmentation. The goal here is to introduce a downscaled form of spatial Keynesianism as a kind of subnational "foreign territory" within a broadly post-Keynesian configuration of national state power. The aggressively competitive logic of post-Keynesian territorial regulation is not interrupted, but its territorial and scalar contours are now recast to establish

---

[71] For a useful critical overview of such discussions, see Gordon MacLeod, "New Regionalism Reconsidered: Globalization, Regulation and the Recasting of Political Economic Space," *International Journal of Urban and Regional Research* 25, no. 4 (2001) 804–29.

partially insulated "enclaves" of enhanced regulatory coordination and spatial redistribution within strictly delimited subnational zones.

In this latest round of rescaling, then, the priorities of ICT-based, post-Fordist industrial growth, territorial competitiveness, crisis management, and sociospatial cohesion are intermeshed uneasily within an increasingly fragmented institutional matrix for urban and regional governance. At present, however, there is little evidence to suggest that such metropolitanized or regionalized rescaling strategies will prove more effective in managing the splintered, scale-relativized, polarized, volatile, and crisis-riven landscapes of post-Keynesian urbanization than the localized strategies of economic development upon which they have been superimposed. On the contrary, this latest round of rescaling appears most likely to further intensify the uneven development of capital, the relativization of scales, the polarization of sociospatial relations, and the geographical differentiation of state power, leading in turn to further cycles of macroeconomic instability, crisis formation, and ad hoc regulatory experimentation within the "lean and mean" geographies of archipelago Europe.

New Economy, New Landscapes of Regulation

This chapter has explored the links between emergent political strategies to promote ICT-based, post-Fordist economic development in European metropolitan regions and the broader rescaling of national state spaces that has been unfolding following the dismantling of spatial Keynesianism in the late 1970s. I have argued that the development of ICT-based, high-technology industries in major metropolitan regions cannot be understood adequately without an examination of the rescaled matrices of national, regional, and local state power within which they are situated and the concerted political strategies through which they have been fostered. Within this rescaled, post-Keynesian configuration of state power, national governments have not simply transferred power downward, but have attempted to institutionalize competitive relations between major subnational administrative units as a means to position major local and regional economies strategically within European and global circuits of capital. In this sense, even as traditional, nationally focused regulatory arrangements have been decentered under conditions of deepening scale relativization, national states have attempted to retain control over strategic urban and regional spaces by integrating them within operationally rescaled, but still nationally coordinated, approaches to territorial development.

Especially since the 1990s, new economy discourse has played a key role in the construction of both new state spaces *and* new urban spaces, for it has served, simultaneously, (1) to naturalize the purported constraints of contemporary "globalization"; (2) to legitimate the retrenchment of inherited, Fordist-Keynesian state institutions and redistributive regional policy relays; (3) to promote the channeling of significant public resources into particular sectors (above all, those based on ICTs, high technology, and finance) and places (above all, global cities and transnationally networked metropolitan regions) instead of others; (4) to further intensify, deepen, and accelerate the ongoing relativization of scales; and (5) to represent the resultant forms of territorial inequality and sociospatial exclusion as the necessary byproducts of globalized, knowledge-driven, informational capitalism. In this sense, the notion of the new economy must be construed as a fundamentally *political* concept: it is best understood less as a self-evident description of an unproblematic empirical reality than as an ideologically refracted product of contentious political strategies oriented toward a specific vision of urban space and how it should be (re)organized.

Like other critical geographers, I have argued that the proliferation of new economy strategies has not entailed the death of distance, the end of geography, or the homogenization of industrial landscapes. Instead, I have interpreted new economy accumulation strategies as important catalysts in generating the unevenly rescaled mosaics of urbanization that have been crystallizing during the last four decades. We have seen, however, that ICT-led strategies of accumulation and urbanization are chronically unstable, for they have perpetuated macroeconomic instability, unfettered uneven spatial development, and wide-ranging crisis tendencies across places, territories, and scales. It is in this context that the production of new, tendentially metropolitanized scales of state spatial regulation since the 1990s can be understood. These metropolitan regulatory experiments have operated both as upscaled institutional arenas for place promotion strategies and as frameworks of crisis management through which at least some of the crisis tendencies, conflicts, and contradictions associated with post-Keynesian capitalism are being institutionally addressed, albeit in inchoate, often ineffectual ways. Figure 5.3 provides a schematic overview of the periodization that flows from this line of argumentation.

In light of this analysis, it seems clear that subnational spaces such as cities and metropolitan regions are key geographical sites in which ICT-based, new economy industries are being cultivated and territorialized. However, such subnational spaces are not only sites for the clustering of new economy firms but are also important institutional arenas in which a variety

---

Spatial Keynesianism: late 1950s–early 1970s
- National states promote economic development by spreading industry, population, and infrastructural investment evenly across the national territory
- Urban managerialism: local states and metropolitan authorities operate mainly as sites of welfare service provision and collective consumption

---

Fordism in crisis (transitional phase): early 1970s–early 1980s
- A new politics of "endogenous" growth emerges in crisis-stricken industrial regions: goal is to mobilize customized policies to confront place-specific forms of economic decline and industrial restructuring
- Various national redistributive policy relays are retrenched, forcing subnational territorial administrations to "fend for themselves" under conditions of intensifying economic uncertainty and accelerating industrial restructuring

---

Post-Keynesian rescaling strategies, round 1: 1980s
- The mobilization of post-Keynesian rescaling strategies: national states promote the reconcentration of economic capacities and infrastructure investments into the most globally networked urban spaces within their territories
- Decentralization of intergovernmental systems to enhance the capacity of subnational institutional levels to promote place-specific conditions for industrial development
- Proliferation of local economic development strategies in response to the new, Europe-wide interspatial competition

---

Post-Keynesian rescaling strategies, round 2: 1990s–present
- The "metropolitanization" and/or regionalization of earlier rescaling strategies: national states increasingly target large-scale metropolitan regions rather than cities or localities as the most appropriate scales for economic rejuvenation
- Crystallization of competitive regionalism: metropolitan institutions are rejuvenated in conjunction with projects to promote interlocality cooperation and regional strategies of economic development
- Metropolitan regions are increasingly viewed as strategic institutional arenas in which new regulatory experiments may be articulated for purposes of economic development and crisis management

---

FIGURE 5.3 State strategies and the political regulation of uneven development: a schematic periodization of the Western European case.

of rescaled regulatory experiments are being mobilized, at once to promote industrial regeneration, to canalize new forms of capital investment, and to manage some of the market failures and governance failures associated with recent rounds of sociospatial restructuring. By way of conclusion, therefore, it may be useful to sketch some of the overarching regulatory problems that have been engendered through this pervasive rescaling of territorial development strategies. In the absence of viable, generalizable solutions to these problems, it is unlikely that ICT-based, new economy industries will provide a stable foundation for urbanization at any spatial scale, within or beyond the European Union.

1. *Intersectoral coordination.* New economy accumulation strategies neglect to address the persistent problems of inherited or revitalized manufacturing industries and the associated infrastructures of social reproduction (including housing, transportation, and education) with which they are connected. As such, these accumulation strategies bracket important sources of employment, land use, and industrial dynamism under contemporary capitalism based on the flawed assumption that the new economy can, in itself, provide an anchor for stable macroeconomic growth. However, in the absence of policy mechanisms designed to facilitate reinvestment and upgrading within inherited manufacturing industries and associated social spaces while articulating them to the growth potentials associated with ICTs, it is unlikely that new economy sectors could provide a basis for long-term economic regeneration.

2. *Interscalar coordination.* New economy accumulation strategies contribute to the deepening fragmentation of regulatory arrangements among diverse institutions, jurisdictions, and scales. Consequently, they undermine the coherence of supralocal institutional arrangements and engender major problems of interscalar coordination among dispersed, increasingly disarticulated organizations, policy regimes, coalitions, and actors. In the absence of such coordination, however, a variety of governance problems—including unfettered interlocality competition; destructive, predatory bidding wars and poaching forays among regional and local states; and intense interterritorial conflicts—may proliferate. Such regulatory crisis tendencies may undermine the social, institutional, and territorial preconditions upon which long-term urban industrial development depends, both in new economy sectors and in other arenas of socioeconomic life.

3. *Territorial inequality and sociospatial exclusion.* New economy accumulation strategies tend to channel investment and public goods not only toward particular sectors, but into specific places and regions that are deemed to be optimal sites for the development of ICT-based sectors. In this manner, new economy accumulation strategies reinforce and accelerate the tendencies of spatial reconcentration, metropolitanization, and interterritorial polarization that have been consistently associated with the post-1980s archipelago economy.[72] In effect, if not always by design, new economy accumulation strategies significantly intensify uneven spatial development and territorial polarization, essentially

---

[72] Veltz, *Mondialisation, villes et territoires.*

abandoning marginalized regions and populations to "fend for themselves" in an aggressively competitive configuration of world capitalism. However, in the absence of politico-institutional mechanisms through which to regulate such intensifying socioterritorial inequalities, the macroeconomic sustainability and political acceptability of ICT-led urban development strategies are subject to serious doubt.

Whether or not ICT-led urban growth can be promoted in a solidaristic, politically negotiated, territorially balanced, and socially equitable form is a matter that remains to be fought out through political struggle and regulatory experimentation, across diverse territories, sites, and scales—including within the strategic urban spaces whose social, infrastructural, and institutional geographies have been most comprehensively transformed through the relentless pursuit of a "new" economic order.

6
Competitive City-Regionalism and the Politics of Scale

THROUGHOUT WESTERN EUROPE, metropolitan regionalism is back on the agenda. Since the early 1990s, new forms of city-suburban cooperation, inter-city coordination, metropolitan institutional reform, and region-wide spatial planning have been promoted in major Western European urban regions. In contrast to the forms of metropolitan regionalism that prevailed during the Fordist-Keynesian period, which emphasized administrative rationalization, interterritorial equalization, and the efficient delivery of public services, this latest round of metropolitan regulatory restructuring has been focused on priorities such as enhancing urban socioeconomic assets, attracting external capital investment, and the competitive positioning of city-regions in transnational economic circuits. In this resolutely post-Keynesian configuration of combined urban and regulatory restructuring, metropolitan regionalism is being mobilized above all as a form of "locational policy" through which urban regions are being promoted as strategic sites for capital accumulation, whether through production, finance, exchange, or consumption.[1]

---

[1] As used here, the notion of locational policy refers to state spatial strategies intended (1) to enhance the structural competitiveness of particular territorial jurisdictions and (2) to position those jurisdictions strategically within supranational circuits of capital. The term "locational policy" is a loose translation of the German word *Standortpolitik*, which gained currency in the context of post-1980s policy debates on *Standort Deutschland* (Germany as an investment

From London, Glasgow, Manchester, the Randstad, Brussels, Copenhagen-Øresund-Malmö, Lille, Lyon, and Paris to Berlin, the Ruhr, Hannover, Frankfurt/Rhine-Main, Stuttgart, Munich, Vienna, Zurich, Geneva, Madrid, Barcelona, Bologna, and Milan, local economic development policies have been linked ever more directly to new forms of metropolitan place marketing, regulatory coordination, infrastructure investment, spatial planning, and territorial forecasting. In these city-regions, and in many others, urban growth coalitions are advocating reinvented forms of metropolitan regionalism as an urgently needed institutional response to the wide-ranging challenges posed by putatively ineluctable trends such as economic globalization, European integration, and intensified interspatial competition. Thus has arisen what critical geographers Kevin Ward and Andrew Jonas have succinctly termed "competitive city-regionalism."[2]

The collective action problems, institutional blockages, and political obstacles associated with such competitive, growth-oriented metropolitan initiatives have been significant and, in some cases, nearly insurmountable.[3] Indeed, many of the most ambitious, politically prominent programs of metropolitan regulation have been implemented only in a relatively "soft" form, and others have been watered down beyond recognition following intense negotiations, contestation, and opposition. Nonetheless, since the 1990s, the proliferation of new metropolitan regionalist strategies has qualitatively transformed inherited scalar frameworks of territorial regulation throughout the Western European urban system. Even in cases of apparent failure, such strategies have played a major role in redefining the political-ideological frame in which questions of urban governance are narrated, negotiated, and fought out, giving unprecedented prominence to the priority of promoting metropolitan-scale economic development. In many instances, the defeat of more comprehensive metropolitan reform initiatives has actually generated renewed momentum for alternative rescaling strategies

---

location). For present purposes, the notion of locational policy is used in a more specific, social scientific sense to describe state strategies oriented toward promoting economic development within a demarcated territorial zone, at any spatial scale. For further elaboration, see Neil Brenner, *New State Spaces: Urban Governance and the Rescaling of Statehood* (New York: Oxford University Press, 2004); as well as Neil Brenner, "Building 'Euro-Regions': Locational Politics and the Political Geography of Neoliberalism in Post-unification Germany," *European Urban and Regional Studies* 7, no. 4 (2000): 319–45.

[2] Kevin Ward and Andrew E. G. Jonas, "Competitive City-Regionalism as a Politics of Space: A Critical Reinterpretation of the New Regionalism," *Environment and Planning A* 36 (2004): 2119–39.

[3] Paul Cheshire and Ian Gordon, "Territorial Competition and the Predictability of Collective (In)action," *International Journal of Urban and Regional Research* 20, no. 3 (1996): 383–99.

that address problems of metropolitan economic development via informal partnerships, interorganizational coordination, multilateral networking, and public-private cooperation. In the face of these realignments, diverse political coalitions, policymakers, corporate elites, planners, and scholars have come to embrace the basic assumption that metropolitan regions, rather than localities or the national economy, represent the natural spatial units in which economic growth may be most effectively stimulated, canalized, coordinated, and sustained. Building upon such assumptions, several prominent contemporary urban thinkers have interpreted such emergent "new regionalisms" as potential institutional anchors for a renewed upswing of worldwide capitalist industrialization and stable territorial development.[4]

Against the background of such metropolitan institutional realignments, regulatory experiments, political struggles, and associated scholarly debates, this chapter confronts two specific tasks, with particular reference to emergent patterns and pathways of competitive city-regionalism in post-Keynesian Europe. First, I situate the new competitive city-regionalism in historical-geographical context by underscoring its qualitative differences from earlier rounds of metropolitan institutional reform. Second, I interpret contemporary metropolitan reform initiatives as expressions of a new politics of scale in which diverse state institutions, territorial alliances, and political coalitions are struggling to reconfigure the scalar organization of urban space *and* regulatory space under conditions of accelerating geoeconomic integration, crisis-induced urban-industrial restructuring, and deepening scale relativization. However, rather than analytically subsuming contemporary metropolitan rescalings under the singular rubric of the "new regionalism," this chapter argues that they have resulted from a variegated, relatively uncoordinated ensemble of political strategies intended to manage some of the major sociospatial dislocations, governance failures, and regulatory crisis tendencies that have crystallized across the urban landscape during the post-Keynesian period. In contrast to the confident forecasts that are often ventured in new regionalist scholarship, this chapter advances a more circumspect interpretation of the apparently enhanced strategic importance of

---

[4] See, for example, Allen J. Scott, *Regions and the World Economy* (London: Oxford University Press, 1998); Philip Cooke and Kevin Morgan, *The Associational Economy* (New York: Oxford University Press, 1998); and the various contributions to Allen J. Scott, ed., *Global City-Regions: Trends, Theory, Policy* (New York: Oxford University Press, 2001). For a systematic critical evaluation, see Gordon MacLeod, "The Learning Region in an Age of Austerity: Capitalizing on Knowledge, Entrepreneurialism and Reflexive Capitalism," *Geoforum* 31 (2000): 219–36; and Gordon MacLeod, "New Regionalism Reconsidered: Globalization, Regulation and the Recasting of Political Economic Space," *International Journal of Urban and Regional Research* 25, no. 4 (2001) 804–29.

city-regions within the uneven, splintered, scale-relativized, and endemically volatile political-economic geographies of contemporary capitalism.

Metropolitan Regionalism and the Historical Geographies of Capitalism

For my purposes here, metropolitan regionalism refers to all strategies to establish regulations, policies, institutions, or modes of coordination at a geographical scale approximating that of the main socioeconomic interdependencies within an urban territory. Thus defined, metropolitan regionalism encompasses a multiplicity of regulatory agendas, governance recalibrations, and institutional reconfigurations—including, for instance, attempts to modify jurisdictional boundaries; proposals to establish supra- or intermunicipal agencies, administrative districts, or planning bodies; legal measures imposed by higher levels of government to regulate urban expansion; and a variety of intergovernmental mechanisms intended to enhance interorganizational and public-private coordination. As such, the political geographies of metropolitan regionalism are likely to vary considerably across contexts and to evolve historically in relation to shifting formations of state institutional organization, modes of territorial regulation, the maneuvers of political coalitions, and the struggles of social movements.

The problem of administrative and jurisdictional fragmentation within large-scale urban regions has long been a topic of intense debate among urbanists. In particular, the spatial mismatch between local administrative units and the functional-economic territory of metropolitan regions has been analyzed from diverse methodological perspectives, including public choice theory, liberal approaches, and radical or Marxian perspectives.[5] David Harvey describes the problem concisely as follows:

> [Local government] boundaries do not necessarily coincide with the fluid zones of urban labor and commodity markets or infrastructural formation; and their adjustment through annexation, local government reorganization, and metropolitan-wide cooperation is cumbersome, though often of great long-term significance. Local jurisdictions frequently divide rather than unify the urban region, thus emphasizing the segmentations (such as that between city

---

[5] Michael Keating, "Size, Efficiency, and Democracy: Consolidation, Fragmentation and Public Choice," in *Theories of Urban Politics*, ed. David Judge, Gerry Stoker, and Harold Wolman (London: Sage, 1995), 117–34.

and suburb) rather than the tendency toward structured coherence and class-alliance formation.[6]

Although metropolitan jurisdictional fragmentation has been considerably more pronounced among major North American urban regions than in their Western European counterparts, scholars have effectively demonstrated the profound consequences of such territorial arrangements for patterns and pathways of urbanization across national contexts, especially in relation to the geographies of collective consumption.[7]

The historical evolution of metropolitan institutional configurations has been tightly intertwined with successive waves of capitalist urbanization. As the reproduction of capital has become more directly dependent upon processes of industrial urbanization, the territorial configuration of cities, city-regions, and their hinterlands has become a focal point of intense regulatory contestation, pitting place-based alliances of classes, class fractions, and other place-dependent social forces against one another in a continual effort to achieve a range of conflicting goals related to production, circulation, and social reproduction. Meanwhile, as the process of urbanization has accelerated, intensified, and expanded, the geographies of the capitalist urban fabric have, in turn, been continuously rewoven. As Edward Soja has argued at length, the broadly monocentric urban regions of the competitive-industrial stage of capitalist development were superseded, after World War II, by the increasingly polynucleated metropolitan regions, urban fields, and megalopolises of Fordist-Keynesian, national-developmentalist, and postcolonial capitalism.[8] Subsequently, and particularly since the neoliberalizing implosions and explosions of worldwide urbanization during the 1980s, the relatively standardized, territorially extended urban-regional matrices of the postwar epoch have been further reworked to form still more colossal, if internally splintered, configurations of territorial development that have been variously described as exopolises, one-hundred-mile cities, galactic metropolises, megacity regions, megapolitan territories, and—in Soja's

---

[6] David Harvey, *The Urban Experience* (Baltimore: Johns Hopkins University Press, 1989), 153.

[7] See, for instance, Max Barlow, *Metropolitan Government* (New York: Routledge, 1991); L. J. Sharpe, ed., *The Government of World Cities: The Future of the Metro Model* (New York: John Wiley & Sons, 1995); Michael Goldsmith, "Urban Governance," in *Handbook of Urban Studies*, ed. Ronan Paddison (London: Sage, 2001), 325–35; and Pieter Terhorst and Jacques van de Ven, *Fragmented Brussels and Consolidated Amsterdam: A Comparative Study of the Spatial Organization of Property Rights*, Netherlands Geographical Studies 223 (Amsterdam: Netherlands Geographical Society, 1997).

[8] Edward Soja, *Postmetropolis* (Cambridge, MA: Blackwell, 2000).

classic formulation—postmetropolitan spaces.[9] Each of these configurations of capitalist urbanization has, in turn, generated contextually specific regulatory dilemmas, governance strategies, territorial conflicts, and sociopolitical struggles within, around, and among major urban regions. It is in relation to this perpetually evolving mosaic of urban spaces, and the problems of territorial regulation it has engendered, that we can begin to decipher successive rounds of metropolitan reform under modern capitalism.

Although consolidated metropolitan institutions had been introduced within several large-scale Euro-American metropolises (notably, New York, London, and Berlin) during the late nineteenth and early twentieth centuries, a broader cycle of metropolitan institution building unfolded across the urbanizing landscapes of North America and Western Europe as of the 1960s and 1970s.[10] During this era, in close conjunction with the expansion of Fordist-Keynesian social engineering projects, welfare policies, and spatial planning systems, debates on metropolitan regionalism focused predominantly on the issues of administrative efficiency, local service provision, land-use planning, infrastructural standardization, and territorial redistribution. Larger units of urban territorial administration were generally seen as being analogous to Fordist forms of mass production insofar as they were thought to generate economies of scale in the field of public service provision.[11] With the growing influence of modernist approaches to territorial planning, consolidated metropolitan institutions were also widely mobilized to help differentiate city-regions functionally among zones of production, housing, transportation, recreation, and so forth. Among the major metropolitan institutions established during this period in Western Europe were the Greater London Council (1963); the Madrid Metropolitan Area Planning and Coordinating Commission (1963); the *Rijnmond* or Greater Rotterdam Port Authority (1964); the *communautés urbaines* in French cities such as Bordeaux, Lille, Lyon, and Strasbourg (1966); the *Regionalverband Stuttgart* (1972); the metropolitan counties in British cities such as Manchester, Birmingham, Liverpool, Leeds, Sheffield, and Newcastle (1974); the *Corporació Metropolitana de Barcelona* (1974); the Greater Copenhagen Council (1974); the *Umlandverband Frankfurt* (1974); and the *Kommunalverband Ruhr*

---

[9] Ibid.

[10] Michael Keating, *The New Regionalism in Western Europe: Territorial Restructuring and Political Change* (Cheltenham, UK: Edward Elgar, 1998).

[11] For example, in a 1969 report to the British government, the Redcliffe-Maud Royal Commission maintained that a population of 250,000 inhabitants was the optimal size "threshold" for effective, efficient local government. See Keating, "Size, Efficiency, and Democracy," 118.

(1975).[12] As discussed in the preceding chapter, these large-scale, technocratic, and highly bureaucratized forms of metropolitan political organization served as key institutional relays within the nationalized system of spatial Keynesianism that prevailed across Western Europe from the 1950s until the late 1970s.

By the early 1980s, however, this managerial formation of city-regionalism had been widely discredited and, in many contexts, was under concerted political attack. Following the crisis of the Fordist-Keynesian interscalar rule regime in the 1970s, urban spaces were dramatically restructured in conjunction with the decline of mass production systems, the mobilization of neo-Fordist and flexible accumulation strategies, the consolidation of new spatial divisions of labor, and the acceleration of geoeconomic and European integration.[13] Under these conditions, as the politico-regulatory infrastructures of spatial Keynesianism were being dismantled, local governments began proactively to mobilize new strategies of endogenous economic development to manage place-specific socioeconomic crises, to adjust to newly imposed fiscal constraints, to stimulate urban industrial regeneration, and to attract new sources of capital investment. In this context of national fiscal retrenchment, proliferating urban entrepreneurialism, aggressive place promotion, and deepening scale relativization, consolidated metropolitan institutions were increasingly viewed as outdated, excessively bureaucratic, and cumbersome vestiges of "big government."[14] Consequently, as Michael Keating explains, "Large-scale local government, like other large-scale organizations, came to be blamed for all manner of problems, and political and intellectual fashion moved back to the 'small is beautiful' philosophy."[15]

Inherited metropolitan institutions such as the Greater London Council, the English metropolitan counties, the Madrid Metropolitan Area Planning and Coordinating Commission, the Barcelona Metropolitan Corporation, the Greater Copenhagen Council, and the *Rijnmond* in Rotterdam were thus summarily abolished. In other major European city-regions, the inherited institutional apparatuses of metropolitan regionalism were maintained but significantly downgraded in operational terms. As of the late 1980s, many scholars of public administration had

---

[12] Sharpe, *Government of World Cities*.

[13] Mick Dunford and Grigoris Kafkalas, eds., *Cities and Regions in the New Europe: The Global-Local Interplay and Spatial Development Strategies* (London: Belhaven Press, 1992).

[14] Barlow, *Metropolitan Government*, 289–98.

[15] Keating, "Size, Efficiency, and Democracy," 122.

concluded that inherited managerial models of city-regionalism were in the midst of a terminal ideological crisis.[16]

This low tide of metropolitan governance in the 1980s resulted not only from the external shocks associated with crisis-induced geoeconomic restructuring and national state retrenchment, but from some of the internal political contradictions of postwar urban territorial administration. Most of the metropolitan authorities created during this era had remained relatively weak; their planning agendas could be readily undermined or blocked by municipalities in an urban region (including both city cores and suburbs) or by regional or central state institutions. Meanwhile, because these managerial city-regionalisms had typically been imposed "from above" and were usually organized according to purely functional criteria such as administrative efficiency, they tended to lack popular legitimacy. Consequently, such metropolitan institutions provided a rather conspicuous governmental target for the expression of simmering territorial conflicts—for instance, between central city cores and wealthy suburban peripheries, and between major urban regions and superordinate levels of the state.[17] For this reason, the managerial city-regionalisms of the postwar era were acutely vulnerable to the dangers of politicization, whereby they could be transformed from putatively neutral governmental service agencies into arenas of direct politico-ideological antagonism between countervailing sociopolitical forces, within and beyond an urban region. As the 1986 abolition of the Labour-dominated Greater London Council by Thatcher's central government paradigmatically demonstrated, the pivotal role of metropolitan institutions in mediating such struggles could expose them not only to intense public criticism, but to the prospect of complete destruction by their opponents.

Toward Competitive City-Regionalism?

Shortly after the high-profile abolitions of the Greater London Council and Rotterdam's *Rijnmond* in the 1980s, proposals to reconstitute metropolitan political institutions began to generate considerable discussion in many major European urban regions. Especially as of the mid-1990s, debates on the need for reinvented forms of metropolitan regionalism have proliferated, in many cases leading to significant changes in region-wide institutional organization, spatial planning, and economic governance. In some cities,

---

[16] Barlow, *Metropolitan Government*; Sharpe, *Government of World Cities*.

[17] Sharpe, *Government of World Cities*, 20–27.

such as London, Bologna, Stuttgart, Hannover, and Copenhagen, entirely new metropolitan institutions were constructed in which significant administrative and planning competencies were concentrated. More frequently, new frameworks of metropolitan coordination were superimposed upon inherited regional political geographies, creating rescaled institutional arenas for political negotiation, regulatory cooperation, strategic intervention, and public debate regarding major issues of urban development. Faced with these proliferating institutional realignments and regulatory experiments, numerous commentators have declared that a major renaissance of metropolitan regionalism is under way.[18]

The post-1990s resurgence of metropolitan regionalism in Western Europe has been multifaceted. As Christian Lefèvre observes, the metropolitan institutional frameworks established since this period have not been designed according to a single model of public administration and imposed from above, but have emerged through contextually embedded regulatory experiments, negotiations, and struggles, "as a product of the system of actors as the process [of institutional change] unfolds."[19] Consequently, each project of metropolitan reform has been powerfully shaped by the multiscalar administrative-constitutional system, framework of territorial regulation, accumulation regime, and formation of urban development in which it has emerged. In particular, across the European urban system, processes of crisis-induced urban restructuring have interacted in unpredictable, place-specific ways with inherited

---

[18] See, for instance, Susanne Heeg, Britte Klagge, and Jürgen Ossenbrügge, "Metropolitan Cooperation in Europe: Theoretical Issues and Perspectives for Urban Networking," *European Planning Studies* 11, no. 2 (2003): 139–53; Christian Lefèvre, "Metropolitan Government and Governance in Western Countries: A Critical Overview," *International Journal of Urban and Regional Research* 22, no. 1 (1988): 9–25; Tassilo Herrschel and Peter Newman, *Governance of Europe's City Regions* (London: Routledge, 2002); Willem Salet, Andy Thornley, and Anton Kreukels, eds., *Metropolitan Governance and Spatial Planning* (London: Spon Press, 2003); Birgit Aigner and Miosga Manfred, *Stadtregionale Kooperationsstrategien*, Münchener Geographische Heft Nr. 71 (Regensburg: Verlag Michael Laßleben, 1994); Werner Heinz, ed., *Stadt & Region—Kooperation oder Koordination? Ein internationaler Vergleich*, Schriften des Deutschen Instituts für Urbanistik, Band 93 (Stuttgart: Verlag W. Kohlhammer, 2000); Bernard Jouve and Christian Lefèvre, *Villes, métropoles: les nouveaux territoires du politique* (Paris: Anthropos, 1999); Guy Saez, Jean-Philippe Leresche, and Michel Bassand, eds., *Gouvernance métropolitaine et transfrontalière: action publique territorial* (Paris: Editions L'Harmattan, 1997); Raymond Saller, "Kommunale Kooperation innerhalb westdeutscher Stadtregionen zwischen Anspruch und politischer Realität," *Raumforschung und Raumordnung* 2, no. 58 (2000): 211–21; Special Edition of STANDORT, "Neubau der Region," *STANDORT—Zeitschrift für Angewandte Geographie* 24, no. 2 (2000); and Sabine Weck, *Neue Kooperationsformen in Stadtregionen— Eine regulationstheoretische Einordnung*, Dortmunder Beiträge zur Raumplanung Nr. 74 (Dortmund: Universität Dortmund, 1995).

[19] Lefèvre, "Metropolitan Government and Governance," 18.

institutional configurations and regulatory geographies, leading to the establishment of "a more bewildering tangle of municipalities, governmental and regional organizations and institutions, and public, private, or informal cooperative approaches with differing actors, functions, and jurisdictions."[20] This "bewildering tangle" of emergent metropolitan regulatory spaces has also been conditioned by, and has in turn engendered, reconstituted geographies of sociopolitical contestation in which diverse actors, organizations, coalitions, and movements are maneuvering across various spatial scales to reshape the dual pathways of institutional reorganization and urban restructuring.

Despite the multiplicity of metropolitan regulatory realignments that have been proposed, debated, and tendentially implemented since the 1990s, several pan-European trends may be discerned:

1. *Metropolitan reform as locational policy.* Contemporary metropolitan regionalist projects have been characterized by an aggressively entrepreneurial orientation: they have been justified primarily as a means to strengthen local economic development strategies by transposing them onto a metropolitan scale. In stark contrast to the Fordist-Keynesian configuration of urbanization, in which debates on metropolitan regulation focused primarily on the problems of administrative efficiency, local service provision, and interterritorial equalization within a relatively coherent national political-economic territory, the metropolitan regulatory reforms of the post-1990s period have been oriented toward the overarching goal of promoting city-regional economic growth in a context of intensifying urban industrial restructuring, European interspatial competition, and geoeconomic integration. In this sense, contemporary metropolitan reform programs represent a significantly upscaled formation of locational policy through which, across various spatial scales, growth coalitions are attempting to enhance the strategic positionality of major urban regions in supranational circuits of capital. In short, following the crisis-induced interscalar realignments and proliferating rescaling projects of the 1970s and 1980s, the managerial forms of metropolitan regionalism that prevailed under spatial Keynesianism have been effectively superseded by competitive city-regionalisms whose central priorities are metropolitan economic development and place promotion.

---

[20] Heinz, *Stadt & Region,* 27.

2. *Narratives of globalization, hypermobile capital, and interspatial competition.*
   Since the run-up to the establishment of the Single European Market in the
   early 1990s, a number of central discursive-ideological tropes have been
   widely repeated among the advocates of competitive city-regionalism:
   - The claim that geoeconomic integration has intensified interplace
     competition for putatively hypermobile capital investment across
     spatial scales
   - The claim that urban regions rather than cities or national economies
     represent the engines of this competition
   - The claim that rampant interplace competition over investment and
     land use within an urban region undermines its aggregate socioeco-
     nomic capacities
   - The claim that new forms of region-wide coordination are required
     to enhance a region's strategic positionality in global and European
     circuits of capital
   - The claim that effective metropolitan economic governance requires
     the incorporation of important economic stakeholders—including
     business associations, chambers of commerce, airport develop-
     ment agencies, transportation authorities, and other local boosterist
     organizations—into newly established institutional platforms for
     planning, guiding, and coordinating urban spatial development
   - The claim that inherited administrative structures, jurisdictional
     boundaries, and modes of spatial planning dissipate a city-region's
     institutional capacities for promoting economic development, and
     thus undermine metropolitan territorial competitiveness
   - The claim that rescaled spaces of metropolitan regulation would
     help enhance region-wide socioeconomic assets, bundle regional
     productive capacities, strengthen regional competitive advantages,
     and stimulate region-wide increasing-returns effects

   Across the European urban system, as well as in other major global
   regions, such claims have crystallized in diverse political inflections,
   including neoliberal, centrist, social democratic, and eco-modernist.
   Taken together, however, they appear to represent a shared, largely
   taken-for-granted ideological *dispositif* on which basis the new spatial
   politics of competitive city-regionalism is currently being articulated
   and fought out.[21]

---

[21] On the various political and ideological modalities of local economic development policy, and
their associated contradictions, see Aram Eisenschitz and Jamie Gough, *The Politics of Local
Economic Development* (New York: Macmillan, 1993). For a parallel line of argumentation with

3. *New regulatory geographies.* In contrast to the hierarchical-bureaucratic frameworks of metropolitan service delivery that prevailed in the 1960s and 1970s, the competitive city-regionalisms of the 1990s have generally been grounded upon a new model of economic governance that "highlights values of negotiation, partnership, voluntary participation and flexibility in the constitution of new structures."[22] Rather strikingly, across Western Europe, this emphasis on "lean and mean" forms of public administration—which is in turn derived from neoliberal discourses on the New Public Management and public choice theory—has replaced the inherited Fordist-Keynesian assumption that large-scale bureaucratic hierarchies would deliver the most efficient allocation of public services. Consequently, "whereas the question of regional government was once addressed mainly in the context of an administrative hierarchy, with an emphasis on vertical relationships, the situation today is one in which the horizontal relations among regions are equally important, as also is a vertical relationship that goes beyond the state."[23] In this manner, metropolitan regulation is being redefined from a vertical, redistributive, and territorially enclosed relationship within a national administrative hierarchy into a horizontal, entrepreneurial, and networked relationship among subnational economic directorates pitted against one another to attract flows of investment within a supranational landscape of capital. Just as importantly, in contrast to the local economic initiatives of the 1980s, which promoted a beggar-thy-neighbor politics of zero-sum competition across the European urban system, the competitive city-regionalisms of the post-1990s period have embraced selective modes of intrametropolitan coordination, cooperation, and networking as an institutional basis for even more aggressive, regionally upscaled strategies of place promotion.[24]

---

reference to the US case, see Neil Brenner, "Decoding the Newest 'Metropolitan Regionalism' in the USA: A Critical Overview," *Cities* 19, no. 1 (2002): 3–21.

[22] Lefèvre, "Metropolitan Government," 18.

[23] Max Barlow, "Administrative Systems and Metropolitan Regions," *Environment and Planning C: Government and Policy* 15 (1997): 410.

[24] On the spatial politics of the "new localism," see Jamie Peck and Adam Tickell, "Searching for a New Institutional Fix," in Amin, *Post-Fordism: A Reader*, 280–315. On the consolidation of regional entrepreneurialism, see Walter Prigge and Klaus Ronneberger, "Globalisierung und Regionalisierung—Zur Auflösung Frankfurts in die Region," *Österreichische Zeitschrift für Soziologie* 21, no. 2 (1996): 129–38; as well as Klaus Ronneberger and Christian Schmid, "Globalisierung und Metropolenpolitik: Überlegungen zum Urbanisierungsprozess der neunziger Jahre," in *Capitales Fatales*, ed. Hansruedi Hitz, Roger Keil, Ute Lehrer, Klaus Ronneberger, Christian Schmid, and Richard Wolff (Zürich: Rotpunktverlag, 1995), 354–78.

4. *A rescaled politics of urban growth.* Across Europe, recent metropolitan reform initiatives have been mobilized by newly rescaled growth coalitions and territorial alliances whose most active participants generally include (a) modernizing national governments; (b) growth-oriented political elites, including mayors and city council members, within fiscally distressed and/or entrepreneurially oriented central cities; (c) local and regional business representatives, property developers, industrialists, and other place entrepreneurs; and (d) political representatives of small- and medium-sized municipalities within a region, often located in close proximity to the city core or to major regional infrastructures such as airports, industrial clusters, office parks, or shopping malls. The most vocal adversaries of competitive city-regionalist projects have generally included (a) representatives of middle-tier or provincial governmental levels that perceive more powerful metropolitan institutions as a threat to their political or administrative authority, (b) residents within large cities that fear a loss of democratic accountability and local political control, and (c) political representatives of wealthier suburban or peri-urban towns that oppose central city dominance, seek to minimize putatively "external" claims on the local tax base, reject regional influence on local land-use decisions, and/or embrace exclusionary localist, xenophobic spatial ideologies.[25] Since the 1990s, the confrontation between these opposed political-economic alliances has significantly reshaped the spatial politics of urban growth and, by consequence, the dynamics of metropolitan governance reform within most major Western European city-regions.

In sum, while there has been a marked discrepancy between demands for comprehensive institutional reforms in many contemporary city-regions and the more modest types of regulatory coordination that have actually been implemented, this general overview suggests that, across diverse politico-institutional contexts, significant rescalings of metropolitan regulatory space have been under way during the last two decades.[26]

---

[25] Heinz, *Stadt & Region*, 21–28.

[26] Peter Newman, "Changing Patterns of Regional Governance in the EU," *Urban Studies* 37, no. 5–6 (2000): 895–908.

The Limits of "New Regionalist" Interpretations

In recent years, the concept of the "new regionalism" has been widely used as a shorthand reference to two major strands of analysis within contemporary geopolitical economy.[27] First, it is often used to refer to studies of the resurgence of regional economies and new industrial districts under conditions of globalized, post-Fordist capitalism.[28] From this perspective, the new regionalism refers to the strategic role of metropolitan agglomeration economies—and their extended regional networks of interfirm relations, innovative milieux, associational linkages, high-technology infrastructural matrices, untraded interdependencies, and forms of institutional thickness—as the engines of economic development under globalizing capitalism. This strand of the new regionalist discussion has focused, in particular, upon certain purportedly paradigmatic industrial districts such as Emilia-Romagna, Baden-Württemberg, Boston's Route 128, Silicon Valley, and Los Angeles/ Orange County, where such networks are thought to have engendered distinctive institutional conditions for post-Fordist forms of industrialization. However, the arguments of this strand of the new regionalism have also been embraced more broadly among national, regional, and local policymakers concerned to find appropriate strategies for promoting industrial regeneration across diverse territorial sites and spatial scales.[29]

Second, the notion of the new regionalism has also been used to describe the new subnational political-economic landscapes—in Udo Bullmann's phrase, the "politics of the third level"—that have emerged within a rapidly integrating European Union.[30] From this perspective, the new regionalism refers to the construction of a "Europe of the regions" through the simultaneous upward and downward rescaling of inherited, nationalized formations of political-economic space. While the notion of a "Europe of the regions" was

---

[27] See John Lovering, "Theory Led by Policy: The Inadequacies of the 'New Regionalism,'" *International Journal of Urban and Regional Research* 23, no. 2 (1999): 379–96; as well as MacLeod, "New Regionalism Reconsidered."

[28] For key engagements with the debate, see Ash Amin, "An Institutionalist Perspective on Regional Economic Development," *International Journal of Urban and Regional Research* 23, no. 3 (1999): 365–78; Michael Storper and Allen J. Scott, "The Wealth of Regions: Market Forces and Policy Imperatives in Local and Global Context," *Futures* 27, no. 5 (1995): 505–26; Scott, *Regions and the World Economy;* and Cooke and Morgan, *Associational Economy.*

[29] For discussion and critical analysis, see the various chapters included in Scott, *Global City-Regions.*

[30] Udo Bullmann, ed., *Die Politik der dritten Ebene. Regionen im Europa der Union* (Baden-Baden: Nomos, 1994); Patrick Le Galès and Christian Lequesne, eds., *Regions in Europe: The Politics of Power* (New York: Routledge, 1998); Keating, *New Regionalism.*

originally articulated as a political counterpoint to the orthodox liberal notion of a "Europe of the corporations," it has more recently come to signify (1) the consolidation of a European framework of multilevel governance in which national governments are but one among many politico-institutional layers involved in the development and implementation of collectively binding policies and (2) the geopolitical strategies of subnational economic spaces to promote endogenous regional development under conditions of intensified geoeconomic and European integration.[31] Accordingly, in this second strand of new regionalist discussion, scholars are concerned to explore the apparent "hollowing out" national political space within the multiscalar administrative hierarchies of the European Union, as well as the increasingly assertive roles of subnational institutions, including regional and local governments, in establishing regulatory infrastructures for economic governance and place promotion within the Single European Market. As Michael Keating explains, the spatial politics of the new regionalism "pits regions against each other in a competitive mode, rather than providing complementary roles for them in a national division of labour."[32]

Taken together, then, the main lines of new regionalist analysis suggest that the institutional architectures of subnational political-economic space are being systematically reworked in the current period, with significant consequences for patterns and pathways of urban development. Whatever their differences of methodology, interpretation, normative orientation, and empirical focus, new regionalist scholars appear to concur that regions—especially metropolitan regions—have become major arenas for a wide range of institutional realignments, regulatory experiments, and political strategies within contemporary capitalism.

Against this background, it might initially seem appropriate to interpret the proliferation of competitive city-regionalisms in post-1990s Europe as an unambiguous verification of the analyses and forecasts advanced in new regionalist scholarship. As we have discussed, recent metropolitan reform initiatives have been justified in significant measure as a means to promote regional economic regeneration in a volatile, crisis-riven, and intensely competitive geoeconomic context. Additionally, such initiatives are often framed with reference to the purported inability of national governments to provide the customized, place-specific regulatory infrastructures that are considered to be most suitable for igniting, guiding, and sustaining

---

[31] Ronneberger and Schmid, "Globalisierung und Metropolenpolitik."

[32] Keating, *New Regionalism*, 73.

regional industrial growth under these conditions. From such a perspective, adopting Alain Lipietz's terminology, one might interpret those urban regions where metropolitan institutional reform has been pushed furthest as "spaces for themselves" in which hegemonic territorial alliances have (1) self-consciously formulated a regional developmental vision or "projected space," (2) embodied that spatial vision in a specific politico-organizational framework or "regional armature," and (3) mobilized these newly created, regionally scaled governance capacities to ignite, intensify, and manage urban economic development, leading to (4) the consolidation of a regionally specific growth model and accumulation strategy.[33] And finally, given the degree to which proponents of metropolitan regulatory reform have been explicitly concerned "to replace the 'imagined community' at the national level with an 'imagined unit of competition' at the regional level,"[34] the resultant subnational regulatory realignments might also be interpreted, following Allen J. Scott's proposal, as the institutional bedrock for a post-Westphalian formation of political space in which city-states, "regional directorates," and supranational trade confederations would tendentially supersede territorially sovereign national states as the hegemonic basis for collective political, economic, and social order.[35]

However, from the vantage point of the theoretical approach to rescaling processes developed in this book, such new regionalist perspectives on metropolitan resurgence appear seriously inadequate. To be sure, new regionalist scholarship has generated a number of salient theoretical insights, research hypotheses, and empirical observations that have considerable relevance for the field of critical urban studies. Nonetheless, these literatures also contain major analytical blind spots that compromise their usefulness for illuminating the contemporary politics of scale, whether in Europe or elsewhere.

For instance, some approaches to the new regionalism have assumed a direct correspondence between official justifications for regional regulatory change and their actual consequences in the spheres of economic governance and territorial development. They have thus tended to interpret nearly any prominent regional political discourses or institutional realignments

---

[33] Alain Lipietz, "The National and the Regional: Their Autonomy Vis-a-Vis the Capitalist World Crisis," in *Transcending the State-Global Divide*, ed. Ronen P. Palan and Barry K. Gills (Boulder, CO: Lynne Rienner Publishers), 27.

[34] Lovering, "Theory Led by Policy," 392.

[35] Scott, *Regions and the World Economy*. For a closely related argument, see also Kenichi Ohmae, *The End of the Nation State: The Rise of Regional Economies* (New York: Free Press, 1995).

as evidence confirming the generic model of regional renaissance that has been postulated in new regionalist theories.[36] However, as more critically attuned accounts have indicated, most contemporary projects of regional institutional restructuring have systematically failed to establish modes of economic governance that enhance local innovative capacities, prevent technological lock-ins, and support long-term socioeconomic dynamism.[37] Indeed, many of the institutional rescalings associated with competitive city-regionalism have, in practice, served mainly to advance neomercantilist place-marketing campaigns that foster wasteful, zero-sum forms of investment poaching, regulatory downgrading, and corporate welfare. Such predatory, beggar-thy-neighbor regional policies are, as Jamie Peck has argued, an important expression of the "widespread tendencies to fiddle with governance while the economy burns."[38] They are also very much at odds with the high-trust, collaborative innovation networks that new regionalist scholars have generally associated with contemporary forms of regional resurgence.

Meanwhile, because new regionalist discourses regarding agglomeration economies, innovative milieux, regional learning, associational networks, territorial competitiveness, and the supposed imperatives of globalization have now been so widely disseminated among policymakers, the use of such arguments to justify subnational regulatory rescalings cannot be viewed simply as an endogenous, "bottom up" response to the new governance imperatives associated with global capitalism or European integration. On the contrary, the proliferation of new regionalist terminology must be understood as a politically mediated outcome of ongoing, transnational forms of policy transfer and ideological contestation that are crystallizing across a volatile, crisis-riven geoeconomic landscape. At the present time, we have only a preliminary grasp of the specific politico-ideological mechanisms and variegated interspatial circuits through which new regionalist keywords, policy recipes, and spatial imaginaries have been disseminated. However, as John Lovering has forcefully argued, any explanation of such trends would

---

[36] Analogous methodological tendencies underpinned early applications of French regulation theory to the study of local politics. In this context, local institutional changes were commonly "read off" from posited macroeconomic shifts, such as the putative "transition" to post-Fordism. For discussion, see Jamie Peck, "Doing Regulation," in *The Oxford Handbook of Economic Geography*, ed. Gordon Clark, Maryann Feldman, and Meric Gertler (New York: Oxford University Press, 2000), 61–82.

[37] See, for instance, Amin, "Institutionalist Perspective"; and Ray Hudson, "Developing Regional Strategies for Economic Success: Lessons from Europe's Economically Successful Regions?," *European Urban and Regional Studies* 4, no. 4 (1997): 365–73.

[38] Peck, "Doing Regulation," 74.

surely need to consider the "instrumental utility [of such notions] to powerful industrial, state and social constituencies."[39] More generally, following
from Lovering's line of critique, it can be argued that the major discursive
tropes associated with the new regionalism have played an important role
in depoliticizing, and thus in normalizing, the profoundly uneven, exclusionary, and often destructive sociospatial consequences of crisis-induced
geoeconomic restructuring in the interests of dominant class fractions,
growth coalitions, and political elites.

These considerations point toward a broader issue that has been almost totally occluded in most approaches to the new regionalism: the neoliberalizing
macropolitical context in which contemporary debates on regional regulatory rescaling are being conducted. Although new regionalist scholars generally acknowledge the progressive erosion of Keynesian welfare national states
and their redistributive intergovernmental policy relays, most have neglected
to theorize explicitly the wide-ranging impacts of such politico-institutional
transformations on the subnational architectures of economic governance, especially within major metropolitan regions. This state-theoretical lacuna in new
regionalist research is particularly problematic because, as Gordon MacLeod
explains, "many of the policy innovations associated with the new regionalism
should be seen as running parallel alongside a deeper political effort to erode
the Keynesian welfarist institutional settlement founded upon the job-for-
life, large-firm centered industrial labor markets and integrated welfare enti-
tlement."[40] This pervasive, tendentially neoliberalizing rescaling of national
political space has, MacLeod suggests, been a "major determinant in actively
shaping the emerging regional world of 'smart' innovation-mediated spaces
and trusting social capital(ism)."[41]

Clearly, it would be a mistake to subsume all aspects of regional economic governance under the rubric of state spatial strategies, whether or
not they are oriented toward neoliberalizing agendas.[42] But it would be
equally problematic to bracket the massive role of rescaled, post-Keynesian
national states in shaping major aspects of urbanization under contemporary conditions, including by facilitating the construction of new, regionally
scaled regulatory architectures for stimulating, managing, and canalizing the

---

[39] Lovering, "Theory Led by Policy," 399.

[40] MacLeod, "Learning Region," 221.

[41] Ibid.

[42] On this danger, see Stefan Krätke, "A Regulationist Approach to Regional Studies,"
Environment and Planning A 31 (1999): 683–704.

process of urban development.[43] It is, in short, through the dismantling of inherited approaches to spatial Keynesianism and the concomitant rescaling of regulatory space that the denationalized vision of "regional motors of the global economy" could displace earlier compensatory, redistributive, and equalizing approaches to territorial development.[44] The consolidation of competitive city-regionalisms in Europe since the 1990s must be understood in direct relation to these wide-ranging rescalings of state space and the intensely contested politics of scale that have at once animated and resulted from them.

State Rescaling and the Regulation of Urbanization

As conceived here, then, contemporary metropolitan institutional reform projects must be interpreted not only through their immediate impacts on local and regional economic development but also with reference to their potentially more durable consequences for the infrastructures of territorial regulation. From this point of view, the rise of competitive city-regionalisms may be viewed as an expression of path-shaping political strategies through which diverse sociopolitical actors, organizations, and coalitions are attempting to "redesign the 'board' on which they are moving and [to] reformulate the rules of the game" that govern the urbanization process.[45] Such strategies are, however, directed less at the urbanization process as such than at the interscalar rule regimes and institutional configurations through which it is politically shaped. It is thus the geography of regulation—especially that

---

[43] For example, in the Dutch, French, Italian, and British contexts, central governments have actually been the driving political and legal forces behind proposals to establish new frameworks for metropolitan governance. Meanwhile, within Germany's federal state, the *Länder* have played the most important role in mobilizing metropolitan institutional reforms in several major urban regions, including Frankfurt/Rhine-Main, Munich, Hannover, Stuttgart, and the Ruhr district. And in nearly all EU states, a broad range of municipal, local, and county-level bodies remain key institutional pillars within the newly proposed or implemented metropolitan regulatory frameworks. In this sense, the spatial politics of competitive city-regionalism have been directly animated by and mediated through inherited architectures of state power, even as the latter are reworked and rescaled in a new geoeconomic context.

[44] The former phrase is from Allen J. Scott, "Regional Motors of the Global Economy," *Futures* 28, no. 5 (1996): 391–411.

[45] Klaus Nielsen, Bob Jessop, and Jerzy Hausner, "Institutional Change in Post-Socialism," in *Strategic Choice and Path-Dependency in Post-Socialism*, ed. Jerzy Hausner, Bob Jessop, and Klaus Nielsen (Brookfield, VT: Edward Elgar, 1995), 6–7. On the interplay between path dependency and path shaping in processes of institutional restructuring, see also Jacob Torfing, "Towards a Schumpeterian Workfare Postnational Regime: Path-Shaping and Path-Dependency in Danish Welfare State Reform," *Economy and Society* 28, no. 1 (1999): 369–402.

of *state* regulation—that forms not only the medium, but the site and the target, of contemporary metropolitan rescaling projects. Once they are operationally mature, these rescaled regulatory spaces (or "regional armatures," in Lipietz's vivid phraseology) are expected to yield significant new politico-institutional capacities through which to stimulate, regulate, and canalize the production of new urban spaces.[46]

The central question that emerges from these considerations is: why has the *metropolitan* scale become such an important force field for these emergent strategies of state rescaling? As argued in the preceding chapter, the consolidation of competitive city-regionalisms during the post-1990s period must be understood in relation to earlier rounds of crisis-induced urban-industrial restructuring, state rescaling, and urban policy reform since the collapse of North Atlantic Fordism in the 1970s. It was in that context, as we have seen, that inherited national intergovernmental systems and relays of spatial redistribution were recalibrated across Europe. This, in turn, constrained municipal governments to engage more directly in market-driven local economic initiatives in an effort simultaneously to address revenue shortfalls, to promote urban-industrial regeneration, and to manage proliferating socioeconomic crises. Under these conditions, European national states also mobilized new forms of locational policy that targeted strategic urban spaces as sites for economic growth, market-oriented territorial planning, splintered infrastructure configurations, and publicly subsidized corporate investment. Consequently, as the priorities of economic growth, territorial competitiveness, and place promotion superseded earlier concerns with collective consumption, infrastructural standardization, and sociospatial equalization, entrepreneurial forms of urban governance were generalized across the European territory.[47]

During the course of the 1980s and subsequently, these entrepreneurial modes of urban governance generated significant, if destabilizing, impacts upon inherited landscapes of territorial regulation and urban development. In particular, as Helga Leitner and Eric Sheppard have explained in a seminal assessment, the proliferation of local economic initiatives contributed to a "general trend towards diverting public resources to support private capital accumulation at the expense of social expenditures [and toward] encouraging the search for short-term gains at the expense of more important longer-term

---

[46] Lipietz, "National and the Regional."

[47] David Harvey, "From Managerialism to Entrepreneurialism: The Transformation of Urban Governance in Late Capitalism," *Geografiska Annaler: Series B Human Geography* 71, no. 1 (1989): 3–17.

investments in the health of cities and the well-being of their residents."[48] Consequently, the entrepreneurial localisms of the 1980s tended to intensify uneven spatial development, to encourage a "race to the bottom" in social service provision, to exacerbate entrenched inequalities within national territorial economies, and to generate new fault lines of politico-territorial conflict at various scales of state power.[49] Although a few European cities were able to ignite short-term bursts of investment due to their relatively early adoption of entrepreneurial urban policies, such first-mover advantages proved ephemeral: almost invariably, they were eroded as the familiar policy recipes of urban entrepreneurialism were diffused across the spatial division of labor.[50] Moreover, the generalization of putatively place-specific, yet often blandly generic approaches to local economic development tended to exacerbate a number of endemic regulatory deficits, governance failures, and coordination problems within the rescaled architectures of post-Keynesian state space. For instance, because entrepreneurial urban policies advanced the geographical differentiation of state regulatory activities without effectively embedding subnational economic development initiatives within an overarching framework of territorial regulation, they tended to undermine the organizational coherence of state institutions and to compromise the operational integration of policy regimes. Additionally, insofar as the resultant intensification of uneven spatial development entailed worsening socioeconomic prospects for significant population segments, the generalization of entrepreneurial approaches to urban development contributed to recurrent legitimation crises for national and local governments.

It is in relation to these wide-ranging institutional rescalings, regulatory realignments, and attendant crisis tendencies that the post-1990s consolidation of competitive city-regionalisms may be deciphered. As my choice of terminology in this chapter underscores, competitive approaches to city-regionalism have continued to privilege the goal of promoting urban economic development and to affirm the politics of aggressive territorial competition among metropolitan regions on European and global scales. However, the project of institutional upscaling associated with competitive city-regionalism has also been grounded upon a concerted critique of purely

[48] Helga Leitner and Eric Sheppard, "Economic Uncertainty, Inter-Urban Competition and the Efficacy of Entrepreneurialism," in *The Entrepreneurial City*, ed. Tim Hall and Phil Hubbard (London: Wiley, 1998), 305.

[49] On each of these outcomes of local economic initiatives and their consequences, see Eisenschitz and Gough, *Politics of Local Economic Development*.

[50] Leitner and Sheppard, "Economic Uncertainty," 303.

localized approaches to urban economic development and an equally resolute affirmation that metropolitan regions, not cities or localities, represent the optimal territorial units for locational policy. Consequently, as discussed earlier, the competitive city-regionalisms of the 1990s promoted a variety of institutional realignments and regulatory strategies that were intended, at the scale of a metropolitan region, (1) to minimize destructive forms of competition among administrative units (generally, municipalities); (2) to coordinate their planning, policy, and governance agendas more effectively; and (3) to create new frameworks for stimulating, managing, and canalizing economic development.

From this perspective, contemporary metropolitan reform initiatives are premised upon the double-edged project of strengthening regional institutional steering capacities, socioeconomic assets, and competitive advantages while also establishing a variety of regulatory flanking mechanisms designed to alleviate some of the most deleterious effects of locally scaled approaches to urban economic development. In effect, the scale of the city-region is to be mobilized as a regulatory pivot between an intraregional realm of enhanced cooperation, administrative coordination, embedded interfirm relations, and territorial solidarity and an extraregional space characterized by aggressive territorial competition, intergovernmental austerity, hypermobile capital flows, and unfettered market relations. By recalibrating the scalar interplay between competitive and cooperative relations within key territories of urban development, competitive city-regionalisms seek to strengthen their strategic positionality in the face of apparently intensifying geoeconomic pressures. Meanwhile, the putative need for "metropolitan solutions to urban problems" has been perceived, politicized, and acted upon in a direct, highly reflexive relation to the endemic limitations of previous rounds of market-oriented local regulatory experimentation within the splintered institutional landscapes of post-Keynesian capitalism. Accordingly, the rescaled regulatory armatures of competitive city-regionalism have also been justified as a means to alleviate or at least to manage some of the major conflicts, dislocations, and crisis tendencies that were triggered through the unrestrained generalization of urban entrepreneurialism during the 1980s.

However, in contrast to official discourses of inclusionary, smart, coordinated, flexible, and sustainable regional development, the de facto spatial politics of competitive city-regionalism have been, in practice, as ineffectual as the beggar-thy-neighbor forms of entrepreneurial urban governance they are ostensibly meant to supersede. As indicated, the common denominator of competitive city-regionalist initiatives is their promotion of the metropolitan scale as a privileged arena and target for new forms of locational policy. Yet, across the European Union, this regionally focused rescaling of state institutional structures and regulatory configurations has been fraught with a number of destructively self-undermining tensions, conflicts, and contradictions.

First, particularly when powerful political-economic interests are tied closely to extant levels of state territorial organization, the project of competitive city-regionalism generates intense struggles between opposed class factions, political coalitions, and territorial alliances regarding issues such as jurisdictional boundaries, institutional capacities, democratic accountability, fiscal relays, and intergovernmental linkages. Relatedly, even when new metropolitan institutions have been successfully established, their capacity to formulate, much less to implement, viable strategies of regional economic development has remained thoroughly problematic. In most European city-regions, the concern to enhance regional distinctiveness is rather decisively counterbalanced by the priority of minimizing investment costs through technological standardization, regulatory downgrading, direct subsidies to capital, and other policies to support a "good business climate." Meanwhile, the priorities of devolving economic governance and enhancing regional institutional flexibility stand in strong tension with the persistent need— in both legal-constitutional and operational terms—for continued political steering, administrative coordination, and fiscal support from superordinate tiers of the state, including national and regional governments. The balance among such diametrically opposed regulatory agendas within any urban region is thus likewise a matter of intense sociopolitical contestation. The process of metropolitan institutional rescaling has not resolved such conflicts but has merely rechanneled and partially reframed them. From this point of view, it would be politically naïve, analytically imprecise, and empirically inaccurate to interpret contemporary forms of competitive city-regionalism as alternatives to the orthodoxies of neoliberal urban governance. On the contrary, even if the rescaled regulatory spaces of contemporary metropolitan regionalism have articulated several countervailing political-ideological impulses, they have been thoroughly infused with, and largely animated by, neoliberalizing institutional agendas, regulatory orientations, and spatial visions.

Second, the spatial politics of competitive city-regionalism have not only failed to supersede the limitations of earlier, localist approaches to economic rejuvenation, but have extended them onto the larger spatial scale of metropolitan regions. This is because, in their current, tendentially neoliberalized forms, metropolitan approaches to locational policy likewise tend to intensify uneven spatial development, zero-sum forms of interspatial competition, and the splintering of territorial regulation, both within and beyond the city-region in which they are mobilized. In this way, by engendering further spirals of economic instability, territorial polarization, urban sociospatial fragmentation, regulatory splintering, and interscalar disorganization, such post-Keynesian rescaling projects have tended to undermine many of the key socio-institutional prerequisites for sustained regional industrial growth and territorial development. Consequently, despite their frequent embrace of solidaristic rhetoric, their modernizing institutional vision, and their explicit attention to problems of interscalar coordination, competitive city-regionalisms appear to have deepened and intensified rather than alleviated the regulatory deficits associated with earlier rounds of post-Keynesian urban restructuring and state rescaling.

Metropolitan Regulatory Space and the Politics of Scale

Perhaps the key analytical question for urban and regional development theory these days is not "Who rules cities?" but rather "At what spatial scale is territorial governance crystallising?"[51]

In his investigation of metropolitan governance restructuring in Los Angeles and Toronto during the 1990s, Roger Keil underscores a key ambiguity within contemporary strategies to rescale urban space.[52] As Keil's analysis demonstrates, broadly allied politico-ideological agendas—neoliberal, social democratic, ecological, and otherwise—may be pursued through diametrically opposed vectors of rescaling. Keil provocatively illustrates this apparent paradox by demonstrating how, during the course of the 1990s, neoconservative political coalitions in Los Angeles and Toronto pursued closely analogous projects of neoliberalization via divergent approaches to the rescaling of urban space. In Los Angeles, conservative secessionist movements pursued a strategy of territorial fragmentation that would have split off the San Fernando Valley, as well as several other nearby areas, from the city core. By contrast, in Toronto, a neoliberal provincial government pursued a consolidationist approach that sought to amalgamate six municipal governments into a single regional megacity. On this basis, Keil suggests that

---

[51] Andrew E. G. Jonas and Kevin Ward, "Cities' Regionalisms: Some Critical Reflections on Transatlantic Urban Policy Convergence" (Working Paper Series, Economic Geography Research Group, 2001), 21.

[52] Roger Keil, "Governance Restructuring in Los Angeles and Toronto: Amalgamation or Secession?," *International Journal of Urban and Regional Research* 24, no. 4 (2000): 758–81.

the real political cleavage in cities is not fundamentally between separationists and consolidationists, but remains one between those who favour democratization, social justice and ecological integrity and those who hope instead to protect the market economy (and the privileges and unequal freedoms associated with it) from what they regard as inappropriate efforts to impose social controls.[53]

In the context of our explorations of emergent metropolitan political strategies in this chapter, Keil's analysis provides a salient cautionary reminder against the reification of particular scales in any terrain of urban research. No scale of territorial regulation can be permanently defined with reference to a singular political project or ideological vision. Conversely, there is nothing intrinsically progressive or, for that matter, inherently reactionary lodged within the metropolitan or regional scale of governance. Indeed, until they are vested with substantive regulatory capacity through intergovernmental relays and activated with political content through regionally specific mobilizations, the institutions of metropolitan governance represent no more than empty organizational shells. Meanwhile, as Keil further explains, "both consolidation and fragmentation can lead to either more closed or more open political processes, to more or less equity and redistributive justice, and to better or worse urban social and natural environments."[54] In this sense, such metropolitan rescaling initiatives must be understood as broadly "compatible strategic options in an attempt to create regional governance at a variety of scales."[55] Strategies of metropolitan rescaling may be pursued by diverse sociopolitical coalitions oriented toward only partially compatible or even directly antagonistic visions of urban space. In turn, the rescaling of metropolitan governance represents only one politico-institutional pathway through which the geographies of capitalist urbanization may be shaped and reshaped.

The preceding discussion of post-Keynesian metropolitan political reform in contemporary Europe offers a further illustration of Keil's insights. As we have seen, the new scalar politics of competitive city-regionalism must be conceptualized not as the embodiment of a singular, internally coherent politico-ideological project, but as the outgrowth of ongoing struggles among diverse sociopolitical forces to manage the regulatory dislocations, conflicts, failures, and crises that have crystallized across the urban landscape since

---

[53] Keil, "Governance Restructuring," 760.

[54] Ibid., 759.

[55] Ibid., 775.

the dissolution of North Atlantic Fordism. While these struggles have contributed to a significant rescaling of inherited urban geographies, they have not established a new, coherently stabilized interscalar rule regime for economic regeneration or territorial development at any spatial scale. Indeed, most of the metropolitan reform initiatives that have crystallized in the post-Keynesian era of deepening scale relativization have offered no more than "partial and temporary responses to the problems they pretend to address."[56] Contemporary patterns and pathways of competitive city-regionalism may therefore be most plausibly interpreted as expressions of the continued, crisis-induced "search for a new institutional fix" via a series of intense yet ad hoc experiments with the scalar (re)configuration of urbanization.[57] Under these conditions, metropolitan regulatory space must be analyzed as a dynamically evolving, spatially polymorphic political force field permeated by recurrent negotiations, maneuvers, conflicts, crises, and struggles.

However, despite the politico-institutional fluidity associated with contemporary metropolitan rescaling projects, it would be short-sighted to dismiss contemporary struggles over the scalar organization of urban space as merely derivative expressions of conflicts over purportedly more essential issues such as economic development, collective consumption, territorial redistribution, democracy, social justice, or ecology. As Erik Swyngedouw has suggested, "the continuous reshuffling and reorganization of spatial scales is an integral part of social strategies and struggles for control and empowerment."[58] As I have argued in previous chapters, this proposition may be fruitfully applied to illuminate a multiplicity of political, institutional, and regulatory rescalings that have powerfully contributed to the production of new urban spaces under post-Keynesian, globalizing capitalism. And, as this chapter has demonstrated, Swyngedouw's concept of the politics of scale has equally salient methodological ramifications for the investigation of emergent forms of competitive city-regionalism. Clearly, the creation of rescaled approaches to metropolitan regionalism has provided neoliberal political alliances with new institutional capacities through which to roll out upscaled forms of locational policy, to impose market-disciplinary forms of urbanization, to insulate the urbanization process from democratic control, and to normalize the intensified patterns of uneven spatial development, territorial enclosure, and geoeconomic volatility that have been unleashed during

---

[56] Ibid., 777.

[57] Peck and Tickell, "Searching for a New Institutional Fix."

[58] Erik Swyngedouw, "Neither Global nor Local: 'Glocalization' and the Politics of Scale," in *Spaces of Globalization*, ed. Kevin R. Cox (New York: Guilford Press, 1997), 141.

the post-Keynesian era. In this sense, the scalar politics of competitive city-regionalism have evidently helped to consolidate, generalize, legitimate, and naturalize neoliberalized spaces of urbanization.

At the same time, however, these rescalings of urban regulatory space may also, at least potentially, open up new institutional arenas through which speculative, profit-driven forms of urban development could be exposed to public scrutiny, subjected to political regulation, subsumed under democratic control, and even superseded through an alternative, more inclusionary vision of urbanization. It is for this reason that contemporary debates on metropolitan institutional reform have remained such important lightning rods for broader struggles over the future patterns and pathways of urbanization. The scalar configuration of urban space is not only a setting for emergent metropolitan regulatory experiments, but one of their very stakes. Under these conditions, even as processes of geoeconomic restructuring, interscalar regulatory contestation, and scale relativization continue to lurch ahead, an urgent task for progressive sociopolitical forces is to explore new ways of harnessing metropolitan institutions to stimulate open public debate on emergent urban transformations; to enhance democratic accountability and community participation; to rein in short-termist, predatory approaches to urban investment; to protect the urban commons against privatization and enclosure; to foster territorially balanced, ecologically sane forms of urban development; and to promote a more egalitarian, socially just distribution of public goods at all spatial scales. Doing so may, in turn, contribute to the imagination—and, ultimately, the *production*—of alternative new urban spaces that would supersede those forged, in recent years, through competitive city-regionalism and a neoliberalizing politics of scale.

7
Urban Growth Machines—But at What Scale?

LIKE ALL COMMODITIES UNDER CAPITALISM, cities are often naturalized, both in scholarly analysis and in everyday life: the social processes required to produce them are forgotten or hidden. The built environment thus acquires the aura of a pregiven materiality, mysteriously devoid of the social relations that engendered it.[1]

In studies of urban governance, this fetish of the city has frequently assumed the form of methodological localism—the tendency of scholars to focus on local political processes without investigating the supralocal state spaces, regulatory frameworks, industrial landscapes, spatial divisions of labor, and socioeconomic flows in which such processes are embedded. To some extent, these localist methodological tendencies stem from the understandable concern of many urban social scientists to legitimate their subfield within disciplinary environments that have long been dominated by methodological nationalism—an equally problematic tendency to naturalize the national scale of political life.[2] Yet, even when this localist orientation stems

---

[1] On the naturalized "aura" of the urban, see Maria Kaika and Erik Swyngedouw, "Fetishizing the Modern City: The Phantasmagoria of Urban Technological Networks," *International Journal of Urban and Regional Research* 24, no. 1 (2000): 120–38.

[2] On methodological nationalism, see Andreas Wimmer and Nina Glick-Schiller, "Methodological Nationalism and Beyond: Nation-State Building, Migration and the Social

from a well-justified concern to circumvent the blind spots of methodological nationalism, it contains serious methodological limitations. Insofar as scholars of urban politics focus predominantly or exclusively on local governance institutions, political coalitions, or regulatory processes, their work is in danger of being ensnared within the formally analogous methodological trap of localism. Within such an epistemological framework, the local or urban scales are taken for granted as pregiven, relatively discrete containers; their supralocal conditions of possibility, contexts of development, and consequences are bracketed. However, to the degree that urban politics are impacted by, and in turn impact, supralocal political-economic conditions, dynamics, and developments, the notion of a discrete "urban" scale of political action is a mystification: it represents various processes that originate outside of cities, and that effectively ricochet through them, as being internally generated or enclosed within their jurisdictional boundaries.

One of the major politico-epistemological agendas of critical urban theory is to deconstruct this fetish of the city by illuminating the variegated, historically specific, and politically contested sociospatial processes that underpin the creation and continual transformation of urban landscapes, including those through which urban governance unfolds.[3] This project of defetishization requires the adoption of a dynamically multiscalar methodological framework through which to investigate, to decipher, and thus to denaturalize those regulatory spaces that are commonly characterized as "urban" or "local." Within such a framework, cities may well remain a central object and terrain of investigation, but they are grasped by being positioned analytically within broader, supraurban political-economic configurations—for instance, of capital accumulation, territorial regulation, socioenvironmental metabolism, and sociopolitical contestation. On the one hand, putatively urban processes are themselves often multiscalar, stretching beyond any single municipality into a tangled jigsaw of metropolises, regions, national or transnational interurban networks, and worldwide spatial divisions of labor. At the same time, cities are in turn shaped by diverse supralocal processes, institutions, and configurations, from worldwide flows of investment, trade, materials, and migration to state jurisdictional boundaries, intergovernmental divisions, various kinds of spatial policies, and planetary-scale

---

Sciences," *Global Networks* 2, no. 4 (2002): 301–34; and John Agnew, "The Territorial Trap: The Geographical Assumptions of International Relations Theory," *Review of International Political Economy* 1, no. 1 (1994): 53–80.

[3] Neil Brenner, *Critique of Urbanization: Selected Essays* (Basel: Bauwelt Fundamente/Birkhäuser Verlag, 2016).

circuits of energy, materials, and ecological flows. This multiscalar method-ological orientation explicitly acknowledges the strategically essential role of cities and the urban scale within modern capitalism but emphasizes their embeddedness within broader landscapes of political-economic activity, ter-ritorial organization, regulatory intervention, metabolic transformation, and social struggle. From this point of view, rather than being seen as a pregiven social fact, the very intelligibility of the city as a discrete arena, terrain, or unit of political-economic life represents a historically contingent, contested *product* of strategies to establish such a formation. In David Harvey's terms, such strategies entail efforts to construct an urbanized "structured coher-ence"—that is, a relatively durable, locally configured framework of institu-tional and sociospatial organization—within otherwise relatively inchoate, multiscalar configurations of capital, infrastructure, population, governance, and ecology.[4]

This chapter explores the implications of such a methodological orienta-tion for deciphering the politics of urban development in the United States. In a first step, I consider the problem of localism, which has been manifested in several recurrent forms within the two major theoretical approaches to the study of US urban politics: urban regime theory and urban growth machine theory.[5] Against methodologically localist interpretations, the growth-oriented character of US urban politics is interpreted here as the product of (histori-cally entrenched but evolving) national state institutions and multiscalar reg-ulatory strategies. On this basis, I elaborate a scale-attuned reading of John Logan and Harvey Molotch's classic 1987 work *Urban Fortunes*. This critical reinterpretation reveals that putatively "local" or "urban" growth machines represent nationalized interscalar constructs rather than internally generated products of place-based mobilizations, coalitions, or alliances.[6] More gener-ally, this analysis suggests that the apparently "urban" character of growth machines, both in the United States and elsewhere, must be carefully investigated and explained, rather than being presupposed. A concluding section summarizes some of the epistemological, methodological, and

---

[4] David Harvey, *The Urban Experience* (Baltimore: Johns Hopkins University Press, 1989).

[5] For overviews of these research traditions, see Mickey Lauria, ed., *Reconstructing Urban Regime Theory: Regulating Urban Politics in a Global Economy* (New York: Sage, 1997); and Andrew E. G. Jonas and David Wilson, eds., *The Urban Growth Machine, Critical Perspectives, Two Decades Later* (Albany: State University of New York Press, 1999).

[6] John Logan and Harvey Molotch, *Urban Fortunes: The Political Economy of Place* (Berkeley: University of California Press, 1987). For an analogous argument on the case of the Netherlands, see Pieter Terhorst and Jacques van de Ven, "The National Urban Growth Coalition in the Netherlands," *Political Geography* 14, no. 4 (1995): 343–61.

comparative implications of the foregoing discussion for developing reflexively multiscalar approaches to the study of urban governance.

Localism in Question

Urban regime theory and growth machine theory are the most influential analytical frameworks through which urban development has been explored within US political science and political sociology, and they have exercised a considerable impact on the fields of urban geography and urban planning as well.[7] Developed as critiques of traditional ecological and structuralist Marxist approaches to urban studies in the 1980s, both theories isolate certain actors, coalitions, and organizations at the urban scale and examine their diverse boosterist activities to promote economic growth. The goal of these research traditions, as Andrew Jonas has explained, is to "uncover rather than merely assert the role of politics in urban theory."[8] In this sense, both theories represent critical reformulations of traditional elite theory in the context of urban politics.[9]

Urban regime theory, as developed influentially by political scientists such as Stephen Elkin, Clarence Stone, and Heywood Sanders, emphasizes (1) the privileged position of business interests in the formation of municipal socioeconomic policies and (2) the changing division of labor between markets and state institutions in processes of urban development.[10] Empirical research within the urban regime framework has examined the ways in which public and private interests mesh together through a range of formal and informal civic arrangements, cooperative alliances, and partnerships that are embodied in, and reproduced through, specific types of urban growth coalition or regime (for instance, pluralist, federalist, or entrepreneurial in Elkin's typology, or caretaker, progressive, or corporate in Stone's framework).[11]

---

[7] Lauria, *Reconstructing Urban Regime Theory*; Jonas and Wilson, *Urban Growth Machine*.

[8] Andrew E. G. Jonas, "A Place for Politics in Urban Theory: The Organization and Strategies of Urban Coalitions," *Urban Geography* 13, no. 3 (1993): 282.

[9] Alan Harding, "Elite Theory and Growth Machines," in *Theories of Urban Politics*, ed. David Judge, Gerry Stoker, and Hal Wolman (London: Sage, 1995), 35–53.

[10] Stephen Elkin, *City and Regime in the American Republic* (Chicago: University of Chicago Press, 1987); Clarence Stone, *Regime Politics: The Governing of Atlanta, 1946–1988* (Lawrence: University Press of Kansas, 1989); and Clarence Stone and Heywood Sanders, eds., *The Politics of Urban Development* (Lawrence: University Press of Kansas, 1987).

[11] Elkin, *City and Regime*; Stone, *Regime Politics*.

Urban growth machine theory, developed in the paradigmatic work of sociologists John Logan and Harvey Molotch, is focused less on policy outcomes than on the process of urban development itself.[12] For Logan and Molotch, the city operates as a growth machine insofar as localized coalitions—generally composed of property owners ("rentiers") and other auxiliary, place-based supporters (developers, universities, local media and newspapers, utility companies, labor unions, small retailers, and the like)—form and attempt to promote land uses that enhance the exchange value of local real estate tracts. Although challenges to the growth agenda and the ideology of "value-free" development may be articulated in the name of use values by neighborhood organizations, slow-growth, and other NIMBYist (not-in-my-backyard) local movements, Logan and Molotch emphasize the overarching power of "place entrepreneurs," generally with the support of municipal government, in circumventing such oppositional forces. On this basis, Logan and Molotch famously contend that urban growth machines have played a key role in shaping the landscapes of urbanization throughout US history. This has remained the case, they argue, despite the deeply polarizing and often socially and environmentally destructive effects wrought by growth machines, both within and among places, throughout the *longue durée* of urban industrial development.

Since the mid-1980s, urban regime theory and growth machine theory have generated an impressive body of research on the politics of local economic development, particularly in the US as well as in comparative international perspective.[13] Consistent with their goal of circumventing the limitations of traditional structuralist approaches, both theories have focused on the activities, alliances, and agendas of local political-economic elites *within* cities. This internalist analytical and empirical focus has, consequently, led several commentators to underscore the problem of "localism" in each of these research traditions. For instance, Alan Harding suggests that both regime theory and growth machine studies are "essentially localist" due to their overwhelming emphasis on intralocal political dynamics: "They often underplay the importance of externally imposed structures that predispose local actors to particular forms of behavior and the role played by

---

[12] Logan and Molotch, *Urban Fortunes.*

[13] Lauria, *Reconstructing Urban Regime Theory;* Jonas and Wilson, *Urban Growth Machine;* Stone and Sanders, *Politics of Urban Development.* For comparative applications, see John Logan and Todd Swanstrom, eds., *Beyond the City Limits: Urban Policy and Economic Restructuring in Comparative Perspective* (Philadelphia: Temple University Press, 1990); and Harvey Molotch and Serena Vicari, "Three Ways to Build: The Development Process in the United States, Japan and Italy," *Urban Affairs Quarterly* 24, no. 2 (1988): 188–214.

more variable non-local sources of influence on urban development, for example the changing demands of higher levels of government or external investors."[14] Similarly, Bob Jessop, Jamie Peck, and Adam Tickell argue that studies of urban growth machines tend to attribute "causal power to local political networks and thereby suggest . . . that spatial variations in urban fortunes are merely a byproduct of the geographies of charismatic city leadership or effective urban networking."[15] In an analogous critique, Andrew Wood suggests that "regime and coalition approaches . . . assert the autonomy of urban or local politics as a legitimate focus for study without properly theorising the basis for that politics. Urban politics is simply politics that takes place in cities rather than being a politics of the city."[16]

Given the multiscalar approach to urbanization developed in this book, these critics' shared emphasis on the supralocal institutional parameters for urban development appears well justified. However, their critique of "localism" requires further theoretical specification. There are at least three analytically distinct ways in which an "urban" analysis may be described as localist:

1. *Ontological* localism entails the claim that local entities, institutions, or processes are in some sense autonomous from, or more causally significant than, entities, institutions, or processes organized at supralocal scales.

2. *Methodological* localism is premised on the assumption that, even though the local may be intertwined with and conditioned by supralocal entities, institutions, or processes, it can and must be isolated from the latter for analytical purposes, as a means to decipher its putatively "internal" structures and determinants. As indicated previously, to the degree that this analytical maneuver is accomplished without explicit justification or explanation, methodological localism may also entail a naturalization of the local scale, that is, its presentation as a pregiven or self-evident site for social scientific inquiry.

3. *Empirical* localism entails the choice of locally scaled entities, institutions, or processes, such as cities, as a focal point for research.

---

[14] Alan Harding, "Urban Regimes in a Europe of the Cities?," *European Urban and Regional Studies* 4, no. 4 (1997): 294.

[15] Bob Jessop, Jamie Peck, and Adam Tickell, "Retooling the Machine: Economic Crisis, State Restructuring and Urban Politics," in Jonas and Wilson, *The Urban Growth Machine*, 144.

[16] Andrew Wood, "Questions of Scale in the Entrepreneurial City," in *The Entrepreneurial City*, ed. Tim Hall and Phil Hubbard (London: Wiley, 1998), 277.

It may, but does not necessarily, entail underlying ontological claims regarding the nature of the local, a naturalization of the local scale, or specific methodological claims about how the local should be most appropriately studied.

In these terms, it can be argued that most proponents of urban regime theory and urban growth machine theory avoid ontological forms of localism. Neither theory is tied intrinsically to the claim that urban processes are ontologically autonomous from, or causally primary over, any other scale(s) of political-economic life. It seems equally clear that both theories do exemplify empirical forms of localism, for the simple reason that they focus on cities or localized modes of governance. This empirical localism appears defensible because, as the literature on US urban political development has demonstrated, cities are indeed important sites of regulatory activity, institutional experimentation, and political contestation. It therefore makes sense to devote intellectual resources to their investigation.

This leaves open the considerably thornier question of methodological localism, which lies at the heart of the critiques raised by the authors quoted previously. To what extent do urban regime theorists and urban growth machine theorists neglect to illuminate the supralocal contexts and determinants of urban development? To what extent do scholars working in these traditions treat the local in isolation from broader political-economic institutions, conditions, forces, and transformations? To what degree do they take the local for granted, as a pregiven or self-evident site? In short, to what extent does the (plausible) empirical localism of urban regime theory and urban growth machine theory slide into a (problematic) methodological localism? To the extent that this occurs, researchers are likely to find themselves ensnared within an urban studies version of the "endogeneity trap" analyzed by Saskia Sassen, in which a site or scale of investigation is explained exclusively with reference to processes assumed to be internal to or coextensive with it.[17]

In contrast to the lines of critique that are advanced in the passages quoted earlier, a close reading of the relevant literatures reveals a more complicated state of affairs, in which authors working in these research traditions frame their objects of investigation and scales of analysis in divergent ways. For

---

[17] Saskia Sassen, *Territory, Authority, Rights: From Medieval to Global Assemblages* (Princeton, NJ: Princeton University Press, 2006). In Sassen's work, the critique of the endogeneity trap focuses mainly on the limits of methodological nationalism and methodological globalism. However, the methodological problem she diagnoses is arguably quite rampant with reference to other scales of investigation as well.

instance, much of the case study–based literature applying regime theory and growth machine theory arguably does veer toward methodological localism, and is thus caught up in the endogeneity trap. Extralocal political-economic parameters are generally presupposed as the analysis focuses primarily on intralocal coalitions and institutional arrangements within a particular city. By contrast, macrohistorical or comparative deployments of these approaches are more likely to avoid methodological localism or to embrace it only in a relatively circumscribed manner. A concern with multiple cities, longer-term temporal frames, or several national contexts also appears to attune scholars more explicitly to the broader sociospatial and institutional fields within which urban politics are constituted. Here, there may be some exploration of endogenous causal chains, but the latter are carefully embedded within a broader, multiscalar explanatory framework that illuminates the supralocal parameters—economic, political, and institutional—that mediate and perhaps directly shape local outcomes.

Whatever their research agenda or methodological orientation, however, theorists of urban regimes and growth machines generally *do* appear to recognize—in more or less detail, and with greater or lesser degrees of reflexivity—the nationally specific "institutional envelope" within which local coalition formation has been configured.[18] The key issue is the extent to which such analyses address the *theoretical* significance of this important empirical observation in the context of their specific arguments about urban political-economic dynamics. The charge of methodological localism is justified only in cases in which the local is unreflexively presupposed and in which, consequently, national institutional configurations and interscalar relays are relegated to an external "background" structure.

The National Institutional Parameters for Urban Development

The concern to avoid methodological localism and the endogeneity trap in urban studies stems from a relatively straightforward proposition: the "localness" of growth politics in US cities, as elsewhere, is not a pregiven or endogenous empirical attribute of the coalitions in question but is a mediated

---

[18] On the notion of "institutional envelopes" and its implications for rethinking growth machine theory, see Murray Low, "Growth Machines and Regulation Theory: The Institutional Dimension of the Regulation of Space in Australia," *International Journal of Urban and Regional Research* 18 (1999): 451–69.

result of national institutional structures, regulatory rule regimes, and political geographies that, quite literally, create a space in which urban growth machines may be established. Indeed, it can be argued that urban growth machines are constructions of the (national) state insofar as national political-institutional frameworks (1) play a major role in delineating the spatial units within which growth coalitions are formed and (2) establish a system of land-use regulations and restrictions that decisively condition local actors' degree of commitment to, and dependence upon, a growth agenda. It is essential, therefore, to situate urban growth coalitions not only within the changing worldwide spatial divisions of labor associated with capitalist systems of production and circulation but also in relation to the evolving spatial divisions of regulation associated with national state institutions, intergovernmental systems, and policy regimes.[19]

These claims can be illustrated with reference to the long-term role of the US national state in mediating the politics of urban development. For present purposes, this discussion brackets the consequences of US cities' evolving positions in geoeconomic divisions of labor and infrastructural supply chains for urban growth machine dynamics.[20] The core concern here is to explore the nationally specific institutional arrangements that have most directly facilitated the proliferation and entrenchment of urban growth machines across the US territory since the nineteenth century:

- *The institutionalized power of private capital.* In the US regulatory system, private property developers are given an inordinate authority to make decisions involving land uses, capital investment, and job locations. This tradition of urban privatism reflects an institutionally entrenched belief that the private sector is best equipped to assess investment opportunities and locations, to organize the technical expertise and management skills required for economic development, and to maximize the efficiency of economic operations. This situation is embodied in, and further exacerbated by, the lack of a major nonbusiness political party in the United States resembling the social democratic, trade union–based parties that have played such an important role in

---

[19] Kevin Cox and Andrew Mair, "Locality and Community in the Politics of Local Economic Development," *Annals of the Association of American Geographers* 78, no. 2 (1988): 307–25.

[20] On such issues, see David Wachsmuth, "Competitive Multi-City Regionalism: Growth Politics beyond the Growth Machine," *Regional Studies* 51, no. 4 (2017): 643–53; and David Wachsmuth, "Infrastructure Alliances: Supply-Chain Expansion and Multi-City Growth Coalitions," *Economic Geography* 93, no. 1 (2017): 44–65.

European municipal politics.[21] For these reasons, in the US context, governmental policies have long been mobilized to create new avenues for privately organized capital investment in cities, whether through urban renewal schemes, housing programs, urban development action grants, or other federal, state, and local incentives. Such policies have directly subsidized capital investment by minimizing private risk and covering key overhead costs, often without subjecting firms to extensive regulatory constraints. Additionally, urban regeneration programs in the United States have prioritized capital-led initiatives to promote (re)investment over labor-oriented policies, generally through the establishment of "partnerships" and other cooperative arrangements between public agencies and business organizations.[22] This institutionalized prioritization of market-led forms of economic governance at each tier of the US state has been an essential precondition for the formation and generalization of urban growth machines. The latter are considerably less likely to crystallize in national states that impose tighter regulatory constraints upon local land markets and local investment decisions.

- *The institutional structure of US federalism.* The federal structure of the US state dictates that political power and responsibilities are shared among multiple administrative levels. Accordingly, subnational political units such as the states and municipalities are allotted important regulatory powers in policy areas such as public health, welfare, education, and economic development, which enable them to influence the locational patterns of industries, infrastructure investment, and population. Although federal urban policies have existed since the New Deal, their implementation is left largely to the states and municipalities.[23] In contrast to most Western European states, there is no nation-wide spatial planning system in the United States, and there are few federal equalization programs that promote the relocation of capital into declining or disadvantaged areas.[24] Within this decentralized political system, the public agencies that are most immediately equipped to influence

---

[21] Alan Harding, "Review Article: North American Urban Political Economy, Urban Theory and British Research," *British Journal of Political Science* 29 (1999): 687.

[22] Peter Eisinger, "City Politics in an Era of Devolution," *Urban Affairs Review* 33, no. 3 (1988): 308–25.

[23] John Mollenkopf, *The Contested City* (Princeton, NJ: Princeton University Press, 1983).

[24] John Friedmann and Robin Bloch, "American Exceptionalism in Regional Planning, 1933–2000," *International Journal of Urban and Regional Research* 14, no. 4 (1990): 576–601.

intranational locational patterns are the states and the municipalities.[25] Economic development initiatives by these subnational tiers of state power intensified considerably after World War II in conjunction with a wave of intranational industrial relocations driven by capital's drive to lower production costs and to seek out nonunionized segments of the workforce. Subsequently, the global economic recession and the acceleration of deindustrialization of the 1970s created a new urgency for external capital investment, particularly within crisis-stricken regions and cities. State-level and local economic development initiatives were markedly intensified during this era and have subsequently become standard policy tools for subnational governments.[26] The federal territorial structure of the US national state must therefore be viewed as a key institutional parameter within which urban growth machines have been recurrently stimulated. Urban growth machines are less likely to form in national states in which municipalities lack such extensive, autonomous powers to influence capital investment and to promote economic development.

- *Decentralized municipal finance.* Municipalities in the United States are heavily dependent upon locally collected taxes—property taxes, in particular—to finance local public goods.[27] Although the structural dependence of the state upon capital for tax revenues is a universal feature of capitalist social formations,[28] this dependency is articulated in a profoundly localized spatial form within the US intergovernmental system due to the decentralized character of local government finance. Because real estate investment provides a crucial source of local property tax revenues, US municipalities are structurally "preprogrammed" to support property-developing growth machine strategies. The strategic importance of property taxes to local government revenue has long underpinned a pattern of "municipal mercantilism" in which US cities compete to encourage land uses within their

---

[25] Peter Eisinger, *The Rise of the Entrepreneurial State* (Madison: University of Wisconsin Press, 1988); Alberta Sbragia, *Debt Wish: Entrepreneurial Cities, U.S. Federalism, and Economic Development* (Pittsburgh, PA: University of Pittsburgh Press, 1996).

[26] Robert Goodman, *The Last Entrepreneurs: America's Regional Wars for Jobs and Dollars* (New York: Simon and Schuster, 1979); Susan Clarke and Gary Gaile, *The Work of Cities* (Minneapolis: University of Minnesota Press, 1998); and Eisinger, *Rise of the Entrepreneurial State.*

[27] Dennis Judd and Todd Swanstrom, *City Politics: Private Power and Public Policy* (New York: Longman, 1998).

[28] Claus Offe, *Contradictions of the Welfare State,* ed. John B. Keane (Cambridge, MA: MIT Press, 1984).

jurisdictions that are considered likely to yield higher tax inputs.[29] Due to the impacts of postwar intergovernmental transfer programs and post-1970s tax revolts, among other factors, the percentage of total municipal revenues derived from property taxes declined steadily during the second half of the twentieth century.[30] Nonetheless, this percentage still remains relatively high in comparative terms. Urban growth machines are less likely to form in national states in which municipal revenues are not directly contingent upon local property values and local economic growth.

- *Bond markets and municipal credit ratings.* Since the mid-nineteenth century, US municipalities have relied extensively on the private bond market to raise credit for major capital improvements in public infrastructure (schools, highways, bridges, hospitals, recreational facilities, and the like). As of the late twentieth century, roughly one-fourth of local spending in US cities was derived from the municipal bond market, and was thus directly contingent upon private investments in local public goods.[31] This arrangement grants important powers to private bond-rating agencies, such as Moody's Investor's Service and Standard & Poor's Corporation, which determine the differential interest rates for municipal bonds within different localities. As Alberta Sbragia explains: "The logic used by [municipal bond] lenders in assessing risk—and the criteria they deem important—is often expressed by groups (business and taxpayer groups especially) that see a city more as a financial enterprise than as a dispenser of services."[32] Insofar as rating agencies' assessments of the local business climate directly impact the cost of municipal bonds, local politicians have an important incentive to promote local economic development and thus to support, stimulate, and participate within urban growth machines.[33] Urban growth machines are less likely to emerge in national states in which private bond markets do not serve as an important source of municipal credit and thus impose such significant constraints upon local state budgetary priorities.

---

[29] Sbragia, *Debt Wish.*

[30] Judd and Swanstrom, *City Politics.*

[31] Ibid., 338.

[32] Alberta Sbragia, "Politics, Local Government and the Municipal Bond Market," in *The Municipal Money Chase: The Politics of Local Government Finance*, ed. Alberta Sbragia (Boulder, CO: Westview Press, 1983), 102.

[33] Ibid.

- *Suburbanization, metropolitan jurisdictional fragmentation, and home rule.* US urban development has long proceeded in tandem with large-scale processes of suburbanization that have continually decentralized the spatial distribution of industry, infrastructure, and population.[34] Until the late nineteenth century, suburban development was managed through municipal annexation strategies, in which suburban zones were incorporated into city cores through the extension of municipal boundaries. During the first quarter of the twentieth century, however, the principle of suburban autonomy, or "home rule," became increasingly predominant.[35] This permitted affluent property owners, as well as industrialists in search of nonunionized labor, to create new municipal units within suburbanizing territories, to introduce various local regulations (such as zoning) to influence land use within these jurisdictions, and thus to protect the value of their property investments. During the postwar period, in conjunction with federal transportation policies, housing programs, and mortgage subsidies, metropolitan jurisdictional fragmentation intensified, and thus deepened the polarization of urban regions among multiple local governmental units competing for capital investment and fiscal resources. Whatever the disagreements between public choice theorists and consolidationists regarding the relative merits of these institutional arrangements, both perspectives concur in their observation that metropolitan jurisdictional fragmentation is likely to localize tax-base competition between governmental units. Indeed, in a national political system in which regulatory capacities are relatively decentralized, in which municipal revenues are heavily contingent upon locally collected taxes, and in which metropolitan areas are jurisdictionally fragmented, local governments would appear to have little choice but to compete for the tax base at both inter- and intraregional scales. In national states that do not permit such an extreme jurisdictional fragmentation of metropolitan areas, especially in conjunction with such extensive fiscal decentralization, it is unlikely that urban growth machines would be consolidated.

---

[34] Kenneth Jackson, *Crabgrass Frontier: The Suburbanization of the United States* (New York: Oxford University Press, 1985); and Robert Fishman, *Bourgeois Utopias: The Rise and Fall of Suburbia* (New York: Basic Books, 1987).

[35] Ann Markusen, "Class and Urban Social Expenditure: A Marxist Theory," in *Marxism and the Metropolis*, ed. William Tabb and Larry Sawers (New York: Oxford University Press, 1979), 90–112.

From this perspective, then, the politics of urban growth machines are derived as much from nationally entrenched, if historically evolving, institutional configurations and rule regimes within the US state apparatus as from the "human activism" of place entrepreneurs.[36] No matter how shrewd the rentiers within US urban growth machines might be in finding new ways to enhance the exchange value of their land, a nationally specific configuration of state spatial organization has been an essential condition of possibility and active impetus for their operations. The growth orientation of US municipalities must therefore be viewed as a key expression and embodiment of the peculiar formation of national state space and territorial regulation that has underpinned successive historical cycles of industrial urbanization since the nineteenth century. This framework of national state power appears to impose an "iron cage" of sorts for local political actors insofar as only a fundamental reform of national political institutions and a radical remaking of national rule regimes could realistically interrupt the logic of aggressive growth politics upon which US urban development has long been grounded.[37]

Growth Machines and the Political Geographies of Urban Development

Building upon the multiscalar mode of analysis proposed previously, it is instructive to revisit the seminal contribution to the study of urban growth machines, John Logan and Harvey Molotch's 1987 book *Urban Fortunes*.[38] Logan and Molotch are most centrally concerned with the political economy of place, understood as a localized land-use nexus whose developmental patterns and pathways are controlled by rentiers, factions of capital with extensive sunk investments in the built environment and their political allies.[39] To develop such an analysis, Logan and Molotch devote extensive attention to the battle among diverse local agents, including members of the growth machine alliance and its opponents, for control over urban land uses. In

---

[36] Logan and Molotch, *Urban Fortunes*, 11.

[37] Contemporary advocates of such a reform include David Rusk, *Inside Game/Outside Game: Winning Strategies for Saving Urban America* (Washington, DC: Brookings Institution Press, 1998); Bruce Katz, "Enough of the Small Stuff: Toward a New Urban Agenda," *Brookings Review* 18, no. 3 (2000): 6–11; and Peter Dreier, John Mollenkopf, and Todd Swanstrom, *Place Matters: Metropolitics for the 21st Century*, 2nd ed. (Lawrence: University Press of Kansas, 2004).

[38] Logan and Molotch, *Urban Fortunes*.

[39] Ibid., 12.

this context, national institutional structures are mentioned mainly to underscore the broader political, legal, and intergovernmental environments in which local power struggles unfold. Accordingly, most commentators have interpreted and appropriated Logan and Molotch's work in methodologically localist terms, as a contribution to the investigation of place-based forms of institutional organization, political alliance formation, and regulatory intervention.

Upon closer examination, however, it becomes evident that Logan and Molotch's analysis avoids the endogeneity trap: it is focused not only on the vicissitudes of place-making, but is permeated with astute observations regarding the national institutional envelope of land-use regulation, the variegated national institutional framework of urban development, and the wide-ranging interscalar consequences of urban growth machine activities.[40] Consequently, in contrast to the localist or endogenous methodological orientation that has generally been attributed to urban growth machine theory, *Urban Fortunes* can be critically reinterpreted as a multiscalar account of the interplay between state space and the politics of urban development, both in the historical and contemporary perspective.[41] A scale-attuned examination of Logan and Molotch's work reveals, in particular, three analytically distinct dimensions of that interplay during the course of US urban history: (1) deep structures of state space and territorial regulation, (2) historically specific regimes of urban spatial policy, and (3) conjunctural struggles over urban spatial development (see Figure 7.1).

1. *Deep structural features of state space and territorial regulation.* On various occasions, Logan and Molotch allude to the entrenched features of the US federal intergovernmental system that were outlined in the previous section. These structurally rooted features of state spatial and institutional organization—in particular, local fiscal and administrative autonomy, metropolitan jurisdictional fragmentation, and the principle of home rule—are said to have played a key role in engendering the formation of urban growth machines and the resultant logic of relentless interlocality tax-base competition throughout US history.[42]

---

[40] The issue is examined in considerable detail in their chapter on "How Government Matters," Logan and Molotch, *Urban Fortunes*, 147–99.

[41] The concept of state space is elaborated at greater length in Neil Brenner, *New State Spaces: Urban Governance and the Rescaling of Statehood* (New York: Oxford University Press, 2004).

[42] Logan and Molotch, *Urban Fortunes*, 2, 27, 147–51, 178–80.

Deep structures of state space and territorial regulation Entrenched features of state spatial organization in the United States that animate, channel, and mediate growth machine activities	• The institutionally entrenched tradition of urban privatism provides business interests with major decision-making powers over urban land uses. • The institutional structure of US federalism provides relatively autonomous capacities to the states and municipalities to engage in economic development initiatives and other strategies to influence the location of capital and population. • The decentralized system of local government finance underpins an extensive reliance of municipalities upon locally collected property taxes and private bond markets. • The jurisdictional fragmentation of metropolitan space and the principle of home rule further intensify interlocality tax-base competition.
Historically specific regimes of urban spatial policy Historical formations of federal and local policies intended to influence the geography of urban land use and thus to enhance the exchange values of places	*Nineteenth-century industrial urbanization* • Growth machines compete for federal subsidies to construct large-scale transportation and communications infrastructures. *Twentieth-century urban expansion and metropolitan fragmentation* • Growth machines mobilize a range of restrictive policies (such as zoning, growth control, and environmental regulations) to influence local land uses within their jurisdictions. • The federal government mobilizes various incentive policies that stimulate the formation of urban growth machines and stratify pathways of urban spatial development. *1980s and beyond* • The federal government attempts to circumvent antigrowth opposition by intensifying fiscal pressures upon localities and by lowering federal standards in policy spheres such as welfare, occupational safety, and environmental protection.
Conjunctural struggles over urban spatial development Strategies and struggles to enhance the use values or exchange values of specific places, often by modifying existent forms of state spatial organization and urban spatial policy	• Pro- and antigrowth forces contest urban/suburban jurisdictional boundaries at various spatial scales. • Pro- and antigrowth forces contest the form, orientation, and geographical distribution of zoning and growth control regulations at various spatial scales. • Pro- and antigrowth forces contest the form, orientation, and geographical distribution of urban policies at various spatial scales.

FIGURE 7.1 The multiscalar historical political geographies of urban growth machines in the United States

2. *Historically specific regimes of urban spatial policy.* Logan and Molotch also explore various ways in which, since the maturation of the nineteenth-century industrial city, federal and local state policies have impacted the geographies of urban development.[43] The resultant regimes of state spatial regulation have decisively molded the political geographies of urban growth machine activities by channeling certain types of development into specific locations, both within and among metropolitan areas. Although Logan and Molotch do not deploy the conceptual vocabulary of regimes, their account implicitly traces three broad historical formations of regularized federal and local land-use policy since the nineteenth century:

- *Nineteenth-century industrial urbanization.* During the early industrial era, urban growth machines jockeyed to attract key federal infrastructural investments (railroads, canals, ports, and the like) and thus to enhance their strategic economic importance within the national economy.[44]
- *Twentieth-century urban expansion and metropolitan fragmentation.* A new formation of urban spatial policies emerged during the period of organized, Fordist-Keynesian capitalism in conjunction with comprehensive planning reform movements, the extension of the urban fabric, the proliferation of suburbanized residential enclaves, and the increasing jurisdictional fragmentation of metropolitan areas. Here, Logan and Molotch trace the role of restrictive local policies (including zoning, growth control, and environmental policies) and federal incentives policies (including housing and urban renewal, urban development action grants, block grants, and tax increment redevelopment) in influencing the geographies of land use and thus in creating a highly stratified urban and suburban hierarchy.[45] This regime of urban spatial policy, which was only fully consolidated during the postwar period, provided national and local politicians with a wide array of policy instruments through which to influence the distribution of local land uses within their jurisdictions and thus "to serve the exchange interests of local elites."[46]

---

[43] Ibid., 147–99.

[44] Ibid., 52–57.

[45] Ibid., 153–99.

[46] Ibid., 178.

- *The post-1980s period.* More briefly, given the historical conjuncture in which their book was written, Logan and Molotch allude to the emergent historical formation of urban spatial policy that was being established under Reagan's New Federalism in the 1980s. Under the Reagan administration, the federal government introduced various new policy strategies that were intended to impel localities to promote local economic development projects—for instance, by diminishing federal urban subsidies and thus tightening local budgetary constraints; by lowering federal standards in welfare, occupational safety, and environmental protection; and through the establishment of deregulated enterprise zones within distressed inner cities. Logan and Molotch interpret these rescaled institutional arrangements as federal governmental strategies to circumvent the forms of antigrowth local resistance that had been consolidated during the preceding two decades.[47]

  Whereas each of the aforementioned federal and local regimes of urban land-use policy facilitated and intensified the activities of urban growth machines, Logan and Molotch suggest that the second and third regimes also met with stiff resistance from an expanding array of antidevelopment forces. Hence, their account implies that national state institutions have long constituted a strategically central arena of political contestation in which the geographies of urban development are fought out. In the US context, Logan and Molotch argue, it is above all through national state institutions and policy regimes that local configurations of land-use regulation are established, enforced, and periodically modified. And it is only within the politico-institutional parameters thus established that urban growth coalitions may crystallize to shape the patterns and pathways of urban development.

3. *Conjunctural struggles over urban spatial development.* Lastly, Logan and Molotch emphasize the role of localized struggles over jurisdictional boundaries and land-use regulations in the context of the more entrenched structures of national state space summarized previously.[48] Growth machines may attempt to rework the organization of state space and territorial regulation at national, metropolitan, and local scales to enhance the exchange values of strategic urban places. Meanwhile,

---

[47] Ibid., 244–47.

[48] Ibid., 37.

antigrowth alliances may attempt to mobilize federal and local state resources, regulations, and restrictions to counter such initiatives and thus to preserve place-based use values. These struggles are always fought out in locally specific patterns that are, in turn, decisively shaped through the distinctive regulatory strategies pursued and the politico-territorial alliances formed by the major actors involved. Issues such as the configuration of jurisdictional boundaries, the structure of zoning and growth control regulations, and the form and distribution of federal urban subsidies thus become central stakes in political struggles over the geographies of urbanization across diverse places and various spatial scales. In this sense, formations of state space and territorial regulation do not merely underpin and animate the activities of urban growth machines, but may themselves be reshaped through the struggles provoked by those activities.

In sum, the configuration of state space has long figured centrally in producing the urban scale as a strategic institutional site for growth machine activities across the US political-economic landscape. Whereas Logan and Molotch's work is focused most directly on explaining how and why the city serves as a *growth machine*, this analysis reveals that, in so doing, they also provide an account of why it is that the *city* serves as a growth machine. The salient point here is thus not only that "the State actively sustains the commodity status of land" but that its spatial and institutional configuration also serves (1) to distribute land uses across national, regional, and local scales and (2) to impel the formation of profoundly localized, growth-oriented territorial alliances.[49] Molotch's subsequent comparative work powerfully reinforces these arguments by showing how nationally specific intergovernmental structures, fiscal arrangements, and land-use regulations in the United States, the United Kingdom, France, Italy, and Japan have entailed significantly divergent rules for rentier participation in local development, leading to major cross-national differences in the geographies of urban development politics.[50] Such comparative investigations make even more explicit an analytical proposition that is subtly interwoven throughout the text of *Urban Fortunes*: the very existence of urban growth machines, and their specific politico-institutional form, hinge upon nationalized rule regimes that impose specific regulatory parameters around processes of

---

[49] Ibid., 27.

[50] See Molotch and Vicari, "Three Ways to Build"; and Harvey Molotch, "Urban Deals in Comparative Perspective," in Logan and Swanstrom, *Beyond the City Limits*, 175–98.

urban development.[51] This interpretation is not intended to diminish the importance of locally rooted political strategies and struggles, which obviously generate place-specific governance arrangements and developmental trajectories. Rather, this mode of analysis is presented as a basis for situating such strategies and struggles within the multiscalar institutional envelope that circumscribes their distinctive capacities for shaping urban space.

The Urban Growth Machine as a Multiscalar Political Strategy

Insofar as urban regime theory and urban growth machine theory have helped illuminate some of the key local political dynamics associated with the production of urban space, they have contributed forcefully to the project of demystifying urban life under modern capitalism. However, due to the methodologically localist tendencies of at least some contributions to these research traditions, they have only partially succeeded in defetishizing the putatively urban dimensions of what is often generically labeled "urban politics." As this discussion has revealed, the operations of urban growth machines cannot be adequately understood as locally generated or self-contained; they are also key moments within the multiscalar processes of state spatial regulation through which the patterns and pathways of capitalist urbanization are forged. Therefore, the fetish character of the city can be fully demystified only through modes of analysis that reflexively illuminate its conditions of production at all spatial scales—from worldwide spatial divisions of labor, resource flows, and metabolic impacts to national institutional configurations and regimes of territorial regulation, subnational governance arrangements, and locally embedded political struggles.

The task of superseding the fetish character of the city is hugely complex: it involves reflexive consideration of the diverse, multiscalar political-economic, institutional, and sociotechnological processes that have produced the uneven, variegated landscapes of urbanization. In this chapter, I have touched upon only one dimension of this wide-ranging research agenda—the need to investigate the role of national state spaces and multiscalar regimes

---

[51] The concept of a rule regime is proposed by Jamie Peck in "Political Economies of Scale: Fast Policy, Interscalar Relations and Neoliberal Workfare," *Economic Geography* 78, no. 3 (July 2002): 332–60. Further elaborations can be found in Chapters 2 and 3 of this book, as well as in Neil Brenner, Jamie Peck, and Nik Theodore, "Variegated Neoliberalization: Geographies, Modalities, Pathways," *Global Networks* 10, no. 2 (2010): 182–222.

of territorial regulation in engendering a highly localized, city-centric form of growth politics during the course of US territorial development. As I have argued, many students of urban growth machines have tended to fall into the endogeneity trap: they take the local scale for granted as the site and target of this growth politics. In contrast, through a critical reading of Logan and Molotch's *Urban Fortunes*, this analysis has critically interrogated that naturalized assumption by demarcating some of the broader politico-institutional conditions of possibility for the formation of growth-oriented territorial alliances at the scale of the city. Logan and Molotch's work productively contributes to that endeavor by elaborating (1) a three-tiered conceptualization of how state spatial structures impact patterns of urban spatial development and (2) a basic periodization of the relationship between state space and urban growth machine dynamics during the history of US industrial urbanization. In this way, their research illuminates the patterns and pathways of US localism through a reflexively nonlocalist mode of analysis: it circumvents the endogeneity trap while recognizing the structural and strategic importance of locality in the spatial politics of urban governance.

This discussion of the national structuration of US urban development builds upon an emergent literature on this issue that includes both historical investigations and contemporary analyses.[52] The central purpose of engaging with this work here has been less to offer a comprehensive overview of the evolving, institutionally variegated national/urban interface in the US context than to underscore its essential epistemological relevance to the very constitution of "urban politics" as a discrete, comparative-historical, and increasingly transnational research field. Indeed, the preceding analysis suggests that the subdisciplinary label "urban politics" is fundamentally misleading insofar as it implies an understanding of the urban as a distinct, self-contained, or pregiven institutional terrain. Against such constructions, the urban has been conceptualized here as a medium, site, and expression of diverse, multiscalar political-economic processes—including strategies of capital accumulation, state regulation, territorial alliance formation, and sociopolitical struggle. This is one sense in which Henri Lefebvre's suggestive conception of the urban as a site of "mediation" can be understood.[53] From

---

[52] See, for example, Gerald Frug, *City-Making: Building Cities without Building Walls* (Princeton, NJ: Princeton University Press, 2002); Dreier, Mollenkopf, and Swanstrom, *Place Matters*; Clarke and Gaile, *Work of Cities*; and Eisinger, *Rise of the Entrepreneurial State*.

[53] Lefebvre, *Urban Revolution*; as well as Stefan Kipfer, "Why the Urban Question Still Matters: Reflections on Rescaling and the Promise of the Urban," in *Leviathan Undone? Towards a Political Economy of Scale*, ed. Rianne Mahon and Roger Keil (Vancouver and Toronto: UBC Press, 2009), 67–86.

this perspective, the urban maintains its "structured coherence"—and, thus, its intelligibility in social science, regulatory struggle, and everyday life—only due to political strategies that attempt to establish it as such. Urban growth machines represent a paradigmatic example of such political strategies.

These epistemological and methodological considerations have particular salience in the contemporary configuration of intensifying scale relativization, in which the national institutional structuration of urbanization processes is being profoundly recalibrated in conjunction with accelerated geoeconomic integration, an increasing neoliberalization of territorial regulation, processes of post-Keynesian state retrenchment, and the proliferation of regionally and locally specific forms of industrial crisis and regulatory response. In the US context, entrepreneurial forms of urban policy have been superimposed upon the distributive land-use regimes, nationally standardized infrastructural configurations, and managerial governance arrangements that prevailed during the industrial, corporate-monopoly, and Fordist-Keynesian accumulation regimes. This intensified activation of local economic development strategies among US cities has been impelled in no small measure through the rescaling of national state spaces—from Reagan's New Federalism in the 1980s to various postfederal programs of welfare devolution and fiscal retrenchment in the 1990s and subsequently.[54] During the last decade, the scalar geographies of this putative "new urban politics" have continued to mutate through the proliferation of multicity growth coalitions that aspire to construct customized infrastructures for regional supply chains and logistics capacity.[55] Consequently, the scalar configuration of "urban" growth machine operations is once again being qualitatively reworked in relation to new accumulation strategies, a new crystallization of the spatial division of labor, various multiscalar politico-institutional realignments, and emergent political strategies to regulate the urbanization process.

As discussed in previous chapters, a closely analogous proliferation of local economic initiatives, likewise animated through combined processes of geoeconomic integration, post-Keynesian state rescaling, and industrial restructuring, has been occurring since the early 1980s across the European Union. Given the long commitment of European welfare states to compensatory regional policies that attempted to integrate local economies within nationalized systems of territorial development and infrastructure provision,

---

[54] Clarke and Gaile, *Work of Cities*; and Eisinger, *Rise of the Entrepreneurial State*. See also, more recently, Paul Kantor, "The End of American Urban Policy—Or a Beginning," *Urban Affairs Review* 52, no. 6 (2016): 887–916.

[55] Wachsmuth, "Competitive Multi-City Regionalism"; and Wachsmuth, "Infrastructure Alliances."

this growth-oriented "new urban politics" represents a rather striking developmental break. In the face of these transformations, and the wide-ranging processes of scale relativization with which they are intertwined, urban growth machines appear to be playing increasingly significant roles in shaping the landscapes of post-Keynesian urbanization across much of Europe.[56] But in the European context as well, the scalar constitution of "urban" growth politics is likewise being significantly reworked through emergent strategies of city regionalism, intercity networking, and new types of regional or interregional infrastructural alliances. Indeed, while property values still matter immensely to the key actors involved in such growth-oriented territorial alliances, the project of increasing ground rents through local land-use intensification is now tightly intertwined with multiscalar political initiatives to construct the customized infrastructural configurations that are thought to facilitate innovation, flexibility, and connectivity under conditions of heightened geoeconomic uncertainty.[57]

The analysis presented here suggests, then, that the consolidation of a new urban politics in the North Atlantic region and beyond must be understood above all in relation to the evolving national institutional envelopes and multiscalar regimes of territorial regulation within which they are embedded. The political arenas of "urban" development are constituted through the continual making and remaking of state spaces across places, territories, and scales. There is indeed a politics of urban growth, and this politics frequently does involve a scale-specific machinery of localized institutions, laws, policies, alliances, strategies, and struggles—but its conditions of possibility lie elsewhere.

---

[56] Alan Harding, "Urban Regimes and Growth Machines: Towards a Cross-national Research Agenda," *Urban Affairs Quarterly* 29, no. 3 (1994): 356–82.

[57] In this sense, the place-based exchange values emphasized by Logan and Molotch can no longer be understood purely in terms of property values; today they encompass a broader spectrum of spatial conditions and infrastructures that impact the positionality of places in global networks. See Jessop, Peck, and Tickell, "Retooling the Machine."

8
A Thousand Layers: Geographies of Uneven Development

RECENT DEBATES ON THE nature and consequences of "globalization" have renewed social scientific interest in questions of worldwide social and spatial inequality. Some commentators have claimed that, under contemporary conditions, geographical differences are being annihilated as new information technologies, transnational corporate strategies, free market politics, and cultural imperialism homogenize the landscapes of everyday life around the world. Most critical geographers have stridently rejected such claims, arguing that late modern capitalism has in fact been premised upon an intensification of differences among places, regions, and territories, even as the mobility of capital, commodities, and populations is enhanced.[1] Rather than superseding geographical differentiation and smoothing out sociospatial inequalities, contemporary processes of geoeconomic integration have entailed a striking reworking, differentiation, and intensification of the patterns of worldwide polarization that have long underpinned and resulted from the process of capitalist development. Meanwhile, struggles for a sense of place, for territorial rootedness, and for a unique geographical

---

[1] See, for example, Kevin Cox, ed., *Spaces of Globalization* (New York: Guilford Press, 1997); Roger Lee and Jane Wills, eds., *Geographies of Economies* (London: Arnold, 1997).

niche remain as intense as ever in a world of sometimes disturbing volatility.[2] Precisely as interconnections among dispersed spaces around the globe are thickened, geographical differences are thus becoming more rather than less profound, at once in everyday life and in the operation of social, political, and economic power. In short, spatial unevenness remains endemic to the contemporary global capitalist (dis)order.[3]

Especially since the 1980s, critical geographical scholarship has confronted the problem of geographical difference in a systematic, theoretically reflexive way. The concept of *uneven spatial development* lies at the heart of such analyses. This concept is derived from Marx's foundational account of capital circulation in *Capital*, where the notion of uneven development was used to describe the existence of differential growth rates among various sectors (or "departments") of the capitalist economy.[4] The concept was reinvented in the early twentieth century by socialist intellectuals such as Lenin, Luxemburg, Bukharin, Trotsky, and (decades later) Mandel, who were concerned to understand the global expansion of the capitalist mode of production through imperialism and colonialism.[5] The concept of uneven *spatial* development was introduced and elaborated by radical geographers in the late 1970s and early 1980s.[6] Through their work on uneven spatial development (USD) and a range of closely related issues—including spatial divisions of labor, industrial restructuring, crisis formation, urbanization, regionalization, and gentrification—radical sociospatial theorists developed new ways of conceptualizing the production and continual reorganization of geographical differences under modern capitalism. The theoretical foundations forged during this period have also proven useful for scholars concerned to analyze various aspects of geographical differentiation that cannot be fully derived from the (il)logics of capital accumulation.[7]

---

[2] Doreen Massey, *Space, Place and Gender* (Minneapolis: University of Minnesota Press, 1996).

[3] Neil Smith, "The Satanic Geographies of Globalization: Uneven Development in the 1990s," *Public Culture* 10, no. 1 (1997): 169–92.

[4] Karl Marx, *Capital*, trans. Ben Fowkes (New York: Penguin, 1976 [1867]).

[5] Anthony Brewer, *Marxist Theories of Imperialism*, 2nd ed. (London: Routledge, 1990).

[6] See Henri Lefebvre, *The Production of Space*, trans. Donald Nicholson (Cambridge: Blackwell, 1991 [1974]); David Harvey, *The Limits to Capital* (Chicago: University of Chicago Press, 1982); Doreen Massey, *Spatial Divisions of Labour* (London: Macmillan, 1985); Neil Smith, *Uneven Development: Nature, Capital and the Production of Space* (New York: Blackwell, 1984); and Edward W. Soja, "Regions in Context: Spatiality, Periodicity, and the Historical Geography of the Regional Question," *Environment and Planning D: Society and Space* 3 (1985): 175–90.

[7] See, for example, Mark Goodwin and Simon Duncan, *The Local State and Uneven Development: Behind the Local Government Crisis* (London: Polity Press, 1988); Jamie Peck, *Work-Place: The*

Building upon this extensive literature, and against the background of the analyses of scale production and rescaling developed in this book, the present chapter considers a specific question: how are the *geographies* of USD to be conceptualized? In his classic contribution on the topic, Neil Smith suggested that USD is deeply imbricated in the production of geographical scale.[8] Indeed, it was Smith's attempt to decipher the see-saw movement of USD under modern capitalism that appears to have led him, in a path-breaking intellectual maneuver, to theorize about geographical scale on its own terms, rather than subsuming it under other geographical concepts such as territory or place. The very differentiation of global, national, regional, and urban scales, Smith proposed, must be understood at once as a medium and a product of the process of USD under capitalism.

Smith's justifiably influential conceptualization inspired a generation of critical geographical scholarship not only on USD, but more generally, on the production of scale and its associated politics. In this chapter, I revisit the intellectual terrain of Smith's initial theorization of USD in the context of more recent attempts to decipher scaling and rescaling processes under modern capitalism. While my analysis builds extensively upon the theoretical foundations constructed by Smith, I propose a broader, polymorphic conceptualization in which scaling and rescaling processes are understood to be tightly interwoven with several other, equally essential dynamics of sociospatial structuration under capitalism—including place-making, territorialization, and networking.[9] Drawing upon Henri Lefebvre's vivid metaphorical description of social space as a *mille-feuille*, I thus interpret the geographies of USD as being composed of "a thousand layers"—a dynamic intermeshing of scale, place, territory, and networks that produces extraordinarily intricate, restlessly mutating configurations of sociospatial organization.[10]

To be sure, Smith's insight that USD is both scale differentiated and scale differentiating remains foundational. However, this chapter underscores

---

Social Regulation of Labor Markets (New York: Guilford, 1996); and Neil Brenner, *New State Spaces: Urban Governance and the Rescaling of Statehood* (New York: Oxford University Press, 2004).

[8] Smith, *Uneven Development.*

[9] A parallel line of argumentation is developed in Bob Jessop, Neil Brenner, and Martin Jones, "Theorizing Socio-Spatial Relations," *Environment and Planning D: Society and Space* 26 (2008): 389–401; and Eric Sheppard, "The Spaces and Times of Globalization: Place, Scale, Networks and Positionality," *Economic Geography* 8 (2002): 307–30.

[10] Henri Lefebvre, *The Production of Space,* 87.

what I have elsewhere termed "the limits to scale."[11] While processes of scaling and rescaling are indeed central to the production of USD under modern capitalism, the theorization presented here is intended to caution against the tendency to overextend scalar concepts in geopolitical economy. Paradoxically, it is precisely the progress of debates on the new political economy of scale during the last three decades, which have generated a nuanced conceptual vocabulary for the analysis of rescaling processes, that now enables us to reconsider the geographies of USD with equal reference to the spatiotemporal dynamics of place-making, territorialization, and networking.

Following a general overview of the theorization of USD that has been developed by radical geographers, I elaborate this polymorphic approach to sociospatial theory through a stylized analysis of the intermeshing of place-making, territorialization, scaling, and networking processes in the production of USD during the *longue durée* geohistory of modern capitalism. In addition to the methodological relativization of scale-centric approaches to USD, this exercise is meant to advance several other core analytical claims:[12]

- USD is not a self-evident fact, an empirical truism, or an ambient background condition of political-economic life under capitalism. It requires active theorization, and continual retheorization, in relation to the restlessly changing historical geographies of capital accumulation, urbanization, state regulation, social reproduction, ecological transformation, and sociopolitical contestation it produces and mediates.
- The geographies, institutional mediations, impacts, and contradictions of USD mutate historically, in close relation to broader configurations of capitalist development, state space, and sociopolitical struggle. Spatial polymorphism is, therefore, not a transhistorical ontological principle, but a pragmatic methodological basis on which to investigate the dynamic historical interplay between place-making, territorialization, scaling, and networking processes; their variegated sociospatial consequences; and their ongoing political contestation.
- The investigation of contextually specific restructuring processes may sometimes require the analytical privileging of particular dimensions of sociospatial relations—scalar, territorial, place-based, networked, or

---

[11] Neil Brenner, "The Limits to Scale? Methodological Reflections on Scalar Structuration," *Progress in Human Geography* 15, no. 4 (2001): 525–48; see also Chapter 3.

[12] See also Jamie Peck, "Macroeconomic Geographies," *Area Development and Policy* 1, no. 3 (2016): 305–17.

otherwise—at least as a starting point for further analysis. However, the appropriate selection and combination of theoretical abstractions in sociospatial investigations is not grounded upon a foundational ontological commitment, but flows from specific explanatory challenges, research questions, and politico-intellectual concerns.

The chapter concludes by specifying some of the wide-ranging implications of the preceding analysis for the conceptualization of the capitalist urban fabric developed in this book. In so doing, it resituates the account of the urban question as a scale question elaborated in previous chapters within a transformed, reflexively polymorphic analytical framework through which the production of new urban spaces may be more precisely investigated.

Foundations

Reflexive theorizing on USD began in the 1970s and has subsequently flourished in the writings of critical geographical political economists.[13] While this literature is quite multifaceted, it contains several core theoretical propositions regarding the nature of USD under modern capitalist conditions, which can be summarized briefly as follows.

Under modern capitalism, the existence of geographical difference is not simply an expression of the discrete qualities of particular places, of inherited differences among regions, or of the fact that sociospatial arrangements are intrinsically heterogeneous. As the division of labor is deepened through sectoral specialization and extended through geographical expansion, spaces throughout the world are simultaneously interconnected and distinguished in a see-saw movement of equalization/differentiation.[14] Rather than extinguishing the distinctiveness of places and territories, this dialectic of simultaneous interconnection/variegation reworks inherited geographical differences, which can now only be understood in relational, intercontextual terms. From this point onward, geographical difference no longer represents the spatialization of particularity. It instead demarcates the distinctive yet constitutively relational positionality of any given space within an evolving, worldwide grid of interdependencies. Contexts, in other

---

[13] For a useful overview of the key positions and arguments in this vast literature, see Jamie Peck, "Uneven Regional Development," in *The International Encyclopedia of Geography*, ed. Douglas Richardson (Oxford: John Wiley and Sons, 2017), online edition, doi:10.1002/9781118786352.wbieg0721.

[14] Smith, *Uneven Development*.

words, are now embedded within *metacontexts*.[15] In the most general terms, then, USD represents the aggregate, macrogeographical expression of such positionalities within each successive configuration of global capitalist development.

Each historical framework of USD entails the differentiation of cores and peripheries—spaces of centrality and marginality, inclusion and exclusion, empowerment and disempowerment, appropriation and dispossession. Accordingly, in this conceptualization, sociospatial positionality refers not simply to absolute terrestrial location, but concerns the relational situatedness of particular spaces within broader, asymmetrically organized frameworks of power.[16] The notion of USD is therefore intended to capture the systematically polarized organization of socioeconomic resources and capacities not only between different populations, but across and among the diverse sociospatial configurations through which the rule of capital is constituted.

Patterns of USD are mediated through large-scale institutional formations (national states, international rule regimes, and subnational regulatory arrangements) and diverse social forces (capitalist firms, business organizations, trade unions, property owners, and place-based social movements). This means that the analysis of geographical difference necessarily entails an inquiry into the politics of space through which historically specific configurations of sociospatial polarization are produced, contested, and remade.[17] Clearly, accumulation strategies play a central role in the structuration of USD, but so too do state institutions, territorially based political alliances, social movements, and other contextually specific struggles.

During the historical evolution of capitalism, certain deep structures of USD have been entrenched. These include the core/periphery division on which the international division of labor has long been grounded, the city/countryside opposition, and the various modalities of ecological appropriation associated with the metabolic rift.[18] Despite this, however, USD is always articulated in historically and contextually specific forms. Global inequality,

---

[15] Neil Brenner, Jamie Peck, and Nik Theodore, "Variegated Neoliberalization: Geographies, Modalities, Pathways," *Global Networks* 10, no. 2 (2010): 182–222.

[16] Sheppard, "The Spaces and Times of Globalization."

[17] Henri Lefebvre, "Reflections on the Politics of Space," in *Henri Lefebvre: State, Space, World: Selected Essays*, ed. Neil Brenner and Stuart Elden (Minneapolis: University of Minnesota Press, 2009 [1970]), 167–84.

[18] Samir Amin, *Capitalism in the Age of Globalization* (London: Zed, 1997); Immanuel Wallerstein, *The Modern World-System I: Capitalist Agriculture and the Origins of the European World-Economy in the Sixteenth Century* (New York: Academic Publishers, 1974); Raymond Williams, *The Country and the City* (Oxford: Oxford University Press, 1973); Jason Moore, *Capitalism and the Web of Life: Ecology and the Accumulation of Capital* (New York: Verso, 2016).

city/non-city divides, and metabolic rifts have remained persistent, durable features of capitalism, but their precise geographical, geopolitical, and geoeconomic contours have been reshaped in manifold ways during the past three centuries. Moreover, even as certain dimensions of USD under capitalism have proven relatively durable, others have been periodically modified, sometimes in quite dramatic ways, during the process of worldwide capitalist development. Examples of the latter include the configuration of urban and regional settlement patterns, city/hinterland relations, the geographies of industrial development, landscapes of infrastructural investment, the organization of political-economic hegemony, and the configuration of worldwide spatial divisions of labor.[19] Patterns of USD can thus be said to crystallize at the interface between inherited sociospatial configurations and emergent spatial strategies intended to transform the latter.

In exploring this wide-ranging constellation of issues, David Harvey's conceptualization of the fixity/motion contradiction under capitalism offers considerable analytical and methodological traction. As we explored in Chapter 2, Harvey argues that the deep structures and *longue durée* trends of USD under capitalism are mediated through struggles to manage historically and geographically specific expressions of the fixity/motion contradiction. Capital accumulation hinges upon the production of historically specific sociospatial configurations, which are internally differentiated and systemically polarized. At the same time, patterns of USD are periodically rearticulated due to capital's impulsion, under conditions of systemic crisis, to creatively destroy established frameworks of territorial organization in pursuit of new spatial fixes for capitalist expansion. Subsequently, as new sociospatial formations for capitalist development are provisionally established, inherited forms of USD are likewise rewoven, generally in ways that preserve some of their inherited contours while restructuring or rupturing others. The shifting patterns and mutating pathways of USD under modern capitalism are thus tightly intertwined with (contextually specific, spatially variegated expressions of) the fixity/motion contradiction.

Geographical differences, then, are not pregiven or immutable features of the social or physical landscape. Under modern capitalism, they are produced, in the form of USD, through historically specific political-economic processes, conflicts, and struggles. It is only through an understanding of such processes, their variegated institutional expressions, and their ongoing contestation that changing historical forms of USD can be deciphered, whether in relation to the challenges of understanding the (il)logics of modern capitalism or with

---

[19] Soja, "Regions in Context."

reference to more specific research terrains, questions, and debates. In this sense, USD is not only the *product* of capitalism, but a basic *precondition* and *medium* for its large-scale, long-term reproduction, intensification, and expansion. As Edward Soja explains, "Capitalism . . . intrinsically builds upon regional or spatial inequalities as a necessary means for its continued survival. The very existence of capitalism presupposes the sustaining presence and vital instrumentality of geographically uneven development."[20]

Mille-Feuille/*A Thousand Layers*

In the discussion thus far, I have deployed the term "space" as a generic category for describing all aspects of geographical difference and a wide range of sociospatial formations, processes, transformations, and conditions. I have thus referred to spaces, spatial differentiation, sociospatial organization, sociospatial relations, sociospatial polarization, sociospatial structuration, and, most generally, uneven spatial development without explicitly delineating the specific geographical patterns in which the latter are articulated. At this stage of the analysis, however, it is necessary to examine more closely the variegated fabric of social space and, specifically, the manifold contours, dimensions, and morphologies of USD. To this end, Lefebvre's emphasis on the polymorphic character of social space within capitalist modernity provides a helpful methodological orientation.[21] From this point of view, the geographies of any social process—urbanization, capital accumulation, social reproduction, state regulation, sociopolitical contestation, uneven development, and so forth—cannot be understood adequately with reference to any singular principle or all-encompassing morphological pattern. Instead, as Figure 8.1 illustrates, several intertwined yet analytically distinct dimensions of sociospatial relations may be distinguished—including place, territory, scale, and networks.[22]

The conceptual abstraction of *place* denotes geographical proximity, clustering, the embedding of sociospatial relations within particular locations, and patterns of areal (horizontal) differentiation.[23] As such, the

---

[20] Edward W. Soja, *Postmodern Geographies* (New York: Verso, 1989), 107.

[21] Lefebvre, *The Production of Space.* See also our discussion of Lefebrve in Chapter 2.

[22] Jessop, Brenner, and Jones, "Theorizing Socio-Spatial Relations"; Sheppard, "The Spaces and Times of Globalization."

[23] Massey, *Space, Place and Gender*; Anssi Paasi, "Place and Region: Looking through the Prism of Scale," *Progress in Human Geography* 28, no. 4 (2004): 536–46; Thomas Gieryn, "A Space for Place in Sociology," *Annual Review of Sociology* 26 (2000): 463–96.

Dimension of sociospatial relations	Mode of sociospatial organization	Resultant patterns of sociospatial relations
Place	Proximity, clustering, spatial embedding, localization of everyday routines and lifeworlds	Agglomeration economies; horizontal differentiation of sociospatial relations among distinct types of locations; spatial divisions of labor; processes of place making and place transformation
Territory	Enclosure, bounding, bordering, parcelization	Areal differentiation of sociospatial relations among bounded zones; inside/outside divides, bordering regimes, and political technologies of calculation; territorialization and reterritorialization processes
Scale	Vertical differentiation, stratification, and/or hierarchization of sociospatial relations among (for instance) global, supranational, national, regional, and/or local levels	Construction of scalar divisions of labor; scalar stratification of political-economic relations; scales of dependence and scales of engagement; scaling and rescaling processes
Networks	Transversal connectivity, circulation and interdependence across geographically dispersed locations or organizational units	Construction of large-scale systems of noncontiguous spatial coordination—for markets, governance, and knowledge; differentiation of sociospatial relations among nodes embedded within dispersed topological systems; network consolidation, rupture, and mutation

FIGURE 8.1 Some key dimensions of sociospatial relations. (Source: Derived from Bob Jessop, Neil Brenner, and Martin Jones, "Theorizing Socio-Spatial Relations," *Environment and Planning D: Society and Space* 26 [2008]: 393.)

concept of place captures an important dimension of each of the aforementioned sociospatial processes, but it cannot illuminate all aspects of their geographies or serve as a generic metaphor for sociospatiality as such. To proceed otherwise would entail the methodological trap of *place-centrism*—that is, the treatment of social space as if it were composed completely and uniformly of places, or the ontological privileging of place over other modalities of sociospatial structuration.

The concept of *territory*, which refers to the enclosure, bordering, and parcelization of sociospatial relations, likewise sets into relief various essential dimensions of macrogeographical development and sociospatial differentiation.[24] However, it would be a serious methodological error to reduce all aspects of social space to this dimension. Indeed, even the geographies of the modern state, which has been routinely defined as a territorial power container, cannot be understood in exclusively territorial terms.[25] This fallacy, which has been quite pervasive within mainstream political studies and international relations theory, may be characterized as *methodological territorialism*.[26]

As I have argued throughout this book, the concept of scale is an essential basis for deciphering the vertical differentiation and stratification of sociospatial relations among (for instance) global, supranational, national, regional, and/ or local levels. As such, scale likewise captures an important, but not comprehensive, dimension of modern sociospatial relations and ongoing sociospatial transformation. To reduce sociospatial relations as a whole to their scalar dimension would lead to the methodological dead end of *scale-centrism*—the overextension of scalar concepts beyond their proper domain of application.[27]

Finally, the concept of the *network* describes the configuration of transversal linkages, interdependencies, forms of circulation, and modes of coordination across geographically dispersed locations or organizational units. These likewise represent an increasingly significant dimension of contemporary sociospatial relations, especially in the age of "informational capitalism."[28] However, the fallacy of *network-centrism* must likewise be avoided insofar as the proliferation of long-distance forms of connectivity and circulation, whether via new information technologies or other

---

[24] See, for example, Robert Sack, *Human Territoriality: Its Theory and History* (New York: Cambridge University Press, 1986); Peter J. Taylor, "The State as Container: Territoriality in the Modern World-System," *Progress in Human Geography* 18 (1994): 151–62.

[25] John Agnew, "The Territorial Trap: The Geographical Assumptions of International Relations Theory," *Review of International Political Economy* 1, no. 1 (1994): 53–80; Neil Brenner, Bob Jessop, Martin Jones, and Gordon MacLeod, eds., *State/Space: A Reader* (Cambridge, MA: Blackwell, 2003); R. B. J. Walker, *Inside/Outside: International Relations as Political Theory* (New York: Cambridge University Press, 1993).

[26] Agnew, "The Territorial Trap"; Brenner, *New State Spaces*.

[27] Brenner, "The Limits to Scale."

[28] See, for example, Peter Dicken, Philip Kelly, Kris Olds, and Henry Yeung, "Chains and Networks, Territories and Scales: Towards a Relational Framework for Analysing the Global Economy," *Global Networks* 1, no. 2 (2001): 89–112; Manuel Castells, *The Rise of the Network Society* (Cambridge, MA: Blackwell, 1996); Ngai- Ling Sum, "Time-Space Embeddedness and Geo-Governance of Cross-Border Regional Modes of Growth," in *Beyond Market and Hierarchy*, ed. Ash Amin and Jerzy Hausner (Cheltenham: Edward Elgar, 1997), 159–95; and Sarah Whatmore and Lorraine Thorne, "Nourishing Networks: Alternative Geographies of Food," in *Globalising Food: Agrarian Questions and Global Restructuring*, ed. David Goodman and Michael Watts (London: Routledge, 1998), 287–304.

infrastructural innovations, does not necessarily erode the importance of place, territory, or scale as co-constitutive dimensions of social space. On the contrary, despite the "flat ontologies" that are often triumphantly embraced within Latourian streams of science and technology studies (STS), assemblage theories, and some branches of poststructuralist urban studies, emergent network geographies are almost invariably tightly intermeshed with place-based, scale-differentiated, and territorialized modes of sociospatial organization.[29]

Thus, in contrast to reductionist, isomorphic, and monodimensional approaches, it is methodologically imperative to view every sociospatial relation, process, and transformation as a crystallization of multiple, mutually entangled geographical dimensions, and consequently, to subject each of the latter to sustained analysis. In *The Production of Space*, Lefebvre develops this point through his thesis of the "superimposition and interpenetration of social spaces."[30] In one particularly vivid formulation, Lefebvre likens the superimposed dimensions of social space to the intricate, asymmetrical layerings within a *mille-feuille* pastry—a powdery French dessert that means, literally, "a thousand leaves" or "a thousand layers" (see Figure 8.2).[31]

While Lefebvre's somewhat fanciful culinary metaphor may distract us momentarily from the challenges of critical sociospatial theory, it has direct methodological implications for the discussion at hand. Like the *mille feuille*, formations of USD are composed of complex, messy articulations among multiple patterns, layers, contours, lines, folds, points, clusters, and edges. Drawing upon the analytical distinction between place, territory, scale, and networks introduced previously, the remainder of this chapter elaborates this proposition through a series of macrogeographical generalizations regarding the evolutionary patterning of USD during the *longue durée* geohistory of capitalism. A schematic summary of this conceptualization is provided in Figure 8.3, which links major accounts of the *sources* of USD under capitalism to the

---

[29] Helga Leitner, "The Politics of Scale and Networks of Spatial Connectivity," in *Scale and Geographic Inquiry*, ed. Eric Sheppard and Robert McMaster (Malden, MA: Blackwell, 2004), 236–55; Harriet Bulkeley, "Reconfiguring Environmental Governance: Towards a Politics of Scales and Networks," *Political Geography* 24 (2005): 875–902; Andrew E. G. Jonas, "Pro Scale: Further Reflections on the 'Scale Debate' within Human Geography," *Transactions of the Institute of British Geographers* 31 (2006): 399–406; and Helga Leitner and Byron Miller, "Scale and the Limitations of Ontological Debate: A Commentary on Marston, Jones and Woodward," *Transactions of the Institute of British Geographers* 32 (2007): 116–25.

[30] Lefebvre, *The Production of Space*.

[31] Ibid., 88.

FIGURE 8.2 Social space as *mille-feuille*? The *mille-feuille* dessert is composed of flaky pastry and (usually) vanilla or crème custard. Its main ingredients are intricately layered to form an elaborate, almost geological, architecture that is readily visible from the side when it is sliced. (Source: Wikipedia Commons.)

analysis of its polymorphic *geographies* that is presented in the remainder of this chapter.

While this analysis devotes a separate section to each of the four dimensions of sociospatial relations just outlined, it should be emphasized that the latter are mutually coformative and thus inextricably intertwined. Accordingly, the distinction between place, territory, scale, and networks must be understood as a purely analytical device for deciphering the intricately interwoven layerings of modern sociospatial relations; it is not an ontological demarcation.[32] After developing this argument on a relatively abstract, geohistorical level, I explicate some of its wide-ranging consequences for historical and contemporary explorations of the urban question.

---

[32] This analysis focuses on place, territory, scale, and networks because, in my view, these conceptual abstractions usefully illuminate important dimensions of USD and its variegated, fluidly mutating geographies under modern capitalism. There are, however, other important dimensions of sociospatial relations—landscape, socionature, and world ecology, for instance— whose exploration could productively complement (and complicate) the analysis presented here.

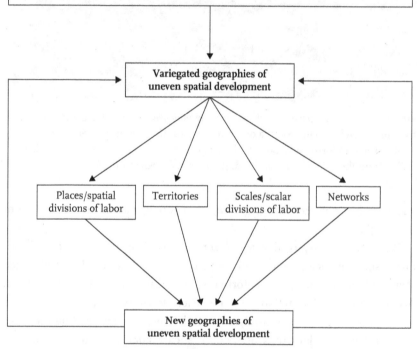

Underlying tendencies and tensions within the geographies of capitalism

- Tension between space-annihilating tendencies of capital (promoting spatial dispersal) and its endemic space dependency (promoting spatial concentration)

- Tension between capital's drive toward equalization (promoting spatial redistribution) and its drive toward differentiation (promoting spatial inequality)

- Endemic tendency toward the creative destruction of sociospatial configurations

- Recurrent quest for a "spatial fix" or "structured coherence" to secure the provisional stabilization of sociospatial configurations

- Chronically unstable, temporary character of spatial fixes: geographies of capitalism remain fundamentally inconstant, discontinuous, and uneven

Variegated geographies of uneven spatial development

Places/spatial divisions of labor | Territories | Scales/scalar divisions of labor | Networks

New geographies of uneven spatial development

FIGURE 8.3 Geographies of uneven spatial development under capitalism.

Places and Uneven Spatial Development

Capitalism emerged within a differentiated geographical landscape inherited from previous historical social formations and modes of production. Key features of the latter included agricultural biomes, precapitalist city-systems, feudal systems of land tenure and surplus extraction, absolutist state structures, and local, interregional, and long-distance trading networks.

Nonetheless, even in its incipient stages, capitalist expansion entailed profound transformations of places, above all through the establishment of new spatial divisions of labor in which dispersed geographical locations acquired specific functional roles within an expanding capitalist world market, and subsequently coevolved relationally within this metacontextual configuration.

Initially, under mercantile capitalism (1600–1750), these spatial divisions of labor were tightly articulated with circuits of precapitalist trade and the geographies of inherited resource endowments—for instance, the locations of waterways, raw materials, mineral supplies, and so forth. However, with the progressive industrialization of capital since the mid-eighteenth century, and the increasing integration of the production process into circuits of accumulation, specifically capitalist spatial divisions of labor emerged that have been based largely upon socially constructed economic assets: agglomeration economies and other forms of capitalist territorial organization designed to intensify, accelerate, and manage surplus value extraction. Consequently, beginning in the core zones of Western Europe and eventually extending throughout the world economy, urbanization processes dramatically accelerated. Capital and labor were concentrated within large-scale, specialized production complexes, and new large-scale, long-distance communications and logistics infrastructures were consolidated to facilitate capital circulation. On a macrogeographical level, these trends entailed the consolidation of a worldwide grid of places differentiated according to their specific functions, specializations, and positions within the spaces of global accumulation.[33] This restlessly evolving, variegated landscape of place-making processes has articulated patterns of USD in several closely intertwined ways.

First, as Friedrich Engels famously noted of nineteenth-century Manchester, new spatial divisions emerged within the expanding metropolitan centers of capitalist production through residential segregation; the functional division of city space; the consolidation of new urban infrastructures for production, social reproduction, and circulation; and successive waves of regionalization. As capitalist urbanization has intensified, accelerated, and expanded, these intraplace divisions have continued to evolve through contextually specific patterns and pathways.[34]

---

[33] Michael Storper and Richard Walker, *The Capitalist Imperative: Territory, Technology and Industrial Growth* (New York: Basil Blackwell, 1989); Dieter Läpple, "Gesellschaftlicher Reproduktionsprozeß und Stadtstrukturen," in *Stadtkrise und soziale Bewegungen*, ed. Margit Mayer, Roland Roth, and Volkhard Brandes (Frankfurt: Europäische Verlagsanstalt, 1978), 23–54.

[34] Peter Marcuse and Ronald van Kempen, eds., *Of States and Cities: The Partitioning of Urban Space* (Oxford: Oxford University Press, 2002).

Second, inherited city/countryside divisions were exacerbated as rapid capitalist industrialization fueled large-scale urbanization and an increasing peripheralization or "underdevelopment" of nonmetropolitan zones. The division between two distinct types of places—capital-rich, industrializing metropolitan centers and capital-poor, predominantly agrarian or extractive peripheries—thus became an essential axis of capitalist USD.[35] Even as patterns and pathways of place-making have been further rewoven, this basic division has persisted, albeit in an evolving form, during the *longue durée* of global capitalist development.[36]

Third, as capitalist industrialization intensified in the global core zones, places across the global periphery were transformed into sites for the primary extraction, processing, and export of raw materials, generally through strategies of accumulation by dispossession in which local resources were coercively enclosed and appropriated. In this manner, spatial divisions of labor articulated a worldwide pattern of USD in which core, capital-rich zones of large-scale industrialization (the "First World" and the "global North") were differentiated from peripheral, capital-poor areas of relative underdevelopment (the "Third World" and the "global South").[37]

Fourth, as industrial restructuring and concomitant rounds of technological innovation accelerated since the nineteenth century, new forms of interplace differentiation rippled across the global capitalist system. The spatial divisions of labor produced through earlier rounds of capitalist industrialization were subjected to successive cycles of creative destruction in conjunction with each subsequent period of crisis-induced restructuring— hence the increasingly chronic instability of places and interplace relations under modern capitalism. As Michael Storper and Richard Walker explain, "Each wave of industrialization brings into existence new growth centers and growth peripheries, stimulates disinvestment in some areas and the radical restructuring of others, and reshuffles spatial production relations and

---

[35] Gunnar Myrdal, *Rich Lands and Poor: The Road to World Prosperity* (New York: Harper, 1958); Williams, *The Country and the City*.

[36] Philip McMichael, "Peasant Prospects in the Neoliberal Age," *New Political Economy* 11, no. 3 (2006): 407–18; Philip McMichael, "Rethinking Globalization: The Agrarian Question Revisited," *Review of International Political Economy* 4, no. 4 (1997): 630–62. In the two final chapters of this book, I revisit the contentious question of whether the city/countryside division can still be described as such in the contemporary moment of planetary urbanization.

[37] Wallerstein, *The Modern World-System I*; Amin, *Capitalism in the Age of Globalization*. On accumulation by dispossession, see David Harvey, *The New Imperialism* (New York: Oxford University Press, 2003).

patterns of territorial income distribution and politics. In so doing, it gives new life to capitalism."[38] Such restructuring processes have, in fact, recurrently unsettled the sociospatial divisions associated with each of the three previously mentioned forms of place-based USD (intrametropolitan, city/countryside, and global core/periphery). The relentless creative destruction of spatial divisions of labor during the last two centuries of capitalist development has not, however, eroded the significance of place as an essential basing point for the articulation of USD.

Fifth, places may become the arenas and stakes of sociopolitical mobilizations that destabilize broader patterns of USD. This is because, even as capital strives to transform places, place-based attachments persist in the form of everyday routines, established lifeworlds, regimes of social reproduction, institutionalized political compromises, and sociocultural identities. Such place-based commitments are often articulated quite sharply when broader processes of capitalist restructuring threaten to destabilize or erode established patterns of place-making and interplace relations. Consequently, capital's impulsion to rework spatial divisions of labor in search of new opportunities for profit making may encounter intense resistance from those whose everyday lives, livelihoods, and identities are tightly enmeshed within particular places. As Harvey has argued, the resultant forms of place-based "revulsion and revolt" may assume reactionary, progressive, or radical forms, but whatever their political valence, the cumulative impact of such place-based insurgencies is to insert a powerful element of friction into capital's drive toward creative destruction.[39] Places, in other words, cannot be creatively destroyed according to the whim of capital; rather, their evolution is an outcome of intense sociopolitical contestation.[40] In this sense, the concrete shape of place-based forms of USD is powerfully mediated through sociopolitical struggles regarding the form, pace, rhythm, and trajectory of capitalist restructuring.

Territories and Uneven Spatial Development

The capitalist space economy emerged in medieval Europe within a fragmented, decentralized mosaic of political-economic spaces. This mosaic

---

[38] Storper and Walker, *The Capitalist Imperative*, 5.

[39] David Harvey, "Money, Time, Space and the City," in *The Urban Experience* (Baltimore: Johns Hopkins University Press, 1989), 165–99.

[40] Ray Hudson, *Producing Places* (New York: Guilford, 2001).

encompassed small city-state enclaves, interurban networks, bishoprics, duchies, principalities, and a patchwork of absolutist state structures lacking fixed territorial boundaries.[41] However, especially following the seventeenth century, territory became an increasingly foundational basis for organizing political life. Despite continued institutional and geographical diversity among them, states were now understood to occupy mutually exclusive, nonoverlapping, contiguous, and sovereign territorial spaces, and were reflexively monitored as such.[42] Borders were now seen clearly to separate the "inside" from the "outside" of states, and the domestic/foreign divide came to serve as a basic reference point for political-economic activity.[43] With the consolidation of mercantile capitalism, this international matrix of state territories was further entrenched as both statesmen and capitalists attempted to expand cross-border trade, to consolidate domestic markets, and thereby to increase national wealth.[44] The territorialization of worldwide political-economic space continued during the first wave of capitalist industrialization through (1) the intensified regulation of interstate boundaries, (2) the increasing internal parcelization of state space among diverse administrative jurisdictions, (3) the development of enhanced infrastructural capacities and intergovernmental relays through which states could attempt to extend their authority over all "points" within their borders, and (4) the imperialist conquest and territorial division of major zones of the world economy.[45]

These territorializations were maintained during subsequent rounds of capitalist industrialization in the nineteenth and twentieth centuries, even through phases of otherwise profound geoeconomic and geopolitical

---

[41] Hendrik Spruyt, *The Sovereign State and Its Competitors: An Analysis of Systems Change* (Princeton, NJ: Princeton University Press, 1994).

[42] John Gerard Ruggie, "Territoriality and Beyond: Problematizing Modernity in International Relations," *International Organization* 47, no. 1 (1993): 139–74. For a critical counterpoint to the influential Westphalian genealogy of territoriality in the international system of states, see Benno Teschke, *The Myth of 1648: Class, Geopolitics and the Making of Modern International Relations* (London: Verso, 2003); and Andreas Osainder, "Sovereignty, International Relations and the Westphalian Myth," *International Organization* 55, no. 2 (2001): 251–87. Another seminal contribution to such debates, which develops the key distinction between territory and territoriality, is Stuart Elden's *The Birth of Territory* (Chicago: University of Chicago Press, 2014).

[43] John Agnew and Stuart Corbridge, *Mastering Space: Hegemony, Territory, and International Political Economy* (New York: Routledge, 1995).

[44] Fernand Braudel, *The Perspective of the World*, trans. Siân Reynolds (Berkeley: University of California Press, 1984).

[45] Henri Lefebvre, "Space and the State," in *Henri Lefebvre: State, Space, World: Selected Essays*, ed. Neil Brenner and Stuart Elden (Minneapolis: University of Minnesota Press, 2009 [1978]), 223–53; Charles Maier, *Once within Borders: Territories of Power, Wealth and Belonging since 1500* (Cambridge, MA: Harvard University Press, 2016).

instability. This is not to suggest that territory, once consolidated, has remained static; its specific modes of organization and operation have in fact evolved significantly within the modern interstate system. The power and wealth containers of early modern territorial states were superseded, during the course of the twentieth century, by new forms of state developmentalism, nationalism, and welfarism that were likewise grounded upon distinctively territorial structures and strategies.[46] Concomitantly, the concrete geographies of interstate borders and intrastate jurisdictional divisions have periodically been modified, whether through warfare, internal rebellions, policy innovations, legal decisions, or social protest. As interstate relations have evolved in relation to the broader dynamics of worldwide capitalist development, new supraregional territorial institutions and frameworks of coordination (for instance, the European Union, the North American Free Trade Agreement [NAFTA], and the Association of Southeast Asian Nations [ASEAN]) have also been introduced that encompass multiple national state spaces and important subnational zones of regulatory activity. Nonetheless, even in the midst of these periodic macrohistorical realignments, territory has persisted as a foundational mode of modern geopolitical organization. Most crucially for this discussion, the differentiated landscapes of state territorial organization have articulated, mediated, and modified forms of USD in at least five key ways.

First, as the modern interstate system has been entrenched and generalized, territory has come to serve as a taken-for-granted category for the understanding of sociospatial organization more generally.[47] As a result, patterns of USD have been widely conceptualized in territorial terms, whether in institutionalized forms of data collection (for instance, in national censuses, Organisation for Economic Co-operation and Development [OECD] statistical tables, or World Bank development reports), in political discourse (for instance, in debates on spatial inequalities within territorially demarcated areas such as Europe, Britain, the South East of England, or London), or in everyday life (for instance, in popular representations of "Africa," the "rust belt," or "the ghetto"). In each case, a unit of analysis is defined with reference to the jurisdictional boundaries of states, territorially demarcated subnational areas, or groups of territorial states. It is then treated as a relatively coherent, integrated whole and contrasted to other,

---

[46] Taylor, "The State as Container."

[47] Agnew, "The Territorial Trap"; Jouni Häkli, "In the Territory of Knowledge: State-Centered Discourses and the Construction of Society," *Progress in Human Geography* 25, no. 3 (2001): 403–22.

formally equivalent units with reference to a particular socioeconomic indicator (for instance, population, unemployment, gross domestic product, or crime rates) or a perceived characteristic (for instance, wealth or poverty, modernity or backwardness, order or disorder). Thus, even though territory represents only one among several constitutive dimensions of USD, it has generally been treated as the most fundamental form in which sociospatial inequalities are organized.

Second, within the modern interstate system, state territorial structures have demonstrated considerable rigidity, and have therefore frequently acted as a drag upon the capitalist impulsion to relocate investment activity. In other words, the territorial borders delineated and controlled by states have been much less malleable than the spatial imprints and infrastructures of capital circulation that interpenetrate them. Consequently, such borders impose determinate locational constraints upon the capitalist drive to creatively destroy established sociospatial configurations. Even when the concrete geographies of capital have been rearranged, the modern interstate system has provided a relatively fixed, stable, and immobile grid of institutionalized sociospatial divisions—a world of parcelized, bordered spaces—for the process of capital circulation. To be sure, state territorial borders and internal jurisdictional arrangements have been modified during the course of capitalist development, in some cases quite significantly (for instance, after major military conflicts, civil wars, or revolutions). Once institutionalized, however, the concrete spatial parcels demarcated by state boundaries are relatively difficult to modify, even as their political-economic operations continue to evolve.[48] As discussed previously, patterns of USD are intimately intertwined with the fixity/motion contradiction under capitalism—the endemic tension between capital's dependence upon fixed sociospatial arrangements and its equally chronic tendency to creatively destroy those very arrangements in pursuit of fresh possibilities for accumulation. The consolidation of state territory as a deep structure of sociospatial organization within modern capitalism directly impacts this contradictory dynamic: it imposes a certain element of fixity, embodied in and layered across the worldwide grid of state territories, upon an otherwise restlessly changing geographical landscape.

Third, actually existing state territorial borders and internal jurisdictional boundaries have direct, durable implications for the concrete forms in which place-based inequalities and spatial divisions of labor are articulated. This is because different types of state territorial structures and regulatory

---

[48] Kevin Cox, "Territorial Structures of the State: Some Conceptual Issues," *Tijdschrift voor Economische en Sociale Geografie* 81 (1990): 251–66.

arrangements organize widely divergent conditions for capital circulation. For instance, the relative costs and availability of labor power, equipment, land, and raw materials; the nature of logistics infrastructures; and the level of taxation and tariffs may diverge significantly among state territories, as well as among intrastate (regional or local) political jurisdictions. Such inter- and intraterritorial differences are likely to have profound ramifications for the locational geographies of capital and, by implication, larger-scale spatial divisions of labor. Capitalists in search of cost-competitive locations are most likely to invest in territories (whether at the scale of localities, metropolitan regions, or national economies) that provide the lowest costs of production and circulation. By contrast, capitalists whose accumulation strategies hinge upon more specialized forms of labor power, interfirm coordination, infra- structural equipment, institutional relays, and technological configurations are more likely to sink investments into territories that provide such re- gionally or locally embedded socioeconomic assets.[49] In this sense, the geographies of (state) territories not only interpenetrate place-based patterns of USD, but directly shape them. As Kevin Cox observes, there is thus fre- quently "some congruence between patterns of geographically uneven devel- opment . . . and the territorial structure of the state."[50]

Fourth, in significant measure due to their territorially centralized institu- tional structures, state institutions have the capacity to influence patterns of USD within and beyond their borders. States may pursue this goal through diverse regulatory strategies, including industrial policies, economic devel- opment initiatives, infrastructure investments, spatial planning programs, labor market policies, regional policies, urban policies, housing policies, international trade agreements, and imperialist interventions, all of which have direct or indirect ramifications for intra- and supranational geographies of production, reproduction, and circulation. For example, early indus- trial states channeled massive public investments into large-scale territorial infrastructures such as railroads, roads, ports, and canals. These state spa- tial strategies were eventually complemented by state-led initiatives to regu- late urban living and working conditions and to establish large-scale public works facilities (such as hospitals, schools, energy grids, mass transportation networks, and waste management systems) within major metropolitan areas. During the course of the twentieth century, across much of the North Atlantic zone, national-developmentalist state institutions promoted their respective national territories as coherently integrated frameworks for economic growth

---

[49] Storper and Walker, *The Capitalist Imperative*.

[50] Kevin Cox, *Political Geography: Territory, State, Society* (Cambridge, MA: Blackwell, 2002), 253.

through a range of redistributive fiscal, industrial, and infrastructural policies. Most recently, across much of the world economy, major urban and regional economies have become strategically important targets for a range of spatially selective policies intended to enhance national competitive advantages in the context of accelerated geoeconomic integration. Throughout these periods, diverse forms of state-led imperialism, colonialism, and neocolonialism also profoundly influenced patterns of USD beyond each state's jurisdictional borders, whether through the expropriation of raw materials, the construction of markets, or the imposition of internal regulatory conditions favorable to foreign direct investment. While the concrete effects of such interventions have varied considerably and have often been considerably at odds with their officially declared political purposes, these examples illustrate the multifaceted ways in which states have attempted to shape and reshape the patterns of USD in which they are enmeshed.

Fifth, the territorial structures of the state provide various overlapping institutional arenas in and through which social movements may attempt to modify inherited forms of USD. Insofar as places represent the most immediate geographical terrain on which many of the most disruptive consequences of capitalist creative destruction are experienced, social movements frequently assume a place-based form. Crucially, however, the "nested hierarchical structures" of the state, with its territorially centralized, bounded, and internally differentiated institutional form, may likewise become important platforms for social forces concerned to confront the dislocations of capitalist creative destruction.[51] Insofar as place-based mobilizations attempt to harness the institutional capacities of the state in pursuit of their agendas, they must often adopt a territorial form. Under these circumstances, state institutions (whether national, regional, or local) may be mobilized against capital's strategies of place-making and place transformation, or at least as a means to reshape the latter to accommodate popular or factional demands. Meanwhile, capitalists may adopt territorial strategies of their own, harnessing state institutions to preserve, modify, or transform the spatial divisions of labor upon which their current or projected accumulation strategies depend. In this manner, the territorial structures of the state become a terrain of intense political contestation in which diverse social forces struggle to influence the geographies and trajectories of capital accumulation.[52] The processes of territorial alliance formation that

---

[51] Harvey, *Limits to Capital*, 430.

[52] Cox, "Territorial Structures of the State."

ricochet throughout all levels of the state apparatus may thus have profound implications for the contextually specific forms in which USD is articulated.

Scales and Uneven Spatial Development

My exploration thus far of places, territories, and the geographies of USD has consistently presupposed a third, equally foundational dimension of sociospatial relations—geographical scale. As I have argued at length in previous chapters, processes of scalar structuration complement the horizontal or areal differentiation of sociospatial relations across places and territories through an equally important vertical dimension, based on their differentiation and stratification among relationally intertwined yet coherently individuated levels, such as the local, the metropolitan, the regional, the national, and the global. Thus understood, like other core macrogeographical processes under capitalism, USD is profoundly scale differentiated. Indeed, all of the aspects of USD discussed previously under the rubric of place and territory are likewise articulated in intensely scale-differentiated, and generally scale-stratified, forms. As with the forms of place-making and reterritorialization discussed earlier, scalar differentiations of USD are likewise historically malleable, through successive rounds of rescaling.

The establishment of capitalist spatial divisions of labor and the territorialization of political power during the course of capitalist industrialization entailed not just the production and transformation of places, the consolidation of new intra- and interplace divisions, the territorial extension of capitalism beyond its North Atlantic heartlands, and the territorial segmentation of sociospatial inequality throughout the capitalist space economy. These developments were also closely intertwined with qualitatively new forms of scalar differentiation and interscalar stratification.

First, the local and regional scales were institutionalized as key spatial niches for specifically capitalist agglomerations of capital, labor, and infrastructure, as embodied in major metropolitan centers and urban regions.[53] This local and regional scaling of USD was constitutively intertwined with the production of the intra- and interplace inequalities described earlier, but cannot be reduced to the latter. It involved not only the internal polarization of metropolitan spatial organization and the further differentiation of cities and city-regions from surrounding hinterlands but also their strategic

---

[53] David Harvey, "The Urbanization of Capital," in *The Urban Experience* (Baltimore: Johns Hopkins University Press, 1989), 17–58.

positioning within a broader, stratified scaffolding of sociospatial relations stretching from the local and the national to the imperial and global scales.

Second, the global scale was consolidated as the ultimate geographical horizon for capitalist expansion, as embodied in the world market.[54] This globalization of capital circulation entailed a violent territorial expansion of the capitalist system into hitherto unincorporated zones and the crystallization of new forms of worldwide core/periphery polarization. It also helped entrench and activate the global scale as an encompassing geographical parameter for an emergent capitalist interscalar hierarchy oriented toward extending the rule of capital in both space and time.

Third, the national scale was further consolidated, tendentially stabilized, and generalized as an institutionalized terrain of mediation within an increasingly worldwide space of intercapitalist competition. This role was most powerfully embodied in the politico-institutional hierarchies, intergovernmental relays, and military apparatuses of the modern interstate system.[55] This nationalized (and *inter*nationalized) scaling of worldwide political-economic space has already been discussed previously, through the analytical lens of (national) territory. It also directly contributed to, and was in turn reinforced by, the various forms of interplace differentiation and territorial inequality that were outlined previously.

In conjunction with the latter trends, processes of USD have also been articulated onto several additional geographical scales, including (1) the neighborhood scale, embodied in intrametropolitan zones of community association and political jurisdiction, and (2) the supranational or imperial scale, embodied in institutionally and/or militarily demarcated spaces of capital circulation, colonization, and political regulation that encompass multiple national states and/or subordinate territories (for example, the European Union or the British Empire). Each of the latter scalings of USD has at once framed and mediated place-based and territorial inequalities. Insofar as each of the aforementioned scales constituted an additional organizational stratum, operational terrain, and stake of contestation within the broader interscalar hierarchies of modern capitalism, it contributed to the further differentiation and stratification of USD.

Because scales are defined relationally, the institutional and spatial coherence of those outlined previously can be grasped only with reference to their distinctive, shifting positions and operations within historically and

---

[54] Marx, *Capital*; Wallerstein, *The Modern World-System I*; Smith, *Uneven Development*.

[55] Smith, "Remaking Scale."

geographically specific, politically contested interscalar configurations. Concomitantly, because the functional activation of scales, interscalar relations, and scalar configurations has evolved historically, through diverse political strategies and struggles, patterns of scalar differentiation should not be treated as mechanistic structural necessities, whether in relation to the process of capital accumulation or the agendas of any other powerful actors, alliances, or organizations. Nonetheless, because the basic differentiation among neighborhood, local, regional, national, supranational, and global scales has been systemically reproduced even as spatial divisions of labor, interplace relations, and territorial configurations have been recurrently creatively destroyed, that interscalar architecture can be viewed as a relatively deep structure within capitalism's unstable geographical landscapes. In this sense, the process of USD under capitalism at once presupposes and reinforces a distinctive formation of scale differentiation and scale stratification, which has been intimately intertwined with place-based and territorial articulations of sociospatial relations.

However, just as place-based and territorial patterns of USD have been profoundly reworked during the geohistory of capitalism, so too have key aspects of its scalar geographies. Beyond the initial wave of scale differentiation outlined earlier, in which specifically capitalist instantiations of interscalar relations were consolidated, the scalar configuration of USD has assumed historically specific forms within the capitalist world economy and has been correspondingly rewoven during the course of capitalist development. Indeed, as I have argued at length in previous chapters, these successive waves of crisis-induced rescaling represent an essential medium and expression of USD under capitalism, both historically and in the current moment of accelerated worldwide sociospatial restructuring.

Mercantile and early industrial capitalism involved a generalized condition of scale relativization in which no single scale prevailed as the dominant stratum of political-economic organization. Patterns of USD were articulated at multiple spatial scales, from the local and the national to the imperial and the global. Within the newly consolidating geographies of early modern capitalism and imperialist expansion, spatial scales provided a relatively malleable scaffolding in and through which USD could be differentiated among diverse types of places, territories, and landscapes.

This situation of scale relativization was rearticulated during the period of national state consolidation that began in the eighteenth century and continued through successive waves of capitalist industrialization and territorial colonization well into the twentieth century. Throughout this *longue durée* period until the eventual erosion of national-developmentalist capitalism in the

1970s, the national scale became increasingly predominant at once as a crystallization point for USD and as an institutional locus for political strategies to manage the latter. As Peter J. Taylor notes, the effort to impose a spatial congruence between economic processes and political organization within each state's territory also entailed a growing nationalization of key aspects of sociospatial relations.[56] To be sure, patterns of USD were also articulated at other spatial scales, from the global and the imperial to the metropolitan and the local, but the increasing territorialization of political-economic life during this epoch was inextricably linked to a generalized nationalization of sociospatial inequality.[57] Consequently, diverse forms and modalities of core/periphery polarization within empires, colonies, states, and metropolitan regions were increasingly understood and acted upon as if they could be neatly aggregated upward or collapsed downward into the national scale of political-economic organization. Despite significant geoeconomic crises, successive waves of industrial restructuring, catastrophic military conflagrations, and violent popular and anticolonial insurgencies that periodically unsettled established sociospatial arrangements, this nationalized interscalar configuration was broadly preserved until the systemic crisis of national-developmentalist capitalism in the late twentieth century.

As I have argued in previous chapters, the post-1970s round of worldwide capitalist restructuring radically destabilized this long entrenched, nationalized scalar fix, leading to a renewed situation of scale relativization. The expansion in the role of transnational corporations and global finance capital since the early 1970s, the consolidation of a new international division of labor, the crystallization of post-Fordist forms of industrial agglomeration, the spatial reconstitution of statehood, the neoliberalization of economic governance, the intensification of international diasporic flows, and the consolidation of new information technologies are among the most dramatic expressions of these wide-ranging rescaling processes. Some scholars have characterized these trends with reference to the purported ascendancy of a single spatial scale—as, for instance, in accounts of the "new globalism," "triadization," "Europeanization," the "new regionalism," the "new localism," or the "local-global nexus."[58] By contrast, the argument proposed

---

[56] Taylor, "State as Container." See also Philip Cerny, "Globalization and the Changing Logic of Collective Action," *International Organization* 49, no. 4 (1995): 595–625; and Michael Mann, *The Sources of Social Power*, vol. 2: *The Rise of Classes and Nation States, 1760–1914* (New York: Cambridge University Press, 1993).

[57] Maier, *Once within Borders*.

[58] For a critical overview of these and related positions, see Lee and Wills, *Geographies of Economies*.

here is that the scalar architecture of capitalism as a whole—and, specifically, of USD—is being contested and reworked in unpredictable, intensely contested, and often haphazard ways.[59] At present, this scale-relativized geography has not ossified into a stabilized sociospatial formation; it more closely approximates a situation of interscalar *flux* than any kind of coherently patterned scalar fix. This line of interpretation builds upon the observation (1) that previously nodal, subordinate, or marginal spatial scales are gaining renewed importance in contemporary political-economic processes, strategies, and struggles and (2) that inherited patterns of individuation and differentiation among previously relatively discrete, coherent scalar strata— the national, the regional, and the local, for instance—are being comprehensively rearticulated through contemporary sociospatial transformations.

The contemporary relativization of scales must not be misconstrued as a transcendence or alleviation of USD as an endemic feature of capitalist space economies. On the contrary, as Neil Smith pointedly argued over two decades ago, "the global restructuring of the 1980s and 1990s embodies not so much an evening out of social and economic development levels across the globe as a deepening and reorganization of existing patterns of uneven geographical development."[60] The key claim here, therefore, is not that the national scale is being dissolved or superseded, or that any other scale has now acquired an operational dominance akin to that of the national during earlier phases of capitalist geohistorical development. The salient point, rather, is that patterns of USD are no longer configured around a predominant scale of political-economic organization, national or otherwise, but are now being produced through an increasingly dense intermeshing of sociospatial relations among previously more coherently individuated scalar strata. These intertwined developments represent the *differentia specifica* of contemporary forms of scale relativization. Deciphering the interplay between contemporary scale relativization processes and these newly emergent geographies of USD arguably represents one of the most urgent analytical tasks for contemporary studies of rescaling.

In sum, this discussion suggests several key ways in which scaling and rescaling processes may influence, and in turn be shaped by, processes of USD.

---

[59] See also Bob Jessop, "The Crisis of the National Spatio-Temporal Fix and the Ecological Dominance of Globalizing Capitalism," *International Journal of Urban and Regional Research* 24, no. 2 (2000): 323–60.

[60] Smith, "Satanic Geographies," 183. See also Amin, *Capitalism in the Age of Globalization*.

- The individuation and differentiation of scales under capitalism generate a hierarchical and stratified, but asymmetrically configured, scaffolding of sociospatial configurations in and through which processes of USD are organized and reproduced.
- Scalar configurations are themselves internally differentiated and stratified insofar as they contain specific divisions of labor among their constitutive tiers or strata (scalar divisions of labor). Across diverse politico-organizational contexts and variegated institutional landscapes, such scalar divisions of labor are among the key scalar expressions of USD.
- Scalar fixes may emerge insofar as interscalar relations are provisionally stabilized around a relatively established scalar division of labor. They thus represent a sociospatial framework in and through which scale-articulated, scale-stratified, and scale-dependent forms of USD may become operational, and may be further entrenched.
- When scalar fixes are destabilized and interscalar relations are unsettled, rescaling processes ensue in which new forms of scale differentiation, new scales of political-economic organization, new interscalar configurations, and new patterns of scale stratification are produced. Rescaling processes may thus destabilize established configurations of USD and generate qualitatively new constellations of sociospatial differentiation, stratification, and inequality.
- Insofar as interscalar arrangements are contested, a politics of scale may emerge in which diverse social forces and political alliances struggle to recalibrate the operational orientations, organizational embodiments, and sociospatial parameters of extant scalar strata, as well as the broader scalar hierarchies in which the latter are relationally embedded. In this sense, much like place and territory, scale may serve as a strategic basing point for social movements concerned with challenging established patterns of USD. The specific configuration of scale-based patterns of USD is thus an arena and stake of sociopolitical contestation.

Networks and Uneven Spatial Development

These considerations bring us to a further dimension of USD that has attracted considerable attention in recent years—namely, the role of networks as the basis for an alternative, topological mode of sociospatial organization based upon "points of connection and lines of flow, as opposed to . . . fixed surfaces and boundaries."[61] For Sarah Whatmore and Lorraine Thorne, networks represent a "mode of ordering of connectivity" in which diverse social spaces are linked together transversally across places, territories, and scales.[62] In closely analogous terms, Helga Leitner argues that networks "span space" by establishing horizontal, capillary-like, or rhizomatic interlinkages among geographically dispersed nodal points.[63] Consequently, "the spatial surface spanned by networks is . . . fluid and unstable" insofar as (1) the degree of connectivity among network nodes may fluctuate, (2) patterns of network membership may fluctuate, and (3) multiple networks may overlap, interpenetrate, and crosscut one another.[64]

Network geographies have long figured centrally in the geohistory of capitalism, and they have been tightly enmeshed with the variegated, uneven geographies of places, territories, and scales in nearly all of their concrete forms. Indeed, interfirm networks, diasporic networks, interlocality networks, infrastructural networks, interstate networks, and network-based social movements have thoroughly interpenetrated, and indeed co-constituted, the place-based, territorial, and scalar geographies of mercantile, industrial, national-developmentalist, and globalizing/neoliberalizing capitalism that were surveyed earlier. Three examples serve briefly to illustrate the role of networks in mediating and animating patterns of USD.

First, the process of capital accumulation has long hinged upon networked relationships among firms. Although many firms within the same sector aggressively compete for profit shares, others engage in cooperative relations through subcontracting, information sharing, technological transfer, and diverse forms of "untraded interdependencies."[65] While the precise nature of such interfirm synergies has evolved during each wave of capitalist industrialization, the latter have generally served to reinforce agglomeration processes and, by implication, to entrench broader matrices of place-based USD during the geohistory of capitalist development.[66]

Second, the consolidation and generalization of the modern interstate system have likewise entailed various types of networked relationships within

---

[61] Whatmore and Thorne, "Nourishing Networks," 289.

[62] Ibid., 295.

[63] Leitner, "The Politics of Scale and Networks of Spatial Connectivity," 248.

[64] Ibid., 248–49.

[65] Michael Storper, *The Regional World: Territorial Development in a Global Economy* (New York: Guilford, 1997).

[66] Allen J. Scott, *Regions and the World Economy* (Oxford: Oxford University Press), 1998.

and among national state apparatuses. Through international organizations, international treaties, international agreements, and other types of regulatory arrangements, judicial agreements, and governance practices, networks have played an important mediating role within the worldwide interstate system.[67] Networks have also long figured centrally in intergovernmental relations within each (national) state apparatus, where they have generally served to coordinate activities among various agencies, branches, and tiers of government, as well as, increasingly, with diverse actors and organizations within civil society. Insofar as these intergovernmental networks and regulatory strategies have influenced the geographies of capital investment, state activities, public service provision, and sociopolitical struggle, they have also necessarily impacted broader patterns of place- and territory-based USD.

Third, in addition to their place-based, territorially grounded, and scale-differentiated forms, social movements have also deployed networked modes of organization to pursue their goals. From the international socialist and feminist movements to ACT UP, the global justice movement, the Arab Spring, the Occupy movement, and #Black Lives Matter, the activities of social movements have depended upon networked ties as a basis for communication, coordination, and mobilization across places, scales, and territories. While the scale and impact of such rhizomatic networking operations have been powerfully enhanced through the contemporary generalization of new information technologies and associated social media, the latter have also been used aggressively, and often covertly, by territorially based institutions such as national states to enhance surveillance, to disseminate propaganda, and to bolster authoritarian forms of political control.[68] Social movement networks are generally embedded within, and intertwined with, places and territories, and they are always articulated in scale-differentiated forms. Yet, their geographies cannot be reduced to any of the latter dimensions of sociospatial relations. Insofar as networking strategies may enhance the capacity of social movements to influence processes of sociospatial restructuring, they are also likely to impact historically specific formations of USD.

In sum, then, networks may articulate, mediate, and influence patterns of USD in several essential ways:

---

[67] James N. Rosenau and Ernst Otto Czempiel, eds., *Governance without Government: Order and Change in World Politics* (Cambridge: Cambridge University Press, 1992).

[68] Manuel Castells, *Networks of Outrage and Hope: Social Movements in the Internet Age*, 2nd ed. (Cambridge: Polity, 2015).

- Networks generally crosscut place-based, territorial, and scalar patterns of USD. In so doing, network formations may reinforce, interrupt, or destabilize intraplace divisions, spatial divisions of labor, territorial borders, interterritorial relations, or scalar configurations. Concomitantly, networks may also reinforce rather than alleviate extant geographies of sociospatial inequality, whether of a place-based, territorial, or scalar nature.[69]

- Contrary to popular representations of networks as nonhierarchical, equalizing, and democratic, most actually existing networks are internally stratified and externally exclusionary. They contain power hierarchies and systems of stratification that marginalize some social actors, organizations, and forces at the expense of others, both within and beyond the network.[70] These may be manifested through the differential abilities of participants to influence network operations; through the establishment of stratified divisions of labor within the network that differentially allocate resources, tasks, and burdens among participants; and/or through the establishment of distinctive rules of closure that limit participation within the network to particular individuals, actors, or organizational entities. While these network-based power relations may be expressed in quite variegated social, political, and organizational forms, they generally entail powerful, wide-ranging impacts on formations of USD and their distinctive geographies.

The question of how emergent network geographies are transforming inherited patterns of USD is a matter of considerable contention in contemporary social theory. Several prominent scholars of contemporary geoeconomic restructuring and new information technologies have suggested that networks are today superseding the entrenched geographies of place, territory, and scale upon which the long-term geohistory of capitalism has been grounded. Alongside predictions that territory is being dissolved or eroded, versions of this position have been advanced through several influential interventions, including Manuel Castells's notion of the "space of flows," Ash Amin's proposals for a "nonscalar" and "topological" interpretation of globalization, and Sallie Marston, J. P. Jones, and Keith Woodward's

[69] Sheppard, "The Spaces and Times of Globalization"; Helga Leitner and Eric Sheppard, "'The City Is Dead, Long Live the Net': Harnessing European Interurban Networks for a Neoliberal Agenda," in *Spaces of Neoliberalism*, ed. Neil Brenner and Nik Theodore (Oxford: Blackwell, 2002), 148–71.

[70] Leitner and Sheppard, "'The City Is Dead, Long Live the Net.'"

radically deconstructive arguments for a "flat ontology."[71] These authors' diverse theoretical, empirical, and political concerns cannot be reduced to the specific *problematique* of USD, but they do commonly imply that inherited formations of territorial inequality are being transcended through a radically new configuration of sociospatial relations—one that is comprehensively based upon a topological, rhizomatic ontology of networks that supersedes all other sociospatial arrangements.

It is not possible to settle here the controversial question of how inherited patterns of USD are being remolded through emergent network topologies, whether of an infrastructural, informational, technosocial, financial, or political character. However, the arguments developed earlier may offer some methodological orientation for such investigations, insofar as they underscore the limitations of any approach that exclusively privileges, overgeneralizes, or fetishizes a singular dimension of sociospatial relations. Thus, rather than pursuing a purely topological analysis of networking—or, for that matter, an exclusively scalar analysis of scalar configurations and rescaling, a methodologically territorialist analysis of territorialization, or a place-centric analysis of place-making—the polymorphic approach proposed here aims to illuminate *and* differentiate the variegated, fluidly mutating dimensions of sociospatial relations within specific historical-geographical contexts. Within such a framework, places, territories, scales, and networks may indeed be demarcated on an abstract, methodological level as key research foci and as analytically distinct dimensions of sociospatial relations. Following their initial construction as such, however, the concrete-empirical investigation of such terrains requires the reflexive combination of these conceptual abstractions in order to decipher the de facto multidimensionality of sociospatial relations.[72]

---

[71] See, for instance, Richard O'Brien, *Global Financial Integration: The End of Geography* (London: Pinter, 1990); Castells, *The Rise of the Network Society*; Ash Amin, "Spatialities of Globalization," *Environment and Planning A* 34 (2002): 385–99; and Sallie Marston, John Paul Jones, and Keith Woodward, "Human Geography without Scale," *Transactions of the Institute of British Geographers* 30 (2005): 416–32.

[72] See Jessop, Brenner, and Jones, "Theorizing Socio-Spatial Relations," Figure 1. As we argued in that text (pp. 382–83): "One dimensionalism arises from taking an abstract-simple entry point and then, through conflation, essentialism, or fetishism, remaining on this terrain. Accordingly, however concrete the analysis may have become, it remains confused within a one-dimensional framework." The point, then, is not to reject the usefulness of abstract-simple entry points for sociospatial research—whether in relation to theories of place, territory, scale, networks, or otherwise. The argument here, rather, is that such abstract entry points remain just that—initial framings of a research agenda and terrain of investigation that, on more concrete-complex levels, will generally require distinctive combinations of abstract concepts, as well as the deployment of supplementary, contextually customized categories of analysis and methodological tactics.

Clearly, then, the observation that networked, topological forms of sociospatial organization are gaining a renewed significance is hugely productive insofar as—much like Neil Smith's initial reflections on scale in the 1980s—it directs scholarly attention to a previously neglected dimension of sociospatial relations that is now being more systematically operationalized and institutionalized in important domains of contemporary sociospatial practice. However, this useful observation does not logically translate into the claim that places, territories, and scales no longer exist, are no longer intermeshed with network geographies, or no longer serve to mediate sociospatial relations. On the contrary, as Eric Sheppard notes, it is essential to explore the "internal spatial structure of and power hierarchies within networks and their considerable resilience and path dependence."[73] Confronting this task, as Sheppard further explains, requires us not only to develop a topological account of the "networks a place participates in," but equally, to elaborate a territorially attuned, scale-differentiated analysis of "how [a place] is positioned within the spaces of those networks."[74] In short, a rigorously polymorphic analysis of networks requires the use of topologically oriented categories, *as well as* reflexively place-based, scalar, and territorial analytics. To proceed otherwise is to engage in the methodological fallacy of network-centrism: it entails a reduction of the radically polymorphic *mille-feuille* of capitalist sociospatial relations into a singular, overgeneralized, or even fetishized form, that of the topological network.

We have only just begun to decipher the emergent sociospatial dynamics, contours, contradictions, and consequences of the latest round of capitalist creative destruction and its wide-ranging implications for patterns and pathways of USD. The conceptual repertoire proposed in this chapter is intended to contribute to that effort by offering a methodologically nominalist counterpoint to the quasi-ontological positions that have gained currency in influential strands of contemporary sociospatial theory. From this point of view, the key issue is not the unilinear replacement of places, territories, and scales by emergent network topologies, but the co-constitutive rearticulation, mutual entanglement, and dense intermeshing of these dimensions of sociospatial practices in relation to one another, through ongoing strategies and struggles over the present and future shape of USD.

---

[73] Sheppard, "The Spaces and Times of Globalization," 318.

[74] Ibid., 317.

Toward a Polymorphic Approach to the Capitalist Urban Fabric

In an incisive article on scale theory published in the late 1990s, Richie Howitt argued against the attempt to attribute "conceptual primacy or conceptual independence" to geographical scale relative to other aspects of sociospatial relations.[75] Just as forcefully, Howitt rejected approaches that treated scale as the mere effect of other, purportedly more fundamental sociospatial processes. At the time of Howitt's intervention, the latter tendency was being vigorously criticized within the burgeoning literature on the production of scale. Meanwhile, however, the former problem—described here under the rubric of scale-centrism—was already becoming widely prevalent as scholars overextended scalar concepts to encompass a variety of other, distinct dimensions of sociospatial relations. Arguing presciently against both conceptions, Howitt insisted that scale deserves a "coequal" status, along with other core geographical concepts such as place and territory, in the "construction and dynamics of geographical totalities."[76]

The analysis presented here resonates closely with Howitt's conceptualization: a coequal understanding of place-making, territorialization, scaling, and networking processes has been elaborated here, on a fairly high level of abstraction, with reference to the problem of deciphering the geographies of USD during the long-run geohistory of capitalism. Like Howitt, I have insisted that scale, while being essential to the uneven historical geographies of capitalist development, represents only one among their most essential dimensions. Just as importantly, the approach to sociospatial theory elaborated here requires us not only to conceptualize scaling processes as being analytically coequal with those associated with place-making, territorialization, and networking processes but also to explore the contextually specific entanglements among the latter that at once forge, reproduce, mediate, and recurrently transform the variegated, constitutively polymorphic fabric of sociospatial relations.[77] The key elements of this line of argumentation are summarized in Figure 8.4.

---

[75] Richard Howitt, "Scale as Relation: Musical Metaphors of Geographical Scale," *Area* 30, no. 1 (1998): 51.

[76] Ibid., 56.

[77] In this sense, my arguments here also resonate closely with more recent writings by Helga Leitner, Eric Sheppard, and Joe Painter, each of whom is likewise concerned to explore how the mutual imbrication of key sociospatial processes—territorialization, scaling, and networking, in particular—produces the uneven political-economic geographies of capitalism. See, for example, Leitner, "The Politics of Scale and Networks of Spatial Connectivity"; Sheppard, "The Spaces and Times of Globalization"; and Joe Painter, "Rethinking Territory," *Antipode* 42, no. 5 (2010): 1090–118.

These considerations have significant implications for the conceptualization of the capitalist urban fabric presented in this book, which is closely articulated to the *problematique* of USD. Beginning with my analysis of capital's fixity/motion contradiction in Chapter 2, I have consistently emphasized the polymorphic character of the capitalist urban fabric—its constitution and transformation through diverse sociospatial processes that involve intermeshed strategies of place-making, territorialization, scaling, and networking, among others. In so doing, however, my main analytical agenda

Dimension of sociospatial relations	Articulations to and crystallizations of uneven spatial development
Place/ place making	• Divisions within places/divisions among places • Differentiation among types of places: city/non-city, production/ reproduction, work/leisure, active/fallow • Spatial divisions of labor: assignment of specific functional roles to different places, or types of places, within a broader system of places • Place-based social movements and struggles may modify patterns of USD
Territory/ territorialization	• Territory as a naturalized unit for the measurement of spatial inequality • Inequalities within territories/inequalities among territories • Differentiation among types of territories: cores vs. peripheries, metropoles vs. hinterlands or colonies • State territories may impose an element of friction upon capital's impulsion toward creative destruction: they introduce and enforce an element of (provisional) fixity upon the restlessly changing landscapes of USD • State territories create differential conditions of capital investment and mobility within their jurisdictions through diverse regulatory strategies • Territory-based social movements may modify patterns of sociospatial inequality

FIGURE 8.4 Key dimensions of uneven spatial development under capitalism.

Scale/scaling	• Place-based and territorial inequalities are always constituted at specific spatial scales (neighborhood, local, regional, national, supranational, and/or global). Patterns of USD are thus always scale articulated and scale differentiated • Scalar divisions of labor: assignment of specific roles to different scales, or types of scales, within a broader interscalar configuration • Individuation, differentiation, and stratification among different types of scales: dominant vs. nodal or subordinate scales • Rescaling: patterns of sociospatial inequality may be reconfigured through broader changes in scalar organization • Politics of scale: contestation of inherited frameworks of scalar organization; creation of new forms of scalar organization and associated stratifications of interscalar relations • Note: divisions and differentiations "within" scales cannot be fully grasped in purely scalar terms; they are generally expressions of place-based, territorialized, and/or networked patterns of sociospatial relations
Networks/ network formation	• Network-based spatial inequalities are closely intertwined with place-based, territorial, and/or scalar divisions; appeals to "pure" network space are generally ideological mystifications • Inequalities within networks and inequalities among different types of networks • Network divisions of labor: assignment of specific functional roles to different nodes within a broader circulatory configuration; internal stratification of nodes in a network through power relations

FIGURE 8.4 Continued

has been to explore the ways in which urbanization processes under modern capitalism have been scale differentiated and scale stratified, especially in relation to successive rounds of state spatial regulation, whose territorial and scalar geographies have, in turn, profoundly imprinted those of the urban fabric. Yet, by proposing to reframe the (contemporary) urban question as a scale question, this investigation has necessarily devoted particular attention to historical scalings of urbanization and, especially, to the role of ongoing rescaling processes in the production of new urban spaces. Thus, while my explorations of global city formation, the world city archipelago, entrepreneurial forms of urban governance, ICT-based strategies of urban economic development, competitive city regionalism, and urban growth machines have engaged with the place-based, territorial, and networked geographies associated with these processes, I have focused above all on their role as animators, mediators, expressions, and products of rescaling, in a geoeconomic and geopolitical context characterized by intensifying scale relativization. In effect, my research agenda here has concentrated less on illuminating the polymorphic character of contemporary urban sociospatial restructuring than on tracking, analyzing, and theorizing the distinctive, if dynamically mutating, scalar dimensions of those processes.

This procedure appears appropriate insofar as it has put into relief a neglected, undertheorized, and yet increasingly strategic dimension of urban restructuring. However, even if such a conceptual maneuver has proven salient in diverse terrains of contemporary urban research, its substantive contributions and future analytical potential must be viewed with considerable caution. Especially in light of the methodological hazards of one-dimensionalism outlined in this chapter, the tendency of scale-attuned modes of analysis to drift into various forms of scale-centrism, scale reductionism, and scalar fetishism must be avoided. Any theoretically reflexive approach to the urban question as a scale question must, therefore, devise methodological strategies for illuminating the scaling and rescaling of urban space, but without overgeneralizing scalar concepts to encompass other, distinct dimensions of urban sociospatial restructuring. In short, the urban question may well have today become a scale question, but it is not *only* that. There are decisive limits to scale, at once as a theoretical concept, as a research tool, and as a dimension of sociospatial practice, strategy, and struggle. The contradictory sociospatial relations that constitute, animate, and relentlessly transform the capitalist urban fabric are constitutively multidimensional; their polymorphic geographies constantly exceed the parameters of any and all conceptual abstractions that might be mobilized to decipher them.

My explorations of the *mille-feuille* of USD under capitalism thus now produce an autocritical methodological counterpoint to the modes of analysis I have elaborated in previous chapters. My claim is not that a scalar perspective on the contemporary urban question is misguided, but that it is likely to be one-sided unless it is reflexively combined with other key analytical categories that illuminate the polymorphic nature of urban space and the multiple dimensions of urban sociospatial restructuring. Rescaling processes, whether of the capitalist urban fabric, state space, social reproduction, sociopolitical mobilization, ecological metabolism, or otherwise, are likely to be intricately entangled with place-based, territorial, and/or networked dynamics of sociospatial restructuring, which likewise require both abstract theorization and concrete-conjunctural modes of analysis. Indeed, as Henri Lefebvre classically insisted in *The Production of Space,* it is essential for critical approaches to sociospatial analysis to avoid the tendency toward a premature totalization of sociospatial relations, be it by fetishizing one of their elements or by implying that they can be represented comprehensively through a "science of space."[78] To the degree that social space might, from some perspectives, appear singular, one-dimensional, transparent, fully knowable, malleable, and thus readily manipulable, this is generally a structural *effect* of politico-ideological strategies that seek to impose authoritarian control over the volatile, politically contested flux of sociospatial relations.[79] Such strategies of politico-ideological totalization and their associated structural effects may assume a range of place-based, territorial, scalar, or networked forms, depending on which dimension of sociospatial relations, or which combination thereof, they seek to instrumentalize.

One-dimensionalism, then, is not merely an arbitrary epistemic error or a contingent methodological blind spot in sociospatial research; it arises from historically specific political strategies, ideological projects, and representational technologies that attempt to mask, and thus to neutralize, the contested, contradictory power relations that inhere within sociospatial configurations. In this sense, emphasizing polymorphism is not only a means to decipher the manifold sociospatial determinations through which the capitalist urban fabric is produced, contested, and transformed. Perhaps more important, it may also serve as a critical methodological resource for the project of destabilizing hegemonic spatial ideologies, especially those that naturalize the intensely contested politics of space upon which urbanization hinges. Polymorphic approaches to sociospatial analysis are, therefore, essential components within the conceptual and methodological arsenal of critical urban theory. As such, they may figure crucially within the broader project of repoliticizing urban knowledge formations in this increasingly

---

[78] Lefebvre, *Production of Space*, 27–30, 90–91, 104 passim. For further elaborations of this anti-totalizing approach to dialectical sociospatial theory, see Gillian Hart, "Relational Comparison Revisited: Marxist Postcolonial Geographies in Practice," *Progress in Human Geography* 42, no. 3 (2018): 371–94; as well as, more generally, Bertell Ollman, *Dance of the Dialectic* (Urbana: University of Illinois Press, 2003).

[79] In an influential analysis, James C. Scott refers to such structural effects as "state simplifications"—but such effects may be produced by nonstate actors and institutions as well, especially by those associated with capital. See James C. Scott, "State Simplifications: Nature, Space and People," *Journal of Political Philosophy* 3, no. 3 (1995): 191–233. A closely related line of analysis that focuses on the scalar simplifications (of both the human and nonhuman world) associated with capitalist supply chains is Anna Lowenhaupt Tsing, "Supply Chains and the Human Condition," *Rethinking Marxism* 21, no. 2 (2009): 148–76. See also Anna Lowenhaupt Tsing, "On Nonscalability: The Living World Is Not Amenable to Precision-Nested Scales," *Common Knowledge* 18, no. 3 (2012): 505–24.

"postpolitical" moment of early twenty-first-century neoliberal capitalist urbanization.[80]

Beyond its general contribution to the work of critical urban theory, several methodologically consequential lines of investigation into urban questions flow from the conceptual framework elaborated in this chapter. Most of the major twentieth-century traditions of urban theory have been premised upon one-dimensional understandings of urban space. For example, much of urban social science, from Chicago school urban sociology to Marxian analyses of agglomeration, has gravitated toward place-centric modes of analysis, albeit often in conjunction with significant explorations of intraplace networks, whether among locally embedded community organizations, capitalist firms, workers, or otherwise. Concomitantly, more recent elaborations of global city theory have tended to embrace various forms of network-centrism, albeit often in conjunction with explorations of how emergent global urban networks animate, and are in turn shaped by, specifically post-Fordist pathways of place-making. Against this background, the arguments presented here provide a critical analytical perspective from which to re-evaluate the geographical imaginaries of these and other major traditions of urban research.

How might a reflexively polymorphic approach to sociospatial theory destabilize the ways in which canonical approaches to urban social science conceptualize their site(s) of theory building, methodological experimentation, and concrete research? How might systematic consideration of the mutual entanglement among place-making, territorialization, scaling, and networking processes reorient the framing questions, conceptual grammar, methodological tactics, and logics of investigation that underpin these research traditions? How, for instance, might an inquiry into early to mid-twentieth-century (re)territorialization and (re)scaling processes reframe Chicago school–inspired approaches to the neighborhood as an arena of urban life, community organization, and human ecology? How might such an inquiry reframe Marxian theories of urban agglomeration and the politics of place during the process of capitalist industrial development?[81] The scale-attuned reading of global city theory

---

[80] Erik Swyngedouw, "The Antinomies of the Post-Political City," *International Journal of Urban and Regional Research* 33, no. 3 (2009): 601–20; Japhy Wilson and Erik Swyngedouw, eds., *The Post-Political and Its Discontents* (Edinburgh: Edinburgh University Press, 2014). On the link between critical urban theory and the critique of spatial ideology, see Neil Brenner, *Critique of Urbanization: Selected Essays* (Basel: Bauwelt Fundamente/Birkhäuser Verlag, 2016).

[81] The relational approach to sociospatial theory developed by Doreen Massey, John Allen, Allan Cochrane, and others at the Open University offers a powerful inroad into precisely such an

presented in Chapter 4 has already explored the ways in which rescaling processes co-constitute, mediate, and rework the place/network relations upon which this literature has been largely focused. This analysis also necessarily presupposed an account of the various forms of territorialization and reterritorialization that have been entangled with both global city formation and the concomitant rescaling of urban governance in globalizing, neoliberalizing metropolitan regions.

In their recent studies of the world city archipelago, Michiel van Meeteren and David Bassens have developed a closely analogous line of critique to that proposed in this chapter.[82] In particular, their work demonstrates that post-1980s processes of global city formation in Europe have involved not only networking and place-making dynamics, but have also been intimately intertwined with the production and transformation of territorialized and scale-stratified sociospatial arrangements. Such processes of reterritorialization and rescaling, they argue, are not secondary byproducts of the world city archipelago but appear to have been essential to its core politico-institutional and geographical operations throughout the post-Fordist, post-Keynesian, and post-developmentalist era. Unless those dimensions of sociospatial relations are systematically considered, van Meeteren and Bassens suggest, the vicissitudes of advanced producer services firms; their variegated circuits of investment, finance, infrastructure, and labor; and their wide-ranging consequences for emergent urbanization processes cannot be adequately understood. This would, in turn, leave the entire global cities literature dangerously "susceptible to the critique of legitimating the very imperatives of global city formation" it ostensibly aspires to subvert.[83] Global city theory is but one among many important terrains of contemporary urban studies in which a reflexively polymorphic methodology may offer a forceful critical counterpoint to the hegemonic projects of spatial totalization associated with contemporary neoliberalizing, financialized capitalism. In precisely this sense, as van Meeteren and Bassens explain:

---

exploration. See, for example, their brilliantly polymorphic study of regionalization and place-making processes in London: John Allen, Allan Cochrane, and Doreen Massey, *Rethinking the Region* (London: Routledge, 1998).

[82] David Bassens and Michiel van Meeteren, "World Cities and the Uneven Geographies of Financialization: Unveiling Stratification and Hierarchy in the World City Archipelago," *International Journal of Urban and Regional Research* 40, no. 1 (2016): 62–81. See also David Bassens and Michiel van Meeteren, "World Cities under Conditions of Financialized Globalization: Towards an Augmented World City Hypothesis," *Progress in Human Geography* 39, no. 6 (2015): 752–75.

[83] Van Meeteren and Bassens, "World Cities and the Uneven Geographies," 77.

it is paramount to analyse processes of legitimization and normalization across spatial scales, by which they [practices and circuits of financialization] are allowed to continue as seemingly benign "post-industrial" growth strategies.

Unveiling the place-, territory- and scale-making aspects of financialized accumulation thus seems to be a project stretching beyond the means of critical urban studies itself to include a societal critique of the dominant accumulation regime.[84]

These arguments are not meant to suggest, a priori, that all dimensions of sociospatial relations will always be equally relevant to all sites, terrains, and *problematiques* of urban research. As I have emphasized, the appropriate combination of categories for urban sociospatial analysis is a relatively contingent matter on which pragmatic but theoretically informed decisions need to be made. Such decisions are likely to hinge upon the context(s), site(s), and purpose(s) of a given research endeavor; they may also require frequent reconsideration as the process of investigation itself unfolds. The point here, then, is that a reflexively polymorphic understanding of urban space may offer a generative basis on which to confront such questions, in marked contrast to the relatively one- (or two-) dimensional conceptualizations of sociospatial relations that underpinned the major traditions of twentieth-century urban research. As such, the approach proposed here may also usefully contribute to ongoing debates regarding the appropriate, if incessantly shifting and essentially contested, spatial parameters of the urban question itself.

A polymorphic framing of the urban question may also generate potentially productive lines of investigation regarding the patterns and pathways of urbanization in specific historical-geographical contexts. Urban researchers have long emphasized the path-dependent character of urban development: inherited historical formations of the built environment, institutional arrangements, growth regimes, and metabolic circuits strongly condition emergent pathways of restructuring. Contextually specific processes of urban transformation result from the collision of such path-dependent sociospatial configurations and emergent strategies of sociospatial creative destruction. The outcomes of such collisions are never structurally preordained but result from contextually embedded crisis tendencies, conflicts, strategies, and struggles, as well as contingencies related to location, jurisdiction, and ecology. In some spatiotemporal contexts, inherited sociospatial arrangements may manifest strongly obdurate, even sclerotic properties, whereas elsewhere they may be transformed with breathtaking

---

[84] Ibid., 77–78.

speed and breadth. The fixity/motion contradiction is thus always articulated and fought out in specific historical-geographical landscapes that decisively shape its spatial expressions, its temporal rhythms, and its variegated impacts upon urban development pathways.[85]

The approach to sociospatial theory proposed here may productively inform the concrete investigation of such path-dependent historical geographies of urban restructuring. From this point of view, there is no singular morphology of "the" city associated with capitalist urbanization, whether in general terms or with reference to its major configurations of world-historical development.[86] The task, rather, is precisely to investigate the polymorphic variegations of the capitalist urban fabric that are forged through contextually specific intermeshings among place-making, territorialization, scaling, and networking processes. This methodological injunction could be fruitfully applied to relatively familiar manifestations of the urban condition (large metropolitan agglomerations or polynucleated urban regions, for instance), leading to new perspectives on the variegated processes through which such spaces have been produced and transformed across space and time. Such an approach might also help guide the geocomparative investigation of many other crystallizations of the capitalist urban fabric around the world, conceived not merely as "deviations" from some putatively universal model but as contextually distinctive, theoretically significant, and relationally interconnected moments within a variegated yet worldwide urbanization process.[87] It is the *longue durée*, path-dependent proliferation of these historically and geographically specific entanglements

---

[85] Christian Schmid, "Specificity and Urbanization: A Theoretical Outlook," in *The Inevitable Specificity of Cities*, ed. ETH Studio Basel (Zurich: Lars Müller Publishers, 2014), 282–97.

[86] Neil Brenner and Christian Schmid, "Towards a New Epistemology of the Urban?," *CITY* 19, no. 2–3 (2015): 151–82.

[87] For some productive inroads into such an investigation that are, in conceptual terms, closely allied with my proposals here, see Roger Diener, Jacques Herzog, Marcel Meili, Pierre de Meuron, and Christian Schmid, *Switzerland: An Urban Portrait*, 4 vols. (Zurich: Birkhäuser, 2001); ETH Studio Basel, ed., *The Inevitable Specificity of Cities* (Zurich: Lars Müller Publishers, 2014); and ETH Studio Basel/Contemporary City Institute, ed., *Territory: On the Development of Landscape and City* (Zurich: Park Books, 2016); as well as Alessandro Balducci, Valeria Fedeli, and Franceso Curci, eds., *Post-Metropolitan Territories: Looking for a New Urbanity* (London: Routledge, 2017). Also highly relevant to such an exploration are, among other works, Alan Berger, *Drosscape: Wasting Land in Urban America* (New York: Princeton Architectural Press, 2006); Patrick Barron and Manuela Mariani, eds., *Terrain Vague: Interstices and the Edge of the Pale* (New York: Routledge, 2013); Thomas Sieverts, *Cities without Cities: An Interpretation of the Zwischenstadt* (New York: Spon Press, 2003); François Ascher, *Métapolis ou l'avenir des villes* (Paris: Editions Odile Jacob, 1995); Lars Lerup, *After the City* (Cambridge, MA: MIT Press, 2001); and Norton Ginsburg, Bruce Koppel, and T. G. McGee, eds., *The Extended Metropolis: Settlement Transition in Asia* (Honolulu: University of Hawaii Press, 1991).

among place-making, territorialization, scaling, and networking processes that, in aggregate, at once constitutes and continually reweaves the capitalist urban fabric as a whole.

Capitalist urbanization, then, is not a process of *pure* flux. As I have argued throughout this book, the drive toward sociospatial creative destruction is but one moment of a dialectic in which capital equally depends upon and seeks to construct relatively fixed and immobile sociospatial configurations that might support its voracious quest to maximize surplus value extraction. To the degree that such a stabilization of sociospatial arrangements is tendentially secured, the urbanization process acquires a coherently patterned, regularized configuration—a "structured coherence," in Harvey's classic terminology.[88] In the analysis of the fixity/motion contradiction under capitalism presented in Chapter 2, I emphasized the distinctively scalar dimensions of this structured coherence: capital's spatial fixes also generally entail scalar fixes insofar as they simultaneously produce and hinge upon contextually specific scalings (and periodic rescalings) of sociospatial relations. To some degree, this line of argumentation involved complementing Harvey's largely place-centered account of the spatial fix in his writings of the 1980s with a more reflexively scale-attuned mode of analysis, one that could connect capital's regionalized circulatory infrastructures to broader scalings and rescalings of sociospatial relations during successive phases of capitalist urbanization. The place-centered notion of structured coherence developed in Harvey's work was thus effectively transformed into a two-dimensional analytical tool, one that permitted a more systematic exploration of (1) the scaling of place-making processes, (2) the place-embeddedness of interscalar configurations, (3) the mutual constitution of historically specific forms of place-making and scale stratification, (4) the role of the latter in forging historically and geographically specific patterns and pathways of urbanization, and (5) the massively destabilizing impacts of contemporary scale relativization processes upon inherited configurations of place-making.

The polymorphic approach to sociospatial theory presented in this chapter at once relativizes and extends that mode of analysis: it offers an expanded conceptual repertoire through which to explore the interplay between path dependency and creative destruction in the production of urbanizing sociospatial configurations. From this point of view, spatial fixes are generally place-based and scale differentiated, but they may also be grounded upon

---

[88] David Harvey, "The Geopolitics of Capitalism," in *Social Relations and Spatial Structures*, ed. Derek Gregory and John Urry (New York: Palgrave, 1985), 128–63; David Harvey, *The Urban Experience* (Baltimore: Johns Hopkins University Press, 1989).

historically specific modes of territorialization and networking as well. The historical geographies of the fixity/motion contradiction—and, by implication, those of the capitalist urban fabric—must thus be subjected to a rigorously polymorphic analysis. How, exactly, is capital's moment of fixity secured across the variegated contexts and configurations of urbanization? To the extent that a structured coherence for capitalist urbanization is provisionally established, does this occur primarily through strategies of place-making, scaling, territorialization, or networking? Or, more probably, does it involve contextually specific intermeshings among place-based, scale-differentiated, territorialized, and networked strategies of sociospatial transformation? Are the major waves of worldwide capitalist urbanization themselves associated with distinctive articulations and entanglements among these dimensions of sociospatial relations? To what degree have contemporary processes of scale relativization been fundamentally, or perhaps only secondarily, intertwined with parallel dynamics of deterritorialization and/or mutations of place-making and/or networking processes? My investigation of the capitalist urban fabric and its rescaling in previous chapters has tentatively opened up such questions with reference to the North Atlantic zone during the Fordist-Keynesian and post-Keynesian waves of urbanization, albeit with a strong methodological emphasis on their scalar parameters. The analysis presented here, however, suggests that more reflexively polymorphic analyses of these, and perhaps other, historical-geographical cycles of urban sociospatial development could prove highly informative.[89]

These reflections return us to one of the core arguments that emerged from my initial presentation of the urban question as a scale question in Chapter 3: the key *explanandum* in the investigation of "urban restructuring," I argued, lies as much in the *urban* component of this phrase as in the process of restructuring. As understood here, the urban is not a merely descriptive label through which to indicate where a restructuring process is unfolding,

---

[89] Parallel questions may also be posed regarding the dynamics of crisis formation that recurrently disrupt established geographies of urbanization. As David Harvey classically argued in his "third cut" theory of crisis in *Limits to Capital*, capital's endemic crisis tendencies are likely to assume a distinctively spatial form, especially due to the operations of place-specific forms of devaluation and consequent strategies of capital switching among investment locations. See *The Limits to Capital* (Chicago: University of Chicago Press, 1982), 424–30. This theorization may likewise be further differentiated in light of the polymorphic approach to sociospatial analysis presented here. During successive stages of capitalist development, the spatialization of crisis and strategic responses to the latter are likely to be articulated not only via place-based, interplace, or interscalar dynamics but also through distinctive projects of (re)territorialization and network formation or reorganization. In other words, the dynamics of crisis formation and the resultant pathways of sociospatial creative destruction that shape the urbanization process are likely to involve intricate, historically and geographically specific entanglements among place-making, scaling, territorialization, and networking strategies.

in a physical-locational sense. Rather, it denotes the *problematique* itself, the central issue under investigation: the urban is not only the locational setting or arena in which urban restructuring unfolds, but its very medium, product, and stake. Given my arguments in this chapter, this proposition now acquires an expanded, more conceptually intricate and potentially generative meaning. As conceived here, the investigation of urban restructuring requires an exploration of how the polymorphic fabric of capitalist urbanization is itself woven and continually rewoven through contextually specific, path-dependent processes of place transformation, rescaling, reterritorialization, and networking. The relentless, volatile intermeshing of such processes facilitates the creative destruction of inherited geographies of urbanization while also anticipating possible future sociospatial configurations in which a renewed structured coherence for the production of urban space might be tendentially secured. This is the polymorphic, systemically patterned but chronically unstable sociospatial terrain on which the future geographies and pathways of capitalist urbanization are being forged and fought out.

9
Planetary Urbanization: Mutations of the Urban Question

IN THE EARLY 1970s, a young Marxist sociologist named Manuel Castells, then living in exile in Paris, began his soon-to-be classic intervention on *The Urban Question* by declaring his "astonishment" that debates on "urban problems" were becoming "an essential element in the policies of governments, in the concerns of the mass media and, consequently, in the everyday life of a large section of the population."[1] For Castells, this astonishment was born of his orthodox Marxist assumption that the concern with urban questions was ideological. The real motor of social change, he believed, lay elsewhere, in working-class action and anti-imperialist mobilization. On this basis, Castells proceeded to deconstruct what he viewed as the prevalent "urban ideology" under postwar managerial capitalism: his theory took seriously the social construction of the urban phenomenon in academic and political discourse but ultimately derived such representations from purportedly more foundational processes associated with capitalism and the state's role in the reproduction of labor power.

Nearly a half century after Castells's classic intervention, it is easy to confront early twenty-first-century discourse on urban questions with a similar

---

[1] Manuel Castells, *The Urban Question: A Marxist Approach* (Cambridge, MA: MIT Press, 1977 [1972]), 1.

sense of astonishment—not because it masks the operations of capitalism but because it has become one of the dominant metanarratives through which our current planetary situation is interpreted, both in academic circles and in the public sphere. Today, advanced interdisciplinary education in urban social science, planning, and design is flourishing in major universities, and urban questions are being confronted energetically by historians, literary critics, and media theorists and in emergent approaches to the environmental humanities. Biogeophysical and computational scientists and ecologists are likewise contributing to urban studies through their explorations of new satellite-based data sources, georeferencing analytics, and geographic information system (GIS) technologies, which are offering new perspectives on the geographies of urbanization across scales, territories, and ecologies.[2] Classic texts such as Jane Jacobs's *The Death and Life of Great American Cities* and Mike Davis's *City of Quartz* continue to animate debates on contemporary urbanism, and more recent, popular books on cities, such as Edward Glaeser's *Triumph of the City*, Jeb Brugmann's *Welcome to the Urban Revolution*, and Richard Florida's *Who's Your City?*, along with documentary films such as Gary Hustwit's *Urbanized* and Michael Glawogger's *Megacities*, are widely discussed in the public sphere.[3] Major museums, expos, and biennales from New York City, Chicago, Venice, and Valparaíso to Christchurch, Seoul, Shenzhen, and Shanghai are devoting extensive attention to questions of urban culture, architecture, design, and development.[4] The notion of the right to the city, developed in the late 1960s by Henri Lefebvre, has now become a popular rallying

---

[2] David Potere and Annemarie Schneider, "A Critical Look at Representations of Urban Areas in Global Maps," *GeoJournal* 69 (2007): 55–80; Shlomo Angel, *Making Room for a Planet of Cities*, Policy Focus Report (Cambridge, MA: Lincoln Institute of Land Policy, 2011); and Paolo Gamba and Martin Herold, eds., *Global Mapping of Human Settlement* (New York: Taylor & Francis, 2009).

[3] Jane Jacobs, *The Death and Life of Great American Cities* (New York: Modern Library, 1965); Mike Davis, *City of Quartz* (New York: Vintage, 1991); Edward Glaeser, *Triumph of the City* (New York: Tantor, 2011); Jeb Brugmann, *Welcome to the Urban Revolution* (New York: Bloomsbury, 2010); Richard Florida, *Who's Your City?* (New York: Basic, 2008); *Urbanized*, directed by Gary Hustwit (2011; London: Swiss Dots, 2011), DVD; and *Megacities*, directed by Michael Glawogger (1998; Vienna: Lotus-Film GmbH, 2006), DVD. For a strong critique of Glaeser, Brugmann, and Florida, among others, see Brendan Gleeson, "The Urban Age: Paradox and Prospect," *Urban Studies* 49, no. 5 (2012): 931–43.

[4] David Madden, "City Becoming World: Nancy, Lefebvre and the Global-Urban Imagination," *Environment and Planning D: Society and Space* 30, no. 5 (2012): 772–87; Gavin Kroeber, "Experience Economies: Event in the Cultural Economies of Capital" (master's thesis, Harvard University Graduate School of Design, 2012); and Jorinde Seijdel and Pascal Gielen, eds., "The Art Biennial as a Global Phenomenon: Strategies in Neoliberal Times," *Cahier on Art and the Public Domain* 16 (2009), https://www.onlineopen.org/the-art-biennial-as-a-global-phenomenon.

cry for social movements, coalitions, and reformers, both mainstream and radical, while also serving as a discursive frame for the activities of diverse global nongovernmental organizations (NGOs), UNESCO, and the World Urban Forum.[5] More generally, metropolitan regions have become basing points and arenas for diverse forms of insurgent mobilization around political rights and democratic citizenship, property relations and the commons, inequality and the infrastructures of social reproduction, anti-austerity politics and migration, and climate resilience and environmental crisis, among many other terrains of political contestation.[6] Finally, debates on planetary climate change are now increasingly emphasizing the strategic importance of urban settlements at once as major sources of environmental degradation and as potential engines of ecological modernization, sustainability, and resilience.[7]

These politico-cultural trends are multifaceted, and their cumulative significance is certainly a matter for ongoing interpretation, investigation, and debate in relation to specific regional contexts of sociospatial restructuring. At minimum, however, they appear to signify that urban spaces have become strategically essential to political-economic and sociocultural life around the world, and to emergent visions of possible planetary futures. For those who have long been concerned with urban questions, whether in the realm of theory, research, or practice, these are obviously exciting developments. But they are also accompanied by new challenges and dangers, not the least of which is the proliferation of deep confusion regarding the specificity of the

---

[5] Margit Mayer, "The 'Right to the City' in Urban Social Movements," in *Cities for People, Not for Profit*, ed. Neil Brenner, Margit Mayer, and Peter Marcuse (New York: Routledge, 2011), 63–85; David Harvey, *Rebel Cities: From the Right to the City to the Urban Revolution* (London: Verso, 2012); and Christian Schmid, "Henri Lefebvre, the Right to the City and the New Metropolitan Mainstream," in *Cities for People, Not for Profit*, ed. Neil Brenner, Margit Mayer, and Peter Marcuse (New York: Routledge, 2011), 42–62.

[6] See, for example, Michael Hardt and Antonio Negri, *Commonwealth* (Cambridge, MA: Harvard University Press, 2009); Andy Merrifield, "The Politics of the Encounter and the Urbanization of the World," *CITY* 16, no. 2 (2012): 265–79; Andy Merrifield, "The Urban Question under Planetary Urbanization," *International Journal of Urban and Regional Research* 37, no. 3 (2013): 909–22; and Margit Mayer, Catharina Thörn, and Håkan Thörn, *Urban Uprisings: Challenging Neoliberal Urbanism in Europe* (London: Palgrave, 2016).

[7] For useful overviews of these debates, see David Wachsmuth, Daniel Aldana Cohen, and Hillary Angelo, "Expand the Frontiers of Urban Sustainability," *Nature* 536 (August 25, 2016): 391–93; and Maria Kaika, "Don't Call Me Resilient Again! The New Urban Agenda as Immunology," *Environment and Urbanization* 29, no. 1 (2017): 89–102. More generally, see Nathan Sayre, "Climate Change, Scale, and Devaluation: The Challenge of Our Built Environment," *Washington and Lee Journal of Energy, Climate and Environment* 1, no. 1 (2010): 92–105; and Timothy Luke, "At the End of Nature: Cyborgs, 'Humachines' and Environments in Postmodernity," *Environment and Planning A* 29, no. 8 (1997): 1367–80.

urban itself, both as a category of analysis for social research and as a category of practice in politics, everyday life, and struggle.[8]

On the one hand, the major contemporary discourses on global urbanism are strikingly city-centric insofar as, in Stephen Cairns's concise formulation, they "regard the city as the defining end point and causal engine of urbanization."[9] The most authoritative institutional source for such conceptions is the UN Habitat Programme's declaration of a historically unprecedented "urban age" due to the world's rapidly increasing urban population, which putatively crossed a majority-urban threshold as of the early 2000s.[10] A city-centric vision of our current geohistorical moment has been further popularized through a series of high-profile Urban Age conferences on questions of urban design, planning, and policy in some of the world's major cities, which have been organized and funded through a joint initiative of the London School of Economics and the Deutsche Bank.[11] More recently, a city-centric conception of urbanization has been further entrenched through the rollout of mainstream global urban policy frameworks such as those associated with the Sustainable Development Goals (SDGs) and the New Urban Agenda (Habitat III) presented in Quito in 2016, in the Paris Agreement of the United Nations Convention on Climate Change (IPCC), and in a host of

---

[8] The distinction between categories of analysis and categories of practice is productively developed by Rogers Brubaker and Frederick Cooper, "Beyond Identity," *Theory & Society* 29 (2000): 1–47. For powerful meditations on its applications to urban questions, see Hillary Angelo, "From the City Lens toward Urbanisation as a Way of Seeing: Country/City Binaries on an Urbanising Planet," *Urban Studies* 54, no. 1 (2016): 158–78; and David Wachsmuth, "City as Ideology," *Environment and Planning D: Society and Space* 32, no. 1 (2014): 75–90; as well as, in an earlier context, Andrew Sayer, "Defining the Urban," *GeoJournal* 9, no. 3 (1984): 279–85.

[9] Stephen Cairns, "Debilitating City-Centricity: Urbanization and Urban-Rural Hybridity in Southeast Asia," in *Routledge Handbook on Urbanisation in Southeast Asia*, ed. Rita Padawangi (London: Routledge, 2019): 115–130.

[10] The key institutional documents from the United Nations are the following: United Nations Department of Economic and Social Affairs, Population Division, *2001 Revision of World Urbanization Prospects* (New York: United Nations, 2002); United Nations Department of Economic and Social Affairs, Population Division, *2011 Revision of World Urbanization Prospects* (New York: United Nations, 2012); United Nations Centre for Human Settlements, *An Urbanizing World: Global Report on Human Settlements* (Oxford: Oxford University Press for the United Nations Centre for Human Settlements [HABITAT], 1996); United Nations Human Settlement Programme, *The State of the World's Cities Report 2006/2007 – 30 Years of Shaping the Habitat Agenda* (London: Earthscan for UN-Habitat, 2007); and United Nations Human Settlement Programme, *The State of the World's Cities Report 2010/2011 – Cities for All: Bridging the Urban Divide* (London: Earthscan for UN-Habitat, 2011). For a detailed analysis, historical contextualization, and critique of the "urban age" hypothesis, see Neil Brenner and Christian Schmid, "The 'Urban Age' in Question," *International Journal of Urban and Regional Research* 38, no. 3 (2013): 731–55.

[11] Ricky Burdett and Deyan Sudjic, eds., *The Endless City* (London: Phaidon, 2006); Ricky Burdett and Deyan Sudjic, eds., *Living in the Endless City* (London: Phaidon, 2010).

national and local policy innovations designed to implement or respond to the latter.[12] Closely aligned versions of such city-centric discourses and policy programs are also being promoted by international business organizations (including the World Economic Forum and the McKinsey Global Institute) and by a range of corporate actors and property developers for whom the construction of "global cities," "smart cities," "creative cities," "sustainable cities," "resilient cities," "eco-cities," and the like is seen as the optimal pathway for ensuring continued economic growth without disrupting the currently hegemonic formation of neoliberalized, financialized accumulation by dispossession.[13] Consequently, as Cairns observes:

> This city-centric perspective on urbanization enjoys remarkable consensus and often forms the basis for long-term sustainable development. For example, each of the United Nations-facilitated frameworks . . . helps set priorities not only for government agencies at all scales, but also multilateral development banks, civil society groups and industry. Although separate initiatives, they cross-reference each other and use mutually recognizable vocabularies to articulate complementary and overlapping agendas that draw on shared forms of evidence on demographic, economic and environmental conditions. . . . Securing the benefits and ameliorating the threats of urbanization, according to these convergent frameworks, is a matter of foregrounding the effects of concentrating and concentrated city settlement types. The policy directions that can follow from such a city-centric understanding of urbanization often prescribe intensification of city settlement: dense, compact, accessible and mixed-used city types.[14]

Paradoxically, however, precisely at a geohistorical moment in which such city-centric conceptions appear to have attained an unprecedented influence in global public discourse, inherited configurations of the capitalist urban fabric are being rewoven in ways that are radically problematizing the inherited definitional equation of urbanization with *city* growth. Indeed, as important as dense spatial concentrations of infrastructure, investment, and population continue to be as sites, expressions, and animators of emergent

---

[12] For overviews and critical contextualization, see Susan Parnell, "Defining a Global Urban Development Agenda," *World Development* 78 (2016): 529–40; Clive Barnett and Susan Parnell, "Ideals, Implementation and Indicators: Epistemologies of the Post-2015 Urban Agenda," *Environment and Urbanization* 28, no. 1 (2016): 87–98; and Kaika, "Don't Call Me Resilient Again!"

[13] Susanne Soederberg and Alan Walks, "Producing and Governing Inequalities under Planetary Urbanization: From Urban Age to Urban Revolution?," *Geoforum* 89 (2018): 107–13.

[14] Cairns, "Debilitating City-Centricity," 1–2.

urbanization processes, the latter are also increasingly superseding inherited spaces of cityness to produce new crystallizations of the capitalist urban fabric that cannot be intelligibly deciphered through, in Hillary Angelo's phrase, "a city lens."[15] As Christian Schmid and I have argued elsewhere, the last four decades have witnessed not only a dramatic spatial expansion of major megacity regions deep into their contiguous hinterlands, but a number of equally far-reaching implosions and explosions of the urban at all spatial scales.[16] These include:

- *The creation of new scales of urbanization.* Extensively urbanized interdependencies are being consolidated within extremely large, rapidly expanding, polynucleated metropolitan regions around the world to create sprawling urban galaxies that stretch beyond any single metropolitan region and often traverse multiple national boundaries. Such megascaled urban constellations have been conceptualized in diverse ways, and the representation of their contours and boundaries remains a focus of considerable research and debate.[17] Their most prominent exemplars include, among others, the classic Gottmannian megalopolis of "BosWash" (Boston–Washington, DC), the "blue banana" encompassing the major urbanized regions in Western Europe, and several urban megaregions in Asia, but also rapidly expanding urban spatial formations such as "San-San" (San Francisco–San Diego) in California, the Pearl River Delta in south China, the Lagos littoral conurbation in West Africa, and other incipient urbanizing territories in Latin America and South Asia.
- *The blurring and rearticulation of urban territories.* Urbanization processes are being regionalized and reterritorialized. Increasingly,

---

[15] Angelo, "From the City Lens toward Urbanisation as a Way of Seeing."

[16] This discussion builds directly upon Neil Brenner and Christian Schmid, "Planetary Urbanization," in *Urban Constellations*, ed. Matthew Gandy (Berlin: Jovis, 2012), 10–13. On the implosion/explosion metaphor, see Chapter 2, as well as Neil Brenner, ed., *Implosions/Explosions: Towards a Study of Planetary Urbanization* (Berlin: Jovis, 2014).

[17] This trend was most famously anticipated in the postwar writings of Jean Gottmann, initially in relation to the densely urbanized Northeastern seaboard region of the United States, and eventually as a worldwide phenomenon, challenge, and threat. For an overview of his evolving reflections on such issues, see Jean Gottmann, *Since Megalopolis: The Urban Writings of Jean Gottmann* (Baltimore: Johns Hopkins University Press, 1990. For more recent analyses of urban territorial expansion and megaregion formation, see Richard Florida, Tim Gulden, and Charlotta Mellander, "The Rise of the Mega-Region," *Cambridge Journal of Regions, Economy and Society* 1 (2008): 459–76; Shlomo Angel, Jason Parent, Daniel Civco, and Alejandro M. Blei, *Atlas of Urban Expansion* (Cambridge, MA: Lincoln Institute of Land Policy, 2012); and Peter Hall and Kathryn Pain, eds., *The Polycentric Metropolis* (London: Earthscan, 2006).

former central functions, such as shopping facilities, corporate head-quarters, multimodal logistics hubs, research institutions, and cultural venues, as well as spectacular architectural forms and other major infrastructural arrangements, are being dispersed outward from historic central city cores into erstwhile suburbanized spaces, among expansive catchments of small and medium-sized towns, and along major transportation corridors such as superhighways and high-speed rail lines.[18]

- *The industrialization of the hinterland.* Around the world, the hinterlands of major cities, metropolitan regions, and urban-industrial corridors are being reconfigured as they are operationalized, infrastructuralized, and enclosed to serve new roles in worldwide supply chains and informational capitalism—whether as back office and warehousing locations, global sweatshops, agro-industrial land-use systems, data storage facilities, energy generation grids, resource extraction zones, logistics hubs and transport corridors, fuel depots, or waste disposal areas.[19]

- *The disintegration of wilderness.* In every region of the globe, erstwhile "wilderness" spaces are being fragmented, transformed, and often degraded through the cumulative socioecological consequences of unfettered worldwide urbanization, or are otherwise being converted into bio-enclaves offering "ecosystem services" to offset destructive environmental impacts generated elsewhere. In this way, the world's oceans, alpine regions, the equatorial rainforests, major deserts, the arctic and polar zones, and even the earth's atmosphere itself are

[18] Edward Soja, "Regional Urbanization and the End of the Metropolis Era," in *The New Blackwell Companion to the City*, ed. Gary Bridge and Sophie Watson (Oxford: Blackwell, 2011), 679–89; Thomas Sieverts, *Cities without Cities: An Interpretation of the Zwischenstadt* (London: Spon Press, 2003); Joel Garreau, *Edge City* (New York: Anchor, 1992); Roger Keil, *Suburban Planet: Making the World Urban from the Outside In* (London: Polity, 2017).

[19] See Martín Arboleda, "Financialization, Totality and Planetary Urbanization in the Chilean Andes," *Geoforum* 67 (2015): 4–13; Mazen Labban, "Deterritorializing Extraction: Bioaccumulation and the Planetary Mine," *Annals of the Association of American Geographers* 104, no. 3 (2014): 560–76; Nikos Katsikis, *"The Composite Fabric of Urbanization: Agglomeration Landscapes and Operational Landscapes; From Hinterland to Hinterglobe: Urbanization as Geographical Organization"* (doctoral diss., Harvard University Graduate School of Design, 2016); Roger Diener, Jacques Herzog, Marcel Meili, Pierre de Meuron, and Christian Schmid, *Switzerland: An Urban Portrait*, 4 vols. (Zurich: Birkhäuser, 2001); Alan Berger, *Drosscapes* (New York: Princeton Architectural Press, 2007); A. Haroon Akram-Lodhi and Cristóbal Kay, eds., *Peasants and Globalization* (New York: Routledge, 2009); Frederick Buttel, Fred Magdoff, and John Bellamy Foster, eds., *Hungry for Profit: The Agri-Business Threat to Famers, Food and the Environment* (New York: Monthly Review Press, 2000); and Swarnabh Ghosh, "Notes on Rurality or the Theoretical Usefulness of the Not-Urban," *Avery Review* 27 (November 2017), http://averyreview.com/issues/27/notes-on-rurality.

increasingly being interconnected with the metabolic circuitry and spatiotemporal rhythms of planetary urbanization.[20]

Rather than being simply concentrated within nodal points or confined within bounded urban territories, then, these imploding/exploding dynamics of capitalist restructuring are producing an intensively variegated urban fabric that is being woven unevenly across vast stretches of the world. This combined rescaling, reterritorialization, and rearticulation of the capitalist urban fabric cannot be understood adequately with reference to population growth trends within the world's largest cities, or as a replication of citylike settlement types across the earth's terrestrial surface. Nor, on the other hand, can traditional notions of the hinterland, the countryside, or the rural adequately capture the emergent patterns and pathways of demographic, sociospatial, infrastructural, legal, financial, and ecological transformation through which many formerly peripheralized or remote spaces are today being enclosed and industrially operationalized to support the dynamic metabolism of the global metropolitan network.

From this point of view, inherited, city-centric approaches to the urban question—whether based on demographic, economic, or morphological indicators—appear to offer an extremely limited basis on which to decipher emergent formations of planetary urbanization: they are locked into a fundamentally unhistorical scalar and territorial ontology—a vision of the urban as localized (or, in some cases, regionalized) and bounded—that precludes exploration of the restlessly evolving, massively consequential links between such "city forming" modes of scalar and territorial individuation and a wide range of closely associated dynamics of sociospatial transformation that may likewise be essential (rather than merely secondary or derivative) expressions of urbanization. Under these conditions, the field of critical urban theory, as

---

[20] See Martín Arboleda, "In the Nature of the Non-City: Expanded Infrastructural Networks and the Political Ecology of Planetary Urbanisation," *Antipode* 48, no. 2 (2016): 233–51; Japhy Wilson and Manuel Bayón, "Concrete Jungle: The Planetary Urbanization of the Ecuadorian Amazon," *Human Geography* 8, no. 3 (2015): 1–23; William Boyd, W. Scott Prudham, and Rachel Shurman, "Industrial Dynamics and the Problem of Nature," *Society and Natural Resources* 14 (2001): 555–70; Neil Smith "Nature as Accumulation Strategy," *Socialist Register* 43 (2007): 1–21; Bill McKibben, *The End of Nature* (New York: Random House, 2006); and Jessica Dempey and Morgan Robertson, "Ecosystem Services: Tensions, Impurities and Points of Engagement within Neoliberalism," *Progress in Human Geography* 36, no. 6 (2012): 758–79. This proposition is further developed in an exhibition of the Urban Theory Lab, *Operational Landscapes* (Melbourne: Melbourne School of Design, 2015). For further details, see "Operational Landscapes Exhibition at Melbourne School of Design," Urban Theory Lab, http://urbantheorylab.net/news/operational-landscapes-exhibition-in-melbourne; as well as Louise Dorignon, "And the Urban Exploded," *Society and Space*, https://societyandspace.org/2015/09/21/and-the-urban-exploded-by-louise-dorignon/.

inherited from the major twentieth-century traditions of both mainstream and radical scholarship, is in a state of disarray, if not outright crisis. If the urban can no longer be understood as a particular kind of place—that is, as a discreet, distinctive, localized, and relatively bounded unit or type of settlement in which specific kinds of social relations obtain—then what could possibly justify the existence of a scholarly field devoted uniquely to its investigation?

Throughout this book, my exploration of the urban question as a scale question has involved a series of concerted theoretical responses to the dislocations of inherited urban epistemologies that were already powerfully reverberating across the field of critical urban studies in the context of late twentieth-century debates on the intertwined *problematiques* of globalization, scale relativization, and the crisis of national-developmentalist capitalism.[21] As I have argued in previous chapters, the elaboration of a reflexively scale-attuned approach to urban theory requires a sustained critique and transcendence of inherited, city-centric approaches to the urban question, as well as a reflexive critical interrogation of the distinctive scalar analytics that are being elaborated in contemporary debates on global urban sociospatial restructuring. A historically dynamic, relationally multiscalar analytical framework positions the recurrent implosions/explosions of the capitalist urban fabric, rather than the growth of the city (or, for that matter, of the agglomeration, the metropolis, or the metropolitan region), as the core focal point and *problematique* of urban research. However, as the preceding overview underscores, the epistemological crisis of urban studies has only deepened in recent years, even though its expressions are often masked by triumphalist discourses that celebrate the accomplishments of contemporary urban "science" and depict the city as the optimal scale for economic growth, innovation, technopolitical management, and/or ecological modernization. Against that background, this chapter considers the prospects for deciphering emergent, early twenty-first-century mutations of the capitalist urban fabric in a geoeconomic context of continued scale relativization, accelerated sociospatial restructuring, and crisis-riven yet deepening neoliberalization.

To this end, I build upon the scale-attuned approach to the capitalist urban fabric developed in previous chapters to present an interpretive counterpoint

---

[21] On the epistemic crises of critical urban studies in the 1970s, see Manuel Castells, "Is There an Urban Sociology?," in *Urban Sociology: Critical Essays*, ed. C. G. Pickvance (New York: St. Martin's Press, 1976), 33–59; Janet Abu-Lughod, *The City Is Dead—Long Live the City* (Berkeley: Center for Planning and Development Research, University of California, 1969); and Sharon Zukin, "A Decade of the New Urban Sociology," *Theory & Society* 9 (1980): 575–601. See, more generally, Edward W. Soja, *Postmetropolis* (Cambridge, MA: Blackwell, 2000).

to contemporary urban age discourse and its "debilitating city-centricity."[22] On this basis, I reflect on the contemporary epistemological crises and possible future pathways for the field of critical urban studies. While a reflexively multiscalar lens remains highly salient for investigating emergent geographies of planetary urbanization, I argue that confronting this challenge also requires us to revisit, and at least partially to revise, some of the foundational spatial assumptions that underpinned twentieth-century urban theory. As the spatialities of the capitalist urban fabric restlessly mutate, so too must we continually reinvent the repertoire of concepts, methods, and cartographies through which its uneven patterns, variegated pathways, crisis tendencies, and contradictions are investigated.

The "Urban Age" and Its Limits

All forms of knowledge and action presuppose interpretive frameworks that permit us to conceptualize and evaluate sociospatial relations, to render intelligible our place in the web of life, and to decipher the flow of change in which we are caught up and to which we contribute. Certain elements of these frameworks are reflexively grasped: we are consciously aware of their role in structuring value, experience, and action, and we may, at times, subject them to critical examination, adjustment, or even reinvention, especially during periods of accelerated restructuring, divisive social conflict, and political turmoil. However, some aspects of these frameworks generally remain hidden from view; they intimately structure our everyday assumptions, interpretations, and practices, but without themselves being accessible for reflexive interrogation. Only in retrospect, when they are being destabilized or superseded, can we more fully grasp the pervasive role of such naturalized *dispostifs* of understanding in the construction of our modes of social life.

Although its lineages can be traced to efforts to decipher the accelerated industrialization of capital, proletarianization of labor, and infrastructuralization of landscape in the "paleotechnic cities" (Lewis Mumford) of nineteenth-century Euro-America and in subsequent, Cold War–era studies of demographic "modernization" spearheaded by American sociologist Kingsley Davis, the notion of a majority-urban world appears to have today become such a *dispostif* of unreflexively presupposed interpretive assumptions.[23] Indeed,

---

[22] Cairns, "Debilitating City-Centricity."

[23] On the historical genealogy of contemporary "urban age" discourse during the post–World War II period, see Brenner and Schmid, "The 'Urban Age' in Question."

much like the catch-all buzzword of "globalization" in the 1990s, the trope of a majority-urban world—an "urban age"—now serves as an epistemological foundation on which a huge array of conditions, dilemmas, conflicts, and crises around the world are being analyzed, and in relation to which diverse public, corporate, civic, and nongovernmental modes of spatial intervention are being mobilized (Figures 9.1 and 9.2).

As Ross Exo Adams has argued, the notion of urbanization has long been used in strikingly atheoretical ways, as if it were a purely descriptive, empirical basis for referencing a natural, quasi-ontological tendency of human spatial organization, one that has existed for millennia but is said to have been accelerating dramatically during the last 150 years:

> Much like the weather, urbanization is [assumed to be] something that exists "out there," a condition far too "complex" to present itself as an object to be examined in its own right and thus something which can only be mapped, monitored compared and catalogued. . . . It thus becomes a term used to

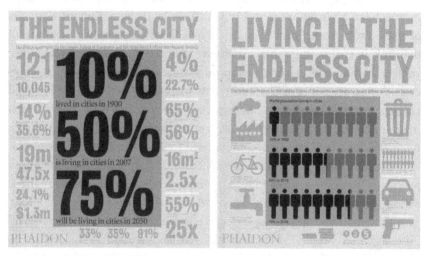

FIGURE 9.1 The "urban age" as a branding device. The currently popular notion of an "urban age" is grounded on the problematic assumption that urbanization can be understood with reference to expanding city population levels, generally as a proportion of total national population. In several influential volumes produced by the Urban Age Project at the London School of Economics, this notion has been invoked to frame and promote a series of conferences on cities and global urban transformation. (Source: Partial book cover images from Ricky Burdett and Deyan Sudjic, eds., *The Endless City* [London: Phaidon, 2006]; Ricky Burdett and Deyan Sudjic, eds., *Living in the Endless City* [London: Phaidon, 2010].)

organize an ever-expanding set of "emerging" problems whose analysis is limited to the particular elements that compose whatever happens to be emerging and the technologies used to register them, leaving the very milieu itself to, once again, remain a neutral background of human existence. At once transhistorical and bound to the immediate present, almost all depictions of the urban treat it as a capacity inherent to the human condition with which we organize ourselves in space.[24]

Despite the forceful warnings of Chicago school urban sociologists such as Louis Wirth against such analytically insubstantial conceptions already in the 1930s, this empiricist, naturalistic, and quasi-environmental understanding of urbanization persisted in various forms throughout the twentieth century. It was paradigmatically embodied in Kingsley Davis's classic, mid-twentieth-century definition of urbanization as the expansion of the

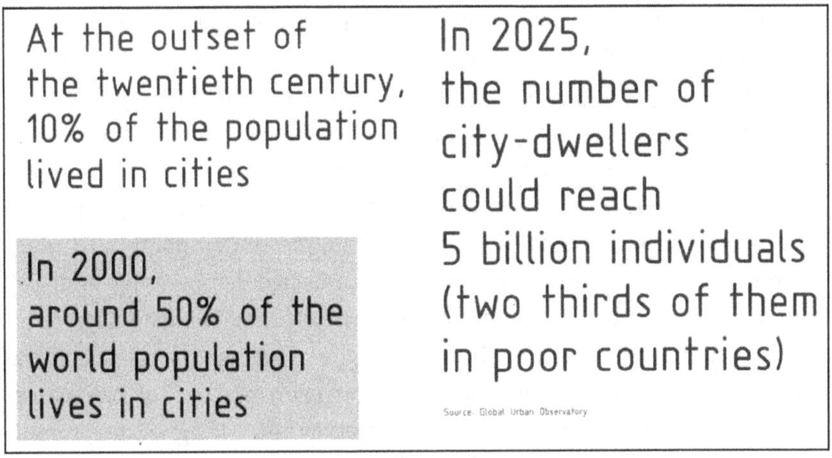

At the outset of the twentieth century, 10% of the population lived in cities

In 2000, around 50% of the world population lives in cities

In 2025, the number of city-dwellers could reach 5 billion individuals (two thirds of them in poor countries)

Source: Global Urban Observatory

FIGURE 9.2 The "urban age" as a dramatic metanarrative. The vision of a majority-urban world is often invoked to frame and dramatize investigations of contemporary urban restructuring. This series of declarations, presented in a double-page spread at the outset of a widely circulated book by Rem Koolhaas and his collaborators, is a typical example. Here, as elsewhere, the vision of a majority-urban world is sourced to UN data, the authority, accuracy, and coherence of which are taken for granted. (Source: Rem Koolhaas, Stefano Boeri, Sanford Kwinter, Nadia Tazi, and Hans Ulrich Obrist, *Mutations: Harvard Project on the City* [Barcelona: Actar, 2000], 1–2.)

---

[24] Ross Exo Adams, "The Burden of the Present: On the Concept of Urbanisation," *Society and Space*, February 11, 2014, https://societyandspace.org/2014/02/11/the-burden-of-the-present-on-the-concept-of-urbanisation-ross-exo-adams/.

city-based population relative to the total national population. Rather than defining cities in social, morphological, or functional terms, Davis famously used arbitrary numerical population thresholds—generally twenty thousand or one hundred thousand—to demarcate their specificity as settlement types.[25] Davis concisely summarized this strictly empirical understanding in the formula $U = P_c / P_t$ (U = urbanization; P_c = population of cities; and P_t = total national population), and he subsequently devoted several decades of careful empirical research to its international application, eventually producing the first comprehensive worldwide survey of city population sizes.[26] In more recent decades, rather than being discredited, naturalistic models of urbanization have acquired a powerful new lease on life in the science of "big data," which tends to regard urban density as a condition that is basically akin to that of a closed biological system—subject to scientific "laws," predictable, and, thus, technically programmable.[27]

Contemporary UN declarations of a majority-urban world, and most major strands of mainstream global urban policy, planning, and design discourse, draw directly upon Davis's midcentury demographic methods, and likewise attempt to grasp the phenomenon of urbanization through some version of this naturalistic, ahistorical, population-based, and empiricist *dispositif*.[28] Here, urbanization is assumed to entail the simultaneous growth and worldwide spatial diffusion of cities, conceived as generic, universally replicable types of human settlement. Thus understood, the contemporary urban age represents an aggregation of various interconnected demographic and socioeconomic trends that have cumulatively increased the populations of large, relatively dense urban centers. In this way, the urban age metanarrative has come to serve as a framework not only of interpretation, but of *justification*, for a multiscalar assortment of spatial interventions designed to promote what geographer Terry McGee classically labeled "city dominance" within a transformed geoeconomic context defined by unfettered financial speculation, widening socioeconomic polarization, proliferating ecological disasters,

---

[25] Kingsley Davis, "The Origins and Growth of Urbanization in the World," *American Journal of Sociology* 60, no. 5 (1955): 429–37.

[26] Kingsley Davis, *World Urbanization: 1950–1970*, vol. 2: *Analysis of Trends, Relationships and Development*, Population Monograph Series No. 9 (Berkeley: Institute of International Studies, University of California, 1972); Kingsley Davis, *World Urbanization: 1950–1970*, vol. 1: *Basic Data for Cities, Countries, and Regions*, Population Monograph Series No. 4 (Berkeley: Institute of International Studies, University of California, 1969).

[27] Brendan Gleeson, "What Role for Social Science in the 'Urban Age'?," *International Journal of Urban and Regional Research* 37, no. 5 (2013): 1839–51.

[28] Brenner and Schmid, "The 'Urban Age' in Question."

and the continued dominance of market-disciplinary governance.[29] Around the world, the shared goal of such urbanization strategies is building the "hypertrophic city"—whether by densifying and extending extant mega-city territories, by creating new urban settlement zones *ex nihilo* in pockets of the erstwhile countryside or along major transportation corridors, or by orchestrating rural-to-urban migration flows through a noxious cocktail of structural adjustment programs, land grabbing, agro-industrial consolidation, ecological plunder, and other forms of accumulation by dispossession that degrade inherited modes of social reproduction outside the large population centers.[30] As Susanne Soederberg and Alan Walks argue, all of these city-building strategies seek further to normalize and entrench rather than to interrupt or supersede the basic commitment to austerity governance, even if some also attempt to address the injustices, contradictions, and crisis tendencies engendered by the latter:

> This [urban age] trope's central message [is that] economic growth is *the* key to unlocking vibrant, sustainable and liveable cities for all. And selectively applying neoliberal policies and best practices from the global North, with requisite modifications for local context, is the best way to ensuring such economic growth. . . . These strategies seek to identify perceived inequalities and social injustices in ways that reinforce a dominant policy rubric based on market freedoms and the preference for private over public consumption—a central premise of neoliberalism and its austerity revival during the last decade.[31]

The ostensibly self-evident message that "the city" has assumed unprecedented planetary importance has thus come to serve as an all-purpose, largely depoliticized ideological rubric around which, in diverse political-economic contexts, aggressively market-disciplinary projects of urban sociospatial transformation and austerity governance are being narrated, justified, and naturalized.[32]

---

[29] Terry McGee, *The Urbanization Process in the Third World* (London: Bell and Sons, 1971).

[30] Max Ajl, "The Hypertrophic City versus the Planet of Fields," in Brenner, *Implosions/Explosions*, 533–50; Mike Davis, *Planet of Slums* (London: Verso, 2006).

[31] Soederberg and Walks, "Producing and Governing Inequalities under Planetary Urbanization," 2.

[32] In this sense, urban age discourse and practice can be viewed as a paradigmatic exemplar of what Erik Swyngedouw has diagnosed as a "postpolitical" technology of governance. See, in particular, Erik Swyngedouw, "The Antinomies of the Post-Political City: In Search of a Democratic Politics of Environmental Production," *International Journal of Urban and Regional Research* 33, no. 3 (2009): 601–20; as well as Japhy Wilson and Erik Swyngedouw, eds., *The Post-Political and Its Discontents* (Edinburgh: University of Edinburgh Press, 2014).

Aside from the highly dubious presentation of market-disciplinary regulation as being at once necessary, optimal, and beyond political challenge, the vision of urbanization as *city* growth contained in such programs is, likewise, anything but self-evident. On a basic empirical level, the limitations of the United Nations' census-based data on urbanization are well known and have long been widely discussed among critical demographers.[33] The simple, but still apparently intractable, problem, to which Kingsley Davis had already devoted extensive critical attention in the 1950s, is that each national census bureau uses its own criteria for measuring urban conditions, leading to serious, persistent, and seemingly absurd inconsistencies in comparative international data on urbanization.[34] In the current decade, for example, among those countries that demarcate urban settlement types based on a population size threshold (101 out of 232 UN member states), the criterion ranges from two hundred to fifty thousand; no less than twenty-three countries opt for a threshold of two thousand, but twenty-one others specify the cutoff at five thousand.[35] A host of comparability problems immediately follow, since "urban" localities in one national jurisdiction may have little in common with those that are identically classified elsewhere. The use of various combinations of additional criteria in the other 131 member states—administrative, density-based, infrastructural, and socioeconomic—adds several further layers of confusion to an already exceedingly heterogeneous international data set. Should certain administrative areas automatically be classified as urban? What population density criterion, if any, is appropriate? Should levels of nonagricultural employment figure into the definition of urban areas (as they do in India, albeit only for male residents)?

In short, even this brief glimpse into the intricacies of the United Nations' data tables reveals that the notion of a majority-urban world is hardly a self-evident fact. It is, rather, a statistical *artifact* constructed through a rather crude aggregation of national census data derived from chronically inconsistent, systematically incompatible definitions of the phenomenon that is supposedly being measured. As such, it also operates as a spatial ideology that seeks to depoliticize the process of capitalist urbanization; to naturalize the contentious accumulation strategies, regulatory architectures, and spatial politics that underpin it; and thus to obscure its constitutively uneven,

---

[33] Tony Champion and Graeme Hugo, eds., *New Forms of Urbanization* (London: Ashgate, 2007).

[34] Davis, "The Origins and Growth of Urbanization."

[35] Chandan Deuskar, "What Does Urban Mean?," World Bank Sustainable Cities (blog), June 2, 2015, http://blogs.worldbank.org/sustainablecities/what-does-urban-mean.

polarizing, and destabilizing consequences for much of the world's population, both within and outside major metropolitan regions.[36]

This is, as development sociologist Max Ajl has pointedly argued, a far cry from the soft-neoliberal techno-utopias of "smart," "sustainable," or "ecological" urbanism that are heralded and hailed in mainstream urban triumphalist discourse. One of the central, if generally unstated, goals of urban age–inspired spatial policies is to promote "the total denuding of the countryside of people, and their increasingly dense enclosure into the *favelas*, barrios and shantytowns of Rio de Janeiro, Caracas, Mumbai, Shanghai, Lagos and Dakar."[37] Just as crucially, Ajl suggests, the urban age metanarrative also serves to legitimate a "double-helix modernization teleology" that celebrates the forced dispossession of the peasantry from inherited systems of social reproduction and smallholding, and the concomitant "development of capital-intense and labor-light agriculture" configured in large-scale industrial enclaves controlled by multinational agribusiness conglomerates.[38] As Ajl further explains, this involves the promotion of a "megacity/agro-export regime" in which cities are considered as a "kind of black box into which one can dump the human population and worry later":

> Bevies of experts, oblivious to the fallout from their forebears' fetishization of capital-intensive agriculture and high-density, high-population urban living, shrugging at the ashes and ruins that lay behind the juggernaut of the development project (which, given the anti-rural bias of such policies, must also be viewed as an *urbanization* project), now peddle a second Green Revolution in agriculture, hoping to structure the sowing of the fields of Africa and Asia on a fully scientific and rational basis: capital-intensive, labor-light, and petroleum-fueled.[39]

In precisely this sense, the "urbanization project" embodied in urban age discourse, data, and practice not only promotes an aggressively market-disciplinary vision of city building as the spatial foundation for our collective

---

[36] Soederberg and Walks, "Producing and Governing Inequalities under Planetary Urbanization."

[37] Ajl, "The Hypertrophic City," 539.

[38] Ibid., 534. For useful overviews of the transformation of global agriculture under a neoliberal food regime, see Tony Weis, *The Global Food Economy and the Battle for the Future of Farming* (London: Zed, 2007); Philip McMichael, "Peasant Prospects in the Neoliberal Age," *New Political Economy* 11, no. 3 (2006): 407–18; and Philip McMichael, *Food Regimes and Agrarian Questions* (Halifax: Fernwood Press, 2013).

[39] Ajl, "The Hypertrophic City," 540, 541, 534.

planetary future, but advocates the subjection of much of the world's erstwhile countryside to some combination of forced depopulation; accelerated land enclosure and privatization of common resources; capital-intensive, export-oriented industrial colonization; and fossil fuel–based ecological devastation in direct support of that goal.[40] In many cases, that urbanization project has sought not only further to industrialize the extraction, cultivation, and processing of food crops and other primary commodities but also to thread advanced infrastructural corridors and special economic zones (SEZs) across erstwhile peri-urban, hinterland, rural, and wilderness zones to "serve as . . . super highways that will help open up as-yet untapped areas of the developing world to private foreign investment, agribusiness expansion, and natural resource extraction."[41]

Interiorizing the Constitutive Outside

Here arises a deeper theoretical problem with contemporary urban age discourse and with the naturalized, city-centric *dispositif* of urbanization from which it is derived. Even if the specificity of city growth relative to other forms of demographic, socioeconomic, and spatial restructuring could somehow be coherently delineated (for instance, through consistently applied, geospatially enhanced indicators for agglomeration),[42] the question

---

[40] One of the great ironies of contemporary discourse on urban "sustainability" is its promotion of putatively "green" technologies within major metropolitan centers while simultaneously "black-boxing" the accelerating industrialization of the erstwhile countryside through fossil fuel–based techno-infrastructures and logistics systems. Both in theory and in practice, this black-boxing of extrametropolitan spaces affirms increasing demand for and extraction of the very fossil fuels that "ecological urbanism" is purportedly trying to supersede. It entails a myopic vision of ecologically sustainable, postcarbon cities directly supported by ecologically catastrophic, petroleum-based industrial hinterlands; unsustainable terrestrial, aerial, and maritime transport systems; and continued, high-technology excavation of increasingly remote subterranean spaces in pursuit of new fossil fuel reserves. For further elaborations on this issue, see Timothy Luke, "Global Cities versus 'Global Cities': Rethinking Contemporary Urbanism as Public Ecology," *Studies in Political Economy* 70 (Spring 2003): 11–33; and Timothy Luke, "Developing Planetarian Accountancy: Fabricating Nature as Stock, Service and System for Green Governmentality," *Nature, Knowledge and Negation* 26 (2009): 129–59.

[41] Ben White, Saturnino M. Borras Jr., Ruth Hall, Ian Scoones, and Wendy Wolford, "The New Enclosures: Critical Perspectives on Corporate Land Deals," *Journal of Peasant Studies* 39, no. 3–4 (2012): 629. See also Michael Levien, "Special Economic Zones and Accumulation by Dispossession in India," *Journal of Agrarian Change* 11, no. 4 (2011): 454–83.

[42] For productive attempts to develop more consistent definitional strategies, see Shlomo Angel, *Planet of Cities* (Cambridge, MA: Lincoln Institute of Land Policy, 2012); as well as Hirotsugu Uchida and Andrew Nelson, "Agglomeration Index: Towards a New Measure of Urban Concentration," Working Paper 29, United Nations University, 2010, https://www.wider.unu.edu/publication/agglomeration-index.

still remains: how to delineate the process of urbanization in *conceptual* terms? Despite its pervasive representation as a neutral, generic, and objective background parameter within which sociospatial relations are situated, the process of urbanization must itself be subjected to careful theoretical scrutiny and critical interrogation.[43] Doing so reveals at least two major epistemological fissures—logically unresolvable yet perpetually recurrent analytical problems—within the hegemonic *dispositif* of city-centric urban knowledge.

First, in the mainstream interpretive framework, urbanization is said to entail the universal diffusion of cities as the elementary units of human settlement. As is widely recognized, however, these supposedly universal units have assumed diverse morphological forms; they have been organized at a range of spatial scales; they have been mediated through a broad array of institutional, political-economic, social, military, and environmental forces; and they have been differentially, unevenly articulated to their surrounding territories, landscapes, and ecologies, as well as to other, more distant population centers. Given the de facto heterogeneity of agglomeration patterns and urban governance configurations, can a universal notion of "the" city still be maintained? If we do reject the hegemonic equation of cityness with singularity, must we not also abandon the vision of urbanization as a universal process of spatial diffusion? Instead, heterogeneity, differentiation, variegation, and, above all, spatial politics would have to be recognized, not simply as unstructured contextual complexity, random empirical diversity, or contextually contingent friction, but as intrinsic, systemically produced aspects of the urbanization process that themselves require abstract theorization.[44]

Second, in the hegemonic *dispositif*, urbanization is defined as the growth of cities, which are in turn conceived as spatially bounded settlement units. This basic conceptual equation (urbanization = city growth), coupled with

---

[43] Neil Brenner and Christian Schmid, "Towards a New Epistemology of the Urban," *CITY* 19, no. 2–3 (2015): 151–82.

[44] Such an approach is forcefully advocated by, among others, Jennifer Robinson, "New Geographies of Theorizing the Urban: Putting Comparison to Work for Global Urban Studies," in *The Routledge Handbook on Cities of the Global South*, ed. Susan Parnell and Sophie Oldfield (New York: Routledge, 2014), 57–70; Ananya Roy, "Worlding the South: Towards a Post-Colonial Urban Theory," in *The Routledge Handbook on Cities of the Global South*, ed. Susan Parnell and Sophie Oldfield (New York: Routledge, 2014), 9–20; and Christian Schmid, "Specificity and Urbanization: A Theoretical Outlook," in *The Inevitable Specificity of Cities*, ed. ETH Studio Basel (Zurich: Lars Müller Publishers, 2014), 282–92. On the systemic production of institutional and spatial variegation, see Neil Brenner, Jamie Peck, and Nik Theodore, "Variegated Neoliberalization: Geographies, Modalities, Pathways," *Global Networks* 10, no. 2 (2010): 182–222; and Jamie Peck, "Cities beyond Compare?," *Regional Studies* 49, no. 1 (2015): 160–82.

the equally pervasive assumption of spatial boundedness, logically requires differentiating the city-like units in question from a putatively non-city (and ipso facto, in this framework, non-*urban*) realm located outside them. However, the demarcation of a coherent city/non-city (and thus urban/non-urban) divide at any spatial scale has proven thoroughly problematic, particularly since the accelerated worldwide industrialization of capital and associated remaking of sociospatial relations in the nineteenth century. Indeed, within the mainstream urban *dispositif*, the delineation of a non-urban "constitutive outside" is at once *necessary*, since it is only on this basis that cities' distinctiveness as such can be demarcated, and *impossible*, since (1) there are no standardized criteria for differentiating city from non-city settlement "types" and (2) the apparent boundaries between urban settlements and their putatively nonurban exterior have been relentlessly imploded and exploded at all spatial scales under capitalism, especially since the acceleration of industrialization in the 1850s.

Despite the persistent naturalization of static, ahistorical settlement typologies (city, suburb, town, rural, countryside, wilderness) in mainstream geographical discourse, the relentless territorial extension of large centers of agglomeration into their surrounding fringes and hinterlands was widely recognized by twentieth-century urban planners and designers, from Ebenezer Howard, Otto Wagner, and Benton MacKaye to Jean Gottmann, Constantinos Doxiadis, Ian McHarg, and John Friedmann. Indeed, although it tends to be marginalized in canonical historical narratives, the process of urban extension and upscaling was arguably one of the formative concerns in relation to which the modern discipline of urban planning was consolidated: it was the signal issue that led the Catalan Spanish planner Ildefons Cerdà to invent the term *urbanización* in his famous 1867 treatise.[45] Rather than being focused simply upon conditions within bounded settlement units, then, several important approaches to modern urban planning and urbanism contained the elements of a relatively dynamic understanding of urban space.[46]

---

[45] See Idefons Cerdà, *A General Theory of Urbanization 1867*, ed. Vicente Guallart (Barcelona: Institute for Advanced Architecture of Catalonia/Actar, 2018 [1967]). For a provocative reading of Cerdà's importance in contemporary debates on urbanization, see Ross Exo Adams, "Natura Urbans, Natura Urbanata: Ecological Urbanism, Circulation and the Immunization of Nature," *Environment and Planning D: Society and Space* 32 (2014): 12–29.

[46] See, in particular, John Friedmann and Clyde Weaver, *Territory and Function: The Evolution of Regional Planning* (Berkeley: University of California Press, 1979). In contrast, Peter Hall's *Cities of Tomorrow* (Cambridge, MA: Blackwell, 2002) embodies a resolutely city-centric approach to urban planning history.

Just as importantly, as Lewis Mumford grimly recognized in his mid-twentieth-century writings on urban history, the developmental pathways of capitalist agglomerations have always been intimately intertwined with dramatic, large-scale, and long-term transformations of extra-metropolitan spaces, often located at a considerable distance from the major centers of capital, labor, and commerce—in particular, landscapes of agricultural production, resource extraction, energy generation, water procurement, and waste management. Mumford described this relation as an interplay between "upbuilding" and "unbuilding" (*Abbau*)—on the one side, the spatial assembly of colossal vertical, horizontal, and subterranean industrial infrastructures, and on the other, the intensifying degradation of surrounding landscapes, ecosystems, watersheds, rivers, seas, and oceans through their intensifying role in supplying cities with labor, fuel, materials, water, and food, and in absorbing their waste products.[47] From the original dispossession of erstwhile rural populations through territorial enclosure to the intensification of land use; the construction of large-scale, capital-intensive infrastructural investments; and the progressive industrialization of hinterland economies to support extraction, cultivation, production, and circulation, the "growth of the city" (Ernest Burgess) under modern capitalism has been directly facilitated through colossal, if unevenly developed sociospatial and ecological upheavals far outside its fluid borders. In precisely this sense, the rural, the countryside, and the hinterland have never been reducible to a mere backstage "ghost acreage" that supports the putatively front-stage operations of large population centers.[48]

Whatever their demographic composition or settlement morphology, then, the variegated spaces of the non-city have been continuously operationalized in support of city-building processes throughout the global history of capitalist uneven development. Such spaces are as strategically central to the forms of territorial organization (and the closely associated processes of

---

[47] Lewis Mumford, "A Natural History of Urbanization," in *Man's Role in Changing the Face of the Earth*, ed. William L. Thomas (Chicago: University of Chicago Press, 1956), 382–98; and "Paleotechnic Paradise: Coketown," in *The City in History* (New York: Harcourt, Brace and World, 1961), 446–81. See also the various contributions to Brenner, *Implosions/Explosions*.

[48] See Álvaro Sevilla-Buitrago, "*Urbs in Rure*: Historical Enclosure and the Extended Urbanization of the Countryside," in Brenner, *Implosions/Explosions*, 236–59; Martín Arboleda, "Spaces of Extraction, Metropolitan Explosions: Planetary Urbanization and the Commodity Boom in Latin America," *International Journal of Urban and Regional Research* 40, no. 1 (2016): 96–112; Mazen Labban, "Deterritorializing Extraction: Bioaccumulation and the Planetary Mine," *Annals of the Association of American Geographers* 104, no. 3 (2014): 560–76; Gavin Bridge, "Resource Triumphalism: Postindustrial Narratives of Primary Commodity Production," *Environment and Planning A* 33 (2001): 2149–73; and Jason Moore, *Capitalism and the Web of Life: Ecology and the Accumulation of Capital* (New York: Verso, 2016).

creative destruction) that underpin the urbanization of capital as are the large, dense metropolitan centers upon which urbanists have long trained their analytical gaze. Today, moreover, such extra-metropolitan landscapes of capital are being comprehensively creatively destroyed through an unprecedented surge of mega-infrastructural investments, land enclosures, and large-scale territorial planning strategies, often transnationally coordinated as speculative responses to global commodity price fluctuations, that are designed to support the accelerated growth of agglomerations around the world.[49] Their developmental rhythms, infrastructural configurations, and political ecologies are thus being linked more directly to those of the global metropolitan network through worldwide spatial divisions of labor, transnational supply chains, and financial circuits; and their continuing commodification, enclosure, industrial transformation, and socioecological degradation are contributing directly to the forms of mass dispossession and displacement that are uncritically catalogued or celebrated in mainstream urban policy discourse under the rubric of "rural to urban" demographic change. Consequently, if we do indeed currently live in an "urban age," this condition must be explored not only with reference to the formation of global cities, metropolitan regions, megacity regions, the world city archipelago, and its inter-metropolitan networks but also in relation to the ongoing, if profoundly uneven, speculative and conflictual industrial operationalization of much of the planet, including terrestrial, subterranean, fluvial, oceanic, and atmospheric space, in support of an accelerating, intensifying, planet-encompassing metabolism of capitalist urbanization.

Urban Epistemologies under Stress

Since its origins in the early twentieth century, the field of urban studies has been regularly animated by foundational debates regarding the nature of the urban question. The intensification of such debates in recent times could thus be plausibly interpreted as a sign of creative renaissance rather than of intellectual crisis. In the early twenty-first century, however, the pervasive fragmentation, disorientation, and downright confusion that permeate the field of urban studies are not merely the result of methodological disagreements (which of course persist) or due to the obsolescence of a particular research paradigm (human ecology, central place theory, Marxism,

---

[49] See Arboleda, "Financialization, Totality and Planetary Urbanization"; Arboleda, "In the Nature of the Non-City"; Wilson and Bayón, "Concrete Jungle"; and Labban, "Deterritorializing Extraction."

regulation theory, global city theory, agglomeration theory, or otherwise). Instead, as the national-developmentalist configuration of postwar world capitalism recedes into historical memory, and as the politico-institutional, spatial, and environmental impacts of various neoliberalized and neo-authoritarian forms of sociospatial restructuring radiate and ricochet across the planet, a more intellectually far-reaching structural crisis of urban studies appears to be under way.

In the late 1960s and early 1970s, the epistemic crises of urban studies involved foundational debates regarding the appropriate categories and methods through which to understand a sociospatial terrain whose basic contours and parameters were a matter of broad consensus. Simply put, that consensus involved the equation of the urban with a specific *spatial unit* or *settlement type*—the city, or an upscaled territorial variant thereof, such as the metropolis, the conurbation, the metropolitan region, the megalop-olis, the megacity, and so forth. Even though radical critics such as Manuel Castells fiercely criticized established ways of understanding this "unit" and offered an alternative, substantially reinvigorated interpretive framework through which to investigate its production, evolution, and contestation, they persisted in viewing the unit in question—the city or agglomeration— as the basic focal point and scale for debates on the urban question. Across otherwise deep methodological and political divides and successive epis-temological realignments, this largely uninterrogated presupposition has underpinned all of the major intellectual traditions in twentieth-century urban studies. Indeed, as my explorations of scalar de- and reconstructions of inherited urban epistemologies throughout this book have suggested, the vision of the urban as a coherently individuated, territorially bounded spatial unit has long been considered so self-evident that it did not require acknowl-edgment, much less justification.

It is this entrenched set of assumptions—along with a broad constella-tion of closely associated epistemological frameworks for confronting and mapping the urban question—that is today being severely destabilized, ar-guably even more comprehensively than had occurred during earlier rounds of debate on the urban question as a scale question in the 1990s and 2000s. The erstwhile boundaries of the city, along with those of larger, metropolitan units of agglomeration, are being exploded and reconstituted as new forms, scales, and pathways of urbanization reshape inherited configurations of territorial organization and macrospatial divisions. Consequently, the contemporary crisis of urban studies is thus not just an expression of epi-stemic perplexity (though the latter is abundantly evident). It stems from an increasing awareness of fundamental uncertainties regarding the very sites, scales, and focal points of urban theory and research under early twenty-first-century capitalism.

In a world of neatly circumscribed, relatively bounded, coherently individuated cities or urban units, whose core socio-morphological properties and interscalar positionalities were a matter of generalized scholarly agreement, urban researchers could burrow into the myriad tasks associated with understanding their underlying social, economic, and cultural dynamics; historical trajectories; intercontextual variations; and the various forms of regulation, conflict, and struggle that emerged within them. But, under contemporary circumstances, these basic conditions of possibility for urban research appear to have been relativized, if not totally superseded. Faced with the relentless interplay between the upbuilding and unbuilding of sociospatial arrangements, along with the perpetual implosion-explosion of urban conditions, relations, and effects across the variegated scalar configurations, territorial formations, and ecological landscapes of global capitalism, can a settlement-based conception of urbanization be maintained? Can the "urban phenomenon," as Henri Lefebvre famously queried, still be anchored exclusively within, and confined to, the city as a more or less bounded unit of analysis?[50] More generally, is there any future for critical urban theory in a world in which urbanization has been "planetarized"?[51]

Among the most specialized, empirically oriented urban researchers, the formidable tasks of data collection, methodological refinement, and place-based investigation continue to take precedence over the challenges of grappling with the field's unstable epistemological foundations and increasingly indeterminate conceptual architecture. Disciplinary and subdisciplinary specialization thus produces what Lefebvre once termed a "blind field" in which concrete investigations of time-honored themes continue to accumulate,

---

[50] Henri Lefebvre, *The Urban Revolution*, trans. Robert Bononno (Minneapolis: University of Minnesota Press, 2003 [1970]).

[51] On the "planetarization" of the urban, see Henri Lefebvre, "Dissolving City, Planetary Metamorphosis," in Brenner, *Implosions/Explosions*, 566–71. The original essay was published in *Le Monde diplomatique* in May 1989 under the title "Quand la ville se perd dans une métamorphose planétaire." For further discussion of this formulation, see Andy Merrifield, "Towards a Metaphilosophy of the Urban," last modified December 15, 2015, https://antipodefoundation.org/2015/12/04/towards-a-metaphilosophy-of-the-urban/. As Merrifield notes:

> The urban doesn't so much spread per se as it becomes a vortex for sucking in everything the planet offers: its capital, its wealth, its culture, and its people. It's this sucking in of people and goods and capital that makes urban life so dynamic, and so menacing, because this is a totalizing force that also "expulses" people, that secretes its residue. And it's this expulsion process that makes urban space expand, that lets it push itself out. It's an internal energy that creates outer propulsion, an exponential external expansion.

even as the "urban phenomenon, taken as a whole" is occluded or completely hidden from view.[52] This generalization also applies to most mainstream applications of GIS and other remote-sensing technologies to the study of urbanization. Despite their impressively wide and increasingly fine-grained lens into emergent geographies of urbanization, scholarly work in this rapidly expanding subfield of urban studies tends to perpetuate a range of blind fields regarding the sociospatial, land-use, and ecological transformations they aspire to illuminate. With a few important exceptions, generally located in the spatial or environmental humanities, the geospatial turn in urban studies has been grounded upon a digitally inflected form of cartographic positivism in which visualizations derived from satellite imagery are presented as if they were a mimetic capture of spatial conditions and distributions "on the ground." Through this "photographic illusion," they render invisible the optical machinery, data-gathering apparatuses, and information-processing protocols, as well as the interpretive frameworks, political strategies, and spatial ideologies, that invariably underpin and mediate all approaches to cartographic representation, whatever their technological foundations.[53]

Meanwhile, among those critical urbanists who are reflexively concerned to wrestle with emergent epistemological crises and interpretive challenges, there is a deepening confusion regarding the analytic foundations and raison d'être of the field as a whole. Even a cursory examination of recent works of critical urban theory—from studies of postmetropolitan, postcolonial, posthuman, neoliberal, relational, ecological, green, assemblage, and Southern urbanism to feminist, queer, critical race-theoretical, anticolonial, decolonial, degrowth, actor-network, and anarchist approaches and investigations of urban metabolism, urban political ecology, urban policy mobility, and global suburbanisms—reveals that foundational disagreements prevail regarding nearly every imaginable issue, from the conceptualization of *what* urbanists are (or should be) trying to study to the justification for *why*

---

[52] The concept of a blind field is borrowed from Henri Lefebvre's ferocious polemic against overspecialization in mainstream urban studies, a situation that in his view contributes to a fragmentation of its basic object of analysis and to a masking of the worldwide totality formed by capitalist urbanization. See Lefebvre, *The Urban Revolution*, 29, 53. For further discussion and elaboration, see Merrifield, "The Urban Question under Planetary Urbanization."

[53] This argument is elaborated at length in Neil Brenner and Nikos Katsikis, *Is the World Urban? Towards a Critique of Geospatial Ideology* (Barcelona: Actar, 2019. For an earlier version of this line of analysis, see Neil Brenner and Nikos Katsikis, "Is the Mediterranean Urban?," in Brenner, *Implosions/Explosions*, 428–59. For a critical theoretical perspective on the use of geospatial data to visualize the geopolitics of urban life, see Laura Kurgan, *Close Up at a Distance: Mapping, Technology, Politics* (Cambridge, MA: Zone Books, 2015).

they are (or should be) doing so and the elaboration of *how* best to pursue their agendas.[54]

In 1980, Sharon Zukin memorably described the evolution of urban sociology during the previous decade as "acephalous"—"all limbs and no head"—due to the absence of an overarching research paradigm, akin to the dominance of human ecology in the mid-twentieth century.[55] A young Manuel Castells had already arrived at the same conclusion in 1968, when he acerbically declared that only the "subject matter" of urban sociology remained "untackled," even as state-directed empirical research on urban topics was being churned out at a breakneck pace across the advanced capitalist world.[56] In the early twenty-first century, urbanists may need to conjure different, albeit no less monstrous, metaphors to characterize the field's transformed intellectual anatomy—a many-headed hydra, perhaps? Today, there is not only a proliferation of diverse streams of concrete research across varied disciplinary and subdisciplinary terrains, but an equally marked explosion of new epistemological frameworks, conceptual explorations, and methodological experiments related to the changing nature of cities, urban conditions, and urban transformations, none of which seem to exert coherent, field-wide coordinating influence, much less paradigmatic dominance. Writing at the turn of the millennium, Edward Soja described the rapidly churning intellectual terrain of urban research as follows:

> The field of urban studies has never been so robust, so expansive in the number of subject areas and scholarly disciplines involved with the study of cities, so permeated by new ideas and approaches, so attuned to the major political and economic events of our times, and so theoretically and methodologically

---

[54] For useful overviews and critical assessments of this state of affairs, see Soja, *Postmetropolis*; and Roy, "The 21st Century Metropolis"; as well as Sharon Zukin, "Is There an Urban Sociology? Questions on a Field and a Vision," *Sociologica* 3 (2011): 1–18. Recent exchanges on the future of urban theory in the pages of journals such as *International Journal of Urban and Regional Research, Urban Studies, Urban Geography*, and *Society and Space* also attest to the extraordinary diversity of epistemological positions, conceptual orientations, and methodological strategies that are currently under development among self-described urban researchers. For early twenty-first-century assessments by some of the founding figures of critical urban studies, see Manuel Castells, "Urban Sociology in the Twenty-First Century," in *The Castells Reader on Cities and Social Theory*, ed. Ida Susser (Cambridge, MA: Blackwell, 2002), 390–406; Saskia Sassen, "Frontiers Facing Urban Sociology at the Millennium," *British Journal of Sociology* 51, no. 1 (2000): 143–59; and Saskia Sassen, "The City: Its Return as a Lens for Social Theory," *City, Culture and Society* 1 (2010): 3–11.

[55] Zukin, "A Decade of the New Urban Sociology," 575.

[56] Manuel Castells, "Is There an Urban Sociology?," in *Urban Sociology: Critical Essays*, ed. Chris Pickvance (London: Tavistock Publications, 1976 [1968]), 33–59.

unsettled. It may be the best of times and the worst of times to be studying cities, for while there is so much that is new and challenging to respond to, there is much less agreement than ever before as to how best to make sense, practically and theoretically, of the new urban worlds being created.[57]

Nearly two decades later, this observation continues to offer an apt characterization of an increasingly diffuse, rapidly evolving intellectual landscape of urban studies.

At one extreme, eminent urban economic geographers defend a monist, universalizing, and narrowly agglomeration-centric conception of urban theory that seeks to demarcate "a common set of genetic forces" underlying urbanization and thus to produce "theoretical generalizations" that apply to "all cities throughout history."[58] Even more starkly universalizing, monist and positivist epistemologies underpin recent, increasingly influential applications of complexity theory, network theory, social physics, and "big data" to develop a "new science of cities" oriented toward revealing putatively transhistorical covering laws.[59] At the other extreme is what Jamie Peck has described as a strongly "particularist drift" associated with influential strands of poststructuralism, Southern theory, actor-network theory, and assemblage urbanism, which entail a rejection of abstract or generalizing categories of the urban; various turns to low-flying descriptivism, naïve empiricism, ethnographic positivism, and/or "case study singularity"; "celebrations of diverse and decentered ordinariness"; and recurrent calls for "open-ended explorations of (singular) urban sites in all their full-spectrum complexity."[60]

---

[57] Soja, *Postmetropolis*, xii.

[58] Michael Storper and Allen J. Scott, "Current Debates in Urban Studies: A Critical Assessment," *Urban Studies* 53, no. 6 (2016): 1114–38, quoted phrases are from page 1116. See also Allen J. Scott and Michael Storper, "The Nature of Cities: The Scope and Limits of Urban Theory," *International Journal of Urban and Regional Research* 39, no. 1 (2015): 1–15. For critical reflections on this position see, among other responses, Richard A. Walker, "Why Cities? A Response," *International Journal of Urban and Regional Research* 40, no. 1 (2016): 164–80; Susan Parnell and Edgar Pieterse, "Translational Global Praxis: Rethinking Methods and Modes of African Urban Research," *International Journal of Urban and Regional Research* 40, no. 1 (2016): 236–46; and Ananya Roy, "Who's Afraid of Postcolonial Theory?," *International Journal of Urban and Regional Research* 40, no. 1 (2016): 200–9.

[59] See, for example, Luis Bettencourt and Geoffrey West, "A Unified Theory of Urban Living," *Nature* 467 (2010): 912–13; Michael Batty, *A New Science of Cities* (Cambridge, MA: MIT Press, 2012); and Geoffrey West, *Scale: The Universal Laws of Growth, Innovation, Sustainability, and the Pace of Life, in Organisms, Cities, Economies, and Companies* (New York: Penguin, 2016). For a critical discussion, see Brendan Gleeson, *The Urban Condition* (London: Routledge, 2014), 55–74.

[60] Peck, "Cities beyond Compare," 159, 167–68. For a critical assessment of assemblage urbanism, in particular, see Neil Brenner, David J. Madden, and David Wachsmuth, "Assemblage Urbanism and the Challenges of Critical Urban Theory," *CITY* 15, no. 2 (2011): 225–40. For some

Between the poles of "spatial fundamentalism" and "empirical particularism," a variety of pragmatically heterodox approaches to the contemporary urban question have been emerging that combine diverse methods (including geopolitical economy, critical development studies, critical GIS, relational comparison, theory-driven case studies, network analysis, and multisited ethnography), occupy a range of epistemological orientations, and focus on divergent sites and scales of investigation across inherited area studies boundaries (including the North/South and East/West divides).[61] In a very general sense, these approaches appear to share a loose conception of urbanization processes as being at once intercontextually patterned *and* contextually embedded. On this basis, they advance what might be understood as "meso-level" conceptual innovations—postmetropolis, splintering urbanism, variegated neoliberalization, worlding cities, global suburbanisms, and peripheral urbanization, for example—oriented toward, in Peck's precise formulation, the "cumulative interrogation of common or connective processes, in conversation across multiple sites."[62] However, despite these broadly aligned epistemic orientations, advocates of such heterodox, midrange approaches to urban theorizing tend to interpret the sources, expressions, parameters, contexts, and consequences of such "common or connective processes" in substantively divergent, if not incompatible, ways. Clearly, then, the field of critical urban theory is percolating with creative, energetic, and eclectic responses to dynamically changing sociospatial conditions, but it also remains quite fragmented among diverse epistemological frameworks and quite a wide range of ontological assumptions regarding the nature of the urban as a site and object of inquiry.

The Field Formerly Known as Urban Studies?

Although this situation of intellectual fragmentation—or is it simply many-headedness?—results from some productive forms of epistemological, conceptual, and methodological experimentation, it is problematic insofar as it limits the field's collective capacity to offer focused, forceful, accessible, and

---

brief reflections on the project of postcolonial urban theory in relation to emerging agendas on planetary urbanization, see Brenner and Schmid, "Towards a New Epistemology of the Urban," 8–13.

[61] The reference to "spatial fundamentalism" is from Roy, "Who's Afraid of Postcolonial Theory?," 207. On the dangers of "empirical particularism," see Peck, "Cities beyond Compare," 169 passim.

[62] Peck, "Cities beyond Compare," 168.

politicized alternatives to the dominant spatial ideologies of our time. As Peck suggests, the projects of critical urban studies "might be losing traction in a protracted moment of deconstructive splintering . . . [and] the proliferation of new urban signifiers [may be associated with] diminishing explanatory returns."[63] And yet, particularly in light of the broad appeal of simplistic urban age reasoning to scholars, planners, designers, and policymakers, and its continued instrumentalization in the service of neoliberalizing and/or neo-authoritarian forms of urban governance, accumulation by dispossession, and techno-environmental manipulation, the development of critical counterpositions and alternative analytic frameworks would appear to be a matter of increasing urgency for all those committed to developing more adequate, critical, and potentially emancipatory ways of interpreting—and, ultimately, of shaping—emergent patterns and pathways of urbanization.

Should urbanists simply affirm the apparent amorphousness of their chosen terrain of investigation and resign themselves to the task of tracking the shifting social life and spatial form of places that are characterized as "urban" based upon contextually specific, common-sense discourses, practices, and protocols? In this conventionalist approach, the notion of the urban is emptied of any substantive theoretical content as an intercontextual or macrospatial category of analysis; it is understood entirely as a category of practice whose deployment in the field of urban studies is contingent upon the vicissitudes of everyday, governmental, and/or corporate settlement taxonomies. Conversely, should urban studies today be pursued using the aspatial framework controversially proposed by Peter Saunders in the 1980s, which emphasized constitutive social processes rather than their materializations in spatial arrangements?[64] For Saunders, collective consumption represented the essential social process that defined urban life, but a contemporary reinvigoration of his aspatial approach to urban sociology could, in principle, yield other definitional demarcations (innovative capacity, or nodality in transportation and communications networks, for instance).

Perhaps, even more radically, it is time to speak of *the field formerly known as urban studies*, consigning work in this realm of inquiry to a phase of capitalist development or human history whose conditions of possibility have now been superseded? In a provocative reflection on such issues, the

---

[63] Ibid., 162. See also, more generally, Neil Brenner, "Debating Planetary Urbanization: Towards an Engaged Pluralism," *Environment and Planning D: Society and Space* 36, no. 3 (2018): 570–90.

[64] Peter Saunders, *Social Theory and the Urban Question*, 2nd ed. (London: Routledge, 1986 [1981]).

eminent urban sociologist Herbert Gans suggests as much, proposing to re-place the inherited *problematique* of urban studies with that of a "sociology of settlements" based upon totally reinvented typologies of human spatial organization and a more fluid understanding of interplace boundaries.[65] Unlike Saunders, Gans insists that this new research field must retain a spatial component, but he opts to renounce the fourfold cartography of urban settlement space (city, suburb, town, rural) that has long underpinned urban sociology, including his own pioneering postwar investigations of sub-urban communities. In Gans's proposal, the urban question is effectively superseded—or, more precisely, abandoned—in favor of a more or less de-scriptive approach to human spatial organization in which new settlement terminologies and taxonomies are to be derived immanently through the research process itself.

Some urban researchers may be tempted to follow Gans's lead, attempting to confront emergent landscapes of urbanization with a more or less blank conceptual slate, devoid of the unwieldy epistemological baggage associ-ated with the last century of debates on cities, metropolitanism, and urban questions. The term "settlements," in Gans's terminology, simply refers to the human tendency to construct durably organized communities by occupying, rearranging, and transforming space. For Gans, the question of how to label these settlements, and how to draw their boundaries, cannot be resolved or even helpfully informed through theoretical abstraction or conceptual speculation; it is a matter to be resolved through concrete, con-textually embedded research. Following this path, however, appears to entail reintroducing a version of Castells's earlier, orthodox Marxist rejection of urban discourse as pure ideology, albeit from a radically empiricist stand-point. Such a position will arguably be very poorly equipped to explain the continued, powerful resonance of the urban across diverse realms of dis-course, debate, and research, as well as its widespread invocation as a site, target, or project in so many arenas of institutional reorganization, political-economic strategy, and popular struggle.

Surely, the intensified, early twenty-first-century engagement with urban questions, projects, and potentialities is indicative of systemic, in-terconnected, and durably recurrent sociospatial transformations under way across the contemporary world, and of the ongoing effort to construct what Frederic Jameson once called a "cognitive map" through which to se-cure some measure of cartographic orientation under conditions of deep

---

[65] Herbert Gans, "Some Problems of and Futures for Urban Sociology: Toward a Sociology of Settlements," *City & Community* 8, no. 3 (2009): 211–19.

phenomenological dislocation.[66] Without systematic exploration and abstract theorization of—to repeat Peck's phrase—the "common or connective
processes, in conversation across multiple sites," that constitute, durably reproduce, and relentlessly transform urban life, it is difficult, if not logically
impossible, to justify the continued existence of a distinct field of "urban"
studies.[67] In her own reflections on possible future pathways of urban studies
in the twenty-first century, Saskia Sassen appears to concur with this assessment, suggesting a conception of the urban as a strategic site for the "inter-
section of major macro-social trends and their particular spatial patterns."[68]

I would defend this position even more assertively. From my point of
view, in the absence of some kind of macrospatial, intercontextual, and
geocomparative agenda for the field of critical urban studies, only two
options are available: the conventionalist pathway mentioned previously, in
which the urban dissolves into its various common-sense, everyday, local
meanings, or the abandonment of urban research as a collective, institutionally based, and critically self-reflexive project of enhancing knowledge in pursuit of more progressive societal futures. In fact, the former pathway is but a
roundabout route to the latter outcome; a purely conventionalist approach to
the urban question will eventually lead to the erosion of criticality; a retreat
into locally circumscribed, hermetically bounded discursive enclaves; and
thus to the dissolution of a distinctively "urban" scholarly agenda.[69]

Reframing the Urban Problematique

Whatever its ideological dimensions, then, the notion of the urban cannot
be reduced to a category of practice; it remains a critical conceptual tool

---

[66] See Frederic Jameson, "Cognitive Mapping," in *Marxism and the Interpretation of Culture*,
ed. Cary Nelson and Lawrence Grossberg (Chicago: University of Illinois Press, 1988), 347–57.
Jameson's neo-Althusserian concept builds upon yet supersedes the strictly phenomenological notion introduced by urban designer Kevin Lynch in his classic text, *The Image of the City*
(Cambridge, MA: MIT Press, 1960). For further elaborations on the interplay between everyday
cognitive maps of the city and critical theorizations of urbanization, see Angelo, "From the City
Lens"; Sayer, "Defining the Urban"; and Wachsmuth, "City as Ideology."

[67] Peck, "Cities beyond Compare," 168.

[68] Sassen, "New Frontiers Facing Urban Sociology," 144. Elsewhere, Sassen advances a version
of the same argument by describing cities and metropolitan regions as "strategic sites where
major macro-social trends materialize and hence can be constituted as an object of study." See
Sassen, "The City: Its Return as a Lens," 3.

[69] On the centrality of epistemological reflexivity to the project of critical urban studies, see
Neil Brenner, *Critique of Urbanization: Selected Essays* (Basel: Bauwelt Fundamente/Birkhäuser
Verlag, 2016).

in any attempt to theorize the uneven, multiscalar, and polymorphic transformations of political-economic landscapes under early twenty-first-century capitalism. As Lefebvre recognized, this process is not confined to any specific place, territory, or scale; it is better understood as a *problematique*, a syndrome of emergent, unevenly interconnected, and discontinuously coevolving conditions, configurations, strategies, and struggles that is engendered through the "prodigious extension of the urban to the entire planet."[70] A case can and must be made, therefore, for the continuation of urban theory, albeit in a critically reinvented form that (1) supersedes narrowly city-centric, settlement-based epistemologies; (2) recognizes the relentlessly dynamic, creatively destructive character of the capitalist form of urbanization; (3) explores homologies, connections, interdependencies, stratifications, and disjunctures among urban(izing) landscapes; and, on this basis, (4) aspires to decipher the unevenly hierarchized, variegated, and path-dependent planetarization of the capitalist urban fabric that is today unfolding. Such an exploration must be attuned to the indelible contextual specificity and constitutive unevenness of the sociospatial transformations wrought through this process while directing equal analytical attention to "commonalities in difference, generalized processes, recurrent patterns, structurally enabled powers and family resemblances."[71]

Despite the hazards of deconstructive splintering mentioned earlier, the consolidation of a planetary formation of urbanization enhances the urgency of developing epistemically heterodox research strategies in the field of critical urban studies. It is precisely the implosion-explosion of worldwide urbanization processes—their simultaneous differentiation, stratification, and relentless extension—that also engenders a de facto multiplication of urban lifeworlds, knowledge formations, interpretive schema, methodological tactics, and research agendas.[72] Consequently, the invention of new approaches

---

[70] Lefebvre, *The Urban Revolution*, 169.

[71] Peck, "Cities beyond Compare," 177.

[72] This argument broadly parallels that of Boaventura de Sousa Santos on the role of epistemological multiplicity in struggles against neoliberal globalization: see, among other works, his book *Epistemologies of the South: Justice against Epistemicide* (Boulder, CO: Paradigm Publishers, 2014). On the challenges of "engaged pluralism" in critical geography, see Trevor Barnes and Eric Sheppard, "'Nothing Includes Everything': Towards Engaged Pluralism in Anglophone Economic Geography," *Progress in Human Geography* 34, no. 2 (2010): 193–214. For applications of this concept to contemporary urban studies debates, see Michiel van Meeteren, David Bassens, and Ben Derudder, "Doing Global Urban Studies: On the Need for Engaged Pluralism, Frame Switching and Methodological Cross-Fertilization," *Dialogues in Human Geography* 6, no. 3 (2010): 296–301; and Brenner, "Debating Planetary Urbanization."

to critical urban theory under early twenty-first-century conditions will require intellectual experimentation and intensive collaboration across research milieu, disciplinary and subdisciplinary specializations, epistemological and methodological divides, and diverse sites and scales of investigation. Summarizing the conclusions reached by an expert panel on the future of urban studies convened at University College London (UCL), Michele Acuto, Susan Parnell, and Karen Seto argue similarly that

> today's urban research . . . remains trapped in the twentieth-century tradition of the systematic study of individual cities and the rise of specialized academic disciplines and professions associated with, amongst others, economics, health, planning, engineering and design. We are far away from understanding the fabric of urban systems. . . . Current urban research on pressing international problems is rudimentary and fragmented at a time when the window of urban transformation demands robust, sophisticated and truly global urban research.[73]

Although the UCL expert panel aspires to produce a "new urban science," I would argue that the undertaking they envision must be resolutely committed to epistemic pluralism in the sense of, as Helga Leitner and Eric Sheppard have proposed, taking seriously "the possibility that no single theory suffices to account for the variegated nature of urbanization and cities across the world."[74] The challenge is precisely to find ways to combine epistemic multiplicity, conceptual adventurousness, methodological heterodoxy, and postdisciplinary sensibilities with a rigorously focused, logically consistent, globally oriented, and contextually grounded analytical orientation that will productively illuminate emergent patterns, pathways, contradictions, and contestations of urban restructuring. Rather than aspiring to construct a singular, monist, authoritative "science" of urban life, then, contemporary urbanists need to embed specialized forms of knowledge production (whether from the social sciences, the spatial and environmental humanities, ecology, or environmental studies) within "engaged pluralist," intercultural modes

---

[73] Michele Acuto, Susan Parnell, and Karen C. Seto, "Building a Global Urban Science," *Nature Sustainability* 1, no. 2–4 (2018).

[74] Helga Leitner and Eric Sheppard, "Provincializing Critical Urban Theory: Extending the Ecosystem of Possibilities," *International Journal of Urban and Regional Research* 40, no. 1 (2016): 230. For further elaborations on epistemic pluralism in the study of planetary urbanization, see Michelle Buckley and Kendra Strauss, "With, against and beyond Lefebvre: Planetary Urbanization and Epistemic Plurality," *Environment and Planning D: Society and Space* 34, no. 4 (2016) 617–36.

of inquiry that reject all forms of intellectual imperialism and promote "ceaseless, even-handed debate among different approaches."[75]

In university environments that are increasingly dominated by corporate-neoliberal agendas and (despite official rhetoric suggesting otherwise) pervasive disciplinary and subdisciplinary fragmentation, there are massive barriers to the construction of such "trading zones" for the development of more inclusive, heterodox, and critical arenas of urban knowledge. Meanwhile, the field of urban studies is being further redefined through the massive impacts of what Peter J. Taylor has termed "corporate social science—"the combined knowledge output on contemporary social relations by self-styled policy think tanks, the research arms of advanced producer service corporations, supplemented by publications by UN institutions and other global players such as NGOs."[76] Such organizations, Taylor suggests, currently "produce publications that constitute a body of knowledge . . . probably at least as large as that of all urban research in universities."[77] Indeed, much of the contemporary public "buzz" around global urbanism has been engendered precisely through the role of corporate social science institutions and affiliated funding sources in global real estate, financial services, accountancy, and data analytics firms in injecting resources into the analysis of strategic urban issues and disseminating the resultant research outputs through their own proprietary communications networks. Given the instrumental, client-oriented, profit-driven, technomanagerial, and depoliticizing orientations of corporate urban studies, its research "products" are obviously grounded upon epistemologies, methods, and substantive agendas that diverge drastically from those that animate the (otherwise internally quite diverse) projects of critical urban researchers.

Under these circumstances, critical urban thinkers must urgently and re-flexively confront the radically transformed politico-institutional conditions for urban knowledge production today. Whether the projects of critical urban

---

[75] Barnes and Sheppard, "'Nothing Includes Everything,'" 199. In the quoted phrase, Barnes and Sheppard are discussing the epistemological position developed by feminist philosopher of science Helen Longino. For a reading of Lefebvre as an engaged pluralist, see Buckley and Strauss, "With, against and beyond Lefebvre." For further discussion of the need for engaged pluralism in the study of planetary urbanization, see Brenner, "Debating Planetary Urbanization." On the relation between modern science and epistemic pluralism, see de Sousa Santos, *Epistemologies of the South*.

[76] Peter J. Taylor, "Corporate Social Science and the Loss of Curiosity," *Items: Insights from the Social Sciences*, Social Science Research Council, August 2, 2016, https://items.ssrc.org/corporate-social-science-and-the-loss-of-curiosity.

[77] Ibid.

studies are situated precariously within the output-driven, impact-oriented research platforms of corporate-neoliberal universities or are animated more directly at the front lines of social activism, protest, and insurgency, their contemporary institutional conditions of possibility are radically different from those that obtained during the waves of academic radicalization and creative politico-epistemic experimentation that flowed forth among critical urbanists in the wake of the worldwide "explosions" of May 1968.[78] While this is not the place to explore the possible politico-institutional parameters that would be required to support the heterodox vision of critical urban studies advocated here, there can be no doubt that radical institutional renewal and reinvention are as essential to the future vibrancy of critical urban studies as are the questions of (re)theorization that have commanded the bulk of my attention in this book.

Of course, these issues are thoroughly intertwined. Critical urban theory cannot flourish in a vacuum: it requires protected institutional spaces for learning, debate, discussion, and outreach; means of public dissemination and open scholarly communication; and financial infrastructures to support independent research, creative reflection, dedicated writing, and ongoing self-criticism. Just as importantly, the creation, renewal, or reinvention of such heterodox institutional spaces for dissident urban knowledge must be informed, if not actively guided, by dynamically evolving critical theories of the urban and urbanization processes, which are themselves closely articulated to emergent *problematiques* of urban restructuring, conflict, aspiration, and struggle across diverse sites and scales, worldwide. As I have argued throughout this book, it is only through the abstractions of theory that the core project(s) of critical urban research can be clarified, but the latter are not arbitrary conceptual or methodological decisions; they represent "real abstractions" of ongoing sociospatial practices, transformations, contestations, insurgencies, hopes, and imaginations. Insofar as visions of possible future politico-institutional configurations for the project(s) of critical urban studies are likely to entail wide-ranging debates about precisely these questions—and, not least, that of *alter-urbanizations*: possible alternative patterns and pathways of urbanization itself—perhaps the lines of theorization elaborated in these pages may offer some orientation for such an endeavor.

---

[78] On the changing geopolitical contexts of urban knowledge production, see Elvin Wyly, "Strategic Positivism," *Professional Geographer* 61, no. 3 (2009): 310–22; as well as Gleeson, "What Role for Social Science in the 'Urban Age.'"

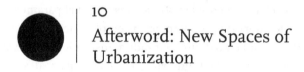

10

Afterword: New Spaces of Urbanization

Penser l'urbain est aujourd'hui une nécessité.[1]

EVEN AMONG THOSE URBAN scholars who broadly concur that emergent landscapes of urbanization are "new" in some qualitatively significant sense, there are myriad disagreements regarding how best to decipher contemporary sociospatial transformations, their sources, and their implications, at once for inherited approaches to the urban question and for future patterns and pathways of urban life. Despite the dangers of theoretical fragmentation and political neutralization discussed in the previous chapter, such disagreements may actually serve to animate renewed intellectual vibrancy within the field of critical urban studies. Indeed, the reflexive engagement with questions of urban *theory* in relation to emergent sociospatial transformations may well represent a common thread that draws together otherwise divergent research cultures around some broadly shared concerns and agendas. Today, across the heterodox epistemic communities of critical urban studies, there is not only a sustained engagement with the challenges

---

[1] Françoise Choay, "Le régne de l'urbain et la mort de la ville," in *La ville, art et architecture en Europe, 1870–1993*, ed. Jean Dethier and Alain Guiheux (Paris: Editions du Centre Georges Pompidou, 1994), 33.

of deciphering the complexities of early twenty-first-century sociospatial transformations within, among, and across contexts. Just as crucially, critical urban scholars are increasingly engaged in a concerted effort to interrogate and, when appropriate, to revise and even to reinvent the very conceptual frameworks through which such restructuring processes are investigated.

This reflexivity regarding the interplay between historical sociospatial transformation and the evolution of modes of theorization is, I have argued, one of the distinctive epistemological commitments of critical approaches to urban questions.[2] Such an approach to urban *theorizing*—an active process, not a fixed stance—requires not only a recognition that all urban knowledges (including the abstractions of theory) are situated, contextually embedded, and contested, but an equally vigilant insistence, by consequence, that theoretical frameworks are radically revisable in relation to their restlessly shifting contexts of emergence and application. Precisely because they are enmeshed within the very sociospatial relations, conditions, and contestations they aspire to illuminate, the interpretive tools of urban studies will themselves require periodic revision and, in some cases, more radical epistemic breaks or paradigm shifts. Thus conceived, the process of urban theorizing is not tied to an underlying ontological foundation through which the intrinsic properties of the urban could somehow be demarcated "once and for all." Rather, in the dialectical, postfoundationalist philosophical traditions in which this book is situated, urban theorizing is always historically constituted and contextually situated. As such, it involves the self-reflexive exploration of a historically developing, geographically uneven process in reflexively dialectical relation to the social production, contestation, and mutation of the very categories of thought (including any number of "real abstractions") mobilized to understand the evolution of that process. In this sense, critical urban theory at once expresses and responds to a *problematique*—a set of concerns, struggles, and aspirations—that emerges from the urbanization process itself. As that process mutates, so too must the conceptual apparatus of urban theory.

It was precisely this dialectic of situated knowledge, sociospatial emergence, spatial politics, and reflexive (re)conceptualization that Henri Lefebvre had in mind when he famously described the urban as a "virtual object."[3] As Lefebvre argued, positivist and technoscientific approaches reduce the urban to extant sociospatial arrangements—the city, the metropolitan region, or

---

[2] Neil Brenner, *Critique of Urbanization: Selected Essays* (Basel: Bauwelt Fundamente/Birkhäuser Verlag, 2016).

[3] Henri Lefebvre, *The Urban Revolution*, trans. Robert Bononno (Minneapolis: University of Minnesota Press, 2003 [1970]).

the administrative territory. Driven by specific strategic imperatives, such as economic growth or state control, these instrumental knowledge formations promulgate a systematically narrowed, depoliticized understanding of urban life that analytically externalizes, and thus renders peripheral or even invisible, any number of essential dimensions of urbanization: the enclosures, dispossessions, and exclusions upon which it is grounded; its extended spatial and ecological dimensions; its contested spatial politics; its relentless sociospatial dynamism; and its powerfully insurgent political potentials. Urban knowledges are thus compartmentalized into "black boxes" and projected across "blind fields" that are designed to mask, or divert attention away from, the depoliticizing distortions upon which this ideologically sanitized vision of sociospatial relations hinges.[4] By contrast, Lefebvre proposed, a revolutionary spatial epistemology would conceive the urban as an open horizon, as a virtuality whose variegated patterns and energetic pulsations are forged precisely through transformative practices, strategies, struggles, experiences, and imaginations, including those oriented toward "differential space"—alternative urbanization processes based upon territorial self-management (in my own terminology, *alter-urbanizations*). In this sense, for Lefebvre, the urban represents an emergent *problematique* rather than a permanently defined, neatly demarcated object of knowledge: it is derived from inherited sociospatial practices; it is enmeshed within present conditions, their contradictions, and their contestation; but it is equally oriented toward a broad spectrum of possible future pathways of sociospatial transformation, from the catastrophic to the emancipatory.

This book has put forward a constellation of epistemological orientations, conceptual tools, and methodological strategies, as well as several more specific lines of interpretation, analysis, and critique through which to explore emergent crystallizations of the urban *problematique*. Although my arguments build upon inherited approaches to critical urban theory (historical-geographical materialist geopolitical economy, in particular), they also align closely with the work of several important strands of early twenty-first-century urban theory (such as postcolonial urbanism) that advocate for major, if not paradigmatic, theoretical renewal—the reinvention of concepts, methods, and cartographies in relation to the dramatically mutating worlds of urbanization they aspire to illuminate. Consequently, while I am sympathetic to certain aspects of Allen J. Scott and Michael Storper's recent, widely discussed call for greater methodological rigor and explanatory coherence

---

[4] Ibid., 26.

in the investigation of urban phenomena across time and space, I strongly reject their equation of definitional exactitude with a monist, universalizing mode of analysis.[5] My theoretical pathway here resonates more closely with what Richard A. Walker, in a productive rejoinder to Scott and Storper's intervention, has described as a "more open and layered approach" to the urban question, one that is attuned precisely to the ways in which the formative elements of intrinsically historical processes, such as urbanization, may themselves mutate through the evolution of sociospatial relations.[6] In the face of such (actual and potential) historical *Gestalt* shifts in the processes under investigation, a universalizing approach to urban theory will likely prove to be an extremely blunt analytical instrument, one that preserves definitional purity only at the very high intellectual cost of restricting a researcher's capacity (1) to recognize ongoing processes of restructuring, emergence, and transformation and, on this basis, (2) to explore possible avenues of (re)conceptualization through which more adequately to decipher the latter in relation to matters of urgent sociopolitical concern.[7]

---

[5] Allen J. Scott and Michael Storper, "The Nature of Cities: The Scope and Limits of Urban Theory," *International Journal of Urban and Regional Research* 39, no. 1 (2015): 1–15.

[6] See Richard A. Walker, "Why Cites? A Response," *International Journal of Urban and Regional Research* 40, no. 1 (2016): 164–80. Despite my broad metatheoretical alignment with Walker on the limits of a universalizing approach to the urban question, my position diverges substantially from his on the question of what a more richly historicized approach to the latter should entail. Among other major points of contention, Walker embraces a conventionally city-centric understanding of urbanization that only partially breaks from the more orthodox, transhistorical version of agglomeration theory embraced by Scott and Storper. Even though he productively recognizes the extrametropolitan forces that shape it, Walker takes as self-evident the notion that "the" city is the exclusive focal point and *explanandum* for a theory of urbanization. By contrast, I have argued throughout this book for a broader conception of (capitalist) urbanization, one that encompasses (multiple scales of) agglomeration, as well as the extended fabric of socioterritorial and ecological infrastructures that support the industrial accumulation of capital. For further elaborations and debates on these issues in relation to my collaborative work with Christian Schmid, see Richard A. Walker, "Building a Better Theory of the Urban: A Response to 'Towards a New Epistemology of the Urban,'" *CITY* 19, no. 2–3 (2015): 183–91; and Neil Brenner and Christian Schmid, "Combat, Caricature and Critique in the Study of Planetary Urbanization," Urban Theory Lab, Harvard Graduate School of Design, April 2015, http://urbantheorylab.net/uploads/Brenner_Schmid_Richard%20Walker_2015.pdf.

[7] It should be noted, however, that there is no *logical* contradiction between the pursuit of a universalizing explanatory agenda and the concern to understand historical variations in the (putatively universal) phenomenon under investigation. Indeed, Scott and Storper appear to believe that the former is a necessary condition of possibility for recognizing the latter. By contrast, like Walker, I contend that it is precisely the universality of Scott and Storper's analytical agenda that restricts its explanatory capacities in relation to historically and geographically specific restructuring processes: by defining the latter, a priori, as mere empirical "variations" of a singular phenomenon, they cannot consider the possibility that the processes under investigation may themselves mutate, in qualitatively significant ways, thus requiring new frameworks of theorization. Just as problematically, Scott and Storper present their own monist approach as the only

As I have argued throughout this book, such *Gestalt* shifts of the urban *problematique* in the modern world are not merely contingent historical disruptions or aberrations from an otherwise linear pathway, but represent intrinsic elements and expressions of the capitalist form of urbanization as such. It is in this sense that the concept of "urban restructuring," as developed throughout this work, refers not simply to changes within predefined spatial containers or fixed units (cities, metropolitan regions, or otherwise) but to a fundamental mutation in the nature of the urbanization process itself, of which successive crystallizations of the capitalist urban fabric are but temporarily stabilized permutations. Much of my theoretical attention here has been devoted to deciphering the dramatic rescaling of the capitalist urban fabric during the post-1980s period; its mediations through scale-articulated, post-Keynesian state spatial strategies; and the wide-ranging consequences of the latter for emergent patterns and pathways of urban development, especially in the older industrialized world. However, my pursuit of these scalar explorations across diverse research terrains has generated insights into a number of additional, if closely interconnected, dimensions of contemporary urban restructuring, including (1) the interplay of rescaling processes with the dialectics of place-making, (re)territorialization, and networking in reshaping the capitalist urban fabric, and (2) the post-1980s consolidation of new, colossally scaled mega-infrastructures of capitalist industrial development across erstwhile territorial hinterlands, leading to a rather dramatic, if systemically uneven, thickening of the capitalist urban fabric in zones that are conventionally classified as nonurban (rural, wilderness, or otherwise).

Crucially, the theoretical lenses into the urban question elaborated in this book have not been derived from an underlying metaphysical position or ontological foundation. Rather, they have been forged in direct relation to the manifold conceptual, methodological, and empirical challenges of deciphering the shifting macrogeographical contexts within which processes

---

viable methodological alternative to the forms of naïve empiricism they are (quite appropriately, in my view) concerned to criticize in contemporary urban studies. In thus proceeding, they either ignore or caricature the wide-ranging methodological contributions of more historically specific modes of intercontextual, macrogeographical analysis, not only of specific cities and intercity relations, but of the extended urban fabric in which the latter are embedded. Notably, Scott and Storper's own foundational contributions to the development of the Los Angeles school of urban studies in the 1980s can be viewed as a powerful example of precisely such an approach. This work offered not a universal theory of agglomeration across human history but an analysis of historically specific tendencies of urban crisis formation, restructuring, and transformation that were crystallizing across the older industrialized world following the collapse of the Fordist accumulation regime. See, for example, Allen J. Scott and Michael Storper, eds., *Production, Work, Territory: The Geographical Anatomy of Industrial Capitalism* (London: Allen & Unwin, 1986).

of urban restructuring have been unfolding under the conditions of intensifying scale relativization that have prevailed since the 1980s. This has required, on the one hand, a concerted rejection of any singular, fixed unit of analysis in the investigation of the urban question, such that historically and geographically specific, scale-differentiated pathways of urban transformation, and their variegated crystallizations within the capitalist urban fabric, could be explored. On the other hand, this has also entailed analytically connecting such scaled patterns and pathways of urban restructuring to a series of macrogeographical formations of capitalist development, their political mediations, their crisis tendencies, and their manifestations in spatial politics, especially in relation to the vicissitudes of the fixity/motion contradiction under capitalism, as theorized in Chapter 2.

It is from this point of view that I have investigated a succession of systemic ruptures within the scalar architectures of the capitalist urban fabric in the North Atlantic zone during the post-1980s period, including (1) the crises of Fordist-Keynesian, national-developmentalist urbanization and the concomitant reshuffling of nationalized interscalar hierarchies, industrialization patterns, and formations of territorial governance and (2) the uneven, crisis-induced and crisis-inducing proliferation of post-Keynesian, market-disciplinary approaches to city building, urban economic development, industrial regeneration, metropolitan regionalism, territorial planning, and interscalar management, leading to a further entrenchment of geo-regulatory instability, an acceleration of patterns of scale relativization, and a pervasive splintering of the inherited urban fabric. These variegated restructuring tendencies have unfolded within, and have actively coshaped, a transformed macrogeographical context of global capitalist development defined by accelerating geoeconomic integration ("globalization"), a consolidating new international division of labor (NIDL), deepening financialization, successive waves of regulatory neoliberalization, and intensifying uneven spatial development.

In the preceding chapter, these lines of analysis flowed into the preliminary demarcation of yet another scale-differentiated formation of macrogeographical transformation, this time manifested in a number of political-economic mutations connected to the dramatic acceleration of late industrial development and associated patterns of large-scale infrastructural investment across strategic zones of the global South. While such transformations have deep, wide-ranging implications throughout the world economy, their imprints have been especially pronounced within the so-called BRICS (Brazil, Russia, India, China, South Africa) territories and along strategic corridors of urban-industrial transformation to which the latter are connected via global supply chains, including in parts of Latin America, Southeast Asia, and Africa, as well as in Eastern Europe and the Middle East.[8] Such trends have received systematic attention in the literatures on radical geopolitical economy, perhaps most foundationally in Giovanni Arrighi's now-classic thesis that they herald the formation of a new, Asia-centric formation of the capitalist world system.[9] However, as several critical geographers have more recently observed, the rise of the BRICS and associated "*new* new international divisions of labor" not only represents a locational shift in the hegemonic centers of world-scale capital accumulation, but heralds the formation of a qualitatively transformed configuration of combined and uneven spatial development under early twenty-first-century conditions.[10]

While this churning maelstrom of capitalist industrial restructuring has in no way reversed the patterns of scale relativization that crystallized during the final decades of the twentieth century, it has arguably quite significantly recast their institutional and sociospatial architecture. According to Ray Hudson, this has occurred through a range of new geopolitical alignments across and within continents and territories; resurgent forms of state-led, export-oriented regional industrial development; and the spatially selective investment operations of newly established multilateral development banks. These politico-institutional shifts and territorial development

---

[8] For an excellent overview and critical evaluation of the rise of the so-called BRICS in the context of anticapitalist, anti-imperialist strategies and struggles, see Patrick Bond and Anna Garcia, eds., *BRICS: An Anti-Capitalist Critique* (London: Pluto, 2015); as well as, more generally, Guido Starostra and Greig Charnock, eds., *The New International Division of Labour: Global Transformation and Uneven Development* (New York: Palgrave, 2016).

[9] Giovanni Arrighi, *The Long Twentieth Century* (London: Verso, 1994); Giovanni Arrighi, *Adam Smith in Beijing: Lineages of the 21st Century* (London: Verso, 2007).

[10] See, for instance, Martín Arboleda, *Planetary Mine: Territories of Extraction in the Fourth Machine Age* (New York: Verso, 2019); Ray Hudson, "Rising Powers and the Drivers of Uneven Global Development," *Area Development and Policy* 1, no. 3 (2016): 279–94; and Jamie Peck, "Macroeconomic Geographies," *Area Development and Policy* 1, no. 3 (2016): 305–22. For the most part, the literature on "late" development is notably silent on the question of the spatial constitution (and reconstitution) of the development models and regimes it investigates. As its prominent use of the temporal label "late" illustrates, research in this literature focuses primarily on the historical timing of industrialization initiatives and the implications of the latter for the nature and extent of state industrial policy coordination and financial support. Consequently, debates on late development leave radically underexplored the question of how the development process itself is spatialized within, across, and among territories, through a broad range of state spatial strategies and spatially selective investments in industrial infrastructures (whether of production, circulation, or reproduction). For an extensive exploration of this and related issues in the context of economic development discourse and struggle in colonial South Asia, see Manu Goswami, *Producing India: From Colonial Economy to National Space* (Chicago: University of Chicago Press, 2004).

projects have, in turn, facilitated the consolidation of new spatial divisions of labor in which advanced, globally networked transport, logistics, communications, energetic, extractive, and manufacturing infrastructures are increasingly being channeled across strategic industrial territories within the BRICS and among various special economic zones and growth corridors within the territories of their regional economic partners.[11] For Hudson, the proliferation of these "new centres of industrial growth," associated megainfrastructures, and territorial development corridors in many parts of the global South has also been intrinsically connected to new forms of accumulation by dispossession, including "a tidal wave of land grabs" that has forced "the conversion of rural dwellers, previously engaged in subsistence agriculture, from a latent labour reserve to become part of a proletarianized factory wage labour force."[12]

Faced with these wide-ranging mutations of inherited capitalist geographies, their confusing politico-institutional mediations, and their uneven infrastructural materializations, Jamie Peck programmatically argues:

> Today, there seems once again to be a pervasive sense that the *Gestalt* of capitalism is in the throes of transformative and indeed structural change. . . . There may also be a shared sense that the extant toolkit of conceptual frameworks and methodological devices is not entirely sufficient for grasping the scope and depth of these transformations. . . . [T]hese radically changed circumstances surely call for a comprehensive renewal (rather than merely a reboot) of the apparatus for making sense of dynamically unfolding processes of combined and uneven development.[13]

It will not suffice, therefore, simply to "replace one 'centric' (radial, or orbital) reading [of capitalist macrogeographies] with another, for instance by positioning China as some *locus novellus*."[14] Rather, Peck proposes, we need to develop rigorously dialectical approaches to macrogeographical restructuring that reflexively theorize the "reciprocal relations between the moving

---

[11] Hudson, "Rising Powers and the Drivers of Uneven Global Development."

[12] Ibid., 290. On the connection between rural land grabs, dispossession, informalization, and urbanization, see also Annelies Zoomers, Femke Van Noorloos, Kei Otsuki, Griet Steel, and Guus Van Westen, "The Rush for Land in an Urbanizing World: From Land Grabbing towards Developing Safe, Resilient, and Sustainable Cities and Landscapes," *World Development* 92 (2017): 242–52.

[13] Peck, "Macroeconomic Geographies," 316.

[14] Ibid., 317.

parts and the evolving whole" of capitalism in a context of inherited but always potentially mutable configurations of spatialized power.[15]

It is precisely in relation to this challenge, I believe, that contemporary approaches to critical urban theory must be forged. Indeed, as I have argued throughout this book, the continued forward motion of capitalist creative destruction constantly requires us to renew our repertoire of concepts and methods, such that newly emergent urbanization processes, their relentless implosions and explosions, their combined and uneven development, their provisionally stabilized sociospatial expressions in the urban fabric, and their ongoing contestation through spatial politics may be critically deciphered. Today, in my view, this theoretical imperative obtains not only in relation to emergent urbanization processes in the BRICS or elsewhere in the global South, but precisely with reference to the restless reconstitution of the urban itself, across diverse, inevitably specific yet relationally interconnected sites and scales, under early twenty-first century capitalism.[16]

Toward a Metatheoretical Synthesis

Against this background, we are now in a position to draw together some of the major metatheoretical positions that flow from our explorations in this book, and that may perhaps prove relevant to confronting the challenges outlined previously. To this end, by way of conclusion, I present a series of synthetic arguments, epistemological perspectives, and conceptual proposals, closely connected to collaborative work with Christian Schmid, which are intended to help orient the ongoing project of deciphering the diverse, variegated, and volatile worlds of urbanization that are proliferating under early twenty-first-century conditions.[17] As with all of my conceptual explorations in this book, those presented here are not intended to "lock in" an ontologically fixed conception of the urban "once and for all," but as provocations for further debate regarding the contemporary planetary urban condition, the state of our intellectual inheritance in the scholarly fields devoted to its investigation, and the prospects for developing new epistemological frameworks, conceptual strategies, methodological tactics, and cartographic perspectives

---

[15] Ibid., 317–18.

[16] On the apparent paradox of "inevitable specificity" amid planetary urban transformation, see ETH Studio Basel, ed., *The Inevitable Specificity of Cities* (Zurich: Lars Müller Publishers, 2014).

[17] See, especially, Neil Brenner and Christian Schmid, "Towards a New Epistemology of the Urban?," *CITY* 19, no. 2–3 (2015): 151–82.

for confronting contemporary sociospatial transformations. In this sense, the ideas presented here are offered as *meta*theoretical proposals. While they suggest a number of epistemological perspectives and methodological orientations for confronting contemporary urban transformations, each of the theses is compatible with a range of substantive conceptions of the urban and urbanization, and with a wide array of concrete research strategies. This endeavor is thus strongly inspired by Lefebvre's call for a metaphilosophy of urbanization—an exploratory, pluralistic epistemology that "provides an orientation . . . , opens pathways and reveals a horizon" rather than advancing definitive pronouncements regarding an actualized condition, a homogeneous structure, or a singular process.[18] As with my scalar explorations of the urban question throughout this book, this line of analysis also builds upon and extends Lefebvre's intellectually dissident insistence on the foundational distinction between the city and the urban. Cities, in this view, represent but one (immensely variegated) sociospatial configuration within the relentlessly mutating, constitutively multiscalar fabric of capitalist industrial urbanization.

More generally, insofar as these proposals simultaneously emphasize systematic, intercontextual, macrospatial patterning *and* contextual differentiation, multiplicity, and specificity, they fall under the broad rubric of the heterodox, meso-level epistemological perspectives outlined in the preceding chapter. The dialectical approach to urban theorizing proposed here thus rejects both poles of the entrenched opposition between spatial fundamentalism (universalizing, positivist, naturalistic, and/or monist theories of city growth) and empirical particularism (naïve objectivist, descriptivist, and/ or contextualist ontologies of the local) in favor of what Bertell Ollman famously described as the "philosophy of internal relations."[19] Here, the crystallization of an increasingly planetarized urban fabric is understood to occur not only through interconnected, coevolving macrogeographical processes (such as territorial enclosure, industrialization, depeasantization, neoliberalization, financialization, mega-infrastructural consolidation, and regulatory rescaling), but through the multiplication of contextually specific,

---

[18] Lefebvre, *The Urban Revolution*, 66.

[19] See, especially, Bertell Ollman, *Dance of the Dialectic* (Urbana: University of Illinois Press, 2003); and Bertell Ollman, *Dialectical Investigations* (London: Routledge, 1993). More recently, see Bertell Ollman and Tony Smith, eds., *Dialectics for the New Century* (New York: Palgrave, 2008). For a provocative reflection on various (Hegelian, post-Hegelian, and anti-Hegelian) approaches to the spatialization of dialectical analysis, see Eric Sheppard, "Geographic Dialectics," *Environment and Planning A* 40 (2008): 2603–12.

territorially embedded patterns and pathways of urban transformation.[20] To paraphrase an incisive formulation on the dialectics of combined and uneven development from historical sociologist Fouad Makki, the point here is not simply that urbanization operates differently in different places, but that the capitalist urban fabric as a whole is itself "differently configured, with correspondingly distinct effects, across the socially uneven political multiplicity of the world."[21] Consequently, the specificity of sociospatial patterns and developmental pathways within the capitalist urban fabric emerges not simply from a pregiven condition of ontological singularity (whether within places, regions, territories, or cultures), or due to the collision of "opposed national and global forces," but crystallizes relationally through the "overdetermined uneven and combined conditions of its existence" in world-historical space-time.[22]

In this specific sense, the evolving conditions of existence for the capitalist urban fabric are at once variegated, path dependent, and relationally interconnected: they cannot be derived from a universal logic, whether of agglomeration, industrialism, globalism, or otherwise, but require historically attuned, reflexively multiscalar, institutionally differentiated, and rigorously relational modes of political-economic and sociospatial inquiry. If deployed with appropriately dialectical attention to the ways in which, as Martín Arboleda notes, "the relation between the parts and the whole [are] in continuous evolution and co-determination," such an approach may help illuminate, simultaneously, the contextual embeddedness *and* intercontextual structuration of urban(izing) spaces and, by consequence, of the capitalist urban fabric as a whole.[23] Figure 10.1 offers a schematic overview of several key conceptual distinctions that are elaborated in our subsequent discussion.

---

[20] A version of this argument is further elaborated in Christian Schmid, "Specificity and Urbanization: A Theoretical Outlook," in ETH Studio Basel, *The Inevitable Specificity of Cities*, 282–97. See also Christian Schmid, Ozan Karaman, Naomi Hanakata, Pascal Kallenberger, Anne Kockelkorn, Lindsay Sawyer, Monika Streuele, and Kit Ping Wong, "Towards a New Vocabulary of Urbanization Processes: A Comparative Approach," *Urban Studies* 55, no. 1 (2018): 19–52.

[21] Fouad Makki, "Reframing Development Theory: The Significance of the Idea of Combined and Uneven Development," *Theory and Society* 44 (2015): 491.

[22] Ibid.

[23] Martín Arboleda, "Financialization, Totality and Planetary Urbanization in the Chilean Andes," *Geoforum* 67 (2015): 5. In this text, Arboleda offers a brilliant synthesis of Ollman and Lefebvre to analyze the urbanization of finance and the financialization of the urban in a gold mining region of the Chilean Andes following the 1993–2013 commodity boom in Latin America. See also Arboleda, *Planetary Mine*.

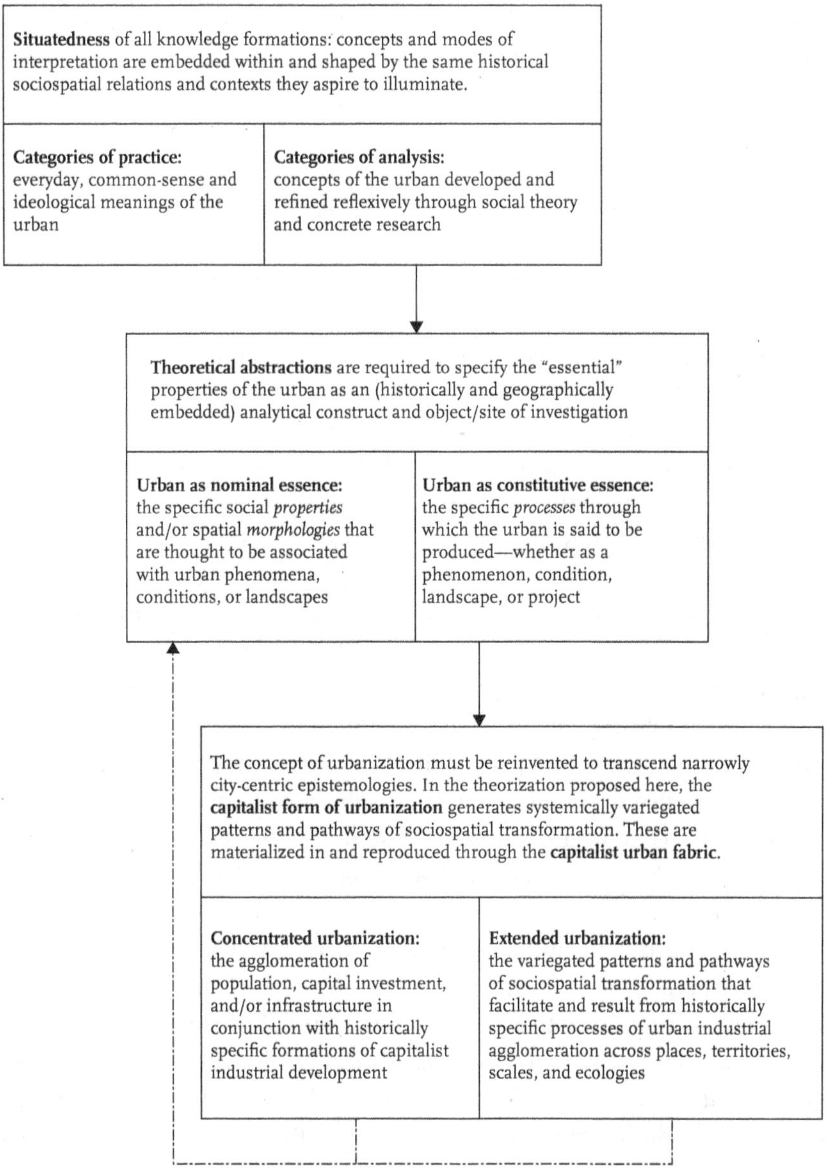

FIGURE 10.1 Some useful distinctions for deciphering contemporary mutations of the urban question.

A Theoretically Reflexive, Process-Based Approach to Urban(izing) Spaces

In mainstream urban studies, cities and urban spaces are generally taken for granted as empirically self-evident sites. Consequently, the urban character of urban research has been conceived simply with reference to the circumstance that it is located within or focused on zones labeled as "cities." However, such naïve empiricist, positivist positions presuppose determinate, if unacknowledged, interpretive assumptions regarding the specificity of cities and/ or the urban that powerfully shape the trajectory of concrete research. In this sense, the urban is not a pregiven, transparently legible arena, site, artifact, or object—its demarcation as a realm of thought, representation, imagination, investigation, or action can only occur through a process of theoretical abstraction, one that is itself embedded within the very sociospatial relations it is meant to grasp. As Andrew Sayer explains, such abstractions condition "how we 'carve up' our object of study and what properties we take particular objects to have."[24] As such, they have a massively structuring impact on concrete investigations of all aspects of sociospatial relations. For this reason, questions of conceptualization lie at the heart of all forms of urban research, even the most apparently empirical, contextual, quantitative, data driven, or detail oriented. They are not mere background conditions or framing devices, but constitute the very interpretive grammar and analytical medium through which urbanists weave together metanarratives, normative-political orientations, methodological tactics, data collection and assembly, concrete analyses, and strategies of intervention. Critical reflexivity in urban studies may be accomplished only if such underlying theoretical assumptions regarding the site, focus, and goals of investigation are made explicit, systematically connected to the historical-geographical contexts in which they are situated, subjected to careful analytical scrutiny, and revised continually in relation to the dynamically evolving geographies of urban development they aspire to illuminate.

Since the formal institutionalization of urban social science in the early twentieth century, the conceptual demarcation of the urban has been a matter of intense debate. Since that time, the trajectory of urban research has involved not only an accretion of concrete investigations in and of urban(izing) spaces, but the continual theoretical rearticulation of their specificity as such. Indeed, during the last century, many of the major creative advances in the field of urban studies have been stimulated precisely through the elaboration of new theoretical "cuts" into the nature of the urban question. Such reconceptualizations have emerged not only through the exigencies of concrete urban research in specific spatiotemporal contexts, but have been powerfully animated by the challenges of deciphering the remaking of the

---

[24] Andrew Sayer, "Defining the Urban," *GeoJournal* 9, no. 3 (1984): 281. See also, more generally, Andrew Sayer, "Abstraction: A Realist Interpretation," *Radical Philosophy* 28 (Summer 1981): 6–15.

world's built and unbuilt environments during periods of intense, often disorienting, sociospatial creative destruction. It is the relentless transformation of urban geographies that engenders the need for a continual revision and even reinvention of the theoretical categories and frameworks of interpretation used to investigate the latter. The abstractions mobilized in the field of critical urban theory are, therefore, not merely devices of conceptual simplification, but are embedded within and shaped by the same restlessly shifting geographies of capitalist urbanization they aspire to illuminate: they are, in this sense, concrete abstractions.[25]

Since its early twentieth-century origins, the field of urban studies has conceived the city as a specific unit and type of settlement space, one that is thought to be fundamentally different and spatially distinct from the non-city zones that lie beyond it—such as suburbs, towns, villages, rural areas, countryside, and wilderness. Chicago school urban sociologists, mainstream land economists, central place theorists, UN urban demographers, neo-Marxian geographers, and global city theorists have understood the basis of this specificity in vastly divergent ways, but all have engaged in the broadly shared analytical maneuver of delineating urban distinctiveness through an explicit or implied contrast of cities to settlement zones and sociospatial conditions located outside their boundaries. It is in this sense that the terrain of the non-city has served as a "constitutive outside" for inherited urban epistemologies. This perpetually present exterior domain stabilizes the very intelligibility of urban studies as a coherent field of research, enabling, anchoring, and, quite literally, *enframing* its persistent focus on the diverse spatial interiors of city life—agglomeration, density, innovation, diversity, creativity, verticality, and so forth. The space of the non-city thus appears simultaneously as the ontological Other of the city/urban, its radical opposite, and as its epistemological condition of possibility, the very basis on which it can be recognized, demarcated, and investigated as such (Figures 10.2 and 10.3).

Much of twentieth-century urban studies has, then, presupposed a settlement-based conception of territorial organization—a world composed of discrete, bounded units, of which "the" city is claimed to be a universally diffused type. In epistemological terms, the construction of such settlement typologies has hinged upon delineating nominal essences through which the

---

[25] See Łukasz Stanek, *Henri Lefebvre on Space: Architecture, Urban Research and the Production of Theory* (Minneapolis: University of Minnesota Press, 2011), 151–56; Christian Schmid, *Stadt, Raum und Gesellschaft: Henri Lefebvre und die Theorie der Produktion des Raumes* (Stuttgart: Franz Steiner Verlag, 2005).

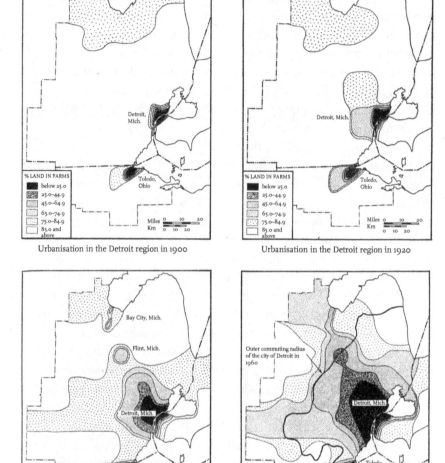

FIGURE 10.2 The urban/rural interface as a function of agrarian land use. In this time-series representation from the early 1970s, Brian Berry used a simple empirical indicator to demarcate the changing urban/rural interface—the percentage of land allocated to agricultural functions. (Source: Brian Berry, *The Human Consequences of Urbanization* [New York: St. Martin's, 1973], 39–42.)

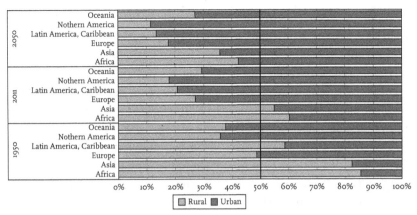

FIGURE 10.3 The urbanization of the world? The United Nations' demographic vision. The United Nations continues to measure urbanization as a function of population growth within "cities": settlement units that, according to national census bureaus, are classified as "urban." This measurement strategy hinges upon the definitional contrast of such units to a vast, putatively nonurban exterior, classified under the homogenizing rubric of "the" rural. This data table is from a major 2012 UN report on urbanization but is typical of the influential approach that has been used by this organization for over four decades. (Source: United Nations Department of Economic and Social Affairs, Population Division, *World Urbanization Prospects, the 2011 Revision* [New York: United Nations, 2012].)

putatively distinctive social and/or spatial characteristics of their key classificatory units (cities, metropolitan regions, towns, villages, rural areas, or otherwise) could be understood. Despite their otherwise significant differences of epistemology, conceptualization, methodology, and politics, this basic theoretical operation underpinned all of the major research traditions in twentieth-century urban studies: the spatial demarcation of distinct, coherently individuated urban "units," whether at local, metropolitan, or regional scales, was accomplished precisely through arguments and assumptions regarding the nominal essences that were thought to inhere within them. By contrast, a revitalized approach to urban theory in the early twenty-first century must prioritize the investigation of constitutive essences—the core *processes* through which urban(izing) geographies are produced, tendentially stabilized, and recurrently transformed.[26] Insofar as a rigorously processual approach deconstructs the forms of settlement fetishism, localism,

---

[26] The distinction between nominal and constitutive essences is derived from Sayer, "Defining the Urban." In this critical realist discourse, "essence" connotes the core analytic elements of a phenomenon, entity, or process, as specified in a historical and geographical context of investigation. They are thus not transhistorical, ontologically fixed essences lodged within what Louis Althusser famously termed an "expressive totality," but emerge through theorists' (contextually

territorialism, and city-centrism that have long been naturalized among urban researchers, it provides a generative epistemological starting point for confronting emergent sociospatial transformations that are currently reworking inherited formations of the capitalist urban fabric.

The point here is not that tendentially stabilized sociospatial configurations no longer exist or should no longer be of interest for urban researchers. On the contrary, as I have argued throughout this book, the establishment of relatively fixed, tendentially stabilized configurations of the capitalist urban fabric is at once an endemic moment within the contradictory metabolism of capital and a strategic goal of state institutions and diverse territorial alliances seeking to position themselves within (or, in some cases, against) that metabolism. Such scaled and territorialized configurations of the urban fabric continue to crystallize under early twenty-first-century conditions through, for example, the formation of metropolitan regions, megalopolises, national territorial matrices, transnational communications networks, continental and intercontinental pipelines and logistics corridors, and a wide range of additional spatial infrastructures of production, circulation, and social reproduction. As such, they must obviously remain a central focal point for critical urban studies. My argument, then, is that the analytical core of the urban question involves theorizing and investigating the underlying *processes* that at once constitute and recurrently destabilize such sociospatial configurations, thus rendering their apparent fixity merely provisional. In large part because they are so volatile and variegated, the nominal essences that may be provisionally materialized within such configurations represent a second-order dimension of the urban *problematique*. The first-order conceptualization of urban processes—the dialectics of urbanization itself—provides the analytical foundation for the subsequent, second-order analysis of their shifting manifestations within historically and geographically specific sociospatial configurations.

---

embedded, socially mediated) attempts to explicate the meaning of problematic concepts for reflexive use in social inquiry. On process-based, relational approaches to sociospatial theory, see Sheppard, "Geographic Dialectics"; as well as David Harvey, *Justice, Nature and the Geography of Difference* (Oxford: Basil Blackwell, 1996); David Harvey, "Space as a Keyword," in *Spaces of Global Capitalism* (New York: Verso, 2006), 117–54; and Doreen Massey, *For Space* (London: Sage, 2005). Variants of the process-based approach advocated here have long underpinned historical-geographical materialist approaches to sociospatial theory, but, with a few major exceptions, their radical implications for the epistemological foundations of urban research have yet to be fully elaborated. For foundational discussions, see David Harvey, "Cities or Urbanization?," *CITY* 1, no. 1–2 (1996): 38–61; and Erik Swyngedouw, "Metabolic Urbanization: The Making of Cyborg Cities," in *In the Nature of Cities*, ed. Nik Heynen, Maria Kaika, and Erik Swyngedouw (New York: Routledge, 2006), 21–62.

Patterns and Pathways of Urbanization, Unbounded

Under early twenty-first-century capitalism, urbanization processes are being consolidated, stratified, differentiated, and multiplied across the planet in ways that problematize inherited conceptions of the city and the urban as interior zones bounded off from, and surrounded by, a vast, nonurban exterior. Under these conditions, the inherited inside/outside dualism offers an impoverished conceptual, methodological, and cartographic foundation for exploring these ongoing sociospatial transformations, whether in abstract analytical terms or with reference to specific world-regional contexts. The claim here is not that a uniform urban skein is being rolled out across the earth to form a continuous, planet-encompassing agglomeration, akin to the Death Star in the *Star Wars* films or the planet of Trantor in Isaac Asimov's classic sci-fi book series *Foundation*, in which there are no morphological striations or density gradients in the built environment. The point, rather, is that our ability to decipher the constitutively uneven, restlessly evolving landscapes of planetary urbanization will be severely constrained if we continue to conceive the world as a patchwork of coherently bounded, discretely individuated settlement units, with the urban understood as one generic, universally diffused type among the latter.[27]

In thus advocating an approach to urban theory that transcends the inherited ontology of bounded spatial units, settlement typologies, and

---

[27] In a previous text, I framed this argument around the notion of an "urban theory without an outside." See Neil Brenner, "Introduction: Urban Theory without an Outside," in *Implosions/Explosions: Towards a Study of Planetary Urbanization*, ed. Neil Brenner (Berlin: Jovis, 2014), 14–35. However, this formulation has proven contentious; it has been widely misunderstood as a call for a universalizing epistemology of the urban based on a masculinist, Eurocentric "god's eye" view of the processes under investigation. In a subsequent exchange, I attempted to clarify this position, in part by replacing my earlier formulation with that of an "urban theory without an inside/outside dualism"—see Neil Brenner, "Debating Planetary Urbanization: Towards an Engaged Pluralism," *Environment and Planning D: Society and Space* 36, no. 3 (2018): 570–90. The key issue at stake here is thus less the reference to an "outside" as such than the conceptual and cartographic demarcation of the urban through the figure of a divide or a border, generally conceived dualistically with reference to the urban/nonurban distinction. My argument is that boundary thinking—the conception of the urban as a discretely individuated spatial unit—severely limits our ability to grasp its variegated, uneven, dynamically mutating sociospatial patterns and pathways. The claim that urbanization cannot be grasped adequately through the spatial ontology of boundedness or territorial enclosure should thus not be misconstrued as an intellectually imperialistic assertion that this process has necessary explanatory primacy over others that may also shape sociospatial relations. There are, of course, many important processes in the world that are not subsumed under or explained by the process of capitalist urbanization, whether at the planetary scale or otherwise. One might, however, reasonably speculate that many significant dynamics of political-economic and ecological transformation are today increasingly likely to coevolve with urbanization in ways that require much closer analytical scrutiny.

interior/exterior divides, Christian Schmid and I have been calling for a broader debate regarding how we might more adequately conceptualize, investigate, and visualize early twenty-first-century processes of urban transformation. Even if these geographies are not coherently enframed within neatly individuated, container-like spatial units, they are still being articulated in determinate territorial patterns and metabolic pathways that require systematic investigation and theorization.[28] From this point of view, recent contributions to urban theory that emphasize or even celebrate the putative indeterminacy, heterogeneity, and unknowability of emergent urban life-forms contain significant epistemic blind spots and political limitations.[29] In effect, they abandon the project of deciphering the "commonalities in difference, generalized processes [and] recurrent patterns" that are crystallizing across the uneven landscapes of planetary urbanization, and in so doing, they render invisible the "structurally enabled powers" associated with ongoing processes of accumulation by dispossession under neoliberalizing capitalism that continue to shape the very phenomena, conditions, and contestations they misrecognize as radical contingencies.[30] One of the major challenges of critical urban studies today is precisely to develop reinvented conceptual, methodological, and cartographic tools through which researchers might more adequately decipher the ongoing production of these new urban spaces and the forms of structural violence, exclusion, and injustice they perpetuate.

Because of its ostensible orientation toward the *problematique* of constitutive essences—processes rather than units—the concept of urbanization would appear to offer an essential basis for confronting this formidable task. To serve this purpose, however, the concept must be systematically reclaimed from the myopically city-centric theorizations that have to date

---

[28] For productive inroads into such an investigation, grounded upon reflexive theorization and concrete, site-specific, and methodologically heterodox research forays, see the foundational contributions by Roger Diener, Jacques Herzog, Marcel Meili, Pierre de Meuron, and Christian Schmid, eds., *Switzerland: An Urban Portrait*, 4 vols. (Zurich: Birkhaüser, 2001); and Alessandro Balducci, Valeria Fedeli, and Francesco Curci, eds., *Post-Metropolitan Territories: Looking for a New Urbanity* (London: Routledge, 2017). Each of these works attempts to analyze emergent patterns and pathways of urbanization (in Switzerland and Italy, respectively) without recourse to inherited urban/rural binarisms or settlement-based understandings of sociospatial differentiation. It remains to be seen whether the concepts and methods elaborated in these books might prove useful, or might at least offer some orientation, for the investigation of patterns and pathways of urban transformation in the BRICS territories or in other zones of incipient or intensifying industrial development.

[29] See, for example, Ash Amin and Nigel Thrift, *Seeing Like a City* (Cambridge: Polity, 2016); and Ignacio Farias and Thomas Bender, eds., *Urban Assemblages: How Actor-Network Theory Changes Urban Studies* (New York: Routledge, 2011).

[30] The quoted phrases are from Peck, "Cities beyond Compare," 177.

monopolized its analytic deployment across the social sciences, the environmental humanities, and the design disciplines. Indeed, with a few notable exceptions, all major inherited approaches to urbanization define this process with reference to its putatively universal spatial *outcome*: the growth of "the" city, along with any nominal essences claimed to be associated with the latter, such as agglomeration economies or large, densely concentrated, diverse populations. In effect, within mainstream approaches, the notion of urbanization is reduced to that of "*city*ization," as more literally conveyed in the German term *Verstädterung*.[31] Within this definitional universe, the question of the urban as such—its specificity as a historical-geographical process, configuration, mediation, and relation—is completely bypassed or black-boxed, or else narrowed to the investigation of those of its sociospatial manifestations that are most immediately connected to the phenomenon of cityness, as the latter is conceived within a particular research tradition. It is logically impossible, on the basis of this city-centric *episteme*, to consider (1) whether urbanization processes might not entail the universalization of a singular spatial form or unit, be it the city or otherwise, and (2) whether urbanization processes might engender essential (rather than merely contingent or secondary) sociospatial manifestations that are not contained within cities or directly expressed in the formation of city-like spatial units.

A reinvented conceptualization of urbanization must systematically explore both of these possibilities, at once as theoretical provocations, as starting points for concrete historical-political inquiry, and as openings toward alternative modes of spatial representation. We need, in short, theories and investigations not simply of "cityization," but of *urbanization*.[32] This

---

[31] In philological terms, the city/urban distinction in English derives from the Latin distinction between *civitas* and *urbs*. Like the Greek concept of *polis*, *civitas* connotes a bounded political space formed by social relationships and public associations, generally among free individuals or citizens (as literally expressed in the French, Italian, and Spanish terms *citoyen*, *cittadino*, and *ciudadano*). By contrast, *urbs* connotes an infrastructure of sociospatial interdependence— including buildings, walls, bridges, roads, and other transport and communications links. As such, the material geographies of the *urbs* extend beyond the boundaries of any specific settlement unit. On these distinctions, their historical evolution, and their possible contemporary manifestations, see Choay, "Le régne de l'urbain et la mort de la ville"; as well as Engin Isin, "Historical Sociology of the City," in *Handbook of Historical Sociology*, ed. Gerard Delanty and Engin Isin (London: Sage, 2003), 312–36; Engin Isin, "The City as the Site of the Social," in *Recasting the Social in Citizenship*, ed. Engin Isin (Toronto: University of Toronto Press, 2008), 261–80; and Pier Vittorio Aureli, *The Possibility of an Absolute Architecture* (Cambridge, MA: MIT Press, 2011).

[32] In an "analytic" proposition, truth is derived simply from the assumed meaning of its constituent terms: the predicate and the subject mutually contain one another, as in "A bachelor is an unmarried man" or "A triangle has three sides." For much of the last century, the proposition that "Urbanization = city growth" has been treated precisely in this way, as a logical truism. By

is, it seems to me, exactly what Françoise Choay had in mind when, over two decades ago, she underscored the urgency of theorizing not only the city but *the urban*.[33] The sociospatial configurations (and, by implication, the nominal essences) that have been associated with cityness *may* in fact be intrinsically connected to historically specific forms of urbanization, but that link must be reflexively interrogated and theoretically clarified rather than being treated as a logical necessity. To the degree that scholars conceive the articulation of urbanization to city building as an a priori definitional essence, they naturalize key elements of the very sociospatial processes that need to be subjected to critical analysis, while marginalizing or rendering invisible other, potentially essential dimensions of urbanization that may not directly materialize within cities or city-like spatial configurations. It is precisely in this sense, as Henri Lefebvre classically argued in *The Urban Revolution*, that the "urban" dimension of urbanization requires reflexive, systematic theoretical interrogation and critical reinvention in relation to the variegated, constitutively multiscalar implosions and explosions of late modern capitalism.[34]

Notably, various versions of this alternative epistemology of the urban were articulated within several largely subterranean traditions of postwar urban theory and research, including in the heterodox writings of architect and planner Constantinos Doxiadis, urban geographer Terry McGee, historical sociologist Charles Tilly, and, of course, Lefebvre himself. For these diverse urban thinkers, the "urban" dimension of urbanization referred less to the spatial generalization of cityness *tout court* than to the consolidation of, among other elements, a specifically modern formation of industrial territorial organization; the extension of large-scale, state-managed sociospatial interdependencies; and accelerated circulation (of labor, commodities, and politico-cultural forms), as well as to the variegated transformations, crises,

---

contrast, I am arguing here that the connection of urbanization to city growth is not established *analytically* through the meaning of either term. While I certainly do not deny the existence and importance of that connection, I insist that both terms of the proposition, and their relationship, require theoretical specification in relation to particular epistemologies of inquiry and the historical-geographical contexts they aspire to illuminate. On analytic propositions and related philosophical debates among Kantians, logical positivists, and critics of the concept such as W. V. Quine, see Edward J. Lowe, "Analytic and Synthetic Statements," in *The Oxford Companion to Philosophy*, 2nd ed., ed. Ted Honderich, (Oxford: Oxford University Press, 2005), 29.

[33] Choay, "Le régne de l'urbain," 33. See also Ross Exo Adams, "Natura Urbans, Natura Urbanata: Ecological Urbanism, Circulation and the Immunization of Nature," *Environment and Planning D: Society and Space* 32, no. 1 (2014): 12–29.

[34] Lefebvre, *Urban Revolution*.

conflicts, and insurgencies induced through those processes.[35] Cities, metropolitan regions, and other zones of agglomeration do indeed crystallize as key, enduring elements within the sociospatial maelstrom of capitalist urbanization, but the latter cannot be defined exclusively with reference to the dynamics of agglomeration or the citylike built environments engendered through that process. While the writings of these and allied authors must obviously be understood in relation to the specific contexts and research traditions in which they were working, such dissident streams of urban theorizing have acquired a renewed significance and fascination in relation to early twenty-first-century sociospatial transformations (Figures 10.4 and 10.5).

Dialectics of Concentrated and Extended Urbanization

Urban theory has long conceived urbanization primarily with reference to the condition of agglomeration—the dense concentration of population, infrastructure, and investment at certain locations on a broader, less densely settled territorial surface. While the morphology of such concentrations is recognized to shift over time, it is above all with reference to this basic sociospatial tendency and its expressions in the built environment that urbanization has generally been defined. However, rather than conceptualizing the spatial expressions of such historically and geographically variegated agglomeration processes under the universal rubric of "the" city, the intellectual horizons of urban theory can be productively expanded through the investigation of variations in the politico-economic causes, institutional mediations, scalar articulations, and sociospatial consequences of agglomeration processes during successive cycles of modern capitalist industrialization, and across diverse geopolitical and world-regional contexts. Contrary to the universalizing epistemologies embraced by many contemporary urban economists and urban economic geographers, such an inquiry is likely to reveal the historical and geographical specificity, and even exceptionalism, of many of the most widely invoked explanatory models of agglomeration, such

---

[35] On Doxiadis, see Nikos Katsikis, "Two Approaches to World Urbanization: R. B. Fuller and C. A. Doxiadis," in Brenner, *Implosions/Explosions*, 480–504. See also Terry McGee, *The Urbanization Process in the Third World* (London: Bell and Sons, 1971); and Charles Tilly, *The Vendée: A Sociological Analysis of the Counter-Revolution of 1793* (Cambridge, MA: Harvard University Press, 1973). For further discussion of Tilly's idiosyncratic but sociologically pathbreaking conceptualization of urbanization, see William Sewell, "Charles Tilly's *Vendée* as a Model for Social History," *French Historical Studies* 33, no. 2 (2010): 307–15.

as that of the Marshallian industrial district.[36] As enduring and fundamental as they are, agglomeration processes vary qualitatively across time and space, in relation to, among other shaping factors, (1) the political economy of capitalist industrialization across sectors, places, and territories; (2) the expanding scales at which external economies are organized; (3) the evolution of state spatial structures and strategies; (4) energetic regimes, their distribution networks, and their geopolitics; (5) shifting modes of surplus extraction and absorption; (6) patterns of uneven spatial development; and (7) ongoing sociopolitical struggles over the general conditions of production, circulation, and reproduction.[37] Accordingly, Christian Schmid and I have introduced the concept of concentrated urbanization to help frame more theoretically reflexive, dialectical, and historically specific modes of inquiry into such systemically patterned spatiotemporal variegations (Figures 10.6 and 10.7).[38]

While the agglomeration question has long monopolized the analytical attention of most urban researchers, considerably less attention has been devoted to what may be characterized as "the hinterland question"—namely, the exploration of how agglomeration processes have been intertwined with wide-ranging sociospatial, infrastructural, and ecological transformations beyond metropolitan centers and their immediately contiguous regions. Though largely ignored or relegated to the analytic background by contemporary urban theorists, the territorial enclosure, demographic fracturing, industrial activation, infrastructuralization, spatial rationalization, ecological

---

[36] See Nicholas Phelps and Terutomo Ozawa, "Contrasts in Agglomeration: Proto-Industrial, Industrial and Post-Industrial Forms Compared," *Progress in Human Geography* 27, no. 5 (2003): 583–604; and Ash Amin and Nigel Thrift, "Neo-Marshallian Nodes in Global Networks," *International Journal of Urban and Regional Research* 16, no. 4 (1992): 571–87.

[37] In developing their foundational argument, Phelps and Ozawa borrow their title from an earlier intervention by urban economist Benjamin Chinitz, which elaborated a closely parallel, midcentury analysis of sectoral specificity in agglomeration processes—see Chinitz, "Contrasts in Agglomeration: New York and Pittsburgh," *American Economic Review* 51, no. 2 (1961): 279–89. See also Walker, "Why Cities?"; as well as Richard Walker and Robert D. Lewis, "Beyond the Crabgrass Frontier: Industry and the Spread of North American Cities, 1850–1950," *Journal of Historical Geography* 27, no. 1 (2001): 3–19; and Edward Soja, "Regional Urbanization and the End of the Metropolis Era," in *The New Blackwell Companion to the City*, ed. Gary Bridge and Sophie Watson (Oxford: Blackwell, 2011), 679–89. Perhaps unexpectedly, these historically oriented approaches to the shifting geographies of agglomeration strongly articulate, in epistemological terms, to Ananya Roy's powerful postcolonial critique of universalizing theories of the city, which likewise advocates for more contextually grounded analyses and explanations of urban sociospatial arrangements—see, for instance, Ananya Roy, "Who's Afraid of Postcolonial Theory?," *International Journal of Urban and Regional Research* 40, no. 1 (2016): 200–9.

[38] Brenner and Schmid, "Towards a New Epistemology of the Urban." For further critical reflections on concentrated urbanization and the limits of inherited approaches to agglomeration theory, see Christian Schmid, "The Agglomeration Question, Revisited," Working Paper, Contemporary City Institute, Department of Architecture, ETH Zurich, July 2018.

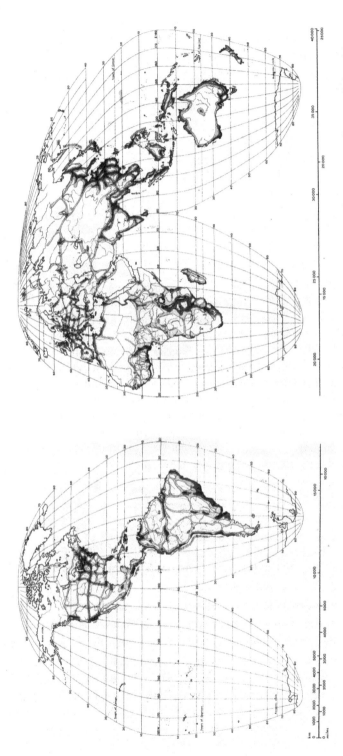

FIGURE 10.4 Doxiadis's speculative vision of a planetary urban fabric. In the early 1970s, Constantinos Doxiadis constructed a speculative vision of world urbanization that postulated the formation of large-scale bands of settlement girding much of the globe, especially along coastlines and major transport corridors. His corresponding map of the worldwide "ecumenopolis" did not depict individual cities or any other discrete settlement units. Instead, it set into relief a rhizomatic proliferation of zones, circuits, and networks whose contours were delineated with reference to differential population densities, connectivity gradients, and corresponding variations in the intensity of human activity. (Source: C. A. Doxiadis and J. G. Papaioannou, *Ecumenopolis: The Inevitable City of the Future* [New York: W. W. Norton, 1974], 368–69.)

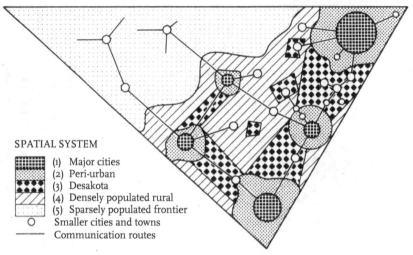

FIGURE 10.5 The extended metropolis in Asia. In developing his critique of "city dominant" approaches to urbanization in Southeast Asia during the 1970s and 1980s, Terry McGee introduced the concept of a *desakota* region (the term literally means "village-city" in Indonesian) to map the uneven boundary between city and non-city spaces. His pioneering work explored the seasonal fluctuation of population levels across this boundary in conjunction with wet-rice harvest cycles and associated patterns of labor migration. In this way, McGee offered a devastating critique of attempts to demarcate a rigidly territorial border separating urban and agrarian lifeworlds. In so doing, he also developed a suggestive alternative mapping of the dense interdependencies among overlapping land-use systems and labor geographies within these extended metropolitan zones. For McGee, the fabric of modern urbanization crosscut the urban/rural divide, and thus problematized both terms of this dualism, at least in their conventional, mainstream meanings. (Source: Terry McGee, "The Emergence of *Desakota* Regions in Asia: Expanding a Hypothesis," in *The Extended Metropolis*, ed. N. Ginsburg, B. Koppel, and T. McGee [Honolulu: University of Hawaii Press, 1991], 6.)

devastation, and periodic, crisis-induced restructuring of hinterland zones has, especially during the last 150 years, been systematically interconnected with processes of concentrated urbanization.

Within this extended field of capitalist industrial transformation, a progressively thickening mesh of large-scale, long-distance infrastructural equipment serves to articulate metropolitan agglomerations ever more tightly to diverse realms of primary commodity production (and associated circulatory relays and metabolic processes) that are traditionally classified as being exterior to the urban condition. The latter include, for example, industrial farmlands, agribusiness corridors, and their extended irrigation infrastructures; terrestrial, subterranean, and maritime landscapes of resource extraction; industrial and plantation forestry; aquaculture and

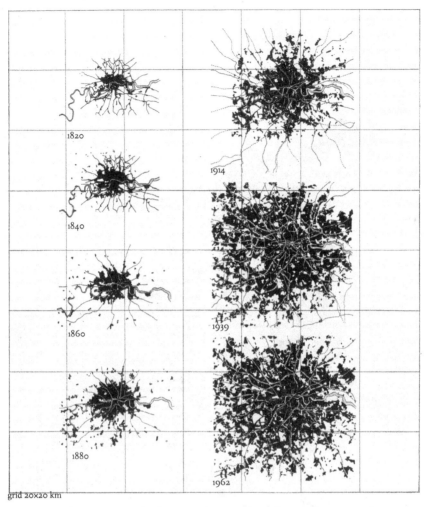

1820

1914

1840

1860

1939

1880

1962

grid 20x20 km

FIGURE 10.6 Concentrated urbanization in London, 1820–1962. During the evolution of modern capitalism, the scale of concentrated urbanization has expanded considerably—as Doxiadis's classic 1968 representation of London's long-term spatial evolution illustrates. With the proliferation of increasingly fine-grained geospatial data sources, the expansion of urban land cover is today among the most well-documented dimensions of contemporary urban sociospatial restructuring. Doxiadis's depiction of this process relied on more conventional, terrestrially grounded data sources, but it yielded a striking time-series visualization that closely resembles those that are now being widely disseminated through the use of satellite-based monitoring systems such as NASA's Landsat. (Source: Constantinos Doxiadis, *Ekistics. An Introduction to the Science of Human Settlements* [New York: Oxford University Press, 1968], 200. For urban Landsat data, see http://sedac.ciesin.columbia.edu/data/set/ulandsat-cities-from-space/maps/2.)

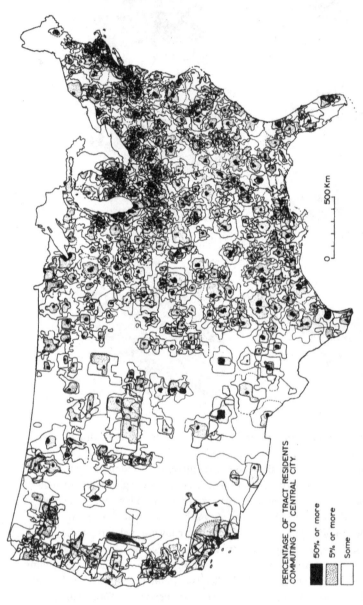

PERCENTAGE OF TRACT RESIDENTS
COMMUTING TO CENTRAL CITY

50% or more

5% or more

Some

FIGURE 10.7 Commuting zones and the concentration of the urban fabric. The process of concentrated urbanization encompasses the daily circulation of workers within and around large-scale agglomerations. Geographer Brian Berry pioneered the systematic mapping of such labor geographies in the 1960s, but he equated them with the decentralization of urban development—a process to which he idiosyncratically referred as "deurbanization." By contrast, as conceived here, these metropolitan geographies of the working day embody the expanding scales on which concentrated urbanization is organized, both in socioeconomic and infrastructural terms. (Source: Brian J. L. Berry, *Geographic Perspectives on Urban Systems* [Englewood Cliffs, NJ: Prentice Hall, 1970], 44–45.)

fishing territories; energy supply infrastructures, including those associated with coal, petroleum, natural gas, nuclear, hydropower, and "renewables," whether on land or sea; canals, dams, irrigation networks, paved waterways, sewage·pipes, and other engineered water management systems; interconti-nental transport corridors (road, rail, air), pipelines, and transoceanic ship-ping lanes; planetary communications grids, data storage infrastructures, information-processing networks, and satellite orbits; and waste disposal systems, garbage dumps, and other zones of industrially induced environ-mental degradation. Rather than relegating these diverse, nonagglomerative spaces of capitalist industrial metabolism to an exterior, nonurban realm of putative "ghost acreage"—whether labeled as hinterland, countryside, rural, wilderness, or otherwise—Christian Schmid and I have proposed to explore the ongoing industrial operationalization of the latter as an essential mo-ment and expression of the capitalist form of urbanization: *extended* urbani-zation (Figure 10.8).[39]

The process of extended urbanization is dialectically intertwined with that of concentrated urbanization, and ever more so as the creatively destructive forward motion of capitalist industrialization intensifies, leading to the con-solidation of more tightly integrated, if chronically volatile, unevenly artic-ulated, and deeply stratified, planetary-scale production networks.[40] In this

---

[39] Brenner and Schmid, "Towards a New Epistemology of the Urban." Although the term "ghost acreage" has a longer lineage connected to postwar, neo-Malthusian studies of food supply shortages, it is used here in the specific sense proposed by critical geographer Gavin Bridge to describe ideological concepts of the hinterland as an "asocial void, a depopulated space without socioecological complexity existing outside time and space"—see Bridge, "Resource Triumphalism: Postindustrial Narratives of Primary Commodity Production," *Environment and Planning A* 33 (2001): 2154. For a more detailed discussion and critique of inherited conceptions of the hinterland as ghost acreage, see Neil Brenner, "Extended Urbanization and the Hinterland Question: Towards the Real Subsumption of the Planet?," Working Paper, Urban Theory Lab, Graduate School of Design, Harvard University, June 2018.

[40] The concept of extended urbanization was first introduced by Roberto-Luis Monte-Mór in his pioneering studies of the production of industrialized urban spaces and networks in the Brazilian Amazon. The term was subsequently used in a different sense by Edward Soja to characterize the changing morphologies of (in our terms) concentrated urbanization under postmetropolitan capitalism. For key texts, see Roberto Luis Monte-Mór, "Extended Urbanization and Settlement Patterns: An Environmental Approach," in Brenner, *Implosions/Explosions*, 109–20; as well as Soja, "Regional Urbanization" and the other contributions to *Implosions/ Explosions*. The conception of extended urbanization proposed here, and in my collaborative work with Christian Schmid, is closest to that developed by Monte-Mór: it refers to the construc-tion and transformation of nonagglomerative, extrametropolitan zones of capitalist industrial activity that at once support and result from the dynamics of metropolitan industrial concen-tration. This entails, in Monte-Mór's precise formulation, "the *de facto* extension of industrial forms of organization onto the configuration of an entire territory, now penetrated by the logics of capitalism" (111). For an incisive overview and contemporary application of Monte-Mór's theory in relation to contemporary international debates, see Rodrigo Castriota and João Tonucci

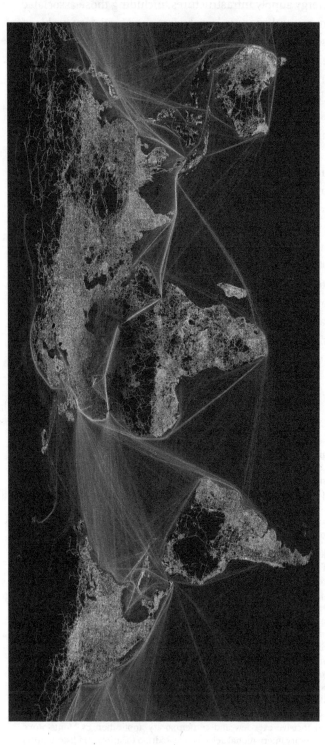

FIGURE 10.8 Veins of the urban fabric: worldwide transportation infrastructures. The development of urban agglomerations hinges upon increasingly dense, worldwide transportation infrastructures: insofar as they constitute a key scaffolding for the capitalist urban fabric's spatial articulation, operationalization, and evolution, they are an essential expression of extended urbanization. Such infrastructures may be viewed as the "veins" through which the sociospatial metabolism of urbanization is stimulated, intensified, reproduced, and reconfigured, albeit always in unevenly variegated, restlessly shifting patterns and pathways. (Source: Nikos Katsikis, Urban Theory Lab, Harvard-GSD; compilation of road, rail, and marine transportation networks. Road and rail networks are based on the Vector Map Level o [VMap0] dataset released by the National Imagery and Mapping Agency [NIMA] in 1997. Marine routes are based on the global commercial activity [shipping] dataset compiled by the National Center for Ecological Analysis and Synthesis [NCEAS], http://www.nceas.ucsb.edu/globalmarine.)

way, the variegated spaces of extended urbanization—their labor markets, property relations, land-use patterns, infrastructural configurations, industrial operations, modes of social reproduction, and metabolic circuits—are more tightly enmeshed within the thickening filaments of the capitalist urban fabric while also being more directly subjected to the pulsating rhythms of implosion-explosion that continually reshape its unstable geographies. They thus represent a key expression of the forms of violent spatial abstraction that at once underpin and result from the industrial metabolism of capital.[41] As such, processes of extended urbanization also serve as a medium and outcome for (historically and geographically specific expressions of) capital's fixity/motion contradiction, as theorized and explored throughout this book.

Crucially, extended urbanization involves not only the private appropriation and commodification of extrametropolitan resources (including labor, land, raw materials, fuel, food and water) to support metropolitan centers, but entails, more specifically, the *industrial* transformation of the hinterland spaces in which such resources are procured and produced. This results in the mutation of those spaces—or specific infrastructural assemblages within them—into what may be termed "operational landscapes": zones whose sociospatial and ecological relations are rationalized, infrastructuralized, and recurrently reorganized to support the metabolism of capitalist industrialization in more or less direct relation to the shifting dynamics of concentrated urbanization.[42] As understood here, the crystallization of operational

---

Filho, "Extended Urbanization in and from Brazil," *Environment and Planning D: Society and Space* 36, no. 3 (2018): 512–28. See also, most recently, Roberto Luis Monte-Mór and Rodrigo Castriota, "Extended Urbanization: Implications for Urban and Regional Theory," in *Handbook on the Geographies of Regions and Territories*, ed. Anssi Paasi, John Harrison, and Martin Jones (London: Edward Elgar, 2018), 332–45. On transnational production networks, see Neil Coe and Henry Yeung, *Global Production Networks: Theorizing Economic Development in an Interconnected World* (New York: Oxford University Press, 2015).

[41] On the abstraction of space under capitalism and its manifold contradictions, see Henri Lefebvre, *The Production of Space*, trans. Donald Nicholson-Smith (Cambridge: Blackwell, 1991 [1974]). See also Stanek, *Henri Lefebvre on Space*; and Japhy Wilson, "The Violence of Abstract Space: Contested Regional Development in Southern Mexico," *International Journal of Urban and Regional Research* 38, no. 2 (2014): 516–38.

[42] Neil Brenner, "Urban Revolution?" and "The Hinterland, Urbanized?," in *Critique of Urbanization*, 192–233. The conception of the (industrializing) hinterland as an operational landscape of urbanization has emerged through years of dialogue with Nikos Katsikis, who coined the phrase. See, in particular, Nikos Katsikis, "The Composite Fabric of Urbanization: Agglomeration Landscapes and Operational Landscapes; From Hinterland to Hinterglobe: Urbanization as Geographical Organization" (doctoral diss., Harvard University Graduate School of Design, 2016); as well as Nikos Katsikis, "The 'Other' Horizontal Metropolis: Landscapes of Urban Interdependence," in *The Horizontal Metropolis between Urbanism and Urbanization*, ed. Paola Viganò, Chiara Cavalieri, and Martina Barcelloni Corte (Berlin: Springer, 2018), 23–46.

landscapes involves the systematic mobilization of modern science and technology, embodied in machinery, infrastructure, territorial organization, and comprehensively engineered land-use configurations, to enhance productivity—not only of labor, but of nature itself—within large-scale, progressively worldwide circuits of capital.[43] In this sense, the construction of operational landscapes involves the reconfiguration of extrametropolitan spatial arrangements and biophysical processes to facilitate increasingly mechanized and/or robotized forms of production and circulation, with correspondingly destructive implications for inherited rhythms of work, land use, and social reproduction, as well as for the ecological web of life, throughout significant swaths of the erstwhile global countryside.[44] For

---

[43] On the industrialization of primary commodity production under capitalism, see William Boyd, W. Scott Prudham, and Rachel Shurman, "Industrial Dynamics and the Problem of Nature," *Society and Natural Resources* 14, no. 7 (2001): 555–70. Insofar as productivity may be enhanced through the acceleration of capital's turnover time and/or the manipulation of biophysical processes to standardize, stabilize, or maximize primary commodity outputs, this formulation includes the moments of production and circulation, as well as the dynamics of ecological transformation. My argument here closely parallels Boyd, Prudham, and Shurman's use of the key Marxian distinction between formal and real subsumption. Whereas Marx deploys that distinction to analyze the transformation of labor exploitation under capitalism (specifically, the shift from absolute to relative surplus-value extraction), Boyd and his colleagues apply it to study the capitalist transformation of nature (specifically, the shift from capitalist production *in* nature to the capitalist production *of* nature). Building upon their insights, I suggest the distinction may also prove helpful for investigating the sociospatial and ecological transformation of extrametropolitan zones during the process of capitalist urbanization. Under capitalism, *hinterlands* are formed through the *formal subsumption* of spatial organization to capital: resources contained therein (such as labor, raw materials, nutrients, and fuel) are appropriated, commodified, and put into market circulation. In contrast, *operational landscapes* (of extended urbanization) are forged through strategies to accomplish the *real subsumption* of spatial organization under capital: here, the configuration of territorial arrangements, land-use systems, infrastructural grids, and metabolic circuits is engineered specifically to maximize surplus-value extraction, and thus to rationalize, intensify, and accelerate the accumulation process. On this reading, it is precisely through the transformation of hinterlands into operational landscapes that extrametropolitan spaces and ecologies become integrally interwoven into the capitalist urban fabric. Whereas hinterlands are configured to channel key sociomaterial inputs into an extrinsically situated process of industrial urban development, operational landscapes are themselves transformed into urban-industrial spaces. As such, they serve as a medium and expression of extended urbanization. This line of argumentation is further elaborated in Brenner, "Extended Urbanization and the Hinterland Question."

[44] See Arboleda, "Financialization, Totality and Planetary Urbanization"; Arboleda, *Planetary Mine*; Zoomers et al., "The Rush for Land in an Urbanizing World"; and Mazen Labban, "Deterritorializing Extraction: Bioaccumulation and the Planetary Mine," *Annals of the Association of American Geographers* 104, no. 3 (2014): 560–76. On the catastrophic ecological dimensions of large-scale industrial development in erstwhile hinterlands, see Saskia Sassen's discussion of "dead land, dead water" in *Expulsions: Brutality and Complexity in the Global Economy* (Cambridge, MA: Harvard University Press, 2014); as well as Naomi Klein's analysis of "sacrifice zones" in *This Changes Everything: Capitalism vs. the Climate* (New York: Simon & Schuster, 2015).

instance, across otherwise diverse historical-geographical contexts, the re-configuration of hinterlands into operational landscapes has been closely intertwined with processes of depeasantization and associated forms of mass population displacement, thus contributing directly to what Farshad Araghi has precisely termed "deruralization": prodigious population decline in rural or formerly rural zones, coupled with a concomitantly dramatic demographic expansion within the world's rapidly expanding megacities.[45] This is but one salient expression of the dialectics of concentrated and extended urbanization in action: labor informalization and autoconstruction practices within megacities are inextricably connected to the dynamics of territorial enclosure, industrial transformation, and mass displacement in the erstwhile countryside.

These considerations suggest, on the one hand, that the everyday metabolic operations of agglomerations (industrial or global cities, metropolitan regions, inter-metropolitan networks, and the like)—including at the planetary scale of the world city archipelago discussed in Chapter 4—must be connected more systematically to the processes of extended urbanization that are today infusing erstwhile hinterland spaces across the world economy.[46] At the same time, this perspective suggests that important institutional, regulatory, infrastructural, financial, and socioenvironmental transformations in zones that are not generally linked to urban conditions, from circuits of agribusiness and extractive landscapes to transoceanic infrastructural networks, underground pipelines, and even satellite orbits, have been more tightly intertwined with the developmental rhythms,

[45] Farshad Araghi, "Global Depeasantization, 1945–1990," *Sociological Quarterly* 36, no. 2 (1995): 337–68. See also, fundamentally, Farshad Araghi, "The Great Global Enclosure of Our Times: Peasants and the Agrarian Question at the End of the Twentieth Century," in *Hungry for Profit: The Agri-Business Threat to Farmers*, ed. Frederick Buttel, Fred Magdoff, and John Bellamy Foster (New York: Monthly Review Press, 2000), 145–60; and Farshad Araghi, "The Invisible Hand and the Visible Foot: Peasants, Dispossession and Globalization," in *Peasants and Globalization*, ed. A. Haroon Akram-Lodhi and Cristóbal Kay (New York: Routledge, 2009), 111–47.

[46] For an earlier, closely parallel version of this argument, see Timothy W. Luke, "Global Cities versus 'Global Cities': Rethinking Contemporary Urbanism as Public Ecology," *Studies in Political Economy* 70 (Spring 2003): 11–33. Here, Luke makes a distinction between "Global Cities" (capital letters) and "global cities" (uncapitalized) that broadly parallels that between concentrated and extended urbanization proposed here:

> Rather than focusing on that handful of Global Cities which serve as the core nodes in networks for global capitalism, this study asks instead about the collective impact of all "global cities." As a planetary system of material production and consumption, these built environments constitute much of the worldwide webs of logistical flows which swamp over the conventional boundaries between the human and the natural with a new biopolitics of urbanism. (15)

speculative logics, and crisis tendencies of metropolitan agglomerations around the world (Figures 10.9 and 10.10). Consequently, whatever their administrative demarcation, population density, sociospatial morphology, or positionality within the maelstrom of capitalist unevendevelopment, such spaces are becoming integral strategic components of an extensively, if unevenly, planetarized urban fabric

This multiscalar dialectic of implosion (industrial concentration, agglomeration) and explosion (socio-infrastructural extension of the urban fabric, intensification of industrial land use, thickening of interspatial connectivity, hyperfinancialized acceleration of capital's metabolism, multiplication of ecological crisis tendencies) is, therefore, an essential analytical, historical-empirical, and political horizon for any critical theory of urbanization in the early twenty-first century. It is, I submit, a more elemental *problematique* for the field of critical urban studies under early twenty-first-century conditions than the recurrent debates on the "future of the city" that continue to dominate mainstream global urban discourse. Indeed, critical urban scholars will arguably be much better positioned to contribute to such debates precisely by connecting agglomeration processes to the broader sociospatial, infrastructural, and ecological transformations upon which they depend and to which they actively, and often quite destructively, contribute. Urgent questions regarding the historical geographies, contemporary configuration, and possible future trajectories of the (capitalist) urban fabric may thus supplant the fetish of the city that has long dominated hegemonic approaches to urban knowledge, policy, and strategy.

State Spatial Strategies and the Remaking of the Urban Fabric

The new formations of the capitalist urban fabric outlined previously have been powerfully shaped through the operations of an array of rescaled state institutions, including entrepreneurial local authorities, national and regional governments, supranational territorial blocs, and multilateral development agencies. Of course, major metropolitan regions around the world remain strategic targets for a wide range of locational policies, advanced infrastructural investments, and economic development initiatives, whether in relation to centrally located megaprojects, peri-urban built environments or at the expanded scale of emergent megaregions and intercity corridors.[47] In this sense, even amid the recurrent rounds of crisis-induced restructuring

---

[47] John Harrison and Michael Hoyler, eds., *Megaregions: Globalization's New Urban Form?* (Cheltenham: Edward Elgar, 2015).

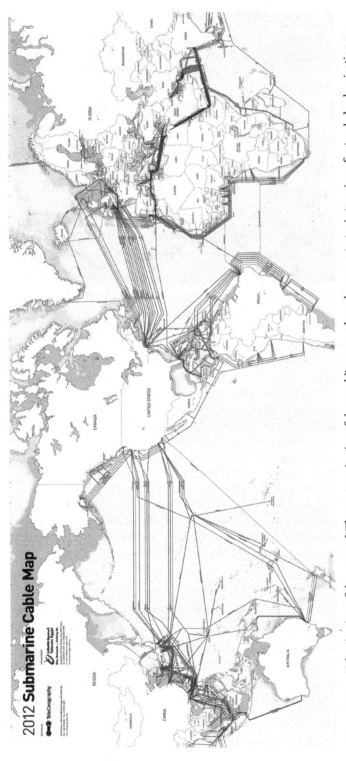

FIGURE 10.9 Urbanization of the oceans? The vast territories of the world's oceans have become strategic terrains of extended urbanization through undersea cable infrastructures (shown here), as well as through shipping lanes and various forms of undersea resource extraction (especially mining and fishing) within and beyond the exclusive economic zones (EEZs) over which national governments command sovereign jurisdictional authority. In this sense, the capitalist urban fabric is not confined to terrestrial space: increasingly, it encompasses, traverses, and transforms a vast array of ecological landscapes, including maritime, fluvial, subterranean, and atmospheric zones. (Source: http://www.telegeography.com.)

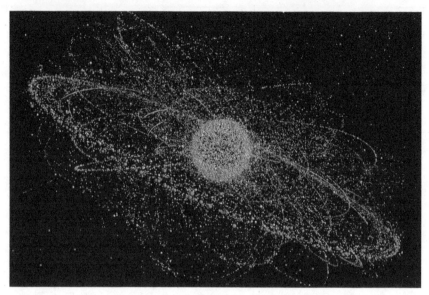

FIGURE 10.10 Space junk as an outer layer of the urban fabric? The field of extended urbanization is being pushed upward and outward into the earth's atmosphere through a thickening web of orbiting satellites and space junk. In
the early twenty-first century, the functional role of such orbital communication
infrastructures—and their detritus—is basically equivalent to that of the clocks
and pocket watches famously invoked by Georg Simmel in 1903 to describe the
elaborate systems of abstract space-time coordination upon which modern metropolitan life then depended. In producing this visualization, artist Michael Najjar
collaborated with the Institute of Aerospace Systems at the Technical University of
Braunschweig (Germany) to capture the extent of space debris that was in circulation across all orbital pathways as of 2012—over 621,000 objects of sizes varying
from one centimeter in diameter to much larger shards of used machinery such as
rocket stages, abandoned satellites, and nuclear reactors. (Source: Michael Najjar
Studio, "Space Debris 2012," with kind permission of the artist, © Michael Najjar.
For Simmel's famous reflections on the universal diffusion of pocket watches and
the cultures of metropolitanism, see George Simmel, "The Metropolis and Mental
Life," in Classic Essays on the Culture of Cities, ed. Richard Sennett [Englewood Cliffs,
NJ: Prentice Hall, 1969], 50–51.)

that have unfolded since the collapse of the Fordist-Keynesian, national-
developmentalist formation of capitalism in the 1970s, the rhythms of
post-Keynesian state rescaling analyzed in previous chapters of this book
continue to reverberate powerfully, if unevenly, across the variegated
terrain of concentrated urbanization. Indeed, even in the wake of the global
financial crisis of 2008, entrepreneurial territorial alliances in metropolitan
regions around the world have steadfastly maintained their commitment
to market-disciplinary, growth-centric, aggressively financialized models of

urban development while imposing new rounds of austerity governance that fracture public infrastructures of social reproduction and thus further entrench post-Keynesian geographies of advanced urban marginality and territorial stigmatization.[48] At this scale, the post-Keynesian splintering of the capitalist urban fabric continues to proceed apace through the persistent state commitment to broadly neoliberalized, market-disciplinary visions of metropolitan growth coupled with a concomitant explosion of intra- and inter-metropolitan sociospatial inequalities resulting from this model's wide-ranging economic, regulatory, social, and ecological contradictions.[49]

Crucially, however, especially in the BRICS zone and in other regions of the global South to which emergent spaces of industrialization are most directly connected via transnational production networks, global city-oriented development agendas are now being much more explicitly articulated to new strategies of macrospatial infrastructural planning at multinational, continental, and even intercontinental scales. As J. Miguel Kanai explains, these projects of "neoliberal territorial design" focus "on creating macro-regional spaces supportive of market-disciplinary societies—which may encompass a vast array of natural areas, regions, cities, regulatory scales and multiple other spatial formations (re)shaped to prioritize access to global markets above any other spatial planning considerations."[50] At present, the most costly, (geo)politically audacious, and colossally scaled exemplars of such neoliberalizing strategies of territorial design are the Initiative for the Integration of Regional Infrastructure in South America (IIRSA), initiated in the early 2000s and rebranded as of 2009 under the rubric of the South American Council of Infrastructure and Planning (COSIPLAN) (Figure 10.11), and China's One Belt, One Road program, initiated in 2013 and recently rebranded as the Belt and Road Initiative (BMI).[51]

---

[48] Susanne Soederberg and Alan Walks, "Producing and Governing Inequalities under Planetary Urbanization: From Urban Age to Urban Revolution?," *Geoforum* 89 (2018): 107–13. On the question of advanced marginality in major Euro-American urban regions, see Loïc Wacquant, "Revisiting Territories of Relegation: Class, Ethnicity and State in the Making of Advanced Marginality," *Urban Studies* 53, no. 6 (2016): 1077–88; and Loïc Wacquant, *Urban Outcasts: A Comparative Sociology of Advanced Marginality* (Cambridge, MA: Polity, 2008). For a productive analysis of emergent forms of intrametropolitan territorial stigmatization, see "Territorial Stigmatization in Action," special issue of *Environment and Planning A: Economy and Space* 46, no. 6 (2014), edited by Loïc Wacquant, Tom Slater, and Virgílio Borges Pereira.

[49] The classic analysis of how metropolitan space is "splintered" under neoliberalizing capitalism is Stephen Graham and Simon Marvin, *Splintering Urbanism* (New York: Routledge, 2001).

[50] J. Miguel Kanai, "The Pervasiveness of Neoliberal Territorial Design: Cross-Border Infrastructure Planning in South America since the Introduction of IIRSA," *Geoforum* 69 (2016): 161.

[51] See, among other overviews, Kanai, "The Pervasiveness"; Felipe Correa, "A Projective Space for the South American Hinterland: Resource-Extraction Urbanism," *Harvard Design Magazine*

FIGURE 10.11 Neoliberal territorial design? The Initiative for the Integration of Regional Infrastructure in South America (IIRSA) project vision for Latin America. New transnational geographies of state intervention into the capitalist urban fabric are emerging, as illustrated in this map of the project portfolio for the IIRSA. Initiated by Brazil in 2000, the IIRSA subsequently evolved into a large-scale, multilateral project of territorial design intended to stimulate, coordinate, and manage the construction of major new logistics, energy, and communication infrastructures across South America. Dominated by corporate interests and market-oriented state elites, the IIRSA has privileged the overarching priority of enhancing connectivity within transnational production networks over agendas such as social inclusion, democratic participation, territorial integration, and ecological conservation. (Source: Map by Felipe Correa/South America Project, Graduate School of Design, Harvard University; used with permission from the designer.)

In postliberalization India, the Delhi-Mumbai Industrial Corridor (DMIC) represents a broadly parallel project of mega-infrastructural territorial planning (under way since 2006), albeit one that is mainly focused on envisioning, planning, and activating an intranational zone of industrial urbanization that is to be articulated across a vast, largely agrarian, and ecologically delicate corridor between two of South Asia's most globally interconnected metropolitan nodes.[52]

In a far-reaching analysis, J. Miguel Kanai and Seth Schindler refer to this striking new (geo)politics of urbanization as the embodiment of an "infrastructure scramble" in which a heterogeneous array of governmental and quasi-governmental bodies—including "regional councils, public works projects, national foreign affairs ministries, multilateral agreements and other ad hoc supranational entities"—are seeking to establish the spatial conditions for "planetwide inter-urban connectivity" by articulating "extensive corridors of territorial development across a continuum of urban-rural conditions that is [consequently] rendered increasingly complex."[53] These developments and their extended infrastructural materializations cannot be adequately explained as endogenous outgrowths of nascent agglomeration economies; they are, in Kanai's precise formulation, "state-mediated processes steered by market-disciplinary logics codified in neoliberal policies."[54] Broadly parallel articulations of this aggressively market-disciplinary, export-oriented political strategy are, Kanai and Schindler suggest, being elaborated by diverse territorial alliances in metropolitan regions, peri-urban peripheries, intercity corridors, and strategic hinterlands across the global South, from Latin America to China, South Asia, Southeast Asia, and Africa. Across otherwise divergent macroregional and national contexts, neoliberal territorial design

---

34 (2011): 174; Xiangming Chen, "Globalisation Redux: Can China's Inside-Out Strategy Catalyse Economic Development and Integration across Its Asian Borderlands and Beyond?," *Cambridge Journal of Regions, Economy and Society* 11 (2018): 35–58; Caroline Filice Smith, "Logistics Urbanism: The Socio-Spatial Project of China's One Belt, One Road Initiative" (MAUD thesis, Harvard University Graduate School of Design, May 2017); and Tom Hancock, "China Encircles the World with One Belt, One Road Strategy," *Financial Times*, May 3, 2017.

52 See Swarnabh Ghosh, "Notes on Rurality or the Theoretical Usefulness of the Not-Urban," *Avery Review* 27 (November 2017), http://averyreview.com/issues/27/notes-on-rurality; Loraine Kennedy and Ashima Sood, "Greenfield Development as Tabula Rasa: Rescaling, Speculation and Governance on India's Urban Frontier," *Economic & Political Weekly*, April 23, 2016, 41–49; and Shriya Anand and Neha Sami, "Scaling Up, Scaling Down: State Rescaling along the Delhi-Mumbai Industrial Corridor," *Economic & Political Weekly*, April 23 2016, 50–58.

53 J. Miguel Kanai and Seth Schindler, "Peri-Urban Promises of Connectivity: Linking Project-Led Polycentrism to the Infrastructure Scramble," *Environment and Planning A: Economy and Space* (forthcoming), doi:10.1177/0308518X18763370.

54 Kanai, "Pervasiveness," 161.

programs and large-scale infrastructural visions are now being "rolled out" in pursuit of the "connectivity imperative" through which, it is widely believed, new industrial spaces may be established within erstwhile marginalized regions and positioned strategically within transnational production networks.

The new infrastructural scramble is an important extension of, and (geo)political counterpart to, the more widely discussed phenomenon of the "global land rush," also known as "land grabbing," a state-activated, aggressively export-oriented "foreignisation of space" that has entailed similarly destructive forms of territorial enclosure, dispossession, displacement, and ecological degradation in vast, primarily agrarian, extractive and biofuel hinterlands across parts of Asia, Africa, and Latin America.[55] The global land rush is composed of several distinct projects of sociospatial transformation and is being articulated in a multiplicity of locational contexts, from the peri-urban fringes of expanding megacities and intercity logistics corridors to fertile, resource-rich hinterland zones, as well as in areas that are officially classified as "barren" or "wasteland." However, one of the most prevalent agendas of these "new enclosures" across many regions in the global South is to enhance land-use productivity, specifically by promoting rapid agrarian industrialization based upon large-scale, capital-intensive, heavily infrastructuralized, monocropped, and export-oriented agribusiness grids.[56] Especially when articulated to the new transnational infrastructural corridors that are being established through neoliberal territorial design strategies, these vast arenas of emergent, export-oriented agro-industrial development are often enclosed within newly established special economic zones (SEZs) intended "to link extractive frontiers to metropolitan areas and foreign markets."[57] The salient point here, then, is not just that—as Annelies Zoomers and her collaborators have productively observed—"large-scale

---

[55] On the "foreignisation" of space through global land grabs, see Annelies Zoomers, "Globalisation and the Foreignisation of Space: Seven Processes Driving the Current Global Land Grab," *Journal of Peasant Studies* 37, no. 2 (2010): 429–47. For useful general overviews of these trends, see also Zoomers et al., "The Rush for Land in an Urbanizing World"; Ben White et al., "The New Enclosures: Critical Perspectives on Corporate Land Deals," *Journal of Peasant Studies* 39, no. 3–4 (2012): 619–47; Saturnino M. Borras Jr., Ruth Hall, Ian Scoones, Ben White, and Wendy Wolford, "Towards a Better Understanding of Global Land Grabbing," *Journal of Peasant Studies* 38, no. 2 (2011): 209–16; and Matias Margulis, Nora McKeon, and Saturnino M. Borras Jr., "Land Grabbing and Global Governance: Critical Perspectives," *Globalizations* 10, no. 1 (2013): 1–23.

[56] White et al., "The New Enclosures," 625–26, 634. In some contexts, the continued role of labor-intensive, smallholder agriculture is also supported, whether as a source of subcontracted but still export-oriented commodity production or as a means to sustain local social reproduction.

[57] Ibid., 629. See also Michael Levien, "The Land Question: Special Economic Zones and the Political Economy of Dispossession in India," *Journal of Peasant Studies* 39, no. 3–4

land investments will often trigger urbanization," or that such investments are "partly a consequence of increasing urban demand and the restructuring of value chains."[58] The analytical framework proposed here suggests, furthermore, that many of the major territorial arenas and targets of the global land rush are themselves being directly intermeshed with emergent geographies of extended urbanization: they are thus becoming integral filaments within the capitalist urban fabric.

Evidently, the variegated manifestations of emergent strategies of neoliberal territorial design and their uneven sociospatial consequences across territories, landscapes, and scales will require further analysis and theorization, not only by scholars of primary commodity production, agrarian environments, rural sociology/geography, political ecology, and global land grabbing, but also by critical urban researchers. Indeed, in the expanded vision of critical urban studies envisioned here, urbanists will need to engage much more systematically with these and related fields of investigation whose spatial foci are conventionally assumed to be extrinsic to their concerns. It remains to be seen whether the scale-attuned, state-theoretical, and territorially expanded perspective on urbanization proposed here, or variations thereof, might offer generative conceptual tools and methodological perspectives for scholars who have long been concerned with developments in agrarian, extractive, pastoral, forested, rural, hinterland, wilderness, or maritime spaces. From my point of view, the potential contribution of such an approach cannot consist in the intellectually imperialistic deployment of "urbanization" (planetary, extended, or otherwise) as a new master concept in relation to which all other processes, transformations, and struggles could somehow be explained. The goal, rather, is to explore possible avenues of cross-fertilization through which the relational coproduction of metropolitan *and* extrametropolitan spaces around the world may be illuminated from diverse intellectual starting points, scales of analysis, and research sites.

(2012): 933–69. As Levien points out, in the contemporary Indian context, many of the new enclosures are driven by real estate speculation and involve the conversion of agrarian land into other industrial, commercial, and residential functions, many of which have speculative, rent-seeking rather than productive impacts upon the local economy. The massively increased demand for nonagricultural land in postliberalization India and the directly consequent intensification of what Levien terms "economic involution" in the erstwhile countryside further underscore the heterogeneity of land transformations associated with the "new enclosures." The industrialization of primary commodity production is but one layer within a multifaceted, contradictory constellation of land-use conversions currently under way across the world's inherited hinterland spaces.

[58] Zoomers et al., "The Rush for Land in an Urbanizing World," 245.

While the conceptualization of the capitalist urban fabric proposed here is tightly articulated to a neo-Lefebvrian theoretical framework and to a systematic concern with the historical and contemporary geographies of capitalist industrial transformation, its reflexively dialectical epistemic foundations are intended precisely to circumvent the methodological hazards associated with economic reductionism, structuralism, and teleology, and thus to avoid the premature interpretive closure of emergent, heterogeneous, uneven, differentially experienced, and contradictory sociospatial relations. Rather than presupposing the prior existence of an encompassing structure, objectified system, or expressive totality into which metropolitan regions or industrializing hinterlands are neatly inserted, the challenge is precisely to explore the relationally coevolving, mutually constitutive interconnections—and the intercontextual mediations—that form and transform such spaces and that, in so doing, simultaneously produce and relentlessly restructure the macrospatial configurations in which they are embedded.[59] Thus understood, the concept of the capitalist urban fabric, and those of planetary and extended urbanization, are not intended to invoke a singular causality or a unified, all-encompassing process; they are put forward precisely as assertive counterpoints to the city-centric, naïve empiricist, diffusionist, and universalizing frameworks that continue to dominate mainstream global urban policy discourse and that are also, it should be noted, still widely presupposed in discussions of land governance, environmental transformation, and sustainable development in putatively "rural" areas. In stark contrast to the widely prevalent tendency to position debates on urban/metropolitan and hinterland/rural restructuring in separate intellectual containers, this heterodox conceptualization offers a possible avenue through which the relational interconnections among such spaces-in-transformation, and indeed their mutual constitution and coevolution, might be more holistically explored.[60]

---

[59] See, especially, Michelle Buckley and Kendra Strauss, "With, against and beyond Lefebvre: Planetary Urbanization and Epistemic Plurality," *Environment and Planning D: Society and Space* 34, no. 4 (2016): 617–36; and Gillian Hart, "Relational Comparison Revisited: Marxist Postcolonial Geographies in Practice," *Progress in Human Geography* 42, no. 3 (2018): 371–94.

[60] There are, of course, any number of parallel avenues of theorization and associated research strategies, derived from different analytical and empirical starting points, through which this challenge may also be confronted. For a number of productive suggestions with reference to the literatures on agrarian environments and global land grabbing, see especially Ghosh, "Notes on Rurality"; and Zoomers et al., "The Rush for Land in an Urbanizing World." Also highly relevant to such an exploration are the "new historical materialism" pioneered by Stephen Bunker and the "lengthened" approach to global commodity chains developed by Paul Ciccantell and David A. Smith. See, for example, Stephen Bunker and Paul Ciccantell, "Matter, Space, Time and Technology: How Local Process Drives Global Systems," *Nature, Raw Materials and Political*

Several broad generalizations may be ventured regarding the significance of emergent forms of neoliberal territorial design and global land grabbing in relation to this book's main arguments. First, states continue to play formative roles in activating, financing, managing, and canalizing the ongoing remaking of the capitalist urban fabric. Emergent spaces and scales of urbanization, both concentrated and extended, are being powerfully shaped through state institutions, legal arrangements, political strategies, and regimes of property rights. For this reason, questions of state theory and state power remain central to the project of critical urban studies. Concomitantly, the investigation of urbanization continues to offer an illuminating, if not essential, analytical lens into the evolution of contemporary statehood, including its variegated, uneven, and dynamically evolving spatialities under late modern, neoliberalizing capitalism.[61]

Second, the problem of creating large-scale, long-term, and relatively fixed infrastructures for capital accumulation appears to be the hegemonic political agenda animating contemporary projects of neoliberal territorial design. Indeed, it seems plausible to interpret the contemporary infrastructural

---

Economy: Research in Rural Sociology and Development 10 (2005): 23–44; and Paul Ciccantell and David A. Smith, "Rethinking Global Commodity Chains: Integrating Extraction, Transport, and Manufacturing," *International Journal of Comparative Sociology* 50, no. 3–4 (2009): 361–84.

[61] This was one of the core theses of Neil Brenner, *New State Spaces: Urban Governance and the Rescaling of Statehood* (New York: Oxford University Press, 2004). Despite a relatively brief resurgence of state-theoretical agendas among Euro-American urbanists around the time in which that book was published, the latter are, unfortunately, today largely absent from the field of critical urban studies. An important exception to this generalization is manifested in recent work on East Asian and Chinese urbanization by critical urban scholars and political geographers, which has explicitly explored the interplay between urban transformation and state spatial restructuring. See, for example, Bae-Gyoon Park, "State Rescaling in Non-Western Contexts," *International Journal of Urban and Regional Research* 37, no. 4 (2013): 1115–22; Fulong Wu, "China's Emergent City-Region Governance: A New Form of State Spatial Selectivity through State-Orchestrated Rescaling," *International Journal of Urban and Regional Research* 40, no. 6 (2016): 1134–51; Zhigang Li, Jiang Xu, and Anthony G. O. Yeh, "State Rescaling and the Making of City-Regions in the Pearl River Delta, China," *Environment and Planning C: Politics and Space* 32, no. 1 (2014): 129–43; Kean Fan Lim, "State Rescaling, Policy Experimentation and Path Dependency in Post-Mao China: A Dynamic Analytical Framework," *Regional Studies* 51, no. 10 (2017): 1580–93; Mahito Hayashi, "Times and Spaces of Homeless Regulation in Japan, 1950s–2000s," *International Journal of Urban and Regional Research* 37, no. 4 (2013): 1188–212; Takashi Tsukamoto, "Neoliberalization of the Developmental State: Tokyo's Bottom-Up Politics and State Rescaling in Japan," *International Journal of Urban and Regional Research* 31, no. 1 (2012): 71–89; and Bae-Gyoon Park, Richard Child Hill, and Asato Saito, eds., *Locating Neoliberalism in East Asia: Neoliberalizing Spaces in Developmental States* (Oxford: Blackwell, 2011). From my point of view, engagement with questions of state power and state spatial transformation could prove essential to contemporary debates on the urban question, not least because doing so could provide a productive basis for deciphering the variegated geographies of urbanization processes, as well as their dynamically evolving (geo)political parameters in a macrospatial context of uneven global neoliberalization.

scramble, as well as significant strands of the global land rush, as state spatial strategies to establish substantially upscaled—multinational, continental, intercontinental, and interoceanic—territorial configurations through which to stimulate, channel, and regulate the circulation of capital within and across global supply chains. Despite their neoliberal rhetoric of unleashing market forces through the dismantling of regulatory constraints on foreign direct investment, the minimization of corporate tax burdens, and the establishment of fast-track, "plug-and-play" infrastructural matrices, contemporary territorial design projects such as the IIRSA, the BRI, and the DMIC can be viewed, in significant measure, as colossally scaled state spatial strategies to upgrade, thicken, and extend the large-scale infrastructural fabric of capitalist urbanization. Insofar as they seek—as Lefebvre prognosticated in the 1970s—to take charge of "the management of space 'on a grand scale,'" they are not merely urban megaprojects, but *megaurbanization* projects: they aim to reconfigure the very land-use matrices, territorial formations, and logistical circuits in and through which the accumulation and circulation of capital are organized at the colossal sale of (expanding) economic super-regions and their intercontinental infrastructural filaments.[62] In precisely this sense, much as Lefebvre postulated, the production of new state spaces does indeed appear to have become a strategic moment in the ongoing, if uneven and stratified, planetarization of the capitalist urban fabric. It is, therefore, impossible to grasp our emergent, planetary moment of urban transformation without systematic consideration of the active role of the state's far-reaching "spatial logistics" in the production and reshaping of inherited territorial configurations, interscalar arrangements, and political ecologies.[63]

---

[62] See Henri Lefebvre, "Space and the State," in *State, Space, World: Selected Essays*, ed. Neil Brenner and Stuart Elden (Minneapolis: University of Minnesota Press, 2009 [1978]), 238. See also Chapter 2. The significance and scale of this contrast can be readily illustrated through some basic cost estimates. A megaproject, in Bent Flyvbjerg's widely accepted definition, typically costs a billion dollars; the project budgets associated with contemporary neoliberal territorial design initiatives are upward of *$100 billion* or more. Although such estimations, like those of all megaprojects, are notoriously unreliable, experts have recently calculated the BRI's current project budget as $340 billion, that of the IIRSA as $158 billion, and that of the DMIC as $100 billion. On megaprojects, see Bent Flyvbjerg, ed., *The Oxford Handbook of Megaproject Management* (New York: Oxford University Press, 2017). For the aforementioned budget estimates (and the challenges associated with calculating them), see Jonathan Hillman, "How Big Is China's One Belt One Road?" Commentary, Center for Strategic and International Studies (CSIS), April 3, 2018, https://www.csis.org/analysis/how-big-chinas-belt-and-road; Japhy Wilson and Manuel Bayón, "Concrete Jungle: The Planetary Urbanization of the Ecuadorian Amazon," *Human Geography* 8, no. 3 (2015): 6; and Ghosh, "Notes on Rurality."

[63] Lefebvre, "Space and the State," 224.

Third, neoliberal design strategies represent a significant deepening and upscaling of the state-induced splintering of the capitalist urban fabric that has been promoted since the dissolution of spatial Keynesian, national-developmentalist approaches to territorial planning in the 1970s. In contrast to the postwar, national-developmentalist discourse of territorial equalization, and also to more recent, market-fundamentalist anticipations of seamless global infrastructural integration, emergent geopolitical strategies to promote "the redesign of vast territories" through the pursuit of competitiveness-driven infrastructural investments are producing what Kanai and Schindler describe as "uneven and complex (rather than homogeneous) urban configurations."[64] By prioritizing customized infrastructural assemblages that are oriented toward selectively enhancing hinterland connectivity and the consolidation of export-led accumulation regimes, they trigger a dramatic upscaling of post-Keynesian, postdevelopmentalist forms of splintering urbanism in conjunction with "the planetary proliferation of infrastructure space."[65] This means that the increasingly pervasive condition of infrastructural "bypass," classically theorized by urban geographers Stephen Graham and Simon Marvin in the early 2000s with reference to the splintering intrametropolitan impacts of advanced information and communication technologies, is now being massively upscaled to rearticulate entire territories and continents within a qualitatively new matrix of uneven spatial development.[66] In precisely this sense, the proliferation of neoliberal approaches to territorial design in the BRICS and beyond appears to be triggering an intensified fracturing, differentiation, and stratification of the capitalist urban fabric rather than fostering a socially inclusive, territorially

---

[64] Kanai and Schindler, "Peri-Urban Promises," 2. Whereas the vision of a "borderless world" dominated mainstream neoliberal imaginations of "globalization" in the 1990s, that vision appears to have been more recently reinvented in the form of "connectography," an idea popularized in a fascinating study by corporate strategist and global policy consultant Parag Khanna—see his *Connectography: Mapping the Future of Global Civilization* (New York: Random House, 2016). Here, the emphasis is not simply on free-floating "flows" of commodities or information, but on the colossal, continent-spanning material infrastructures that enable the latter. Despite his productive infrastructural spatializations, however, the familiar neoliberal fantasy of seamless, market-based sociospatial integration remains more or less unchanged in Khanna's analysis. On the massive, hugely consequential disjuncture between ideological fantasy and grim everyday materiality associated with emergent, large-scale projects of territorial design and mega-infrastructural transformation, see Japhy Wilson and Manuel Bayón, "Fantastical Materializations: Interoceanic Infrastructures in the Ecuadorian Amazon," *Environment and Planning D: Society and Space* 35, no. 5 (2017): 836–54.

[65] Kanai and Schindler, "Peri-Urban Promises," 5.

[66] On the consolidation of intrametropolitan infrastructural bypasses under neoliberal urbanization, see Graham and Marvin, *Splintering Urbanism*.

integrative, or ecologically balanced mode of development at any spatial scale. As Kanai explains:

> Infrastructure supplies neoliberal globalization's material backbone, enabling select territorial enclaves to harness strategic flows and circulations. These world-class nodes gain centrality, while other, bypassed geographies are peripheralized. . . . Thus specific places decouple from location—Global South vs. Global North, for instance; and their home country's aggregate economic output—and, instead, are shaped by relative degrees of centrality within cross-border networks of global extent and differential articulation.[67]

The establishment of new vectors of infrastructural connectivity for transnational circuits of capital also translates directly into a wide range of exclusions, deprivations, disruptions, vulnerabilities, and dispossessions for large population segments within the dispersed hinterland regions into which major investments are being projected. Kanai and Schindler describe this new macrogeography of injustice as follows:

> There is a proliferation of connectivity conditions laying geographically outside the morphologically consolidated urban zone, sometimes very distant from the city, but spread along vectors of infrastructure provision. These places and their inhabitants may not fully benefit from urban centrality (economic development, access to services, comprehensive infrastructure support). Yet they are still impacted by the spatial effects of urban extension that are counterpart to increased agglomeration in cities, receiving various surpluses such as increased traffic, waste and pollutants, and are subject to new forms of dispossession and violence.[68]

Fourth, and finally, the consolidation of neoliberal territorial design projects has engendered newly rescaled, rewoven intermeshings between the capitalist urban fabric and state space itself. To unpack this somewhat speculative proposition and its import for this book's core argument, it is necessary to recall the reading of Lefebvre's concept of the state mode of production (SMP) that was explicated at length in Chapter 2.[69] In that context, I discussed Lefebvre's observation that the intensification of state spatial logistics during the course of twentieth-century capitalist

---

[67] Kanai, "Pervasiveness," 161.

[68] Kanai and Schindler, "Peri-Urban Promises," 5. For further discussion along similar lines in the contemporary Indian context, see Kennedy and Sood, "Greenfield Development as Tabula Rasa."

[69] See the section of Chapter 2, "State Space, Scalar Fixes, and the Fabric of Urbanization," pages 79–84.

industrial development had established a progressively more intricate intermeshing of state space with the capitalist urban fabric—so much so that, on Lefebvre's high-modernist reading, state space and the space of urbanism were becoming practically indistinguishable, at least on the phenomenological level of everyday experience. I argued, however, that Lefebvre advanced this proposition through an empirically questionable "spatial imprinting" hypothesis: he appears to have believed that twentieth-century states had effectively managed to configure the urban fabric into morphologies that were not only bureaucratically legible, and thus politically manageable, but isomorphic with the spatial architectures of state power itself. For Lefebvre, this progressive statization (*étatisation*) of the capitalist urban fabric was paradigmatically embodied in the tight articulation between nationally centralized formations of state territorial power and the concomitant nationalization of spatial planning systems, interregional circulatory infrastructures, and the public equipment of both production and social reproduction. It was similarly manifested, he believed, in the symmetrical intermeshing of precision-nested intergovernmental relays with homologously scale-differentiated national urban hierarchies. Thus, despite Lefebvre's consistent emphasis on the tendential, uneven, polymorphic, contradictory, and contested dimensions of such technomanagerial state spatial strategies, his notion of the SMP appears to have been premised, at core, upon the high-modernist expectation that the emergent, planetarized formation of the capitalist urban fabric would continue to crystallize in a "statist" (*étatique*) form: it would thus become increasingly isomorphic with the territorial and scalar architectures of state space itself.

As I have argued throughout this book, Lefebvre's analytical framework helpfully illuminates the central role of state spatial strategies in shaping and reshaping the capitalist urban fabric across diverse sites and scales. However, his spatial imprinting hypothesis has, at best, only limited applicability: it appears to be contextually bound to the Fordist-Keynesian, national-developmentalist, high-modernist configuration of capitalism in which it was developed; and even in that context, it probably overstates the degree to which any isomorphism between state space and urban space was actually established. More important for my purposes here, the last four decades of post-Keynesian, postdevelopmentalist state rescaling and capitalist implosion-explosion have effectively obliterated any such spatial isomorphism that might have been even tendentially accomplished through previous rounds of local, regional, and industrial policy intervention and nationally standardizing public infrastructure investment. Indeed, rather than molding urban space into modernist-statist territorial and interscalar morphologies, the predominant trajectory of the state spatial strategies explored in this book has been precisely to invert this classic postwar, national-developmentalist priority: it is now state space itself that is being reshaped to conform more directly to the (speculatively projected) future spatial imprints of (urbanizing) transnational capital.

Despite their many differences in contexts of emergence, locational targets, methods of intervention, politico-ideological valence, and substantive goals, this is the common thread among the wide-ranging state spatial strategies explored in previous chapters: all seek to establish customized, place-, territory-, and/or scale-specific institutional frameworks—"urbanisms of exception," in Martin Murray's more recent terminology—through which to enhance the locational assets of particular urban zones (high-technology industrial districts, global cities, informational cities, global city-regions, special economic zones) in relation to circuits of transnational capital.[70] The configuration of state space is thus transformed into a politico-institutional basis for strategies to enhance urban territorial competitiveness.[71] Under these circumstances, exceptionalized regulatory geographies serve as political strategies for reshaping the capitalist urban fabric, not according to a modernist-statist template for progressive national societal development, but as a means to bring state space more directly into conformity with the projected infrastructural requirements of capital circulation within global supply chains.

Contemporary projects of neoliberal territorial design and global land grabbing do not appear to counteract or interrupt these powerful, post-1980s tendencies of state spatial restructuring, but they may well signal a qualitatively significant evolution of the latter. As indicated, neoliberal territorial design entails a dramatic upscaling of earlier forms of urban locational policy, and thus of state space itself, in relation to current or projected transnational circuits of capital. Here, the goal is not simply to create zones of advanced infrastructure and market-disciplinary regulatory arrangements within urbanizing districts, enclaves, regions, or corridors, but to redesign the very macrogeographical frameworks in and through which the urbanization of capital occurs—including both the concentrated *and* extended moments of that process, as well as the variegated infrastructural fabric through which

---

[70] See Martin J. Murray, *The Urbanism of Exception: The Dynamics of Global City Building in the Twenty-First Century* (New York: Cambridge University Press, 2016).

[71] On the discourse, politics, and ideology of territorial competitiveness, see Neil Brenner and David Wachsmuth, "Territorial Competitiveness: Lineages, Practices, Ideologies," in *Planning Ideas That Matter*, ed. Bishwapriya Sanyal, Lawrence Vale, and Christina Rosen (Cambridge, MA: MIT Press, 2012), 179–206.

the latter are articulated. Thus, in addition to the intensified emphasis on large-scale logistics infrastructure, this emergent constellation of state spatial strategies also appears to give renewed (geo)political priority to the hinterland question—specifically, to the political, regulatory, and financial challenges of converting hinterlands into operational landscapes of extended urbanization. While the BRI, the IIRSA, and the DMIC certainly continue to target major metropolitan regions, industrial clusters, ports, and other logistics centers for a range of infrastructural projects, they also seek to transform (parts of) inherited peripheries, rural areas, and hinterlands into zones of advanced infrastructural equipment, export-oriented industrial intensification, and seamless transnational connectivity. This is also, as discussed earlier, a central goal of many global land-grabbing initiatives, especially in peripheral agrarian and extractive zones. Of course, projects of rural industrialization have a long, beleaguered, and often brutally violent history under modern capitalism.[72] The question—very much an open one, at the present time—is whether the new state spatial strategies sketched here might signal a new historical formation of the latter, now tied more directly than previously to the political challenges of (re)designing the fabric of capitalist urbanization itself, and the spatially variegated infrastructural filaments out of which it is woven.

It is worth considering, finally, whether contemporary neoliberal territorial design projects and global land-grabbing initiatives signal a new politico-spatial configuration of the "internationalized state" to which Nicos Poulantzas and other Marxian state theorists first drew attention in the late 1970s.[73] While the major BRICS national states continue to play strategic geopolitical roles in the construction and implementation of such projects, the latter also appear to involve a more complex spatial distribution of state operations—across regions, territories, and scales—oriented toward the transnational circulation of capital. This, in turn, appears to be establishing new layers of state power—institutional arrangements, regulatory operations, legal codes, and financial relays—that are much more tightly enmeshed with the splintered infrastructural topographies of the capitalist urban fabric than with inherited relays of territorial sovereignty, legitimacy, democratic accountability, and political

---

[72] See, for example, Raj Patel, "The Long Green Revolution," *Journal of Peasant Studies* 40, no. 1 (2013): 1–63.

[73] See, above all, Nicos Poulantzas, *State, Power, Socialism*, trans. Patrick Camiller (London: New Left Books, 1978); as well as Sol Picciotto, "The Internationalisation of the State," *Capital & Class* 15, no. 1 (1991): 43–63. For a spatially attuned overview of these neo-Marxian debates, see Jim Glassmann, "State Power beyond the 'Territorial Trap': The Internationalization of the State," *Political Geography* 18 (1999): 669–96.

deliberation.[74] The political consequences of such a development remain to be articulated and fought out across the variegated, uneven, and stratified landscapes in which this latest formation of the capitalist urban fabric is being formed. For present purposes, it must suffice simply to recall Lefebvre's foreboding observation that the "space of catastrophe"—the possibility of systematic rupture—is an endemic possibility within any institutional project that seeks to impose a fixed, stabilized order upon the restless flux of sociospatial relations.[75] The very attempt to mask or suppress the politics of space thus triggers its intensified (re)politicization, often giving further momentum to insurgent political forces that seek to construct alternative forms of territorial organization, societal development, and everyday life.

Critical Urban Theory and the "City Effect"

What, then, remains of the category "city" in the approach to critical urban theory proposed here? Insofar as the field of urban studies has long presupposed the bounded, unitlike character of the city or has sought to explain it with reference to certain nominal essences that putatively inhere within the organization of settlement space or agglomeration economies, the existence of cities has largely been naturalized rather than being viewed as a puzzle requiring reflexive theorization, geohistorical contextualization, and geocomparative analysis. In this sense, my arguments in this book lend further support to Lefebvre's much-debated assertion that "the concept of the city no longer corresponds to a social object. Sociologically it is a pseudoconcept."[76] To the degree that urbanists perpetuate such

---

[74] This line of argumentation diverges from Keller Easterling's provocative reading of emergent mega-infrastructures of urbanization as a form of "extrastatecraft" that is thought to lie outside, while also supplementing, inherited formations of state power—see her *Extrastatecraft: The Power of Infrastructure Space* (London: Verso, 2016). As I have argued throughout this book with reference to Lefebvre's concept of the "secret of the state," one of the signal features of state spatial strategies under modern capitalism is precisely to (attempt to) obscure or mask their pervasive role in the structuration of social space, including urban space. A first step in (re)politicizing such spaces is to find ways to decipher the wide-ranging, if contradictory, role of state institutions in their establishment and ongoing reproduction. From this point of view, the apparent absence of state operations from emergent infrastructural geographies—the "extra" in Easterling's concept of extrastatecraft—may actually signify a highly aggressive politics of space at work and the concomitant formation of new urban spaces *and* new state spaces. See Henri Lefebvre, "Reflections on the Politics of Space," in *State, Space, World: Selected Essays*, ed. Neil Brenner and Stuart Elden (Minneapolis: University of Minnesota Press, 2009), 167–84.

[75] Henri Lefebvre, "Space and the State," 235–36.

[76] Lefebvre, *Urban Revolution*, 57.

chaotic conceptions, or pseudoconcepts, through their unreflexive choice of categories of analysis, the field of urban studies is likely to remain trapped within an epistemological matrix that at once narrows its vision of the core *problematique* under investigation and obscures the manifold determinations, mediations, and contestations that underpin the very spatial arenas it takes for granted. These epistemological tendencies are strikingly analogous to those that constrained studies of nationalism prior to the radically historical, process-oriented interventions of critical scholars such as Nicos Poulantzas, Benedict Anderson, and Étienne Balibar, among others, in the 1980s.[77] Much like the nation-form, as analyzed by such radical critics, the city under capitalism may be viewed as an ideological *effect* of contextually specific spatial practices, institutional arrangements, and modes of representation that create the structural appearance of territorial distinctiveness, singularity, boundedness, and coherence within a broader, worldwide maelstrom of relentless sociospatial transformation and implosion-explosion.[78]

The critical investigation of such "city effects" can proceed coherently neither by preserving the city concept as a transhistorically self-evident category of analysis nor by jettisoning it entirely as a pure mystification. Instead, as David Wachsmuth has cogently argued, the notion of the city must be treated above all "as a category of practice: a *representation* of urbanization processes that exceed it."[79] Consequently, "any tenable concept of the city will look less like a scientific abstraction and more like a cognitive map"—in other words, it will serve as a "phenomenal category, not an analytical one."[80] The challenge, from this point of view, is precisely to decipher how contextually specific experiences, discourses, and representations of cityness are actively constructed through diverse projects of sociospatial transformation (including scale-making, territorialization, place-making, and network formation) that emerge and coevolve within the broader, unevenly woven topographies of the capitalist urban fabric.

---

[77] See, for example, Poulantzas, *State, Power, Socialism*; Benedict Anderson, *Imagined Communities: Reflections on the Origin and Spread of Nationalism* (London: Verso, 1983); and Étienne Balibar, "The Nation Form: History and Ideology," in *Race, Nation, Class: Ambiguous Identities*, ed. Étienne Balibar and Immanuel Wallerstein (London: Verso, 1991), 86–106.

[78] On the nation-form under capitalism and associated scholarly debates among critical theorists of nationalism, see Manu Goswami, "Rethinking the Modular Nation Form: Toward a Sociohistorical Conception of Nationalism," *Comparative Studies in Society and History* 44, no. 4 (2002): 770–99.

[79] David Wachsmuth, "City as Ideology," *Environment and Planning D: Society and Space* 32, no. 1 (2014): 76, italics in original.

[80] Ibid., 78, 79.

While such city effects may derive from diverse (inter)contextual sources and historical geographies, it seems plausible to expect that they will crystallize in a relatively tight articulation to the strategies of modern states to shape sociospatial relations (along scalar, territorial, place-based, and networked dimensions), as well as through recurrent sociopolitical insurgencies. Indeed, in the modern world, the city concept serves, in significant measure, as a governmental and legal category (the same could be argued for that of the "rural"), and this in turn has powerful structuring impacts upon spatial politics and everyday life.[81] Insofar as the notion of the city is directly implicated in specific projects of political management, territorial alliance formation, and concomitant sociospatial transformation—and also in the ideological distortion of those very operations—it must be critically unpacked in relation to the broader politico-institutional configurations in which it is strategically inscribed. Just as importantly, myriad projects of insurgent sociospatial transformation may explicitly mobilize visions of "the city"—for instance, of municipal governmental institutions or the spaces they enclose—as their arena, medium, and target.[82] The point here, then, is not to dismiss such city-oriented discourses, representations, imaginaries, strategies, alliances, and struggles as illusory or unimportant, but to advocate a more theoretically reflexive, historically grounded, and spatially polymorphic interrogation of the variegated contexts, transformations, and contestations in relation to which they emerge. In contrast to the widely pervasive, naïve objectivist treatment of the city concept as an unproblematic, self-evident, and sociologically neutral tool, it is the "city lens" itself that must thus be subjected to critical analytical scrutiny.[83]

---

[81] Pierre Bourdieu has astutely theorized the role of state institutions in generating, disseminating, and naturalizing everyday categories of practice: "One of the major powers of the state," he notes, "is to produce and impose . . . categories of thought that we spontaneously apply to all things of the social world—including the state itself." See Pierre Bourdieu, "Rethinking the State: Genesis and Structure of the Bureaucratic Field," *Sociological Theory* 12, no. 1 (1994): 1. This observation arguably also applies to the construction of everyday spatial categories and cognitive maps. On the role of state institutions and legal frameworks in shaping everyday meanings of the city and the urban, see Ananya Roy, "What Is Urban about Critical Urban Theory?," *Urban Geography* 37, no. 6 (2016): 810–23; and Gerald Frug, *City Making: Building Cities without Building Walls* (Princeton, NJ: Princeton University Press, 2001).

[82] See, for example, Doreen Massey, *World City* (Cambridge: Polity, 2007); Harvey, "Cities or Urbanization?"; and Andy Merrifield, *Dialectical Urbanism: Social Struggles in the Capitalist City* (New York: Monthly Review Press, 2002). For a helpful critical discussion of such issues, see Mark Davidson and Kurt Iveson, "Beyond City Limits: A Conceptual and Political Defense of 'the City' as an Anchoring Concept for Critical Urban Theory," *CITY* 19, no. 5 (2015): 646–64.

[83] Hillary Angelo, "From the City Lens toward Urbanisation as a Way of Seeing: Country/City Binaries on an Urbanising Planet," *Urban Studies* 54, no. 1 (2016): 158–78.

What spatial practices and modes of representation produce the persistent, if also quite variegated, experiential effect of "the" city's scalar individuation, place-based singularity, territorial boundedness, networked nodality, and, more generally, its apparent structured coherence? How do such unit-demarcating effects vary across places, scales, and territories, and according to the differential positionalities of social actors within multiscalar formations of spatialized power relations? How have such practices and representations, and their unevenly distributed sociospatial consequences, been transformed during the course of capitalist industrial development, through successive regimes of state power and in the contemporary moment of crisis-induced restructuring? How have they served to promote or contest specific urbanization projects, whether centered on the capitalist growth imperative (the "city as a growth machine"), the geopolitics of state domination, governmentality *dispositifs*, technoscientific simplifications, or insurgent political mobilizations for spatial justice and the urban commons (the "right to the city")? Such questions regarding the persistent "urban sensorium," which at once inheres within, systematically obscures, and yet also continually reshapes the capitalist urban fabric, must surely figure crucially within any approach to critical urban theory.[84] Under conditions of planetary urbanization, in which the gulf between everyday cognitive maps of city making and worldwide landscapes of sociospatial, institutional, and ecological implosion-explosion appears to be rather dramatically widening, the critical interrogation of such city effects appears to have acquired particular urgency.[85]

Of course, the project of deciphering the interplay between emergent patterns and pathways of urbanization and configurations of uneven

---

[84] Kanishka Goonewardena, "The Urban Sensorium: Space, Ideology, and the Aestheticization of Politics," *Antipode* 37, no. 1 (2005): 46–71. A wide-ranging historical, epistemological, and institutional research agenda flows from the frameworks of analysis proposed by Wachsmuth, Roy, Angelo, and Goonewardena, not only on how the city lens is produced across geohistorical contexts, but on how it mediates the construction and transformation of sociospatial categories, in relation to the study of city *and* non-city landscapes, at once in scholarly discourse, governmental practice, political struggle, and everyday life.

[85] These reflections on city effects are also inspired by earlier debates on the "state effect" among neo-Foucauldian and neo-Marxian state theorists. See, for example, Timothy Mitchell, "The Limits of the State: Beyond Statist Approaches and Their Critics," *American Political Science Review* 85, no. 1 (1991): 77–96; and Bob Jessop, *State Theory: Putting the Capitalist State in its Place* (London: Polity, 1990). For a closely related discussion of the "territory effect," see also Neil Brenner and Stuart Elden, "Henri Lefebvre on State, Space, Territory," *International Political Sociology* 3, no. 4 (2009): 353–77.

spatial development remains as urgent as ever. However, the methodologically localist, territorialist notions of the city that continue to prevail in the field of urban studies are increasingly blunt conceptual tools for that purpose. In precisely this sense, as Ananya Roy has forcefully argued, this would appear to be an especially opportune moment in which "to blast open new theoretical geographies" to forge a rejuvenated, reflexive, and relational approach to critical urban studies.[86] This does not mean abandoning or dismissing inherited discourses of the city (or, it should be added, of the "rural"), but treating them as categories of practice that require critical analytical scrutiny and geopolitical contextualization in relation to state spatial strategies, the politics of space, and everyday life. Like Roy, however, I have argued here for a radical reassessment and reinvention of the categories of analysis through which the project(s) of critical urban studies are to be pursued. The notion of the *urban*, as reimagined here, may offer some generative epistemological openings for that endeavor, but only if its analytical content is precisely distinguished from the unreflexively city-centric semantic matrix in which it has long been entrapped.

Once the rigid analytical constraints imposed by the methodologically pointillist, localist, and territorialist assumptions of twentieth-century urban studies are relaxed, a host of static, ahistorical dualisms (interior/exterior, city/countryside, urban/rural, society/nature, local/global, endogenous/exogenous, place/space) may be productively superseded. Through such dialectical explorations, the geographies of capitalist urbanization may be reconceptualized in ways that have the potential to illuminate not only the variegated patterns and pathways of agglomeration but also the continuous, multiscalar production and transformation of an unevenly woven urban fabric across the many terrains of extended urbanization that are today still being widely misclassified on the basis of exteriorizing ideologies of the countryside, the rural, and the wilderness. By offering a strongly relational epistemological counterweight against all forms of spatial fetishism, such a perspective may also illuminate, and thus help to politicize, the formative yet too-often-hidden connections between metropolitan strategies of neoliberalization and various projects of market-disciplinary sociospatial transformation, enclosure, austerity

---

[86] Ananya Roy, "The 21st Century Metropolis: New Geographies of Theory," *Regional Studies* 43, no. 6 (2009): 820.

Categories of practice	Categories of analysis
• ideologies of "the" city and city growth • "urban age" discourse; majority-urban world • urban triumphalism • urban/rural binarism	• fixity/motion contradiction • scale; rescaling; scalar fix • state spatial strategies • urban fabric • planetary urbanization • politics of space

Urban as nominal essence: tendential stabilization of the capitalist urban fabric through	Urban as constitutive essence: core processes shaping the production and relentless transformation of the capitalist urban fabric, including
• construction of interscalar configurations and scalar fixes; • spatially selective political strategies to promote "growth" or "competitiveness" • geopolitics of territorial alliance formation, scale-making, place-making, network alliance formation, and various combinations thereof	• crisis-induced creative destruction of territorial organization and interscalar configurations; • implosions/explosionsof sociospatial relations through the contradictory dynamics of territorialization, scaling, place-making, and networking; • mobilization of state spatial strategies to (re)shape the fabric of urbanization • spatial politics of urban restructuring

Concentrated urbanization: the agglomeration question ...	Extended urbanization: the hinterland question...
• implosion-explosions of sociospatial relations to produce site- and scale-specific clustering effects • changing geographies of agglomeration (along territorial, place-based, scalar and networked dimensions) in relation to cycles of capitalist industrial development • role of state spatial strategies and spatial politics in mediating and contesting patterns and pathways of agglomeration	• implosions-explosions of sociospatial relations to support, and as a result of, processes of capitalist industrial agglomeration • Changing geographies of non-city land use, territorial organization, and sociometabolic dynamics in relation to cycles of capitalist industrial development • role of state spatial strategies and spatial politics in mediating and contesting the industrial operationalization of hinterland zones

Struggles to appropriate (privately or collectively) the sociopolitical and sociotechnical **capacities and potentialities** produced through earlier rounds of urbanization

Variegated, uneven historical geographies of the **capitalist urban fabric**

FIGURE 10.12 Toward an investigation of the planetary urban fabric. [Note: this figure builds on Figure 10.1; see p. 345]

governance, accumulation by dispossession, and ecological plunder that have been imposed across many of the world's hinterland zones in recent decades. Figure 10.12 provides a synthetic overview of the major conceptual and methodological proposals that have been put forward in this discussion.

Coda: Planetary Metamorphosis and the Urban Question

We thus return to the classic question posed by Manuel Castells in *The Urban Question* over four decades ago, and with which we opened our explorations of the urban question as a scale question in this book: "Are there specific urban units?"[87] Under conditions in which the capitalist form of urbanization is being generalized on a planetary scale, this question must be reformulated as: "Is there an urban *process*?" Here, I have answered that question affirmatively, with reference to the distinctive, restlessly unstable, systemically uneven, and intensely variegated spatialities of capitalist industrialization, as theorized throughout this book with reference to the fixity/motion contradiction, its evolving scalar articulations and stratifications, its mediations through state spatial strategies and spatial politics, and its polymorphic, path-dependent politico-infrastructural expressions in the capitalist urban fabric.

In the terms proposed here, it is the relentless implosion-explosion of sociospatial relations through capitalist industrial development—across territories, places, scales, and ecologies—that must today be positioned at the analytical epicenter of critical urban theory. The *problematique* of planetary urbanization has emerged precisely through the uneven extension of this creatively destructive process of implosion-explosion—the industrial metabolism of capital, brutally spatialized—onto the scale of the entire planet. This transformation has, in turn, generated wide-ranging, often profoundly destabilizing consequences not only for processes of city building and metropolitan development but also for the far-flung operational landscapes—the erstwhile hinterlands of the world—whose sociospatial relations, land-use patterns, infrastructural configurations, and ecological dynamics are now being remade through emergent circuits of capitalist industrialization and the planetary supply chains that support them.

In this sense, the hinterland question is no longer exterior to the urban question, but represents a core dimension of the latter. Today, it is impossible to grasp the essential elements of the urban question except in relation to the diverse, extrametropolitan zones of the world that are now being enframed within and subordinated to the (il)logics of capital's industrial metabolism, and which directly support the "growth of the city" upon which urbanists have for so long focused their analytical gaze. Insofar as many of the world's hinterland spaces—extraction zones, agrarian environments,

---

[87] Manuel Castells, *The Urban Question: A Marxist Approach* (Cambridge, MA: MIT Press, 1977 [1972]), 101.

logistics landscapes, and waste management sites—are being transformed into territories of accelerated, large-scale industrialization, they are increasingly crosscut by and more tightly interwoven within the capitalist urban fabric. Consequently, as new formations of territorial enclosure, population displacement, infrastructural connectivity, industrial land-use intensification, financialization, and metabolic acceleration rework inherited rhythms of "rural" life—the erstwhile "outsides" of urbanism—the hinterland cannot be construed as a peripheralized realm of ghost acreage or as a remote "sacrifice zone" where the "dirty work" of supporting metropolitan life is consigned. Rather, formerly exteriorized hinterland spaces mutate into operational landscapes: strategic sites and circuits of industrial transformation that are being woven directly into the capitalist urban fabric. The hinterland thus becomes a strategic territory, medium, and expression of the urban *problematique* itself.

Paradoxically, even as the myriad "menaces" generated by this "planetary metamorphosis"—the consolidation, at the dawn of the third millennium, of a planetarized formation of the capitalist urban fabric—loom ever larger over social existence, significant strands of contemporary urban studies remain mired in a "debilitating city-centrism."[88] This stubbornly entrenched yet increasingly obsolescent epistemology reduces the urban *problematique* to that of city growth, and thus externalizes—analytically, cartographically, and politically—the vast, variegated, and dynamically mutating geographies of extended urbanization through which the latter is constituted, and with which it dialectically coevolves. In stark contrast, I have argued here that contemporary discourses and debates on the majority-urban world, the power of agglomeration, the triumph of the city, and the world city network severely narrow our horizons for deciphering the colossal scale and the menacing, potentially devastating consequences of emergent urban transformations worldwide. The claim, in other words, is not only that various extrametropolitan territories of industrial development must today be construed as strategically essential elements within the capitalist urban fabric, but that our ability to grasp even the more conventionally defined sites of urban life—such as global cities,

---

[88] On the "menace" of planetarized urbanization, see Henri Lefebvre, "Dissolving City, Planetary Metamorphosis," in Brenner, *Implosions/Explosions*, 569. This enigmatic text, one of Lefebvre's final writings, was originally published as "Quand la ville se perd dans une métamorphose planétaire," *Le monde diplomatique*, May 1989. On "debilitating city-centrism," see Stephen Cairns, "Debilitating City-Centricity: Urbanization and Urban-Rural Hybridity in Southeast Asia," in *Routledge Handbook on Urbanisation in Southeast Asia*, ed. Rita Padawangi (London: Routledge, 2019): 115–130, 1; as well as our discussion of such issues in the preceding chapter.

megacities, and metropolitan regions—is seriously compromised in the absence of systematic, reflexively relational analysis of such erstwhile exterior zones: the terrain of extended urbanization. The concept of the capitalist urban fabric, as elaborated in this book via a series of scalar explorations, through a concomitant consideration of place-making, territorialization, and networking processes, and with reference to emergent approaches to extended urbanization, represents one possible basis on which the horizons for urban theory may today be broadened in relation to the wide-ranging challenges of analyzing emergent spaces of urbanization. Perhaps still more important, such a conceptual reorientation may also prove useful for deciphering, and perhaps also for informing, ongoing strategies and struggles over the reconstitution of urban—and, thus, planetary—life itself.

Indeed, the expanded, reinvigorated approach to critical urban theory proposed in these pages is offered not only to help wrest open new perspectives for investigating the historical and contemporary geographies of urbanization under capitalism. It is also put forward in the hope of contributing to the collective project of imagining and, ultimately, pursuing alternative forms and pathways of urbanization at all spatial scales, from the most locally circumscribed to those of emergent, planet-wide webs of interdependence. In these grim times of entrenched market fundamentalism, naturalized austerity governance, consolidating identitarian violence, resurgent technoscientific authoritarianism, unfettered socioecological plunder, and looming environmental catastrophe, it seems especially urgent to harness the tools of critical urban theory toward the imagination of *alter-urbanizations*: approaches to the production and transformation of space that are focused not on maximizing capitalist profitability, but on the common appropriation of the multifaceted potentials—for development without growth; for social and political emancipation; for shared life (both human and nonhuman) and nonviolent being-in-common; for ecological justice, sanity, (re)diversification, and stewardship; and for cultural multiplicity and experimentation—that are embedded within, and yet systemically suppressed by, the process of urbanization itself.

Recent debates on the right to the city are, of course, centrally relevant to that project, and they also wrestle with the persistent challenge of deciphering where—in what site(s) and at what scale(s)—emergent struggles for alter-urbanizations might be crystallizing, or might be likely to emerge in the future.[89] In the neo-Lefebvrian framework elaborated here, there can be

---

[89] For overviews of the relevant literature, see Neil Brenner, Peter Marcuse, and Margit Mayer, eds., *Cities for People, Not for Profit: Critical Urban Theory and the Right to the City* (New York: Routledge, 2011).

no singular, definitive answer to that question, because the struggle within and over the urban emerges precisely in relation to the restlessly shifting challenges of appropriating *and* transforming the multifaceted potentials produced through urbanization, across the variegated places, territories, scales, and ecologies that form the urban fabric. As the geographies of the capitalist urban fabric mutate, so too is the politics of space rearticulated, a process that, in turn, entails a recomposition of emergent visions not only of how, but of *where* the spaces and the potentials of the urban might be appropriated and productively transformed. Consequently, as David J. Madden explains, the very idea of the "right to the city" is deeply ironic, since the approach to urban theory that underpins it actually posits the continual creative destruction of any and all fixed sociospatial arrangements, at all spatial scales, under modern capitalism:

> This paradoxical claim—that the city is over but some new, truer urbanism has in fact not yet even begun—is the center of Lefebvre's critical stance. . . . [I]t is only in this context that one can properly understand Lefebvre's notion of the "right to the city." It is often glossed over as the "right to urban life" or the right to inhabit . . . and discussed as a desired but not yet established claim to centrality, place, equality, public space, participation, and citizenship. But the right to the city must be more than a demand for the good life. It is arguably only against the background of the end of the city, and its replacement by urban society, that the concept . . . can be seen in its fully ironic originality. Lefebvre is not urging some sort of return to the existing city. He is challenging urban inhabitants to develop *new* spaces, institutional forms and political frames.[90]

In this sense, the struggle for the right to the city must be understood as a form of insurgent spatial politics oriented not just toward a more equitable distribution of, and access to, extant urban spaces and potentials. It involves, far more radically, the collective appropriation of the social power to produce urban life itself, across a multitude of scales, places, territories, and networks, within a thoroughly interdependent, if brutally stratified, planetary web of life. This power also lies at the heart of the notion of alter-urbanizations, which refers not simply to the possibility of a more democratic, just, inclusive, or ecological redesign of extant spaces, either within or beyond metropolitan regions, but to the prospect for a collective appropriation, political self-organization, and ongoing transformation of the very

---

[90] David J. Madden, "City Becoming World: Nancy, Lefebvre and the Global-Urban Imagination," *Environment and Planning D: Society and Space* 30, no. 5 (2012): 782.

capacity to urbanize—that is, to produce the "new spaces, institutional forms and political frames" whose conditions of possibility and utopian promise are engendered through the relentless forward motion of the urbanization process itself.[91]

Against this background, the foregoing analysis strongly affirms the enduring importance of the politics of space, the proliferation of radically democratic regulatory experiments, and the ongoing struggle for the commons within the world's metropolitan regions, the densely agglomerated zones associated with processes of concentrated urbanization. At the same time, my explorations here suggest that such struggles must be more explicitly and reflexively linked to a broader (geo)politics of the planetary commons that is also being fought out elsewhere, by peasants, small landholders, indigenous peoples, and other dispossessed, displaced, or residualized populations (including many of those employed in industrial agriculture, mining, and logistics) across the variegated landscapes of extended urbanization, as well as within inherited hinterlands that, while not directly subsumed within capital's industrial metabolism, are still threatened by its destructive socioecological impacts. Here too, in the force field of emergent strategies of neoliberal territorial design, land grabs, lengthening global supply chains, and consolidating transnational logistics networks, the dynamics of capitalist implosion-explosion are unleashing creatively destructive effects upon inherited social and spatial divisions of labor, land-use configurations, systems of social reproduction, ecological landscapes, and practices of everyday life. These processes and their variegated sociospatial and ecological consequences are, in turn, being politicized by a range of social movements, coalitions, and advocacy networks that seek to contest, among other issues, the neocolonial land enclosures, intensifying social immiseration, generalized labor precarity, cascading ecological plunder, rampant population displacement, and persistent everyday violence inflicted through capital's relentlessly speculative, aggressively financialized, and maniacally growth-centric spatiotemporal (il)logics.[92] As Martín Arboleda observes, such contestations often build upon, and may also seek to appropriate and transform, the very

---

[91] Ibid.

[92] See, for example, Martín Arboleda, "Financialization, Totality and Planetary Urbanization"; Martín Arboleda, "Spaces of Extraction, Metropolitan Explosions: Planetary Urbanization and the Commodity Boom in Latin America," *International Journal of Urban and Regional Research* 40, no. 1 (2016): 96–112; Stefan Kipfer, "Pushing the Limitations of Urban Research: Urbanization, Pipelines and Counter-Colonial Politics," *Environment and Planning D: Society and Space* 36, no. 3 (2018): 474–93; Elizabeth A. Sowers, Paul S. Ciccantell, and David A. Smith, "Labor

infrastructures of communication and transportation that have been forged through processes of extended urbanization:

> In so far as urbanization implies a multiscalar process of production and re-production of the built environment in which global structures of capital and everyday practices become interlinked . . . these operational landscapes—besides fostering marginalization and oppression—also provide new centralities and opportunities for encounter between previously isolated communities or individuals. . . . Thus, it is precisely in the opening of avenues for increased communication and interaction where the emancipatory promise of planetary urbanization lies. Along with energy transmission lines and roads, contemporary techniques for resource extraction require sophisticated telecommunications infrastructures, meaning that extended urbanization . . . has not only fostered physical mobility (via road infrastructures) but also communication among local communities, in themselves a crucial precondition for political action.[93]

---

and Social Movements' Strategic Usage of the Global Commodity Chain Structure," in *Choke Points: Logistics Workers Disrupting the Global Supply Chain*, ed. Jake Alimahomed-Wilson and Immanuel Ness (London: Pluto Press, 2018), 19–34; and Alberto Toscano, "Lineaments of the Logistical State," *Viewpoint Magazine*, September 27, 2014, https://viewpointmag.com/2014/09/28/lineaments-of-the-logistical-state/.

[93] Arboleda, "Spaces of Extraction," 107. As Arboleda points out, these observations regarding the new political potentialities unleashed through the establishment of advanced connectivity infrastructures beyond metropolitan centers resonate productively with a classic but widely misunderstood passage in Marx and Engels's *Communist Manifesto* on the transformation of the countryside under modern capitalism: "The bourgeoisie has subjected the country to the rule of the towns. It has created enormous cities, has greatly increased the urban population as compared with the rural, and has thus rescued a considerable part of the population from *the idiocy of rural life*"; see Karl Marx and Friedrich Engels, "Manifesto of the Communist Party," in *Marx/Engels Selected Works*, vol. 1 (Moscow: Progress Publishers, 1969 [1848]), 17, italics added. ·As Hal Draper has pointed out, the use of the term "idiocy" in the English translation of this passage is a major error: *isolation* is the correct rendering. The German word *Idiotismus* does not mean stupidity (for which there is a distinct German term, *Idiotie*); rather, it connotes "privatized apartness," or separation from social intercourse and political life (see Draper's masterful book, *The Adventures of the Communist Manifesto* [Alameda, CA: Center for Socialist History, 2004], 220–21). In this sense, Marx and Engels are suggesting that the forward motion of capitalist industrial transformation in such extrametropolitan spaces obliterates the relative isolation of rural life, embedding it more directly within the thickening web of sociospatial and ecological relations that forms the capitalist spatial division of labor, and modern political life more generally. Not least through the gigantic infrastructural circuits upon which such transformations hinge, they may consequently open up new horizons for political subjectivity, collective action, and territorial transformation. Such classical arguments are highly relevant to contemporary explorations of extended urbanization and the politics of emergent operational landscapes. An incisive analysis of this constellation of issues also lies at the heart of Andy Merrifield's powerful intervention, *The Politics of the Encounter: Urban Theory and Protest under Planetary Urbanization* (Athens: University of Georgia Press, 2013). For productive contemporary reflections on the city/country *problematique* in Marxian thought, see also Timothy Brennan, "On the Image of the Country and the City," *Antipode* 49, no. 1 (2017): 34–51.

Increasingly, then, such contestations of capital's extended built environments, sociospatial matrices, logistical operations, metabolic circuits, and neocolonial logics resonate with, and occur in direct parallel to, those that are percolating within and around globally networked metropolitan regions, which are likewise grounded upon, and may attempt to appropriate, the variegated techno-infrastructural capacities embedded within the capitalist urban fabric.[94] The approach proposed here thus opens up a perspective for critical urban theory in which connections are made, both analytically and strategically, among the various forms of sociospatial transformation, spatial politics, and grassroots activism that are being relationally, if unevenly, coproduced across the planetary landscape.

Despite the brutal injustices and the devastating social and ecological violence with which they are indelibly intertwined, the potentials unleashed through the capitalist form of urbanization may also contain the traces of radically different modes of urbanization: alter-urbanizations in which social and ecological spaces are produced, shared, appropriated, and continually transformed in common, through collective societal self-management and a mode of territorial development that has been uncoupled from the capitalist growth imperative. By offering conceptual tools through which to decipher the multiplication of such potentials, even as they are instrumentalized in support of capital accumulation, tranquilized to bolster state control, or enclosed for private, exclusionary, or repressive purposes, critical urban theory has an important, if necessarily circumscribed, role to play in the ongoing, collective imagination of such alter-urbanizations, and in struggles to actualize them.

---

[94] An argument along these lines is suggested in the literature on the "new enclosures," especially Massimo De Angelis, *The Beginning of History: Value Struggles and Global Capital* (London: Pluto, 2007). For wide-ranging analyses of emergent forms of contestation over the global commons (including issues related to the appropriation of land, water, air, and food), see Nik Heynen, James McCarthy, Scott Prudham, and Paul Robbins, eds., *Neoliberal Environments* (New York: Routledge, 2007); Fred Magdoff and Brian Tokar, eds., *Agriculture and Food in Crisis: Conflict, Resistance, and Renewal* (New York: Monthly Review Press, 2011); and Richard Peet, Paul Robbins, and Michael J. Watts, eds., *Global Political Ecology* (New York: Routledge, 2011).

ACKNOWLEDGMENTS

The idea for this book has been brewing since at least 2004, when I published an earlier work, *New State Spaces*. It has taken me quite a while to weave together the various threads of my thinking on scale and the urban question, which has meanwhile continued to evolve in relation to my own research agendas, intellectual collaborations, and broader scholarly debates. I hope this book will productively complement and extend my earlier lines of argumentation on the interplay between state rescaling and urban restructuring, while also clarifying and consolidating some of the methodological foundations of more recent work on planetary urbanization. I owe a massive debt to Martín Arboleda, Álvaro Sevilla-Buitrago, Stuart Elden, and David Wachsmuth for their comradely encouragement, and for offering consistently wise counsel on key editorial decisions. Deepest thanks are also due to Peter Marcuse and Margit Mayer for their friendship, comradeship, and inspiration over the many years in which this project has gestated.

The ideas developed in these pages have been shared extensively in conferences, colloquia, lectures, panels, and seminars, mainly in Europe and North America, but also in parts of Latin America, Asia, and Australia. Sincere thanks are due to my friends and colleagues in the fields of critical urban studies, radical geography, and geopolitical economy for the opportunity to report on my research and for many generous engagements, challenging debates, and wide-ranging critiques over the years, which have offered massive intellectual stimulus for my work in urban theory. For such invitations and associated discussions, I am grateful to Lisa Brawley, Ayşe Çağlar, James DeFilippis, Shelly Feldman, Stephen Gill, Brendan Gleeson, Nina Glick-Schiller, Miriam Greenberg, Anne Haila, Alan Harding, Erik Harms, Nik Heynen, Jinn-yuh Hsu, Yuri Kazepov, Roger Keil, Alison Landsberg, Susan Larson, Takashi Machimura, Rianne Mahon, Tomislav

Medak, Bae-Gyoon Park, Paolo Perulli, Francisco Quintana, Hugh Raffles, Jenny Robinson, Miguel Robles-Durán, Ananya Roy, Asato Saito, Rodrigo Salcedo, Bish Sanyal, Saskia Sassen, Nathan Sayre, Eric Sheppard, Manfred Steger, Pelin Tan, Lawrence Vale, Kevin Ward, and David Wilson.

I benefited immensely from the opportunity to serve as visiting professor at several outstanding institutions—the Department of Geography, Bristol University (Benjamin Meaker Visiting Professorship); the Amsterdam Institute for Metropolitan and International Development Studies (AMIDST), University of Amsterdam (Wibaut Chair in Urban Studies); and the Department of Geography, National University of Singapore (Lim Chong Yah Visiting Professorship). Deepest thanks to my colleagues in these universities—especially to Wendy Larner and Adam Tickell (Bristol); Robert Kloosterman and Ewald Engelen (Amsterdam); and Neil Coe, Tim Bunnell, and Jamie Gillen (Singapore)—for their friendly welcome, generous support, and critical intellectual engagement.

I would like to express particular appreciation for the powerfully interdisciplinary scholarly community associated with the Research Committee on Urban and Regional Development (RC21) of the International Sociological Association and the closely allied journal, the *International Journal of Urban and Regional Research* (*IJURR*), on whose editorial board I had the privilege to serve for nearly a decade. In the contested, often ideologically fraught landscapes of contemporary urban studies, RC21 and *IJURR* continue to provide an essential intellectual anchor—and, indeed, a safe harbor—for many generations of critical, heterodox urbanists. They have certainly offered me considerable orientation and inspiration during the course of my own urban explorations, and for that I remain deeply appreciative.

My approach to critical urban theory has been forged through several sustained collaborations during the last fifteen years—in particular, with Nik Theodore, Jamie Peck, and Christian Schmid. Working together with such brilliant, creative, and dedicated thinkers has been one of the great privileges of my work as an urbanist, and I am enormously grateful to each of them for their intense energies and intellectual generosity in so many shared endeavors. My thinking about the interplay between territory, place, scale, and networks has also been helpfully informed by earlier work with Bob Jessop, Martin Jones, and Gordon MacLeod, to whom I remain thankful for an intensely generative collaboration in the early 2000s.

During my years teaching Sociology and Metropolitan Studies at New York University (NYU), a remarkable group of doctoral students in Sociology, History, and American Studies provided intense intellectual stimulation and critical dialogue on diverse themes in critical sociospatial theory.

All deserve my warmest thanks and my deepest respect—especially Hillary Angelo, Daniel Aldana Cohen, David J. Madden, Michael McQuarrie, Stuart Schrader, and David Wachsmuth. Among my many wonderful colleagues on the NYU faculty, I would like to express particular gratitude to Vivek Chibber, Arlene Davila, Manu Goswami, Eric Klinenberg, Harvey Molotch, Anne Rademacher, Andrew Ross, and Danny Walkowitz for many years of fruitful interaction on a wide range of shared labors. Beyond NYU, Andrea Kahn, Andy Merrifield, Hugh Raffles, and Miguel Robles-Durán were always generous, thoughtful, and challenging interlocutors.

Since 2011, I have been fortunate to work closely with a wonderfully creative group of theoretically minded urbanists, critical cartographers, designers, and architects affiliated with the Urban Theory Lab (UTL), a research platform and doctoral workshop I established upon joining the faculty of Harvard University's Graduate School of Design (GSD). For their shared commitment to the project of developing critical, heterodox, postdisciplinary, and politically relevant approaches to the urban question, and for critical intellectual engagement in so many arenas, I thank all of the GSD and MIT students who have taken my classes, participated in our colloquia, and contributed to our emerging ideas, agendas, and aspirations. Among the many urbanists who have played a role in this collaborative endeavor, particular thanks are due to Kian Goh, Daniel Ibañez, Nikos Katsikis, and Mariano Gomez Luque, as well as to frequent visiting scholar Álvaro Sevilla-Buitrago of the Universidad Politécnica de Madrid. Martín Arboleda, who joined us for several productive years as Urban Studies Foundation Postdoctoral Fellow, quickly became a vibrantly energetic presence within the UTL, as well as a close colleague, collaborator, and friend.

Thanks are due to my colleagues at the Harvard GSD for their sustained intellectual engagement, which has challenged me to expand, and often to rethink, many of my core epistemological assumptions regarding the urban question. Particular appreciation goes to Sai Balakrishnan, Pierre Bélanger, Eve Blau, Diane Davis, Sonja Dümpelmann, Rosetta Elkin, Susan Fainstein, Jerold Kayden, Sanford Kwinter, Rahul Mehrotra, Kiel Moe, Robert G. Pietrusko, Peter Rowe, Hashim Sarkis, and Krzysztof Wodiczko. I have also benefited from productive dialogues with Gerald Frug of Harvard Law School about the issues explored in this book.

I owe a warm thank you to many other friends and colleagues in the fields of critical urban studies and radical geography who have, over the years, helped me think through a number of issues explored in this book. These include Ross Exo Adams, Adrian Blackwell, Tim Bunnell, Ben Derudder, Kanishka Goonewardena, Stephen Graham, Mahito Hayashi, Jinn-yuh Hsu,

Yuri Kazepov, Roger Keil, Stefan Kipfer, Mazen Labban, Patrick Le Galès, Helga Leitner, Michiel van Meeteren, Jason W. Moore, Bae-Gyoon Park, Teresa Pullano, Xuefei Ren, Jenny Robinson, Ananya Roy, Nathan Sayre, Eric Sheppard, Tom Slater, Łukasz Stanek, Erik Swyngedouw, Damian White, Japhy Wilson, Matthew W. Wilson, and Oren Yiftachel.

Martín Arboleda and Álvaro Sevilla-Buitrago generously read and commented on countless drafts of several key chapters. Their critical feedback has been essential to my progress on this project and to my ability, finally, to finish it.

I wish to express my deepest respect, admiration, and appreciation for three of my teachers who passed away during the final years in which this book was being written—John Friedmann, Edward Soja, and Moishe Postone. During some of the formative moments of my own intellectual development, I was absolutely privileged to have the opportunity to learn from and dialogue with each of these formidable thinkers. I will always be profoundly grateful for that—and I will miss each of them immensely. Their fearlessly dissident energies and path-breaking intellectual legacies will persist, I am certain, through the many generations of students and colleagues whose work and lives they impacted, and through the enduring power of their ideas.

At OUP, James Cook offered expert editorial advice, calm professionalism, and steadfast encouragement during this book's long, winding pathway toward completion. I deeply appreciate his support—and his patience. I am also very grateful to Amanda Miller, a Master of Design Studies (MDes) student (now alumna) at the Harvard GSD, for providing impeccably precise bibliographic, editorial, and administrative assistance amid her own busy academic and professional schedule.

Thank you, friends and colleagues, for helping me bring this project to fruition.

This book is for Ignacia, Ivan, and Izar.

Sources

The author gratefully acknowledges the publishers of the original texts for permitting their use in this book. All have been substantially reworked and expanded for this publication.

- Chapter 2: partially derived from a text published in *Environment and Planning D: Society and Space* 16, no. 5 (1998): 459–81.

- Chapter 3: *Critical Planning* 16 (2009): 60–79.
- Chapter 4: *Review of International Political Economy* 5, no. 1 (1998): 1–37.
- Chapter 5: Kurt Hübner, ed., *The Regional Divide: Rethinking the "New Economy."* London and New York: Routledge, 2005, 151–86.
- Chapter 6: *DISP* 152, no. 1, (2003): 15–25.
- Chapter 7: Richardson Dilworth, ed., *The City in American Political Development.* New York: Routledge, 2009, 121–40.
- Chapter 8: Roger Keil and Rianne Mahon, eds., *The New Political Economy of Scale.* Vancouver: University of British Columbia Press, 2009, 27–49.
- Chapters 9 and 10: partially derived from a text published in *Public Culture* 25, no. 1 (2013): 85–114.

BIBLIOGRAPHY

Abu-Lughod, Janet. *The City Is Dead—Long Live the City*. Berkeley: Center for Planning and Development Research, University of California, 1969.

Acuto, Michele, Susan Parnell, and Karen C. Seto. "Building a Global Urban Science." *Nature Sustainability* 1, no. 2–4 (2018).

Adams, Ross Exo. "The Burden of the Present: On the Concept of Urbanisation." *Society and Space*. February 11, 2014. http://societyandspace.org/2014/02/11/the-burden-of-the-present-on-the-concept-of-urbanisation-ross-exo-adams.

Adams, Ross Exo. "Natural Urbans, Natural Urbanata: Ecological Urbanism, Circulation and the Immunization of Nature." *Environment and Planning D: Society and Space* 32 (2014): 12–29.

Adorno, Theodor. "Resignation." In *Critical Models: Interventions and Catchwords*, translated by Henry W. Pickford, 289–93. New York: Columbia University Press, 2005.

Aglietta, Michel. *A Theory of Capitalist Regulation*. New York: Verso, 1979.

Agnew, John. "Representing Space: Space, Scale and Culture in Social Science." In *Place/Culture/ Representation*, edited by James Duncan and David Ley, 251–71. London: Routledge, 1993.

Agnew, John. "The Territorial Trap: The Geographical Assumptions of International Relations Theory." *Review of International Political Economy* 1, no. 1 (1994): 53–80.

Agnew, John, and Stuart Corbridge. *Mastering Space: Hegemony, Territory, and International Political Economy*. New York: Routledge, 1995.

Aigner, Birgit, and Miosga Manfred. *Stadtregionale Kooperationsstrategien*. Münchener Geographische Heft Nr. 71. Regensburg: Verlag Michael Laßleben, 1994.

Ajl, Max. "The Hypertrophic City versus the Planet of Fields." In Brenner, *Implosions/Explosions*, 533–50.

Akram-Lodhi, A. Haroon, and Cristóbal Kay, eds. *Peasants and Globalization*. New York: Routledge, 2009.

Albrechts, Louis, ed. *Regional Policy at the Crossroads: European Perspectives*. London: Jessica Kingsley, 1989.

Allen, John. "Powerful City Networks: More Than Connections, Less Than Domination and Control." *Urban Studies* 47 (2010): 2895–911.

Allen, John, Allan Cochrane, and Doreen Massey. *Rethinking the Region*. London: Routledge, 1998.

Altvater, Elmar. "Fordist and Post-Fordist International Division of Labor and Monetary Regimes." In Storper and Scott, *Pathways to Industrialization and Regional Development*, 21–45.

Amin, Ash. "An Institutionalist Perspective on Regional Economic Development." *International Journal of Urban and Regional Research* 23, no. 3 (1999): 365–78.

Amin, Ash, ed. *Post-Fordism: A Reader*. Cambridge, MA: Blackwell, 1994.

Amin, Ash. "Regions Unbound: Toward a New Politics of Place." *Geografiska Annaler* 86 (2003): 33–44.

Amin, Ash. "Spatialities of Globalization." *Environment and Planning A* 34 (2002): 385–99.

Amin, Ash, and Nigel Thrift. *Cities: Reimagining the Urban*. London: Polity, 2002.

Amin, Ash, and Nigel Thrift. "Neo-Marshallian Nodes in Global Networks." *International Journal of Urban and Regional Research* 16, no. 4 (1992): 571–87.

Amin, Ash, and Nigel Thrift. *Seeing Like a City*. Cambridge: Polity, 2016.

Amin, Ash, and Nigel Thrift. "Territoriality in the Global Political Economy." *Nordisk Samheallgeografsk Tidskrift* 20 (1995): 1–36.

Amin, Samir. *Capitalism in the Age of Globalization*. London: Zed, 1997.

Anand, Shriya, and Neha Sami. "Scaling Up, Scaling Down: State Rescaling along the Delhi-Mumbai Industrial Corridor." *Economic & Political Weekly*, April 23 2016, 50–58.

Anderson, Benedict. *Imagined Communities: Reflections on the Origin and Spread of Nationalism*. London: Verso, 1983.

Anderson, James. "The Shifting Stage of Politics: New Medieval and Post-Modern Territorialities?" *Environment and Planning D: Society and Space* 14 (1996): 133–53.

Angel, Shlomo. *Making Room for a Planet of Cities (Policy Focus Report)*. Cambridge, MA: Lincoln Institute of Land Policy, 2011.

Angel, Shlomo. *Planet of Cities*. Cambridge, MA: Lincoln Institute of Land Policy, 2012.

Angel, Shlomo, Jason Parent, Daniel Civco, and Alejandro M. Blei. *Atlas of Urban Expansion*. Cambridge, MA: Lincoln Institute of Land Policy, 2012.

Angelo, Hillary. "From the City Lens toward Urbanisation as a Way of Seeing: Country/City Binaries on an Urbanising Planet." *Urban Studies* 54, no. 1 (2016): 158–78.

Angelo, Hillary, and David Wachsmuth. "Urbanizing Urban Political Ecology: A Critique of Methodological Cityism." *International Journal of Urban and Regional Research* 39, no. 1 (2015): 16–27.

Ansell, Chris. "The Networked Polity: Regional Development in Western Europe." *Governance* 13, no. 3 (2000): 303–33.

Appadurai, Arjun. *Modernity at Large: Cultural Dimensions of Globalization*. Minneapolis: University of Minnesota Press, 1996.

Appelbaum, Richard, and William L. Robinson, eds. *Critical Globalization Studies*. New York: Routledge, 2005.

Araghi, Farshad. "Global Depeasantization, 1945–1990." *Sociological Quarterly* 36, no. 2 (1995): 337–68.

Araghi, Farshad. "The Great Global Enclosure of Our Times: Peasants and the Agrarian Question at the End of the Twentieth Century." In Buttel, Magdoff, and Foster, *Hungry for Profit: The Agri-Business Threat to Farmers*, 145–60.

Araghi, Farshad. "The Invisible Hand and the Visible Foot: Peasants, Dispossession and Globalization." In Akram-Lodhi and Kay, *Peasants and Globalization*, 111–47.

Arboleda, Martín. "Financialization, Totality and Planetary Urbanization in the Chilean Andes." *Geoforum* 67 (2015): 4–13.

Arboleda, Martín. "In the Nature of the Non-City: Expanded Infrastructural Networks and the Political Ecology of Planetary Urbanisation." *Antipode* 48, no. 2 (2016): 233–51.

Arboleda, Martín. *Planetary Mine: Territories of Extraction in the Fourth Machine Age.* New York: Verso, 2019.

Arboleda, Martín. "Revitalizing Science and Technology Studies: A Marxian Critique of More-Than-Human Geographies." *Environment and Planning D: Society and Space* 35, no. 2 (2017): 360–78.

Arboleda, Martín. "Spaces of Extraction, Metropolitan Explosions: Planetary Urbanization and the Commodity Boom in Latin America." *International Journal of Urban and Regional Research* 40, no. 1 (2016): 96–112.

Arrighi, Giovanni. *Adam Smith in Beijing: Lineages of the 21st Century.* London: Verso, 2007.

Arrighi, Giovanni. *The Long Twentieth Century.* London: Verso, 1994.

Arthur, W. Brian. *Increasing Returns and Path Dependence in the Economy.* Ann Arbor: University of Michigan Press, 1994.

Ascher, François. *Métapolis ou l'avenir des villes.* Paris: Editions Odile Jacob, 1995.

Aureli, Pier Vittorio. *The Possibility of an Absolute Architecture.* Cambridge, MA: MIT Press, 2011.

Aydalot, Philippe. *Dynamique spatiale et développement inégal.* Paris: Economica, 1976.

Balducci, Alessandro, Valeria Fedeli, and Franceso Curci, eds. *Post-Metropolitan Territories: Looking for a New Urbanity.* London: Routledge, 2017.

Balibar, Etienne. "The Nation Form: History and Ideology." In *Race, Nation, Class: Ambiguous Identities* by Etienne Balibar and Immanuel Wallerstein, 86–106. London: Verso, 1991.

Barlow, Max. "Administrative Systems and Metropolitan Regions." *Environment and Planning C: Government and Policy* 15 (1997): 399–411.

Barlow, Max. *Metropolitan Government.* New York: Routledge, 1991.

Barnes, Trevor, and Eric Sheppard, "'Nothing Includes Everything': Towards Engaged Pluralism in Anglophone Economic Geography." *Progress in Human Geography* 34, no. 2 (2010): 193–214.

Barnett, Clive, and Susan Parnell. "Ideals, Implementation and Indicators: Epistemologies of the Post-2015 Urban Agenda." *Environment and Urbanization* 28, no. 1 (2016): 87–98.

Barron, Patrick, and Manuela Mariani, eds. *Terrain Vague: Interstices and the Edge of the Pale.* New York: Routledge, 2013.

Bassens, David, and Michiel van Meeteren. "World Cities and the Uneven Geographies of Financialization: Unveiling Stratification and Hierarchy in the World City Archipelago." *International Journal of Urban and Regional Research* 40, no. 1 (2016): 62–81.

Bassens, David, and Michiel van Meeteren. "World Cities under Conditions of Financialized Globalization: Towards an Augmented World City Hypothesis." *Progress in Human Geography* 39, no. 6 (2015): 752–75.

Batty, Michael. *A New Science of Cities*. Cambridge, MA: MIT Press, 2012.

Beauregard, Robert. "What Theorists Do." *Urban Geography* 33, no. 4 (2012): 477–87.

Bender, Thomas. "Reassembling the City: Networks and Urban Imaginaries." In Farías and Bender, *Urban Assemblages*, 303–23.

Benko, Georges, and Michael Dunford, eds. *Industrial Change and Regional Development: The Transformation of New Industrial Spaces*. London: Belhaven, 1992.

Berger, Alan. *Drosscape: Wasting Land in Urban America*. New York: Princeton Architectural Press, 2006.

Berndt, Christian. "The Rescaling of Labour Regulation in Germany: From National and Regional Corporatism to Intrafirm Welfare?" *Environment and Planning A* 32, no. 9 (2000): 1569–92.

Berry, Brian J. "City Size Distributions and Economic Development." *Economic Development and Cultural Change* 9 (1961): 573–87.

Berry, Brian, and Frank E. Horton, eds. *Geographic Perspectives on Urban Systems*. Englewood Cliffs, NJ: Prentice Hall, 1970.

Bettencourt, Luis, José Lobo, Dirk Helbing, Christian Kühnert, and Geoffrey West. "Growth, Innovation, Scaling and the Pace of Life in Cities." *Proceedings of the National Academy of Sciences* 104, no. 17 (2007): 7301–6.

Bettencourt, Luis, and Geoffrey West. "A Unified Theory of Urban Living." *Nature* 467 (2010): 912–13.

Bird, Jon, Barry Curtis, Tim Putnam, George Robertson, and Lisa Tickner, eds. *Mapping the Futures: Local Cultures, Global Change*. New York: Routledge, 1993.

Bond, Patrick, and Anna Garcia, eds. *BRICS: An Anti-Capitalist Critique*. London: Pluto, 2015.

Borras Jr., Saturnino M., Ruth Hall, Ian Scoones, Ben White, and Wendy Wolford. "Towards a Better Understanding of Global Land Grabbing." *Journal of Peasant Studies* 38, no. 2 (2011): 209–16.

Boudreau, Julie Ann, Pierre Hamel, Bernard Jouve, and Roger Keil. "New State Spaces in Canada: Metropolitanization in Montreal and Toronto Compared." *Urban Geography* 28, no. 1 (2007): 30–53.

Bourdieu, Pierre. *Acts of Resistance: Against the Tyranny of the Market*. New York: New Press, 1998.

Bourdieu, Pierre. *Outline of a Theory of Practice*. Cambridge: Cambridge University Press, 1977.

Bourdieu, Pierre. "Rethinking the State: Genesis and Structure of the Bureaucratic Field." *Sociological Theory* 12, no. 1 (1994): 1–18.

Boyd, William, W. Scott Prudham, and Rachel Shurman. "Industrial Dynamics and the Problem of Nature." *Society and Natural Resources* 14, no. 7 (2001): 555–70.

Boyer, Robert, and J. Rogers Hollingsworth. "From National Embeddedness to Spatial and Institutional Nestedness." In *Contemporary Capitalism: The Embeddedness of Institutions*, edited by J. Rogers Hollingsworth and Robert Boyer, 433–84. New York: Cambridge University Press, 1997.

Braudel, Fernand. *The Perspective of the World*. Translated by Siân Reynolds. Berkeley: University of California Press, 1984.

Brennan, Timothy. "On the Image of the Country and the City." *Antipode* 49, no. 1 (2017): 34–51.

Brenner, Neil. "Beyond State-Centrism: Space, Territoriality and Geographical Scale in Globalization Studies." *Theory & Society* 28 (1999): 39–78.

Brenner, Neil. "Building 'Euro-regions': Locational Politics and the Political Geography of Neoliberalism in Post-Unification Germany." *European Urban and Regional Studies* 7, no. 4 (2000): 319–45.

Brenner, Neil. "Critical Urban Theory, Reloaded?" In Brenner, *Critique of Urbanization*, 268–89.

Brenner, Neil. *Critique of Urbanization: Selected Essays*. Basel: Bauwelt Fundamente/Birkhäuser Verlag, 2016.

Brenner, Neil. "Debating Planetary Urbanization: Towards an Engaged Pluralism." *Environment and Planning D: Society and Space* 36, no. 3 (2018): 570–90.

Brenner, Neil. "Decoding the Newest 'Metropolitan Regionalism' in the USA: A Critical Overview." *Cities* 19, no. 1 (2002): 3–21.

Brenner, Neil. "Extended Urbanization and the Hinterland Question: Towards the Real Subsumption of the Planet?" Working Paper, Urban Theory Lab, Graduate School of Design, Harvard University, June 2018.

Brenner, Neil. "Global, Fragmented, Hierarchical: Henri Lefebvre's Geographies of Globalization." *Public Culture* 10, no. 1 (1997): 135–67.

Brenner, Neil. "The Hinterland, Urbanized?" In Brenner, *Critique of Urbanization*, 212–33.

Brenner, Neil, ed. *Implosions/Explosions: Towards a Study of Planetary Urbanization*. Berlin: Jovis, 2014.

Brenner, Neil. "Introduction: Urban Theory without an Outside." In Brenner, *Implosions/Explosions: Towards a Study of Planetary Urbanization*, 14–35.

Brenner, Neil. "The Limits to Scale? Methodological Reflections on Scalar Structuration." *Progress in Human Geography* 15, no. 4 (2001): 525–48.

Brenner, Neil. *New State Spaces: Urban Governance and the Rescaling of Statehood*. New York: Oxford University Press, 2004.

Brenner, Neil. "The *Problematique* of Critique." In Brenner, *Critique of Urbanization*, 16–24.

Brenner, Neil. "State Territorial Restructuring and the Production of Spatial Scale: Urban and Regional Planning in the Federal Republic of Germany, 1960–1990." *Political Geography* 16, no. 4 (1997): 273–306.

Brenner, Neil. "Urban Revolution?" In Brenner, *Critique of Urbanization*, 192–211.

Brenner, Neil. "What Is Critical Urban Theory?" In Brenner, *Critique of Urbanization*, 25–41.

Brenner, Neil, and Stuart Elden. "Henri Lefebvre on State, Space, Territory." *International Political Sociology* 3, no. 4 (2009): 353–77.

Brenner, Neil, and Stuart Elden. "Introduction: State, Space, World. Lefebvre and the Survival of Capitalism." In *State, Space, World: Selected Essays*, edited by Neil Brenner and Stuart Elden, 1–50. Minneapolis: University of Minnesota Press, 2009.

Brenner, Neil, Bob Jessop, Martin Jones, and Gordon MacLeod, eds. *State/Space: A Reader*. Cambridge, MA: Blackwell, 2003.

Brenner, Neil, and Nikos Katsikis. "Is the Mediterranean Urban?" In Brenner, *Implosions/Explosions*, 428–59.

Brenner, Neil, and Nikos Katsikis. *Is the World Urban? Towards a Critique of Geospatial Ideology*. Barcelona: Actar, 2019.

Brenner, Neil, and Roger Keil. "From Global Cities to Globalized Urbanization." In Brenner, *Critique of Urbanization*, 69–84.

Brenner, Neil, and Roger Keil, eds. *The Global Cities Reader*. New York: Routledge, 2006.

Brenner, Neil, David J. Madden, and David Wachsmuth. "Assemblage Urbanism and the Challenges of Critical Urban Theory." *CITY* 15, no. 2 (2011): 225–40.

Brenner, Neil, Margit Mayer, and Peter Marcuse, eds. *Cities for People, Not for Profit*. New York: Routledge, 2011.

Brenner, Neil, Jamie Peck, and Nik Theodore. "After Neoliberalization?" *Globalizations* 7, no. 3 (2010): 313–30.

Brenner, Neil, Jamie Peck, and Nik Theodore. "Variegated Neoliberalization: Geographies, Modalities, Pathways." *Global Networks* 10, no. 2 (2010): 182–222.

Brenner, Neil, and Christian Schmid. "Combat, Caricature and Critique in the Study of Planetary Urbanization." Urban Theory Lab, Harvard Graduate School of Design, April 2015. http://urbantheorylab.net/uploads/Brenner_Schmid_Richard%20Walker_2015.pdf.

Brenner, Neil, and Christian Schmid. "Planetary Urbanization." In *Urban Constellations*, edited by Matthew Gandy, 10–13. Berlin: Jovis, 2012.

Brenner, Neil, and Christian Schmid. "Towards a New Epistemology of the Urban?" *CITY* 19, no. 2–3 (2015): 151–82.

Brenner, Neil, and Christian Schmid. "The 'Urban Age' in Question." *International Journal of Urban and Regional Research* 38, no. 3 (2013): 731–55.

Brenner, Neil, and Nik Theodore. "Cities and the Geographies of 'Actually Existing Neoliberalism.'" In Brenner and Theodore, *Spaces of Neoliberalism*, 2–32.

Brenner, Neil, and Nik Theodore, eds. *Spaces of Neoliberalism: Urban Restructuring in North America and Western Europe*. Oxford: Blackwell, 2002.

Brenner, Neil, and David Wachsmuth. "Territorial Competitiveness: Lineages, Practices, Ideologies." In *Planning Ideas That Matter*, edited by Bishwapriya Sanyal, Lawrence Vale, and Christina Rosen, 179–206. Cambridge, MA: MIT Press, 2012.

Brewer, Anthony. *Marxist Theories of Imperialism*. 2nd ed. London: Routledge, 1990.

Bridge, Gavin. "Resource Triumphalism: Postindustrial Narratives of Primary Commodity Production." *Environment and Planning A* 33 (2001): 2149–73.

Brubaker, Rogers, and Frederick Cooper. "Beyond Identity." *Theory & Society* 29 (2000): 1–47.

Brugmann, Jeb. *Welcome to the Urban Revolution*. New York: Bloomsbury, 2010.

Brunet, Roger. *Les villes 'europeenes.'* Paris: DATAR, 1989.

Buckley, Michelle, and Kendra Strauss. "With, against and beyond Lefebvre: Planetary Urbanization and Epistemic Plurality." *Environment and Planning D: Society and Space* 34, no. 4 (2016): 617–36.

Bulkeley, Harriet. "Reconfiguring Environmental Governance: Towards a Politics of Scales and Networks." *Political Geography* 24 (2005): 875–902.

Bullmann, Udo, ed. *Die Politik der dritten Ebene. Regionen im Europa der Union*. Baden-Baden: Nomos, 1994.

Bullmann, Udo. *Kommunale Strategien gegen Massenarbeitslosigkeit. Ein Einstieg in die sozialökologische Erneuerung*. Opladen: Leske and Budrich, 1991.

Bunker, Stephen, and Paul Ciccantell. "Matter, Space, Time and Technology: How Local Process Drives Global Systems." *Nature, Raw Materials and Political Economy: Research in Rural Sociology and Development* 10 (2005): 23–44.

Bunnell, Tim, and Anant Maringanti. "Practicing Urban Research beyond Metrocentricity." *International Journal of Urban and Regional Research* 34, no. 2 (2011): 415–20.

Burdett, Ricky, and Deyan Sudjic, eds. *The Endless City: The Urban Age Project by the London School of Economics and Deutsche Bank's Alfred Herrhausen Society.* London: Phaidon, 2006.

Burdett, Ricky, and Deyan Sudjic, eds. *Living in the Endless City.* London: Phaidon, 2010.

Butler, Chris. "Abstraction Beyond a 'Law of Thought': On Space, Appropriation and Concrete Abstraction." *Law Critique* 27, no. 3 (2016): 247–68.

Buttel, Frederick, Fred Magdoff, and John Bellamy Foster, eds. *Hungry for Profit: The Agri-Business Threat to Famers, Food and the Environment.* New York: Monthly Review Press, 2000.

Cairns, Stephen. "Debilitating City-Centricity: Urbanization and Urban-Rural Hybridity in Southeast Asia." In *Routledge Handbook on Urbanisation in Southeast Asia,* edited by Rita Padawangi. London: Routledge, 2019): 115–130.

Castells, Manuel. *Networks of Outrage and Hope: Social Movements in the Internet Age.* 2nd ed. Cambridge: Polity, 2015.

Castells, Manuel. *End of Millennium.* Cambridge, MA: Blackwell, 1998.

Castells, Manuel. *The Informational City.* Cambridge, MA: Blackwell, 1989.

Castells, Manuel. "Is There an Urban Sociology?" In *Urban Sociology: Critical Essays,* edited by C. G. Pickvance, 33–59. New York: St. Martin's Press, 1976.

Castells, Manuel. *The Power of Identity.* Cambridge, MA: Blackwell, 1997.

Castells, Manuel. *The Rise of the Network Society.* Cambridge, MA: Blackwell, 1996.

Castells, Manuel. *The Urban Question: A Marxist Approach.* Cambridge, MA: MIT Press, 1977 [1972].

Castells, Manuel. "Urban Sociology in the Twenty-First Century." In *The Castells Reader on Cities and Social Theory,* edited by Ida Susser, 390–406. Cambridge, MA: Blackwell, 2002.

Castree, Noel. "The Anthropocene and the Environmental Humanities: Extending the Conversation." *Environmental Humanities* 5 (2014): 233–60.

Castree, Noel. "Geographic Scale and Grass-Roots Internationalism: The Liverpool Dock Dispute, 1995–1998." *Economic Geography* 76, no. 3 (2000): 272–92.

Castree, Noel, and Derek Gregory, eds. *David Harvey: A Critical Reader.* Malden, MA: Blackwell, 2006.

Castriota, Rodrigo, and João Tonucci Filho. "Extended Urbanization in and from Brazil." *Environment and Planning D: Society and Space* 36, no. 3 (2018): 512–28.

Cerny, Philip. "Globalization and the Changing Logic of Collective Action." *International Organization* 49, no. 4 (1995): 595–625.

Chakrabarty, Dipesh. "The Climate of History: Four Theses." *Critical Inquiry* 35, no. 2 (2009): 197–222.

Champion, Tony, and Graeme Hugo, eds. *New Forms of Urbanization.* London: Ashgate, 2007.

Charnock, Greig, and Guido Starosta, eds. *The New International Division of Labor: Global Transformation and Uneven Development.* New York: Palgrave Macmillan, 2016.

Chen, Xiangming. "Globalisation Redux: Can China's Inside-Out Strategy Catalyse Economic Development and Integration across Its Asian Borderlands and Beyond?" *Cambridge Journal of Regions, Economy and Society* 11 (2018): 35–58.

Cheshire, Paul, and Ian Gordon. "Territorial Competition and the Predictability of Collective (In)action." *International Journal of Urban and Regional Research* 20, no. 3 (1996): 383–99.

Chinitz, Benjamin. "Contrasts in Agglomeration: New York and Pittsburgh." *American Economic Review* 51, no. 2 (1961): 279–89.

Choay, Françoise. "Le régne de l'urbain et la mort de la ville." In *La ville, art et architecture en Europe, 1870–1993*, edited by Jean Dethier and Alain Guiheu, 26–38. Paris: Editions du Centre Georges Pompidou, 1994.

Christaller, Walter. *Central Places in Southern Germany*. Translated by Carlisle W. Baskin. Englewood Cliffs, NJ: Prentice Hall, 1966 [1933].

Ciccantell, Paul, and David A. Smith. "Rethinking Global Commodity Chains: Integrating Extraction, Transport, and Manufacturing." *International Journal of Comparative Sociology* 50, no. 3–4 (2009): 361–84.

Clarke, Susan, and Gary Gaile. *The Work of Cities*. Minneapolis: University of Minnesota Press, 1998.

Clout, Hugh D., ed. *Regional Development in Western Europe*. 2nd ed. New York: John Wiley & Sons, 1981.

Coe, Neil, and Henry Yeung. *Global Production Networks: Theorizing Economic Development in an Interconnected World*. New York: Oxford University Press, 2015.

Cohen, R. B. "The New International Division of Labor, Multinational Corporations, and Urban Hierarchy." In *Urbanization and Urban Planning in Capitalist Society*, edited by Michael Dear and Allen J. Scott, 287–315. London: Methuen, 1981.

Collinge, Chris. "Flat Ontology and the Deconstruction of Scale." *Transactions of the Institute of British Geographers* 31 (2006): 244–51.

Collinge, Chris. "Self-Organization of Society by Scale: A Spatial Reworking of Regulation Theory." *Environment and Planning D: Society and Space* 17 (1999): 557–74.

Collinge, Chris. "Spatial Articulation of the State: Reworking Social Relations and Social Regulation Theory." Unpublished manuscript, Centre for Urban and Regional Studies, Birmingham, 1996.

Connolly, William E. "Democracy and Territoriality." *Millennium* 20, no. 3 (1991): 463–84.

Cooke, Philip, and Kevin Morgan. *The Associational Economy*. New York: Oxford University Press, 1998.

Correa, Felipe. "A Projective Space for the South American Hinterland: Resource-Extraction Urbanism." *Harvard Design Magazine* 34 (2011): 174–85.

Cox, Kevin. "The Difference That Scale Makes." *Political Geography* 15 (1996): 667–70.

Cox, Kevin. *Political Geography: Territory, State, Society*. Cambridge, MA: Blackwell, 2002.

Cox, Kevin. "'Rescaling the State' in Question." *Cambridge Journal of Regions, Economy and Society* 2, no. 1 (2009): 107–21.

Cox, Kevin, ed. *Spaces of Globalization*. New York: Guilford Press, 1997.

Cox, Kevin. "Territorial Structures of the State: Some Conceptual Issues." *Tijdschrift voor Economische en Sociale Geografie* 81 (1990): 251–66.

Cox, Kevin, and Andrew Mair. "Levels of Abstraction in Locality Studies." *Antipode* 21 (1989): 121–32.

Cox, Kevin, and Andrew Mair. "Locality and Community in the Politics of Local Economic Development." *Annals of the Association of American Geographers* 78, no. 2 (1988): 307–25.

Cronon, William. *Nature's Metropolis: Chicago and the Great West*. New York: W. W. Norton, 1991.

Crouch, Colin, and Patrick Le Galès. "Cities as National Champions?" *Journal of European Public Policy* 19, no. 3 (2012): 405–19.

Cunningham, David. "The Concept of Metropolis: Philosophy and Urban Form." *Radical Philosophy* 133 (September/October 2005): 13–25.

Daniels, Peter, Andrew Leyshon, Michael Bradshaw, and Jonathan Beaverstock, eds. *Geographies of the New Economy: Critical Reflections*. London: Routledge, 2009.

Davidson, Mark, and Kurt Iveson. "Beyond City Limits: A Conceptual and Political Defense of 'the City' as an Anchoring Concept for Critical Urban Theory." *CITY* 19, no. 5 (2015): 646–64.

Davies, Howard. "Will London Survive as a Financial Centre after Brexit?" *The Guardian*, April 26, 2017.

Davis, Kingsley. "The Origins and Growth of Urbanization in the World." *American Journal of Sociology* 60, no. 5 (1955): 429–37.

Davis, Kingsley. *World Urbanization: 1950–1970*, vol. 1: *Basic Data for Cities, Countries, and Regions*. Population Monograph Series No. 4. Berkeley: Institute of International Studies, University of California, 1969.

Davis, Kingsley. *World Urbanization: 1950–1970*, vol. 2: *Analysis of Trends, Relationships and Development*. Population Monograph Series No. 9. Berkeley: Institute of International Studies, University of California, 1972.

Davis, Mike. *City of Quartz*. New York: Vintage, 1991.

Davis, Mike. *Planet of Slums*. London: Verso, 2006.

De Angelis, Massimo. *The Beginning of History: Value Struggles and Global Capital*. London: Pluto, 2007.

De Angelis, Massimo. *Omnia Sunt Communia: On the Commons and the Transformation to Postcapitalism*. London: Zed, 2017.

Delaney, David, and Helga Leitner. "The Political Construction of Scale." *Political Geography* 16 (1997): 93–97.

Dempey, Jessica, and Morgan Robertson. "Ecosystem Services: Tensions, Impurities and Points of Engagement within Neoliberalism." *Progress in Human Geography* 36, no. 6 (2012): 758–79.

Deuskar, Chadan. "What Does Urban Mean?" World Bank Sustainable Cities (blog). June 2, 2015. http://blogs.worldbank.org/sustainablecities/what-does-urban-mean.

Dicken, Peter, Philip Kelly, Kris Olds, and Henry Yeung. "Chains and Networks, Territories and Scales: Towards a Relational Framework for Analysing the Global Economy." *Global Networks* 1, no. 2 (2001): 89–112.

Dickinson, Robert. *City and Region: A Geographical Interpretation*. London: Routledge and Kegan Paul, 1964.

Dieleman, Frans, and Sako Musterd, eds. *The Randstad: A Research and Policy Laboratory*. Dordrecht: Kluwer, 1992.

Diener, Roger, Jacques Herzog, Marcel Meili, Pierre de Meuron, and Christian Schmid. *Switzerland: An Urban Portrait*. 4 vols. Zurich: Birkhaüser, 2001.

Dijkink, Gertjan. "Metropolitan Government as Political Pet? Realism and Tradition in Administrative Reform in the Netherlands." *Political Geography* 14, no. 4 (1995): 329–41.

Dorignon, Louise. "And the Urban Exploded." *Society and Space*. http://societyandspace.com/material/commentaries/dorignon/.

Dorling, Danny. "Brexit: The Decision of a Divided Country." *British Medical Journal*, July 6, 2016.

Doxiadis, Constantinos, and J. G. Papaioannou. *Ecumenopolis: The Inevitable City of the Future*. New York: W. W. Norton, 1974.

Draper, Hal. *The Adventures of the Communist Manifesto*. Alameda, CA: Center for Socialist History, 2004.

Dreier, Peter, John Mollenkopf, and Todd Swanstrom. *Place Matters: Metropolitics for the 21st Century*. 2nd ed. Lawrence: University Press of Kansas, 2004.

Duncan, Simon, and Mark Goodwin. *The Local State and Uneven Development*. London: Polity, 1988.

Dunford, Michael, and Diane Perrons. "Regional Inequality, Regimes of Accumulation and Economic Development in Contemporary Europe." *Transactions of the Institute of British Geographers* 19 (1994): 163–82.

Dunford, Mick, and Grigoris Kafkalas, eds. *Cities and Regions in the New Europe: The Global-Local Interplay and Spatial Development Strategies*. London: Belhaven Press, 1992.

Dunford, Mick, and Grigoris Kafkalas. "The Global–Local Interplay, Corporate Geographies and Spatial Development Strategies in Europe." In Dunford and Kafkalas, *Cities and Regions in the New Europe*, 3–38.

Dunkley, Emma. "Six Cities in Search of London's Business after Brexit." *Financial Times*, June 8, 2017.

Easterling, Keller. *Extrastatecraft: The Power of Infrastructure Space*. London: Verso, 2016.

The Economist. "Financial Centres Survey." May 1998, 17.

Eisenschitz, Aram, and Jamie Gough. "The Contradictions of Neo-Keynesian Local Economic Strategy." *Review of International Political Economy* 3, no. 3 (1996): 434–58.

Eisenschitz, Aram, and Jamie Gough. *The Politics of Local Economic Development*. New York: Macmillan, 1993.

Eisinger, Peter. "City Politics in an Era of Devolution." *Urban Affairs Review* 33, no. 3 (1988): 308–25.

Eisinger, Peter. *The Rise of the Entrepreneurial State*. Madison: University of Wisconsin Press, 1988.

Elden, Stuart. *The Birth of Territory*. Chicago: University of Chicago Press, 2014.

Elden, Stuart. "Land, Terrain, Territory." *Progress in Human Geography* 34, no. 6 (2010): 799–817.

Elden, Stuart. "Missing the Point: Globalisation, Deterritorialisation and the Space of the World." *Transactions of the Institute of British Geographers* 30 (2005): 8–19.

Elden, Stuart. "The Space of the World." *New Geographies* 4 (2011): 26–31.

Elden, Stuart. *Understanding Henri Lefebvre: Theory and the Possible*. New York: Continuum, 2004.

Elkin, Stephen. *City and Regime in the American Republic.* Chicago: University of Chicago Press, 1987.

Escobar, Arturo. "The 'Ontological Turn' in Social Theory." *Transactions of the Institute of British Geographers* 32 (2007): 106–11.

Esser, Josef, and Joachim Hirsch. "The Crisis of Fordism and the Dimensions of a "Postfordist" Regional and Urban Structure." *International Journal of Urban and Regional Research* 13, no. 3 (1989): 417–37.

ETH Studio Basel, ed. *The Inevitable Specificity of Cities.* Zurich: Lars Müller Publishers, 2014.

ETH Studio Basel/Contemporary City Institute, ed. *Territory: On the Development of Landscape and City.* Zurich: Park Books, 2016.

Fainstein, Susan. "Resilience and Justice." *International Journal of Urban and Regional Research* 39, no. 1 (2015): 157–67.

Faludi, Andreas, and Arnold Van der Valk. *Rule and Order: Dutch Planning Doctrine in the Twentieth Century.* Dordrecht: Kluwer Academic Publishers, 1994.

Farías, Ignacio. "Introduction: Decentering the Object of Urban Studies." In Farías and Bender, *Urban Assemblages,* 1–24.

Farías, Ignacio, and Thomas Bender, eds. *Urban Assemblages: How Actor-Network Theory Changes Urban Research.* New York: Routledge, 2010.

Feagin, Joe, and Michael Peter Smith. "Cities and the New International Division of Labor: An Overview." In Smith and Feagin, *The Capitalist City,* 3–34.

Fishman, Robert. *Bourgeois Utopias: The Rise and Fall of Suburbia.* New York: Basic Books, 1987.

Florida, Richard. *Who's Your City?* New York: Basic, 2008.

Florida, Richard, Tim Gulden, and Charlotta Mellander. "The Rise of the Mega-Region." *Cambridge Journal of Regions, Economy and Society* 1 (2008): 459–76.

Flyvbjerg, Bent, ed. *The Oxford Handbook of Megaproject Management.* New York: Oxford University Press, 2017.

Fox-Przeworski, Joanne. "Changing Intergovernmental Relations and Urban Economic Development." *Environment and Planning C: Government and Policy* 4, no. 4 (1986): 423–39.

Friedmann, John. "Where We Stand: A Decade of World City Research." In Knox and Taylor, *World Cities in a World-System,* 21–26.

Friedmann, John. "The World City Hypothesis." *Development and Change* 17 (1986): 69–83.

Friedmann, John, and Robin Bloch. "American Exceptionalism in Regional Planning, 1933–2000." *International Journal of Urban and Regional Research* 14, no. 4 (1990): 576–601.

Friedmann, John, and John Miller. "The Urban Field." *Journal of the American Planning Association* 31, no. 4 (1965): 312–20.

Friedmann, John, and Clyde Weaver. *Territory and Function: The Evolution of Regional Planning.* Berkeley: University of California Press, 1979.

Friedmann, John, and Goetz Wolff. "World City Formation: An Agenda for Research and Action." *International Journal of Urban and Regional Research* 6 (1982): 309–44.

Fröbel, Folker, Jürgen Heinrichs, and Otto Kreye. *The New International Division of Labor: Structural Unemployment in Industrialized Countries and Industrialization in Developing Countries.* Translated by Pete Burgess. New York: Cambridge University Press, 1980.

Frug, Gerald. *City-Making: Building Cities without Building Walls*. Princeton, NJ: Princeton University Press, 2002.

Galison, Peter. "The Limits of Localism: The Scale of Sight." In *What Reason Promises: Essays on Reason, Nature and History*, edited by Wendy Doniger, Peter Galison, and Susan Neiman, 155–70. Berlin: De Gruyter, 2016.

Gamba, Paolo, and Martin Herold, eds. *Global Mapping of Human Settlement*. New York: Taylor & Francis, 2009.

Gandy, Matthew. *The Fabric of Space: Water, Modernity and the Urban Imagination*. Cambridge, MA: MIT Press, 2016.

Gans, Herbert. "Some Problems of and Futures for Urban Sociology: Toward a Sociology of Settlements." *City & Community* 8, no. 3 (2009): 211–19.

Garreau, Joel. *Edge City*. New York: Anchor, 1992.

Geddes, Patrick. "A World League of Cities." *Sociological Review* 26 (1924): 166–67.

Ghosh, Swarnabh. "Notes on Rurality or the Theoretical Usefulness of the Not-Urban." Avery Review 27 (November 2017). http://averyreview.com/issues/27/notes-on-rurality.

Giddens, Anthony. *The Constitution of Society: Outline of the Theory of Structuration*. Cambridge: Polity, 1984.

Giddens, Anthony. *A Contemporary Critique of Historical Materialism*. Berkeley: University of California Press, 1985.

Gieryn, Thomas. "City as Truth-Spot: Laboratories and Field-Sites in Urban Studies." *Social Studies of Science* 36, no. 1 (2006): 5–38.

Ginsburg, Norton, Bruce Koppel, and T. G. McGee, eds. *The Extended Metropolis: Settlement Transition in Asia*. Honolulu: University of Hawaii Press, 1991.

Glaeser, Edward. *Cities, Agglomeration and Spatial Equilibrium*. New York: Oxford University Press, 2008.

Glaeser, Edward. *Triumph of the City*. New York: Tantor, 2011.

Glassmann, Jim. "State Power beyond the 'Territorial Trap': The Internationalization of the State." *Political Geography* 18 (1999): 669–96.

Gleeson, Brendan. "The Urban Age: Paradox and Prospect." *Urban Studies* 49, no. 5 (2012): 931–43.

Gleeson, Brendan. *The Urban Condition*. London: Routledge, 2014.

Gleeson, Brendan. "What Role for Social Science in the 'Urban Age'?" *International Journal of Urban and Regional Research* 37, no. 5 (2013): 1839–51.

Go, Julian. *Postcolonial Thought and Social Theory*. New York: Oxford University Press, 2016.

Goldsmith, Michael. "Urban Governance." In *Handbook of Urban Studies*, edited by Ronan Paddison, 325–35. London: Sage, 2001.

Goodman, Robert. *The Last Entrepreneurs: America's Regional Wars for Jobs and Dollars*. New York: Simon and Schuster, 1979.

Goodwin, Mark, and Simon Duncan. *The Local State and Uneven Development: Behind the Local Government Crisis*. London: Polity Press, 1988.

Goodwin, Mark, and Joe Painter. "Local Governance, the Crises of Fordism and the Changing Geographies of Regulation." *Transactions of the Institute of British Geographers* 21 (1996): 635–48.

Goonewardena, Kanishka. "The Urban Sensorium: Space, Ideology, and the Aestheticization of Politics." *Antipode* 37, no. 1 (2005): 46–71.

Goonewardena, Kanishka, Stefan Kipfer, Richard Milgrom, and Christian Schmid, eds. *Space, Difference, Everyday Life: Reading Henri Lefebvre*. New York: Routledge, 2008.

Goswami, Manu. *Producing India: From Colonial Economy to National Space*. Chicago: University of Chicago Press, 2004.

Goswami, Manu. "Rethinking the Modular Nation Form: Toward a Sociohistorical Conception of Nationalism." *Comparative Studies in Society and History* 44, no. 4 (2002): 770–99.

Gottdiener, Mark. *The Social Production of Urban Space*. 2nd ed. Austin: University of Texas Press, 1985.

Gottdiener, Mark. "Space as a Force of Production." *International Journal of Urban and Regional Research* 11 (1987): 405–16.

Gottmann, Jean. *Megalopolis*. Cambridge, MA: MIT Press, 1961.

Gottmann, Jean. *Since Megalopolis: The Urban Writings of Jean Gottmann*. Baltimore: Johns Hopkins University Press, 1990.

Gough, Jamie. "Changing Scale as Changing Class Relations." *Political Geography* 23, no. 2 (2004): 185–211.

Gough, Jamie. "The Contradictions of Neo-Keynesian Local Economic Strategy." *Review of International Political Economy* 3, no. 3 (1996): 434–58.

Gough, Jamie, and Aram Eisenschitz. "The Construction of Mainstream Local Economic Initiatives: Mobility, Socialization and Class Relations." *Economic Geography* 72, no. 2 (1996): 178–95.

Graham, Stephen. "Cities in the Real-Time Age: The Paradigm Challenge of Telecommunications to the Conception and Planning of Urban Space." *Environment and Planning A* 29 (1997): 105–27.

Graham, Stephen, and Simon Marvin. *Splintering Urbanism*. New York: Routledge, 2001.

Greenfield, Adam. *Against the Smart City*. New York: Do projects, 2013.

Gregory, Derek, and John Urry, eds. *Social Relations and Spatial Structures*. New York: Palgrave, 1985.

Hahne, Ulf. *Regionalentwicklung durch Aktivierung intraregionaler Potentiale*. Schriften des Instituts für Regionalforschung der Universität Kiel, Band 8. Munich: Florenz, 1985.

Häkli, Jouni. "In the Territory of Knowledge: State-Centered Discourses and the Construction of Society." *Progress in Human Geography* 25, no. 3 (2001): 403–22.

Hall, Peter. *Cities of Tomorrow*. Cambridge, MA: Blackwell, 2002.

Hall, Peter. *The World Cities*. New York: McGraw-Hill, 1966.

Hall, Peter, and Kathryn Pain, eds. *The Polycentric Metropolis*. London: Earthscan, 2006.

Hall, Stuart. "Marx's Notes on Method: A 'Reading' of the '1857 Introduction.'" *Cultural Studies* 17, no. 2 (2003): 113–49.

Hall, Tim, and Phil Hubbard, eds. *The Entrepreneurial City: Geographies of Politics, Regime and Representation*. London: Wiley, 1998.

Hall, Tim, and Phil Hubbard. "The Entrepreneurial City: New Politics, New Urban Geographies." *Progress in Human Geography* 20, no. 2 (1996): 153–74.

Hancock, Tom. "China Encircles the World with One Belt, One Road Strategy." *Financial Times*, May 3, 2017.

Harding, Alan. "Elite Theory and Growth Machines." In Judge, Stoker, and Wolman, *Theories of Urban Politics*, 35–53.

Harding, Alan. "Review Article: North American Urban Political Economy, Urban Theory and British Research." *British Journal of Political Science* 29 (1999): 673–98.

Harding, Alan. "Urban Regimes and Growth Machines: Towards a Cross-National Research Agenda." *Urban Affairs Quarterly* 29, no. 3 (1994): 356–82.

Harding, Alan. "Urban Regimes in a Europe of the Cities?" *European Urban and Regional Studies* 4, no. 4 (1997): 291–314.

Hardt, Michael, and Antonio Negri. *Commonwealth*. Cambridge, MA: Harvard University Press, 2009.

Harrison, John, and Michael Hoyler, eds. *Megaregions: Globalization's New Urban Form?* Cheltenham: Edward Elgar, 2015.

Hart, Gillian. "Denaturalizing Dispossession: Critical Ethnography in the Age of Resurgent Imperialism." *Antipode* 38, no. 5 (2006): 977–1004.

Hart, Gillian. "Relational Comparison Revisited: Marxist Postcolonial Geographies in Practice." *Progress in Human Geography* 42, no. 3 (2018): 371–94.

Harvey, David. "Cities or Urbanization?" *CITY* 1, no. 1–2 (1996): 38–61.

Harvey, David. *The Condition of Postmodernity*. Cambridge, MA: Blackwell, 1989.

Harvey, David. "From Managerialism to Entrepreneurialism: The Transformation in Urban Governance in Late Capitalism." *Geografiska Annaler: Series B Human Geography* 71, no. 1 (1989): 3–17.

Harvey, David. *The Enigma of Capital: And the Crises of Capitalism*. New York: Oxford University Press, 2010.

Harvey, David. "The Geopolitics of Capitalism." In Gregory and Urry, *Social Relations and Spatial Structures*, 128–63.

Harvey, David. *Justice, Nature and the Geography of Difference*. Oxford: Basil Blackwell, 1996.

Harvey, David. *The Limits to Capital*. Chicago: University of Chicago Press, 1982.

Harvey, David. "Money, Time, Space and the City." In Harvey, *The Urban Experience*, 165–99.

Harvey, David. "Neoliberalism as Creative Destruction." *Annals of the American Academy of Political and Social Science* 610 (2007): 22–44.

Harvey, David. *The New Imperialism*. New York: Oxford University Press, 2003.

Harvey, David. *Rebel Cities: From the Right to the City to the Urban Revolution*. London: Verso, 2012.

Harvey, David. *The Seventeen Contradictions of Capitalism*. New York: Oxford University Press, 2014.

Harvey, David. "Space as a Keyword." In *Spaces of Global Capitalism*, 117–54.

Harvey, David. *Spaces of Capital: Towards a Critical Geography*. New York: Routledge, 2001.

Harvey, David. *Spaces of Global Capitalism*. London: Verso, 2006.

Harvey, David. *The Urban Experience*. Baltimore: Johns Hopkins University Press, 1989.

Harvey, David. "The Urbanization of Capital." In Harvey, *The Urban Experience*, 17–58.

Harvey, David. *The Urbanization of Capital: Studies in the History and Theory of Capitalist Urbanization*. Baltimore: Johns Hopkins University Press, 1985.

Hayashi, Mahito. "Times and Spaces of Homeless Regulation in Japan, 1950s–2000s." *International Journal of Urban and Regional Research* 37, no. 4 (2013): 1188–212.

Heeg, Susanne, Britte Klagge, and Jürgen Ossenbrügge. "Metropolitan Cooperation in Europe: Theoretical Issues and Perspectives for Urban Networking." *European Planning Studies* 11, no. 2 (2003): 139–53.

Hegel, G. W. F. "Preface." In *The Philosophy of Right*, translated by Alan White. Indianapolis: Focus-Hackett, 2002 [1820].

Heinz, Werner, ed. *Stadt & Region—Kooperation oder Koordination? Ein internationaler Vergleich*. Schriften des Deutschen Instituts für Urbanistik, Band 93. Stuttgart: Verlag W. Kohlhammer, 2000.

Held, David. *Democracy and the Global Order: From the Modern State to Cosmopolitan Governance*. Cambridge: Polity, 1995.

Herod, Andrew. "Labor's Spatial Praxis and the Geography of Contract Bargaining in the US East Coast Longshore Industry, 1953–1989." *Political Geography* 16, no. 2 (1997): 145–69.

Herod, Andrew. "The Production of Scale in United States Labour Relations." *Area* 23 (1991): 82–88.

Herod, Andrew. *Scale*. New York: Routledge, 2011.

Herrschel, Tassilo, and Peter Newman. *Governance of Europe's City Regions*. London: Routledge, 2002.

Heynen, Nik, Maria Kaika, and Erik Swyngedouw, eds. *In the Nature of Cities: Urban Political Ecology and the Politics of Urban Metabolism*. New York: Routledge, 2006.

Heynen, Nik, James McCarthy, Scott Prudham, and Paul Robbins, eds. *Neoliberal Environments*. New York: Routledge, 2007.

Hillman, Jonathan. "How Big Is China's One Belt One Road?" Commentary, Center for Strategic and International Studies (CSIS). April 3, 2018. https://www.csis.org/analysis/how-big-chinas-belt-and-road.

Hirschman, Albert. *The Strategy of Economic Development*. New Haven, CT: Yale University Press, 1958.

Horkheimer, Max. "Traditional and Critical Theory." In *Critical Theory: Selected Essays*, translated by Matthew O'Connell, 188–243. New York: Continuum, 1982 [1937].

Howitt, Richard. "Scale as Relation: Musical Metaphors of Geographical Scale." *Area* 30, no. 1 (1998): 49–58.

Hudson, Ray. *Producing Places*. New York: Guilford, 2001.

Hudson, Ray. *Production, Places and Environment*. London: Routledge, 2014.

Hudson, Ray. "Rising Powers and the Drivers of Uneven Global Development." *Area Development and Policy* 1, no. 3 (2016): 279–94.

Hudson, Ray, Mick Dunford, Douglas Hamilton, and Richard Kotter, "Developing Regional Strategies for Economic Success: Lessons from Europe's Economically Successful Regions?" *European Urban and Regional Studies* 4, no. 4 (1997): 365–73.

Isin, Engin. "The City as the Site of the Social." In *Recasting the Social in Citizenship*, edited by Engin Isin, 261–80. Toronto: University of Toronto Press, 2008.

Isin, Engin. "Historical Sociology of the City." In *Handbook of Historical Sociology*, edited by Gerard Delanty and Engin Isin, 312–36. London: Sage, 2003.

Jackson, Kenneth. *Crabgrass Frontier: The Suburbanization of the United States*. New York: Oxford University Press, 1985.

Jacobs, Jane. *The Death and Life of Great American Cities.* New York: Modern Library, 1965.

Jameson, Frederic. "Cognitive Mapping." In *Marxism and the Interpretation of Culture,* edited by Cary Nelson and Lawrence Grossberg, 347–57. Chicago: University of Illinois Press, 1988.

Jameson, Fredric. *The Hegel Variations: On the Phenomenology of Spirit.* New York: Verso, 2014.

Jessop, Bob. "Conservative Regimes and the Transition to Post-Fordism: The Cases of Great Britain and West Germany." In *Capitalist Development and Crisis Theory,* edited by Mark Gottdiener and Nicos Komninos, 261–99. New York: St. Martin's Press, 1989.

Jessop, Bob. "The Crisis of the National Spatio-Temporal Fix and the Ecological Dominance of Globalizing Capitalism." *International Journal of Urban and Regional Research* 24, no. 2 (2000): 323–60.

Jessop, Bob. "Fordism and Post-Fordism: A Critical Reformulation." In Storper and Scott, *Pathways to Industrialization and Regional Development,* 46–69.

Jessop, Bob. *The Future of the Capitalist State.* London: Polity, 2002.

Jessop, Bob. "The Narrative of Enterprise and the Enterprise of Narrative: Place-Marketing and the Entrepreneurial City." In Hall and Hubbard, *The Entrepreneurial City,* 77–102.

Jessop, Bob. "Post-Fordism and the State." In Amin, *Post-Fordism: A Reader,* 251–79.

Jessop, Bob. *State Theory: Putting the Capitalist State in Its Place.* London: Polity, 1990.

Jessop, Bob, Neil Brenner, and Martin Jones. "Theorizing Socio-Spatial Relations." *Environment and Planning D: Society and Space* 26 (2008): 389–401.

Jessop, Bob, Kurt Nielson, and Ove Pedersen. "Structural Competitiveness and Strategic Capacities: Rethinking State and International Capital." In *Institutional Frameworks of Market Economies,* edited by Jerzy Hausner, Bob Jessop, and Kurt Nielsen, 23–44. Brookfield, VT: Avebury, 1993.

Jessop, Bob, Jamie Peck, and Adam Tickell. "Retooling the Machine: Economic Crisis, State Restructuring and Urban Politics." In Jonas and Wilson, *The Urban Growth Machine: Critical Perspectives Two Decades Later,* 141–61.

Johnson, Robert, and Rianne Mahon. "NAFTA, the Redesign, and Rescaling of Canada's Welfare State." *Studies in Political Economy* 76 (Autumn 2005): 7–30.

Jonas, Andrew E. G. "A Place for Politics in Urban Theory: The Organization and Strategies of Urban Coalitions." *Urban Geography* 13, no. 3 (1993): 280–90.

Jonas, Andrew E. G. "Pro Scale: Further Reflections on the 'Scale Debate' within Human Geography." *Transactions of the Institute of British Geographers* 31 (2006): 399–406.

Jonas, Andrew E. G. "The Scale Politics of Spatiality." *Environment and Planning D: Society and Space* 12 (1994): 257–64.

Jonas, Andrew E. G., and Kevin Ward. "Cities Regionalisms: Some Critical Reflections on Transatlantic Urban Policy Convergence." Working Paper Series, Economic Geography Research Group, 2001.

Jonas, Andrew E. G., and David Wilson, eds. *The Urban Growth Machine: Critical Perspectives Two Decades Later.* Albany: State University of New York Press, 1999.

Jouve, Bernard, and Christian Lefèvre. *Villes, métropoles: les nouveaux territoires du politique.* Paris: Anthropos, 1999.

Judd, Dennis, and Todd Swanstrom. *City Politics: Private Power and Public Policy*. New York: Longman, 1998.

Judge, David, Gerry Stoker, and Hal Wolman, eds. *Theories of Urban Politics*. London: Sage, 1995.

Kahn, Andrea. "Defining Urban Sites." In *Site Matters: Design Concepts, Histories, and Strategies*, edited by Carol Burns and Andrea Kahn, 281–96. New York: Routledge, 2005.

Kaika, Maria. "Don't Call Me Resilient Again! The New Urban Agenda as Immunology." *Environment and Urbanization* 29, no. 1 (2017): 89–102.

Kaika, Maria, and Erik Swyngedouw. "Fetishizing the Modern City: The Phantasmagoria of Urban Technological Networks." *International Journal of Urban and Regional Research* 24, no. 1 (2000): 120–38.

Kanai, J. Miguel. "The Pervasiveness of Neoliberal Territorial Design: Cross-Border Infrastructure Planning in South America since the Introduction of IIRSA." *Geoforum* 69 (2016): 160–70.

Kanai, J. Miguel, and Seth Schindler. "Peri-Urban Promises of Connectivity: Linking Project-Led Polycentrism to the Infrastructure Scramble." *Environment and Planning A: Economy and Space* (forthcoming). doi:10.1177/0308518X18763370.

Kantor, Paul. "The End of American Urban Policy—Or a Beginning." *Urban Affairs Review* 52, no. 6 (2016): 887–916.

Karaman, Ozan. "An Immanentist Approach to the Urban." *Antipode* 44, no. 4 (2011): 1287–306.

Katsikis, Nikos. "The Composite Fabric of Urbanization: Agglomeration Landscapes and Operational Landscapes; From Hinterland to Hinterglobe: Urbanization as Geographical Organization." Doctoral diss., Harvard University Graduate School of Design, 2016.

Katsikis, Nikos. "The 'Other' Horizontal Metropolis: Landscapes of Urban Interdependence." In *The Horizontal Metropolis between Urbanism and Urbanization*, edited by Paola Viganò, Chiara Cavalieri, and Martina Barcelloni Corte, 23–46. Berlin: Springer, 2018.

Katsikis, Nikos. "Two Approaches to World Urbanization: R. B. Fuller and C. A. Doxiadis." In Brenner, *Implosions/Explosions*, 480–504.

Katz, Bruce. "Enough of the Small Stuff: Toward a New Urban Agenda." *Brookings Review* 18, no. 3 (2000): 6–11.

Keating, Michael. "The Invention of Regions: Political Restructuring and Territorial Government in Western Europe." *Environment and Planning C: Government and Policy* 15 (1997): 383–98.

Keating, Michael. *The New Regionalism in Western Europe: Territorial Restructuring and Political Change*. Cheltenham: Edward Elgar, 1998.

Keating, Michael. "Size, Efficiency, and Democracy: Consolidation, Fragmentation and Public Choice." In Judge, Stoker, and Wolman, *Theories of Urban Politics*, 117–34.

Keil, Roger. "Governance Restructuring in Los Angeles and Toronto: Amalgamation or Secession?" *International Journal of Urban and Regional Research* 24, no. 4 (2000): 758–81.

Keil, Roger. *Suburban Planet: Making the World Urban from the Outside In*. London: Polity, 2017.

Keil, Roger, and Peter Lieser. "Frankfurt: Global City—Local Politics." In *After Modernism: Global Restructuring and the Changing Boundaries of City Life*, edited by Michael Peter Smith, 39–69. New Brunswick, NJ: Transaction Publishers, 1992.

Keil, Roger, and Rianne Mahon, eds. *Leviathan Undone? The New Political Economy of Scale*. Vancouver: University of British Columbia Press, 2010.

Kelly, Philip F. "Globalization, Power and the Politics of Scale in the Philippines." *Geoforum* 28 (1997): 151–71.

Kennedy, Loraine, and Ashima Sood. "Greenfield Development as Tabula Rasa: Rescaling, Speculation and Governance on India's Urban Frontier." *Economic & Political Weekly*, April 23, 2016, 41–49.

Khanna, Parag. *Connectography: Mapping the Future of Global Civilization*. New York: Random House, 2016.

King, Anthony D. *Global Cities: Post-Imperialism and the Internationalization of London*. New York: Routledge, 1990.

King, Anthony D. *Urbanism, Colonialism and the World Economy*. New York: Routledge, 1991.

Kipfer, Stefan. "Pushing the Limitations of Urban Research: Urbanization, Pipelines and Counter-Colonial Politics." *Environment and Planning D: Society and Space* 36, no. 3 (2018): 474–93.

Kipfer, Stefan. "Why the Urban Question Still Matters: Reflections on Rescaling and the Promise of the Urban." In Keil and Mahon, *Leviathan Undone?*, 67–86.

Klein, Noami. *This Changes Everything: Capitalism vs. the Climate*. New York: Simon & Schuster, 2015.

Knox, Paul L., and Peter J. Taylor, eds. *World Cities in a World-System*. New York: Cambridge University Press, 1995.

Krätke, Stefan. "A Regulationist Approach to Regional Studies." *Environment and Planning A* 31 (1999): 683–704.

Krätke, Stefan. *Stadt, Raum, Ökonomie*. Basel: Birkhäuser Verlag, 1995.

Krätke, Stefan. "Stadtsystem im internationalen Kontext und Vergleich." In *Kommunalpolitik*, edited by Roland Roth and Hellmut Wollmann, 176–93. Opladen: Leske Verlag, 1993.

Krätke, Stefan, and Renate Borst. *Berlin: Metropole im Wandel*. Berlin: Leske + Budrich, 1999.

Krätke, Stefan, Susanne Heeg, and Rolf Stein. *Regionen im Umbruch*. Frankfurt: Campus, 1997.

Krätke, Stefan, and Fritz Schmoll. "Der lokale Staat—'Ausführungsorgan' oder 'Gegenmacht'?" *Prokla* 68 (1987): 30–72.

Kroeber, Gavin. "Experience Economies: Event in the Cultural Economies of Capital." Master's thesis, Harvard University Graduate School of Design, 2012.

Kurgan, Laura. *Close Up at a Distance: Mapping, Technology, Politics*. Cambridge, MA: Zone Books, 2015.

Labban, Mazen. "Deterritorializing Extraction: Bioaccumulation and the Planetary Mine." *Annals of the Association of American Geographers* 104, no. 3 (2014): 560–76.

Läpple, Dieter. "Gesellschaftlicher Reproduktionsprozeß und Stadtstrukturen." In *Stadtkrise und soziale Bewegungen. Texte zur internationale Entwicklung*, edited by Margit Mayer, Roland Roth, and Volkhard Brandes, 23–54. Frankfurt: Europäische Verlagsanstalt, 1978.

Latour, Bruno, and Emilie Hermant. *Paris: Invisible City*. Translated by Liz Carey-Libbrecht. 2006 [1998]. http://www.bruno-latour.fr/virtual/EN/index.html.

Lauria, Mickey, ed. *Reconstructing Urban Regime Theory: Regulating Urban Politics in a Global Economy*. New York: Sage, 1997.

Le Galès, Patrick, and Christian Lequesne, eds. *Regions in Europe: The Politics of Power*. New York: Routledge, 1998.

Leborgne, Danièle, and Alain Lipietz. "Two Social Strategies in the Production of New Industrial Spaces." In Benko and Dunford, *Industrial Change and Regional Development*, 27–49.

Lee, Roger, and Jane Wills, eds. *Geographies of Economies*. London: Arnold, 1997.

Lefebvre, Henri. *De l'État*. 4 vols. Paris: Union Generale d'Editions, 1976–78.

Lefebvre, Henri. "Dissolving City, Planetary Metamorphosis." In Brenner, *Implosions/Explosions*, 566–70. Originally published as "Quand la ville se perd dans une métamorphose planétaire," *Le monde diplomatique*, May 1989.

Lefebvre, Henri. *La production de l'espace*. 4th ed. Paris: Anthropos, 2000 [1974].

Lefebvre, Henri. *The Production of Space*. Translated by Donald Nicholson. Cambridge: Blackwell, 1991 [1974].

Lefebvre, Henri. "Reflections on the Politics of Space." In *State, Space, World: Selected Essays*, edited by Neil Brenner and Stuart Elden, 167–84. Minneapolis: University of Minnesota Press, 2009 [1970].

Lefebvre, Henri. "The Right to the City." In *Writings on Cities*, edited and translated by Eleonore Kofman and Elizabeth Lebas, 63–184. Cambridge: Blackwell, 1996 [1968].

Lefebvre, Henri. "Space and Mode of Production." In *State, Space, World: Selected Essays*, edited by Neil Brenner and Stuart Elden, 210–22. Minneapolis: University of Minnesota Press, 2009 [1980].

Lefebvre, Henri. "Space and the State." In *State, Space, World: Selected Essays*, edited by Neil Brenner and Stuart Elden, 223–53. Minneapolis: University of Minnesota Press, 2009 [1978].

Lefebvre, Henri. *State, Space, World: Selected Essays*. Edited by Neil Brenner and Stuart Elden. Translated by Gerald Moore, Neil Brenner, and Stuart Elden. Minneapolis: University of Minnesota Press, 2009 [1964–86].

Lefebvre, Henri. *The Survival of Capitalism*. Translated by Frank Bryant. New York: St. Martin's Press, 1976 [1973].

Lefebvre, Henri. *The Urban Revolution*. Translated by Robert Bononno. Minneapolis: University of Minnesota Press, 2003 [1970].

Lefèvre, Christian. "Metropolitan Government and Governance in Western Countries: A Critical Overview." *International Journal of Urban and Regional Research* 22, no. 1 (1998): 9–25.

Leitner, Helga. "The Politics of Scale and Networks of Spatial Connectivity." In Sheppard and McMaster, *Scale and Geographic Inquiry*, 236–55.

Leitner, Helga. "Reconfiguring the Spatiality of Power." *Political Geography* 16 (1997): 123–43.

Leitner, Helga, and Byron Miller. "Scale and the Limitations of Ontological Debate: A Commentary on Marston, Jones and Woodward." *Transactions of the Institute of British Geographers* 32 (2007): 116–25.

Leitner, Helga, and Eric Sheppard. "'The City Is Dead, Long Live the Net': Harnessing European Interurban Networks for a Neoliberal Agenda." In Brenner and Theodore, *Spaces of Neoliberalism*, 148–71.

Leitner, Helga, and Eric Sheppard. "Economic Uncertainty, Inter-Urban Competition and the Efficacy of Entrepreneurialism." In Hall and Hubbard, *The Entrepreneurial City*, 285–308.

Leitner, Helga, and Eric Sheppard. "Provincializing Critical Urban Theory: Extending the Ecosystem of Possibilities." *International Journal of Urban and Regional Research* 40, no. 1 (2016): 228–35.

Leitner, Helga, Eric Sheppard, and Kristin Sziarto. "The Spatialities of Contentious Politics." *Transactions of the Institute of British Geographers* 33, no. 2 (2008): 157–72.

Lerup, Lars. *After the City*. Cambridge, MA: MIT Press, 2001.

Levien, Michael. "The Land Question: Special Economic Zones and the Political Economy of Dispossession in India." *Journal of Peasant Studies* 39, no. 3–4 (2012): 933–69.

Levien, Michael. "Special Economic Zones and Accumulation by Dispossession in India." *Journal of Agrarian Change* 11, no. 4 (2011): 454–83.

Li, Zhigang, Jiang Xu, and Anthony G. O. Yeh. "State Rescaling and the Making of City-Regions in the Pearl River Delta, China." *Environment and Planning C: Politics and Space* 32, no. 1 (2014): 129–43.

Lim, Kean Fan. "State Rescaling, Policy Experimentation and Path Dependency in Post-Mao China: A Dynamic Analytical Framework." *Regional Studies* 51, no. 10 (2017): 1580–93.

Lipietz, Alain. "The Local and the Global: Regional Individuality or Interregionalism?" *Transactions of the Institute of British Geographers* 18, no. 1 (1993): 8–18.

Lipietz, Alain. *Mirages and Miracles*. London: Verso, 1987.

Lipietz, Alain. "The National and the Regional: Their Autonomy Vis-à-Vis the Capitalist World Crisis." In *Transcending the State-Global Divide*, edited by Ronen P. Palan and Barry K. Gills, 23–44. Boulder, CO: Lynne Rienner Publishers, 1994.

Lobao, Linda, and Lazarus Adua. "State Rescaling and Local Governments' Austerity Policies across the USA, 2001–2008." *Cambridge Journal of Regions, Economy and Society* 4, no. 3 (2011): 419–35.

Loftus, Alex. "Violent Geographical Abstractions." *Environment and Planning D: Society and Space* 33 (2015): 366–81.

Logan, John, and Harvey Molotch. *Urban Fortunes: The Political Economy of Place*. Berkeley: University of California Press, 1987.

Logan, John, and Todd Swanstrom, eds. *Beyond the City Limits: Urban Policy and Economic Restructuring in Comparative Perspective*. Philadelphia: Temple University Press, 1990.

Lovering, John. "Theory Led by Policy: The Inadequacies of the 'New Regionalism.'" *International Journal of Urban and Regional Research* 23, no. 2 (1999): 379–96.

Low, Murray. "Growth Machines and Regulation Theory: The Institutional Dimension of the Regulation of Space in Australia." *International Journal of Urban and Regional Research* 18 (1999): 451–69.

Lowe, Edward J. "Analytic and Synthetic Statements." In *The Oxford Companion to Philosophy*, 2nd ed., edited by Ted Honderich, 29. Oxford: Oxford University Press, 2005.

Luke, Timothy. "At the End of Nature: Cyborgs, 'Humachines' and Environments in Postmodernity." *Environment and Planning A* 29, no. 8 (1997): 1367–80.

Luke, Timothy. "Developing Planetarian Accountancy: Fabricating Nature as Stock, Service and System for Green Governmentality." *Nature, Knowledge and Negation* 26 (2009): 129–59.

Luke, Timothy. "Global Cities versus 'global cities': Rethinking Contemporary Urbanism as Public Ecology." *Studies in Political Economy* 70 (Spring 2003): 11–33.

Luke, Timothy. "Neither Sustainable nor Development: Reconsidering Sustainability in Development." *Sustainable Development* 13 (2005): 228–38.

Lyall, Sarah. "Will London Fall?" *New York Times*, April 11, 2017.

Lynch, Kevin. *The Image of the City*. Cambridge, MA: MIT Press, 1960.

Machimura, Takashi. "The Urban Restructuring Process in Tokyo in the 1980s: Transforming Tokyo into a World City." *International Journal of Urban and Regional Research* 16, no. 1 (1992): 114–28.

MacLeod, Gordon. "The Learning Region in an Age of Austerity: Capitalizing on Knowledge, Entrepreneurialism and Reflexive Capitalism." *Geoforum* 31 (2000): 219–36.

MacLeod, Gordon. "New Regionalism Reconsidered: Globalization, Regulation and the Recasting of Political Economic Space." *International Journal of Urban and Regional Research* 25, no. 4 (2001): 804–29.

Madden, David. "City Becoming World: Nancy, Lefebvre and the Global-Urban Imagination." *Environment and Planning D: Society and Space* 30, no. 5 (2012): 772–87.

Magdoff, Fred, and Brian Tokar, eds. *Agriculture and Food in Crisis: Conflict, Resistance, and Renewal*. New York: Monthly Review Press, 2011.

Maier, Charles. "Consigning the Twentieth Century to History: Alternative Narratives for the Modern Era." *American Historical Review* 105, no. 3 (2000): 807–31.

Maier, Charles. *Once within Borders: Territories of Power, Wealth and Belonging since 1500*. Cambridge, MA: Harvard University Press, 2016.

Makki, Fouad. "Reframing Development Theory: The Significance of the Idea of Combined and Uneven Development." *Theory and Society* 44 (2015): 471–97.

Mann, Michael. *The Sources of Social Power*, vol. 2: *The Rise of Classes and Nation States, 1760–1914*. New York: Cambridge University Press, 1993.

Marcuse, Peter, and Ronald van Kempen, eds. *Globalizing Cities: A New Spatial Order?* Cambridge, MA: Blackwell, 2001.

Marcuse, Peter, and Ronald van Kempen, eds. *Of States and Cities: The Partitioning of Urban Space*. Oxford: Oxford University Press, 2002.

Marden, Peter. "Geographies of Dissent: Globalization, Identity and the Nation." *Political Geography* 16 (1997): 37–64.

Margulis, Matias, Nora McKeon, and Saturnino M. Borras Jr. "Land Grabbing and Global Governance: Critical Perspectives." *Globalizations* 10, no. 1 (2013): 1–23.

Markusen, Ann. "Class and Urban Social Expenditure: A Marxist Theory." In *Marxism and the Metropolis*, edited by William Tabb and Larry Sawers, 90–112. New York: Oxford University Press, 1979.

Marston, Sallie. "The Social Construction of Scale." *Progress in Human Geography* 24, no. 2 (2000): 219–42.

Marston, Sallie, John Paul Jones, and Keith Woodward. "Human Geography without Scale." *Transactions of the Institute of British Geographers* 30 (2005): 416–32.

Martin, Ron. "Making Sense of the 'New Economy': Realities, Myths and Geographies." In Daniels, Leyshon, Bradshaw, and Beaverstock, *Geographies of the New Economy*, 15–31.

Martin, Ron, and Peter Sunley. "The Post-Keynesian State and the Space Economy." In Lee and Wills, *Geographies of Economies*, 278–89.

Martindale, Don. "Prefatory Remarks: The Theory of the City." In *The City, by Max Weber*, edited and translated by Don Martindale, 9–64. New York: Free Press, 1958.

Martinelli, Flavia, and Erica Schoenberger. "Oligopoly Is Alive and Well: Notes for a Broader Discussion of Flexible Accumulation." In Benko and Dunford, *Industrial Change and Regional Development*, 117–33.

Marx, Karl. *Capital*. Translated by Ben Fowkes. New York: Penguin, 1976 [1867].

Marx, Karl. *Grundrisse: Foundations of the Critique of Political Economy*. Translated by Martin Nicolaus. New York: Penguin Books, 1973 [1857].

Marx, Karl. "Introduction." In Marx, *Grundrisse: Foundations of the Critique of Political Economy*, 81–114.

Marx, Karl, and Friedrich Engels. "Manifesto of the Communist Party." In *Marx/ Engels Selected Works*. Vol. 1. Moscow: Progress Publishers, 1969 [1848].

Massey, Doreen. *For Space*. London: Sage, 2005.

Massey, Doreen. "Power-Geometry and a Progressive Sense of Place." In Bird et al., *Mapping the Futures: Local Cultures, Global Change*, 59–70.

Massey, Doreen. *Space, Place and Gender*. Minneapolis: University of Minnesota Press, 1996.

Massey, Doreen. *Spatial Divisions of Labour*. London: Macmillan, 1985.

Massey, Doreen. *World City*. Cambridge: Polity, 2007.

Mayer, Margit. "Contesting the Neoliberalization of Urban Governance." In Leitner, Peck, and Sheppard, *Contesting Neoliberalism: Urban Frontiers*, 90–115.

Mayer, Margit. "Post-Fordist City Politics." In Amin, *Post-Fordism: A Reader*, 316–37.

Mayer, Margit. "The 'Right to the City' in Urban Social Movements." In Brenner, Mayer, and Marcuse, *Cities for People, Not for Profit*, 63–85.

Mayer, Margit. "The Shifting Local Political System in European Cities." In Dunford and Kafkalas, *Cities and Regions in the New Europe*, 255–76.

Mayer, Margit, Catharina Thörn, and Håkan Thörn. *Urban Uprisings: Challenging Neoliberal Urbanism in Europe*. London: Palgrave, 2016.

McFarlane, Colin. "Assemblage and Critical Urbanism." *CITY* 15, no. 2 (2011): 204–24.

McFarlane, Colin. "The City as Assemblage: Dwelling and Urban Space." *Environment and Planning D: Society and Space* 29 (2011): 649–71.

McGee, Terry. *The Urbanization Process in the Third World*. London: Bell and Sons, 1971.

McGee, Terry. "The Urbanization Process: Western Theory and Third World Reality." In McGee, *The Urbanization Process in the Third World*, 12–34.

McKibben, Bill. *The End of Nature*. New York: Random House, 2006.

McMichael, Philip. *Development and Social Change*. London: Sage, 1996.

McMichael, Philip. *Food Regimes and Agrarian Questions*. Halifax: Fernwood Press, 2013.

McMichael, Philip. "Peasant Prospects in the Neoliberal Age." *New Political Economy* 11, no. 3 (2006): 407–18.

McMichael, Philip. "Rethinking Globalization: The Agrarian Question Revisited." *Review of International Political Economy* 4, no. 4 (1997): 630–62.

Meeteren, Michiel van, David Bassens, and Ben Derudder. "Doing Global Urban Studies: On the Need for Engaged Pluralism, Frame Switching and Methodological Cross-Fertilization." *Dialogues in Human Geography* 6, no. 3 (2010): 296–301.

Megacities. Directed by Michael Glawogger. 1998. Vienna: Lotus-Film GmbH, 2006. DVD.

Merrifield, Andy. *Dialectical Urbanism: Social Struggles in the Capitalist City.* New York: Monthly Review Press, 2002.

Merrifield, Andy. *Metromarxism.* New York: Routledge, 2002.

Merrifield, Andy. *The Politics of the Encounter: Urban Theory and Protest under Planetary Urbanization.* Athens: University of Georgia Press, 2013.

Merrifield, Andy. "The Politics of the Encounter and the Urbanization of the World." *CITY* 16, no. 2 (2012): 265–79.

Merrifield, Andy. "Towards a Metaphilosophy of the Urban." Last modified December 15, 2015. https://antipodefoundation.org/2015/12/04/towards-a-metaphilosophy-of-the-urban/.

Merrifield, Andy. "The Urban Question under Planetary Urbanization." *International Journal of Urban and Regional Research* 37, no. 3 (2013): 909–22.

Miller, Byron. "Is Scale a Chaotic Concept? Notes on Processes of Scale Production." In Keil and Mahon, *Leviathan Undone?*, 51–66.

Miller, Byron. "Political Action and the Geography of Defense Investment." *Political Geography* 16 (1997): 171–85.

Mitchell, Timothy. "The Limits of the State: Beyond Statist Approaches and Their Critics." *American Political Science Review* 85, no. 1 (1991): 77–96.

Mollenkopf, John. *The Contested City.* Princeton, NJ: Princeton University Press, 1983.

Mollenkopf, John, and Manuel Castells, eds. *Dual City: Restructuring New York.* New York: Russell Sage Foundation, 1991.

Molotch, Harvey. "Urban Deals in Comparative Perspective." In Logan and Swanstrom, *Beyond the City Limits*, 175–98.

Molotch, Harvey, and Serena Vicari. "Three Ways to Build: The Development Process in the United States, Japan and Italy." *Urban Affairs Quarterly* 24, no. 2 (1988): 188–214.

Monte-Mór, Roberto Luis. "Extended Urbanization and Settlement Patterns: An Environmental Approach." In Brenner, *Implosions/Explosions*, 109–20.

Monte-Mór, Roberto Luis de Melo. "Modernities in the Jungle: Extended Urbanization in the Brazilian Amazon." PhD diss., Department of Urban Planning, University of California Los Angeles, 2004.

Monte-Mór, Roberto Luis de Melo. "What Is the Urban in the Contemporary World?" *Cadernos de Saúde Pública* 21, no. 3 (2005): 942–48.

Monte-Mór, Roberto Luis, and Rodrigo Castriota. "Extended Urbanization: Implications for Urban and Regional Theory." In *Handbook on the Geographies of Regions and Territories*, edited by Anssi Paasi, John Harrison, and Martin Jones, 332–45. London: Edward Elgar, 2018.

Moore, Jason W., ed. *Anthropocene or Capitalocene? Nature, History and the Crisis of Capitalism.* Oakland, CA: PM Press/Kairos, 2016.

Moore, Jason W. *Capitalism in the Web of Life: Ecology and the Accumulation of Capital*. New York: Verso, 2016.

Moore, Jason W. "The Capitalocene, Part I: On the Nature and Origins of Our Ecological Crisis." *Journal of Peasant Studies* 4, no. 3 (2017): 594–630.

Morgan, Glenn. "Supporting the City: Economic Patriotism in Financial Markets." *Journal of European Public Policy* 19, no. 3 (2012): 373–87.

Mouritzen, Paul E. *Managing Cities in Austerity*. London: Sage, 1992.

Mumford, Lewis. *The City in History*. New York: Harcourt, 1961.

Mumford, Lewis. "A Natural History of Urbanization." In *Man's Role in Changing the Face of the Earth*, edited by William L. Thomas, 382–98. Chicago: University of Chicago Press, 1956.

Mumford, Lewis. "Paleotechnic Paradise: Coketown." In Mumford, *The City in History*, 446–81.

Murray, Martin J. *The Urbanism of Exception: The Dynamics of Global City Building in the Twenty-First Century*. New York: Cambridge University Press, 2016.

Myrdal, Gunnar. *Economic Theory and Under-Developed Regions*. London: Gerald Duckworth, 1957.

Myrdal, Gunnar. *Rich Lands and Poor: The Road to World Prosperity*. New York: Harper, 1958.

Newman, Peter. "Changing Patterns of Regional Governance in the EU." *Urban Studies* 37, no. 5–6 (2000): 895–908.

Nielsen, Klaus, Bob Jessop, and Jerzy Hausner. "Institutional Change in Post-Socialism." In *Strategic Choice and Path-Dependency in Post-Socialism*, edited by Jerzy Hausner, Bob Jessop, and Klaus Nielsen, 3–46. Brookfield, VT: Edward Elgar, 1995.

O'Brien, Richard. *Global Financial Integration: The End of Geography*. London: Pinter, 1990.

Offe, Claus. *Contradictions of the Welfare State*. Edited by John B. Keane. Cambridge, MA: MIT Press, 1984.

Offe, Claus. "'Crisis of Crisis Management': Elements of a Political Crisis Theory." In Offe, *Contradictions of the Welfare State*, 35–64.

Offe, Claus. "Zur Frage der "Identität der kommunalen Ebene." In *Lokale Politikforschung*, edited by Rolf-Richard Grauhan, 2:303–9. New York: Campus, 1975.

Ohmae, Kenichi. *The End of the Nation State: The Rise of Regional Economies*. New York: Free Press, 1995.

Ollman, Bertell. *Dance of the Dialectic*. Urbana: University of Illinois Press, 2003.

Ollman, Bertell. *Dialectical Investigations*. London: Routledge, 1993.

Ollman, Bertell, and Tony Smith, eds. *Dialectics for the New Century*. New York: Palgrave, 2008.

Ong, Aihwa. "The Chinese Axis: Zoning Technologies and Variegated Sovereignty." *Journal of East Asian Studies* 4 (2004): 69–96.

Ong, Aihwa. "Graduated Sovereignty in South-East Asia." *Theory, Culture and Society* 17, no. 4 (2000): 55–75.

"Operational Landscapes Exhibition at Melbourne School of Design." *Urban Theory Lab*. http://urbantheorylab.net/news/operational-landscapes-exhibition-in-melbourne.

Osainder, Andreas. "Sovereignty, International Relations and the Westphalian Myth." *International Organization* 55, no. 2 (2001): 251–87.

Paasi, Anssi. "Place and Region: Looking through the Prism of Scale." *Progress in Human Geography* 28, no. 4 (2004): 536–46.

Painter, Joe. "Rethinking Territory." *Antipode* 42, no. 5 (2010): 1090–118.

Palumbo-Liu, David, Nirvana Tanoukhi, and Bruce Robbins, eds. *Immanuel Wallerstein and the Problem of the World: System, Scale, Culture.* Durham, NC: Duke University Press, 2011.

Panitch, Leo. "Globalization and the State." In *Socialist Register 1994,* edited by Ralph Miliband and Leo Panitch, 60–93. London: Merlin Press, 1994.

Park, Bae-Gyoon. "State Rescaling in Non-Western Contexts." *International Journal of Urban and Regional Research* 37, no. 4 (2013): 1115–22.

Park, Bae-Gyoon, Richard Child Hill, and Asato Saito, eds. *Locating Neoliberalism in East Asia: Neoliberalizing Spaces in Developmental States.* Oxford: Blackwell, 2011.

Park, Robert, and Ernest Burgess, eds. *The City.* Chicago: University of Chicago Press, 1967 [1925].

Parkinson, Michael. "The Rise of the Entrepreneurial European City: Strategic Responses to Economic Changes in the 1980s." *Ekistics* 350 (1991): 299–307.

Parnell, Susan. "Defining a Global Urban Development Agenda." *World Development* 78 (2016): 529–40.

Parnell, Susan, and Sophie Oldfield, eds. *The Routledge Handbook on Cities of the Global South.* London: Routledge, 2014.

Parnell, Susan, and Edgar Pieterse. "Translational Global Praxis: Rethinking Methods and Modes of African Urban Research." *International Journal of Urban and Regional Research* 40, no. 1 (2016): 236–46.

Patel, Raj. "The Long Green Revolution." *Journal of Peasant Studies* 40, no. 1 (2013): 1–63.

Peck, Jamie. "Cities beyond Compare?" *Regional Studies* 49, no. 1 (2015): 160–82.

Peck, Jamie. "Doing Regulation." In *The Oxford Handbook of Economic Geography,* edited by Gordon Clark, Maryann Feldman, and Meric Gertler, 61–82. New York: Oxford University Press, 2000.

Peck, Jamie. "Macroeconomic Geographies." *Area Development and Policy* 1, no. 3 (2016): 305–22.

Peck, Jamie. "Political Economies of Scale: Fast Policy, Interscalar Relations and Neoliberal Workfare." *Economic Geography* 78, no. 3 (2002): 332–60.

Peck, Jamie. "Struggling with the Creative Class." *International Journal of Urban and Regional Research* 29, no. 4 (2005): 740–70.

Peck, Jamie. "Uneven Regional Development." In *The International Encyclopedia of Geography,* edited by Douglas Richardson et al., 1–17. Oxford: John Wiley and Sons, 2017.

Peck, Jamie. *Work-Place: The Social Regulation of Labor Markets.* New York: Guilford, 1996.

Peck, Jamie, and Adam Tickell. "Neoliberalizing Space." In Brenner and Theodore, *Spaces of Neoliberalism,* 33–57.

Peck, Jamie, and Adam Tickell. "Searching for a New Institutional Fix: The After-Fordist Crisis and the Global-Local Disorder." In Amin, *Post-Fordism: A Reader,* 280–315.

Peck, Jamie, and Adam Tickell. "The Social Regulation of Uneven Development: Regulatory Deficit,' England's South East, and the Collapse of Thatcherism." *Environment and Planning A* 27 (1995): 15–40.

Peet, Richard, Paul Robbins, and Michael J. Watts, eds. *Global Political Ecology.* New York: Routledge, 2011.

Phelps, Nicholas, and Terutomo Ozawa. "Contrasts in Agglomeration: Proto-Industrial, Industrial and Post-Industrial Forms Compared." *Progress in Human Geography* 27, no. 5 (2003): 583–604.

Picciotto, Sol. "The Internationalisation of the State." *Capital & Class* 15, no. 1 (1991): 43–63.

Pinson, Gilles. *Gouverner la ville par project: urbanisme et gouvernance de villes européenes.* Paris: Presses de Sciences Po, 2009.

Potere, David, and Annemarie Schneider. "A Critical Look at Representations of Urban Areas in Global Maps." *GeoJournal* 69 (2007): 55–80.

Poulantzas, Nicos. *State, Power, Socialism.* Translated by Patrick Camiller. London: New Left Books, 1978.

Pred, Allan. *City-Systems in Advanced Economies.* London: Hutchinson, 1977.

Prigge, Walter, and Klaus Ronneberger. "Globalisierung und Regionalisierung—Zur Auflösung Frankfurts in die Region." *Österreichische Zeitschrift für Soziologie* 21, no. 2 (1996): 129–38.

Radice, Hugo. "The National Economy: A Keynesian Myth?" *Capital and Class* 22 (1984): 111–40.

Rautenstrauch, Lorenz. "Frankfurt und sein Umland: Planung, Politik, Perspektiven im Bereich des Umlandverbandes Frankfurt." In *Verdichtungsregionen im Umbruch,* edited by Manfred Streit and Hans-Arthur Haasis, 233–98. Baden-Baden: Nomos, 1990.

Reinert, Hugo, and Erik Reinert. "Creative Destruction in Economics: Nietzsche, Sombart, Schumpeter." In *Friedrich Nietzsche 1844–2000: Economy and Society,* edited by Jürgen Georg Backhaus and Wolfgang Drechsler, 55–85. Boston: Kluwer, 2006.

Rhodes, Martin. "'Subversive Liberalism': Market Integration, Globalization and the European Welfare State." *Journal of European Public Policy* 2, no. 3 (1995): 384–406.

Robinson, Jennifer. "Comparative Urbanism: New Geographies and Cultures of Theorizing the Urban." *International Journal of Urban and Regional Research* 40, no. 1 (2016): 187–99.

Robinson, Jennifer. "Global and World Cities: A View from off the Map." *International Journal of Urban and Regional Research* 26, no. 3 (2002): 531–54.

Robinson, Jennifer. "New Geographies of Theorizing the Urban: Putting Comparison to Work for Global Urban Studies." In Parnell and Oldfield, *The Routledge Handbook on Cities of the Global South,* 57–70.

Robinson, Jennifer. *Ordinary Cities.* London: Routledge, 2006.

Rodriguez-Pose, Andres. *The Dynamics of Regional Growth in Europe.* Oxford: Clarendon Press, 1998.

Ronneberger, Klaus. "Kontrollierte Autonomie und rigide Norm: zur neoliberalen Restrukturierung des Sozialen." *Widersprüche* 69 (1998): 129–50.

Ronneberger, Klaus, and Roger Keil. "Ausser Atem—Frankfurt nach der Postmoderne." In *Capitales Fatales: Urbanisierung und Politik in den Finanzmetropolen*, edited by Hansruedi Hitz, 208–84. Zürich: Rotpunktverlag, 1995.

Ronneberger, Klaus, and Christian Schmid. "Globalisierung und Metropolenpolitik: Überlegungen zum Urbanisierungsprozess der neunziger Jahre." In *Capitales Fatales: Urbanisierung und Politik in den Finanzmetropolen Frankfurt und Zürich*, edited by Hansruedi Hitz, Roger Keil, Ute Lehrer, Klaus Ronneberger, Christian Schmid, and Richard Wolff, 379–98. Zürich: Rotpunktverlag, 1995.

Rosenau, James N., and Ernst Otto Czempiel, eds. *Governance without Government: Order and Change in World Politics*. Cambridge: Cambridge University Press, 1992.

Roy, Ananya. "The 21st Century Metropolis: New Geographies of Theory." *Regional Studies* 43, no. 6 (2009): 819–30.

Roy, Ananya. "What Is Urban about Critical Urban Theory?" *Urban Geography* 37, no. 6 (2016): 810–23.

Roy, Ananya. "Who's Afraid of Postcolonial Theory?" *International Journal of Urban and Regional Research* 40, no. 1 (2016): 200–9.

Roy, Ananya. "Worlding the South: Toward a Post-Colonial Urban Theory." In Parnell and Oldfield, *The Routledge Handbook on Cities of the Global South*, 9–20.

Roy, Ananya, and Aihwa Ong, eds. *Worlding Cities: Asian Experiments and the Art of Being Global*. Oxford: Wiley-Blackwell, 2011.

Ruggie, John Gerard. "Territoriality and Beyond: Problematizing Modernity in International Relations." *International Organization* 47, no. 1 (1993): 139–74.

Rusk, David. *Inside Game/Outside Game: Winning Strategies for Saving Urban America*. Washington, DC: Brookings Institution Press, 1998.

Sack, Robert. *Human Territoriality: Its Theory and History*. New York: Cambridge University Press, 1986.

Saez, Guy, Jean-Philippe Leresche, and Michel Bassand, eds. *Gouvernance métropolitaine et transfrontaliére: action publique territorial*. Paris: Editions L'Harmattan, 1997.

Said, Edward. "Traveling Theory." In *The World, the Text and the Critic*. Cambridge, MA: Harvard University Press, 1983.

Salet, Willem, Andy Thornley, and Anton Kreukels, eds. *Metropolitan Governance and Spatial Planning*. London: Spon Press, 2003.

Saller, Raymond. "Kommunale Kooperation innerhalb westdeutscher Stadtregionen zwischen Anspruch und politischer Realität." *Raumforschung und Raumordnung* 2, no. 58 (2000): 211–21.

Santos, Boaventura de Sousa. *Epistemologies of the South: Justice against Epistemicide*. Boulder, CO: Paradigm Publishers, 2014.

Sarkis, Hashim. "The World According to Architecture: Beyond Cosmopolis." *New Geographies* 4 (2011): 104–8.

Sassen, Saskia. *Cities in the World Economy*. London: Sage, 1993.

Sassen, Saskia. "The City: Its Return as a Lens for Social Theory." *City, Culture and Society* 1 (2010): 3–11.

Sassen, Saskia. *Expulsions: Brutality and Complexity in the Global Economy*. Cambridge, MA: Harvard University Press, 2014.

Sassen, Saskia. "Frontiers Facing Urban Sociology at the Millennium." *British Journal of Sociology* 51, no. 1 (2000): 143–59.

Sassen, Saskia. *The Global City: New York, London, Tokyo.* Princeton, NJ: Princeton University Press, 1991.

Sassen, Saskia. *Losing Control? Sovereignty in an Age of Globalization.* New York: Columbia University Press, 1996.

Sassen, Saskia. "Territory and Territoriality in the Global Economy." *International Sociology* 15, no. 2 (2000): 372–93.

Sassen, Saskia. *Territory, Authority, Rights.* Princeton, NJ: Princeton University Press, 2006.

Saunders, Peter. *Social Theory and the Urban Question.* 2nd ed. London: Routledge, 1986 [1981].

Saunders, Peter. *Urban Politics: A Sociological Interpretation.* London: Heinemann, 1979.

Sayer, Andrew. "Abstraction: A Realist Interpretation." *Radical Philosophy* 28 (Summer 1981): 6–15.

Sayer, Andrew. "Behind the Locality Debate: Deconstructing Geography's Dualisms." *Environment and Planning A* 23, no. 3 (1991): 283–308.

Sayre, Nathan. "Climate Change, Scale, and Devaluation: The Challenge of Our Built Environment." *Washington and Lee Journal of Energy, Climate and Environment* 1, no. 1 (2010): 92–105.

Sayer, Andrew. "Defining the Urban." *GeoJournal* 9, no. 3 (1984): 279–85.

Sayre, Nathan. "Ecological and Geographical Scale: Parallels and Potential for Integration." *Progress in Human Geography* 29, no. 3 (2005): 276–90.

Sayer, Andrew. *Method in Social Science.* 2nd ed. London: Routledge, 1992.

Sayer, Andrew. "Postfordism in Question." *International Journal of Urban and Regional Research* 13, no. 3 (1989): 666–95.

Sbragia, Alberta. *Debt Wish: Entrepreneurial Cities, U.S. Federalism, and Economic Development.* Pittsburgh, PA: University of Pittsburgh Press, 1996.

Sbragia, Alberta. "Politics, Local Government and the Municipal Bond Market." In *The Municipal Money Chase: The Politics of Local Government Finance,* edited by Alberta Sbragia. Boulder, CO: Westview Press, 1983.

Scharpf, Fritz W. *Crisis and Choice in European Social Democracy.* Ithaca, NY: Cornell University Press, 1991.

Schmid, Christian. "The Agglomeration Question, Revisited." Working Paper, Contemporary City Institute, Department of Architecture, ETH Zurich, July 2018.

Schmid, Christian. "Henri Lefebvre, the Right to the City and the New Metropolitan Mainstream." In Brenner, Mayer, and Marcuse, *Cities for People, Not for Profit,* 42–62.

Schmid, Christian. "Journeys through Planetary Urbanization: Decentering Perspectives on the Urban." *Environment and Planning D: Society and Space* 36, no. 3 (2018): 591–610.

Schmid, Christian. *Patterns and Pathways of Global Urbanisation: Towards a Comparative Analysis.* Zurich: Urban Theory Lab ETH Zurich, 2012.

Schmid, Christian. "Specificity and Urbanization: A Theoretical Outlook." In ETH Studio Basel, *The Inevitable Specificity of Cities,* 282–97.

Schmid, Christian. *Stadt, Raum und Gesellschaft: Henri Lefebvre und die Theorie der Produktion des Raumes.* Stuttgart: Franz Steiner Verlag, 2005.

Schmid, Christian. "Theory." In Diener et al., *Switzerland: An Urban Portrait,* 1:163–224.

Schmid, Christian. "The Urbanization of the Territory: On the Research Approach of ETH Studio Basel." In ETH Studio Basel/Contemporary City Institute, *Territory: On the Development of Landscape and City,* 22–48.

Schmid, Christian, Ozan Karaman, Naomi Hanakata, Pascal Kallenberger, Anne Kockelkorn, Lindsay Sawyer, Monika Streule, and Kit Ping Wong. "Towards a New Vocabulary of Urbanization Processes: A Comparative Approach." *Urban Studies* 55, no. 1 (2018): 19–52.

Scott, Allen J., ed. *Global City-Regions: Theory, Trends, Policy.* New York: Oxford University Press, 2001.

Scott, Allen J. "Regional Motors of the Global Economy." *Futures* 28, no. 5 (1996): 391–411.

Scott, Allen J. *Regions and the World Economy.* Oxford: Oxford University Press, 1998.

Scott, Allen J. *The Urban Land Nexus and the State.* London: Pion, 1980.

Scott, Allen J., and Michael Storper. "Industrialization and Regional Development." In *Pathways to Industrialization and Regional Development,* edited by Allen J. Scott and Michael Storper. New York: Routledge, 1992.

Scott, Allen J., and Michael Storper. "The Nature of Cities: The Scope and Limits of Urban Theory." *International Journal of Urban and Regional Research* 39, no. 1 (2015): 1–15.

Scott, Allen J., and Michael Storper, eds. *Production, Work, Territory: The Geographical Anatomy of Industrial Capitalism.* London: Allen & Unwin, 1986.

Scott, James C. "State Simplifications: Nature, Space and People." *Journal of Political Philosophy* 3, no. 3 (1995): 191–233.

Scott, Joan. "The Evidence of Experience." *Critical Inquiry* 17, no. 4 (1991): 773–97.

Seijdel, Jorinde, and Pascal Gielen, eds. "The Art Biennial as a Global Phenomenon: Strategies in Neoliberal Times." *Cahier on Art and the Public Domain* 16 (2009). https://www.onlineopen.org/the-art-biennial-as-a-global-phenomenon.

Sevilla-Buitrago, Álvaro. "*Urbs in Rure*: Historical Enclosure and the Extended Urbanization of the Countryside." In Brenner, *Implosions/Explosions,* 236–59.

Sewell, William. "Charles Tilly's *Vendée* as a Model for Social History." *French Historical Studies* 33, no. 2 (2010): 307–15.

Sewell, William. "A Theory of Structure: Duality, Agency and Transformation." *American Journal of Sociology* 98, no. 1 (1992): 1–29.

Sharpe, L. J., ed. *The Government of World Cities: The Future of the Metro Model.* New York: John Wiley & Sons, 1995.

Sheppard, Eric. "Geographic Dialectics." *Environment and Planning A* 40 (2008): 2603–12.

Sheppard, Eric. "The Spaces and Times of Globalization: Place, Scale, Networks and Positionality." *Economic Geography* 33, no. 3 (2002): 307–30.

Sheppard, Eric, and Robert McMaster, eds. *Scale and Geographic Inquiry.* Malden, MA: Blackwell, 2004.

Sieverts, Thomas. *Cities without Cities: An Interpretation of the Zwischenstadt.* New York: Spon Press, 2003.

Smith, Caroline Filice. "Logistics Urbanism: The Socio-Spatial Project of China's One Belt, One Road Initiative." Master's thesis, Harvard University Graduate School of Design, May 2017.

Smith, Michael Peter, and Joe Feagin, ed. *The Capitalist City*. Cambridge, MA: Blackwell, 1989.

Smith, Neil. "Dangers of the Empirical Turn." *Antipode* 19 (1987): 59–68.

Smith, Neil. "Geography, Difference and the Politics of Scale." In *Postmodernism and the Social Sciences*, edited by Joe Doherty, Elspeth Graham, and Mo Malek, 57–79. New York: St. Martin's Press, 1992.

Smith, Neil. "Homeless/Global: Scaling Places." In Bird et al., *Mapping the Futures: Local Cultures, Global Change*, 87–119.

Smith, Neil. "Nature as Accumulation Strategy." *Socialist Register* 43 (2007): 1–21.

Smith, Neil. "Remaking Scale: Competition and Cooperation in Prenational and Postnational Europe." In *Competitive European Peripheries*, edited by Heikki Eskelinen and Folke Snickars, 59–74. Berlin: Springer Verlag, 1995.

Smith, Neil. "The Satanic Geographies of Globalization: Uneven Development in the 1990s." *Public Culture* 10, no. 1 (1997): 169–92.

Smith, Neil. "Scale Bending and the Fate of the National." In Sheppard and McMaster, *Scale and Geographic Inquiry*, 192–212.

Smith, Neil. *Uneven Development: Nature, Capital and the Production of Space*. New York: Blackwell, 1984.

Smith, Neil, and Cindi Katz. "Grounding Metaphor: Towards a Spatialized Politics." In *Place and the Politics of Identity*, edited by Michael Keith and Steve Pile, 67–83. London: Routledge, 1993.

Smith, Neil, and Dennis Ward. "The Restructuring of Geographical Scale: Coalescence and Fragmentation of the Northern Core Region." *Economic Geography* 63, no. 2 (1987): 160–82.

Soederberg, Susanne, and Alan Walks. "Producing and Governing Inequalities under Planetary Urbanization: From Urban Age to Urban Revolution?" *Geoforum* 89 (2018): 107–13.

Soja, Edward W. "Economic Restructuring and the Internationalization of Los Angeles." In Smith and Feagin, *The Capitalist City*, 178–98.

Soja, Edward W. "Inside Exopolis: Scenes from Orange County." In *Variations on a Theme Park: The New American City and the End of Public Space*, edited by Michael Sorkin, 94–122. New York: Noonday Press, 1994.

Soja, Edward W. "The Postfordist Industrial Metropolis." In Soja, *Postmetropolis*, 156–88.

Soja, Edward W. *Postmetropolis*. Cambridge, MA: Blackwell, 2000.

Soja, Edward W. *Postmodern Geographies*. New York: Verso, 1989.

Soja, Edward W. "Regional Urbanization and the End of the Metropolis Era." In *The New Blackwell Companion to the City*, edited by Gary Bridge and Sophie Watson. Oxford: Blackwell, 2011.

Soja, Edward W. "Regions in Context: Spatiality, Periodicity, and the Historical Geography of the Regional Question." *Environment and Planning D: Society and Space* 3 (1985): 175–90.

Soja, Edward W. *Seeking Spatial Justice*. Minneapolis: University of Minnesota Press, 2010.

Soja, Edward W., and Miguel Kanai. "The Urbanization of the World." In Burdett and Sudjic, *The Endless City*, 54–69.

Sowers, Elizabeth A., Paul S. Ciccantell, and David A. Smith. "Labor and Social Movements' Strategic Usage of the Global Commodity Chain Structure." In *Choke Points: Logistics Workers Disrupting the Global Supply Chain*, edited by Jake Alimahomed-Wilson and Immanuel Ness, 19–34. London: Pluto Press, 2018.

Spruyt, Hendrik. *The Sovereign State and Its Competitors: An Analysis of Systems Change*. Princeton, NJ: Princeton University Press, 1994.

Staeheli, Lynn. "Empowering Political Struggle: Spaces and Scales of Resistance." *Political Geography* 13 (1994): 387–91.

STANDORT. "Neubau der Region." *STANDORT—Zeitschrift für Angewandte Geographie* 24, no. 2 (2000): 5–8.

Stanek, Łukasz. *Henri Lefebvre on Space: Architecture, Urban Research and the Production of Theory*. Minneapolis: University of Minnesota Press, 2011.

Stanek, Łukasz, Christian Schmid, and Ákos Moravánszky, eds. *Urban Revolution Now: Henri Lefebvre in Social Research and Architecture*. London: Routledge, 2014.

Starostra, Guido, and Greig Charnock, eds. *The New International Division of Labour: Global Transformation and Uneven Development*. New York: Palgrave, 2016.

Stavrides, Stavros. *Common Space: The City as Commons*. London: Zed, 2016.

Stöhr, Walter, and David R. Taylor. *Development from Above or Below? The Dialectics of Regional Planning in Developing Countries*. New York: Wiley, 1981.

Stone, Clarence. *Regime Politics: The Governing of Atlanta, 1946–1988*. Lawrence: University Press of Kansas, 1989.

Stone, Clarence, and Heywood Sanders, eds. *The Politics of Urban Development*. Lawrence: University Press of Kansas, 1987.

Storper, Michael. "The Resurgence of Regional Economies, Ten Years Later: The Region as a Nexus of Untraded Interdependencies." *European Urban and Regional Studies* 2, no. 3 (1995): 191–221.

Storper, Michael. *The Regional World: Territorial Development in a Global Economy*. New York: Guilford, 1997.

Storper, Michael, and Allen J. Scott. "Current Debates in Urban Studies: A Critical Assessment." *Urban Studies* 53, no. 6 (2016): 1114–38.

Storper, Michael, and Allen Scott. "The Geographical Foundations and Social Regulation of Flexible Production Complexes." In Wolch and Dear, *The Power of Geography*, 24–27.

Storper, Michael, and Allen J. Scott, eds. *Pathways to Industrialization and Regional Development*. New York: Routledge, 1992.

Storper, Michael, and Allen J. Scott. "The Wealth of Regions: Market Forces and Policy Imperatives in Local and Global Context." *Futures* 27, no. 5 (1995): 505–26.

Storper, Michael, and Richard Walker. *The Capitalist Imperative: Territory, Technology and Industrial Growth*. New York: Basil Blackwell, 1989.

Strange, Susan. "The Defective State." *Daedalus, Journal of the American Academy of Arts and Sciences* 124, no. 2 (1995): 55–74.

Sum, Ngai-Ling. "Time-Space Embeddedness and Geo-Governance of Cross-Border Regional Modes of Growth." In *Beyond Market and Hierarchy*, edited by Ash Amin and Jerzy Hausner, 159–95. Cheltenham: Edward Elgar, 1997.

Swyngedouw, Erik. "The Antinomies of the Post-Political City: In Search of a Democratic Politics of Environmental Protection." *International Journal of Urban and Regional Research* 33, no. 3 (2009): 601–20.

Swyngedouw, Erik. "The Heart of the Place: The Resurrection of Locality in an Age of Hyperspace." *Geografiska Annaler B* 71 (1989): 31–42.

Swyngedouw, Erik. *Liquid Power: Contested Hydro-Modernities in Twentieth Century Spain.* Cambridge, MA: MIT Press, 2015.

Swyngedouw, Erik. "The Mammon Quest: 'Glocalisation,' Interspatial Competition, and the Monetary Order: The Construction of New Scales." In Dunford and Kafkalas, *Cities and Regions in the New Europe,* 39–68.

Swyngedouw, Erik. "Metabolic Urbanization: The Making of Cyborg Cities." In Heynen, Kaika, and Swyngedouw, *In the Nature of Cities,* 21–62.

Swyngedouw, Erik. "Neither Global nor Local: 'Glocalization' and the Politics of Scale." In Cox, *Spaces of Globalization,* 137–66.

Swyngedouw, Erik. "Reconstructing Citizenship, the Re-Scaling of the State and the New Authoritarianism: Closing the Belgian Mines." *Urban Studies* 33 (1996): 1499–521.

Swyngedouw, Erik. "Territorial Organization and the Space/Technology Nexus." *Transactions of the Institute of British Geographers* 17 (1992): 417–33.

Swyngedouw, Erik, and Nik Heynen. "Urban Political Ecology, Justice and the Politics of Scale." *Antipode* 35, no. 5 (2003): 898–918.

Swyngedouw, Erik, Frank Moulaert, and Arantxa Rodriguez. "Neoliberal Urbanization in Europe: Large-Scale Urban Development Projects and the New Urban Policy." In Brenner and Theodore, *Spaces of Neoliberalism,* 195–229.

Taylor, Peter J. "Corporate Social Science and the Loss of Curiosity." *Items: Insights from the Social Sciences.* Social Science Research Council. August 2, 2016. https://items.ssrc.org/corporate-social-science-and-the-loss-of-curiosity.

Taylor, Peter J. "Embedded Statism and the Social Sciences: Opening Up to New Spaces." *Environment and Planning A* 28 (1996): 1917–28.

Taylor, Peter J. "Geographical Scales within the World-economy Approach." *Review* 5, no. 1 (1981): 3–11.

Taylor, Peter J. "Is the UK Big Enough for Both London and England?" *Environment and Planning A* 29, no. 5 (1997): 766–70.

Taylor, Peter J. "A Materialist Framework for Political Geography." *Transactions of the Institute of British Geographers* 7 (1982): 15–34.

Taylor, Peter J. "The Paradox of Geographical Scale in Marx's Politics." *Antipode* 19 (1994): 387–91.

Taylor, Peter J. *Political Geography: World-Economy, Nation-State and Locality.* New York: Longman, 1985.

Taylor, Peter J. "The State as Container: Territoriality in the Modern World-System." *Progress in Human Geography* 18 (1994): 151–62.

Taylor, Peter J. "Understanding the 1980s, Part 1a." *Review of International Political Economy* 1, no. 2 (1994): 365–73.

Taylor, Peter J. "World Cities and Territorial States: The Rise and Fall of Their Mutuality." In Knox and Taylor, *World Cities in a World-System,* 48–62.

Taylor, Peter J. *World-City Network.* London: Routledge, 2004.

Taylor, Peter J., and Ben Derudder. "Porous Europe: European Cities in Global Urban Arenas." *Tijdschrift voor Economische en Sociale Geografie* 95, no. 2 (2004): 527–38.

Taylor, Peter J., and Michael Hoyler. "The Spatial Order of European Cities under Conditions of Contemporary Globalization." *Tijdschrift voor Economische en Sociale Geografie* 91, no. 2 (2000): 176–89.

Terhorst, Pieter, and Jacques van de Ven. *Fragmented Brussels and Consolidated Amsterdam: A Comparative Study of the Spatial Organization of Property Rights, Netherlands Geographical Studies 223.* Amsterdam: Netherlands Geographical Society, 1997.

Terhorst, Pieter, and Jacques van de Ven. "The National Urban Growth Coalition in the Netherlands." *Political Geography* 14, no. 4 (1995): 343–61.

Teschke, Benno. *The Myth of 1648: Class, Geopolitics and the Making of Modern International Relations.* London: Verso, 2003.

Thom, René. *Modèles Mathémathiques de la Morphogénèse: Recueil de Textes sur la Theorie des Catastrophes et ses Applications.* Paris: Union Générale d'Editions, 1974. Translated by W. M. Brookes and D. Rand as *Mathematical Models of Morphogenesis* (New York: Halsted Press, 1983).

Thomas, Gieryn. "A Space for Place in Sociology." *Annual Review of Sociology* 26 (2000): 463–96.

Tilly, Charles. *Coercion, Capital and European States, AD 990–1990.* Oxford: Blackwell, 1990.

Tilly, Charles. *The Vendée: A Sociological Analysis of the Counter-Revolution of 1793.* Cambridge, MA: Harvard University Press, 1973.

Tömmel, Ingeborg. "Decentralization of Regional Development Policies in the Netherlands—A New Type of State Intervention?" *West European Politics* 15, no. 2 (1992): 107–25.

Tömmel, Ingeborg. "Internationale Regulation und lokale Modernisierung." *Zeitschrift für Wirtschaftsgeographie* 40, no. 1–2 (1996): 44–58.

Torfing, Jacob. "Towards a Schumpeterian Workfare Postnational Regime: Path-Shaping and Path-Dependency in Danish Welfare State Reform." *Economy and Society* 28, no. 1 (1999): 369–402.

Toscano, Alberto. "Lineaments of the Logistical State." *Viewpoint Magazine.* September 27, 2014. https://viewpointmag.com/2014/09/28/lineaments-of-the-logistical-state/.

Toscano, Alberto. "The Open Secret of Real Abstraction." *Rethinking Marxism* 20, no. 2 (2008): 273–87.

Tsing, Anna Lowenhaupt. *Friction: An Ethnography of Global Connection.* Princeton, NJ: Princeton University Press, 2005.

Tsing, Anna Lowenhaupt. "On Nonscalability: The Living World Is Not Amenable to Precision-Nested Scales." *Common Knowledge* 18, no. 3 (2012): 505–24.

Tsing, Anna Lowenhaupt. "Supply Chains and the Human Condition." *Rethinking Marxism* 21, no. 2 (2009): 148–76.

Tsukamoto, Takashi. "Neoliberalization of the Developmental State: Tokyo's Bottom-Up Politics and State Rescaling in Japan." *International Journal of Urban and Regional Research* 31, no. 1 (2012): 71–89.

Uchida, Hirotsugu, and Andrew Nelson. "Agglomeration Index: Towards a New Measure of Urban Concentration." Working Paper 29, United Nations University, 2010. https://www.wider.unu.edu/publication/agglomeration-index.

United Nations Centre for Human Settlements. *An Urbanizing World: Global Report on Human Settlements.* Oxford: Oxford University Press for the United Nations Centre for Human Settlements (HABITAT), 1996.

United Nations Department of Economic and Social Affairs, Population Division. *2001 Revision of World Urbanization Prospects.* New York: United Nations, 2002.

United Nations Department of Economic and Social Affairs, Population Division. *2011 Revision of World Urbanization Prospects.* New York: United Nations, 2012.

United Nations Human Settlement Programme. *The State of the World's Cities Report 2006/2007—30 Years of Shaping the Habitat Agenda.* London: Earthscan for UN-Habitat, 2007.

United Nations Human Settlement Programme. *The State of the World's Cities Report 2010/2011—Cities for All: Bridging the Urban Divide.* London: Earthscan for UN-Habitat, 2011.

Upmeyer, Bernd, ed. "Non-Urbanism." *MONU* 16 (2012).

Urban Theory Lab. *Operational Landscapes* exhibition. Melbourne: Melbourne School of Design, 2015.

Urbanized. Directed by Gary Hustwit. London: Swiss Dots, 2011. DVD.

Vale, Lawrence J. "The Politics of Resilient Cities: Whose Resilience and Whose City?" *Building Research & Information* 42, no. 2 (2014): 191–201.

Veltz, Pierre. "The Dynamics of Production Systems, Territories and Cities." In *Cities, Enterprises and Society on the Eve of the 21st Century*, edited by Frank Moulaert and Allen J. Scott, 78–96. London: Pinter, 1997.

Veltz, Pierre. "European Cities in the World Economy." In *Cities in Contemporary Europe*, edited by Arnaldo Bagnasco and Patrick Le Galés, 33–34. New York: Cambridge University Press, 2000.

Veltz, Pierre. *Mondialisation, villes et territoires: L'économie d'archipel.* Paris: Presses Universitaires de France, 1993.

Wachsmuth, David. "City as Ideology." *Environment and Planning D: Society and Space* 32, no. 1 (2014): 75–90.

Wachsmuth, David. "Competitive Multi-City Regionalism: Growth Politics beyond the Growth Machine." *Regional Studies* 51, no. 4 (2017): 643–53.

Wachsmuth, David. "Infrastructure Alliances: Supply-Chain Expansion and Multi-City Growth Coalitions." *Economic Geography* 93, no. 1 (2017): 44–65.

Wachsmuth, David. "Three Ecologies: Urban Metabolism and the Society-Nature Opposition." *Sociological Quarterly* 53, no. 4 (2012): 506–23.

Wachsmuth, David, Daniel Aldana Cohen, and Hillary Angelo. "Expand the Frontiers of Urban Sustainability." *Nature* 536 (August 25, 2016): 391–93.

Wachsmuth, David, David J. Madden, and Neil Brenner. "Between Abstraction and Complexity: Meta-Theoretical Observations on the Assemblage Debate." *CITY* 15, no. 6 (2011): 740–50.

Wacquant, Loïc. "Revisiting Territories of Relegation: Class, Ethnicity and State in the Making of Advanced Marginality." *Urban Studies* 53, no. 6 (2016): 1077–88.

Wacquant, Loïc. *Urban Outcasts: A Comparative Sociology of Advanced Marginality.* Cambridge, MA: Polity, 2008.

Wacquant, Loïc, Tom Slater, and Virgílio Borges Pereira, ed. "Territorial Stigmatization in Action." Special issue, *Environment and Planning A: Economy and Space* 46, no. 6 (2014).

Walker, R. B. J. *Inside/Outside: International Relations as Political Theory*. New York: Cambridge University Press, 1993.

Walker, Richard A. "Building a Better Theory of the Urban: A Response to 'Towards a New Epistemology of the Urban.'" *CITY* 19, no. 2–3 (2015): 183–91.

Walker, Richard A. "Why Cities? A Response." *International Journal of Urban and Regional Research* 40, no. 1 (2016): 164–80.

Walker, Richard A., and Robert D. Lewis. "Beyond the Crabgrass Frontier: Industry and the Spread of North American Cities, 1850–1950." *Journal of Historical Geography* 27, no. 1 (2001): 3–19.

Wallerstein, Immanuel. *The Modern World-System I: Capitalist Agriculture and the Origins of the European World-Economy in the Sixteenth Century*. New York: Academic Publishers, 1974.

Wallerstein, Immanuel, ed. *Open the Social Sciences: Report of the Gulbenkian Commission on the Restructuring of the Social Sciences*. Stanford, CA: Stanford University Press, 1996.

Wallerstein, Immanuel. *Unthinking Social Science: The Limits of 19th Century Paradigms*. Cambridge: Polity, 1991.

Ward, Kevin, and Andrew E. G. Jonas. "Competitive City-Regionalism as a Politics of Space: A Critical Reinterpretation of the New Regionalism." *Environment and Planning A* 36 (2004): 2119–39.

Weck, Sabine. *Neue Kooperationsformen in Stadtregionen—Eine regulationstheoretische Einordnung*. Dortmunder Beiträge zur Raumplanung Nr. 74. Dortmund: Universität Dortmund, 1995.

Weis, Tony. *The Global Food Economy and the Battle for the Future of Farming*. London: Zed, 2007.

Weiss, Linda. *The Myth of the Powerless State*. London: Policy, 1998.

West, Geoffrey. *Scale: The Universal Laws of Growth, Innovation, Sustainability, and the Pace of Life, in Organisms, Cities, Economies, and Companies*. New York: Penguin, 2016.

Whatmore, Sarah, and Lorraine Thorne. "Nourishing Networks: Alternative Geographies of Food." In *Globalising Food: Agrarian Questions and Global Restructuring*, edited by David Goodman and Michael Watts, 287–304. London: Routledge, 1998.

White, Ben, Saturnino M. Borras Jr., Ruth Hall, Ian Scoones, and Wendy Wolford. "The New Enclosures: Critical Perspectives on Corporate Land Deals." *Journal of Peasant Studies* 39, no. 3–4 (2012): 619–47.

Williams, Raymond. *The Country and the City*. Oxford: Oxford University Press, 1973.

Wilson, Japhy. "The Violence of Abstract Space: Contested Regional Development in Southern Mexico." *International Journal of Urban and Regional Research* 38, no. 2 (2014): 516–38.

Wilson, Japhy, and Manuel Bayón. "Concrete Jungle: The Planetary Urbanization of the Ecuadorian Amazon." *Human Geography* 8, no. 3 (2015): 1–23.

Wilson, Japhy, and Manuel Bayón. "Fantastical Materializations: Interoceanic Infrastructures in the Ecuadorian Amazon." *Environment and Planning D: Society and Space* 35, no. 5 (2017): 836–54.

Wilson, Japhy, and Erik Swyngedouw, eds. *The Post-Political and Its Discontents.* Edinburgh: University of Edinburgh Press, 2014.

Wimmer, Andreas, and Nina Glick-Schiller. "Methodological Nationalism and Beyond: Nation-State Building, Migration and the Social Sciences." *Global Networks* 2, no. 4 (2002): 301–34.

Wirth, Louis. "Urbanism as a Way of Life." In *Classic Essays on the Culture of Cities*, edited by Richard Sennett, 143–64. Englewood Cliffs, NJ: Prentice Hall, 1969 [1937].

Wolch, Jennifer, and Michael Dear. *The Power of Geography: How Territory Shapes Social Life.* London: Unwin Hyman, 1989.

Wu, Fulong. "China's Emergent City-Region Governance: A New Form of State Spatial Selectivity through State-Orchestrated Rescaling." *International Journal of Urban and Regional Research* 40, no. 6 (2016): 1134–51.

Wyly, Elvin. "Positively Radical." *International Journal of Urban and Regional Research* 35, no. 5 (2011): 889–912.

Wyly, Elvin. "Strategic Positivism." *Professional Geographer* 61, no. 3 (2009): 310–22.

Zoomers, Annelies. "Globalisation and the Foreignisation of Space: Seven Processes Driving the Current Global Land Grab." *Journal of Peasant Studies* 37, no. 2 (2010): 429–47.

Zoomers, Annelies, Femke Van Noorloos, Kei Otsuki, Griet Steel, and Guus Van Westen. "The Rush for Land in an Urbanizing World: From Land Grabbing towards Developing Safe, Resilient, and Sustainable Cities and Landscapes." *World Development* 92 (2017): 242–52.

Zukin, Sharon. "A Decade of the New Urban Sociology." *Theory & Society* 9 (1980): 575–601.

Zukin, Sharon. "Is There an Urban Sociology? Questions on a Field and a Vision." *Sociologica* 3 (2011): 1–18.

INDEX

Page numbers followed by *f* indicate figures.

437

Angel, Shlomo, 300–2, 305, 316–17
Angelo, Hillary, 13–14, 300–3, 304–5, 384
Ansell, Chris, 192–93
Anthropocene era, 32–33, 48–49
anthropology, cultural, 49–50
Appadurai, Arjun, 127–28
Appelbaum, Richard, 17–18
APS (advanced producer service) firms,
    121–24, 125–26, 149–51
Arab Spring, 284
Araghi, Farshad, 363–65
Arboleda, Martín, 14, 32–33, 306–7, 319–
    20, 339–40, 344, 392–93
archipelago economy, 189–90. *See also*
    world city archipelago
area studies, 99–100
Arrighi, Giovanni, 339
Arthur, W. Brian, 107–8
Ascher, François, 296–97
ASEAN (Association of Southeast Asian
    Nations), 272–73
Asia, 305, 358*f*, 372–73
Asimov, Isaac, 351
assemblage urbanism, 36, 137, 265–66
Association of Southeast Asian Nations
    (ASEAN), 272–73
Aureli, Pier Vittorio, 352–53
autonomy, suburban, 245
Aydalot, Philippe, 57–58

Baden-Württemberg, Germany,
    122–23, 219
Balducci, Alessandro, 296–97, 351
Balibar, Étienne, 382–83
Barcelona Metropolitan
    Corporation, 212–13
Barlow, Max, 189, 210
Barnes, Trevor, 330–31
Barnett, Clive, 303–4
Barron, Patrick, 296–97
Bassand, Michel, 213–14
Bassens, David, 14–15, 120–25, 149–51,
    294–95, 330–31
Batty, Michael, 325
Bayón, Manuel, 306–7, 375–78
Beauregard, Robert, 38–39

Belgium, 188–89
Belt and Road Initiative (BRI), 369,
    375–76, 380–81
Bender, Thomas, 351–52
Berger, Alan, 296–97, 306
Berndt, Christian, 108–9
Berry, Brian, 4, 139, 348*f*
Bettencourt, Luis, 38–39, 325
big data, 291–92, 311–12, 325
big government, 212
black boxes, 335–36
#BlackLivesMatter, 284
Blei, Alejandro M., 305
blind fields, 322–23, 335–36
Bloch, Robin, 242–43
blue banana region, 190–92, 305
Bologna, Italy, 213–14
bond markets, 244
Bond, Patrick, 339
borders and boundaries, 351, 377–78
    jurisdictional, 250–51
    territorial boundaries, 271–75, 305–6
    village-city *(desakota)* regions, 358*f*
Borras, Saturnino M., Jr., 315–16, 372–73
Borst, Renate, 197–98
Boston, Massachusetts, 219, 305
BosWash (Boston–Washington, DC), 305
Boudreau, Julie-Anne, 174–75
boundaries. *See* borders and boundaries
Bourdieu, Pierre, 49–50, 173, 384
Boyd, William, 306–7, 363–65
Boyer, Robert, 97–98
Braudel, Fernand, 119–20, 167, 271–72
Brazil, Russia, India, China, South
    Africa (BRICS) territories,
    339, 361–63
Brennan, Timothy, 393
Brenner, Neil, 5–6, 8–11, 17–19, 29–30,
    42–43, 48–49, 51–52, 53–54, 62,
    69–70, 71–73, 97, 106–7, 113, 115–16,
    132–33, 137, 146, 158–59, 173–74,
    206–7, 233–34, 251–52, 258–59,
    260–61, 264–65, 293, 296–97,
    304–5, 316–17, 322–23, 325–27,
    335–37, 342–43, 351, 358–65, 375,
    380, 385, 390–91

Brewer, Anthony, 257
Brexit, 155–56
BRI (Belt and Road Initiative), 369, 375–76, 380–81
BRICS (Brazil, Russia, India, China, South Africa) territories, 339, 340–41, 351, 369, 377–78, 381–82
Bridge, Gavin, 319–20, 358–61
British Empire, 278
Brookes, W. M., 63–64
Brubaker, Rogers, 302–3
Brugmann, Jeb, 300–2
Brunet, Roger, 190–92
Brussels, Belgium, 152
Bücher, Karl, 119–20
Buckley, Michelle, 27–28, 331–32, 374
Bukharin, Nikolai, 257
Bulkeley, Harriet, 100, 265–66
Bullmann, Udo, 187–88, 219–20
Bundesbank, 156–57
Bunker, Stephen, 374
Bunnell, Tim, 34
Burdett, Ricky, 303–4
Burgess, Ernest, 1–2, 319
Butler, Chris, 41–42
Buttel, Frederick, 306

Cairns, Stephen, 303–4, 389–90
capital
  accumulation of, 23, 31–32, 41–42, 51–52, 54–58, 59–62, 70–71, 76–77, 83–86, 95, 97–98, 102, 106–8, 121, 122–23, 126, 145–46, 155–56, 173–74
  foreign, 147
  hypermobile, 216
  institutionalized power of, 241–42
  private, 241–42
capitalism
  competitive, 65
  contemporary, 102–3, 134
  early industrial, 279
  fixity/motion contradiction under, 52, 53–62, 75–76, 262, 297–98
  geographical differences under, 261–63
  geopolitics of, 51, 57–58

global, 125–26
  historical geography of, 5, 59, 209–13, 269–71, 275–76, 279–81, 283
  industrialization under, 270, 271–73
  informational, 265–66
  mercantile, 269–71, 279
  modern, 2–3, 29–30, 66–67, 279, 359f, 380–81, 390–91, 393
  nation-form under, 382–83
  neocapitalism, 65, 67
  neoliberalizing, 375
  new economy of, 172
  new phase of, 172
  post-Fordist, 125, 149–51
  postmetropolitan, 361–63
  postmodern, 17–18
  restructuring under, 176–77
  scales under, 102–3, 105–6, 113, 282
  space under, 71–72, 143–44, 361–63
  spatial units of, 92–93
  state space under, 71–72, 143–44
  territorial organization under, 53, 60, 61–62, 125, 137, 271–77
  transformation of nature under, 363–65, 367f
  uneven development under, 256–99, 268–90f
  urbanization under, 15–17, 21–22, 26–27, 41–42, 45, 52, 59–60, 69–71, 74–79, 80–81, 141, 147, 168–69, 288–99, 290f, 336–37, 359f, 374–76, 378–79, 380–81, 389–90, 394
  world, 120, 339
Capitalocene era, 32–33
cartography, 328–29
  connectography, 377–78
  horizontal, 2–3
Castells, Manuel, 6–7, 34, 46, 91–95, 118–19, 121–22, 127–28, 130–31, 169, 181–82, 265–66, 284, 285–86, 300, 308, 321, 323–24, 388
Castree, Noel, 32, 55–56, 108–9
Castriota, Rodrigo, 361–63
catastrophe, 68, 81, 381–82
central place theory, 4

horizontal cartography, 2–3
Horkheimer, Max, 35
Howard, Ebenezer, 318
Howitt, Richard, 100, 288
Hoyler, Michael, 149–51, 190–91, 366–69
Hubbard, Phil, 147–48, 187–88
Hudson, Ray, 173–74, 221–22,
    271, 339–41
Hugo, Graeme, 314
Hustwit, Gary, 300–2
Hymer, Stephen, 121–22
hypermobile capital, 216
hyperproductivism, 148
hypertrophic cities, 312–13

ICTs (information and communications
    technologies), 171–75, 189–90,
    197–98, 200, 201–5,
    280–81, 377–78
IIRSA (Initiative for the Integration
    of Regional Infrastructure in
    South America), 369, 370f,
    375–76, 380–81
immanentist methodology, 38–39
imperial scale, 278. See also
    supranational scale
imperialism, 53, 279
import substitution industrialization
    (ISI), 121–22
India, 339, 371–73. See also BRICS
    (Brazil, Russia, India, China, South
    Africa) territories
industrial cities, 57, 59–60
industrial decline, 133–34
industrial districts, 147, 355–56
industrialization, 363–65
    capitalist, 270, 271–73
    of commodity production, 372–73
    deindustrialization, 121–22
    global, 54–55
    hinterland, 300.
    import-substitution, 121–22
    neo-Fordist, 124–25
    new centres, 340–41
    new economy industries, 23–24

nineteenth-century, 249
post-Fordist, 124–25
and regional development, 189–90
rural, 380–81
inequality. See uneven spatial
    development
information and communications
    technologies (ICTs), 171–75,
    189–90, 197–98, 200, 201–5,
    280–81, 377–78
infrastructures, 75, 362f, 371–73, 375–78,
    381–82, 393
Initiative for the Integration of Regional
    Infrastructure in South America
    (IIRSA), 369, 370f, 375–76, 380–81
injustice, 394
innovation hubs, 147
institutional envelopes, 240
institutions, 240–46
intergovernmental relations, 152–55
interiorization, 316–20
internal relations, 343–44
international financial centers, 151
International Journal of Urban and
    Regional Research, 323–24
international relations, 99–100
interscalar configurations, 58, 59, 106
interscalar coordination, 204
interscalar organization, 105–6
interscalar rule regimes, 106–7
intersectoral coordination, 204
interspatial competition, 216
IPCC, 303–4
ISI (import substitution
    industrialization), 121–22
Isin, Engin, 352–53
islands, metropolitan, 11, 14–15. See also
    world city archipelago
isolation of rural life, 393
Italy, 122–23, 158–59, 223–24,
    251–52, 351
Iveson, Kurt, 384

Jackson, Kenneth, 245
Jacobs, Jane, 300–2